Don Moon

INTERNATIONAL YEARBOOK
OF POLITICAL BEHAVIOR RESEARCH

GENERAL EDITOR: Heinz Eulau, *Stanford University*

International Year Book of Political Behavior Research

Quantitative International Politics: Insights and Evidence

CONTRIBUTORS

Chadwick F. Alger, *Northwestern University*
Hayward Alker, Jr., *Yale University*
Richard A. Brody, *Stanford University*
Michael Haas, *University of Hawaii*
Ole R. Holsti, *Stanford University*
Charles A. McClelland, *University of Michigan*
Robert C. North, *Stanford University*
Donald Puchala, *Columbia University*
James N. Rosenau, *Rutgers University*
J. David Singer, *University of Michigan*
Melvin Small, *Wayne State University*
Rudolph J. Rummel, *University of Hawaii*
Bruce M. Russett, *Yale University*
Dina A. Zinnes, *Indiana University*

Quantitative International Politics:
Insights and Evidence

Edited by **J. David Singer**

THE FREE PRESS, New York

COLLIER-MACMILLAN LIMITED, London

Collier-Macmillan Canada, Ltd., Toronto, Ontario
Library of Congress Catalog Card Number: 66-23083
Second printing November 1968

Preface

The appearance of the quantitative, empirical studies brought together by J. David Singer in this sixth volume of the *International Yearbook of Political Behavior Research* represents an exciting scientific event, not just in the field of international politics, but in the discipline of political science as a whole. The significance of these new researches for the scientific study of world politics is made sufficiently explicit by the editor of this volume in his own introduction and does not require further elaboration. Their importance for political science as a whole and the other social sciences warrants some additional observations.

The satisfaction one derives from publishing the kind of enterprise like the *International Yearbook* is, above all, that it gives one an opportunity to share, if only as an observer, in the lively developments at the frontiers of one's discipline. When, some twelve years ago, some of us first discussed the feasibility of a special publication devoted to behavioral researches on politics, our immediate concern was with facilitating communication among behaviorally oriented colleagues and with creating an outlet for the rapidly growing number of behavioral studies.[1] For, at that time, the editors of most political science journals were still generally hostile to the newer tendencies. But we also hoped that the studies published in a special medium would stimulate further efforts along behavioral science lines. Of all volumes in this series published so far, perhaps none is better suited to this purpose than the present book. I expect it to find wide acceptance as a tool of instruction by those teachers of international politics for whom the daily papers and weekly journals are not the alpha and omega of political information or wisdom.

Interestingly, when the *Yearbook* series was finally planned in 1957, international politics was not one among the ten topics suggested for inclusion by our consultants.[2] There was good reason for this. In a review of the political science literature I prepared about that time, only the early works of Karl Deutsch and Richard Snyder could be cited as evidence of the behavioral orientation in the

1. The communication and publication problem was first discussed by Robert E. Lane, Robert E. Agger and myself during the Summer Seminar in Political Behavior conducted at the Survey Research Center of the University of Michigan in 1954. Letters to some twenty-five members of the profession were sent out to test the sentiment regarding a political behavior journal or some other means of facilitating communication. The matter was further discussed at the 1954 meeting of the American Political Science Association in Chicago. But there was much apprehension that a separate "behavioral" publication would have schismatic consequences and, after an association committee reported negatively, the idea of securing official sponsorship was dropped. But two events followed. Alfred de Grazia, supported by Deutsch and Snyder, began the publication of PROD (Political Research: Organization and Design) in September, 1957 (now *American Behavioral Scientist*). And the idea of the *Yearbook* series developed in the same year, after a number of political sociologists, notably Morris Janowitz and Seymour Martin Lipset, expressed support. The first volume, planned for publication in 1959, was delayed and did not appear until 1961.

2. The same was true, by the way, of "judicial behavior." See the Preface in Glendon Schubert, ed., *Judicial Decision-Making* (New York: Free Press, 1963), p. vii.

study of international politics proper.[3] Reviewing the state of the field again in 1961, I found "many behavioral rumblings in the study of international behavior in recent years, but most of the rumblings have been theoretical rather than empirical".[4] And, a year later, I observed that "there seems to be an inverse relationship between theorizing as an independently creative activity and the empirical accessibility of the phenomena theorized about. I find that the most exciting theoretical work in potential behavioral research now being done centers about the range of problems traditionally of interest to the student of international relations—precisely the area where access to behavioral data is perhaps most difficult to come by."[5] The paucity of rigorous empirical research in the field was also reflected in the first "modern," behavior-oriented reader in the field, James N. Rosenau's *International Politics and Foreign Policy*, and this paucity was certainly not due to any lack of diligence in searching out such studies on the part of the editor of that excellent collection.[6]

All this, as the present volume shows, has changed a good deal. But what has also changed, it seems to me, is the level of self-confidence that has come to characterize political scientists as symbolized by the present editor's decision to invite only political scientists and (almost unbelievable) historians to prepare studies for this book. Only a few years ago it would have been unthinkable to exclude, so purposefully, political sociologists, social psychologists, or cultural anthropologists from this kind of endeavor, so great was their prestige among those political scientists who were dissatisfied with the state of their discipline. What, one wonders, has happened? For it certainly cannot be our intention at this late date to set up barriers to interdisciplinary discourse that are even higher than those imposed by the conventional academic departmentalization.

My answer is simple and short. It is that political scientists have learned the language and methods of behavioral science. Political scientists, at long last, have become social scientists. I am quite confident, for instance, that the contributors to this volume, without exception, would feel as much at home at meetings of the American Sociological Association or the American Psychological Association as they are comfortable at the meetings of the American Political Science Association. While this volume, then, has been written *by* political scientists and historians, it is written *for* all social scientists interested in international political phenomena, regardless of their professional affiliation. It looks as if the time has come, finally, when political scientists can pay back to their fellow social scientists in the other disciplines some of the intellectual debts owed for so long. Whether they will pay back so much as they borrowed only the future can tell.

HEINZ EULAU

Stanford, California
August, 1965

---

3. Heinz Eulau, "Political Science," in Bert F. Hoselitz, ed., *A Reader's Guide to the Social Sciences* (New York: Free Press, 1959), pp. 115–120.

4. Heinz Eulau, *Recent Developments in the Behavioral Study of Politics* (Stanford, Calif.: Dept. of Political Science, Standford Univ., 1961), p. 9.

5. Heinz Eulau, "Segments of Political Science Most Susceptible to Behavioristic Treatment," in James C. Charlesworth, ed., *The Limits of Behavioralism in Political Science* (Philadelphia: American Academy of Political and Social Science, 1962), p. 37.

6. New York: Free Press, 1961.

Contents

Contents of Chapters

Quantitative International Politics: Insights and Evidence

Editor's Introduction[1]

Every intellectual discipline seems to pass through a number of stages on the road from folklore to science. The same general pattern that has characterized the evolution of the physical and biological sciences seems to be repeating itself today in the social sciences. For centuries, the curious and the scholarly tend to seek understanding via the route of speculation, and even though such speculation often rests heavily on deduction from the orthodox cosmology of the time and place, it is not without its experiential and inductive aspects. Eventually, certain dissenters begin to doubt whether speculation and impression are, after all, a satisfactory route to knowledge, and the consequence often is an effort to improve the methods of observation. They discover that we cannot explain and we cannot predict until we can *describe*, and that satisfactory description, in turn, requires relatively systematic observational procedures. More specifically, such procedures must be standardized, visible, explicit, and repeatable; in other words, they must be operational.

On the other hand, there must be compelling grounds for deciding which phenomena are to be subjected to these operational observational procedures. Such grounds are, of course, a function of the theoretical predilections of the would-be observer. But if these theoretical predilections are to be anything

1. Although all contributors to this *Yearbook* have had an opportunity to criticize this Introduction, and several of them entered dissents of varying intensity and scope, the statement remains that of the editor alone. That is, all of the suggestions were considered, but not all were followed. My justification was two-fold: (1) beyond certain fundamentals, philosophies of science must and do differ widely, with some of the issues remaining largely a matter of individual preference or style; and (2) at this point in the development of the discipline, it seems worthwhile to slightly *overstate* certain considerations, even at the risk of appearing somewhat extreme. I would also like to thank Karl W. Deutsch for his frank and discerning comments on the Introduction and several of the substantive papers, and Susan Jones for her assistance in editing, proofreading, and preparation of the Indexes.

1

other than idiosyncratic bias or the conventional wisdom of the moment, they need to flow from a coherent and developing theoretical framework.

The emerging discipline of world politics is, today, short on both counts. Woefully lacking in operational indicators of political and diplomatic variables, our theory is not much better. This latter weakness, while partially attributable to the discipline's intellectual heritage from history and international law, as well as the strong tendency towards ethnocentrism among scholars in any nation, is by no means independent of the data deficiency. On the contrary, it could be argued that data-less theorizing is—despite some important exceptions—largely sterile, and that in the absence of empirically observed statistical regularities, little progress on the theoretical front can be expected.

While recognizing that there are many roads to knowledge and that all are partly complementary, we might postulate three broad and discernible ones here. The first such road is the deductive: from a relatively broad (if not always explicit) theory, we deduce, via logical procedures, certain limited generalizations. The second, intimately connected, is the road of analogy; from theories and generalizations that seem compelling in *another* empirical realm we analogize to that of world politics. Both these intellectual procedures are indispensable to the acquisition of knowledge, but neither is sufficient. Rather, deduction and analogy should be viewed as important sources of hypotheses: propositions which must still be put to the test. This leads, in turn, to the third general path—that of induction. But the inductive process is impossible in the absence of data.

THE USES OF DATA

It may be argued that historians, political scientists, and international lawyers—if they have done nothing else—have been gathering and codifying data for decades. It depends, of course, on what we mean by "data." Our argument here is that a great many *facts* and an impressive body of *information* (in the colloquial rather than the cybernetic sense) have indeed been generated by the scholarly efforts of these disciplines, but that very few *data* have been produced. Data, it may be argued, only emerge after large and unassorted heaps of facts have been screened and codified by the systematic application of consistent, visible, and replicable procedures for observation and classification. When such operational and scientific procedures have been so utilized, we may speak of *data-making*, as distinguished from the more anecdotal and intuitive procedures of fact-accumulating and information-gathering.[2] To put it another way, empiricism does not inevitably generate data—which *are* theoretically useful—and it often generates nothing more than facts or impressions—which, while valuable, are not yet in the form required for hypothesis-testing. A final note in this connection is that even if a key variable is not going to be quantified in a particular study, it pays to approach it *as if* an operational measure were being sought. The mere consideration of how it *might* be operationalized can often lead to a clarification of familiar concepts which, while rich in nuance and insight, turn out on closer examination to be vague and imprecise.

2. My definition of data and my distinction between data-making and data-analysis may be slightly unorthodox, but the intent is to clarify and differentiate in an area that often seems to be one of conceptual confusion. For a fuller explication, see the review article on "Data-Making in International Relations" (Singer, 1965).

MIDDLE-RUN OBJECTIVES

This, then, is the theme of the present volume. Our hope is that the data generated here and the resulting generalizations will carry our discipline a step further away from the folklore end of the spectrum, and a discernible degree closer to the scientific end. Our justification is not, however, a purely intellectual one. Though the acquisition and codification of knowledge provide sufficient grounds for any scholarly enterprise, there is in the case of world politics (or its more restricted version, international politics) an additional motivation: reducing the likelihood of unintended war. If we think of interactions among nations in scientific as well as normative terms, rather than in the latter fashion alone, it becomes evident that *some* portion of the variance is accounted for by factors having little to do with the conventional warlike versus peacelike classification of the national actors. That is, an appreciation of such other phenomena as the organization of the international system, the prior interdependence of the protagonists, or their alliance commitments would seem equally critical. Once a process gets underway or a system begins to take on structure, the effects of conscious human intervention upon any future state of affairs are appreciably reduced. As long as neither the scholar nor the policy maker has a particularly strong understanding of the dynamics of war and its many preconditions, we will have only the haziest notion of whether the limited degree of behavior which *is* susceptible to our influence or control is or is not increasing the probability of war. In other words, war may be highly analogous to industrial accidents, epidemics, or economic depressions, and it may well be that the type of research which has produced greater understanding and reduced incidence of these social disasters is also relevant to international politics in general and war in particular.

SHORT-RUN OBJECTIVES

In addition to these middle-run scientific and policy objectives, we are motivated by a more instrumental consideration. Given the remarkable amount of skepticism, hostility, and apathy still prevalent among scholars of world politics regarding the possibility (and/or desirability) of a scientific discipline, we conceive of this collection as a demonstration. It is intended to demonstrate that political scientists can use rigorous, quantitative methods to examine important theoretical questions in the field of world politics.[3] It is intended to help dispel the pessimism in our field which often avers that the really important and interesting problems of international relations and world politics are not susceptible to quantitative treatment: "If it can be measured, it must be trivial." This pessimism has been further buttressed by the belief that even if operational and quantitative procedures *are* relevant to the central problems of the field, they are so complex and elusive that no traditionally trained political scientist can possibly master them.

3. There is certainly no intention here of suggesting that no quantitative work of such a nature has yet been done. As the Bibliography makes clear (Part 1A) *some* research meeting these criteria has already been undertaken.

SELECTION CRITERIA

This brings us then to the backgrounds of our contributors and the mode of selection. Taking the latter first, only two criteria were applied in inviting participation: (1) Was the individual a political scientist and/or historian? (2) Had he or she demonstrated an interest in and capacity for rigorous methodology? While some excellent work is being done by other social scientists, especially those in social psychology (see Parts IIA and IIB in the Bibliography), to have included them would have diluted the impact of an all-political-science effort. The intention was certainly to recruit the more interdisciplinary scholars, but mere knowledge of, and interest in, sociology, psychology, anthropology, or economics would not suffice. While recognizing the critical importance of the *findings* and *concepts* of these disciplines, our preoccupation here was with the adaptation and utilization of their *methods* and *techniques*. Thus, as Part IB of the Bibliography shows, quite a few of our colleagues are borrowing in a creative and fruitful way from related disciplines, but their non-quantitative work was not meant to be included here.

With these considerations in mind, and with somewhat more than two years' lead time allowed, two recruiting procedures were used. First, all of the established scholars who were known to be engaged in, or planning, quantitative research were approached and invited to undertake an empirical study for eventual inclusion in the volume. In more casual and subtle form, the considerations they were asked to keep in mind were: (1) The choice of substantive problems should be explicitly justified on theoretical and/or policy grounds. (2) The choice of independent and dependent variables should be explicitly justified on theoretical grounds. (3) The operations which are utilized to convert the variables from a verbal, qualitative form to numerical, quantitative form should be justified on logical and empirical as well as technical grounds. (4) These operations should be so explicitly described that the procedure can be understood by the reader who has never conducted a similar operation, and can be replicated by that reader with a minimum of technical advice or by using a well-known and highly standardized procedure.

Of the ten people originally invited, eight accepted; of these latter, three subsequently found that they could not meet the deadline, and withdrew somewhere along the way. It was in anticipation of this likelihood, therefore, that a supplementary procedure was used. An additional ten or so of the younger scholars, whose graduate training indicated both an interest and competence in quantitative methods, were also approached. But whereas the original invitees were virtually assured that their papers would be included, the others were encouraged to submit their work on a competitive basis. While all expressed interest, several withdrew and some teamed up with one another or with one of the original invitees.

AUTHORS' FORMAL TRAINING

Returning then to the matter of whether or not political scientists can indeed learn and utilize the quantitative techniques already familiar to related disciplines and to such political research as voting and survey studies, it is instructive to note the training and background of the contributors who emerged from our recruiting process. We ended up with fourteen authors and co-authors of the ten papers, and of these, only eight (Alker, Brody, Haas, Holsti, Puchala, Rummel, Russett, and Zinnes) attended graduate school at times and places which would have provided formal training in social science methodology.[4] The remaining six (Alger, McClelland, North, Rosenau, Singer, and Small) were trained in political science or history before the quantitative approaches had found their way into the graduate curricula of their departments. Therefore, while recognizing the importance of such formal preparation, it is evident that these methods and techniques are by no means so exotic or mysterious that they cannot be more or less self-taught after graduate school or even well after a scholar's research and teaching career has assumed fairly definitive form.[5]

DATA-MAKING PROCEDURES

So much for our authors and their training in quantitative methodology. What sorts of methods did they use in the studies at hand? None of the ten studies is exclusively a data-analysis operation; all required some mixture of data-making and data-transformation prior to the search (via data-analysis) for theoretically meaningful patterns. Treating them in the order of increasing necessity for the conversion of raw information into numerical indicators, perhaps the one that comes closest to finding its data ready-made is the Haas inquiry into the relationship between domestic stress and strain on the one hand and a nation's tendency to engage in military behavior on the other. His problem was one of locating reliable figures on unemployment and on rates of increase in electric power consumption for his ten sample nations and three time periods, and then treating these as his indicators of *stress*. For a domestic *strain* index, he had to do the same thing for suicide, homicide, and alcoholic death rates, while the dependent variable of military behavior was measured by defense expenditure levels, war-involvement frequency, and war-initiation frequency. Likewise, Alker and Puchala, in their effort to measure trends toward economic integration in the North Atlantic area found their data in relatively ready-made form, but had then to convert their import and export figures into an index of "relative [economic] acceptance" by use of an equation (adapted from Savage and Deutsch, 1960) which takes account of the share of each nation's trade which

4. Several of these younger scholars did their undergraduate or Master's work in mathematics, economics, or one of the physical sciences, thus acquiring some competence in, and predisposition toward, rigorous methods and procedures. Worth noting also is the fact that all eight of the more recently trained authors graduated from only three schools: Northwestern, Stanford, and Yale. As to the universities out of which the studies have come, the ten are distributed as follows: three from Yale, and one each from Hawaii, Indiana, Michigan, Northwestern, Rutgers, Stanford, and Southern California. Since completion of the studies, however, McClelland has moved from Southern California to Michigan, and Rummel from Yale to Hawaii.

5. Extremely useful, but unfortunately terminated after a very few years, were two Ford Foundation programs. One provided for summer-long seminars in which unfamiliar methods and concepts were described by visiting lecturers from a variety of disciplines. The other offered full-year fellowships to political scientists interested in "tooling up" in related disciplines or to other social scientists eager to acquire some expertise in the international relations field. Now might be a propitious time for such programs to be reinstituted.

could be normally expected if there *were* no trading preferences. Although Russett's effort to identify meaningful political regions in the global system also proceeded from existing quantitative indicators (systematically accumulated by the Yale Data Project and reported in Russett, *et al.*, 1964) it was again essential to transform these data into meaningful indicators of intra-regional similarity and dependence via factor analysis procedures. Turning to the Alger project, a few of the variables were more or less ready at hand (national contributions to, and votes in, the United Nations), but most required systematic personal observation and classification. That is, the frequency and type of interpersonal interaction in the sessions of the Fifth Committee had to be visually observed, classified, and recorded, while the evaluations of the delegates by one another required personal interviews.

In the midrange, methodologically, are the McClelland, Rummel, and Singer-Small studies. In these three, contemporary or archival sources had to be culled and the materials coded in an effort to identify and classify specific types of political and military events; once the facts had been reliably ascertained, they had to be combined and aggregated into structural and behavioral indices. Finally, the Rosenau, Zinnes, and Holsti-North-Brody studies were presented with the greatest gap between raw material and useful quantitative indicators. Relying largely upon governmental records and diplomatic communications, all three resort to content analysis as a major data-making procedure.

DATA-ANALYSIS PROCEDURES

As the reader is well aware, large amounts of quantitative data may be very useful in providing more accurate, standardized, and therefore comparable descriptions; however, normally the purpose is to go beyond description and toward prediction and/or explanation. The moment we move into either of these enterprises, we become involved automatically in the search for correlation: is there any stable and consistent relationship between two or more sets of variables when they are compared over and over again? The presence or absence of such a relationship is ascertained by various modes of data-analysis, all of which, in one fashion or another, are searches for a statistical correlation strong enough not to have occurred by sheer chance.

Data-analysis techniques need not, of course, be used only to test hypotheses or confirm empirical generalizations of the "if _____, then _____" variety. They may also be used for combining, sorting, distilling, or transforming relatively raw quantitative data into more theoretically useful measures or indices of variables (Janda, 1965). Such is the case with two of our ten papers. As indicated in the previous section, Russett utilizes a factor analysis procedure to ascertain which nations are most similar to, and dependent upon, which other nations, and which nations are least similar and interdependent. Similarly, Alker and Puchala employ a programmed equation which converts raw import and export figures into a much more meaningful indicator called "relative [economic] acceptance." The Rummel contribution, although addressed to the comparison of correlations between a number of domestic attributes and the nations' involvement in external conflict, emerges from a larger project in which factor analysis is the major technique for transforming a multitude of socioeconomic-political quantities into a smaller number of more theoretically meaningful dimensions.

As to the balance of the studies reported here, Haas, Alger, and Holsti-North-Brody use Spearman's rank difference correlation (*rho*) to measure the coincidence of their independent and dependent variables; the latter two also employ the chi-square and Mann-Whitney *U*-tests for this purpose. Rosenau relies primarily on the *t*-test, while Rummel, Singer-Small, and Zinnes lean heavily on the Pearson product-moment correlation (*r*); and McClelland uses the standard Log_2 (log base 2) tables to compare his crisis events with their likelihood of occurring by sheer chance. Finally, Zinnes uses the scatter diagram as well as the Pearson *r*-measure in order to discern the presence and strength of her correlations.

Lest the reader be put off by this host of unfamiliar statistical tests, it should be emphasized that not all of us need fully understand the mathematical intricacies which underlie them, but must be sufficiently informed to know which test is most appropriate and meaningful for a given type of research design.[6] The point is that the general strength and direction of a linear relationship can often be estimated via such visual displays as the simple matrix or the scatter diagram; the statistical test may give a more precise indication, or reveal a patterning which, because of the data's extensiveness and complexity, might not otherwise be evident.

Also germane is the fact that these widely used and highly standardized techniques may not always be adequate for testing more complex theoretical formulations. Eventually, we must advance from correlations between two sets of variables to more complex statistics of a multivariate and non-linear nature, and thence on to the search for "fit" between several sets of distributions and the equation or mathematical model which allegedly predicts to the empirically observed outcomes.

This might also be the appropriate juncture at which to anticipate a not unlikely criticism. It will no doubt be said that "those people" ought to spend less time talking about their methods and more time getting on with the substance of their research. Five or so years from now, that should (hopefully) be a legitimate complaint, but today it is premature. At every stage in any discipline's development, certain problems and preoccupations are likely to be dominant, and these will lead to a certain amount of awkward self-consciousness. The discipline of world politics is no exception, and if we recognize it as now at the threshold between the pre-scientific and the scientific stage, we need not be surprised (or annoyed) by this preoccupation with method.[7]

TIME FRAME

Turning now from method to broader elements of research design we should consider some of the dimensions along which a study might be classified. Critical among these is that of temporal focus; a key issue when contemplating a new

6. One of our authors, however, has recently published a book which should go a considerable distance in clarifying the reasoning behind them; see Alker (1965). A comparable effort is found in another of our contributors' papers; see Rummel (1965a).

7. On the other hand, there would seem to be no scientific discipline that does not require a small group of scholars who continue to specialize in methodology; hence, the existence of such important journals as *Econometrica, Psychometrika,* and *Sociometry.*

empirical undertaking is whether to utilize one or more case studies, the cross-sectional approach, or longitudinal analysis. It is evident that we cannot generalize from a single case; yet if that discrete case is so analyzed as to produce a large number of observations of a restricted number of variables, it takes on considerably greater scientific value.[8] Thus, even though the Holsti-North-Brody and the Zinnes papers are literally case studies of the outbreak of World War I, each is based on a large number of observations of a limited number of perceptual and behavioral variables, and they may therefore be treated as longitudinal studies, albeit embracing a highly restricted time frame.

Two other contributions that might also be thought of as case studies are those by Russett and Rummel. But since each is relatively indifferent to time, and neither examines a particular episode or sequence of events, they might better be classified in an intermediate category known as the cross-sectional analysis. In these studies, there is little or no preoccupation with a sequence or flow of events, but the concern is rather with the uniformities observed at a given time. Similar in this regard are the Alger and Rosenau contributions, which focus upon one or two (respectively) spatial-temporal settings of relatively brief duration; again, the element of sequence or time lag is of minimal importance in all three.

Closer to the other end of the continuum are the Haas and the Singer-Small investigations. In both of these, we have what might be called comparative cross-sectional analyses, with three and twenty-five sets of observations respectively providing the sequence of time-slice readings at which the correlations are sought. Still more sequential is McClelland's interaction analysis during the many Berlin confrontations. Lastly, the Alker-Puchala study is explicitly concerned with the changes which occur in trading patterns over time, and clearly falls into the longitudinal category.

LEVELS OF ANALYSIS

Another way of classifying these studies—and the one adopted as the basis of organization here—is according to the units or levels of analysis at which either the observations are made or the variables are located. This distinction, though seldom made explicit, is important, since the social scientist will often observe and measure phenomena at one level of analysis as a basis for describing (by a modest inferential leap) the conditions at another level. Illustrative here are the Russett, Singer-Small, and Alker-Puchala papers. The first infers a systemic property (regionalism) from the attributes of the sub-systemic or national level; the next infers systemic properties (alliance aggregation and war) from observation of national behaviors and relationships; and the last infers a systemic property (integration) from the trade behavior of nations.

Given the awkwardness of trying to distinguish in a compelling and systematic way among the multitude of independent variables used in this collection, we will differentiate on the basis of our dependent variables only. That is, about what classes of phenomena are the contributors seeking to generalize, and to what

8. A brief analysis of the implications of a high N/V ratio (number of cases over number of variables) is in Deutsch, Singer, and Smith (1965).

types of variables at what levels of analysis are they trying to predict? In Part I, three are primarily concerned with the behavior of foreign policy decision makers; the individual is their unit of analysis. Of these, Rosenau seeks to predict how American Senators will behave vis-à-vis the Secretary of State from knowledge regarding their party membership and committee assignment; Alger examines the extent to which a United Nations delegate's behavior vis-à-vis his Fifth Committee colleagues can be predicted from his own role and status in the committee and from his nation's fiscal and administrative role in the organization; and Zinnes examines the interdependence between and among the articulations and perceptions of the policy-making elites in the governments most involved in the crisis which preceded World War I.

In Part II, Holsti-North-Brody also focus upon the reciprocal perceptions and articulations of the 1914 decision makers, but they attempt to correlate these role behaviors with the national military actions and economic transactions which accompany the conflict-escalation process. Closely related to these latter processes are those described by McClelland as he codifies the interaction sequences of the Soviet Union and the United States in a series of Berlin confrontations between 1948 and 1960. Quite comparable also are the Rummel and the Haas studies; each attempts to predict the military or foreign conflict behavior of the nation on the basis of various internal attributes of the nation.

In Part III, we shift to a third level of analysis—that of the system. Here Singer-Small examine the correlations between alliance aggregation patterns in the international system and the amount of war which the system experiences. Although neither the Alker-Puchala nor the Russett studies are, strictly speaking, hypothesis-testing operations, each recombines descriptive material so as to enhance our understanding of the present and future international system. The former scrutinizes the trends toward and away from economic integration in the North Atlantic region, while the latter examines the traditionally defined geographical regions in order to ascertain the extent to which they constitute meaningfully coherent sub-systems.

In a general sense, these studies are an excellent reflection of the substantive interests of the field as a whole, and it is especially worth noting that the individual human being is by no means the sole object of our attention. Not surprisingly, the myth has gotten around that those of us who utilize the behavioral sciences in our research are only interested in individuals and that we are hostile to any focus upon institutions and indifferent to groups or social systems. The evidence here clearly refutes that impression, and none of us is oblivious to the theoretical and methodological liabilities of the individual as a basic unit of analysis, especially at this stage in the discipline's development (Eulau, 1963). At the same time, we are all aware of the significance of role and socialization for a nation's foreign policy, and appreciate that nothing approaching a fully explanatory theory can ignore individual psychology.

THE FINDINGS

One of the more frequent criticisms of the behavioral science approach to research in our field is that it generates a great deal of methodological and conceptual verbiage as well as a fair amount of numbers, but that it seldom adds much to our substantive knowledge. To put it in the baseball metaphor of my colleague, Inis Claude, there's a lot of fancy wind-up, but we never get around to the pitch. As I suggested above, there *is* something to the charge; we must be more self-conscious not only about our methods now than we will be later, but about our selection of constructs, their measurement, and the conceptual formulations we use to give order and coherence to our research.

Despite these demands of the transition from pre-scientific to scientific work, our research has not been without its immediate empirical payoffs. As section IA of the Bibliography will show, a modest amount of data-based evidence bearing on a range of substantive problems has already begun to appear. That the present single volume increases that amount by perhaps (and this would be most difficult to measure) five or ten percent is merely an indication of how far we have to go on the road to data-based theory. What, then, are some of the findings which emerge from the ten studies presented here?

In the opening paper, Rosenau generates and analyzes sufficient data to demonstrate that United States Senators in the Acheson and Dulles eras tended to be much more responsive to the constraints of party affiliation and Foreign Relations Committee membership than to their own personal views when it came to working with the Secretary of State. The argument over the relative potency of individual and role variables has been a critical one in political science generally, and Rosenau's findings—despite the limited empirical domain—give impressive support to those who have urged greater attention to the predictive power of role variables in the policy process. In Alger's study of another class of decision makers, he demonstrates that those delegates in the Administrative and Budgetary Committee in 1962 who engaged in the most interpersonal interactions there, were not only from the larger-sized missions and from nations with high GNP per capita and high contribution to the United Nations, but were also the ones whose Committee colleagues rated as highest in relevant knowledge and general competence. Returning to decision-makers in their own national capitals again (but in an earlier era) Zinnes' data further confirm the proposition that foreign policy elites tend to reciprocate, in their articulations, their perceptions of hostility toward them, but not within any discernibly regular time period.

Shifting from the individual to the national level of analysis, Holsti-North-Brody used essentially the same perceptual phenomena as did Zinnes, but coded and scaled them into different variables and combined them with a number of national *actions*. In measuring the changing frequency and intensity of expressions as well as perceptions, they found a discernible escalation in both over the six weeks of crisis, but that the Dual Alliance nations showed a markedly greater and earlier tendency to over-react than did the Triple Entente members. Examining a similar type of diplomatic and military process in the 1948–1963 time frame, McClelland focused primarily on national actions during the recurring Berlin confrontation, and found that three distinct crises could be identified by the increasing frequency of certain classes of actions contrasted to a hypothetical "expected" frequency. He further found that these crises were relatively brief in duration, averaging about three months, and that crisis behavior tends toward increasing routinization.

Also at the national level, but focusing on the relationship between a society's attributes and its propensity to become involved in foreign conflict, Rummel demonstrates that in the mid-1950's there was no significant covariation between the two sets of variables. Looking at a similar problem, Haas also found that a variety of internal stresses and strains failed (during the 1900–1960 period) to covary with several indicators of national aggressiveness.

At the level of the international system, Singer and Small discovered that the greater the number of alliance commitments operative in the system, the more war there will be in the years immediately following, but that this finding only holds true for the twentieth century; during the nineteenth, they found almost as strong an *inverse* relationship. Among the findings in the Alker-Puchala study are the demonstrated rise, plateau, and fall of intra-European economic interdependence coupled with a dramatic economic growth rate and an increasing share of global trade. Finally, Russett's data demonstrate that while the geographical notion of region makes some sense, proximity is too simple an indicator of international groupings, and that several measures of structural and behavioral similarity and interdependence reveal somewhat different groupings in the contemporary international system. Only a few of these reveal sufficiently high scores to show much promise for their political integration.

A PROPOSAL

In sum, our hope is that these empirical studies, despite their methodological disparity and the lack of theoretical coherence, will provide a needed impetus to research and teaching in world politics. Beyond the methodological demonstrations which they provide, the findings which emerge here, as well as from the larger projects of which the studies are a part, are not without value. Though several of us are working with relatively hard data for the first time, our hope is that we have not become so involved in them (and the procedures which produced them) that the theoretical implications have been ignored. The accumulation and codification of empirical generalizations, as already noted, represents an indispensable element in the growth of theory, and we conclude, therefore, with a proposal reflecting this conviction.

As this volume goes to press, political scientists have demonstrated not only their increasing awareness of the importance of data, but have made appreciable progress in procedures for its storage and retrieval as well as its generation. At present, there are several research groups which serve, *inter alia*, as data storage centers, among which are the Inter-University Consortium for Political Research at Michigan's Survey Research Center; the International Data Library at Berkeley's Survey Research Center; the Yale Political Data Program; the International Development Research Center's Data Archive at Indiana; and the Cross-National Data Bank in the Public Affairs Research Institute at San Diego State College; in addition, there is the more specialized Roper Public Opinion Research Center at Williams College.[9] All of these units have begun to store, on cards or tape in quickly accessible form, politically relevant data, including, but not restricted to, voting and public opinion materials going back varying lengths of time into the past. Beyond these archives, a number of volumes have

9. A useful summary of these and other centers, most of which concentrate on survey and polling data, is in Bisco (1966).

been published, of which two are particularly relevant: Russett *et al.*, *World Handbook of Political and Social Indicators* (1964), and the Banks and Textor *Cross-Polity Survey* (1963). Preceding these by more than a decade was Cantril's *Public Opinion, 1935–1946* (1951) bringing together survey results from twenty-three polling organizations in sixteen countries.

Although some of the data found in these places may be of interest to students of world politics—especially those who focus on what we might call comparative foreign policy—most are primarily intended for the student of national or comparative politics.[10] It is by no means too early for world politics scholars to undertake a similar venture for the storage and retrieval of data most relevant to our discipline.

But raw data must still, however, be manipulated, rearranged, and combined in order to be theoretically useful. That is, data on one variable must be compared and correlated with data measuring other variables, both for purposes of cross-validation among apparently similar variables and for the production of empirical generalizations. At this writing, sufficiently few such correlations have been attempted, but five years from now, this body of information may well be not only massive, but scattered in all sorts of fugitive places and therefore retrievable only at great cost in time and money. For such long-established scientific disciplines as sociology and psychology, it would now be a nearly impossible task to collect and collate all the inter-variable correlations and data-based propositions that have been recorded, despite the real value of such a central source for these disciplines as a whole or for their general sub-disciplines. As the compilers of the most comprehensive inventory to be attempted in those two disciplines remind us, the operation was "so formidable that we would not have attempted the task were we not convinced of the need for the product" (Berelson and Steiner, 1964, p. 3). Had their job been undertaken even as late as 1948 when Shils (ibid., p. 4) urged that "nothing is more necessary at present than the systematic collation and 'shaking down' of American sociological research results to discover what they amount to," it would have been a somewhat more manageable mission. The point is that we are still close enough to the beginning to make a comparable enterprise quite tractable; five or ten years from now, the difficulties will be considerably greater.

Though it might be desirable if all of us meant the same thing by the same words, and employed the same operations to measure the same variables, this is by no means necessary; cross-indexing of comparable and closely related variables could solve the retrieval problem while permitting maximum individuality. At the same time, of course, the researcher could first ascertain whether the operations used by others satisfy his needs, and if so, he could use the same indicators for the same variables, thus saving himself great expense and permitting maximum comparability and cumulativeness.

The proposal, then, is that we organize a combined data and correlational archive. On each file card or under each variable in the catalog could be the information relevant to the basic data: (1) the verbal name given to the measure by its original designer, the generally used synonyms, and cross references to

---

10. Of greater interest to us are the pioneering efforts of Quincy Wright in *A Study of War* (1942) and Lewis F. Richardson in his *Statistics of Deadly Quarrels* (1960) and *Arms and Insecurity* (1960). The more recent quantitative studies are listed in the Selected Bibliography.

those synonyms which have also been operationalized by others; (2) the data-making or operational procedures; (3) the raw materials which were screened and processed to make the data; and (4) the spatial-temporal setting, or sample therefrom, which is embraced. Beyond this, the catalog might go on to identify: (5) all other variables (in the data bank or not) against which the subject variable had been correlated; (6) the spatial-temporal range for each such pairing; (7) the correlational statistic used; and (8) the files in which the procedures and results can be found.

Though a system such as this would not be inexpensive, by initiating it now we would be saved a great deal of effort and expense later. More important, however, would be the scientific payoffs in the short-run. First, the tremendous costs of data-making would be spread over several projects rather than having the results used by only one researcher. Second, individual scholars with limited personnel and money would be able to do quantitative work, rather than being required to limp along with such anecdotes and impressions as provide the "poor man's substitute for data." Third, the comparability and therefore the cumulativeness of our research findings would rise dramatically. Fourth, research would be consciously replicated rather than unknowingly repeated.

Other virtues of an arrangement such as this come to mind, but the point should be sufficiently clear by now. The projects which led to the studies presented in this volume are an important beginning, a data and findings archive can accelerate the process considerably, and both together should encourage other scholars to join in one of the most intellectually exciting and humanly important enterprises of our time: building a science of world politics.

One

The Decision Maker's Level

James N. Rosenau

Private Preferences and Political Responsibilities: The Relative Potency of Individual and Role Variables in the Behavior of U.S. Senators[1]

In order to develop a science of international politics and foreign policy, certain initial steps have to be taken. As in any science, an integrated body of tested or testable propositions about the dynamics of international life is necessarily an end product, a final stage in the lengthy processing of the materials of the field. Only after the relevant variables have been identified and their relative potency assessed through quantitative analysis is it possible to fashion a coherent body of empirical theory. If these initial steps are neglected and efforts to build integrated theory undertaken directly, there are likely to be as many theories as there are theorists, and the convergence around a common set of concepts and findings, which is necessary to the evolution of a unified science, is not likely to occur. To be sure, students of international phenomena need not have similar interests or work on similar problems. However, for all their diverse efforts to be cumulative—for them to permit the integration of the various pieces into a larger whole—the raw data of the field must undergo an initial processing which renders them sufficiently comparable to be fused and unified. Just as hides are processed into leather before shoes can be made and trees into lumber before houses can be built, so must international phenomena be made ready for theory-building.[2]

1. This paper is part of a general inquiry into the dynamics of international politics and foreign policy in which I am engaged with the support of the Center of International Studies at Princeton University. I am grateful for the facilities the Center has placed at my disposal. No less helpful has been the support of the Research Council of Rutgers University, which made possible the gathering and processing of the empirical data presented in the paper. The assistance and counsel of my wife Norah has also been invaluable. Neither she nor the Center nor the Council, however, are responsible for the emphases and interpretations contained in the paper.
    2. For an elaboration of this reasoning, see Rosenau (1964a, Part III).

17

Although recent years have witnessed considerable progress in the specification of relevant international variables, the same cannot be said for the other initial task of assessing their relative potency. Stated differently, a variety of causal agents has been identified, but confusion and contradiction still prevail with respect to the degree to which, and the circumstances under which, each agent is causal. The literature on military relations and strategy is but one of many examples that can be cited. In it ambitious individuals, technological break-throughs, particular ideologies, certain types of elites, spiraling mechanisms of the international system, and aggressive forms of government are varyingly posited as prime movers in the generation and sustenance of arms races. All of these variables may indeed be sources of an arms race, but analysts are far from a consensus on where to locate each one in the process. Even worse, the literature is totally lacking in any effort to determine which variables are likely to prove more potent when two or more of them come into conflict.

In large part, the field is in this condition because of insufficient quantitative analyses. To describe the causal potency of a variable is to make a probability statement about its effects, and such a statement can only be made if the operation of the variable is observed in a number of instances. A science of international politics, like any other science, seeks to explain and predict not particular events but general patterns; not single occurrences but the probable times out of, say, one hundred that a given stimulus will give rise to a given response.[3] Scientific analysis is thus more than merely systematic analysis. One can systematically analyze a single situation by carefully examining and interrelating its constituent parts, but such an inquiry does not become a scientific enterprise until the situation is treated as one of many that might occur under specified conditions. Hence a science of international politics must be founded on quantitative data analyzed in terms of the laws of probability (that is, statistically). Most research in the field, however, amounts to little more than analyses of single situations. Consequently, as illustrated by the literature on military policy, most attempts to contrast the causal strength of two variables are necessarily speculative, and often more confusing than clarifying.

It must be emphasized that the generation and analysis of quantitative data is not the end goal of scientific inquiry. The ultimate goal is—to repeat—general, unified, and empirical theory. Assessing the relative potency of key variables is an initial, and not the final, step toward this goal. It involves comparing the causal strength of variables prior to linking them up in causal sequences. It is to raise, for example, the question as to whether greater influence should be attributed to the functional requirements of international stability or to the motivation of officials, but it is not to ask how systemic requirements and official motives *combine* to produce a series of events. To assess the relative potency of variables, in short, is to fashion the initial propositions upon which integrated theory is built and not to construct the theory itself.

---

3. Perhaps it bears repeating that the same is true of the physical sciences. Contrary to a widely held belief, the physicist is unable to account for the behavior of every atom, nor intent upon doing so. Rather, his capacities and goals are limited to probability statements about how *most* atoms will respond to different kinds of stimuli.

QUANTITATIVE HISTORICAL COMPARISON

A variety of quantitative methods can be used to contrast the potency of two or more variables that might serve as causes of the same event. Controlled experiments, simulations of actual conditions, and survey techniques are perhaps the methods that have been most frequently used for this purpose. The method employed here, however, has not been explicitly developed elsewhere and thus we need to examine its utility and limitations in some detail. For want of a better label, we shall call it the method of "quantitative historical comparison." Four basic steps are involved in any application of the method. First, it is necessary to identify and observe a sequence of behavior that (a) was repeatedly undertaken by a number of actors in some past era; (b) occurred in such a way as to be measurable (i.e., each instance of it was recorded in the documents of the era); and (c) could reasonably be assumed to have been generated by at least the two (or more) variables which the analyst wishes to compare. Second, on the basis of the patterns discerned in the repeated occurrences of the behavior, the analyst develops an initial impression of the relative potency of the two variables and then translates these impressions into testable hypotheses which predict how the sequence of behavior would unfold if the order, operation, and/or presence of one or both of the variables in the sequence were altered. Third, the analyst finds and compiles the records of another era that is essentially comparable to the first in all respects except for the two variables being examined, these being essentially different in ways that are consistent with the hypotheses.[4] Finally, the assessment of the relative potency of the variables is made by examining whether the behavioral sequences of the second era are, to a statistically significant extent, patterned differently from those of the first era and in the directions predicted by the hypotheses. If, as may well be the case, the findings are not so clear as to confirm or negate the hypotheses unmistakably, then of course the analyst moves on to a third comparable period which is so structured as to allow for further confirmation or disconfirmation.

Any sequence of political behavior in which voting is a crucial step provides an obvious example of the phenomena to which the method of quantitative historical comparison can be readily and fruitfully applied. Whether the sequence occurs in an electorate, a legislature, or an international organization, voting involves a number of actors engaging in the same behavior; hence it is readily quantified. Usually the votes represent important choices for the people of an era, and key political variables are thus likely to be operative. Since important matters are at stake, moreover, the written records of the era will usually contain a tabulation of how each of the actors voted; therefore, the behavior is especially susceptible to accurate measurement even though it cannot be directly observed. Furthermore, whatever the site of the voting, it ordinarily occurs in the context of standardized procedures. Consequently, the number of factors that comprise the setting for behavior and that vary from one era to the next are likely to be fewer for voting sequences than for other types, and comparison between eras is made that much easier.

4. This is not to say that everything else about the two eras must be equal or even virtually so. As will be indicated, exact equivalence can never be achieved, so that emphasis must be placed on the essentiality of the similarities and the differences.

Although a number of students of international politics and foreign policy have already demonstrated that voting lends itself especially well to quantitative historical comparison (Alker and Russett, 1965; Haas, E., 1962; Hovet, 1960, 1963; Rieselbach, 1960; Singer and Sensenig, 1963), it is not the *only* kind of activity that can be subjected to this method of analysis. Data on other aspects of international behavior are not so readily available as voting statistics, but they do exist and can be accumulated. As long as the behavior under investigation is recurrent and recorded, quantitative comparison is possible. If the behavior is verbal, such as is found in legislative debates, state papers, and newspaper editorials, then the technique of counting recurrent phrases or themes—known as content analysis—can be used to sort out the relative potency of the variables giving rise to the behavior (Holsti, 1962; Pool, 1952; Singer, 1964; Zinnes, North, and Koch, 1961). If the behavior is of a grosser kind, such as the maintenance of an international relationship or the occurrence of violence within and between societies, then mass media, census tracts, and a wide variety of other types of public records can be used for quantitative historical comparison (Rummel, 1963; Russett, 1963; Tanter, 1964).

Notwithstanding the adaptability of various types of historical materials to quantitative comparison, this method of analysis is inflexible in certain important respects. Most notably, there is a rigid requirement that the hypotheses derived from inspection of the data of the first era be formulated before the data of the second era are examined. Indeed, ideally the data of the second era should not even be gathered until after the hypotheses have been formulated and made ready for testing. The researcher must be totally ignorant of how the data will be patterned in the second era. To be sure, he has to be sufficiently familiar with the general circumstances of the second era to know that it is comparable to the first in all major respects except for the variables he is contrasting. What quantitative patterns the data will reveal, however, must be a mystery to him. In this way the hypotheses can be fairly tested. The researcher will be neither consciously tempted nor subconsciously inclined to formulate his hypotheses on the basis of prior knowledge which will insure their confirmation. Like the experimenter in the laboratory, he must undergo the exquisite pleasure (or is it pain?) of waiting to see whether or not his predictions will be borne out by future events. For the laboratory researcher the "future" actually lies ahead in time, because he must conduct his experiment again in order to test his hypotheses. But, by clearly separating his research into two stages, the user of quantitative historical comparison can also anticipate "future" events even though they actually transpired in the past.

But the case for this method of inquiry can be overstated. It is not a perfect instrument of research, free of defects and easily applied. Two drawbacks are particularly noteworthy. One concerns the possibility that crucial aspects of the variables which the analyst wishes to assess may not have found their way into the documented records of an era. This problem is particularly acute whenever foreign policy decision-making at the highest levels of officialdom is encompassed by the variables being assessed. State papers may be obtainable in archives, but modern techniques of telecommunications have diminished the extent to which high-level deliberations, either within or between national decision-making units, are recorded in writing.[5] Even if an adequate written record has been

---

5. For a useful enumeration and analysis of the many difficulties that are encountered when one attempts to develop data on high-level decision-making, see Snyder and Paige (1958).

kept, moreover, there remains the additional problem that the archives may not be open to the researcher. Any effort to assess the relative potency of variables pertaining to the foreign policy behavior of officials in closed societies, for example, would prove to be an extremely arduous task for the user of quantitative historical comparison. It forces him to assess their potency in the context of more remote processes for which documentation *is* available. Indeed, whenever there is a scarcity of decision-making records, be it in relatively open or closed societies, comparison must move to the less reliable procedure of quantifying the events that both preceded and succeeded decision and then inferring the potency of decisional variables from variations in the stimulus-response patterns.

The second difficulty with this method of research is no less troublesome. It concerns the twofold question of whether the functioning of the variables being contrasted is sufficiently different in the two eras and whether these time periods are otherwise sufficiently similar to justify the assumption that quantitative comparison of the two sets of data constitutes measurement of the relative potency of the variables. From a certain perspective, it is obvious that no two eras of history can be regarded as identical, or even similar. Regardless of how brief the time which an era is defined as spanning, it is always possible to demonstrate that people differ, leaders change, technologies advance, norms evolve, and institutions alter from one era to the next if the analyst is inclined to view social processes idiographically. In the absolute sense, history does not repeat itself in *any* respect, much less in all respects but two. Yet no science, not even those that focus on physical matter, deals with absolutes. To repeat, science is concerned with the general and not the particular, which means, in effect, that it ignores small differences in order to discern large similarities. It is only in this sense, after all, that the experimental method has any meaning. In absolute terms, each run of an experiment involves different and uncontrolled conditions. One might control for the sex and size of the rats that are stimulated in one run of the experiment, but those stimulated in the next run are, like the people in two eras of history, not exactly the same rats, or, if they are, they are older, less agile, wiser, and otherwise different in a multitude of ways compared to what they were when the experiment was first conducted. Likewise, the planet whose path in space is charted is not the same object each time its location is recorded. From one day to the next it ages and is, to the extent of the differences that occur with the passage of time, as unlike the way it was as a society in two adjacent eras of history. Because their orientations are nomothetic, however, the rat psychologist and the astronomer ignore such differences and assume either that these differences are not central to the phenomena being measured or that they are distributed at random among the phenomena. So it is with quantitative historical comparison. The user of this method views history through nomothetic and not idiographic eyes. Thus in assessing the potency of variables pertaining to the English crown, to use an oversimplified example for purposes of emphasis, he would ignore the fact that it was worn by a man in one era and by a woman in the next, preferring instead to proceed on the assumption that he is measuring the operation of the monarchy when he contrasts the activities of the two individuals.

This is not to imply, however, that the problem of comparable eras can simply be wished away under the banner of scientific legitimacy. There still remains the need to demonstrate that the two *eras* are sufficiently *similar* and the assessed *variables* sufficiently *different* to warrant the conclusions derived from the quantitative comparison. There is no easy solution to this problem; it is a matter of consensus-building. Like the psychologist and the astronomer, the student of international politics must demonstrate to his colleagues that his assumptions and procedures were sound, and that therefore the conditions which he claims to have controlled and the variables which he claims to have measured were in fact subjected to his manipulations. The task of building a consensus in international politics is more difficult than in other sciences because so much still remains unknown. But it is possible. The researcher will know that he has succeeded when his case for the legitimacy of his quantitative historical comparison has been accepted and his findings are integrated into the subsequent work of his colleagues.

Of course, no method of empirical analysis is ideally suited to the scientific study of international politics and foreign policy. Each has special characteristics that make it appropriate to some kinds of problems and inappropriate to others. The researcher must thus remain flexible and let the method (or combination of methods) he employs, be a consequence, and not a determinant, of the purposes of his research and the kinds of data available to him.

THE RELATIVE POTENCY OF INDIVIDUAL AND ROLE VARIABLES

The method of quantitative historical comparison is particularly suited to the main purpose of this inquiry—that of assessing the relative potency of role and individual variables in the behavior of top foreign policy officials. By analyzing the recurrent actions of *different* individuals who occupy the *same* roles during two *similar* historical eras, and by also focusing on the *same* individuals as they occupy *different* roles in the two eras, it should be possible to test hypotheses that predict the extent to which foreign policy behavior derives from (1) the requirements of high office on the one hand, and (2) from personal conviction and idiosyncratic experience on the other.

Comparison of individual and role variables is long overdue in the study of international politics and foreign policy.[6] The literature of the field is pervaded by inarticulate premises and contradictory assumptions about the contribution which such variables make to the behavior of nations and other international actors. Widespread, for example, is the tendency to depict one American President as bound by the limits of his office, while describing another's actions as stemming from an aggressive personality. In the same manner a De Gaulle might be posited as freewheeling and unencumbered by the limitations of role, while a Khrushchev is viewed as restricted by the need to maintain support at home.[7] On the other hand, exactly the opposite interpretations have been put forward to explain previous French and Soviet leaders. Similarly, even as Anthony Eden's personality is cited as the source of England's behavior in the Suez crisis of 1956, so it is also asserted that postwar British foreign policy is

---

6. For a recent analysis that should help to correct this situation, see Edinger (1964).

7. Contrast, for example, the accounts of the two leaders in Carleton (1963, pp. 278–279 and 351–352).

founded on both the need and the reluctance to reduce its overseas commitments.[8] Endless examples of this kind of inconsistency could be cited. Most students in the field have not consciously made even a mental assessment, much less a quantitative historical comparison, of the relative strength of the two types of variables.

A primary consequence of this situation is the tendency of many researchers to attribute high potency to individual variables and either to ignore or to discount role variables. Lacking a clear-cut conception of relative potency, many observers find it easier to fall back on the notion that each moment of history is a function of the individuals—their talents, outlooks, and backgrounds—who made it, than to consider the possibility that the action of the moment arises out of considerations which *any* individual—or at least any within a wide range of talents, outlooks and backgrounds—would have found impelling. Research into international behavior thus tends to focus on the unique aspects and experiences of particular leaders, groups, or nations; on what attitudes and capabilities they bring to their roles rather than on the attitudinal and behavioral demands which the roles make of them.

Yet a strong case can be made for a contrary position that accords greater, or at least as much, potency to role as to individual variables. Human beings are not free-floating entities who respond compulsively and unpredictably to situations in terms of uncontrollable drives and needs. Rather, their drives and needs are tamed through socialization, and the counterargument thus asserts that throughout life most people learn and practice the habit of acceding to the major expectations of the roles they occupy. As has been persuasively argued (Brim, 1964), there is adult as well as infant socialization, which means, in effect, that individual variables are constantly giving way to, and being reshaped by, role variables. Stated differently, people act out their roles as well as their impulses. Those whose impulses lead them to resist the requirements of a role usually are removed from it or, much less frequently, bring about changes in it with the tacit or explicit consent of the holders of the expectations that comprise the role. Thus do families endure, impersonal organizations persist, societies cohere. Role phenomena, in other words, are a major reason for the fact that human affairs are characterized by constancy as well as variety.

The application of this line of reasoning to the conduct of foreign policy is easily made. Policy makers occupy roles in the same sense that being a father or a child constitutes occupancy of a role. Such positions embrace certain responsibilities that have to be performed and expectations that have to be met if their occupants are to remain in them. Whatever prior experiences an official may have had, and regardless of the outlooks and talents he may have previously developed, he has to make some adjustments which render his attitudes and behavior compatible with the formal and informal requirements of his policy-making responsibilities. It is the process whereby these adjustments are made that comprises the socialization of foreign policy officials. Note that the process encompasses a much more precise and limited set of phenomena than is usually associated with the general concept of socialization. It is not a lifelong process, but rather its duration is confined to the term of office. It begins not when a person is born, but when he takes up his duties as a foreign policy official and undergoes the attitudinal and behavioral changes that they require. Just as a man is not

8. A typical instance of this discrepancy can be found in Murphy (1964, pp. 380 and 382).

socialized into the role of father until children enter the family, so the socialization of foreign policy officials begins only after they enter upon their jobs.[9]

The importance of this process can be readily indicated. Presumably it is a primary reason why the broad bases of a nation's foreign policy do not ordinarily undergo profound change from one generation of leaders to the next. It has even been argued that the shift from the Stalin to the post-Stalin era in Russia did not produce significant change in Soviet foreign policy (Shulman, 1963). Likewise, to cite but one more of many examples that could be listed, presumably role-induced attitudes underlie the fact that, despite differences in temperament, party, and social background, all four postwar American presidents have been vigorous champions of the foreign aid program.

To be sure, personalities do vary and these variations are not necessarily filtered out by the requirements of role, as the argument for attributing greater potency to role variables would concede. Presidents and presidencies do differ and, no doubt, so do the performances of any two occupants of the same role. Every role allows *some* leeway for individual interpretation and it is in this area of the role that personality and background variables are operative. Indeed, it seems reasonable to presume that the higher a role is located in a political system, the fewer the formal and informal demands it will make of its occupant (thus, for example, an American President can probably pursue his personal policy preferences much further than can, say, a civil servant in the Department of State). Nevertheless, concludes the argument, this leeway for individual interpretation is extremely small compared to the attitudinal and behavioral requirements that high office imposed upon its occupants. Even the President must function within narrowly prescribed limits,[10] so much so that it would be easier to predict the behavior of any President from prior knowledge of the prevailing state of that role than from data pertaining to his past accomplishments, orientations, and experiences.

One thing is clear from the juxtaposition of these two contradictory lines of reasoning: the problem is essentially empirical and not philosophical.[11] It is not a matter of whether temperament and ideology lead the analyst to attribute more potency to individual or role variables, but rather a matter of what empirical data reveal to be the case. If they reveal, as seems probable, that both individual and role variables contribute to the attitudes and behavior of foreign policy

9. This point is somewhat overstated in order to differentiate the socialization of foreign policy officials from that of people in general. Of course, some socialization occurs even before officials occupy their roles. Through observing their predecessors-to-be and anticipating their own occupancy, officials can begin to undergo some of the changes necessary to perform the role before they actually assume it. Similarly, anticipatory socialization occurs in the case of the father when the existence of a pregnancy is verified and the requirements of the new role thereby become imminent.

10. As one advocate of this line of reasoning puts it, "The President may be the most powerful man in the country, but relatively speaking he has less control over his cabinet than a lowly VA section chief has over his clerks or a corporal over his squad" (Huntington, 1961, p. 148).

11. This point is a reversal of a position taken in an earlier essay (Rosenau, 1966, p. 44). At that time too much weight was accorded to the fact that there would always be some analysts who would reject quantitative findings indicating a high potency for role variables, and that they would do so by advancing a philosophy of history which ascribed primary potency to individual variables. While any findings would no doubt meet resistance of this sort, it now seems obvious that differences in potency are subject to empirical verification and that therefore the problem is not a philosophical one.

officials, the question is still an empirical one. For then the problem becomes one of determining whether one set of variables is more potent than the other, and to what degree.

Before turning to these empirical problems, let us briefly elaborate the key distinctions between individual and role variables implicit in the foregoing discussion. By an *individual* variable is meant any aspect of an actor which characterized him prior to his assumption of policy-making responsibilities and which did not necessarily characterize any other person who might have occupied, through election, appointment, or other means, the same position. Contrariwise, a *role* variable refers to any aspect of the actor derived from his policy-making responsibilities and which is expected to characterize any person who fills the same position. Thus both an individual variable and a role variable can be a behavioral trait, a possessed quality, or a mental orientation, depending on whether the trait, quality, or orientation was unique to the person or required by his position. An agile mind, a legal training, and an upper middle-class childhood are illustrative of the different types of individual variables that might characterize a high executive official of the United States, whereas a practice of consulting Congress, a lifelong record of accomplishment, and internationalist attitudes toward foreign policy exemplify role variables that might be inherent in his position. The key to the distinction is the word *necessary* in the foregoing formulation. An aspect of an official reflects individuality if there is no reason to presume that his predecessor or successor would have *necessarily* possessed a similar trait, quality, or orientation. Thus, even more concrete examples of individual variables would be the fact that Eisenhower was a Protestant Republican over sixty years of age who was educated at West Point, spent his earlier career in military service, and developed a deep commitment to a balanced federal budget, whereas Kennedy was a Catholic Democrat in his forties who was educated at Harvard, spent his adult life in elective politics, and developed a concern for the welfare of the underprivileged. That both men were whites over thirty-five, born in the continental United States, and committed to American participation in the North Atlantic community, on the other hand, is reflective of the state of the presidency at the time they occupied it in the mid-twentieth century.

It is worth emphasizing the notion that attitudes as well as behavior are conceived to be aspects of role. The idea that occupancy of a position requires a person to act in certain ways has long been accepted by social scientists, but the inclusion of the psychological processes which underlie behavior among the requirements of a role is less widespread. Since so much of politics involves the expression of attitudes, however, expansion of the concept to embrace this dimension serves as a valuable tool in explaining behavior that might otherwise seem inconsistent or hypocritical. When political actors move from being candidates to officeholders, from the opposition to the government, from minority to majority, from weakness to strength—to mention but a few of the more obvious instances—their perceptions of the world and its problems undergo profound change and even complete reversal. The change in role increases or lessens their responsibilities and thus alters their perspective on relevant objects in their environment, making these appear more or less salient, desirable, and manageable. Responsibility, so to speak, breeds responsibility, with the result that both men and nations become more broad-minded and less aggressive the more responsibility they acquire for the course of events.[12] Few, for example, would accuse an American President of hypocrisy if his inaugural address championed reduced tariffs even though earlier he had written his predecessor protesting tariff decreases on goods produced in his state. Such a reversal is extremely plausible in the context of role-induced attitude change, and it is in this sense that psychological processes are considered to be part and parcel of the requirements of office.

The inclusion of attitudes among role phenomena is often misinterpreted as indicating that a man is deprived of *all* freedom of choice and thought when he enters a new role. No such meaning is here intended. As previously suggested, a role is conceived to consist of three interrelated parts: its formal requirements, its informal requirements, and a range of choice within which the occupant can give expression to his talents, training, and convictions without either being removed from the role or bringing about significant changes in it. By *formal* role requirements is meant those aspects of a position which are constitutionally, statutorily, or in some other legal manner prescribed by the system in which the position is located. *Informal* requirements are conceived to be those behavioral and attitudinal prescriptions to which a role occupant must adhere, not because they have been recorded in the law books, but because they have evolved as unwritten norms which have, in political terms, the "force of law." It is true that, by definition, this conception makes the formal and informal aspects of a role deterministic. Its occupant *must* perform them, and if he is disinclined to do so, he *must* develop attitudes which, at the very least, do not prevent him from performing them. This is obvious in the case of the formal requirements, but it is no less the case for the informal requirements. There is nothing in the United States Constitution, for example, that says a Secretary of State must consult with allies abroad and members of Congress at home. Yet every Secretary of State since World War II has devoted considerable energy to both pursuits and there is every reason to expect that these informal requirements will continue to be inexorable parts of the office in the future.[13]

Notwithstanding the inexorable nature of the requirements, however, there does remain the third area of a role in which individual discretion is permissible. Here the occupant can not only express the capabilities and beliefs which are uniquely his own, but he can also exercise discretion with respect to the extent to which he wishes to press close to that outer limit of the role where he will either change the role or be removed from it. In addition, and no less important, the *range of choice* allows the individual some opportunity to decide which set of

12. Presumably the diminution of responsibility precipitates a contrary process, albeit the process would appear to be slowed by the experience of having once held greater responsibility. The criticism which former American Presidents make of their successors of the opposite party, for example, is never so unrestrained as that voiced by colleagues in their party who have not occupied the White House.

13. A recent instance of these requirements provides a good example of the extent to which a role can modify behavior and attitudes. Before he became Secretary of State, Dean Rusk delivered a series of lectures on the policy-making process and, in one of them, advocated an interpretation of the secretaryship in which its occupant should spend more time attending to matters at home and less to servicing alliances through travel abroad. By the time his secretaryship was several months old, however, Mr. Rusk logged a record number of miles of overseas travel. Subsequently he conceded this discrepancy between his advocated and actual behavior by observing that, "Fortunately, the lecture on the Secretary of State was not published" (U.S. Congress, 1961, p. 1285).

formal and informal requirements he will follow when those pertaining to two of the roles he occupies are in conflict. Only the Secretary of State, for example, can decide whether to favor allies or Congressmen whenever incompatibility develops between the formal or informal requirements of the two relationships. This area of individual discretion available to role occupants is perhaps even more clearly illustrated by the popular tendency to describe American Presidents as "strong" or "weak": such characterizations refer not to the physical prowess of those who reside in the White House, but to two alternative ways in which they interpret the requirements of, and resolve the conflicts among, the various roles they occupy as President.

In sum, it is only certain aspects of a role, and not the role itself, that deprives the occupant of choice. But, it must immediately be asked, how wide is this third area of policy-making positions? Is there greater room for individual discretion or are the opportunities for role occupants to express their talents and convictions few in number and narrow in scope? Posed diagrammatically, if the three aspects of a position are conceived as concentric circles, with the inner one representing the proportion of its scope covered by the formal requirements, the middle one the coverage of the informal requirements, and the outer one the range of free choice, will the position be more accurately portrayed by pattern A or B?

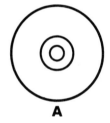 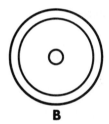

A **B**

So we return to the empirical problem. These questions cannot be answered conceptually, but only through the accumulation and analysis of data on a variety of policy-making roles. Many different ones must be examined, because the relative potency of role and individual variables is not likely to be the same in different political systems. Just as the leeway for individual discretion is probably greater the higher a position is located in a system, so it may be that the range of choice is greater for a top policy-making position the more democratic the system in which it is located. Likewise, the relative potency of role and individual variables may differ for developed and underdeveloped systems, the former type of system being more bureaucratized than the latter and thus more likely to have explicit and elaborate role requirements to which its policy makers must conform.[14] Before a general theory of foreign policy can be developed, in other words, separate theories of the international behavior of particular types of societies will have to be fashioned. The task of assessing relative potency is in reality a sequence of empirical problems, rather than a single problem.

Here, however, we have confined ourselves to an assessment of role and individual variables in one specific political system, that of the United States. Our

14. For a further discussion of how the relative potency of variables must be reranked to account for the degree to which a system is politically and economically developed, see Rosenau (1966, pp. 47–48).

method was that of quantitative historical comparison and our data were processed through the technique of content analysis.[15] The data themselves consist of the behavior of United States Senators in a particular foreign-policy-making role, that of friend or critic of the Secretary of State. Hypotheses were derived from their recurrent behavior in the years 1949–1952, when Dean Acheson occupied the secretaryship, and these were then tested in the 1953–1956 period, when the post was held by John Foster Dulles.[16] Henceforth we shall refer to the former as the "Acheson era" and to the latter as the "Dulles era," but it should be remembered throughout that our focus is on the behavior of Senators and not of Secretaries of State.

THE ACHESON AND DULLES ERAS COMPARED

It is not difficult to argue that the Acheson and Dulles eras were sufficiently similar in broad outline to justify use of quantitative historical comparison. The international environment toward which American foreign policy was directed did not undergo vast change during the eight-year period. The bipolar organization of world politics which emerged from World War II had not yet been undermined by either the fragmentation of the two blocs or the emergence of a coherent group of neutral nations. Although Stalin passed from the scene in the second month of the Dulles era, it was not until the end of that era that the policies of the Soviet Union turned from minimal involvement with the non-Communist world to reliance on foreign-aid programs, personal diplomacy, cultural exchange, and other non-military techniques to gain influence abroad. Cold War rivalry during Acheson's secretaryship and the first four years of Dulles's was conducted in essentially military terms. To be sure, the Korean War began in the middle of the Acheson era and ended early in the Dulles era, but the situation in the Far East was far from peaceful during the latter period even though American troops were not actually involved in combat. In addition, throughout both eras the United States had a clear-cut superiority in atomic weapons and the capacity to use them at long range. The problems—and changes —fostered by nuclear stalemate had yet to become manifest when that part of the Dulles secretaryship which concerns us came to a close.

The essential constancy of the international environment evoked an essentially uniform response from the United States throughout the eight-year period. Continuity rather than change marked the transition from the Acheson to the Dulles era. Both Secretaries repeatedly warned against the aggressive policies of the Communist world. Both sponsored efforts to strengthen and unify the network of alliances in which the United States became inextricably involved after World War II. Just as Acheson nurtured NATO into being, for example, so did Dulles encourage the formation of SEATO and other treaty arrangements which, like

15. A full discussion of both the procedures and categories employed to gather and organize the data will be found in Rosenau (1957, Chaps. 1–2 and Appendix I). So as to facilitate comprehension and evaluation of the material presented here, brief explanations of the major categories and the rules governing their use are provided in footnote form where appropriate.

16. In fact, Dulles held the post until early in 1959. But, in order to avoid the confounding effects of extraneous variables (such as those that are associated with a reelected administration), only the first four years of his secretaryship have been included in the comparison, thereby making the two periods equal in length and coterminous with one presidential term.

NATO, committed the United States to the defense of its allies in the event of attack.

Admittedly the two eras were sharply differentiated in terms of the rhetoric with which American policy was articulated. The Dulles era was marked by catchy slogans designed, apparently for domestic political reasons, to suggest that major policy innovations were being introduced. Such phrases as "agonizing reappraisal," "massive retaliation," "brinkmanship," and "liberation in Eastern Europe" were used for this purpose and in fact did represent new ways of describing the ends and means of American action abroad. Leaving aside their descriptive labels, however, the actual contents of the policies pursued in the Dulles era were not significantly different from those followed in the 1949–1952 period. As Hans Morgenthau put it,

Although Dulles consistently strove to make it appear that his foreign policies were different from, and superior to, the foreign policies of his predecessors, it is a historic fact that he essentially continued those very policies. Refusal to recognize the legitimacy of the *status quo* in [Eastern] Europe and defense of the *status quo* in [Western] Europe and elsewhere through containment, as well as foreign aid, were the cornerstones both of his and his predecessors' foreign policies (1961, p. 306).

Similarly, another close student of the secretaryship observed that,

Whatever may have been their abstract philosophies of international politics, both Acheson and Dulles met the pressing problems of their administrations with realism. With their Presidents, they gave more heed to the national security and to power politics than any secretary had since William Seward. Both spoke and acted from a conviction that the welfare of the nation can be served at this juncture in history only by power, ethically used, to prevent Soviet Russia from imposing on all a form of society in which ideals, ethics, and religion would be forever lost (Hill, 1963, p. 162).

Nor does the essential similarity between Acheson and Dulles end with the contents of the policies they sponsored. Both men were sons of ministers; both were born and brought up on the Eastern seaboard; both attended Ivy League colleges; both went through law school and eventually became partners in large firms specializing in corporation law. Perhaps even more important, both brought to the secretaryship extensive prior experience in the foreign affairs field at both the governmental and nongovernmental levels. Indeed, Dulles's previous tour of duty in officialdom included nearly two years as a special adviser to Secretary Acheson. Together the two men successfully conducted the negotiations which culminated in the ratification of the Japanese Peace Treaty by forty-eight nations in September 1951, and its acceptance by the United States Senate in March 1952 (see Cohen, 1957; Dunn, 1963).

The personal qualities of the two men, too, had much in common. Both were men of strong convictions. Both had agile minds and considerable forensic ability. Partly as a consequence of these qualities, the tenure of both men in the secretaryship was marked by stormy controversy. Neither, however, was abandoned by the President whom he served. They both consistently and unqualifiedly enjoyed the support and encouragement of their respective chiefs.

In short, a member of the Senate during the 1949–1956 period would have found it difficult to distinguish between the problems, policies, and activities of the two Secretaries of State. To be sure, their personalities were different and their style of administering the State Department and selling policies to the public and Congress diverged in notable respects.[17] However, in terms of the more basic stimuli, namely, the efforts of the Secretary of State to cope with a relatively constant and hostile international environment, Senators were similarly exposed during the Acheson and Dulles eras.

What, then, was the major difference between the two eras that permits us to assess the relative potency of role and individual variables? If the international environment, American policies towards it, and the Secretaries responsible for the policies were essentially comparable over the eight-year period, what factor was so sharply altered halfway through the period as to justify dividing it into two separate eras and analyzing the recurring behavior of Senators through quantitative historical comparison? The answer is simple. From the perspective of a Senator perceiving the conduct of American foreign policy, the major difference lay in the party affiliations of the responsible officials: for the first four years policy was formulated and implemented by a Democratic Secretary of State under a Democratic President, whereas a Republican Secretary of State under a Republican President shouldered the burden during the last four years.

That this shift in party responsibility facilitates an assessment of the relative potency of role and individual variables becomes readily apparent as we turn now to specifying—and defining operationally—which of the many variables that underlie the behavior of Senators have been contrasted. In order to simplify the analysis, only two role and two individual variables have been subjected to empirical examination. One of the role variables, which we shall call the *party role*, is of a general nature, while the other is highly specialized and will be known as the *committee role*.[18] The essential components of the former (party role) are conceived to be all the norms, both formal and informal, that have long obliged Senators to support the officials of the executive branch when it is controlled by their party and to criticize them when the opposition is in control. The latter (committee role) refers to all the expectations which require—as a consequence of informal and continuous contact with the personnel and problems of the State Department—Senators on the Foreign Relations Committee to feel that they have a special responsibility for defending the Secretary of State or at least avoiding excessive criticism of him in public. The two individual variables are also of a

17. Acheson is deemed to have been much more concerned about and attentive to the adequacy of decision-making processes in the State Department than was Dulles, whereas the latter was more sensitive to congressional demands for tougher action against "security risks" than was the former. Indeed, most biographers of Dulles emphasize that his greater readiness to cater to congressional sensibilities in this respect stemmed from a conscious effort to avoid some of the legislative difficulties which Acheson had experienced after Senator Joseph R. McCarthy precipitated wholesale attacks on the loyalty of department officials in February, 1950.

18. This is not to imply that these are the only role variables that can shape Senatorial orientations toward the Secretary of State. It may well be that, say, the representational role—which requires Senators to be attentive to the needs of their constituencies and the values of their regions—is equally or more important as a source of their behavior. Unfortunately, however, space limitations do not permit additional breakdowns that would facilitate a refinement of the analysis along these lines. Strictly speaking, therefore, it must be admitted that in measuring the potency of party and committee affiliations we may also be assessing the operation of other, unidentified role variables. On the other hand, the findings presented below are readily explicable within this framework and do not suggest the need to search for the influence of other variables. For an incisive discussion of the many other roles that legislators occupy, as well as of the applicability of the role concept to legislative behavior, see Wahlke, Eulau, Buchanan, and Ferguson (1962, pp. 7–28).

general and a specific kind. The former, which we shall call *personal policy beliefs,* takes two forms, a positive form in which the private convictions of a Senator generally correspond to the aforementioned foreign policies pursued in the Acheson and Dulles eras, and a negative form in which a Senator's views are essentially contrary to the general policy line followed by the two Secretaries. The specific individual variable, consisting of what will be called *personalizing tendencies*, also takes a positive and a negative form. The former encompasses the inclinations of Senators to commend the Secretary's personal qualities as well as, or even apart from, his performances. The negative form of personalization refers to the practice whereby Senators find fault with the Secretary's personal qualities or condemn him as a symbol of evil forces at work, irrespective of whether or not they criticize him for his actions or his failures to act.

Plainly, both the general role and individual variables were operative for every Senator during the Acheson and Dulles eras.[19] Senators were either Democrats or Republicans[20] and they generally either agreed with or dissented from the containment policies pursued by the Secretary of State. The simultaneous operation of two of these variables thus placed every Senator in a conflictive position in at least one of the eras: during the Acheson era a conflictive situation was experienced by Republicans with positive policy beliefs and Democrats with negative policy beliefs, whereas Democrats with positive policy beliefs and Republicans with negative policy beliefs underwent the same conflict during the Dulles era. Republicans on the Foreign Relations Committee and Democrats with negative personalizing tendencies were exposed to an additional dimension of conflict during the Acheson era, as were Democratic Committee members and Republican personalizers during the Dulles era.[21]

19. I am indebted to Leroy N. Rieselbach for posing the question of whether this point is as self-evident as I have suggested. Noting that the importance of partisanship declined markedly when the "man-above-party" Eisenhower replaced the "hard-hitting" Truman in the White House, Rieselbach queries the propriety of presuming that the definition of the party role remained constant throughout the eight-year period. Without disputing the historical accuracy of this observation, its relevance to the formulation developed here seems doubtful. There can be no question that Eisenhower's presidency did introduce a nonpartisan tone into the conduct of party competition, but there is no evidence that this tone was so dominant as to drown out the basic expressions whereby Senators indicate their party loyalties. Certainly this was not the case with Eisenhower's Secretary of Agriculture, Ezra Taft Benson (see Adams, 1961, Chap. 11). A period of nonpartisanship may allow a Senator to agree with the policies of the opposition, but surely it is not in itself sufficient to permit an obfuscation of party lines to the point where he is inclined either to praise his opponents for their behavior or to criticize the performances of the executive leaders of his own party. "We can do it better" is a time-honored theme of party competition that even the cordiality of the Eisenhower years did not diminish, and it is this theme that underlies the definition of the party role used here.

20. There was one exception: Wayne Morse of Oregon, who was a Republican in the first four Congressional sessions examined, an Independent in the next two, and a Democrat in the last two. To simplify statistical analysis, however, here the middle phase has been ignored and Morse's standing as a Democrat is assumed to have spanned the entire Dulles era.

21. It should be noted that under four specialized (and rare) conditions, a Senator could have either avoided or undergone these conflicts during both eras. If in late 1952 or early 1953 he changed party allegiances, received an assignment to the Foreign Relations Committee, reversed his personal policy benefits, or acquired personalizing tendencies, then he would have avoided or undergone, depending on the direction of the shifts, simultaneous exposure to conflicting variables throughout the eight-year period. Only the first two of these conditions, however, have been accounted for in the ensuing analysis. Although Senator Morse's change of party affiliation and the assignment of new members to the Foreign Relations Committee

How Senators resolved these conflicts depended on whether role or individual variables were more potent. It will be recalled, however, that to assess their potencies we must first examine the data of the Acheson era. To formulate hypotheses at this stage in the analysis would be to engage in little more than guesswork. Knowledge about how policy makers resolve conflicts between their jobs and their beliefs is too scant to permit such a procedure. But if the data of the Acheson era suggest hypotheses which can be tested in the Dulles era, then the method of quantitative historical comparison can be used to good advantage. Fortunately this is the case.

DERIVING THE HYPOTHESES: THE ACHESON ERA

The data of the Acheson era have been summarized elsewhere (Rosenau, 1959) and their major patterns need only be noted here. Of the hundred and twenty-one persons who served in the Senate during the thirty-six legislative months of the 1949–1952 period, ninety-two Senators engaged in some behavior with respect to the Secretary of State[22] and, of these, thirty-four engaged in recurrent behavior.[23] This latter group, which we shall henceforth designate the Articulates, consisted of only 28 per cent of the Senate membership, but it recorded 89 per cent of the 3,502 references to Acheson made on the floor of the Senate during his secretary-

in 1953 is a matter of historical record, alterations in personal policy beliefs and personalizing tendencies are not so easily identified and are much less likely to occur. Perhaps a profound religious revelation or a traumatic psychological experience can produce sharp changes in certain kinds of personal convictions, but political beliefs are not usually the subject of such changes, at least not in the United States. To be sure, personal political beliefs can, as noted above, undergo permanent alteration as a result of adult role socialization, but alterations arising out of this source are of course merely an indication of the potency of role variables. Hence for the purposes of this inquiry it seems reasonable to presume that any differentiation in the patterns of criticism or approval which Senators exhibit in the two eras stem from role considerations rather than from sudden shifts in personalizing tendencies or personal beliefs.

22. It is perhaps of interest that one of these was John Foster Dulles, who held a Senate seat for four months in 1949 and who made five references (defined below) to Acheson, of which two were classified as favorable and three as neutral.

23. This behavior was "observed" in the *Congressional Record* and consisted of everything Senators said about the Secretary during recorded debate for the four-year period. The unit employed to measure the behavior was a "reference" and any Senator who served more than ten legislative months during the Acheson era and who averaged more than 0.07 references per month was considered to have engaged in recurrent behavior. The limits of a reference were determined by the limits of five mutually exclusive categories corresponding to the ways in which Senators identified Acheson as an object in their environment. That is, a reference is not equatable to every time Acheson's name was mentioned by a Senator. Rather *one* reference was defined as existing whenever a Senator mentioned *one* personal quality, or *one* performance, or *one* authority of Acheson's, or *one* symbol-collectivity performance or quality, or *one* of three complexes subsumed under a residual category. (Only the first, second, and fourth of these categories are relevant to the ensuing analysis and their nature is noted below in footnote 24.) Thus a reference might be a word, a phrase, a sentence, or several paragraphs in length (by procedural definition; however, it could not be longer than one column of the *Congressional Record*). In addition to being coded in substantive categories, each reference was also categorized in terms of whether the quality, performance, authority, and such, appeared to be cited by the Senator in favorable, unfavorable, or neutral terms. For the exact rules governing the coding of references in each substantive and directional category see Rosenau (1957, pp. 26–43, 847–854).

TABLE 1. *Distribution of References by Party in the Acheson Era (in Percentages)*

	(N)	Favorable	Unfavorable	Neutral	Total
Republicans	(2,665)	5	70	25	100
Democrats	(837)	48	6	46	100

ship. Of the total references, 15 per cent were classified as favorable, 55 per cent as unfavorable, and 30 per cent as neutral. The references to *personal* qualities were substantially fewer (18 per cent) than those that were made to Acheson's *performances* (61 per cent).[24]

That these raw data lend themselves to the formulation of hypotheses becomes immediately apparent when they are broken down in terms of party affiliation. Far from engaging in similar behavior, the Republicans and Democrats sharply diverged in both quantity and quality of their reactions to Acheson. Stated succinctly, the Republicans were both more active and more hostile with respect to him than were the Democrats: while Republicans comprised only 45 per cent of the Senators, they accounted for 76 per cent of the total 3,502 references and 97 per cent of the 1,921 unfavorable references. On the other hand, the Democrats were considerably more cordial toward Acheson, accounting for 74 per cent of the 537 favorable references. These differences between the parties are depicted even more sharply in Table 1, which presents a directional breakdown of the references made by each group.

Hardly less distinctive are the patterns discernible in the data for the seventeen Senators of both parties who served on the Foreign Relations Committee during this 1949–1952 period. Of their 526 references, 45 per cent were classified as favorable, 9 per cent as unfavorable, and 46 per cent as neutral. This amounts to much greater cordiality toward Acheson than that exhibited by the 104 Senators who were not members of the committee, 10 per cent of whose 2,976 references were recorded as favorable, 63 per cent as unfavorable, and 27 per cent as neutral.

While the foregoing patterns suggest hypotheses that ascribe greater potency to role than to individual variables, further inspection of the data indicate that the patterns are not as one-sided as they may seem at first glance. Sufficient differentiation can be discerned within the ranks of each party to suggest that individual variables are not totally lacking in potency. These intraparty phenomena are especially manifest in the reference patterns of the twenty-four Republican and ten Democratic Senators who engaged in recurrent behavior, and thus it is to these Articulates that we now turn our attention.

24. The distinction between personal qualities and performances has been adapted from Parsons and Shils (1952, p. 57). References in which Senators identified Acheson in terms of what he *was*, *is*, or *should be* were classified in the personal qualities category, whereas those to what he *did*, *does*, or *should do* were treated as performance references. If Senators identified the Secretary neither as a complex of personal qualities nor as a complex of performances, but as a symbol of some phenomenon or collectivity (the "Acheson approach" or the "Dulles crowd") such identifications were treated as separate references. However, since the symbol-collectivity references were not too numerous and apparently stemmed from the same sources as did those to personal qualities, the presentation here has been simplified by combining them into the personal qualities category.

TABLE 2. *The Articulates in the Acheson Era (1949–1952).*

Senator	Party	References per Month of 1949-52 Senate Tenure	Total References to the Secretary of State	Proportion of References Recorded as			Proportion of Favorable References of Cordial Senators, or of Unfavorable References of Hostile Senators, to			Form of Hostility or Cordiality
				Favorable	Unfavorable	Neutral	Personal Qualities	Performances	Other Aspects	
THE HOSTILE ARTICULATES										
Welker	R	1.0	16	—	100.0	—	43.7	31.2	25.1	Ind.
Jenner	R	5.8	210	—	96.2	3.8	20.3	58.9	20.8	Ind.
McCarthy	R	9.0	324	—	95.4	4.6	38.9	53.7	7.4	Ind.
Malone	R	9.6	346	—	90.8	9.2	12.4	63.7	23.9	Ind.
Dirksen	R	1.6	26	—	84.6	15.4	22.7	63.6	13.7	Ind.
Taft	R	2.3	82	—	84.1	15.9	14.5	81.2	4.3	Ind.
Bridges	R	2.2	79	—	83.5	16.5	34.9	45.4	19.7	Ind.
Wherry	R	8.8	264	0.4	79.1	20.5	16.3	57.9	25.8	Ind.
Kem	R	4.1	149	—	78.5	21.5	23.1	57.3	19.6	Ind.
Capehart	R	1.6	58	—	77.6	22.4	20.0	66.7	13.3	Ind.
Bricker	R	0.8	28	—	75.0	25.0	23.8	71.4	4.8	Dis.
Brewster	R	2.4	88	9.1	69.3	21.6	8.2	82.0	9.8	Ind.
Mundt	R	1.6	58	1.7	69.0	29.3	17.5	72.5	10.0	Ind.
Langer	R	1.4	51	11.8	60.8	27.4	12.9	61.3	25.8	Ind.
Cain	R	3.5	127	5.5	58.3	36.2	8.1	82.4	9.5	Dis.
Knowland	R	3.6	130	7.7	54.6	37.7	4.2	80.3	15.5	Dis.
Ferguson	R	1.9	68	—	47.1	52.9	3.1	84.4	12.5	Dis.
Morse	R	2.8	99	10.1	45.5	44.4	2.2	71.1	26.7	Dis.
Watkins	R	2.2	80	1.3	43.7	55.0	2.9	97.1	—	Dis.
McCarran	D	1.0	35	2.9	37.1	60.0	7.7	92.3	—	Dis.
Donnell	R	2.4	47	—	34.0	66.0	—	100.0	—	Dis.

TABLE 2—Continued.

THE CORDIAL ARTICULATES

Benton	D	3.8	98	75.5	2.1	22.4	21.6	43.2	35.2	Ind.
McMahon*	D	1.2	44	75.0	—	25.0	42.4	42.4	15.2	Ind.
Pepper	D	0.7	14	71.4	—	28.6	60.0	40.0	—	Ind.
Lehman	D	2.1	54	68.5	—	31.5	32.4	46.0	21.6	Ind.
Vandenberg*	R	1.8	44	69.2	—	31.8	53.3	26.7	20.0	Ind.
Humphrey	D	1.7	62	66.1	—	33.9	46.3	24.4	29.3	Ind.
Connally*	D	4.1	146	54.1	—	45.9	43.0	39.2	17.8	Ind.
Wiley*	R	1.4	51	49.0	—	51.0	28.0	56.0	16.0	Ind.
Lucas	D	2.8	55	46.5	—	54.5	4.0	52.0	44.0	Dis.
Fulbright*	D	1.6	57	40.4	17.5	42.1	39.1	8.7	52.2	Ind.
Hickenlooper*	R	1.5	54	35.2	27.8	37.0	84.2	5.3	10.5	Ind.
Kefauver	D	0.9	32	25.0	18.8	56.2	—	62.5	37.5	Dis.
Smith (N.J.)*	R	1.3	48	20.8	14.6	64.6	30.0	50.0	20.0	Ind.

Key: *Member of the Committee on Foreign Relations. R = Republican; D = Democrat; Ind. = Indiscriminate (more than 10 per cent of directional references classified in the personal qualities category); Dis. = Discriminate (less than 10 per cent of the directional references classified in the personal qualities category).

As can be seen in Table 2, the Articulate Republicans engaged in three distinct forms of behavior. Four of them made more favorable than unfavorable references (a pattern that shall henceforth serve as our operational definition of *cordial* behavior and as the distinguishing characteristic of Cordial Senators). All the other Articulate Republicans engaged in *hostile* behavior (operationally defined as more unfavorable than favorable references and hereafter attributed to Hostile Senators), but differed considerably in the extent to which they confined their hostility to Acheson's performances. Thirteen did not distinguish Acheson the actor from Acheson the person and registered more than 10 per cent of their unfavorable references in the latter category, behavior which shall henceforth be defined as *indiscriminate* hostility. On the other hand, seven Hostile Republicans directed their criticism largely at Acheson's actions and made only a minimum (less than 10 per cent) of their unfavorable references to his person. Hereafter we shall refer to this pattern of criticism as *discriminate* hostility. Needless to say, it is highly relevant that *all* four of the Cordial Republicans and none of their twenty Hostile colleagues were members of the Foreign Relations Committee.

Although not nearly so pronounced, differentiation can also be discerned among the ten Articulate Democrats listed in Table 2. One of them (McCarran) diverged from the general cordiality of Democrats towards Acheson and recorded a pattern of discriminate hostility. Among the Cordial Democrats, moreover, a notable distinction can again be drawn between those who confined their reactions to Acheson's performances and those who engaged in the positive form of personalization. Using the same operational cutoff point employed in the case of Hostile Senators,[25] two of the Cordial Democrats engaged in what shall be called *discriminate* cordiality by directing a preponderant proportion of their praise at Acheson's performances and having less than 10 per cent of their references coded in the personal qualities category. On the other hand, seven of the Cordial Democrats were not so selective in their approval and indicated support of Acheson as both an actor and a person. Indeed, not only did seven Democrats engage in *indiscriminate* cordiality (as we call the behavior of Cordial Senators who directed more than 10 per cent of their favorable references at the Secretary's personal qualities), but five of them praised Acheson's person as much as or more than they did his performances. It is noteworthy that among these latter five were all three of the Articulate Democrats who held seats on the Foreign Relations Committee.

Eleven main hypotheses have been derived from these data for the Acheson era. The first seven arise out of the initial indication that, in general, role variables are more important than individual variables. Let us consider first the party role. It seems highly doubtful that the Republicans and Democrats would have engaged in such sharply different behavior, both quantitatively and qualitatively, if personal policy beliefs had been the predominant variable. Private convictions

---

25. It must be emphasized that the use of this cutoff point is not founded on the imputation of a magical quality to the quality of 10 per cent. Such a percentage is an arbitrary demarcation which was employed by way of permitting a more concrete analysis of what were regarded as significant, albeit relative, differences among the Hostile and Cordial Articulates. It was employed because it happened to fall approximately at the midway point in the widest gap near the center of the distribution of the two groups of Articulates, and thus it more nearly separated them then would have any other percentage.

can arise out of a variety of sources and experiences, and although some differences in the social backgrounds of Republicans and Democrats have been uncovered (Matthews, 1960, Chap. 2), these are not so great as to suggest a rationale that would systematically link the differences to the differential party behavior that was directed at Acheson. In the absence of such a rationale, it seems reasonable to presume that on chance grounds alone, the Hostile and Cordial Articulates would have been more equally divided among Senators from both parties if individual variables had been the prime source of behavior. To be sure, party affiliation and personal policy beliefs can often be mutually reinforcing, but to view such a process as operative in this case necessitates a presumption that Republican legislators personally rejected the postwar policy of containment, that Democratic Senators uniformly approved it, and that therefore the same patterns which prevailed in the Acheson era would also be manifest in the Dulles era. Such reasoning however, violates common sense. As indicated by the continuity of American foreign policy through the Truman and Eisenhower administrations, the two parties were not so far apart in their general orientations for all Senators to have found reinforcement for their personal beliefs in the party alignment of the 1949–1952 period. Rather it makes far greater sense to interpret the data as indicating that the potency of the party role was sufficient to lead Senators of both parties to subordinate those personal beliefs which were contrary to role requirements, with the result that Republicans voiced repeated criticism of the Secretary of State or avoided praising him while, to a lesser extent, Democrats either registered approval or avoided registering disapproval. Accordingly, keeping in mind the premise that American foreign policy was essentially the same in both eras, it is now possible to derive our first four predictions about the distribution of the data to be expected during the 1953–1956, or Dulles, period. We shall call them the "party hypotheses," and they would seem to be self-evident if our comprehension of the Acheson era is sound and the attribution of greater potency to the party role thus proves accurate:

Hypothesis 1: Democrats were more active with respect to Dulles than were Republicans (they averaged significantly more[26] references per month of Senate tenure than did the Republicans and they also had a higher proportion of their group among the Articulates than did the Republicans).

Hypothesis 2: Republican Senators engaged in more cordial behavior with respect to Dulles than did their Democratic colleagues (the former averaged a significantly greater excess of favorable over unfavorable references than did the latter).

Hypothesis 3: Republican Senators engaged in cordial behavior with respect to Dulles (they averaged a significantly greater number of favorable than unfavorable references to him).

Hypothesis 4: Democratic Senators engaged in hostile behavior with respect to Dulles (they averaged a significantly greater number of unfavorable than favorable references to him).

26. That is, "significantly more" in the statistical sense, by which is here meant the .05 level of probability ($P < .05$). Henceforth such words as *more, less, greater,* and *fewer* will be used only if the comparison will be or was tested in this way. Stated differently, an hypothesis will be viewed as confirmed only if the data are so clearly distributed in the predicted direction that the probabilities of such a distribution occurring by chance are less than five out of one hundred.

But the potency of the party role is not absolute. The findings of the Acheson era plainly indicate that the requirements of *party* affiliation are susceptible to modification when they conflict with those of the *committee* role. The close association of the Secretary and Senators on the Foreign Relations Committee, along with the sense of responsibility committee members acquire as a result of participating in the State Department's deliberations, apparently give rise to a set of expectations that are strong enough to restrain committee members in the opposition party from fulfilling the demands of their party role. Indeed, the committee role would seem to be so potent that it also leads members who are in the Secretary's party to feel especially obliged to come to the defense of both his policies and his person. This interpretation brings us to the next set of predictions, which we shall call the "committee hypotheses" and which are not so obvious:

Hypothesis 5: Members of Foreign Relations Committee were more cordial toward Dulles than were non-members (the former averaged a significantly greater excess of favorable over unfavorable references than did the latter).

Hypothesis 6: Democrats on the Foreign Relations Committee were less hostile toward Dulles than were Democrats not on the committee (the former averaged a significantly smaller excess of unfavorable over favorable references than did the latter).

Hypothesis 7: Republicans on the Foreign Relations Committee were more cordial towards Dulles than were Republicans not on the committee (the former averaged a significantly greater excess of favorable over unfavorable references than did the latter).

Hypothesis 8: Republicans on the Foreign Relations Committee were more indiscriminately cordial towards Dulles than were Republicans not on the committee (the former averaged a significantly greater number of favorable references in the personal qualities category than did the latter).

The task of deriving hypotheses pertaining to the operation of individual variables is not an easy one. That such variables are potent under certain conditions is clear from the presence of one Democrat (McCarran) among the Hostile Senators and from the fact that thirteen Republican Senators extended their criticism to embrace Acheson's personal qualities. The opposition party role encourages its occupants to voice criticism of the Secretary, but certainly it does not require Senators to engage in *indiscriminate* hostility. Presumably such behavior stems from individual factors which incline Senators to go beyond the opposition party role. What these factors are and how they operate, however, is far from clear. Negative personalization may have stemmed from unusually strong negative policy beliefs. Or it may have stemmed from a variety of background and personality variables that were in no way linked to personal policy beliefs. The difference between these two sources is extremely important because they lead to different and contradictory predictions about behavior in the Dulles era.

Let us first consider personal policy beliefs as a source of negative personalizing tendencies. To posit such a linkage is to make the not implausible assumption that when opposition to a set of policies is very intense, criticism becomes emotional and extends beyond the policies themselves to everything that is associated with them. Under circumstances of high attitudinal intensity, in other words, Senators are sufficiently agitated to fuse the contents and the makers of policy into an indistinguishable mass and, in so doing, to engage in behavior which goes well beyond the necessities of their role as members of the opposition party. Viewed in this way, the indiscriminate hostility toward Acheson can be interpreted as having been undertaken by a few remaining Republicans who still clung to the hope that prewar "normalcy" could be restored, and whose personal policy beliefs were therefore so strongly opposed to the postwar extension of American commitments that they could not contain their discontent within the requirements of their party role. If this was the source of their behavior, such Senators were not likely to be any more impressed with a Secretary from their own party than they were with Acheson. Certainly their strong policy beliefs would have prevented them from shifting to the ranks of the Cordial Articulates. Rather, at most, the requirements of their new party role would have had no greater effect than to induce them to remain passive[27] and, at least, it probably would have had the effect of removing the indiscriminate dimension from their hostility. Furthermore, if it is assumed that the residue of longing for prewar normalcy was limited to a handful of Republicans, whose party had once been identified with such a state of affairs, then it also follows that Democrats would not tend to hold personal policy beliefs strong enough to produce indiscriminate hostility toward Dulles. Additional support for this derivation is provided by the presence of only one Democrat among Hostile Senators in the Acheson era.

The foregoing line of reasoning gives rise to two "individual hypotheses" that the data for the Dulles era ought to confirm:

Hypothesis 9: Republicans among the Hostile Articulates were discriminate rather than indiscriminate in their hostility towards Dulles (their average proportion of unfavorable references in the personal qualities category was not significantly greater than 10 per cent).

Hypothesis 10: Democrats among the Hostile Articulates were discriminate rather than indiscriminate in their hostility toward Dulles (their average proportion of unfavorable references in the personal qualities category was not significantly greater than 10 per cent).

Quite a different prediction, however, results if indiscriminate hostility is viewed as stemming from a variety of background and personality characteristics that are unrelated to policy beliefs and that are spurred by—or at least not inhibited by—the opposition party role to produce an especially aggressive mode of criticism. If this is the case, then Dulles' replacement of Acheson was bound to have a significant effect on those Republicans who possessed one or another of these characteristics. Such Senators were likely to find other outlets for their personalizing tendencies, because their new party role restrained them from expressing hostility and either encouraged them to engage in cordiality toward Dulles or permitted them to turn to other matters and remain passive with

27. Sustained hostility toward Acheson is one form such passivity could take. Checked by their new role as members of the new Secretary's party, these Republicans may have found an outlet for their strong negative policy beliefs by continuing to blame Acheson for everything that had happened, was happening, and would happen. A separate record of the references to Acheson during the Dulles era was kept and is noted in the analysis of the data.

respect to him.[28] In addition, if this interpretation is correct, then it must be further assumed that the advent of the Dulles secretaryship relieved Democrats who possessed similar characteristics from the obligations of their opposition party role and allowed them to engage in indiscriminate hostility. While Democrats may not have held policy beliefs strong enough to result in negative personalization, there is no reason to assume that they differed from Republicans in their susceptibility to whatever nonpolicy variables might encourage such behavior. Accordingly, a third "individual hypothesis" was derived:

Hypothesis 11: The Hostile Articulates consisted only of Democratic Senators who were indiscriminate rather than discriminate in their hostility toward Dulles (the Hostile Articulates did not include any Republicans and the average proportion of unfavorable references recorded in the personal qualities category by its Democratic members was significantly greater than 10 per cent).

Although hypotheses 9 and 10 on the one hand and hypothesis 11 on the other are mutually exclusive, neither of the rationales on which they are based is so compelling as to warrant eliminating either the former or the latter. On the contrary, our comprehension of the sources of negative personalization is so scanty that they seem equally logical. In the absence of any basis for choosing between the two interpretations, therefore, it seems preferable to adopt the less rigorous procedure of letting all the hypotheses stand and seeing which are upheld by the data of the Dulles era.

It will be noted that in neither the derivation of hypotheses 9 and 10 nor in the interpretation leading to hypothesis 11 have we treated indiscriminate hostility as symmetrical with indiscriminate cordiality. The sources of negative personalization may be obscure in the data for the Acheson era, but at least some reasonable speculation as to its nature proved possible. This is not the case with respect to the positive form of personalization. Beyond the conclusion that the committee role conduces to indiscriminate cordiality (hypothesis 8), we are not able to discern any other factors that foster such behavior. Conceivably the same individual variables that underlie indiscriminate hostility are also operative for those at the cordial extreme, but there is nothing in the data that justifies hypothesizing such a symmetry. Hopefully, the dynamics of indiscriminate behavior will become more manifest as we turn now to the data for the Dulles era.[29]

TESTING THE HYPOTHESES: THE DULLES ERA

The data comprising Senatorial behavior toward Dulles are presented in Table 3 and analysis of them resulted in confirmation of seven of the hypotheses, while three were not confirmed and one was actually negated. Those that were

28. The additional possibility noted in the previous footnote is also relevant here. Republicans with personalizing tendencies may have found that Acheson continued to serve as a useful focus of their intense hostility.

29. It must be emphasized that following the basic rule of quantitative historical comparison, the data for the Dulles era were not inspected by the researcher until after the analysis up to this point was written. Well-trained student assistants had previously gathered the data (using the same rules of procedure as were employed for the earlier study of the Acheson era), but all eleven of the hypotheses were derived before the data were examined.

Senator	Party	References per Month of 1953-56 Senate Tenure	Total References to the Secretary of State	Proportion of References Recorded as			Proportion of Favorable References of Cordial Senators, or of Unfavorable References of Hostile Senators, to			Form of Hostility or Cordiality
				Favorable	Unfavorable	Neutral	Personal Qualities	Performances	Other Aspects	
THE HOSTILE ARTICULATES										
Jenner	R	1.9	60	—	91.7	8.3	16.4	80.0	3.6	Ind.
Malone	R	3.3	106	6.6	82.1	11.3	9.2	73.6	17.2	Dis.
Fulbright*	D	2.3	72	9.7	76.4	13.9	12.7	81.8	5.5	Ind.
O'Mahoney	D	1.3	41	2.5	70.7	26.8	10.3	86.2	3.5	Ind.
Morse*	D	4.3	137	7.3	61.3	31.4	14.3	78.6	7.1	Ind.
Douglas	D	2.3	72	16.7	59.7	23.6	11.6	83.7	4.7	Ind.
McCarran	D	2.7	43	11.6	58.2	30.2	4.0	88.0	8.0	Dis.
Humphrey*	D	8.4	268	19.0	57.5	23.5	3.2	93.5	3.3	Dis.
Lehman	D	1.7	53	17.0	52.8	30.2	7.1	89.3	3.6	Dis.
McCarthy	R	2.3	74	17.5	51.4	31.1	—	100.0	—	Dis.
Gillette*	D	1.2	20	25.0	50.0	25.0	—	100.0	—	Dis.
Bricker	R	2.0	65	36.9	41.6	21.5	7.4	88.9	3.7	Dis.
Mansfield*	D	4.9	157	33.8	40.1	26.1	3.1	90.6	6.3	Dis.
Langer*	R	2.3	75	38.7	40.0	21.3	10.0	90.0	—	Dis.
THE CORDIAL ARTICULATES										
Thye	R	0.8	26	88.5	—	11.5	17.4	60.9	21.7	Ind.
Ferguson*	R	1.4	23	78.3	—	21.7	—	77.8	22.2	Dis.
Hicklenlooper*	R	0.9	29	75.9	—	24.1	18.2	63.6	18.2	Ind.
Wiley*	R	5.3	168	75.6	—	24.4	22.8	70.9	6.3	Ind.
Knowland*	R	3.6	116	74.1	2.6	23.3	22.1	74.4	3.5	Ind.
Smith (N.J.)*	R	7.1	228	71.9	1.3	26.8	12.8	76.2	11.0	Ind.
Capehart*	R	1.0	31	71.0	—	29.0	9.1	72.7	18.2	Dis.
Neuberger	D	0.7	11	54.5	18.2	27.3	—	100.0	—	Dis.
Dirksen	R	1.1	34	53.0	2.9	44.1	50.0	38.9	11.1	Ind.
Cooper	R	1.2	21	47.6	19.1	33.3	20.0	70.0	10.0	Ind.
Sparkman*	D	1.1	34	47.0	11.8	41.2	12.5	75.0	12.5	Ind.
Kefauver	D	1.8	56	41.1	28.5	30.4	—	100.0	—	Dis.

Key: *Member of the Committee on Foreign Relations. R = Republican, D = Democrat; Ind. = Indiscriminate (more than 10 per cent of directional references classified in the personal qualities category); Dis. = Discriminate (less than 10 per cent of directional references classified in the personal qualities category).

confirmed included two party (2 and 4), three committee (5, 7, and 8), and two individual (9 and 10) hypotheses. Two party (1 and 3) and one individual (11) hypothesis comprised those that were not confirmed by the data. The fourth committee hypothesis (6) was not only not confirmed, but in fact the data were significantly arrayed in the opposite direction from the one that had been hypothesized. Before interpreting these findings, let us outline them in greater detail.

Although the pattern of activity in the Dulles era was sharply different from that which marked the Acheson era, the differences did not conform to the expectation (contained in hypothesis 1) that Senators in the opposition party would be more active than those in the Secretary's party. Of 2,531 references to Dulles, 1,282 were made by Democrats and 1,249 by Republicans. In absolute terms, the former were more active than the latter, but this difference did not prove to be a statistically significant one ($t = .024$; $df = 119$).[30] Furthermore, of the twenty-six Senators who formed the Articulates in the Dulles era,[31] fourteen were Republicans and twelve were Democrats, a difference which was neither significant ($\chi^2 = .159$; $df = 1$) nor in the predicted direction.

TABLE 4. *Distribution of References by Party in the Dulles Era (in percentages)*

	(*n*)	Favorable	Unfavorable	Neutral	Total
Republicans	(1,249)	52	22	26	100
Democrats	(1,282)	21	50	29	100

In terms of their evaluative content, on the other hand, the reference patterns did yield important distinctions between the two parties. The prediction (2) that the Republicans would be more cordial toward Dulles than would the Democrats was amply confirmed by the data ($t = 2.70$; $df = 119$; $P < .01$); the former accounted for 71 per cent of the 925 favorable references, whereas the latter tallied 70 per cent of the 918 unfavorable references. Stated in comparative terms, the mean Republican excess of favorable over unfavorable references was 6.31, whereas the equivalent figure for the Democrats was −6.32. A further measure of the effects of the role shift occasioned by the Dulles era is provided by the contrast between the directional breakdown of the references made by each group (Table 4) and the equivalent data for the Acheson era (Table 1).

Yet, for reasons noted below, the anticipated performance of the party role

30. Except as indicated in the one case when a chi square (χ^2) test was more appropriate to the question being asked (because proportions rather than means were being compared), a *t*-test was used throughout to assess statistical significance. Tables indicating when different values of t and χ^2 are significant for various degrees of freedom (*df*) can be found in any textbook on statistics.

31. These twenty-six Senators comprised 21 per cent of the one hundred and twenty-one persons (sixty-one Republicans and sixty Democrats) who served in the Senate during the thirty-two months of the 1953–1956 period and they accounted for 80 per cent of all the references to Dulles. It will be recalled that the equivalent figures for the Acheson era involved thirty-four Articulates who constituted 28 per cent of the Senate and made 89 per cent of the references.

was not confirmed as fully as the foregoing might suggest. The expectation that the Republicans would engage in cordial behavior with respect to Dulles (hypothesis 3) was not upheld by the data. Although they averaged more favorable than unfavorable references, the difference did not prove to be significant ($t = 1.55$; $df = 61$). The Democrats, on the other hand, did conform to expectations (hypothesis 4) by engaging in hostile behavior toward Dulles. Their mean of 10.6 unfavorable references was significantly greater than their mean of 4.4 favorable ones ($t = 2.88$; $df = 60$; $P < .01$).

With one important exception, the data pertaining to the committee role were patterned along the lines that had been hypothesized. The expectation (hypothesis 5) that the nineteen Senators who served on the Foreign Relations Committee during the 1953–1956 period[32] would be more cordial toward Dulles than the one hundred and two Senators who were not members of the committee was plainly upheld by the findings: the former averaged 14.3 more favorable than unfavorable references, whereas the equivalent mean for the latter was -2.5. This difference proved to be a significant one ($t = 2.69$; $df = 122$; $P < .01$). Stated in the same form as the findings for the Acheson era cited above (p. 33), the committee members had 47, 27, and 26 per cent of their 1,329 references to Dulles classified as, respectively, favorable, unfavorable, and neutral, whereas the equivalent figures for the 1,202 references made by non-members were 25, 47, and 28 per cent. Similarly, the predictions that Republican committee members would be both more cordial (hypothesis 7) and more indiscriminately cordial (hypothesis 8) than Republican non-members were confirmed by the data. While the former averaged 44.8 more favorable than unfavorable references, the mean difference for the latter was -1.2, and the difference between these means was indeed significant ($t = 5.12$; $df = 61$; $P < .001$). Likewise, the greater indiscriminate cordiality of Republican committee members is evident in the difference between the mean of 8.6 favorable references which they recorded in the personal qualities category and the equivalent figure for non-members of 0.6. This difference also proved to be significant ($t = 5.40$; $df = 61$; $P < .001$).

On the other hand, the behavior of the Democrats on the Foreign Relations Committee was strikingly contrary to what had been anticipated (hypothesis 6). They were not less hostile toward Dulles than their fellow Democrats, but, in fact, the mean difference between their favorable and unfavorable references indicated significantly greater hostility: the mean for the nine committee members was -19.7, while that for the fifty-two non-members was -3.9 ($t = 2.73$; $df = 59$; $P < .01$).

As for the individual variables, the findings support the interpretation (hypotheses 9 and 10) that personal policy beliefs would lead both Republicans and Democrats to engage in hostile behavior, but that in neither case would the beliefs be so strong as to foster indiscriminate hostility. In the Dulles era the Articulates consisted of fourteen Hostile Senators and twelve Cordial ones. The former group was composed of nine Democrats and five Republicans. While four of the Democrats and one of the Republicans compiled a record of indiscriminate hostility (Table 3), in each case the margin of unfavorable references

32. Two Republican Senators joined the committee in 1954 and one Democrat joined it in 1955. In the statistical calculations, the references for these Senators were broken down in terms of the years in which they were made and allocated to the committee and non-committee totals accordingly.

in the personal qualities category was only slightly in excess of 10 per cent, so that the over-all averages for both the Democrats and the Republicans conformed to the predictions set forth in hypotheses 9 and 10 and failed to uphold the expectation contained in hypothesis 11. That is, neither the Democrats nor the Republicans in the Hostile Articulate group averaged significantly more than 10 per cent of their unfavorable references in the personal qualities category ($t = 1.53$; $df = 8$ for the former, and $t < 1$; $df = 4$ for the latter). On the contrary, the average for both groups was actually less than the cutoff point: the nine Democrats averaged 7.4 unfavorable references to Dulles's personal qualities and the equivalent figure for the five Republicans was 8.6.

Several other aspects of the data contained in Table 3 need to be pulled together and noted. Particularly relevant is the fact that all five of the Hostile Republicans in the Dulles era had engaged in indiscriminate hostility during the Acheson era. Likewise, we shall have occasion to comment on the fact that five of the nine Hostile Democrats were members of the Foreign Relations Committee.[33] Pertinent, too, is the finding that of the nine Republicans among the Cordial Articulates, six were members of the committee[34] and four of the six engaged in indiscriminate cordiality.

Although not covered by any hypotheses or included in Table 3, one other set of findings can usefully be summarized before we attempt to interpret the data. As previously indicated, a record of the references to Acheson during the Dulles era was kept and these reveal some interesting and highly relevant patterns. All told, forty Senators made 284 references to Acheson during the 1953–1956 period. Of these, 12 per cent were classified as favorable, 73 per cent as unfavorable, and 15 per cent as neutral. Democrats accounted for 19 per cent of all the references, 85 per cent of the favorable references, 5 per cent of the unfavorable references, and 37 per cent of the neutral references. Contrariwise, Republicans made 81 per cent of all the references, 15 per cent of the favorable references, 95 per cent of the unfavorable references, and 63 per cent of the neutral references. Most notably, 172 unfavorable references, or 83 per cent of all the unfavorable references, were made by the eleven Republican Senators who continued to hold a Senate seat in the Dulles era, after having engaged in indiscriminate hostility during the Acheson era.[35] Indeed, four of these eleven Senators actually made more unfavorable references to Acheson than to Dulles during the 1953–1956 period.

INTERPRETING THE RESULTS

Interpretation of empirical findings is rarely easy. Only when every prediction is upheld by the data does interpretation become simple. Under such circumstances the researcher needs merely to restate the reasoning that led to the

33. Of the four other Democrats on the committee, one engaged in indiscriminate cordiality and the other three did not engage in sufficient behavior to be classified among the Articulates.

34. One of the four other Republicans who served on the committee was indiscriminately hostile and the other three were insufficiently active to be grouped with the Articulates.

35. Only Wherry and Kem of the thirteen Republicans who were indiscriminately hostile toward Acheson did not serve in the Senate during the 1953–1956 period. The former died in 1951 and the latter lost a bid for reelection in 1952.

predictions and emphasize that the empirical data demonstrate its validity. Such complete validation, however, is usually confined to situations in which the various parts of a theory have been previously tested and refined. Otherwise it is an extraordinary, and perhaps even a suspicious, event when an entire series of hypotheses is confirmed. Knowledge of the behavior of public officials is far from the point where each hypothesis in a complex framework is proven accurate by the distribution of previously unexamined data.

Considered in this context, the fact that four of our hypotheses failed of confirmation is not as discouraging as it might otherwise seem. The fact that seven were confirmed indicates that the rationale for ascribing greater potency to role rather than individual variables has considerable merit. On the average, Senators from both parties did reverse themselves and behave differently toward Dulles than they had toward Acheson. The shift to the opposition role did lead the Democrats to engage in hostile behavior. The contrary shift did result in the Republicans being more cordial toward Dulles than were the Democrats, and it also appears to have curbed the personalizing tendencies of the most hostile Republicans. Members of the Foreign Relations Committee did engage in behavior which distinguished them from other Senators, albeit in the case of the Democratic committee members, the nature of their distinctive behavior was quite unexpected.

Furthermore, the general reasoning which gave rise to the predictions is not undermined by the two party (1 and 3) and one individual (11) hypotheses that were not confirmed. These three findings can be readily explained without altering the ascription of greater potency to role than to individual variables. In the case of hypothesis 1, which was unlike all the others in that it dealt with the quantitative dimension of Senatorial behavior, it is now clear that we erred in presuming that role variables shape the extent of behavior in the same way that they affect its direction. No doubt there is some relationship between the quantitative and qualitative dimensions of policy-making roles, but there is no reason to assume that the relationship is a simple one in which high activity is associated with hostility and low activity with cordiality. More important, whatever the nature of the relationship, it is not of central concern here. Our attempt to assess the relative potency of role and individual variables would hardly have been hindered if hypothesis 1 had not been formulated in the first place.

Nor does the failure of hypotheses 3 and 11 present a serious problem. In both cases such a result was logically necessitated by the confirmation of other hypotheses. It will be recalled that hypothesis 11 was explicitly posited as contrary to 9 and 10, so the fact that it was not upheld is not so much a failure as a confirmation of an alternative line of reasoning. The confirmation of hypothesis 9, moreover, necessitated the failure of hypothesis 3. The latter predicted that the Republicans would be cordial toward Dulles, a prediction which could not have been supported if, as anticipated in hypothesis 9, strong policy beliefs led a segment of Republican ranks to continue the hostility toward the Secretary of State which had marked the Acheson era. If hypothesis 11, which reasoned that other than strong policy beliefs underlay the negative personalization, had proven valid, then such Republicans would not have sustained their hostility and hypothesis 3 would have been confirmed. As it was, these Senators siphoned off some of their antagonism by continuing to berate Acheson throughout the

Dulles era. If they had not made 172 unfavorable references to Acheson during the four years *subsequent* to his secretaryship, probably their behavior toward Dulles would have been much more hostile than it was, and hypothesis 3 might then have been negated rather than simply not confirmed. In other words, the fact that hypothesis 3 was not confirmed serves as a measure of the extent to which the potency of role variables can be offset by the strength of individual variables, but at the same time the fact that the data for hypothesis 3 were arrayed in the predicted direction (though not significantly so) rather than reversed is an indication of how role considerations can mitigate and redirect individual tendencies.

Of course, there does remain the need to adjust our assessment of role and individual variables to the fact that hypothesis 6 was reversed. This is an important finding. No logical relationship between the hypotheses can be cited to explain the fact that Democrats on the Foreign Relations Committee actually compiled a record of substantial hostility toward Dulles. Clearly, our conception of role variables must be adjusted to account for this wholly unexpected result.

But this finding can also be viewed as an opportunity—as a chance to deepen our comprehension of the interplay between role and individual variables beyond what it would have been if all the hypotheses had been confirmed. For the lesson of hypothesis 6 is plain: we assumed too readily that the requirements of the committee role operate similarly upon all Senators who enter it. The data make it clear that in fact the requirements are subject to reinterpretation under special conditions. Note that we do not view the data as indicating that there are conditions which will make the requirements of committee membership subject to replacement by individual variables. Such an explanation might be justified if hypothesis 6 had merely fallen short of confirmation. In this event one might have concluded that no systematic differences prevailed between Democratic committee members and Democratic non-members, and that therefore the role requirements did not overcome the individual inclinations of Democratic Senators. However, and to repeat, hypothesis 6 was not only not confirmed, but it was negated. There was a significant difference between Democratic committee members and Democrats not on the committee, only the difference was one in which the latter were less hostile toward Dulles than were the former. Hence, even though different than those which prevailed in the Acheson era, role requirements, and not individual variations, can be presumed to have been operative. Unless individual variables functioned identically for all the Democrats on the committee during the Dulles era, a highly unlikely circumstance, the significance of the difference uncovered by the data could only mean that role variables were operative.

An examination of the content of the unfavorable references made by Democratic members of the Foreign Relations Committee provides at least a partial explanation of their unexpected behavior. Repeatedly, and vigorously, they complained about Dulles's manner of dealing with the committee. They contended that he either misinformed the committee or failed to keep it informed, and that instead he used other means of enunciating new departures or interpretations of American foreign policy. In effect, a recurring theme of their unfavorable references was that they were being used—rather than consulted—by the Secretary of State. The following excerpts from reactions to a single episode are typical of the way committee Democrats expressed their annoyance:

MR. MANSFIELD: Mr. President, the Secretary of State has set in motion a review and reappraisal of the foreign policy of the United States. I do not know whether that was his intention when he gave an interview to a reporter for *Life* magazine. It seems to me that if it were, he might have found a more appropriate method. If he wished to discuss the achievements of American foreign policy with the public, he had only to request an open hearing with the Committee on Foreign Relations (U.S. Congress, 1956, p. 971).

MR. HUMPHREY: If the *Life* magazine article is correct as to what Mr. Dulles's role was in the Indochina war, then the Secretary misinformed the Senate Committee on Foreign Relations. I was present during his testimony, and I say that Mr. Dulles had better say to this Congress that he told the truth to the Foreign Relations Committee or that he told the truth to the reporter for *Life* magazine, because he cannot have both stories. He cannot have *Life* magazine's report of his role in Indochina and, at the same time, his testimony before the Foreign Relations Committee, because they are diametrically opposite. I say regretfully that they are unalterably opposed (U.S. Congress, 1956, p. 394).

MR. FULBRIGHT: If there is anything to a bipartisan policy, it means co-operation between the administration and the legislative branch, so that the people of the country may be enlightened and their support enlisted. The Senator from Montana (Mansfield) and I do not get the same attention in the press as does the administration, and if we tell the people one story and the Secretary of State tells a different story, it creates an impossible situation for us (U.S. Congress, 1956, p. 974).

The recurrence of comments such as these suggest that hypothesis 6 was reversed, not because Democrats on the Foreign Relations Committee were resistant to the requirements of their role, but because they felt, rightly or wrongly, that Dulles's behavior altered their role requirements and relieved them of the responsibility to defend him in public. As previously indicated, the informal requirements of the committee role derive from special opportunities to participate in the making of foreign policy and the sense of responsibility that is fostered by the chance to work closely with the Secretary of State. Convinced that Dulles had not permitted these conditions for the performance of the role to come into being, the Democrats on the committee had even more reason to be critical of him than the non-members of their party, and they thus compiled a record of greater hostility than did other Democrats.

Additional support for this explanation of the outcome of hypothesis 6 is provided by the fact that the Democrats on the committee evidenced a keen awareness of the requirements of the role and a deep regret that they could not abide by them. Time and again they referred to the excessive Congressional criticism of Dulles' predecessor and to the need to give the Secretary of State the benefit of any doubt. In the end, however, the restraints of the committee role gave way to the perception that Dulles had failed to provide justification for restraint. Both the conflict and its resolution is plainly manifest in this typical observation:

MR. FULBRIGHT: . . . I have no desire to vilify a Republican Secretary of State, as a recent Democratic Secretary of State was vilified because he did not reverse every world current that was adverse to America. Apart from the wrong to the person involved, we have seen all too clearly how this kind of partisanship makes the whole of America its victim. What we want and what we will support is the truth, however unpleasant. What we want and what we will support is a Secretary of State who will not treat us as children ready to clap in delight at every fairy story, however fanciful. What we want and what we will support is a Secretary of State who will come to us, not with packaged solutions to every ill that plagues the world, but who will come to us, instead, with a statement of facts about the nature of those ills. Such a Secretary of State would win our respect for his courage, and for the respect he himself showed the truth (U.S. Congress, 1956, p. 3369).

Presumably the repeated expressions of this conflict would not have occurred if individual rather than role variables had underlain the reversal of hypothesis 6.

CONCLUSIONS

Since they involve an intricate series of assumptions and procedures, quantitative historical comparisons are bound to give rise to questions about the validity, relevance, and generalizability of the findings which they generate. What has been measured? How accurate are the measurements? What do they mean? Such questions always seem especially pertinent when a quantitative study comes to an end, and this inquiry is no exception: Do the findings demonstrate that role variables are more potent than individual variables for all kinds of foreign policy officials, or only for United States policy makers? Indeed, should our conclusions be limited only to Senators, or is it appropriate to presume that, say, officials of the executive branch are as circumscribed by role considerations as are their counterparts in the Congress? And what about the limited relevance of Senatorial behavior toward the Secretary of State? Is it not possible that the relative potency of role and individual variables would have been different, or even reversed, if reactions to more salient and central objects in the international environment, such as the Soviet Union or NATO, had been examined?[36]

It will be recalled that the answer to the first two of these questions had already been indicated. Yet it bears repeating that we have assessed the potency of role and individual variables only with respect to the foreign policy officials of one society in a limited historical period. One can think of other policy-making systems, particularly underdeveloped ones, that would not be likely to reveal, if analyzed in the same way, such potency accruing to role variables.

But does not this finding also emphasize that our assessment is limited to Senatorial posts and inapplicable to the behavior of all American foreign policy

36. A host of more specific questions also come to mind: Is the behavior of Senators on the Senate floor an adequate sample of their total behavior? Are not their activities outside the Senate chamber just as significant and, if so, what happens to the findings if, as is quite possible, such activities are different from and somewhat contrary to those that transpire on the floor of the Congress? In addition, by quantifying references in the way we did, have we not measured such irrelevant characteristics as loquaciousness, seniority, and illness rather than the potency of individual and role variables? Unfortunately, space limitations do not permit consideration of these more specific types of questions. However, a discussion of them can be found in Rosenau (1957, Chap. 1).

officials? Here the answer is less clear. Strictly speaking, we have dealt only with legislative roles. The tasks Senators perform as makers of foreign policy are not the same as those undertaken by officials in the State Department and other executive agencies. By definition, both formally and informally, the legislative approach to foreign affairs is more partisan and less intellectual than the executive approach, and thus an assessment of executive positions might well yield a different balance of relative potency than the one uncovered here. On the other hand, it must also be noted that interpretations of the leeway for individual discretion in a role are, at least in part, culturally derived, and that, to the extent that this is the case, two officials in the same political culture will be similarly inclined to place role requirements ahead of individual preferences, even though the requirements be legislative in one instance and executive in the other. The formal and informal responsibilities of Senators and high State Department officials, in other words, differ in a variety of important ways, and for most analytic purposes these differences are crucial; but, in the absence of relevant data, it does not seem inappropriate to generalize upon the findings of this study and to presume that the potency of role variables is equally great for foreign policy makers in both branches of the government.

As for the question of whether this conclusion would have to be altered if reactions to more salient objects in the international environment had been examined, here again the case can be argued along contradictory lines. Certainly it is true that Senatorial behavior toward the Secretary of State is of limited significance compared to most of the activities in which foreign policy officials engage. The daily press may make much of Congressional antagonism to the Secretary and his colleagues in the State Department, but in fact neither the content of policies nor the course of events are likely to be greatly affected by such matters. Furthermore, there are a multitude of choices which foreign policy officials have to make that do not involve their standing as Republicans or Democrats. If less partisan and more important forms of behavior had been investigated, therefore, the analysis might have revealed a different set of potencies accruing to role and individual variables.

On the other hand, it must also be observed that the conflicts between role and individual variables examined here are of a classic kind and in certain respects closely resemble many of the choices which foreign policy officials are called upon to make. At a higher level of generalization, we examined the question of how policy makers adjust to external changes which result in contradictions between objects in the environment that had been harmoniously linked prior to the changes. We found that policy makers do not accept the disharmony created by the changes and instead achieve balance by acquiescing to the requirements of role variables. In the absence of data on other types of behavior, it thus seems appropriate to presume that such a conclusion would hold up for a wide range of activities in addition to the reactions of Senators to the Secretary of State. Given the change occasioned by De Gaulle's divisive policies in NATO, for example, the findings of this inquiry point to the prediction that American policy makers would minimize their personal preferences with respect to De Gaulle or France and would instead engage in behavior that was consonant with the requirements of the role of a NATO member. Or take the change which occurred when two allies of the United States, Greece and Turkey, threatened each other over Cyprus. It would seem that American officials reacted not in terms of their personal beliefs as to where the blame should be placed, but rather in terms of the requirements of their role as allies of both parties to the dispute. Such a reaction is not inconsistent with the patterns revealed by the data analyzed here. Similarly, to take a third situation, when a duly elected regime is overthrown by a military junta in a country on which the United States relies for support against Communist advances in Asia or for contributions to the Alliance for Progress, the requirements of the role of military ally in Asia or of socioeconomic ally in Latin America usually leads American policy makers to put aside their individual distaste for the downfall of democratic institutions. Again,

such behavior is predictable on the basis of how Senators reacted to a Democratic and Republican Secretary of State.

Ideally, of course, these generalizations upon the findings of this inquiry should themselves be tested empirically. As previously indicated, the validity of an interpretation depends upon the degree to which a consensus prevails among other researchers, and doubtless these generalizations would be more widely accepted if additional data were available to support them. In the absence of such data, however, it is hoped that the findings of this study will incline more researchers to proceed on the basis of the general assumption that role variables are substantially more potent than individual variables insofar as the makers of American foreign policy are concerned. Or, if this is asking too much, then hopefully the findings might at least spur efforts to treat clashes between role and individual variables as an important source of international political behavior.

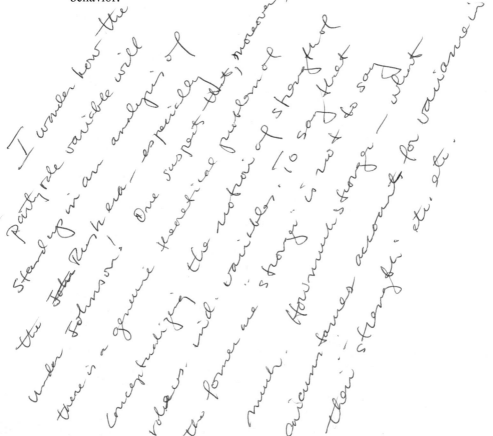

Chadwick F. Alger

Interaction in a Committee of The United Nations General Assembly[1]

INTRODUCTION

Scholars have devoted much attention to the significance of public sessions in international organizations for both the practice of diplomacy and the condition of relations between nations. They have not, however, taken much account of the dramatic way in which "public diplomacy" provides them with greater access to the phenomena they are studying than is the case with more traditional diplomacy. The access consists of opportunities both for observation and for direct contact with participants. This paper will be concerned primarily with observation. As an exploration in the systematic collection of observational data on a main committee of the U.N. General Assembly, it is part of a larger effort to study the political process in the United Nations.

The research data described here were collected in 1962. At that time the seven main committees of the General Assembly—all committees of the whole—each had a hundred and ten nations as members. The committees are the setting in which the major work of the General Assembly is achieved, and their decisions are, for the most part, later accepted by plenary sessions of the Assembly. The members of the committees are seated at spots designated by their nation's name on two large horseshoe desks, one located inside the other. National delegations are seated in alphabetical order, with each nation moving five places

1. Data for this paper were collected while the author was Visiting Professor of United Nations Affairs at New York University. Generous research support for this professorship was provided by the Rockefeller Foundation. Analysis of the data was made possible by a grant from the Carnegie Corporation to the International Relations Program of Northwestern University. Valuable research assistance was contributed by Dr. Robert Weiner of New York University and Mrs. Jean Jacobsohn, Mrs. Lucille Mayer, and Mr. Allen Wilcox of Northwestern. I am grateful to Professors Harold Guetzkow, Kenneth Janda, and Raymond Tanter of Northwestern University for helpful criticism.

51

to the right at the first session of each week. One person from each delegation sits at a desk, each of which is equipped with a microphone, with other members of his delegation seated directly behind him.

The observer of the main committees of the Assembly, and other public United Nations bodies as well, soon becomes aware that two kinds of activity are simultaneously taking place before his eyes. There is a continuous flow of *public* debate heard by all in the room, and there are frequent *private* conversations between two or more delegates that are only heard by those involved. The public debate consists of prepared general statements on each agenda item followed by statements introducing resolutions and amendments and discussion of these, sometimes concluding with voting and explanation of votes. As the debate on an item proceeds, it tends to pass through a cycle in which the earlier portion often consists of monotonous statements and restatements of national positions, often addressed to audiences outside the committee room. Only the final stage includes interchange that can be called debate. It is clear to the observer that much debate and discussion has gone into the drafting of resolutions and development of support for them that is not voiced in the public debate.

Only occasionally do all the members of a committee focus their attention on the public speaker. As in other parliamentary bodies, members daydream, read, nap, and engage in chitchat with their neighbors. They also move about the chamber talking to other colleagues. Although public debate is the ostensible purpose for a committee meeting—indeed, it cannot meet if delegates are not willing to speak—members come not only to hear the speeches but also to carry on private negotiation and to circulate among other members in order to keep in touch with what is going on. Chairmen recognize the importance of private conversation when they try to keep the debate going in a committee at times when delegates are reluctant to inscribe their names on the speaker's list. Usually the chairmen do not believe that yet another public speech will help the committee reach consensus, but they do believe that, while the committee is in session, private lines of communication are established and members are encouraged to work on committee problems.

Therefore, as in all parliamentary bodies, the fate of items on agendas of General Assembly committees is affected not only by public debate, but also by private debate, negotiation, and discussion in and out of the committee chamber. Outcomes are affected by the characteristics of the parliamentary society that develops around the concerns of a committee, such as the nature of the internation communication system, development of leadership roles, availability of expertise, and length of time participants have served together. Outcomes, in terms of effects on relations among member nations, are not always revealed by votes and may not be reflected in public debate at all. It is not uncommon for a delegate to begin a speech like this: "While my delegation is not completely happy with the resolution, we have agreed to support it, because it appears to be the most feasible arrangement under existing conditions. Therefore, in the spirit of cooperation . . . ." Such statements often come after hours of negotiation in small groups, efforts to obtain support of informally circulated alternative draft resolutions, regional group meetings, and frantic pleas to foreign offices for changes in instructions.

But the political scientist finds his efforts to study this process time-consuming and expensive, even after establishment of the personal contacts necessary for gathering data. One problem is that certain aspects of the political process may have to be studied as they occur, because participants tend to forget and over-rationalize past behavior in response to interviews administered sometime after events occur. But it is exceedingly difficult for a researcher to study an issue as it is processed by a committee. Which of the over one hundred members should he contact? Should he extend his contacts to include additional members as the process moves forward? Since the more he knows the more he can find out, how can he increase knowledge before talking to contacts? Research reported here explores how intensive observation can help answer such questions.

The first task is to describe briefly the milieu of the Fifth Committee. Then the 3,475 observed interactions in the Fifth Committee are analyzed in terms of: (1) relation of interaction to the legislative process, (2) interactions of individual nations, (3) relation of interaction to national public speaking, (4) regional group interaction, (5) relation between group interaction and voting, (6) relation between non-committee roles of individuals and interaction, and (7) relation between individual reputation for being capable and informed and interaction. While attempting to limit exposition to moderate length, an effort will be made to offer richness in describing the context of observed interactions. Hopefully, readers will be enabled to join in the development of strategies for generating significant knowledge from observation of parliamentary behavior.

THE FIFTH COMMITTEE MILIEU

The observational data reported here were collected during the meetings of the Administrative and Budgetary Committee (Fifth Committee) of the U.N. General Assembly in the fall of 1962. This committee held seventy meetings between October 1 and December 20. With the exception of two night meetings in the last two weeks of the session, meetings were held at 10:30 A.M. and 3:00 P.M. The length of sessions ranged from half an hour to three and one-half hours, with most sessions lasting two to three hours.

In order to collect data, all but one of the sessions of the committee were attended,[2] the observer sitting in the first row of the press section, which is approximately ten feet from delegate seats on one side of the outer horseshoe desk. The activities of the observer included recording in a notebook: (1) length of public speeches; (2) participants in private conversations, length of each conversation, and name of initiator; and (3) number of delegates in attendance for each nation. In addition, the observer held conversations with delegates whenever they approached him in the chamber. A record of these conversations reveals a hundred and sixty-seven with delegates from twenty-seven nations. Activity also included contact with delegates between sessions in corridor, lounge, bar, and dining room. Outside the committee room, conversations were held with forty-seven members of the committee. Of these, twenty-two were contacted three or more times. Although this paper focuses on observations made in the committee chamber, conversations with delegates in and outside the chamber helped in relating observed behavior to the wider political process, and offered some information about the content of private conversations in the chamber.

2. In the midst of the Cuban missile crisis, one meeting was missed because of attendance at a Security Council meeting. Some members of the Fifth Committee also attended.

In the 1962 fall session, the work of the Fifth Committee ranged from routine details of Secretariat operations to highly controversial and widely reported decisions on the financing of peace-keeping operations.[3] All resolutions passed by the committee were accepted by the plenary. In December the committee voted to "accept" the advisory opinion of the International Court of Justice declaring that all members were obligated to pay assessments levied against them to cover expenses for peace-keeping operations in Suez and the Congo.[4] The committee also approved continued expenditures for the Suez and Congo operations, proposed the establishment of a Working Group of Twenty-one to study problems of peace-keeping finance, and passed a resolution calling for a special session of the General Assembly devoted solely to financial problems of the organization. The committee had a debate on geographic representation in the Secretariat, controversy centering on the appropriate methods for insuring that all member nations were adequately represented and on the preference of some nations for having a higher percentage of fixed term appointments in contrast to career appointments.

The more routine business of the committee included budget estimates for the coming year, supplementary budgets for the current year,[5] reports from auditors, appointments of members to administrative and budgetary subsidiary bodies, and miscellaneous administrative and personnel problems. In much of the debate on these items, the committee, displaying attitudes typical of national parliamentary committees, gave microscopic examination to the expenditures of international bureaucrats under its scrutiny: Are these printing charges out of line? Do we really need a new telephone exchange in the Geneva headquarters? Why don't all members of the Secretariat travel economy class? Although delegates from all parts of the world engaged in a game intended to keep the Secretariat economy-minded, budgetary debate revealed deep disagreement whenever expansion of the scope of United Nations activities arose. The poorer nations of Africa, Asia, and to some degree Latin America, continually pushed for an extension of the services of the organization to members, while the Soviet Union and Eastern European countries resisted. The smaller developed nations tended to be supportive of the underdeveloped nations, with the larger developed nations less supportive, but not overtly as negative as the Soviet group. Thus, the Fifth Committee debates on administrative and budgetary issues are also discussions in which members define the role of the organization.

Though all nations in the United Nations are members of each main committee, there is much variation in the interest different nations demonstrate in particular committees. Because the work of the seven main committees is conducted simultaneously, small delegations may have difficulty being present at all meetings. A count of number of *delegates* present was made in the middle of forty-two of the Fifth Committee sessions under observation, and the number present ranged from seventy to 148. But because some nations are always represented by more than one delegate, the number of *nations* represented varied from

3. Summary records of the debates may be found in United Nations, General Assembly, Seventeenth Session, Fifth Committee, *Official Records*, 914th meeting to 983rd meeting (Oct. 1 to Dec. 20, 1962).

4. The advisory opinion is published in *ICJ Reports*, 1962, pp. 151–181.

5. See Singer (1961, pp. 96–121) for more detailed discussion of the role of the Fifth Committee in the United Nations budget process.

forty-five to 105. The number of delegates present surpassed one hundred (approximately seventy nations) on only one third of the occasions on which attendance was taken. Attendance rose and fell in cycles related to progress being made with items on the agenda, with the high figure of 148 reached on December 12, when the committee voted on the advisory opinion of the International Court of Justice.

Daily attendance for most nations involves one or two delegates, with the major powers often having three or four present and sometimes as many as five. The United States offers an example of how division of labor within a delegation may occur when there is high representation. A Senator or member of the House of Representatives usually sits in the Fifth Committee, delivering all major speeches and handling most of the public debate. He is advised by one or two members of the U.S. Permanent Mission who prepare speeches and handle most of the contact with other delegations. Depending on the specific issue being debated, one or two advisers from the State Department may be present. If they have had United Nations experience, or if they stay for a number of weeks, they, too, may get involved in relations with other delegations. A nation that can afford to assign a number of persons to a committee has advantages over those which cannot. Such a nation has more opportunities to keep in touch with what other nations are thinking and doing, has more chance to influence other delegations, and has a greater supply of manpower for devising proposals consistent with its interests. On the other hand, in a fast-moving parliamentary process, a four or five man team may have difficulty in coordinating and in presenting a consistent image of their nation's intentions. This may produce misunderstandings with other delegations that sometimes engender lack of confidence.

Eighteen of the seventy meetings were observed primarily to learn the identity of committee members. Therefore, the 3,475 interactions[6] included in the analysis that follows were recorded during the last fifty-two meetings of the committee. In recording interactions, it was possible to identify ninety-one delegates by nation and actual name and thirty-four by nation and coded name designation. Thus a total of 125 delegates were identified.

It is certain that interactions were missed, particularly very short ones between delegates who were sitting next to each other in locations distant from the observer. Those missed because of distance from the observer are probably rather evenly distributed among the committee membership because of the five-place weekly rotation of seats of nations. A few interactions were also missed when the observer occasionally talked with delegates as they walked past. Such opportunities were always given priority over observation because of their importance in providing information needed in interpreting interaction data. Discussions with participants took only three of the 137 hours spent in observing the committee.

The 3,321 interactions resulted from 2,840 interaction situations in which the number of participants ranged from two to nine. Where there were more than

6. This total, and the analysis that follows, includes the interactions of 96 nations. The remaining 14 nations engaged in a total of only 13 interactions. The total also includes the 167 interactions of the observer which, distributed among 27 nations, are included in the nation totals. In cases where total number of interactions is reported as 3,321, these interactions have been excluded.

two participants in an interaction situation, it was broken up into all possible pairs for counting purposes. The frequency distribution of number of participants in interaction situations is as follows:

2 participants	2,662	situations
3 participants	158	situations
4 participants	16	situations
5 participants	1	situation
6 participants	1	situation
8 participants	1	situation
9 participants	1	situation
Total	2,840	situations

Interactions take place between delegates sitting next to each other, by a delegate getting up and going over to the seat of another delegate, or by a discussion that takes place at a spot in the committee room other than at the seat of one of the participants. Fifth Committee delegates did most, although not all, of their talking at the seat of one of the participants:

At own seat	3,995
At seat of another	1,611
Another place in room	1,028
Total	6,634

Since these figures are on individual participants, N is $2 \times 3,321$, or 6,642, with 8 unknown.

INTERACTION AND THE LEGISLATIVE PROCESS

In a highly informative description of United Nations parliamentary activity two delegates comment: "Frequently formal meetings are used chiefly as a place where individual delegates can be reached at a certain time so as to arrange informal meetings." They also observe that these "informal" meetings sometimes take place "at the back of the committee chamber itself" (Hadwen and Kaufmann, 1962, p. 50). But there are very few references in the literature to private conversation in public diplomacy and no systematic analysis. A UNESCO study of *The Technique of International Conferences* (1951) contains a lengthy check list of potential subjects for systematic study of international conferences that even extends to nonverbal communication. But there is an intriguing oversight in the fact that many conferences have a simultaneous two-level dialogue and no recognition of the fact that national units in international conferences often have more than one spokesman. It is even more surprising that a search of the conference literature, including the experimental literature in other areas of social behavior, also reveals no recognition of the simultaneous two-level phenomenon.

The widely known social interaction analysis of Bales could be utilized for analysis of public debate; yet his categories cannot be used for analysis of interaction data, because the content of conversations is not known (Bales, 1950).

This makes the one known exception, a 1938 paper by Garland C. Routt, all the more remarkable. He recorded contacts of eleven members of the Illinois Senate during the first fifteen minutes of each hour the body was in session, a total of eighty-six sample periods.[7] As a result of discussions with Senators, he found a "general estimate" that at least seventy-five per cent of conversations on the floor of the Senate were about legislation. He concluded from "preliminary inspection of the tabulations" that "contacts tended to center around individuals who by other indices were shown to play important roles in the process of legislation" (Routt, 1938, p. 132).

No estimate of the percentage of Fifth Committee private conversation that was related to issues before the committee has been made, but the observer was drawn to those delegates playing important roles in the legislative process by discerning who was very active in private conversation. The observer's judgment is that those delegates taking initiative requiring them to leave their seats were most involved in drafting and obtaining support for legislation and in working for a committee consensus.

It is difficult to go beyond the contributions of Routt in relating to the legislative process interaction data that do not include the content of conversations. There may be some advantage, however, in working with data from continuous observation over long periods of time, in contrast to samples of portions of meetings. When a delegate who has previously been inactive starts a round of conversations, the observer is stimulated to develop hypotheses about new developments that are not yet (and perhaps never will be) reflected in the public debate and to direct questions to participants about these inferences. For example, during the debate on the International Court of Justice advisory opinion, a Ceylon delegate suddenly became active as follows:

11:25 a.m.	Ceylon to Czechoslovakia
11:29 a.m.	Ceylon to U.S. No. 2
11:31 a.m.	Ceylon to U.S. No. 1
11:42 a.m.	Ceylon to Czechoslovakia
11:44 a.m.	Ceylon to Czechoslovakia
11:45 a.m.	Ceylon to U.S. No. 3
11:45 a.m.	Ceylon to Czechoslovakia, both proceed to an adjacent small conference room and are joined by U.S. No. 3
12:29 p.m.	Czechoslovakia and U.S. No. 3 return to the committee room

This pattern suggests, in the light of knowledge of the issues being debated,

7. Although their work is not based on observation in legislative chambers, the work of Samuel Patterson (1959) and Wayne L. Francis (1962) on state legislators and Alan Fiellin (1962) on the New York delegation to the U.S. House of Representatives have common concerns with Routt and the author of this paper. Particularly relevant is Francis' effort to obtain information on interaction patterns of state legislators through interviews.

that Ceylon is trying to mediate disagreements between the United States and the Soviet group. Armed with such evidence, the observer can say to a participant, "What kind of compromise is Ceylon trying to achieve between the Soviet group and the West?" If the respondent is cognizant of the activities of the Ceylon delegate (he may know less than the observer), it is almost certain that his response will extend the knowledge of the observer. But it is doubtful that a participant would volunteer information about this quiet Ceylon mediation effort were it unsolicited.

In this case the observer was correct in guessing the nature of the mission of the Ceylon delegate. Why did Ceylon choose Czechoslovakia instead of the Soviet Union: Possibly because of acquaintance facilitated by seating proximity. Should this effort be taken very seriously? Evidence tending to indicate that this was a serious effort was offered when the Czechoslovak delegate returned from the "back room" conference and moved as follows:

12:31 p.m.	Czechoslovakia to U.S.S.R.
12:33 p.m.	Czechoslovakia to Ukraine
12:34 p.m.	Czechoslovakia to Romania
12:34 p.m.	Czechoslovakia to Poland
12:35 p.m.	Czechoslovakia to Bulgaria
12:38 p.m.	Czechoslovakia to Mongolia

This suggests that the Ceylon effort was important enough to merit the attention of other members of the Soviet group. Since the Czechoslovak did not stop long enough with each delegate to discuss the matter, it is guessed that he was arranging a later meeting. The Czechoslovak pattern also reveals who is in the Soviet consultation group. Although Albania and Cuba always voted with the group in this session, the interaction pattern in the committee reveals that these two delegations were not in on group consultations (Byelorussia and Hungary were probably absent in the example described above).

Might the analysis of change in rate of interaction over two months of observation indicate a relationship between interaction and the legislative process? Table 1 reveals that the interaction rate, based on analysis of those items to which the committee devoted more than one hour, is not the same for all agenda items. Rankings, based on interactions per minute for agenda items, roughly correspond to rankings, based on the observer's judgment, of controversy generated in the committee. It seemed that UNEF and ONUC expenditures, the ICJ advisory opinion, and geographic distribution of the Secretariat generated the most controversy. These items rank highest in number of interactions per minute. They also rank highest when variation in number present is taken into account by dividing interactions per minute by average attendance. On the other hand, Soviet group dissatisfaction with the scale of assessments on members seemed to generate more controversy over this item than its low place in the rankings indicates. A Soviet Union resolution on this issue was withdrawn, while resolutions on ICJ, UNEF-ONUC, and geographic distribution of the Secretariat all received wide support. Therefore, the data suggest that the more controversial an issue, the greater the interaction that accompanies the successful passage of a resolution. The data also indicate that interaction is vitally related to the parliamentary process.

TABLE 1.   *Number of Interactions During Debate of Major Agenda Items*[a]

Agenda Item	Minutes per Item[b]	Inter-actions per item	Average Attendance per item	Inter-actions per Minute	Interactions per Minute Av. At'd'ce
UNEF-ONUC	86	60	88.00	0.70	0.0080
ICJ Advisory Opinion	1210 (20 hrs.)	979	104.25	0.81	0.0078
Geographic Distribu-tion of Secretariat	941 (16 hrs.)	597	97.33	0.63	0.0065
International School	83	39	85.00	0.47	0.0055
Budget Estimates	2775 (46 hrs.)	1356	92.29	0.49	0.0053
Scale of Assessments	541 (9 hrs.)	216	79.00	0.40	0.0049
Pattern of Conferences	68	6	101.00	0.09	0.0009

[a]All figures in this table based on last 52 or 70 meetings of Fifth Committee, UN General Assembly, 17th Session.

[b]All over 60 minutes.

INTERACTION OF INDIVIDUAL NATIONS

A tally of total interactions by nation reveals heavy concentration of activity in the delegations of a few nations. Only one nation, the United States, had over 600 interactions; the next highest interactors, the Netherlands and Ireland, were in the 400–500 range; Canada, the United Kingdom, and Israel were in the 300–400 range; New Zealand, Iraq, and Secretariat personnel, in the 200–300 range: the U.S.S.R., Australia, Brazil, Norway, Yugoslavia, Czechoslovakia, Poland, and Argentina experienced between 100 and 200 interactions; and the remaining 94 delegations scored fewer than 100. As Table 2 shows, approximately half of the 3,475 recorded interactions were accounted for by ten delegations and the Secretariat. Worth noting is the dominance of the Western parliamentary democracies, and the absence of any African delegations from the high interactor list; also interesting is the fact that five of these ten high interacting nations (the Netherlands, Ireland, Israel, New Zealand, and Iraq) rarely had more than one man present at committee meetings.[8]

Conversations between seatmates accounted for 1,240 of the 3,475 interactions.

8. For all delegations there is a Spearman rank correlation of 0.49 between attendance and amount of interaction ($N = 96$). Attendance was measured by summing the number of delegates present for each nation for all of the forty-two occasions on which attendance was taken.

TABLE 2. *Highest Interactors in Rank Order*[a]

Total	Total Minus Seatmates	Initiatives Taken	Total Interaction Time in Minutes	No. of Nations Contacted	Pairs	Pairs Minus Seatmates
U.S. 621	U.S. 436	U.S. 201	U.S. 2415	U.S. 61	U.K.-U.S.[b] 158	Can.-U.S. 52
Netherlands 443	Canada 317	Canada 178	Canada 1451	(Sec.) 50	Ire.-Israel[b] 150	(U.S.-Sec.) 45
Ireland 418	Netherlands 252	Ireland 131	U.K. 1436	Brazil 37	Neth.-N.Z.[b] 148	Nor.-U.S. 34
Canada 344	(Sec.) 215	U.K. 114	Mexico 971	Yugoslavia 36	Iraq-Ire.[b] 108	Neth.-U.S. 31
Israel 317	Ireland 173	Netherlands 108	Liberia 968	Netherlands 36	Ukr.-U.S.S.R.[b] 66	Can.-U.K. 30
U.K. 309	U.K. 157	Israel 75	Chile 936	Canada 33	Israel-Italy[b] 56	Can.-Neth. 28
N.Z. 250	Norway 145	Australia 71	Netherlands 931	Iraq 31	Can.-U.S. 52	Israel-Neth. 28
(Sec.) 222	Brazil 137	Norway 71	Ireland 753	U.K. 31	(Sec.-U.S.) 45	Poland-Rom. 27
Iraq 220	Australia 123	Brazil 70	Norway 710	Australia 27	Afghan.-Yugo.[b] 45	Australia-U.S. 26
U.S.S.R. 196	U.S.S.R. 117	(Sec.) 68	N.Z. 557	Czech. 27	Austria-Bel.[b] 43	Czech.-U.S.S.R. 24
Australia 176	Czech. 116	U.S.S.R. 66	Denmark 517	Argentina 23	Nepal-Neth.[b] 41	Ireland-Neth. 23
Brazil 165	Israel 116	Yugoslavia 60	(Sec.) 443	U.S.S.R. 23	U.S.-Nor. 34	Australia-Neth. 21
Norway 157	Iraq 115	Czech. 55	Czech. 411	Ceylon 22	Neth.-U.S. 31	Ire.-N.Z. 21
Yugoslavia 154	Yugoslavia 109	Ceylon 45	Israel 387	Chile 22	Can.-U.K. 30	Ire.-U.S. 21
Czech. 135	N.Z. 103	Iraq 40	Pakistan 350	India 21	Can.-Neth. 28	Arg.-Brazil 19
Poland 113	Poland 101	Chile 37	Yugoslavia 313	Mexico 21	Isr.-Neth. 28	Can.-Ireland 19
Argentina 101	Denmark 84	Poland 37	Sweden 278	Ireland 20	Pol.-Rom. 27	Can.-N.Z. 18
Denmark 97	Argentina 80	Colombia 34	Ceylon 273	Pakistan 20	Hon.-Hung.[b] 27	Can.-Cey. 18
Austria 90	India 77	N.Z. 34	Australia 260	Poland 20	Australia-U.S. 26	Den.-Sweden 17
India 89	Ceylon 75	Argentina 33	India 242	Mali 19	Czech.-U.S.S.R. 24	(U.K.-Sec.) 16
Chile 78	Mexico 67	India 24	U.S.S.R. 238	Norway 19	Ire.-Neth. 23	Den.-Norway 16
						Can.-Denmark 16

[a] Includes first twenty nations and Secretariat.

[b] Seatmates.

If the most frequent interacting pairs are ranked, it is found that the first six pairs are all seatmates.[9]

U.K. and U.S.	158 interactions
Ireland and Israel	150 interactions
Netherlands and New Zealand	148 interactions
Iraq and Ireland	108 interactions
Ukraine and U.S.S.R.	66 interactions
Israel and Italy	56 interactions
	(see also Table 2, column 6)

It is likely that much of the talk between seatmates is not on committee business, though this does not necessarily mean that the relationship that develops between seatmates does not create communication patterns and rapport that have political effects. The amount of seatmate conversation may vary because of individual personalities and political and cultural differences existing between delegations. It is likely that the second ranking pair, Ireland and Israel, talked a great deal because they were both gregarious individuals. Had they not been seatmates, it is most unlikely that this pair would have ranked very high. On the other hand, the United States and the United Kingdom would have had close liaison, although probably only about one third the number of recorded conversations, no matter where they sat.

When rankings are made that do not include conversations with seatmates, the American lead over the number-two nation drops from a ratio of 6:4 to 4:3. In this ranking, Canada, with only fifteen conversations with its neighbors from Cameroon and Central African Republic, moves into second position (see Table 2).

The active role of Canada in committee interaction is brought out more clearly when nations are ranked on the basis of initiatives taken (see Table 2). Canada ranks second, only twenty-three behind the 201 recorded for the United States. Since initiatives in seatmate conversations are often not discernible to the observer, Canada's high ranking is partially attributable to her lack of seatmate interaction. Thus, a higher percentage of Canada's initiatives were recorded than in the case of the United States. Nevertheless, this figure does indicate that the Canadian delegation had the greatest mobility—conversations in which Canada went to the seat of another delegate.

Committee interaction can also be measured by the number of nations with which a nation is observed talking. When rankings are made on this basis in contrast to total interactions, Austria, Denmark, Israel, and New Zealand drop out of the first twenty and are replaced by Ceylon, Mali, Mexico, and Pakistan. The United States still leads the rankings, showing conversations with sixty-one nations, followed by the Secretariat with fifty, Brazil with thirty-seven, and Yugoslavia and the Netherlands with thirty-six. Brazil and Yugoslavia attract attention, because they rank eleven and thirteen in total interactions, but two and three in number of nations contacted.

Figure 1, showing the interaction links between the first twenty pairs of nations,

9. Total interactions for all interacting pairs of nations were compiled, after data were punched on IBM cards, by using NUCROS, a general cross-classification program. See Janda (1965), Chap. 6, for a discussion of this program; on pp. 40–42, he describes how NUCROS was used.

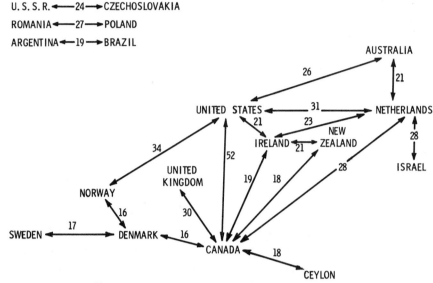

FIGURE 1. *Diagram of interaction between first twenty ranked nonseatmate pairs.*

eliminating seatmates, offers a useful view of the most used communication links. The most active network links together nations from North America, Europe, the Commonwealth, and Israel. One Latin American pair and two Eastern European pairs are in the first twenty, but are not tied to other nations. It is remarkable that no African or Arab nations are included. The figure reveals the nations that have a number of very active links.

Canada	7
United States	5
Netherlands	5
Ireland	4

Interaction between nonseatmates is used in Figure 1 because it is felt that the nonseatmate relationships more adequately reflect purposeful legislative activity than seatmate conversations. This caused ten seatmate pairs to be dropped from the figure—United Kingdom–United States, Ireland–Israel, Netherlands–New Zealand, Iraq–Ireland, Ukraine–U.S.S.R., Israel–Italy, Afghanistan–Yugoslavia, Austria–Belgium, Nepal–Netherlands, and Honduras–Hungary. In the observer's judgment, three of these pairs would fall above the minimum number of interactions for pairs in Figure 1, even if they had not been seated next to each other—United Kingdom–United States (about fifty), Ireland–Israel (about twenty), and the Netherlands–New Zealand (about twenty). These could be added to the diagram and would increase the number of spokes running to the hubs of the wheels accordingly:

Canada	7
United States	6
Netherlands	6
Ireland	5

Why are some nations higher interactors than others? At first glance at the diagram of high interactors, it might be concluded that there is a relationship between committee interaction and nations with Western democratic institutions. The fact that the Soviet Union and Eastern European nations are not linked into the major interaction network, as defined in Figure 1, tends to support comments that have been made on Soviet diplomatic behavior. C. Chaumont and Walter Sharp have suggested that there is a relationship between Soviet domestic institutions and their diplomatic behavior (Chaumont, 1953, p. 273; Sharp, 1963, p. 333). Philip Mosely observes:

The important network of informal communication among the "western" powers as well as the moderate latitude given to their representatives, makes for a swift pace of negotiation which arouses bewilderment and suspicion among their Soviet colleagues (Mosely, 1951, p. 276).

Data are not available in this study on the latitude of decision given to representatives nor on Soviet attitudes toward the "informal communication" among Western nations. On the other hand, the data do not tend to indicate that there are great differences between the parliamentary activity of Soviet and Western nations. In number of interactions and in interaction initiatives, the Soviet Union ranks in the first ten nations and the Eastern European nations are well represented. Four out of eleven Soviet group nations are listed in the high-interactor diagram. On the other hand, a major Western nation, France, does not appear at all.

Observation of the Fifth Committee and examination of data collected suggest a number of factors that might help to explain the amount of nation interaction in the committee: (1) interest in an issue, particularly in terms of desire to get certain resolutions enacted; (2) national policies on issues that are close enough to the view of the majority to permit negotiation of and agreement with a negotiated consensus; (3) number of nations with whom close ties are maintained outside the organization; (4) working relationships established between individuals; and (5) characteristics of individual participants. Relevant characteristics of individuals appear to be: (1) personality traits that affect the capability and desire for establishing and maintaining personal contacts, (2) knowledge of issues under consideration, and (3) perception of United Nations parliamentary processes.

Delegate perceptions of parliamentary processes in the world body might be influenced by the characteristics of legislatures in their own nations and their role in governmental decision-making. But their perceptions are also shaped by the kinds of roles delegates have themselves performed in their own governmental system. Upon first encountering United Nations parliamentary activity, some Western bureaucrats and foreign service officers appear to be no more attracted to its norms and procedures than their Soviet and Eastern European counterparts. Many modify their view to some degree, because participation also shapes delegate perception of the very parliamentary processes.[10]

10. For more extended discussion, see Alger (1963), and C. Chaumont, who asserts: "The international conference is one means of cultural adaptation" (1953, p. 277).

TABLE 3. Spearman Rank Correlations Between Nation Participation in Fifth Committee, Nation Investment of Men and Money in the UN, and Nation Characteristics[a]

		1	2	3	4	5	6	7	8	9	10	11	12	13	14	15	16	17	18	19	20	21	22	23	24	25	26	27
1 Time spent in interact.	(N = 97)																											
2 No. interactions	(N = 97)	92																										
3 No. interactions (ns.)[a]	(N = 97)	86	91																									
4 Initiatives taken	(N = 97)	85	91	91																								
5 Initiatives received	(N = 97)	86	92	90	83																							
6 Initiatives taken (ns.)	(N = 97)	84	86	92	95	82																						
7 Initiatives rec'd (ns.)	(N = 97)	83	87	90	81	97	82																					
8 No.res.&amend. spons'd	(N = 97)	41	34	38	30	39	34	44																				
9 No. of speeches	(N = 97)	63	70	73	65	77	67	75	34																			
10 Length of speeches	(N = 97)	60	70	72	64	77	64	74	32	96																		
11 Questions asked[b]	(N = 97)	32	38	42	35	44	40	46	29	65	58																	
12 Questions answered[b]	(N = 97)	46	48	54	48	51	51	52	40	58	55	60																
13 Total citations[b]	(N = 97)	55	64	70	59	73	62	73	33	91	90	61	50															
14 Neutral citations[b]	(N = 97)	59	69	73	63	76	65	75	30	87	87	56	48	95														
15 Positive citations[b]	(N = 97)	49	56	60	50	65	55	64	37	85	82	59	47	94	82													
16 Negative citations[b]	(N = 97)	44	53	60	50	61	51	62	31	80	78	66	57	82	79	73												
17 No. in Perm. Mission	(N = 96)	36	38	42	36	37	35	35	22	29	30	14	36	31	33	28	23											
18 No. in GA delegation	(N = 96)	41	48	48	50	49	43	46	19	40	43	21	39	39	43	35	26	69										
19 Total attendance	(N = 96)	38	49	48	46	51	44	51	09	49	50	21	35	46	49	44	29	50	69									
20 Voluntary contrib.	(N = 96)	51	53	52	52	52	46	50	30	38	39	13	39	37	39	35	24	56	67	59								
21 % reg. budg. contrib.	(N = 96)	52	59	59	59	55	52	52	17	43	45	17	40	41	45	36	31	62	81	66	82							
22 UN payments/GNP	(N = 93)	14	14	18	17	14	13	13	17	11	07	08	18	05	05	04	13	-03	06	04	30	12						
23 % total UN contrib.	(N = 93)	55	60	59	58	56	50	51	20	45	46	18	42	42	44	36	34	60	79	62	88	96	30					
24 Population	(N = 90)	23	29	29	28	32	23	29	04	34	35	20	33	33	33	31	21	64	66	54	61	75	-13	71				
25 GNP	(N = 90)	46	54	52	53	51	44	48	10	40	42	18	39	40	41	36	29	60	76	64	77	94	07	92	80			
26 GNP/population	(N = 90)	46	53	53	59	40	52	38	16	20	23	-01	21	28	32	21	22	32	47	33	56	65	21	63	18	56		
27 Date of independence[c]	(N = 90)	-26	-25	-16	-23	-13	-14	-09	-13	-05	-01	[10]	-10	-07	-08	-05	-07	-25	-26	-15	-35	-41	-25	-47	26	40	47	

[a]Nonseatmates.
[b]Coding of these data not checked for reliability. Included for exploratory purposes only.
[c]Earliest date ranked first.

64

COMPARISON OF PUBLIC SPEAKING AND INTERACTION PERFORMANCE OF NATIONS

Interaction data, it has been shown, reveal some information about the legislative process that is not reflected in public debate. But it is necessary to investigate further differences between the two sources of data because of the differential costs in data collection. Collecting interaction data on legislative bodies as large as that under analysis is a time-consuming and tedious task. If the same information could be obtained from public debate, perhaps summary records of the Fifth Committee might even be substituted for attendance at sessions. In order to face this issue forthrightly, data were collected on participation in public debate and compared with interaction data. In order to see the relative relationship of these two measures of United Nations participation with other measures, both were compared with attendance, resolution sponsorship, size of delegations, and financial contributions. In addition, correlations were computed between both interaction and public speaking and a few characteristics of nations, such as gross national product (GNP) and population. Spearman rank correlations relating a total of twenty-seven variables with each other are provided in Table 3.[11]

In order to check whether choice of one of several measures of participation in interaction would make a great deal of difference, several measures were used: time consumed in interactions, total number of interactions, and number of interactions minus those with seatmates. Because total interactions correlates over .9 with the other two measures, it is a useful single measure of amount of interaction. There was similar concern whether total length of a nation's speeches would result in a quite different ranking for a nation than number of speeches. Rankings for these two measures correlated .96, so either could be used.

A correlation of .70 between rankings of nations according to number of speeches and rankings based on number of interactions indicates that public debate records are quite a helpful indicator as to who is active in private conversation. When number of speeches is plotted against number of interactions in a scatter diagram, however, it is discovered that much of the unexplained variation is accounted for by a few nations who are high interactors. Canada, Ireland, Israel, the Netherlands, and New Zealand are among the first seven interactors, but rank between seventeen and thirty-five in number of speeches.

11. Spearman rank correlations are used because the distributions for a number of variables are not of the same form. Thus the Pearson product-moment correlation could not reach the maximums of -1.0 and $+1.0$. Ranking the data prior to calculating the product moment results in the distributions generally having the same form, although some information is sacrificed (Guilford, 1956, p. 287).

Less than 0.20	Slight; almost negligible relationship
0.20–0.40	Low correlation; definite but small relationship
0.40–0.70	Moderate correlation; substantial relationship
0.70–0.90	High correlation; marked relationship
0.90–1.00	Very high correlation; very dependable relationship (Guilford, 1956, p. 145)

(Since Guilford's guidelines apply only to significant r's, Kerlinger's rule of thumb for significance of Pearson r is helpful. "With about 100 pairs of measures" an r of 0.20 is significant at the 0.05 level and an r of 0.25 is significant at the 0.01 level [Kerlinger, 1964, p. 171].)

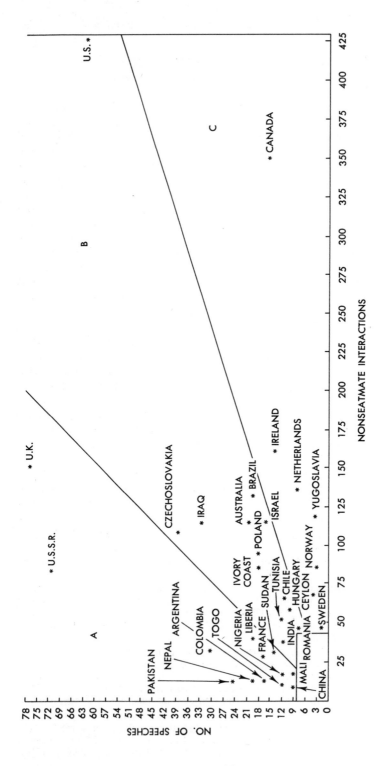

FIGURE 2. *Public speaking and nonseatmate interaction.*

66

The differences in their rank for speaking and rank for interacting vary from fourteen to thirty ranks. Thus, despite a generally high correlation between rankings for speaking and interaction, public speaking data do not draw attention to a group of deviant cases that are very active interactors and seem to be highly important participants in the political process. There are also deviant cases that rank much higher in public speaking than they do in interaction.

If interactions with seatmates are removed from the interaction/public-speaking scatter diagram, the deviant cases are more noticeable. A scatter diagram reveals a striking tendency for high participants in public speaking and/or interaction to have one of three styles of participation. One group, falling near a line that cuts through the *B* sector in Figure 2, has balanced participation in both public speaking and interaction. Here are found Tunisia, India, Romania, Hungary, Chile, the Ivory Coast, Poland, Australia, Brazil, and, far out on the top right, the United States. Near a line cutting the *A* sector are nations that speak much more than they interact—China, Mali, Nigeria, Togo, the Sudan, France, Liberia, Argentina, Nepal, Pakistan, Colombia, the U.S.S.R., and the U.K. Near a line passing through the *C* sector are nations that interact more than they speak—Sweden, Ceylon, Norway, Yugoslavia, the Netherlands, and Ireland. Canada appears deviant even from this group, having more interaction in relation to its amount of speaking than the others, and thus falling below the line.

The relationship between nation rank in public speaking and rank in inter-action can be further probed by comparing the degree to which several indices of interaction relate to public speaking. Rank order correlations between number of public speeches and interactions are as follows:

Total interaction time	.63
Initiatives taken	.65
Total interactions	.70
Initiatives received	.77

Thus the strongest relationship is between number of speeches and initiatives received. It sounds plausible that those who give the most speeches may receive initiatives consisting of questions, replies, congratulations, and so on. Initiatives received also correlates more closely with citations in public debate of the speeches of others (.73), than with other measures of interaction.[12] This, too, seems plausible in that it would be expected that those who mention the speeches of others in their public assertions would receive initiatives related to these citations.

Although these findings are plausible, research hypotheses proposed a different, and also plausible, kind of relationship between public and private conversations. Instead of the interaction between private and public discourse suggested by the above correlations, it was hypothesized that the two kinds of activity would be mirrors of each other i.e., nations high as to interaction time would be high in public-speaking time (actual correlation .60), and nations with a high

12. Reliability checks have not been done on the data acquired through analysis of speeches: questions asked, questions answered, and citations of speeches of others. The primary value of conclusions based on these data is as an aid in making the judgment that additional resources should not be invested in this type of content analysis. Number of speeches not only has a higher correlation to number of interactions than these measures of debate content, but also can be obtained with much less research effort and expense.

number of interactions would deliver a high number of speeches (actual correlation .70). But these correlations between public speaking and interaction are both lower than that between public speaking and initiatives received (.77).

An alternative research hypothesis was tested by content analysis of speeches for citations of speeches of other committee members. It was predicted that high interactors would more often cite speeches of other committee members. It was expected that high interactors would be more immersed in an interchange of ideas that would also be reflected in their public speaking. The correlation between citations of others and number of interactions is quite high (.64), but not as high as the correlation between number of interactions and number of speeches (.70). It was also expected that the number of questions asked in public debate might be more related to interaction initiatives than number of speeches, but this was not confirmed. Initiatives taken is much more closely related to number of speeches (.65) than it is to questions asked (.35).

In an effort to probe the relationship between roles in the legislative process and amount of activity in the public arena, the number of resolutions and amendments sponsored by each nation were correlated with the number of speeches and number of interactions. It was thought that this might give a useful comparison of speeches and interactions as related to the legislative process. But neither number of speeches (.34) nor number of interactions (.34) is closely related to sponsorship of resolutions and amendments. The probable explanation for the low correlations is that resolution sponsorship by a nation often is not accompanied by active participation in the preparation of the resolution. Sponsors are selected often from various geographic and interest groups of nations in order to encourage support from other nations in these groups.

Table 4 indicates how nation ranks for number of speeches and number of interactions relate to other measures of participation (manpower and money allocated to the United Nations) and a few characteristics of nations. The table shows that interaction is generally more closely related to such phenomena than is public speaking. Manpower invested can be measured in terms of actual attendance at meetings, number in General Assembly delegations, and number permanently stationed at headquarters. The expectation that these measures

TABLE 4. *Comparison of Speaking and Interaction Rank Correlations with Nation Investment of Men and Money in the UN and National Characteristics*

Variable	No. of Interactions	No. of Speeches
No. in Permanent Mission	0.38	0.29
No. in General Assembly	0.48	0.40
Committee Attendance	0.49	0.49
Voluntary Contributions	0.53	0.38
Regular Budget	0.59	0.43
Total UN Contributions	0.60	0.45
UN Payments/GNP	0.14	0.11
GNP	0.54	0.40
GNP/Population	0.53	0.20
Population	0.29	0.34

would be related in this order to committee participation is supported, but the relationship is not very strong. The closer relationship between monetary contributions and committee activity was not expected. It was expected that manpower in the committee room would be more related to activity than financial contributions.

Monetary contributions were measured in four ways: total contributions, contributions to the regular budget (not including peace-keeping operations, most economic programs, and refugee relief), voluntary contributions (primarily for peace-keeping operations, economic programs, and refugee relief), and total contributions over gross national product. It was expected that voluntary contributions would be more closely related to public speaking and interaction than total contributions. This was based on the assumption that voluntary contributions reflect an interest and concern with the United Nations that would be related to degree of participation in public speaking and interaction. The expectation is not supported by data. United Nations payments/GNP was included to see whether costs of participation in terms of capacity to pay would be more related to debate and interaction activity than absolute figures on payments. There is virtually no correlation.

Because population and GNP are popular measures of "national power" in the international relations literature, it is interesting to discern their relationship with United Nations activity. Population has rather low correlations with interactions (.29) and speeches (.34), but it is the only item in the table that is more correlated with speeches than interactions. GNP is more closely related to interaction (.54) than public speeches (.40). The relationships here are not far below total contributions and regular budget contributions. This is not surprising, because GNP is an important factor in the determination of national assessments for UN budgets. GNP/population is also included, because it was noted while collecting observational data that a number of the higher interacting nations were those with high per-capita incomes. Although GNP/population (.53) has about the same relationship to interactions as does GNP (.54), GNP/population has only a .20 relation to public speeches while GNP has a .40 relationship. Furthermore, a most interesting characteristic of GNP/population is the great difference between its degree of relationship to interactions and its relationship to public speeches, a difference of .33. This is over twice the difference for any other item in the table.

The consistently higher relationship between interaction, in contrast to public speaking, and measures of number of men in missions and delegations, United Nations financial support, and GNP of nations is important evidence of the significance of interaction data. Had the reverse been true, it would have encouraged doubts about the significance of interaction behavior. Had there been no difference between the relation of interaction and public speaking to these variables, it would have suggested that the greater effort required to obtain interaction data is not justified, since the public debate data are easier to compile. It is not known, of course, whether the same pattern of relationships would be evident in other main committees of the Assembly. Because United Nations budgets are considered in the Fifth Committee, it could be that there is a higher relationship between budgetary contributions and committee activity in this committee than in other committees. If an issue-related phenomenon has been uncovered, instead of one that holds across all committees, then it might be found that interaction in other committees is related to other variables. For example, in the Trusteeship and Non-Self-Governing Committee, interaction might be more closely related to date of independence (the more recent the date of independence, the more interaction) than to monetary contributions to the United Nations.[13]

INTERACTION OF REGIONAL GROUPS

Table 5 provides data on the number of nations in each of eight regional groups that engaged in one hundred or more interactions. The information indicates low activity on the part of African, Arab, and Asian nations, with only one nation of the forty-one interactors from these regions having more than one

TABLE 5. *Number of Interactions for Nations in Regional Groups*

Regional Group (and No. of Nations)[a]	Under 50	50 to 99	100 or more
NATO (13)	5	3	5 (38%) Canada, Netherlands, Norway, U.K., U.S.
Commonwealth (12)	6	2	4 (33%) Australia, Canada, New Zealand, U.K.
Soviet (10)	4	3	3 (30%) Czechoslovakia, Poland, U.S.S.R.
Western Europe (15)	6	5	4 (27%) Ireland, Netherlands, Norway, U.K.
Latin America (18)	12	4	2 (11%) Argentina, Brazil
Arab (12)	10	1	1 (8%) Iraq
Asia (13)	9	4	—
Sub-Sahara Africa (16)	15	1	—

[a]Includes only nations for which interactions are recorded.

hundred interactions. With only two high interactors out of eighteen, the Latin American group is not much different in this respect from the Arab group. NATO, the Commonwealth, the Soviet group, and Western Europe do not vary a great deal in the percentage of interaction leaders, ranging between 27 and 38 per cent. The relatively low activity of the African, Arab, Asian, and Latin American nations is also confirmed by Table 6, where total interactions are

13. It was expected that participation in public debate and interaction in the Fifth Committee would be related inversely to date of independence (the more recent the date of independence, the less a nation's activity). This was based on the belief that delegations of new nations would not have the technical competence and background of experience enabling them to take an active role in Fifth Committee affairs. Table 3 indicates a consistent negative correlation between date of independence and committee activity, but all correlations are very low.

presented for regional groups. Though Latin America has about one hundred more interactions than the Soviet group, their rate per active nation (47) is lower than that of the Soviet group (75). All other groups (Western Europe, NATO, and Commonwealth) average over one hundred interactions per nation.

Table 6 shows the degree to which members of regional groups confine their interactions to members of their own group. Latin America has the largest percentage of intragroup interactions, 64 per cent, which is 3 per cent above that of the Soviet group. NATO is the only other group with a reasonably high figure (44 per cent). Asia (28 per cent), Western Europe (25 per cent), and the Commonwealth (24 per cent) are clustered below groups with high internal interactions. Sub-Sahara Africa (18 per cent) and the Arab nations (16 per cent) have a remarkably low percentage of communication with other nations in their group.

TABLE 6.   *Interactions of Regional Groups*

Regional Group (and No. of Nations)[a]	Total Inter-actions	Average per Nation	Total in Group	Per Cent in Group
Latin America (18)	842	47	542	64
Soviet (10)	746	75	456	61
NATO (13)	2,185	168	972	44
Asia (13)	467	36	92	20
Western Europe (15)	1,819	121	455	25
Commonwealth (12)	1,395	116	340	24
Sub-Sahara Africa (16)	313	20	56	18
Arab (12)	393	33	62	16

[a]Includes only those nations for which interactions are recorded.

There is great variation in performance by nations within regional groups. In the Latin American group only Brazil (165), Argentina (101), Chile (78), Mexico (77), Colombia (61), and Honduras (51)[14] have more than fifty interactions. In contrast to 64 per cent intragroup interaction for the Latin American group as a whole, these nations performed as follows: Colombia (34 per cent), Brazil (44 per cent), Honduras (45 per cent), Chile (51 per cent), Argentina (53 per cent), and Mexico (70 per cent). Brazil stands out in intergroup activity, having contact with twenty-seven nations, with the other high intergroup inter-actors ranging between ten and fourteen. In comparison, ten of the eighteen Latin American nations have more than 85 per cent of the interactions within their own group.

Though the Soviet group, as a whole, has about the same percentage of intra-group activity as the Latin Americans, most nations in this group perform nearer the group norm. The major interactors in the group are U.S.S.R. (196), Czecho-slovakia (135), and Poland (113). Czechoslovakia leads in number of nations contacted outside the group (19), with both U.S.S.R. and Poland contacting fourteen.

14. Twenty-seven of Honduras' interactions were with seatmate, Hungary.

Members of the Arab group are in general not very active, with only two nations having more than twenty-five interactions: Iraq (220) and Tunisia (56). Both have less than 20 per cent of their interactions within the Arab group, with Iraq talking to twenty-four other nations and Tunisia talking to only ten. Whereas Tunisia's contacts are largely centered on Africa, Iraq's are rather widely spread.

The activity of the NATO group presents a dramatic contrast: United States—621, the Netherlands—443, Canada—344, United Kingdom—309, Norway—157, and Denmark—97. Examining the interactions of the four highest outside the group, little variation is found in number of nations contacted for Canada (28), the Netherlands (28), and the United Kingdom (25). The United States offers a striking contrast with fifty nations contacted. Only Brazil had more interactions with Latin America than the United States, and no Arab nation contacted other Arabs as often as did the United States. Interactions between the United States and regional groups are as follows: Western Europe—60, Latin America—56, Asia—38, Soviet—24, Sub-Sahara Africa—24, and Arab—23.

Notably absent from the group of high interactors is France, with a total of only twenty-five interactions. France's participation in public debate was also lower than would be expected, with France ranking fifteenth (17 speeches) and the United Kingdom (76 speeches), Soviet Union (72 speeches), and United States (61 speeches) in the first three ranks. The interaction record in this case is a realistic portrayal of French conduct in negotiations and discussions outside the committee chamber. France refused to participate in the very active negotiations that took place on the International Court's advisory opinion, authorization of further UNEF and ONUC spending, and future plans for handling problems of peace-keeping finance.

Western Europe includes one high interactor which was not in NATO: Ireland, with 418 interactions. A striking aspect of Western European interaction is the contrast between two Benelux partners, the Netherlands and Belgium. The Netherlands participated in 443 interactions, 15 per cent within the Western European group; and Belgium participated in 57 interactions, 86 per cent intragroup. If this region is divided into its Common Market and Scandinavian subgroups, a further contrast emerges. Among the Common Market nations, a mere 22 out of 608 interactions for these nations were within the group (4 per cent), whereas Scandinavia had 106 out of 348 interactions taking place within the group (30 per cent). The contrast may possibly be the consequence of the split in the Common Market group over peace-keeping finance, with France and Belgium largely out of step with the Assembly majority and not participating, and Italy and the Netherlands in step with the majority and participating.

Notable in the Sub-Sahara Africa group is the fact that no interactions are recorded for nine nations and, of the sixteen that had interactions, none had more than fifty-three. The highest interactor was Liberia, whose delegate was vice president of the committee.[15] Following Liberia were Mali (45), Nigeria (43), and the Ivory Coast (31). Only 17.9 per cent of the interactions of nations in this group were intragroup.

With 28 per cent of their activity intragroup, the Asian nations had slightly more intragroup interaction than the Arabs, Sub-Sahara Africa, and Western

15. It is not customary for the chairman to serve also as delegate from his nation. In this session of the Fifth Committee, a Dutch delegate was elected chairman, but then ceased to represent his nation on the committee.

Europe. Only four nations in the group had more than fifty interactions: India (89), Nepal (81), Ceylon (76), and Afghanistan (53). It is the only regional group beside Sub-Sahara Africa that does not have a nation with over one hundred interactions. With about half of Afghanistan and Nepal's interactions occurring with their seatmates, actually only Ceylon and India reveal significant involvement in the private consultations in the chamber.

The highest interactors in the Commonwealth are the members of the so-called old Commonwealth: Canada (344), United Kingdom (309), New Zealand (250), and Australia (176). India with eighty-nine and Ceylon with seventy-six are the only other nations with over fifty interactions. The fact that the Commonwealth nations have more intragroup interactions than Sub-Sahara Africa and the Arabs is surprising (24 per cent). It is also surprising that those Commonwealth nations with the highest percentage of intragroup interactions are not old Commonwealth, but proved to be Pakistan (44 per cent), Ceylon (36 per cent), and Nigeria (35 per cent). They are followed by Canada (28 per cent), India (26 per cent), Australia (22 per cent), New Zealand (21 per cent), United Kingdom (21 per cent), and Ghana (10 per cent). Other Commonwealth nations do not have enough interactions to make percentages meaningful.

It is difficult to place Yugoslavia in any group, although she most often collaborates with the underdeveloped nations, particularly those from Afro-Asia. Yugoslavia's interaction pattern tends to mirror this non-group status. The single Yugoslav delegate was observed in contact with thirty-seven nations (only two nations contacted more) and these contacts were spread among a number of groups: Arab (28), Sub-Sahara Africa (18), Asia (17 plus 45 with seatmate Afghanistan), Soviet (15), Latin America (13), and Western Europe (3).

VOTING IN REGIONAL GROUPS AND ITS RELATION TO INTERACTION

Virtually all of the rigorous empirical work done on United Nations politics has been devoted to the analysis of roll call votes. It will be of interest, therefore, to relate interactional behavior to voting behavior by investigating whether regional groups with the highest percentage of intragroup interaction tend to be more in agreement in voting. The Fifth Committee had eight roll call votes during the Seventeenth Session. One roll call was taken on proposed emergency assistance of $2 million to Rwanda and Burundi for the construction of roads and government buildings. Controversy arose because the assistance was for capital expenditures of a character not previously included in the regular budget of the United Nations. In the voting (Yes—50, No—0, Abstain—37) none would vote against the assistance, though those disagreeing on principle abstained. Abstentions came from Latin America, the West, and the Soviet group. Exceptions to this pattern were the affirmative votes of Mexico, Colombia, and Chile from Latin America and those of Austria, Belgium, and the Netherlands from Europe.

Three roll call votes concerned geographic distribution of the Secretariat. One vote passed a resolution sponsored by Brazil, Iraq, Nigeria, Sudan, Syria, and Tunisia that offered general guidelines to the Secretary-General for achieving more equitable geographic distribution. The support for the resolution was overwhelming (Yes—84, No—10, Abstain—2) with only the Soviet group opposing. The other two votes on geographic distribution were on amendments to this resolution offered by Poland and not passed by the committee. They would have tended to extend that portion of the Secretariat covered by principles of geographic distribution, implied lessening of support for a career service, and removed a portion of the resolution indicating that nations with no more than five nationals in the Secretariat are not overrepresented. The Polish amendments received little support outside the Soviet group. Voting on one was Yes—14, No—44, and Abstain—36, and voting on the other was Yes—11, No—39, and Abstain—46.

The final four roll calls were concerned with problems of peace-keeping finance. Three were related to the aforementioned advisory opinion of the International Court of Justice which stated expenditures for UNEF and ONUC peace-keeping operations are expenses of the organizations for which all members can be legally assessed. The fourth established the Working Group of Twenty-one and asked it to submit a report to the Assembly on peace-keeping finance problems.

The committee voted overwhelmingly to "accept" the opinion of the Court, with a vote of Yes—75, No—17, and Abstain—14. (A quite similar roll call vote was taken on just the operative paragraph of this resolution and on the resolution establishing the Working Group of Twenty-one.) Voting in the negative were the Soviet group, four Arab nations, France, and South Africa. Abstaining were six Arab nations and a few close African neighbors plus Belgium, Spain, and Yugoslavia. A third vote on the Court's opinion came earlier when Jordan submitted an amendment that asked the General Assembly "to take note of" the opinion rather than "accept" it. Jordan's amendment was rejected by a 28-61-14 vote, being supported by the Soviet and Arab groups, and also Guinea, Mali, Madagascar, Indonesia, Yugoslavia, and Belgium.

A measure of the voting cohesiveness of each regional group was obtained through calculating an index of agreement for each pair in the group and averaging the indices for all pairs. The index of agreement used is that proposed by Arend Lijphart which takes into account the three voting alternatives in the United Nations: yes, no, and abstain. The Lijphart procedure makes it possible for an index of agreement between two nations on a single vote to have three conditions: (1) Nation A and nation B may be in complete agreement by both voting in favor, both voting against, or both abstaining; (2) A and B may be in complete disagreement, that is, when A votes in favor and B against, or vice versa; (3) A and B may be in partial agreement, that is, one of them votes either in favor or against, and the other abstains. Lijphart's formula for calculating an index of agreement (IA) is as follows:

$$IA = \frac{f + \frac{1}{2}g}{t} \times 100\%$$

in which t equals the total number of votes under consideration, f equals the number of votes on which A and B are in full agreement, and g equals the number of votes on which they agree only in part. An index of agreement of 100 per cent indicates full agreement on all roll call votes and an index of zero indicates that the two countries always vote opposite. When one of a pair of nations is absent for a vote, no index is calculated for that pair on that vote (Lijphart, 1963, p. 910).

Table 7 provides the average indices of voting agreement for regional groups.[16] Voting agreement for all groups is above 80 per cent. The Soviet group and Latin America stand out at the top of the rankings, with voting agreement indices of 98 and 92 respectively. The other six groups cluster between 80 and 84. There is not a significant rank correlation between voting agreement of groups and percentage of intragroup interaction of groups (Spearman rank correlation, .50). On the other hand, the fact that the Soviet and Latin American groups are both widely separated from the other groups in percentage of voting agreement and intragroup interaction suggests that there may be a relationship between these two variables. This relationship should be investigated further in a committee where group voting agreement scores are more dispersed.

TABLE 7.   *Comparison of Regional Group Voting and Interaction*

Regional Group (No. of Nations)[a]	Voting Agreement	(Rank)	Intragroup Interaction	(Rank)
Soviet (11)	97.99	1	0.61	2
Latin America (18)	92.07	2	0.64	1
Western Europe (15)	84.54	3	0.25	5
Sub-Sahara Africa (16)	84.03	4	0.17	7
Commonwealth (12)	83.39	5	0.24	6
NATO (13)	83.37	6	0.44	3
Arab (11)	82.85	7	0.16	8
Asia (13)	80.11	8	0.28	4

Spearman rank correlation = 0.50
(not significant at 0.05 level)
$N = 8$

[a]Applies to voting data only. Number of nations for whom interactions are recorded is provided in Table 6.

EFFECT OF NON-COMMITTEE ROLES ON INDIVIDUAL BEHAVIOR

Individual delegate characteristics, such as personality, past experiences, and non-committee roles, appear to have an effect on committee activity. Observation has revealed cases where change in delegates alters a nation's rate of participation in a committee from high to low, without evident change in policy. With different representation a nation's influence on the parliamentary process may change considerably. Some delegates seem not to have the qualities necessary for becoming mobile operators in a parliamentary body, while others thrive on it. But some who are mobile are more effective than others. Delegates often mention the importance of trust in their relationship with other delegates. Trust between delegates seems not to be strongly related to the state of relations

16. Indices were computed by a program written for the CDC 3400 computer by Allen R. Wilcox, Department of Political Science, Northwestern University.

TABLE 8. *Interactions and Public Speaking by Post*[a]

Post	No. of Interactors	Observed Average	Expected Average
Total Interactions			
Permanent Mission	41	59.4	44.7
Foreign Office	26	65.8	44.7
Overseas Post	13	49.3	44.7
Parliamentarian	5	21.6	44.7
Other Government Post	2	17.0	44.7
Private Citizen	4	55.0	44.7
	91	268.1	

$\chi^2 = 46.7$ (5 degrees of freedom, significant at .001 level)

Post	No. of Interactors	Observed Average	Expected Average
Initiatives Taken			
Permanent Mission	41	18.2	14.7
Foreign Office	26	21.3	14.7
Overseas Post	13	14.8	14.7
Parliamentarian	5	5.6	14.7
Other Government Post	2	3.5	14.7
Private Citizen	4	25.0	14.7
	91	88.4	

$\chi^2 = 25.2$ (5 degrees of freedom, significant at .001 level)

Post	No. of Interactors	Observed Average	Expected Average
Initiatives Received			
Permanent Mission	41	14.0	12.3
Foreign Office	26	17.2	12.3
Overseas Post	13	16.8	12.3
Parliamentarian	5	4.8	12.3
Other Government Post	2	5.0	12.3
Private Citizen	4	15.8	12.3
	91	73.6	

$\chi^2 = 13.7$ (5 degrees of freedom, significant at .02 level)

Post	No. of Interactors	Observed Average	Expected Average
Speeches			
Permanent Mission	41	7.0	7.6
Foreign Office	26	7.8	7.6
Overseas Post	13	7.5	7.6
Parliamentarian	5	5.8	7.6
Other Government Post	2	3.0	7.6
Private Citizen	4	14.5	7.6
	91	45.6	

$\chi^2 = 9.7$ (5 degrees of freedom, significant at .10 level)

[a]Chi square one sample test used, a goodness-of-fit test used to test whether a significant difference exists between an *observed* distribution and a distribution that would be *expected* by chance (Siegel, 1956, pp. 42–47).

between their nations. Irrespective of nationality, some delegates have the confidence of other delegates who trust that their promises will be kept and that information they offer is accurate. The trust seems to be based both on the qualities of the presentation of self to others and on performance in parliamentary activity.

Participants in General Assembly delegations come not only from national permanent missions at the United Nations but also from other posts. In the Fifth Committee, permanent mission personnel participated in 2,436 interactions, with officials from other posts participating in 2,758. If the officials coming from other posts are separated into categories, the distribution is as follows:

Post (*No. of Interactors*)		*No. of Interactions*
UN Permanent Mission	(41)	2,436
Foreign Office	(26)	1,728
Overseas Missions	(13)	651
Private Citizens	(4)	221
Parliamentarians	(5)	114
Other Government Post	(2)	44
Unknown		1,448
Total		6,642

The high number of interactions by permanent mission personnel fulfilled expectations. As permanent participants in United Nations activities, they know each other, are inclined to be informed on substantive issues, and are experienced in United Nations parliamentary activity.

Another perspective on the relationship between post and interaction is obtained if the number of interactors from each post is taken into account. Table 8 shows that the ninety-one identified interactors come primarily from permanent missions (41), foreign offices (26), and other foreign posts (13). The foreign office personnel have the highest rate of interaction (66), in contrast to sixty for permanent missions, and fifty for those from other posts. A chi square one sample test reveals that the post of a delegate is positively related to the amount of his interaction, with only a .001 probability that the observed relationship occurred by chance. The high interaction rate of foreign office personnel on the Fifth Committee could be partially explained by the fact that many come from foreign office bureaus where they work on Fifth Committee problems. Furthermore, many have had prior service on this committee. The importance of length of service in the Assembly to interaction is supported by the fact that the ten highest interactors participated in the Assembly an average of 4.2 years, while the other eighty-one delegates served an average of only 2.5 years.

Similar differences between posts are found for interaction initiatives taken and initiatives received. Once again foreign office personnel have the highest rate, followed by permanent mission delegates and those from other overseas posts. There are greater differences among posts in regard to initiatives taken than in regard to initiatives received. Nevertheless, differences among posts for both initiatives taken and initiatives received are significant with chi square one sample tests showing the significance level to be .001 for initiatives taken and .02 for initiatives received.

Table 8 reveals that foreign office, permanent mission, and other overseas post personnel all intervened in public debate an average of seven to eight times. The relationship between public speaking and post is not significant at the .05 level. Thus, at least in the Seventeenth Session of the General Assembly, the Fifth Committee interaction data give the researcher a greater ability to discriminate between the activity of delegates from different posts than is the case with public speaking data.

Eleven delegates who served on the committee are members of the Advisory Committee on Administrative and Budgetary Questions, the total membership of the body except for its chairman, although one member was only present for part of the session. They serve on the committee as individual experts in closed meetings, giving detailed attention to budgetary and administrative requests of the Secretary-General. After detailed examination of his requests, they make recommendations to the Assembly, and the recommendations, along with the Secretary-General's requests, are considered by the Fifth Committee. The recommendations of the ACABQ carry much weight and generally are accepted with few modifications. Because members of the ACABQ—in the formal sense at least—serve as individuals, nations have no obligation to appoint them to the Fifth Committee. Since the experts are drawn from permanent missions, and occasionally foreign offices, however, it is convenient for nations to use their expertise in the latter committee. Here they are no longer individual experts, but serve as representatives of their governments. In this capacity, they may occasionally take different positions than they did in meetings of the ACABQ. In the Fifth Committee meetings, the ACABQ is represented by its chairman, who sits at the chairman's desk and occasionally explains the position of the ACABQ, but never speaks for his nation.

Trygve Lie thought that membership in the Advisory Committee should disqualify a person from service in the Fifth Committee. It did not seem appropriate to him that Advisory Committee members "also represent their Governments [in the General Assembly] . . . where they act as advocates for the Advisory Committee or may argue or vote against its recommendations" (Singer, 1957, p. 402). On the other hand, it might be considered beneficial to have the expertise of ACABQ members injected into Fifth Committee deliberations. It is not the purpose of this paper to render a judgment, but to extend knowledge of their committee behavior as it compares to other members'.

It appears to the observer of the Fifth Committee that some members of the ACABQ demonstrate superior knowledge of a number of items on the committee agenda, that other members of the Fifth Committee acknowledge their expertise, and that members of the ACABQ manifest interest in obtaining acceptance of their recommendations. On the basis of general impressions of the session under examination, five members appeared to be quite active committee members (Argentina, Iraq, U.K., U.S., U.S.S.R.), three moderately active (Nigeria, Pakistan, and Sudan), and three engaged in little activity (Chile, France, and Romania). But over-all it would be expected that members of the ACABQ interact more and speak more than members of the committee that are not on the ACABQ. Furthermore, if members of the ACABQ interact more than other members, this would tend to support argument for the importance of interaction to the legislative process.

The data reveal that ACABQ members do indeed engage in more interactions and make more speeches than other members of the committee. Based on the ninety-one identified committee members who participated in interaction, it is found that ACABQ members interact an average of ninety-nine times, whereas other members of the committee interact only fifty-one times. In addition, ACABQ members speak an average of twenty-four times, whereas non-ACABQ members speak an average of five times. Chi square one sample tests reveal that both of these differences are significant at the .001 level. It is noted, however, that whereas ACABQ members speak over four times as much as their colleagues, they interact only twice as much.

INDIVIDUAL REPUTATION FOR BEING CAPABLE AND INFORMED

It would be expected that members of the ACABQ would receive greater respect from their colleagues in the committee than other members, and a modest effort was made to ascertain the extent to which this is so. Since reliable information on this question can best be obtained from delegates with whom the researcher has had considerable contact and rapport, only seven such persons were interviewed to obtain the information, of whom six were willing to name individuals. Each was asked to name the delegates in the Fifth Committee considered to be the "most informed on Fifth Committee business" and those considered to be the "most capable in obtaining their objectives." Each of the six delegates who supplied names was from a different nation, with two from North America, two from Europe, one from the old Commonwealth, and one from Africa. With each respondent permitted to name as many delegates as he wished, they cited twenty-five persons as being capable and twenty as being well-informed. All but two of those on the informed list are on the capable list as well, but eight of those on the latter are not on the former. This indication that a reputation for being informed is harder to achieve than recognition of being capable is further supported by the fact that a total of seventy-one nominations were made for capable delegates (with the highest individual score being seven) and a total of only thirty-eight nominations were made for informed delegates (with the highest individual score being five).

Returning to the ACABQ, it is found that its members are more likely to be given credit for being informed and capable than are nonmembers. When the number of ACABQ members receiving nominations is compared with those of the other eighty identified interactors, we find that ACABQ members are more frequently identified as highly capable and informed than are nonmembers, and less frequently identified as noncapable and noninformed. Whereas six of the eleven ACABQ members were identified as informed, only fourteen of eighty nonmembers were nominated. Nine of the eleven ACABQ members were identified as capable but only seventeen of the eighty nonmembers. Chi square tests[17] show ACABQ members to be significantly different from other committee members in both cases, with a .02 significance level for "informed" and a .001 significance level for "capable." It was expected that more ACABQ members would receive nominations for being capable and informed than other committee

17. Chi square tests for 2×2 tables with correction for continuity (Siegel, 1956, pp. 107–109).

TABLE 9. *Average Number of Nominations of ACABQ and Non-ACABQ for Capable and Informed List*

	Capable		Informed	
	No. of Delegates	Average Number of Nominations	No. of Delegates	Average Number of Nominations
ACABQ	9	3.67	6	3.00
Non-ACABQ	17	2.29	14	1.43
	Mann-Whitney $U = 57$ *not* significant at .05		Mann-Whitney $U = 74$ significant at .01	

members, but it was not expected that ACABQ members would be distinguished from other members more on the basis of capability than on the basis of knowledge about committee business.

This kind of test of ACABQ repute for being informed and capable is not completely satisfying, because persons nominated receive equal weight no matter how many times they are mentioned. A complementary approach is to work only with the population of persons nominated as capable or informed, and ask: Did individual members of the ACABQ or individual non-ACABQ members receive a higher number of nominations? Table 9 reveals that individual members of the ACABQ are nominated more often as both capable and informed; however, when the question is asked in this form, the ACABQ members are distinguished from the rest of the committee more for their reputation for being informed. When the Mann-Whitney U Test[18] is applied to the data to determine whether ACABQ scores (average number of times each member is nominated) are larger than non-ACABQ scores, there is not a significant difference at the .05 level for *capable* scores, but there is a significant difference at the .01 level for the *informed* scores.

The data on the reputation of ACABQ members for being capable and informed must be handled with restraint, since it represents the judgment of only six committee members. Nevertheless, it does support observer judgment and fits in with conclusions based on other legislative bodies. Richard Fenno, writing of the Appropriations Committee of the United States House of Representatives, concludes:

Within the Committee, respect, deference and power are earned through subcommittee activity and, hence to a degree, through specialization. Specialization is valued further because it is well suited to the task of guarding the Treasury. Only by specializing, Committee members believe, can they unearth the volume of factual information necessary for the intelligent screening of budget requests (Fenno, 1962, p. 316).

The ACABQ is the guardian of the United Nations treasury, and specialization permits it to achieve its goal.

18. Mann-Whitney U Test is used as a nonparametric alternative to the parametric t-test for difference between means (Siegel, 1956, pp. 116–126).

So far as budgetary and administrative questions are concerned, observer judgment is that the members of the ACABQ have not only the respect of their colleagues, but they also have considerable influence. Their recommendations are rarely challenged by the full committee. Though many of these recommendations are accepted without resolutions sponsored by delegations, an effort was made to find out whether delegations with ACABQ members have greater success in getting resolutions and amendments they sponsor accepted. It was found that delegations with ACABQ members are more involved in sponsorship, with ten of eleven delegations sponsoring an item, whereas only forty-four of the other ninety-nine were sponsors. But delegations with ACABQ members differ little from other delegations in ratio of successes to failures (80 per cent of the ACABQ delegations had 100 per cent success and 84 per cent of other delegations had 100 per cent success). With forty-five of fifty-four sponsoring delegations having complete success, successful sponsorship is not a very useful basis for discriminating among delegations in this session of the Fifth Committee.

It was expected that those named as capable and informed would be more active participants in the Fifth Committee than other members. This is the case, with delegates named as either capable and informed giving significantly more speeches and participating in significantly more interactions than delegates not so named. Table 10 reveals that those delegates named as capable and/or informed have a mean interaction rate of 130 compared to 26 for other committee members. Those nominated as capable and/or informed speak an average of seventeen times compared to four for other committee members. The strong relationship between a reputation for being capable and/or informed and rate of participation in both private conversation and public debate conforms to findings in a number of natural and experimental settings that are summarized by Collins and Guetzkow (1964, pp. 155–156). Particularly relevant is the finding by Bates (1952) and by Borgatta and Bales (1956) that amount of communication sent and reputation for "who contributed the most to carrying out the assigned task of the group" are highly correlated.

TABLE 10. *Speaking and Interaction of Capable and Informed Compared to Other Delegates*

	Delegates Named as Capable and/or Informed (N = 27)		All Other Delegates (N = 64)		
	Mean	Total	Mean	Total	
Interactions	129.78	3,504	25.67	1,643	Mann-Whitney *U* Test = 2.63 (significant at .004 level)
Speeches	16.66	450	3.61	231	Mann-Whitney *U* Test = 4.84 (significant at .00003 level)

SUMMARY AND CONCLUSION

Observation in the United Nations General Assembly supports Garland Routt's assertion, based on observation of interaction in the Illinois Senate, that high interactors play important legislative roles.[19] An observer attempting to follow the legislative process finds that high interactors are those who seem to be most active in drafting resolutions and obtaining support for them. But interaction is not highly correlated with the sponsorship of resolutions and amendments, apparently because many sponsors neither write resolutions and amendments nor take major responsibility for the development of support of them.

Variation in the interaction rate that accompanies different issues indicates relationship between interaction and the legislative process. More controversial items appear to generate a higher rate of interaction. Further evidence of relationship between interaction and legislative activity is provided by patterns that give the observer cues to mediation efforts. In addition, proof that interaction gives useful cues to the observer is provided when a nation such as France, which would normally be expected to play a prominent role, is not active in interaction and is also inactive in the parliamentary process that extends outside the chamber.

Observation of the Fifth Committee tended not to support explanations of differences between Soviet and Western behavior, in "informal" parliamentary activity that are based solely on cultural differences. It is suggested that Soviet interactional behavior, and that of all nations, might more effectively be explained by a number of factors: (1) degree of issue interest, (2) national policy (whether close enough to majority to permit negotiation), (3) national ties outside the organization, (4) working relationships of individuals in different delegations, and (5) individual delegate characteristics (perception of parliamentary process, knowledge of issues, personality).

Amount of nation interaction is more related to a number of other measures of United Nations participation than is public speaking. Measures for participation used are number in permanent mission, number in Assembly delegation, voluntary financial contributions, regular budget contributions, total United Nations financial contributions, and total payments/GNP. Attendance at Fifth Committee meetings is related equally to public speaking and interaction. Comparison based on national characteristics shows interaction to be more related to GNP and GNP/population, and public speaking to be more related to population. The stronger relationship between most of these variables and interaction suggests that interaction may better reflect some aspects of national activity in the United Nations than records of public debate.

This hunch is given further support by an examination of a scatter diagram on which public speaking by nation is plotted against interaction. Although interaction and public speaking correlate .70, there is an important group of deviant cases that is high in interaction (ranking from 2 to 7) and relatively lower in public speaking (ranking 17 to 35). Three of these nations (Canada, Ireland,

19. Further confirmation of this assertion has been obtained through analysis of interaction in a 1963 session of the Fifth Committee and comparing it with participation in negotiation outside the committee chamber (Alger, 1966a and 1966b).

and the Netherlands) rank in the first four of nations with the largest number of intensive interaction relationships. That is, for those pairs of nations that have more than sixteen interactions, these nations are hubs of communication wheels. They are also known to be important participants in the legislative process. However, it is unlikely that their important role would be discerned from records of public debate.

Of all the measures of interaction available, number of initiatives received correlates most highly with public speaking. This finding offers some support for a hypothesis, developed out of an earlier study, that interaction serves as a feedback system for public debate. This hypothesis was generated by analysis of interaction data collected during brief observation of the Security Council (Alger,.1961). It is of considerable interest because of reports from experimental research with small groups indicating that opportunity for feedback increases the accuracy of reception of messages and increases receiver and sender confidence in their part in the communication process. These factors in turn increase amity, whereas the absence of feedback engenders greater hostility (Leavitt and Mueller, 1955).

Considerable variation is found in the percentage of intra-group interaction among regional groups, with the Latin American and Soviet groups having a much higher percentage of such interaction than all others. These two groups also had much higher indices of voting agreement than all others, with little difference between the voting agreement of the other six. Though the rank correlation between voting cohesion and intragroup interaction scores for all groups was not significant, the performance of the Latin American and Soviet groups suggests that there may be some relationship between these two variables. This relationship might be revealed more clearly in committees where group scores on voting cohesion are more dispersed.

There is a significant relationship between the permanent roles of General Assembly delegates and their quantity of interaction, with foreign office personnel being the most active, followed by members of UN permanent missions. Though there is a similar tendency in public speaking, it is not significant at the .05 level. Delegates that rank high in interaction have had more years of Assembly service than others. Delegates considered to be capable and informed by other delegates have significantly more interactions than other delegates. They also deliver significantly more speeches.

Members of the Advisory Committee on Administrative and Budgetary Questions have significantly more interactions and also deliver significantly more speeches than other nonmember delegates. They also have a reputation among their colleagues for being more capable and more informed. The eleven individuals on the ACABQ nominated to a list of capable and a list of informed delegates received a higher average number of nominations than other delegates. Their average number of nominations for being informed is significant at the .05 level, while their average number of nominations for being capable is not significant. In general, the findings on ACABQ members tend to conform with data collected on the roles of specialists in other parliamentary bodies.

In conclusion, this study of interaction in a General Assembly committee has tended to indicate that in some respects the parliamentary process in an international organization is similar to that found in the parliamentary bodies of nations and their subdivisions. There are also indications that social processes in international parliamentary bodies are, in some respects, similar to those found in face-to-face groups operating in quite different settings.

There is considerable evidence that many of the interactions observed during meetings of the Fifth Committee are significantly related to the handling of the issues before it. The researcher obtains a different appraisal of the activity of some delegates through observing interaction than he does through listening to the public debate. Cues to important actions never discussed in public debate can be discerned through observation. If these kinds of data appear important to the researcher, he should consider adding the collection of interaction data to his research strategy. This conclusion seems to be applicable not only to international parliamentary bodies, but also to those found in a variety of other political units.

Dina A. Zinnes

The Expression and Perception of Hostility in Prewar Crisis: 1914[1]

Explanations for the hostile behavior of states have long been a primary interest of the student of international relations. Why does a state sever diplomatic contact with another state; under what conditions does a state increase its military expenditures; when will one state establish a naval blockade against a second state; why does a state declare war? The present study was designed to probe into some of the determinants of belligerent state behavior. In particular, it will explore the extent to which a state's hostile behavior is a function of its perception of a hostile environment, and the accuracy of the proposition that the more hostility a state perceives, the more hostility it will express. This basic generalization will be reduced to four different hypotheses that will be tested using the messages exchanged between heads of state during the prewar crisis of 1914.

INTRODUCTION

Since I will be using traditional concepts in a somewhat unorthodox fashion, it is perhaps important to note at the outset what is meant by *a state, state behavior,* and *hostile state behavior.* The *state,* for the purpose of this discussion, refers to the group of *key decision makers* and their associates and subordinates. A *key decision maker* is an individual who, by virtue of his governmental position, has the power to make and implement decisions binding on the

1. This research was supported in part by the Stanford Studies in Conflict and Integration and the Esther Caukin Branauer Fellowship awarded by the American Association of University Women. The author wishes to thank Dr. Robert C. North, Dr. Philip Buck, and Dr. Bernard Cohen for their ideas and suggestions in the preparation of this study. Thanks must also be accorded the Carnegie Study Group on Measurement Problems Relative to Development at Indiana University for their help in preparing the manuscript.

population of his state. Since this study is concerned with a state's behavior in international rather than domestic affairs, key decision makers can only include those individuals capable of making or directly influencing foreign policy decisions (thus excluding such policy makers as the minister for economic affairs). Examples of key decision makers include the Prime Minister, President, royal heads of government, Secretary of State for War, and Secretary of State for Foreign Affairs. *Associates and subordinates* of key decision makers are those individuals who advise the key men, implement their decisions, and represent them in their absence: clerks, secretaries, undersecretaries. The *state*, then, consists of those individuals who determine and initiate courses of action binding on the remainder of the population.

A state *behaves* when its key decision makers issue threats, declare war, or negotiate treaties. *Hostile behavior* occurs when decision makers *attempt to injure* the inhabitants of another state, regardless of whether the attempt is successful. State x's act may not in fact be injurious to state y, but if it was so intended it is considered a hostile act on the part of x. Since there are many manifestations of hostile state behavior—cessation of diplomatic contact, increasing military expenditures, initiating a blockade, declaring war, to name only a few—it is necessary to specify the form or type of hostility to be investigated. This study will be concerned with perceptions and expressions of hostility by key decision makers as they were written in the diplomatic communications exchanged within and between states during the 1914 crisis.

Two variables are central to this study: (1) a state's *expression of hostility* toward another state, and (2) a state's perception that it is the target of another state's hostility, which will be termed a *perception of hostility*. It should be noted that whether or not a state is in fact the object of another state's hostility is irrelevant to the second variable. A hostile expression by state x is of the form: "We will bomb y"; while x's perception of hostility would be of the form: "y threatens to bomb our territory."

The four hypotheses postulate the following relationships between these two variables:

1   *If x perceives itself to be the object of hostility, then x will express hostility.* In this hypothesis, neither the source nor the object of hostility is specified. In particular, any of five situations could occur according to this hypothesis: (a) state x could be incapable of determining the apparent source of hostility and might express hostility at random to any other state; (b) x might specify the apparent source of hostility but still express hostility randomly; (c) x could be incapable of determining the source but express hostility toward a specific state; (d) x could perceive itself the target of y's hostility but express hostility to a specific third state z (displacement); or, finally (e) x could perceive itself the target of y's hostility and express hostility to y.

For the purposes of simplicity in the ensuing discussion, the following notation will be used to state this hypothesis. If we let xP indicate that x perceives itself the object of hostility and xE indicate that x expresses hostility, then hypothesis (1) can be stated:

$$\text{If } xP \text{ then } xE. \tag{1}$$

2   *If x perceives that it is the object of y's hostility, then x will express hostility toward y.* If we let xPy indicate that x perceives itself the object of y's hostility

and let xEy indicate that x expresses hostility to y, then the hypothesis can be stated:

$$\text{If } xPy \text{ then } xEy. \tag{2}$$

Clearly, hypothesis (2) is a special case of hypothesis (1), namely the fifth alternative described above in which both source and object are specified. Since it was not possible to test all five of the above alternatives we chose the most intuitively relevant one.

3 *If x expresses hostility toward y, then y will perceive that it is the object of x's hostility.* In notational form this becomes:

$$\text{If } xEy \text{ then } yPx. \tag{3}$$

4 *If x expresses hostility toward y, then y will express hostility toward x;* that is,

$$\text{If } xEy \text{ then } yEx. \tag{4}$$

Hypotheses (1) and (2) postulate the internal mechanism of hostile expression. These two hypotheses maintain that if a state *perceives* itself the object of hostility it will express hostility, regardless of whether it is in fact the object of hostility. The first two hypotheses then are concerned only with a state's perception, not with the reality of that perception. Hypotheses (3) and (4), on the other hand, explore the interactions between states. These latter two hypotheses maintain that what a state perceives is a function of reality, or events in the international community, rather than, for example, manifestations of psychological states of mind of decision makers. If x expresses hostility to y, (xEy), y correctly perceives this fact (yPx), or if x does not express hostility to y, then y does not perceive hostility.

Using hypotheses (2) and (3) we can diagram the following chain reaction:

Hypothesis (2)		Hypothesis (3)		Hypothesis (2)
xPy ———————→	xEy	———————→	yPx	———————————→
If x perceives that it is the object of y's hostility, then x will express hostility toward y		If x expresses hostility toward y, then y will perceive itself the object of x's hostility		

Although support for both hypotheses (2) and (3) would necessarily imply support for hypothesis (4), the failure of either hypothesis (2) or (3) implies no specific result for hypothesis (4). It was therefore necessary to test hypothesis (4) separately.

DATA SOURCES

The four hypotheses were tested using the documents from the pre–World War I crisis of 1914. These documents are the internal and international communications which were authored by the key decision makers of Germany, Austria-Hungary, France, England, Russia, and Serbia in the six-week period prior to the outbreak of war, June 28 through August 4, 1914.

The key decision makers in 1914 for each of these six states, along with their "appendages" were as follows:

GREAT BRITAIN
Prime Minister and Secretary of State for War   ....Mr. Asquith
Secretary of State for War (succeeded Mr. Asquith,
   Aug. 6, 1914) ....Earl Kitchener, of
                                                        Khartoum
Lord High Chancellor ....Viscount Haldane
Secretary of State for Foreign Affairs...................Sir Edward Grey
Permanent Undersecretary of State for Foreign Affairs ....Sir A. Nicolson

FRANCE
President of the Republic...........................M. Poincaré
President of the Council ....M. Réné Viviani

Ministers of Foreign Affairs ....
- 1. M. Jonnart
- 2. M. Stephen Pichon
- 3. M. Réné Viviani
- 4. M. Bienvenu-Martin (Acting)
- 5. M. Doumergue
- 6. M. Delcassé

Political Director ....M. de Margerie
Political Director (Acting) ....M. Berthelot

RUSSIA
Tsar Nicholas
Minister for Foreign Affairs ....M. Sazonof
Minister for War ....M. Suchomlinof

GERMANY
Kaiser Wilhelm
Imperial Chancellor ....Dr. von Bethmann-
                                                        Hollweg
Secretary of State ....Herr von Jagow
Undersecretary of State.............................Herr von Zimmermann

AUSTRIA-HUNGARY
Emperor Franz Joseph
Secretary of State for Foreign Affairs .... Count Berchtold
Undersecretaries of State for Foreign Affairs............
- Baron Macchio
- Count Forgach

President of the Ministry of Austria ....Count Sturgkh
President of the Ministry of Hungary...................Count Tisza

SERBIA
Crown Prince Alexander
Prime Minister ....M. Pashitch
Acting Prime Minister and Minister for Foreign Affairs....Dr. Laza Patchou

Several noteworthy features of the 1914 documents make them a good source of data for this study. First, they are readily accessible in collated volumes, all of which are available in the Hoover Institution on the Stanford campus. Second, considerable hostility existed during this crisis period, so that an adequate amount of data exists for testing the hypotheses. Finally, one of the principal difficulties of working with historical documents, namely determining the authenticity and completeness of document collections, has been, in large part, resolved in the case of the 1914 documents.[2] The 1914 crisis received considerable attention from many prominent historians, who spared no pains determining (1) which documents or collections had been falsified, and (2), approximately how many and what types of documents might be missing. Furthermore, following (and in one case during) the war, the governments of three of the major state participants were overthrown: Germany, Austria-Hungary, and Russia. The new governments, in their rush to discredit the old, published all documents related to the war, particularly those which might incriminate the previous government. These documents, and the absence of comparable documents for England and France, seemed to imply that these two countries had something to hide. "Revisionist historians" subsequently charged England and France with direct responsibility for the outbreak of war. Before long, England and France also felt compelled to publish most of the documents from the six-week crisis period. As a result of these events a reasonably complete set of documents exists for the six-week period prior to the outbreak of war.

However, although a reasonably complete set of documents exists, we must acknowledge two important and possibly significant omissions. Although England felt compelled to publish some of the relevant documents, by law she was not permitted to release the bulk of the collection until fifty years after the event, in 1964. Hence, when the study was begun, not all of the British documents for this period were available. The percentage and significance of this omission has not yet been systematically investigated. On the other hand, various cross-checks, using Austrian, German, and Russian documents (determining, for example, whether British messages referred to in the German collection were published in the British collection), seem to indicate that most of the important communications were available when the study began. The second difficulty was more serious—namely, the almost complete lack of documents for one of the original contenders in the dispute, Serbia. While an attempt was made to compensate for this defect, as discussed hereafter, it did remain a source of difficulty.

The five document collections together contain from 4,000 to 5,000 interstate and intrastate communications for the six major participants in the 1914 crisis.[3] Only about half of this number were used in the present study. As discussed earlier, only documents authored by key foreign policy decision makers were analyzed. There was, however, one important exception to this rule. Since very few Serbian documents were available, secondary sources were used to obtain additional statements made by Serbian decision makers. In this one instance, all statements imputed to Serbian decision makers, either by decision makers of other states or by ambassadors, were assumed to be accurate reflections of official Serbian opinion.

2. For a complete discussion of this problem see this author's "Documents as a Source of Data," in North *et al.*(1963), pp. 17–36.
3. The collections from which data were acquired were the following: for Germany, Montegelas and Schucking (1924); for the Austro-Hungarian Monarchy, Ministerium des K. und k. Hauses und des Aeusseren (1930); for Russia, Komissiia po izdaniiu dokumentov epokhi imperializma (1934); for France, Commission for the Publication of Documents Relative to the War of 1914 (1936); for Great Britain, Foreign Office (1926).

DATA COLLECTION PROCEDURES

Data to test the hypotheses were collected by means of content analysis. As suggested by its name, this is a method for rigorously analyzing the content of written materials. Variables of interest are operationalized by composing a list of words, symbols, or themes which are synonymous with the variables. Certain simple tests of hypotheses can then be made by counting the frequency with which these words (symbols or themes) appear in a given text (Berelson, 1954; Pool, 1959).

An initial problem faced in the course of this study was the choice between the three analytical units—word, theme, or symbol. Since a cursory examination of the documents seemed to indicate that it might be difficult to compose a list of words synonymous with diplomatic expressions of hostility, the first choice fell to the theme. The documents were then coded by counting the number of hostile themes, or phrases. But it was soon discovered that the reliability between coders (agreement as to what constituted a hostile theme) was unreasonably low, probably because of poor training procedures. The word was then tried as the unit, and the same documents were recorded. Although several word lists were utilized, this unit also proved to have difficulties. Even though *reliability* (agreement between coders) was high (since coders simply counted the occurrences of words on the word list), the coders complained that rigid adherence to the word list caused them to code items which, from the context of the material, were clearly not manifestations of hostility; that is, the *validity* of the coding results was low. Thus while *thematic* content analysis appeared to be relatively valid but inadequately reliable, *word* content analysis led to low validity but high reliability.

The solution finally adopted consisted of a combination of word and thematic content analysis procedures. A list of *tip-off* words was devised to alert the coder to the possibility of a relevant theme.[4] The coder, however, was not compelled to count every tip-off word, only those in which the context revealed a manifestation of hostility. Intensive training sessions helped the coder determine which contexts were appropriate. This procedure led to a minute breakdown of themes, as shown in the forms in Figures 1, 2a and 2b, since only one tip-off word could appear in a theme.[5]

4. Since the documents originated in several different languages and represented expressions and perceptions of people with different cultural backgrounds, it might be argued that certain countries would appear more hostile than others because more hostile modifiers, or tip-off words, tend to appear in one language than another. While this is a problem, and could be controlled for, it should be kept in mind that this study is interested in the behavior of states in general, not with the behavior of particular states. As long as similar behavior is observed over all six states (for example, that all states express hostility when they perceive themselves the object of hostility), whether some states express and perceive more hostility than others is not of immediate relevance. Furthermore, the most hostile state in the 1914 crisis was, as one would expect on the basis of the origin of the crisis, Austria-Hungary. While this result might be attributable to cultural differences, it should be noted that the Austrian and German languages are almost identical, while the differences between the two in terms of frequency or intensity of expression or perception of hostility is considerable, as can be seen from Figures 12 and 13.

5. In retrospect, of course, one always sees a better method. The test document was labeled as such, so that the coders were probably more "on their toes"; undoubtably several test

The original document collections appear in four different languages: English, French, German, and Russian. Since content analysis procedures are heavily dependent on nuances or shadings of meanings, it was obviously desirable to content-analyze the documents in their original language text. On the other hand, to permit the subsequent scaling of hostility themes, it was necessary to translate the themes into English. This was done on the code sheet. Thus every hostility theme used in the analysis appeared in English on a code sheet. A potential coder, therefore, had to pass a language proficiency test which tested both his ability to grasp nuances of words and to translate a text into English. A coder usually only coded in one language.

Before the actual coding began, the coders participated in a one-week training session in which the hostility theme was defined both conceptually and by way of example. Using 1914 documents the coders were shown samples of hostility themes. The coders then made a series of dry runs in which they were given sample documents to code. When these documents were completed, the coding instructor checked the coding and discussed any errors with the coders. Only when the coder demonstrated his ability to code a sample document faultlessly was he permitted to begin the actual coding.

A final check on all the coders was made before the coding began. The degree of agreement between any two coders, that is, a measure of the reliability of the coding, was ascertained. The reliability formula frequently used for these purposes, namely the Pearson correlation coefficient, could not be used in this instance. According to this formula, if two coders code ten documents and each coder arrives at the same *number* of hostility themes for each document, the intercoder reliability would be 1.0, indicating perfect agreement. But in fact it could be the case that the themes picked up by each coder were entirely different, so that agreement is really zero. Thus it was necessary to devise a different formula.

The new formula was a function of two considerations. First, since several variables were being coded at the same time for purposes of related studies, the coder was simultaneously coding perceptions of power, frustration, hostility, satisfaction, and friendship (Figure 2a). The similarity of several of these variables (frustration and hostility) was a potential source of error, with the possibility of a coder correctly picking up a theme, but then coding it incorrectly by placing it in the wrong variable category. The second factor affecting the reliability formula was that the code sheets were consistently checked (or spot-checked) to maintain high reliability as the coding proceeded. Since the coder was required to copy the verbatim text from which he abstracted a theme (see later discussion), the checker could determine whether the appropriate context existed for the tip-off word, and whether the theme had been properly coded in terms of the relevant variable (for example, that a hostility theme had not been incorrectly labeled as a frustration theme). Note that this checking procedure only insures against errors of commission, and not against errors of omission. If a hostility theme was missed in the document, it was lost for good, since the checker never reread the original documents.

---

documents should have been slipped in at different points during the coding procedure to determine whether, for example, fatigue factors have any appreciable effect. However, the consistent checking of the coding alleviated some of this difficulty by discovering errors of commission, for instance, the improper labeling of themes.

These two considerations determined the following procedure for measuring the reliability of the coding. A test document was selected and two individuals who had worked closely with the training of coders noted together which statements in the document represented themes appropriate for each variable. The coders then coded the test document. A coder's score was computed on the basis of a point system. If a coder correctly coded a theme, which meant that he had both correctly discovered a theme *and* assigned it to the appropriate variable category (found a hostility theme and labeled it correctly), he received one point. If the coder found a theme but put it in the wrong variable category (found a hostility theme but incorrectly coded it as, say, a frustration theme), he was partially penalized by receiving only half a point, the argument being that the checker would most likely catch this error of commission and correct it. Failure to perceive a theme netted the coder no points. Since errors of omission would never be caught by the checker, the reliability formula ought to demonstrate the extent to which these errors were occurring. The reliability quotient was then formed by adding the number of points each coder acquired and then dividing this by the total number of possible points (as determined by the instructors) multiplied by the number of coders. Using this formula, the reliability score for the coding of the 1914 documents was .67. Considering the conservative nature of the reliability formula (since most errors of commission would be caught by the checker), .67 was felt to be adequate to permit coding to begin.[6]

The coding procedure included the following steps (see Figures 1, 2a, and 2b).

FIGURE 1. *Examples of coding perceptions of hostility.**

AFFECTIVE PERCEPTIONS: *D   E   F   G   H 5*
Author of document *A–H* (*Berchtold*)   Person quoted
Recipient of document *A–H* (*Franz Joseph*)   Interlocutor
Source *Oe-U, VIII,* # *10126, 8 July 1914*

"Perceiver": Auth. *X* Recip.   Pers. quoted   Interloc.   Other
"Perceived": Auth.   Recip.   Pers. quoted   Interloc.   Other   *Serbia*
"Target" of perception   *Austria-Hungary*

This perception is stimulated by an event in the PAST   PRESENT *X* FUTURE

Text:
We cannot remain indolent bystanders, when Serbia is agitating against us, when our own subjects are incited to commit treason and murder-plots are prepared. The statements made not only by the Serbian press but also by Serbian diplomats further such a hatred and represent such a lack of international decorum and the impression made by them at home and at abroad affects the estimation of our power and energy in such a way that for the sake of our prestige and security, serious and energetic steps have to be taken in Belgrade.

Capsule statement(s):

H.1. "Serbia is agitating AGAINST us . . . "

H.2. ". . . our own subjects ARE INCITED to commit treason . . . "

*Note minute breakdown of themes, that is, that every tip-off word signals the onset of a *separate* theme.

6. A more detailed account of this procedure can be found in Zinnes (1963c).

FIGURE 1—*cont.*

H.3. " . . . murder-plots ARE PREPARED . . . "

H.4. "The statements made not only by the Serbian press but also by Serbian diplomats further such a HATRED."

H.5. "The statements made not only by the Serbian press but also by Serbian diplomats . . . (adversely) AFFECT the estimation of our power and energy . . . "

D: PERCEPTION OF POWER   *E:* PERCEPTION OF SATISFACTION
F: PERCEPTION OF FRUSTRATION *G:* PERCEPTION OF FRIENDSHIP
H: PERCEPTION OF HOSTILITY

FIGURE 2a.   *Examples of coding expressions of hostility.*

AFFECTIVE PERCEPTIONS: *D*   *E*   *F1*   *G1*   *H4*

Author of document *Germany* (*Wilhelm II*)   Person quoted

Recipient of document *A-H* (*Franz Joseph*)   Interlocutor

Source *Kautsky # 503, 31 July, 1914*

"Perceiver": Auth. *X* Recip.   Pers. quoted   Interloc.   Other

"Perceived": Auth. *X* Recip.   Pers. quoted   Interloc.   Other   *Serbia*

         G 1-Austria   *H 4-France*

"Target" of perception   *H 1-General*; *H 2-Russia*; *H 3-France*; *F 1-Russia*

This perception is stimulated by an event in the PAST   PRESENT   FUTURE *X*

Text:

The introductory mobilization of my entire army and the navy which I have ordered today will be followed shortly by the actual mobilization. I am planning on the second of August as the first day of mobilization and I am prepared in fulfillment of the obligations of my alliance, to start war at once against Russia and France. It is of utmost importance in this grave struggle that Austria oppose her principal forces to Russia and not splinter her strength by a simultaneous offensive against Serbia. This is of all the more importance as a great part of my army will be employed against France. Serbia plays in this gigantic fight which we are entering shoulder to shoulder a very ordinate role, which requires of us only the defensive measures absolutely necessary.

Capsule statement(s):

H.1. "The introductory mobilization of my entire army and the navy which I have ordered today will be followed shortly by the ACTUAL MOBILIZATION."

H.2. "I (Wilhelm II) am prepared . . . TO START WAR at once against Russia . . .*"

H.3. "I (Wilhelm II) am prepared . . . TO START WAR at once against . . . France . . . "*

F.1. "It is of utmost importance in this GRAVE struggle . . . "**

H.4. " . . . a great part of my army will be EMPLOYED AGAINST France . . . "

G.1. "I (Wilhelm II) am prepared, in fulfillment of the OBLIGATION OF MY ALLIANCE, to start war . . . "**

D: PERCEPTION OF POWER   *E:* PERCEPTION OF SATISFACTION
F: PERCEPTION OF FRUSTRATION   *G:* PERCEPTION OF FRIENDSHIP
H: PERCEPTION OF HOSTILITY

*Note that a new theme exists when either perceiver, perceived, or, in this case, target changes. It should also be mentioned that when no direction is implied a theme is coded in both directions: "Austria and Serbia are at WAR" is coded *both* as an expression of hostility by Austria and an expression of hostility by Serbia.

**Note that themes for several variables were put on the same code sheet.

FIGURE 2b. *An expression of hostility sent by the Russian foreign office to its four ambassadors.*

AFFECTIVE PERCEPTIONS: *D   E   F   G   H 1*

Author of document *Russia (Sazanov)*   Person quoted

Recipient of document *Russia (Svorbeev, Isvolsky, Benckendorff, Shebeko)* Interloc.

(Berlin, Paris, London, Vienna)

Source: *MO III V5 #279, 30/17 July 1914*

"Perceiver": Auth. *X* Recip.   Pers. quoted   Interloc.   Other

"Perceived": Auth.   Recip.   Pers. quoted   Interloc.   Other *H 1 Russia*

"Target" of perception *H 1 Austria*

This perception is stimulated by an event in the PAST   PRESENT   *X*   FUTURE

Text:

Until receipt through the German government of a fully satisfactory answer of Austria, we will continue our armaments.

Capsule statement(s):

H.1. " . . . we will continue our ARMAMENTS."

D: PERCEPTION OF POWER   *E:* PERCEPTION OF SATISFACTION

F: PERCEPTION OF FRUSTRATION *G:* PERCEPTION OF FRIENDSHIP

H: PERCEPTION OF HOSTILITY

Beneath the title of the code sheet, on the first line labeled *Author of document*, the coder indicated the state where the communication originated and then in parentheses the name of the decision maker(s) who had signed the document. In Figure 1 the author is Austria-Hungary, and the writer is Berchtold. At an early point in the study an attempt was made to distinguish between documents which were authored by different decision makers, hoping that one might detect differences between decision makers. However, a study of the foreign offices and the documents themselves led to the conclusion that this was an unprofitable enterprise. In some cases documents had no author—they were simply sent out by the foreign office. In other cases it was learned that a document had been drawn up by one man but signed by another, or that several individuals had written the communication together and all appended their signatures. Therefore, since it was frequently not possible to distinguish between the expressions and perceptions of different decision makers in one state, we assumed that all statements of the key decision makers of a particular state represented the consensus of sentiment for that state.

On the second line of the code sheet, labeled *Recipient of document*, the coder noted the *home state* of the individual who received the communication. Since most of the communications sent by the decision makers of a state went to that state's ambassadors or representatives stationed abroad, the "recipient of document" was frequently the same as the author, as shown in Figure 2b. In this Figure, Sazanov has written to Russia's four ambassadors stationed in Berlin, Paris, London, and Vienna, hence both author and recipient are given as Russia. In parentheses, the coder indicated the name of the representative involved (Svorbeev, Isvolsky, Benckendorff, Shebeko) and the country in which the representative was stationed, and this was later recorded as a com- munication *between* the two countries, whereas that shown in Figure 1 is an *intra*-state communication.

The *source of the document* gives all information necessary for locating the document coded on the sheet. The *perceiver, perceived,* and *target* categories can perhaps best be understood in terms of the general hostility statement:

x perceives that *y* is hostile to *z*

In this statement *x* is known as the *perceiver*, *y* the *perceived*, and *z*, the *target*. For example, if Austria's decision makers said "The Serbian government tolerated anti-Austrian propaganda," the perceiver would be Austria, the perceived, Serbia, and the target Austria. The remaining categories on the top of the code sheet (*person quoted, interlocutor*) are not relevant for the present study.

The coder, having filled in the categories in the top one-third of the page, then copied, verbatim, the portion of the text from which his statement(s) would be extracted. This text might be as long as a paragraph or as short as a sentence; longer reproductions usually occurred when several themes were being coded from the same text. The purpose of copying the text verbatim was twofold. It provided the context for checking the coding, as discussed earlier, and was subsequently used in scaling the hostility themes (see later discussion).

After the verbatim text was copied, the coder "capsulized" the hostility theme(s) by abstracting a statement from the text in the form of the general hostility theme: "*x* perceives *y* hostile to *z*," though often the perceiver is understood and therefore not stated. When capsulizing a statement, the coder capitalized the tip-off words, but continued to use the actual words in the text. For example, the sentence: "In a general manner, it seems as though the Austrian government feeling itself overwhelmed by its press and by the military party, seeks to obtain the maximum from Serbia, through a preliminary intimidation, direct and indirect, and relies upon Germany to this effect," in capsulized form becomes two hostility themes: " ... the Austrian government ... seeks to OBTAIN THE MAXIMUM from Serbia ..." and "... the Austrian government . . . seeks to obtain the maximum from Serbia through a preliminary INTIMIDATION . . ." Each abstracted theme was labeled with the appropriate variable, i.e. hostility, friendship, frustration, etc., and the number of themes per variable was indicated on the top of the code sheet. Five hostility themes, for example, were abstracted from the text shown in Figure 1 and this is shown by the "5" after the "H" or hostility category on the top of the page.

The number of themes that could appear on a single code sheet was limited by space and the requirement that all themes on that sheet for a particular variable have the same perceiver, perceived and target. In Figure 1, the perceiver is Austria, the perceived Serbia, and the target Austria for *all five hostility* themes. The length of a theme—that is, where one theme ended and another began—was determined by the occurrence of a new tip-off word or a change in either the perceiver, perceived or target. Figures 1 and 2 demonstrate this break down of textual material into minute themes, each containing a single tip-off word. Figure 2a further shows (see H2 and H3) how a single statement can become two hostility themes.

On the basis of the code sheet it is possible now to determine measures for xP, xPy, xE, and xEy. Recall the general hostility statement:

x perceives y hostile to z.

If perceiver and target are the same, then we can rewrite the general statement to read:

x perceives y hostile to x.

This form of the general hostility statement is known as a *perception of hostility* by x, or xPy. Examples of perceptions of hostility can be found in Figure 1. Similarly, if perceiver and perceived are identical, we have:

x perceives x hostile to y,

which we term an *expression of hostility*. Actually in this case x does not really perceive itself—this is simply the form the coding took. Figures 2a and 2b give examples of expressions of hostility.

It will be noted that two other types of statements are logically possible, namely:

x perceives x hostile to x,

x perceives y hostile to z.

These two types were not used in this study.

Scaling

Any of the four variables (xP, xPy, xE, xEy) could be measured by counting the frequency with which the specified type of statement described above occurred within given time intervals. This procedure implicitly assumes that all hostility statements are of equal intensity since all statements contribute equally to the total result. Yet we often find dramatic differences between the content of two hostility statements. Should the same weight be given a statement expressing anger over propaganda as to a statement threatening annihilation? To alleviate this problem two types of scaling procedures were used. The first assigned to each hostility theme a weight from one to twelve, to reflect the intensity of hostility in that statement. The second categorized hostility themes into two mutually exclusive groups: threats and actions.

Intensity weights were assigned hostility statements on the basis of the following procedure. Eleven random samples were selected from a universe of more than 2,000 hostility statements, each sample containing between ten and sixteen statements. For a given sample—let us assume that it contained ten hostility statements—all possible pairs were generated: $\dfrac{n(n-1)}{2} = \dfrac{10(9)}{2} = 45$.

For each pair a judge, assuming himself to be the decision maker of the target state, made a decision as to which of the two statements represented the most hostile statement.

The most hostile statement received a "vote". In this fashion, when all pairs had been judged, a series of votes resulted that then permitted the rank-ordering of the statements—the most hostile statements having the largest number of votes. The results are as shown in Table 1.

TABLE 1. *Pair Comparison Judgments on a Selection of Twelve Hostility Statements from the 1914 Crisis Statements*

	No. Votes Received	Rank Order
1. Austria-Hungary wants to undermine the great moral credit which Serbia enjoys in Europe today.	2	3
2. Austria-Hungary wants to exploit politically against Serbia the insane deed of an exalted young fanatic.	1	2
3. The Austro-Hungarian press is for purely political reasons placing a heavy responsibility for the crime of an Austrian subject on Serbia and the entire Serbian peoples.	0	1
4. The Russian Pan-Slavists' object is the weakening of the Triple Alliance.	11	12
5. The Sarajevo affair was the result of a well-organized conspiracy the threads of which can be traced to Belgrade.	9	10
6. Serbia's policy is responsible for such crimes against Austria.	8	9
7. Romania permits within her own confines an agitation against us which is just as hateful as that tolerated by Serbia.	4	5
8. Romania permits within her own confines an agitation against us which is just as hateful as that tolerated by Serbia.	3	4
9. All the other participants of the Council of the Ministers share the opinion of provoking a war with Serbia in order to settle our accounts with that arch-enemy of the monarchy at last.	10	11
10. Serbia is agitating against us.	5	6
11. Our own subjects are incited to commit treason.	7	8
12. Murder plots are prepared against us.	6	7

This procedure has two advantages. First, if perfect or near-perfect rank-ordering results, one can be reasonably confident that the judgments are being made along a single dimension and are being made consistently. One therefore has a certain amount of faith in the use of the concept of "hostility". Second, the results of these judgments provide the material for the generation of a "yardstick" against which the remaining hostility statements can be judged. Thus the eleven samples which were used were combined, and all statements given the lowest rank order were analyzed, then the next lowest, and so on. In this way, a common denominator was discovered for each level that produced the following abstract scale.

1. Shirking obligations
2. Preventing press from misleading public opinion, denying, putting an end to
3. Using events against opponent, refusal, making others responsible, mis-representation, spreading false news
4. Cool relationship, undermining credit of opponent, undermining opponent's position in world

5. Tolerating agitation against others, weakening opponent directly, warning opponent, possibility of intervention, will not tolerate
6. Reproaching, agitating against opponent, anti-x feeling, difficulties
7. Conspiracy, committing crimes against opponent or so implicated, provoking, inciting others against enemy
8. Making demands, diplomatic ruptures, démarche, danger, conflict, taking steps
9. Getting maximum, intimidating, humiliating, ultimatums, menace
10. Mobilization, troop concentrations, troop movements
11. Declaration of war, attacks, bombing
12. Destruction, annihilation, disposal

This abstract scale, which reflects the rank ordering of each of the samples, was then used to scale the remaining hostility statements. A statement was scaled by comparing it with the "yardstick" and answering the question: Which of the twelve degrees of the general scale does this statement most resemble? The answer to this question determined the scale value of the statement.

Several reliability checks were made of this scaling. Since only one judge was used to scale the statements, the reliability was computed for the same individual over time.[7] One hundred and ninety-five statements were scaled twice with one week intervening, using the general abstract scale. The correlation was .95. A similar correlation was computed at the end of the scaling process and was found to be .98. Both, of course, were significant beyond the .01 level.[8]

The other type of scaling was nominal. It placed the statements into two mutually exclusive categories on the basis of whether they were threats or actions. A threat statement was a statement in the future tense, and an action (or report) statement was one made in the present or past tense. Examples of some threat statements are:

1. Germany would probably not wait for a pretext for attacking us.
2. The Russian military districts against Austria will be mobilized.
3. I shall be overwhelmed by the pressure brought upon me and forced to take extreme measures which will lead to war.
4. I am prepared to start war at once against Russia.
5. This, however, only can be possible when Serbia is eliminated as a factor of political power.
6. Serbia can, however, by no means permit the Austro-Hungarian press to mislead the public opinion of Europe.
7. The Serbs must be disposed of and that right soon.
8. I was disturbed by what the Ambassador has told me about the form that anti-Serbian feeling might take in Serbia.

7. There is, of course, no problem in using only one judge to compute the reliability score. The question of reliability is one of consistency, and if only one judge judges all statements, one simply wants to know whether he is consistent over time. On the other hand, a problem does exist in the use of only one judge to make the pair-comparison judgments. To what extent does the abstract scale represent the idiosyncracies of one individual? This question can only be answered by comparing the pair-comparison judgments of several judges. Unfortunately, the limitations of the study did not permit this analysis.

8. The scale generated by this procedure is an absolute scale. One of the characteristics of an absolute scale is that its intervals are equal. See Suppes and Zinnes (1963).

9. I spoke to M. Cambon of the great apprehension felt as to what Austria was going to demand of Serbia.
10. For the sake of our prestige and security serious and energetic steps have to be taken in Belgrade.

Examples of action statements are:

1. The Austrian note reproaches the Serbian government.
2. The Serbian government tolerated anti-Austrian propaganda.
3. England has maintained a reserved attitude to the Triple Entente ever since the Balkan crisis.
4. Military action against Serbia has been decided.
5. An order for mobilization against Austria was given in Serbia.
6. Austria declared war on Serbia.
7. The object of that action was to crush Serbia and make her a vassal of Austria.
8. In the Italian question Vienna seems to disregard our advice.
9. The English fleet protects France's northern coast by tying up our fleet.
10. The whole war is plainly arranged between England, France, and Russia for the annihilation of Germany.

Note that these examples are not necessarily for only one type of variable; that is, they could be either for perception or expressions of hostility (xPy or xEy). The reliability score for this scaling was computed by categorizing the statements twice, with a week intervening, and then determining the number of disagreements between the first and second scaling. Using 195 statements, there were 12 disagreements or $12/195 = 94$ per cent agreement.

RESEARCH DESIGN

Each of the hypotheses, it should be noted, can and will be tested under six different conditions, depending on (1) which statements are counted, and (2) whether we use the non-weighted (mere frequency count) or a weighted intensity score. The consequent conditions would then be:

1. Frequency count of all statements
2. Frequency count of threat statements only
3. Frequency count of action statements only
4. Intensity score of all statements
5. Intensity score of threat statements only
6. Intensity score of action statements only

Let us now consider how hypothesis (1)—that there is a relationship between a state's perception of hostility and its expression of hostility—could be tested under condition (1) (using all statements and only using frequency measures), using correlation procedures. For a given state x we would determine, for each day, the number of xP statements made (its perceptions of hostility) and the number of xE statements made (its expressions of hostility). Having completed this tabulation for state x we would go on to states y, z, and so on, and perform similar computations. Then, since we are not concerned with the behavior of any particular state, we would combine the results for all states x, y, z, and so on. Since there were thirty-eight days in the crisis and six different states were involved, if there was a value for xP and xE on each day, at the conclusion of the process $6 \times 38 = 228$ pairs of numbers would be obtained, one set for xP and one set for xE. It is then a simple matter to correlate these two sets of numbers.

But consider now the implication of such a computed correlation. The assumption implicit in this design (as is true in any correlation design, since the events being correlated must be independent) is that the value of xP (or xE) on a given day is unaffected by, and *independent* of, the values of xP (or xE) for any other day. The meaning of this assumption can perhaps be more graphically demonstrated by way of an example. At the end of a day, a key decision maker sits at his desk and makes notes concerning the following. First, he lists on his memo pad the number of times during the day that he felt his state was the object of another state's hostility. Then he allows himself free rein and expresses hostility toward other states, indicating these feelings on his note pad. Having accomplished these two tasks, the results are tossed in the wastebasket (though thoughtfully not torn up), the decision maker takes a good stiff drink, wipes from his memory all that he has just done and goes off to bed. The following morning he arrives at the office with a clean memory ready to begin the day anew. None of the miseries of the previous day remain to plague him. At the end of the day he repeats the process, and then once again retires with a clean memory. And so he continues from day to day. Thus the correlation procedure described above assumes that the events of the previous day have no effect on the events of the present day.

This is not a totally implausible assumption, but a more realistic one would admit the existence and operation of memory. One obvious modification of this independence assumption is to assume that the events of the immediately preceding day do affect the events of the present day. This assumption would produce the following modification in the correlation design described above. To determine xP for a given day n we would add the xP values for day n to those for the preceding day, that is for day $(n-1)$, and then divide the result by two. This new averaged value for xP would then be compared with the xE value for day n. Using this procedure we would once again generate two sets of numbers, one for xP and a corresponding one for xE. A correlation coefficient could then be easily computed to determine the degree of relationship between the two sets of values. Obviously, in a similar fashion one could introduce an infinite number of modifications by permitting the previous two, three, four, etc., days to affect a particular day.

The calculations described introduce a second assumption. They imply that the previous $(n-m)$ days affect day n equally. That is to say, we simply added the xP value for day $(n-1)$ to the xP value for day n and divided by two; the values for each day were given equal weight. Since recent events are usually more vivid than those of several weeks earlier, this is not the most realistic assumption that could be made. This second assumption could therefore be modified by allowing the days to contribute differentially to the measure of xP, that is, by weighting the most recent day, day n, more heavily than the previous day, day $(n-1)$, and so on. As was the case with the first assumption, there exist an unlimited number of variations which could be introduced in terms of the weights one wishes to assign to the preceding days.

Thus the above discussion indicates that there are two assumptions implicit in using the correlation design to test the hypotheses: (1) the assumption concerning the effects of the previous days, or the *memory span* assumption, and (2) the assumption which determines the differential effects of the previous days, the *accuracy of memory* assumption. Since all possible variations of each assumption could not be studied, three variations of the first assumption (memory span) and two variations of the second (accuracy of memory) were analyzed using three models.

Model I, known as the *no memory model*, assumes, as discussed above, that each day is independent of every other day; the events of the previous days have no effect on day n. In this case the correlation is computed in a manner similar to that described above.

Model II is known as the *imperfect memory model*. In this case, the memory span is assumed to be four days. The decision maker on day n recalls days $(n-1)$, $(n-2)$, and $(n-3)$ but cannot remember beyond day $(n-3)$. Furthermore, he does not remember these days equally well. This model assumes that day $(n-1)$ has a greater effect on day n than does day $(n-2)$, while day $(n-2)$ has a greater effect than day $(n-3)$. These differential effects are reflected in the use of weights. The xP value for day n is multiplied by four, the xP value for day $(n-1)$ is weighted by a factor of three, day $(n-2)$ is given a weight of two, and day $(n-1)$ receives a weight of one. The correlation design consisted of averaging the xP values (adding the weighted values for four days and dividing by the sum of the weights, $1 + 2 + 3 + 4 = 10$) over a group of four days and then comparing this value with the xE value on the fourth day. The values for the fifth day would be determined by summing the xP values (with their weights) for days two through five, averaging this result and comparing it with the xE value for the fifth day; and so on. The use of a four-day memory span was somewhat arbitrary, though it did represent an attempt to use a memory span that approximated an individual's capacity to remember previous events.

Model III is known as the *perfect memory model*. This model assumes that *all* previous days affect the behavior of a decision maker on a given day. Furthermore, this model assumes that the effects of these earlier days are equal. The decision maker not only remembers all previous days but he remembers every day equally well. The correlation design in this case consisted of averaging the values of xP for the first n days and then comparing this value with the xE value on day n. For example, on day three, the xP values for days one, two, and three would be summed, averaged, and then compared with the xE value for day three; for day four, the xP values for days one, two, three, and four would be averaged and compared with the xE value for day four; and so forth.

Thus far we have not considered a factor which could prove to be important, namely the time lag between perceptions and expressions and consequent expressions of hostility. In the above discussion of correlation designs, the xP value for day n, or the averaged xP value for $(n-m)$ days, was compared with the xE value for day n. This design assumes that one day is sufficient time for xP (perception of hostility) to have an effect on xE (expression of hostility). This is not an unreasonable assumption in this instance, since xP and xE are both expressed by the same state. But the assumption is somewhat stronger when applied to hypotheses (3) and (4), ($xEy{\rightarrow}yPx$; $xEy{\rightarrow}yEx$). The application of this design to these two hypotheses assumes that one day is sufficient time for an xEy (x's expression of hostility to y) to be received by y and have some effect on y's perception of x, namely yPx. The case is similar for hypothesis (4). Again, this is not an unreasonable assumption to make for an historical period in which the telegraph, particularly in times of crisis, was heavily relied upon. However, it does suggest the possibility of making other assumptions which allow for a greater time interval.

For this reason, then, three subsidiary models were constructed; Models Ia, IIa, and IIIa. These models are essentially the same as described above except that the correlation computed is a lag correlation. In Model Ia, the xP value for day n is compared with the xE value the day after, i.e. for day ($n + 1$), the xP value for day ($n + 1$) is compared with the xE value for day ($n + 2$), and so on. This is similarly the case for Models IIa and IIIa.

In summary, then, the hypotheses will be examined under all of the earlier mentioned six conditions, and applying all six of these memory-lag models, providing thirty-six different opportunities for the testing of the hypotheses.

RESULTS AND INTERPRETATION

Figures 3 through 8 describe the range of values for the perception and expression of hostility throughout the crisis. The values, as can be seen from the graphs, were obtained by pooling the data over states, (the values represent the total perception or expression of hostility by all states) and then grouping the resulting data into sets of four days.[9] Figures 3 and 4 demonstrate the overall rise in frequency and intensity for both perceptions and expressions of hostility; Figures 5 through 8 give these data for the threat and action categories separately. Note that while there is a general tendency for both perceptions and expressions of hostility to increase over the entire period, regardless of condition, one finds that the frequency and intensity conditions are not mirror images of one another. The intensity of perceptions and expressions appears to rise consistently over the crisis period for the total, threat, and action conditions, while the frequency measure is less consistent from one condition to the next and often appears to decline in the later days of the crisis.

---

9. It is, of course, possible to question the assumptions inherent in pooling the data over the six states. Explicitly, this procedure assumes that the states exhibit similar behavior, or that they would exhibit similar behavior if we could observe them for an unlimited period of time. Whether or not this assumption is valid must depend in part on the results—if we obtain good results, we would consider the assumption warranted, if not, we might wish to revise it. A similar question might be raised concerning the use of raw scores, rather than standard scores, in computing the correlation over six states: should not the data be standardized within each state and then correlations computed using these scores? If the initial assumption, stated above, can be granted, then there is obviously no need to standardize. If not, then the only answer that can be given at this stage is that the present analysis represents a first approximation in testing the hypotheses. Standardization within countries is just one of a multitude of possible refinements (for example, standardization per day per country) that could be made in future analyses, provided, of course, that adequate data existed to allow for such operations (which is not presently true for the 1914 data). The present analysis has sought only to determine how far one might go in predicting expressions or perceptions by using a mininum number of parameters.

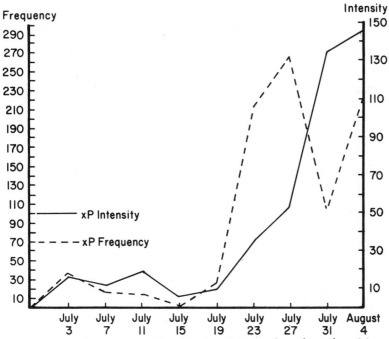

FIGURE 3. *Perceptions of hostility by all states throughout the crisis.*

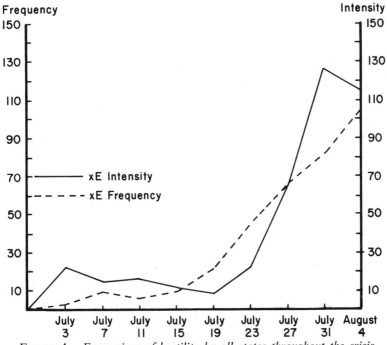

FIGURE 4. *Expressions of hostility by all states throughout the crisis.*

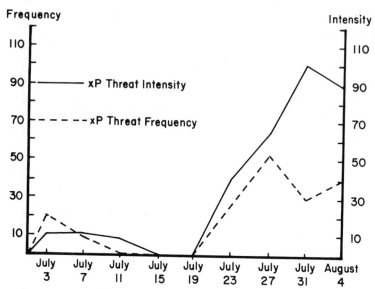

FIGURE 5.   *Perceptions of threat by all states throughout the crisis.*

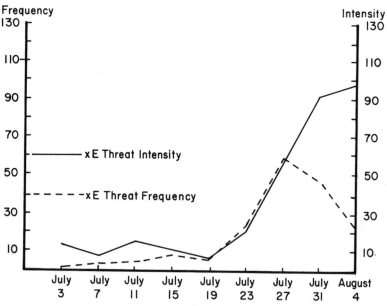

FIGURE 6.   *Expressions of threat by all states throughout the crisis.*

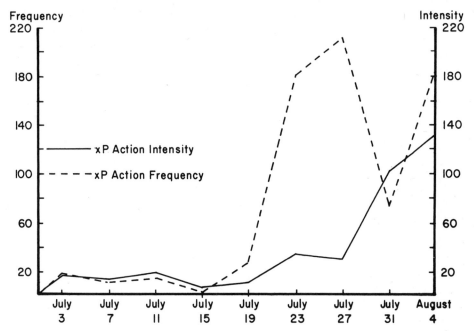

FIGURE 7.   *Perceptions of hostile actions by all states throughout the crisis.*

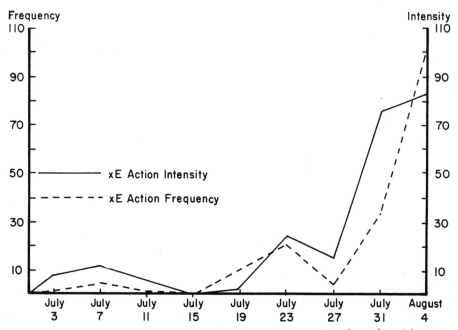

FIGURE 8.   *Expressions of hostile actions by all states throughout the crisis.*

Figures 9 through 14 demonstrate similar results for each state independently. In these graphs, however, only condition (1) is shown (frequency, using all statements). These graphs demonstrate the differences between Models I, II, and III. Since any model affects only the xP (perception of hostility) variable, there is only one curve for the xE (expression of hostility) variable, while there are three for the xP variable (representing Models I, II, and III). One notes again the consistency of the behavior of the variables for each state, with the exception of Serbia. The chaotic nature of this graph (Figure 14) is undoubtedly due to the use of secondary source material and probably indicates that this should be discarded in future analyses. The similarity of behavior for the other five states is of interest, since the states do not contribute equal amounts of data to the correlation design.

HYPOTHESES (1) $(xP \rightarrow xE)$ AND (2) $(xPy \rightarrow xEy)$

Hypotheses (1) and (2) are concerned with the relationship between a state's perception of hostility and its subsequent expression of it. Table 2 reports the correlations for these two hypotheses for the two best versions, Models I (no memory) and II (imperfect memory) over the six conditions. The r column designates the correlations obtained, the n column the number of cases involved (days on which a state either perceived or expressed hostility; days on which neither occurred were omitted since they would unduly inflate the correlation)

TABLE 2.   *Results for Hypotheses (1) and (2)*

	Model II (Imperfect Memory)					
	Hypothesis 1			Hypothesis 2		
Condition	r	n	Sign.	r	n	Sign.
Frequency						
1. All statements	0.59	93	1%	0.61	159	1%
2. Threat statements	0.60	77	1%	0.63	129	1%
3. Action statements	0.26	74	5%	0.28	115	1%
Intensity						
4. All statements	0.41	93	1%	0.36	159	1%
5. Threat statements	0.31	77	1%	0.15	129	—
6. Action statements	0.51	74	1%	0.54	115	1%
	Model I (No Memory)					
Frequency						
1. All statements	0.55	66	1%	0.56	96	1%
2. Threat statements	0.25	54	—	0.32	86	1%
3. Action statements	0.29	49	5%	0.30	64	5%
Intensity						
4. All statements	−0.02	66	—	−0.14	96	—
5. Threat statements	−0.20	54	—	−0.35	80	1%
6. Action statements	0.11	49	—	0.07	64	—

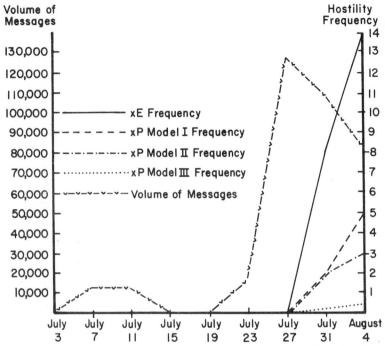

FIGURE 9.   *England. Frequency of perception and expression of hostility for models I, II, and III.*

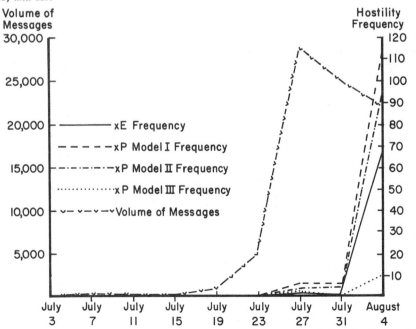

FIGURE 10.   *France. Frequency of perception and expression of hostility for models I, II, and III.*

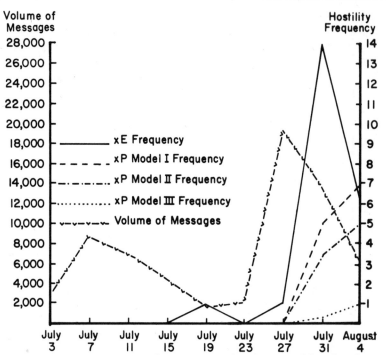

FIGURE 11.   *Russia. Frequency of perception and expression of hostility for models I, II, and III.*

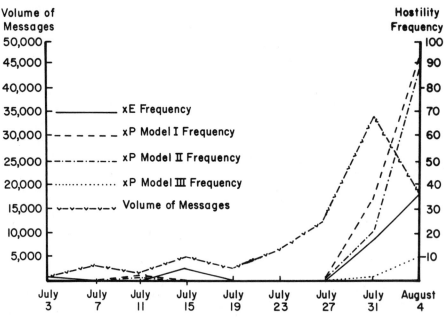

FIGURE 12.   *Germany. Frequency of perception and expression of hostility for models I, II, and III.*

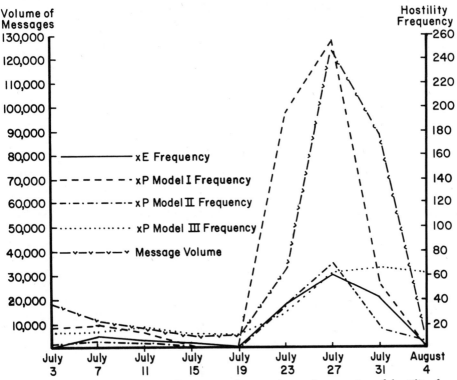

FIGURE 13. *Austria-Hungary. Frequency of perception and expression of hostility for models I, II, and III.*

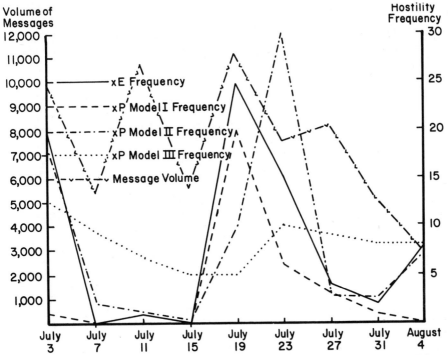

FIGURE 14. *Serbia. Frequency of perception and expression of hostility for models I, II, and III.*

and the significance column reports the significance of the obtained correlation.[10] Although both hypotheses are supported by the data under Model II (except for hypothesis (2) under condition (5)) there are important differences between the conditions.[11] For both hypotheses the highest correlation is found under condition (2), which used the *frequency measure* and only *threat* statements: the correlation was .60 for hypostheis (1) and .63 for hypothesis (2). The second best condition, again for both hypotheses, was condition (1), also a frequency measure but not using all statements. Since condition (2) (threat statements) is only a subset of the data used in condition (1) (threats plus actions), undoubtedly the results for condition (1) are principally due to the relationship obtained with only threat statements. Interestingly, the third best condition was (6) in which the *intensity measure* was used but only *action* hostility statements were employed. In this instance the correlations were .51 and .54 for hypotheses (1) and (2) respectively.

We can therefore conclude, that in terms of frequency or intensity of threats or actions, when a state perceives itself the object of another state's hostility, it expresses hostility (hypothesis 1) and it both identifies, and expresses hostility toward the offending state (hypothesis 2). Furthermore, since the results for hypotheses (1) and (2) under Model III or any of the lag models were considerably poorer, it is clear that the best model assumption is that of an "imperfect memory," namely Model II. The best results are obtained when we assume that the decision maker expresses hostility on the basis of the events of the past four (unequally remembered) days.

Several other features of the results found in Table 2 are also noteworthy. The similarity of the correlations for hypotheses (1) and (2) is of interest. It seems reasonable, on the basis of these results, to conclude that of the five possible causes which might produce a relationship between xP and xE (as discussed earlier), one of the important components is the relationship between xPy and xEy. In other words, when a state feels it is the object of another state's hostility, it is generally capable of identifying the offending state and then expressing hostility toward it, rather than displacing vis-à-vis some third state. This, however, is not to say that the five other possibilities do not also occur. Lacking perfect correlation between xPy and xEy, it is still possible that on some of the occasions in which x perceives y hostile to itself, it expresses hostility toward some other state, or that part of the time x is unable to determine its persecutor.

Table 2 also demonstrates that the frequency conditions, (1), (2), and (3),

10. The applicability of significance tests is possibly questionable since it is not clear whether the sample can be considered random.

11. The significance of a given correlation was determined throughout this study by consulting the appropriate tables under $n–2$ degrees of freedom. To maintain that a correlation reaches the 0.05 (or 0.01) level of significance is to say that that correlation could have been obtained by chance in five out of a hundred trials (or one in a hundred), when the actual correlation is zero. Hence, on the basis of significance tests one can conclude, if the correlation is significant, that *some* relationship exists between the variables under study. However, the exact nature or extent of that relationship cannot be determined on the basis of the significance tests. Throughout the discussion in the remaining sections, statements will be made concerning the confirmation or refutation of an hypothesis on the basis of significance tests. These statements should be read in light of the meaning of significance tests; to say, on the basis of a significance test, that the data support the hypothesis is to say that some relationship obtains between the variables.

produce better results than their corresponding intensity conditions, (4), (5), and (6). This is somewhat surprising since the time-series graphs indicated greater consistency for the intensity condition. However, this should not be seen as a contradition, since Figures 3 through 8 plot the *total* perception and expression of hostility for all states combined, and do not take into account the relationship between variables per condition for the individual states—a factor of critical importance in the computation of the correlation. Finally, it is also of interest to note the differences obtained between the total condition, the threat condition, and the action condition. For Model II, the hypotheses are best supported by the threat-frequency condition.

Although hypotheses (1) and (2) appear to be supported by the data, one must guard against uncritical acceptance of these results. One of the difficulties of using correlations to test hypotheses is that it is impossible to demonstrate beyond a shadow of a doubt that the relationship obtained is not due to some unknown third variable. The present study harbors just such a third variable in the form of the *volume* of messages. Since hostility cannot be expressed or perceived unless a message is written, it is possible that the relationships obtained between xP and xE (for hypothesis 1) and xPy and xEy (for hypothesis 2) might be due to message volume. That is to say, it is conceivable that as the numbers of messages exchanged increases, the number of perceptions and expressions in those messages increases. Obviously the more messages exchanged the greater opportunity a decision maker has for perceiving or expressing hostility. Note, however, that message volume could only affect the three frequency conditions, not the intensity measures. In a series of tests using different measures of message volume (number of messages, number of punctuation marks to measure phrases, number of words), partial correlations were computed for both hypotheses (1) and (2)—namely, between expression and perception of hostility on the one hand, and the volume of messages on the other. Although these tests were computed in several different ways (for hypothesis 2 it was computed between xPy, xEy, and xVy, as well as between xPy, xEy, and xV, where xVy indicates that x sends messages to y and xV merely indicates the total number of messages sent by x, it was found that the partial correlations only slightly lowered the original correlations obtained for hypothesis (1) and had no effect on the original correlations computed for hypothesis (2).[12] The results for hypothesis (1) are shown in Tables 3, 4, and 5.

It must be admitted, however, that the use of the partial correlation in the present problem is questionable. Usually, when a third variable is partialled out, correlations are computed between all pairs of the three variables *using the same population;* hence the n for each of the correlations is the same. In this study, however, the n's varied for each correlation, because it was possible for messages to be sent without any hostility being expressed or perceived. This raises a question concerning both the interpretation of the partial correla-

12. Although the number of messages does appear to rise corresponding to the variable it can be reasonably argued that this measure of message volume could not be the cause of the relationship between perception and expression of hostility. To partial out the effects of message volume it is necessary to operationalize message volume in a manner corresponding to thematic content analysis. An analysis of the documents demonstrates that documents almost invariably contain more than one theme. Hence, measuring message volume simply by counting documents would not make the message volume variable comparable to the expression and perception of hostility variables.

tions and the use of significance tests. Which n should be used in determining the significance of an obtained partial correlation? As can be seen from Tables 3, 4, and 5 we adopted the most conservative (lowest) n (since the greater the n the greater the significance of a given correlation). Thus, to assure ourselves that message volume is not playing a critical role we must further refer to the graphs of the individual states—Figures 9 through 14—where the volume of words (the measure of message volume most comparable to thematic content analysis) has been plotted over the days of the crisis and can be compared with

TABLE 3.   *Comparison of Results for Hypothesis (1) Under Condition (1)*

Model	Original Correlation			Partial Correlation		
	r	*n*	*Sign.*	*r*	*Low n*	*Sign.*
No memory: I	0.55	66	1%	0.49	66	1%
Imperfect memory: II	0.59	93	1%	0.55	93	1%
Perfect memory: III	0.35	127	1%	0.30	127	1%
Lag Models						
No memory: Ia	0.32	72	1%	0.31	72	1%
Imperfect memory: IIa	0.45	91	1%	0.42	91	1%
Perfect memory: IIIa	0.27	124	1%	0.24	124	1%

TABLE 4.   *Comparison of Results for Hypothesis (1) Under Condition (2)*

Model	Original Correlation			Partial Correlation		
	r	*n*	*Sign.*	*r*	*Low n*	*Sign.*
No memory: I	0.25	54	—	0.14	54	—
Imperfect memory: II	0.60	77	1%	0.52	77	1%
Perfect memory: III	0.37	126	1%	0.33	126	1%
Lag Models						
No memory: Ia	0.30	56	5%	0.22	56	—
Imperfect memory: IIa	0.63	76	1%	0.63	76	1%
Perfect memory: IIIa	0.31	123	1%	0.29	123	1%

TABLE 5.   *Comparison of Results for Hypothesis (1) Under Condition (3)*

Model	Original Correlation			Partial Correlation		
	r	*n*	*Sign.*	*r*	*Low n*	*Sign.*
No memory: I	0.29	49	5%	0.29	49	5%
Imperfect memory: II	0.26	74	5%	0.25	74	5%
Perfect memory: III	0.10	111	—	0.05	111	—
Lag Models						
No memory: Ia	0.03	53	—	0.04	53	—
Imperfect memory: IIa	0.11	73	—	0.10	73	—
Perfect memory: IIIa	0.05	108	—	0.02	108	—

the frequency of perceptions and expressions of hostility. Considering these graphs, we find that during the latter period of the crisis, when considerable hostility was being expressed and perceived, the volume of messages decreases.[13] It would therefore seem reasonable to conclude that message volume, as measured by the volume of words exchanged, is not the cause of the relationships obtained for hypotheses (1) and (2).

HYPOTHESES (3) $(xEy \to yPx)$ AND (4) $(xEy \to yEx)$

While hypotheses (1) and (2) were concerned with the intrastate mechanism of a state's expression of hostility (that the decision makers expressed hostility as a consequence of their perceptions), hypotheses (3) and (4) consider the interactions between states, and in particular the effects of one state's hostility on another state's perception and expression of hostility.

It might be worthwhile to consider the interpretation of the models when applied to hypotheses (3) and (4). Under *Model I, the no-memory model*, hypothesis (3) says: when x expresses hostility toward y on day n, on that same day n, y perceives that it is the object of x's hostility. *Model Ia* (the no memory lag model) maintains that x's expression on day n makes y perceive itself the target on the following day. *Model II, the imperfect memory model*, says that it is the cumulative, weighted set of expressions (over four days) by x to y that determines the extent of y's perception that it is the object of x's hostility. *Model IIa* follows Model II except that it states that y's perception occurs on the following, or fifth day. The *perfect memory model, Model III*, says that y's perception of self as target is a function of all the previous days of x's expression of hostility, considered equally (that is, the days are not weighted as in Model II). *Model IIIa* again introduces the time lag factor.

For hypothesis (4) the interpretation of the models is similar. *Model I:* when x expresses hostility on day n, y replies in kind on that same day; *Model Ia:* x's expression on day n elicits an expression from y on the following, $n + 1$, day; *Model II:* x's expression over four days, with weight factors, determines y's expression back to x; *Model IIa:* similar to Model II, but with a lag; *Model III:* all of x's past expressions taken together equally affect y's expression back to x; *Model IIIa:* similar to Model III, with a lag.

The differences between the models interpreted in terms of hypotheses (3) and (4) can be explained slightly differently. Model I (and to some extent Model Ia) essentially maintains that a state's perception or behavior is an *immediate* consequence of another state's hostile expressions. In other words, Model I says that a state immediately perceives itself the target (hypothesis 3) and/or immediately responds to hostility with hostility (hypothesis 4), and further, once it perceives or responds, it then forgets the events of that day and goes on to the next as if nothing had ever happened. Hence, interpretatively speaking, Model I assumes that a state reacts suddenly and without much

---

13. See footnote 9 above. It should also be noted in this context that standardization within countries as opposed to standardization over countries (as was done here) might, but need not, necessarily increase poor correlations. Depending on the relationship of the means and variances for the two variables, standardization within countries could either increase or decrease a correlation originally computed over all countries using raw data.

planning or presence of forethought, but that once it responds it doesn't hold a grudge.

Models II and III on the other hand, could be thought of as postulating more calculated or planned, rather than immediate or emotional, behavior. Models II and III say that y's perception or expression of hostility is a function of x's expression of hostility over several days. In other words, these models assume that states do not perceive or behave solely on the basis of a single day's experience, but react, rather, in terms of the accumulation of experience acquired over a number of days. Since the behavior is less instantaneous and more a function of time, it might be argued that these models postulate more rational or more carefully planned behavior on the part of a state. Admittedly, the term rational is being used very loosely in this context.

The results for hypotheses (3) and (4) bear striking contrast to those found for hypotheses (1) and (2). First, unlike hypotheses (1) and (2), very few high correlations were obtained. Second, the best model for hypotheses (3) and (4) is Model Ia, the no memory lag model, Model I being a close second. The results for Models Ia and I are given in Table 6. On the basis of the Table it is unquestionably the case that the frequency/intensity conditions and the threat/action categorization have a pronounced and significant effect on the results—far more so than was the case with hypotheses (1) and (2). High and significant correlations are obtained only under condition (5), when the intensity of threat statements is used (the exception being for hypothesis 4, condition 4): the correlation here for hypothesis (3) is $-.49$ and for hypothesis (4) it is $-.72$. Note that for hypotheses (1) and (2) the frequency conditions produced the best results, while for hypotheses (3) and (4), in line with what

TABLE 6.   *Results for Hypotheses (3) and (4)*

| Condition | Model Ia (No Memory—Lag) | | | | | |
| | Hypothesis 3 | | | Hypothesis 4 | | |
Frequency	*r*	*n*	*Sign.*	*r*	*n*	*Sign.*
1. All statements	0.04	112	—	−0.16	56	—
2. Threat statements	−0.16	86	—	−0.27	47	—
3. Action statements	−0.01	79	—	−0.21	30	—
Intensity						
4. All statements	−0.19	108	5%	−0.50	56	1%
5. Threat statements	−0.49	86	1%	−0.72	47	1%
6. Action statements	−0.19	79	—	−0.33	30	—
	Model I (No Memory)					
Frequency						
1. All statements	0.02	108	—	0.02	55	—
2. Threat statements	−0.19	90	—	−0.25	49	—
3. Action statements	0.08	77	—	0.17	30	—
Intensity						
4. All statements	−0.20	112	5%	−0.21	55	—
5. Threat statements	−0.41	90	1%	−0.50	49	1%
6. Action statements	−0.14	77	—	−0.07	30	—

was anticipated from the time series graphs, it is the intensity condition which provides considerably better results. The differences between the threat and action conditions, as discovered in the case of the first two hypotheses, is also evident here. In particular, significant results are only obtained for the threat category. Again, compare the results for the first two hypotheses in which, using the intensity measure, the action category provided the best results. For hypotheses (3) and (4) under the intensity condition, the best correlations, in absolute value, are only acquired for threat statements. Thus the results for hypotheses (3) and (4) differ significantly from those found for hypotheses (1) and (2).

The most surprising result, however, as shown in Table 6, is the existence of *negative* correlations. In fact, those correlations which are high are always negative. This poses some perplexing questions of interpretation: what is the meaning and significance of negative correlations in this context?

A search for the explanation of the negative correlations should turn to a consideration of the procedure used to acquire a correlation under hypotheses (3) and (4). Consider for the moment a possible example. Suppose we wish to construct a scatter diagram between two particular countries, x and y, for hypothesis (3), Model I, using all statements and the frequency measure. The scatter diagram might appear as shown in Figure 15. The values along each axis represent frequencies of the given variable and range from zero—no statements made—to some indefinite number. A mark in any of the squares represents a day; that is, a mark in the square which intersects the xEy variable at eight and the yPx variable at three says that there was one day on which x expressed hostility eight times to y and y felt it was the object of x's hostility three times (note that we are here working with Model I), two marks in that

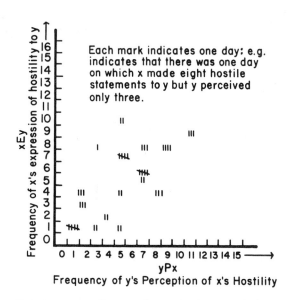

FIGURE 15. *Sample scatter diagram demonstrating correlation computation for two countries for hypothesis (3).*

square would indicate that this situation occurred on two different days, and so forth.

Suppose now that x expressed varying amounts of hostility to y on ten different days, but that on none of those ten days did y explicitly perceive x's hostility. Since we are working with Model I, those ten days would then fall along the xEy axis—they would fall in the zero column for yPx. A similar situation would occur if on ten *different* days y perceived itself the object of x's hostility even though x was not expressing any hostility toward y. In this latter situation the ten days would fall along the yPx axis—along the zero row for xEy. If only one of these situations occurred, that is, there existed only values for the xEy, or only values for the yPx variable, it would not be possible to compute a correlation, since one would eventually have to divide by zero in the correlation formula. However, if *both* situations occur, a negative correlation could result, as shown in Figure 16.

Pursuing this possibility, several scatter plots were made for pairs of individual countries in those cases in which good negative correlations were obtained, namely, Models I and Ia under condition (5). The results of these plots verified the supposition: when x expressed hostility to y, y did not perceive this fact on the same or following day (as proposed by the models); however, on days on which x did not express hostility, y perceived itself the object of x's hostility. Two sample scatter plots for the pairs Germany-Serbia and Russia-Austria are shown in Figures 17 and 18. A similar phenomenon occurs for hypothesis (4).

On the basis of these scatter plots, the negative correlations must lead us to two conclusions. First, it is reasonable to suppose that some relationship *does* exist between x's expression of hostility and y's perception of self as target. If no relationship existed, then we would expect a low correlation; or in the

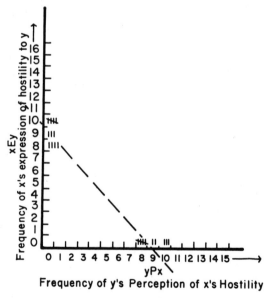

FIGURE 16.   *Sample scatter diagram demonstrating negative correlation for hypothesis (3.)*

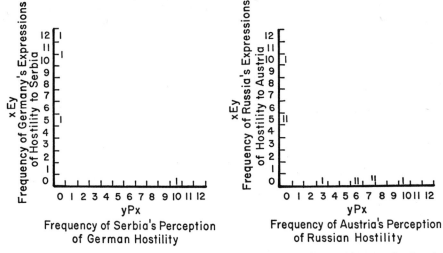

FIGURE 17. *Scatter diagram for Germany and Serbia for hypothesis (3).*

FIGURE 18. *Scatter diagram for Russia and Austria for hypothesis (3).*

extreme case described above, we would be unable to compute the correlation (if only values for one variable existed). Furthermore, the relationship most probably exists when threat statements are used with the intensity measure; but it may also occur under any of the other five conditions. Second, the relationship which exists must not be that hypothesized by any of the models—the models are *inadequate* for the purpose of testing hypotheses (3) and (4). This last statement can be demonstrated by reconsidering one of the sample plots shown previously, namely, Figure 17 for the pair Germany-Serbia. Note that there was one day on which x's expressions of hostility toward y had an average intensity of eleven, but on that day y did not perceive x's hostility; note also that there was one day on which x did not express hostility to y, but y felt it was the object of x's hostility, which it perceived had an average intensity of ten. If the proper model could be found these two days could be combined, thereby turning a negative correlation into a potentially (if other days could similarly be combined) positive one. For example, instead of the models used in this study one might try a model in which x's expression of hostility to y is hypothesized as perceived by y three days later. Of course, it is conceivable that an adequate model does not exist. This situation would occur if, for example, to combine one set of two points into one, as described above, one assumption must be made (the three-day lag assumption, possibly); but in order to combine another pair of points, a different assumption must be made (a four-day lag, for instance). On the other hand, it is possible that with a proper model good correlations could be obtained for all conditions.

The results for hypotheses (3) and (4) cannot, therefore, be used as the basis for any conclusions concerning these hypotheses. Despite the fact that the data may not support the hypotheses, the inadequacy of the models prohibits any firm conclusion. It thus remains for future studies to explore other models in greater detail.

CONCLUSION

Although we have seen hypotheses (1) and (2) supported by the data and have suggested that the results for hypotheses (3) and (4) are not entirely discouraging, it is still reasonable to question the overall significance of these findings. To what extent have we answered questions about hostile state behavior, or about conflict between states. Can we draw any conclusion at all about state behavior on the basis of *written* expressions and perceptions? Furthermore, is this study anything more than an extended case study? Are the results applicable to other states in other historical periods?

Although an attempt has been made to go beyond a case study by using and combining the data for six different states, still it must be admitted that a sample of six is highly inadequate for drawing any general conclusions about hostile state behavior. We also acknowledge the severe limitations of the short span of time covered and note that this time period was characterized by a major crisis which ended in war. Perhaps other periods of time, or other crises which do not resolve into war, might produce different results. Obviously these suppositions can only be confirmed by further research, using other states and other historical time periods. However, two recent studies which tend to support the results for the first hypothesis provide some reassurance.

Rudolph Rummel did a factor analytic study of measures of foreign and domestic conflict for seventy-seven nations during 1955–1957 (Rummel, 1963). The factor analysis required the computation of correlations between all pairs of indices. For our purposes only the correlations between the foreign conflict measures are of interest. Although the operationalization of the variables is not identical, there is considerable similarity between his measure of *accusation* and our measure of xP (perception of hostility). An accusation is defined as "any official diplomatic or governmental statement by the executive leaders of a country which makes a charge or allegation against another country . . ." Furthermore, his other measures of foreign conflict could be interpreted as various measures of our variable, expression of hostility (xE). If this comparison is granted, then we find a series of interesting correlations between accusations on the one hand (comparable to xP in the present study) and various forms of hostile expression on the other (comparable to xE). These correlations are as follows for the different equivalents: Negative Sanctions, .48; Protests, .69; Severence of Diplomatic Relations, .39; and Threats, .81. For the xE equivalents, they are: Military Action, .65; War, .56; Troop Movements, .62; Mobilizations, .46; and Foreign Killed, .70.[14]

Several points should be stressed concerning these correlations. First, the correlations are all reasonably high and therefore strongly indicate that a relationship does exist between xP, the perception of hostility, and xE the expression of hostility. Since these correlations are based on data for a larger number of nations for a longer period, it appears possible to suggest that the 1914 results for hypothesis (1) might be generalized beyond the six states in that crisis to apply to other states in other historical periods.

14. Since the N for each correlation is seventy-seven, most of the correlations would be significant if the variables had been normally distributed, which, according to Rummel, they were not.

Second, they show that there is an important difference between one of the xE measures and all the remaining xE measures. In particular, *threats* are defined as "any official diplomatic communication or governmental statement by the executive leaders of a country which states or implies that a particular country will incur certain negative sanctions if it acts in a certain way." They therefore, like our measure of xE, represent *written expressions* of hostility. In contrast, the other variables represent *actions* by a state, not written statements. With this difference in mind, we note that the threat-accusation correlation is highest, but that other correlations, such as protests or foreign killed, are also relatively high. It would seem reasonable, then, to conclude that, while differences exist between physical behavior and written expression, these differences are not appreciable; by measuring the relationship between xP and xE in our study, we have measured and analyzed certain aspects of hostile behavior.

A second study is also of related interest. Using the first hypothesis, along with several others, George Zaninovich has been comparing perceptions with actions in the current Sino-Soviet conflict (Zaninovich, 1964). His data come from two sources. Perceptions were coded from official Chinese and Soviet communications, while actions were determined from reports made by outside observers, namely, the *New York Times*, the *London Times*, and *Deadline Data*. His results corroborate the findings of the present study; perceptions of hostility and actions are positively related. Again, the differences in data source— different states and time periods—gives us further evidence that the findings of the present study do not represent unique situations. In addition, Zaninovich finds high positive correlations between written statements on the one hand and actions on the other, a result similar to that noted in Rummel's study.

It seems reasonable to conclude, then, on the basis of the present analyses as well as the results of the Rummel and Zaninovich studies, that a relationship does exist between a state's perception of itself as the target of hostility and its subsequent expression of hostility—namely, that hypothesis (1) is confirmed. Conclusions for hypothesis (2) cannot be made as positively, since in this instance we have only the results from the 1914 crisis. Nevertheless, the 1914 data do strongly suggest that if a state feels persecuted by a particular state it will express hostility toward that state. Unfortunately, similar conclusions cannot be made for hypotheses (3) and (4). Whether or not states correctly perceive reality and exchange hostility must be further tested in subsequent analyses.

Two

The National Level

Ole R. Holsti, Robert C. North, and
Richard A. Brody

Perception and Action
in the 1914 Crisis[1]

INTRODUCTION

The Archduke Francis Ferdinand, heir apparent to the throne of Austria-Hungary, was assassinated June 28, 1914, in Sarajevo by a young Serbian nationalist. Within a week, imperial Germany had promised "blank check" support of the Vienna government in its policy to punish Serbia for the crime. On July 23 the Austro-Hungarians presented Serbia with an ultimatum, and five days later Vienna declared war against its neighbor. On July 29, the day following the declaration of war, imperial Russia—acting to support a small, fellow Slav nation and to "deter" Austria-Hungary—ordered and then cancelled a general mobilization. Efforts were made to shape a mobilization clearly directed against Austria-Hungary, but technical difficulties of communication intervened, and on July 30, St. Petersburg reversed its decision in favor of general mobilization —in spite of German warnings and misgivings. The Berlin government then proclaimed a "state of threatening danger of war" on July 31 and dispatched to St. Petersburg a twelve-hour ultimatum demanding a cessation of Russian preparations on the German frontier. On the following day Germany ordered mobilization, and at 7:00 P.M. declared war on Russia, which had not replied to Berlin's ultimatum.

Foreseeing a two-front war, in the east with Russia and in the west with France, the Berlin government tried to gain an initial advantage by invading Luxembourg and demanding permission of Belgium to cross Belgian territory. On August 3, Germany declared war against France, and the following day Great Britain declared war against Germany. Within three weeks what began as a local Balkan dispute—a "limited" war—had exploded into a major European war, and in the years that followed a large part of the world became involved. When the fighting finally stopped in the latter part of 1918, the Austro-Hungarian Empire

1. The authors gratefully acknowledge the helpful comments and suggestions of Professors James N. Rosenau and J. David Singer on an earlier draft of this paper.

was in dissolution and imperial Germany was on the edge of collapse. Essentially, then, two wars began in the summer of 1914: a war between Austria-Hungary and Serbia, which most European statesmen of the time hoped to keep localized, and a major "world war," which escalated from the smaller conflict in spite of universal intentions to the contrary.

What purpose if any, can be served by a re-examination of a situation that, from at least some perspectives, can be considered a part of "ancient"—that is, pre-nuclear—history? What relevance does such a historical crisis have for the present? Clearly the circumstances are different, the nations and leaders are different, and the weapons are different. Why dig into the half-forgotten past?

Like many historical situations, the events culminating in World War I have been studied for a multitude of purposes. Early studies were largely characterized by single-minded searches for a culprit or culprits upon whom to lay full blame for the war. Among the most important of these were the analyses made by Lenin and Hitler, each of whom was using history in order to support the necessity for activist political movements. Whatever the shortcomings of their analyses in terms of scientific objectivity and rigor, their practical effect cannot be denied; our present world has been shaped in large part by the movements led by Lenin and Hitler.

As archives containing the documentary evidence were opened and the passions aroused by the war subsided, historians searching for scapegoats were largely superseded by scholars who were more concerned with determining "what really happened" rather than "who was to blame." Here the work of Sydney B. Fay (1928) and Luigi Albertini (1953) stands out.

More recently the events of 1914 have been re-examined with the purpose of discovering possible recurring patterns of decision-making behavior in crisis (Abel, 1941; Russett, 1962). These social science approaches to historical situations are based upon the fundamental assumption that there are patterns, repetitions, and close analogies throughout the history of human affairs. The circumstances and paraphernalia will differ between the Peloponnesian War and World War II, but the patterns of human fears and anxieties and perceptions of threat and injury may not be dissimilar. A fundamental part of the problem lies in identifying the levels of abstraction at which problems or events that are widely separated in time and space are found to be similar.

There are important advantages in using historical situations for this kind of research. With the whole sweep of human history to choose from, the scholar can select situations where the archives are open and documentation is relatively complete and illuminating. Clearly, in view of security restrictions, it is impossible to obtain materials of this quality in a more contemporary situation. Attempts at developing a theory of international behavior will almost of necessity, then, depend on the examination of historical evidence.

Beyond this, historical situations offer the advantages of an algebra book with the answers in the back. A scholar thus enjoys the possibility of working at a problem—even making a "prediction"—and comparing his "answer" with the way things really turned out.[2] In this way he can compare in most minute detail what statesmen have said with what they have actually done—and determine what perceptions have shaped their decisions.

2. A related suggestion is that of testing hypotheses by way of sealed predictions, which will be opened some years in the future (Snyder and Robinson, 1961).

History provides the sole key we have into the future: "The only way to judge what will happen in the future is by what has happened in the past" (Horst, 1963, p. 12). Wisdom about the present and future is derived wholly from what we have experienced—or learned about—in the past. It is by comparing new problems with old experiences, by looking for similarities and differences, that we move into the future. "Other things being equal, the more frequently things have happened in the past, the more sure you can be they will happen in the future" (*ibid.*). As human beings without occult pre-vision, we have no other way of assessing, judging, and deciding.

Essentially, then, it is by projecting past experience into the future that human beings make decisions; and statesmen, in this respect, are not exceptions. Foreign policy decisions, like other human decisions, imply not only an abstraction from history, but also the making of "predictions"—the assessment of probable outcomes. These two operations may be undertaken almost unconsciously, but they are nonetheless real and inescapable. The Marshall Plan was based upon a prediction, derived from some combination of experience, that systematic aid to European nations would bring about certain consequences. Viewed in retrospect, this prediction seems to have been generally sound. The basic prediction inherent in Khrushchev's decision to establish long-range missiles in Cuba, on the other hand, was much less accurate.

The weeks just prior to the outbreak of war in 1914 offer a particularly useful setting for studying the behavior of states, the processes of international conflict, and the escalation of limited war into major war. Embedded in archival data lies something close to a prototype of crisis against which a contemporary crisis—or future crisis—can be measured profitably. A primary goal throughout this study has been to develop an empirical model of inter-state behavior. The relatively complete nature of the 1914 data makes it an ideal situation in which to undertake initial testing and modification of such a model.

In order to carry out these studies we have moved on three fronts: (1) the collation of relevant social-psychological, psycholinguistic, and political science theory into a hopefully coherent and testable model of state behavior in the international system; (2) the development of techniques for assessing behavior, attitudes, values, and other psycho-political phenomena in the absence of direct access to the subject of our assessments; and (3) the detailed analysis of a series of international political situations, using these techniques to explore, amend, and further refine our theoretical model.

There have always been two fundamental requirements for the advancement of systematic knowledge in any discipline—an adequate model or theory of the phenomena under study, and tools for accurate measurement. The rapid development of chemistry from alchemy, for example, followed Mendeleev's atomic chart, which placed all the elements within one framework. This development also depended upon the invention of progressively more sophisticated instruments of measurement. A similar pattern is discernible in the other physical sciences, and more recently, to some degree, in several of the social sciences.

If we are to move—however falteringly—toward a science of international relations, our models and techniques should facilitate investigations which are comparable, replicable, and cumulative. They should permit the student to investigate international transactions, examine how they were initiated and received, and compare them in situations that are widely separated in time and circumstance. They should encompass concepts and measures that will yield un-biased and accurate comparisons and findings trans-nationally, trans-culturally, and trans-historically.

Second, the model and techniques should be capable of encompassing various levels of human society—from the interpersonal to the international. This requirement stems from both theoretical and practical considerations. The student of international politics is concerned with the behavior of individuals, groups, and organizations, all of which must ultimately be linked into a viable theory. At the same time, one could bring a strong case for the proposition that nowhere are the behavioral sciences as weak as in the ability to link existing knowledge at various levels. In order to overcome this weakness, investigation of interstate behavior will need to adapt and integrate concepts and findings from a number of other disciplines. This is not a plea for undiscriminating eclecticism. But a theory which ignores, or is incompatible with, the findings of such disciplines as psychology, social psychology, cybernetics, and communica-tions theory, as well as knowledge of politics at the local or national level, is almost certain to be inadequate. To paraphrase Russell Ackoff (1960, p. 6), human behavior is not organized into disciplines in the same way that universities are.

Third, the techniques should yield quantifiable data wherever possible. Not all data are capable of statistical testing, nor are qualitative data necessarily inferior; but where inferences are based on statistical techniques, confidence in them is enhanced. The accumulation of quantifiable data may make it possible to develop further, test, and draw closer to the real world a body of rigorous mathematical models for the study of international relations. With better instruments of measurement, the efforts of such pioneers as Richardson (1960), Abelson (1963), Wright (1955), Riker (1962), and Boulding (1962) can be pushed further.

Finally, there must be an intimate relationship between the model and the research techniques out of which will emerge what Eulau (1963, p. 27) calls "empirically relevant" propositions: "It is the theoretician's responsibility not only to assert that his propositions can be tested, but to suggest how they can be tested"—and, one may add, to test them. A theory which fails to satisfy this criterion will not advance the cause of systematic knowledge very far—whatever the power of its internal logic.

THE UNIT OF ANALYSIS

The systematic study of international relations presents special difficulties. Who and what, for example, are the primary perceiving, deciding, and acting units in international politics? Is an individual human being—the king or prime minister or dictator or president—essentially the embodiment of the state? Or is state behavior the consequence of a corporate decision that is somehow different from the decision of any single person? Upon which unit should the analyst focus—decision-maker or the nation-state (Wolfers, 1962; Singer, 1961)? Each level of aggregation or organization—for example, nation-states, popula-tions, or decision-making groups—can be considered a potentially useful choice, but for different research tasks. Each alternative, moreover, carries with it potential advantages and disadvantages and its own peculiar set of assumptions that the analyst must adopt with his choice of a research focus.

The arguments for choosing the nation-state are in many respects persuasive. The primacy of the state in international law is unquestioned: until very recently the individual had little or no status in law. The important interactions on the international level—the exchange of ambassadors, signing of treaties, or declarations of war—moreover, are all undertaken legally in the name of the nation. In addition, the institutions most relevant to international politics, such as foreign offices or armed forces, are those of the state. Thus it is hardly surprising that the state has been the key unit of analysis for the legal-institution—or, what Wolfers calls the "traditional"—approach to international politics.

At the same time, however, the state as the primary unit appears to provide an insufficient basis for building a comprehensive theory of international relations (Angell, 1955). Although we habitually reify nation-states—by referring to Russian actions or American policies—this in fact is but a convenient shorthand for identifying decisions made by individuals in Moscow or Washington or elsewhere who have the power to commit the resources of their respective states to the pursuit of policy goals at the international level. The "levers of state" are tended by individuals, alone or in groups, and not by some corporate concept. If we rely upon the state as a unit of analysis we run the risk of failing to account for people—and how they perceive and how they respond to what they perceive.

A common characteristic of many recent attempts to formulate a framework for the systematic study of international politics has been a focus on the individual as a major unit of analysis. International politics, like any social activity, involves people. It follows, if people are involved in operating the international system, that individual, group, and organizational psychological factors may aid in explaining the behavior that men, organized into nations, exhibit toward each other.

These recent approaches embrace a concern for subjective as well as objective factors in the policy process. One important contribution of "decision-making" models (Simon, 1958; March and Simon, 1958; Snyder, *et al.*, 1962) has been an emphasis on the perspective of the actor—and upon *his* definition of the situation—rather than upon the perspectives and situational definitions of the investigator. Without neglecting the analysis of organizations and institutions, these studies begin with the basic assumption that "Nation-state action is determined by the way in which the situation is defined subjectively by those charged with the responsibility for making choices" (Snyder, *et al.*, 1962, p. 212).

It would be a mistake, however, to assume that selection of the decision-maker as the primary unit of analysis commits the investigator to a neglect of larger units such as institutions or nations. The top foreign policy leaders of a nation are not just men—they are men in socially defined roles which may constrain their behavior. Neither do they represent merely decision sub-routines which weigh "national" interest" and "national power" against the opportunity for "national gain" to arrive at policy. National leaders *are* individuals making policy choices for their nations in a complex of highly articulated group, organizational, societal, and inter-social systems. The task of the behavioral scientist studying international politics is to gain understanding of how these systems fit together and how they affect the choice behavior of individuals in leadership roles.

Perhaps the strongest case for the selection of decision-makers as the unit of analysis is that it does not exclude the consideration of larger units; rather it enriches the study of institutions. In describing the fundamental premises of the "behavioral persuasion," Eulau has written (1963, p. 15):

The political behaviorist concentrates on the behavior of individuals whose interactions and transactions make up collective behavior, even if he is concerned with describing and explaining the actions of groups, organizations or other large collectivities. Groups, organizations or nations have no independent status apart from the conduct of the individuals who are related by behaving toward each other in certain ways. But, from the behavioral perspective, these collectives exist and behave the way they do only insofar as the people composing them act in certain ways.

When we study transactions between nation-states we are focusing on decisions which are arrived at and initially implemented by a small group of leaders who have reached high status and are performing their roles as an outcome of an elective, appointive, or some other highly differentiating selective process. In systemic terms this group may be viewed as a specialized, functional sub-system or component of the national system. In fact, the sub-system is still a collection of individuals, however, and thus decision-makers remain the fundamental unit of analysis.

The individual decision-maker within any large organization, including a nation-state, is embedded, of course, in a considerable number of more or less nesting and overlapping groups each with its own roles, statuses, expectations, and preferences. He also has carried with him into office a complex of personal habits, memories, attitudes, inclinations, and predispositions. In performing his decision-making role he is to one degree or another aware of pressures and limitations emanating from these sources, and also from public opinion and expectation; the interests and policies of other components of his government; advice from military, scientific, and other specialized advisers; institutional memories; and the history and traditions of the organization. Essentially, then, the behavior of a decision-maker cannot be considered without reference to the organization of which he is a part.[3]

THE IMPORTANCE OF PERCEPTIONS

Foreign-policy-making may be viewed as a search for satisfactory alternatives from among the range of those perceived by leaders who choose for their respective nation-states. The key concept in this approach is the *perception*, the process by which decision-makers detect and assign meaning to inputs from their environment and formulate their own purposes or intents. For an individual to respond to a person, object, or event, there must first be the *detection* of signals, which is a function of our senses. In addition, however, we must have some code—a set of concepts or images—which permits us to *interpret* the meaning of the stimulus.

For all human beings these codes are largely a product of experience and training. The infant with normal hearing can detect the sound waves created by

3. The data analyzed in subsequent sections of this paper are the product of individual and organizational processes, but no effort is made here to separate the impact of the two factors. For a theoretical discussion of the contribution of psychological and sociological factors to foreign policy making, see Snyder, *et al.* (1962) and Brody (1966).

human voices. But there is little understanding, and therefore limited influence on the behavior of the child, until he learns the code (language) which permits him to organize and interpret the sound waves into meaningful patterns. These concepts become the "lenses" through which each of us makes sense of the otherwise unmanageable number of signals from the environment with which we are bombarded. Some concepts are relatively simple and may be subject to little variation across individuals or time. Other concepts are more complex and open to misinterpretation or disagreement. And, as Snyder (1962, p. 104) has pointed out, complexity, ambiguity, and lack of stability are a few of the characteristics which tend to be more pronounced in foreign policy decision-making than in other settings. Perceptions appear to be equally crucial to studies of conflict and studies of coalition, organization, federation, or other unification.

Our studies to date have also reinforced our belief in the necessity of taking perceptual variables into account and for correlating them with more "objective" indices. For human beings do not always respond to the same stimuli in the same way. A phenomenon may be perceived by one actor as positive (acceptable, rewarding) and by another as negative (unacceptable, punishing). Similarly, the same actor may view the same stimulus as positive in one situation—that is, when associated with one set of accompanying stimuli—and negative in another situation. In any case, the essential point is that the actor's response will be shaped *by his perception* of the stimulus and not necessarily by qualities objectively inherent in it. This means that my behavior—in terms of my perceptions—may appear perfectly rational and appropriate to me (subjective rationality), whereas you—*in terms of your perceptions*—may consider my behavior utterly mad. This is a major reason why the rights and wrongs in conflicts on all levels—between husband and wife, between labor and management, and between opponents in the cold war—are frequently so difficult to establish.

THE PROBLEM OF ACCESS: THREE APPROACHES

But if the human being is the unit of analysis, how are we to get at the decision-maker embedded in such a vast and somewhat exclusive institutional structure as a modern state? Clearly the standard method of attitude measurement—the personal interview, the questionnaire, or the direct observation of decision-makers in action—can rarely be used by the social scientist who seeks to study human behavior at the international level.[4]

The problem of access has been approached in a number of ways: (1) through aggregate data analyses, (2) through direct access to analogous situations, and (3) through indirect analyses of actual situations.

Those who emphasize the aggregate data approach are basically concerned with two problems: determining the typical interaction among types of nations, and ascertaining the factors predicting the direction of changing relationships among nations.

There are today over a hundred and twenty nations capable of carrying on some sort of international relations (that means over seven thousand dyads and endless triads and tetrads). On the assumption that not all of the differences which distinguish these nations are relevant for their international politics, there

4. For an exception to this statement, see Pruitt (1962).

have been undertaken a series of studies that seek to establish the minimum number of factors describing nations and yielding the maximum explanatory power in describing their inter-relations with other nations (Deutsch, 1960; Rummel, 1963). Aggregate data analyses have also been employed to explain the waxing and waning of alliances and to test Deutsch's theory of the conditions under which different degrees of coalition emerge (Deutsch, 1954; Deutsch, *et al.*, 1957; Russett, 1963).

Rummel (1964a, 1963) and Tanter (1964) have employed factor analysis and multivariate analysis of aggregate data to determine the relationship between domestic and international conflict (it is a surprisingly weak one) and to select predictors of both types of conflict. Rummel reports ". . . . the independent variables were most able to account for the lack or low level of foreign conflict behavior on the part of the world's nations, but not the higher magnitudes (1963b, p. 36)." We have found (Holsti and North, 1965; North, *et al.*, 1964; Holsti, Brody, North, 1965; Holsti, 1965), that at high levels of tension, perceptual factors become increasingly important This correspondence is certainly not conclusive, but suggests the need for combining aggregate data and perceptual data approaches.

A second strategy, that of examining an *analogous* social system, is a relatively new approach for students of international politics (Guetzkow, *et al.*, 1963). The logic of this approach calls for building into the simulated setting enough of the contextual elements found in the actual system so that behavior observed in the former will replicate behavior observed in the latter. If this is accomplished or substantially approximated, the rewards are rich indeed.

A research team recently used simulation to play groups of live decision-makers against the events which led to the outbreak of war in 1914. The investigators divided their subjects by psychological test into separate groups—one group that more or less matched the persons who made major decisions in the 1914 crisis, and one group that did not match. Each was divided into decision-making teams to correspond with leadership roles in major European capitals nearly five decades earlier, and then placed in semi-laboratory situations analogous to 1914. As simulated events unfolded, the subjects were given historical messages which had been "masked," so that items revealing the particular crisis would be suitably camouflaged, but which carried the same general message as the historical document. After the two separate groups had worked their way through the crisis simulation, their own records were subjected to the same processes of content analysis that had been used on documents from the outbreak of World War I. In this particular case study, a striking similarity emerged between the real actors of 1914 and the psychologically matched simulation teams. The non-matched teams found other ways of handling their conflicts: they negotiated, called a conference, and avoided war (Hermann and Hermann, 1962).

Many more such studies must be completed before conclusions can be drawn, but these simulation experiments open a whole new range of possible ways for linking history with the present and for closing at least a part of the gap between the abstractions of simulations and game theory on the one hand, and behavior in the real world on the other hand.

Simulations have also been used to examine the spread of nuclear weapons (Brody, 1963); the effect of strategic doctrines on international stability (Crow and Soloman, 1962; Crow, 1963); the effect of weapon system characteristics on national policy (Raser and Crow, 1964). All of these studies indicate the relevance of psychological variables in the complex intergroup processes present in internation simulation. The results of the validation experiments (if they are positive) will add to the confidence with which similar findings can be expected in the actual international system.

The third approach has proceeded on two distinguishable paths: (1) the retrospective reconstruction of decision processes and (2) the analysis of manifest content to determine underlying attitudes. These solutions to the problems of analysis at a distance are generally called "decision-making analysis" and "content analysis" (North, *et al.*, 1963; Holsti, *et al.*, 1964b) respectively.

The "decision-making approach," typified by the work of Richard C. Snyder and his associates (Snyder, *et al.*, 1962; Snyder and Paige, 1958) has relied heavily on the retrospective reports of actual participants as to who and what was involved in a given foreign policy decision. The interviews in which these reports are developed are constructed to focus attention on motivation, perceptions of the situation, group and organizational process, the sources of initiative and alternatives, and like topics. Throughout this work there is a conscious effort to gauge the relevance of psychological studies of decision-making. Snyder refers to the attempt to "embrace two levels of analysis in a single framework—the sociological level (organizational factors) and the psychological level (individual or personality factors)" as a "central feature" of his analytic scheme (1963, p. 243).

There are difficulties attendant to the retrospective interview approach. Two seem particularly relevant in the present context: (1) access to decision-makers is largely restricted to one side of the cold war, (2) the dependence on recall in self-reporting is a formidable source of error. The first difficulty, of course, disappears if the decision was made by a nation to whose leaders the analyst has access. The difficulties with recall data have been overcome by supplementing these data with materials not produced retrospectively—diaries, speeches, and such. Nevertheless, awareness of these difficulties has led to an alternative approach—the content analysis of verbal and written materials contemporaneous to the decision and originating with the decision-makers.

Content analysis—described as an "attempt to infer the characteristics and intentions of sources from inspection of the messages they produce" (Osgood, *et al.*, 1957, p. 275)—is not a new approach. In the study of literature, content analysis has been used to solve questions of disputed authorship. During World War II social scientists used it to study propaganda, and some United States intelligence information was derived from analyses of enemy broadcasts and other communications channels (George, 1959). More recently, content analysis has become a major tool of psycholinguistics for analyzing the relationship between messages and the characteristics of their users. Much early content analysis depended upon counting the frequency with which certain attributes were present or absent in a given body of material. The attribute—such as hostility, for example—might be looked for in individual words or in themes, but in either case it was the frequency of appearance or non-appearance of specified classes and categories that was measured. But there are circumstances when frequency counts are not sufficiently sensitive for differentiating subtle changes of content. Pilot studies using content analysis for the study of international politics suggested, for example, that measures of *intensity*—as well as frequency—are needed if we are to differentiate crisis from non-crisis situations, or escalating from non-escalating crises, or a tendency to cooperate or ally or unify as contrasted with a tendency to oppose or fragment or disintegrate. Selection—for cruciality—among attributes, that is, deciding which ones account for the greater proportion of variance in behavior, requires the use of scales. In view of the non-substantial nature of the attributes that appear to be crucial, however, the construction of scales presents special difficulties.

RELATING PERCEPTIONS TO BEHAVIOR: THE INTERACTION MODEL

We are interested not only in what national decision makers *perceive*—or say they perceive—about themselves and others. We are also interested in what they actually *do*. How are these perceptual and action elements to be brought together systematically and correlated for meaningful analysis? Basically, we are interested in inter-nation "communication" in the sense that this concept can be used to characterize all transactions between nations. This indicates that both the verbal *and* the physical acts have information potential. The acts of one nation can be considered as inputs to other nations. The basic problem is this: given some input to a nation, what additional information do we need to account for the nation's foreign policy response?

The conceptual framework we have selected for such analysis is a two-step mediated stimulus-response ($S–r : s–R$) model. These elements are as follows: A stimulus (S) is an event in the environment which may or may not be perceived by a given actor, and which two or more actors may perceive and evaluate differently. A stimulus may be a physical event or a verbal act. The stimuli relevant to international politics tend to originate with the acts of other nations (or are perceived as) directed toward a nation in question. This is not to say that domestic problems (for example, pressure for tariffs) have no relevance. Rather, it is to assert that the impetus for most decisions, especially in crisis, is extra-national. Input behavior (S) can be described in terms of the clarity and salience of the stimulus. Clarity is a function of both the nature of the act, and its intensity. Is the act physical or verbal? Is it at a high or low level of intensity? These characteristics may play a considerable part in determining the manner in which the nation-state responds (R). On the other hand, physical acts of moderate to high intensity may have a low level of salience; even a very clear stimulus may find the actors focused elsewhere. For example, during the early weeks of the 1914 crisis, British decision makers were primarily concerned with the Ulster situation rather than the events on the Continent.

A response (R) is an action of an actor, without respect to his intent or how either he or other actors may perceive it. Both S's and R's are non-evaluative and non-affective. For example, on July 29, 1914, Russia, in response to the declaration of war, ordered a partial mobilization of the southern district (R). Although the intention behind it was only to deter Austria-Hungary from invading Serbia, this action served as a stimulus (S) to Germany, which, within hours, responded by threatening a mobilization of its own (R).

In the model, the perception (r) of the stimulus (S) within the national decision system corresponds to the "definition of the situation" in the decision-making literature (Snyder, *et al.*, 1962; March and Simon, 1958).[5] For example, during the crisis leading up to World War I, Germany perceived that Russia was threatening German borders. Finally, (*s*) represents the actor's expressions of his own intentions, plans, actions, or attitude toward another actor; for example, Germany asserted an intention of supporting Austria-Hungary. Both (*r*) and (*s*) carry evaluative and affective loadings. In the case of the Russian partial mobilization (*R*), although the intent behind it (*s*) was aimed solely at Austria-Hungary, it was perceived (*r*) as a serious threat by German decision-makers, who expressed their own intent (*s*) to take similar action. Three days later Germany ordered a general mobilization (*R*).

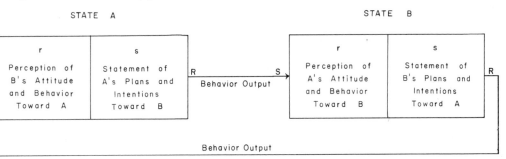

FIGURE 1. *The Interaction Model.*

Operationally, it would be much simpler, of course, to confine oneself only to *S* and *R*, as do many traditional theories of international politics. In many situations and for many decision-makers the best predictor of state A's action response toward state B will be the nature of state B's actions. If the latter were unambiguously dangerous, one would expect them to be negatively valued by almost any individual or group in a decision-making role. Predicting President Roosevelt's response to the attack on Pearl Harbor would not be difficult. However, not all—or even most—inter-nation actions are so unambiguous. Consider, for example, Chamberlain's and Churchill's perceptions of Hitler's invitation to confer at Munich on the fate of Czechoslovakia.

There have been serious doubts about the feasibility of quantifying perceptual and affective data, and the inclination, until recently, has been to emphasize "hard" variables and aggregate data: to measure gross national products and populations, or to count troops or planes or ships or megatons, and assume that decision-makers respond to the "objective" value assigned to these capabilities by the investigator. As important as these "objective" data are, they may fail to take into sufficient account how human beings react to the factors discussed above. Many of the crucial problems of international politics concern such questions as decision-making, communication, and negotiation under varying conditions of stress. For this purpose, valuable indicators of tension are subjective ones, that is, those revealed by the decision-makers themselves. "Objective" indicators of tensions, such as rising defense budgets, while useful as supplementary information, may not indicate that a particular decision-maker felt himself to be under

5. This is an application of the "Thomas Theorem": "If men define situations as real, they are real in their consequences" (W. I. Thomas, quoted in Merton, 1957, p. 421).

the pressure of high stress. Moreover, objective data are usually compiled on an annual, quarterly, or monthly basis. These indices may well be used to reveal the trend toward an environment conducive to crisis (Wright, 1957; K. J. Holsti, 1963; Deutsch, 1960; Russett, 1963)—such as Europe in 1914 or the cold war since 1945—but are less useful for the intensive study of a *short* time period. Thus it is particularly important for the investigator who seeks to analyze short-term changes in the international system—such as the crisis situation—to incorporate subjective data into his model.

COLLECTING THE PERCEPTUAL DATA

The selection of the 1914 crisis as the initial case in which to attempt rigorous quantitative analyses of conflict at the international level was based on several considerations. The available documentation relating to the outbreak of World War I surpasses that of any crisis of similar magnitude. Among the major nations involved, only the Serbian archives have remained relatively inaccessible to the investigator. Moreover, a generation of careful scholarship has produced published and readily accessible document collections of unquestioned authenticity, including those of Austria-Hungary (1930), France (1936), Great Britain (1926), Germany (Montgelas and Schücking, 1924), and Russia (1934). The forged, altered, or incomplete collections—produced by the various governments while passions and charges of "war guilt" still ran high—have been superseded. Finally, the crisis is a classic example of war through escalation. The minor war between Austria-Hungary and Serbia—which crisis-hardened European diplomats expected to remain localized—engulfed nearly the entire continent within ten days. The existing international system—still referred to by many as the classic example of a functioning "balance of power" system—was unable to cope with the situation as it had previously done in the recurring Balkan crises. While extensive war plans had been drawn up by the various general staffs, there is little evidence that any European decision maker wanted or expected a general war—at least in 1914.[6]

The perceptual data were derived in whole from documents authored by selected British, French, Russian, German, and Austro-Hungarian decision makers. Those persons filling key roles such as head of state, head of government, or foreign minister were selected, unless there was a clear indication—from such standard sources as Fay (1928) or Albertini (1953)—that the person had no part whatsoever in the formulation of decisions. In addition, certain other persons who played a prominent part in the events were added. The complete list of decision-makers whose messages were subjected to content analysis is found in Table 1.

One issue that must be resolved in a satisfactory manner in research which is so heavily dependent upon diplomatic documents is that of *sampling*. Three potential sources of error are present. First, do the published documents represent a faithful sample of the communication between decision-makers? One difficulty

---

6. Prince von Bülow recalled Chancellor Bethmann-Hollweg's reaction to the outbreak of war: "At last I (Bülow) said to him: 'Well, tell me, at least, how it all happened.' He raised his long, thin arms to heaven and answered in a dull exhausted voice: 'Oh—if I only knew' " (Bülow, 1931, p. 166).

TABLE 1. *1914 Decision Makers Selected for Documentary Content Analysis*

Position[a]	Austria-Hungary	Germany	England	France	Russia
Head of State	Franz Joseph	Wilhelm II	George V	Poincaré	Nicholas II
Head of Government	Stürgkh[b] Tisza	Bethmann-Hollweg	Asquith	Viviani	
Secretary for Foreign Affairs	Berchtold	Jagow	Grey	Viviani	Sazonov
Undersecretary for Foreign Affairs	Forgach Macchio Hoyos	Zimmer-mann Stumm	Nicolson	Bienvenu-Martin Berthelot Ferry	
Minister of War/ Chief of General Staff	Conrad	Moltke		Messimy	Sukhomlinov
Others			Haldane[c]		

[a]Position refers to functionally equivalent roles, not to formal titles, which vary from nation to nation.
[b]Stürgkh was Austro-Hungarian Minister-President; Tisza was Hungarian Prime Minister.
[c]Lord Chancellor.

is represented by that portion of communication which is not recorded—for example, face-to-face conversations, telephone messages, or conferences in which no official minutes are recorded. While the basic "sense" of such communication can often be cross-checked against diaries, memoirs, or other such sources, this type of communication represents a source of sampling error of generally unknown proportions.

A second potential source of sampling error is found in the adequacy of document collections themselves. Possible sources of loss are those attributable to mis-filing or destruction of documents—either intentionally or inadvertently—and bias or carelessness by those commissioned to collect and publish them. Even in the case of intentionally destroyed documents, however, the historian or social scientist is not helpless. For example, if A destroys his copy of a message sent to B, it should still be found among B's documents.

The documents published in various collections used in this study of the 1914 crisis appear to be complete. For example, according to the introduction to the British documents by J. W. Headlam-Morely, Historical Adviser to the Foreign Office, the question of sampling was decided as follows:

When it had been determined that a new edition should be issued, the question had to be considered on what principle this should be prepared. It would have been possible simply to publish in its original and unparaphrased form the complete text of the documents already published [in the White Paper of 1914], inserting those passages which had been omitted and adding to them such documents of obvious political importance as had not been included. This would not have been satisfactory. It certainly would not have satisfied the criticisms and stilled the suspicions which had been aroused. The only thing to do was to publish the whole correspondence, including every telegram and dispatch, however unimportant and incorrect, in any way relating to the origins of the war. This is the course which has been pursued, and *the reader has before him in this edition everything, within the specified dates, contained in the Foreign Office records which appeared to have a bearing on the origin and outbreak of the war. He is in possession of all the documentary material which the Secretary of State and his advisers had before them at the time* (Great Britain, 1926, p. vii, italics added).

Similar criteria appear to have been used in the various other collections.

A third source of potential sampling error is in the selection of documents for content analysis by the investigator. The data in the present paper are derived from the *complete* universe, rather than a sample thereof: the *verbatim text* of published documents meeting the criteria of authorship and time (June 27–August 4).

The initial step in the exploitation of these documents was to devise perceptual units that could be defined, recognized by separate investigators, counted, and ranked along scales of more-to-less intensity. The units used in these analyses of international crisis—the *perceptions*—have been abstracted from the documents in terms of the following elements: *the perceiving party or actor; the perceived party or actors; the action or attitude; and the target party or actor.*[7] For example, the assertion by a Russian decision maker that "The Austrian, as well as German, hope is for the ultimate annihilation of Serbia," was coded as follows:

Perceiver	Perceived	Action or Attitude	Target
Russia	Austrian	hope is for the ultimate annihilation of	Serbia
Russia	German	hope is for the ultimate annihilation of	Serbia

The 1914 documents yielded over 5,000 such cognitive and affective perceptions.

The analysis of these data has gone through three fairly distinctive states: (1) the use of only *frequency* of perceptions; (2) the recoding of the documents, and scaling of the perceptions for the *intensity* of various attributes; and (3) correlational analyses between perceptions and the various types of "*hard*" and *action* data.

Using frequency of themes as a technique of analysis, an initial paper tested two basic hypotheses about the relationships between perceptions of threat and perceptions of capability in international crisis (Zinnes, North, Koch, 1961). Theodore Abel, in his survey of decisions to go to war—including the case of 1914—had concluded that, "in no case is the decision precipitated by emotional tensions, sentimentality, crowd behavior, or other irrational motivations" (1941, p. 855). The evidence presented in that initial study strongly supported a contrary hypothesis: *If perceptions of anxiety, fear, threat, or injury are great enough, even the perception of one's own inferior capability will fail to deter a nation from going to war.*

Using perceptual data—but no action data—from the 1914 crisis, Dina A.

7. For a full description of this technique of coding and scaling documentary data see Robert C. North, *et al.*, 1963. The reliability coefficient used in this coding of perceptions was computed as follows:

$$R = \frac{2\,(C_{1,2})}{C_1 + C_2}$$

It required not only that all coders pick up the same number of statements, but also that they agree on the identity of each statement. The composite reliability for the various categories of perceptions gathered—hostility, friendship, frustration, satisfaction, and so forth—was .67. The reliability figure for coding hostility—the variable upon which the analysis in subsequent sections of this paper is based—was above .80 in every case. This level of agreement can be illustrated by a hypothetical example. Assume that in a given document, the first coder (C_1) extracted 13 perceptions and the second coder (C_2) found 12. If they agreed on structure (perceiver-perceived-action/attitude-target) as well as the proper category of 10 of the perceptions, this would result in a reliability level of .80.

Zinnes tested four hypotheses about the relationships between perceptions of hostility and expressions of hostility by key decision-makers (Zinnes, 1963).[8] In the 1914 case it was found that a nation-state tends to express hostility to the degree that it sees itself to be the target of another state's hostility; and such a nation-state, on identifying the source of perceived injury, tends then to express hostility toward the perceived offending state.

Although these studies reinforced the belief that content analysis of documentary material provides a rich source of data, they also revealed the importance of measuring *intensity* as well as *frequency* of perceptions. Thus the entire set of documents was recoded for perceptions of: hostility, friendship, frustration, satisfaction, and desire to change the *status quo*. Each item was next typed on a separate card and masked to conceal the identity of the various actors. Thus the example cited above would appear as:

> *X's* hope is for the ultimate annihilation of Z.
> *Y's* hope is for the ultimate annihilation of Z.

The entire set of cards for each category (for example, hostility) was then scaled for intensity by a series of three judges on a forced-distribution scale of 1 to 9 by the Q-Sort technique (Block, 1961).[9] The quantitative results were then aggregated into twelve time periods, each containing approximately one twelfth of the documentation.

After the complete recoding and scaling of the 1914 documents, the hypotheses relating perceptions of capability and injury were re-examined. It was found that decision-makers of each nation most strongly felt themselves to be the victims of injury precisely at that time when its leaders were making policy decisions of the most crucial nature (Holsti and North, 1965). As mentioned, perceptions of its inferior capability did not deter a nation such as Germany from going to war. The Kaiser's desperate reaction to the events which were engulfing him—perhaps best characterized by his assertion, "If we are to bleed to death, England shall at least lose India" (Montgelas and Schücking, 1924, p. 350)—is the reaction of a decision-maker under such severe stress that any action is preferable to the burden of the sustained tension.[10]

8. The following four hypotheses were tested: (1) *If x perceives itself the object of hostility, then x will express hostility*; (2) *if x perceives itself the object of y's hostility, then x will express hostility toward y*; (3) *if x expresses hostility toward y, then y will perceive that it is the object of x's hostility*; (4) *if x expresses hostility toward y, then y will express hostility toward x*. Zinnes tested each hypothesis under various time-lag models, using both frequency and intensity of statements. Only hypotheses one and two were supported at statistically significant levels in her study. One interpretation of these findings might be that in crisis "actions speak louder than words"; that is, in hypotheses one and two, *x*'s perceptions are probably based on both *y*'s *actions* and *y*'s expressions. Hypotheses three and four, however, are concerned only with the relationship of expressions of attitude and perceptions of these attitudes. Thus, Zinnes' study suggests the limitations of working solely with perceptual data, to the exclusion of action data.

9. The Q-Sort technique requires judges to place the entire universe of statements into nine categories with a distribution approximating normality: 5%-8%-12%-16%-18%-16%-12%-8%-5%. In all cases inter-judge agreement was better than the .70 level suggested by Block (1961). This level of agreement indicates an average discrepancy of approximately 1.5 categories per statement.

10. These findings appear to support Russett's assumption that "the outbreak of war, at least on a scale involving several major powers, was an accident rather than the result of a deliberate aggressor's plot" (Russett, 1962, p. 4). This does not preclude the possibility of "accident proneness."

This reaction in the face of an adversary's greater capabilities—a reaction strikingly familiar to instances in the Peloponnesian Wars, the wars between Spain and England during the sixteenth century, and the Japanese decision to strike at Pearl Harbor (Holsti, 1963)—are not unrelated to the dilemmas of our own age of missiles and nuclear warheads. These findings underscore the need for re-examining that "common sense" and almost irresistible "conventional wisdom" which argues that deterrence is merely a matter of piling up more and/or better weapons than the opponent can amass.

COLLECTING THE BEHAVIORAL DATA

These initial studies were based solely on perceptual data, without a systematic attempt to correlate them against other data. Critics of content analysis have frequently pointed to the lack of studies in which inferences based on content data are tested against independent material (Berelson, 1952, p. 74–75). For example, is there any significant relationship between what policy makers say and write, and the actual decisions they make? If there is not, then the value of content analysis as a research technique is placed in serious doubt. The next reasonable step, therefore, was to examine the relationship between perceptions and a series of "hard" indices. Financial data such as stock and bond prices, gold movements, commodity futures, interest rates, and other items lend themselves to this purpose. Reliable data on these indicators, measured and reported on a daily basis, are readily accessible.[11]

The relationship between the level of tension, revealed through the content analysis of documents, and political decision-making may be investigated directly or indirectly. The direct approach involves a search for correlation between the results of the content analysis and such actions as troop movements, mobilization, breaking of diplomatic relations and the like. The indirect approach involves a correlation of the "soft" variables with a set of indices which are presumed to be sensitive to international tension levels.

The financial indicators discussed here are of the latter type. Although they respond to events other than international political crises, the history of 1914 rules out other causes of fluctuation. Given fluctuations of financial indicators, correlated with increases and decreases in international tension, these indicators can be used to check the validity of content analysis data. If the latter covary both with the political/military actions of nations participating in the crisis and with the fluctuations of financial indicators that respond to the tensions born of these actions, confidence in the content analysis techniques is substantially enhanced.

The results of the investigation of these indirect relationships follow.

THE FLOW OF GOLD

Any study of the flow of gold involving the major actors in the 1914 crisis must center on London—"the financial center and the free market for gold" (Jaeger, 1922). Whereas notes could be redeemed for gold to an unlimited extent in the

11. Data have been gathered from the following sources: the *Times* (London), the *Economist* (London), the *Wall Street Journal*, *Le Temps* (Paris), and from Hirst (1915). Comparisons of the financial and perceptual data were initially reported in Holsti and North, 1965.

Bank of England, the government banks of Berlin, St. Petersburg, and Paris had been hoarding gold for a considerable period of time prior to the assassination of Francis Ferdinand (Hirst, 1915, pp. 281, 290).[12] As late as July 25, the influential London *Economist* opposed demands from some British bankers that England take official steps to prevent a run on gold in times of panic (*Economist*, July 25, 1914, p. 169). Thus fluctuations in the influx or exflux of gold from London took place in a market free—until July 31—of any governmental interference. *But not w/o expectations thereof !*

Table 2 shows the daily average net flow of gold in and out of London. As the crisis developed, there was first a marked decrease in the influx of gold, followed by a wave of withdrawals when war broke out on the Continent. Only on August 1 was there any abatement. Late in the previous day the bank rate had been raised to an almost unprecedented 8 per cent; on August 1 the rate was increased again to 10 per cent. Thus the drop in net outflow from £1,204,000 on July 31 to £60,000 is less the result of a restoration of confidence than of a consciously adopted policy on the part of the British to take remedial steps by abolishing the free market in gold.

When the movement of gold is compared to the daily fluctuations in the intensity of perceived hostility[13] there is a significant correlation ($r_s = .85$). It is interesting to note, for example, that the drop in perceiver hostility on Monday, July 27, is matched by a sharp rise in the influx of gold. During the preceding weekend many observers and participants, including the Kaiser and Winston Churchill, had felt that the Serbian reply to the ultimatum marked the end of the crisis.[14] Similarly the steady rise in hostility starting on July 28 corresponds to the withdrawal of gold in panic proportions.

The comparison of content analysis data with financial indices is greatly strengthened if evidence can be introduced to show that the latter are in fact sensitive "barometers" of the course of international politics. Is there any evidence that the exflux of gold was related to the European crisis? Table 2 reveals that the great bulk of outbound gold was in fact shipped to the Continent. The net outflow for the period was £1,440,000; included however, are British purchases of £1,703,000 in bars and the receipt of £803,000 from various nations in South America. The net direct outflow (June 27–August 1) to continental Europe, excluding neutral Switzerland, was £3,011,000; the net exflux to the Continent from July 27 to August 1, a period encompassing the outbreak of war, was £3,018,000. Thus, gold shipments to the Continent from the entire period account for 75 per cent of all *gross* outflow and for 211 per cent of *net* outflow.

12. By the law of July 3, 1913, the Bank of Germany was authorized to build up a gold-silver war reserve of 240 million marks. At the same time the French were building up a counterpart to the German fund (*Economist*, July 25, 1914, p. 169; Aug. 15, 1914, pp. 216, 321).

13. By all perceivers (decision makers of France, England, Russia, Germany, and Austria-Hungary).

14. In the margin of his copy of the text of the Serbian reply to Austria, the Kaiser wrote, "A brilliant performance for a time limit of only forty-eight hours. This is more than one could have expected! A great moral victory for Vienna; but with it every reason for war drops away, and Giesl might have remained quietly in Belgrade! On the strength of this *I* should never have ordered mobilization" (Montgelas and Schücking, 1924, p. 254). Churchill wrote, "On Saturday afternoon the news came in that Serbia had accepted the ultimatum. I went to bed with a feeling things might blow over . . . we were still a long way, it seemed, from any danger of war. Serbia had accepted the ultimatum, could Austria demand more?" (Churchill, 1928, p. 208).

TABLE 2. *Gold Influx* (+) *and Exflux* (−) *from London* (in £ thousands)

Source or Destination	June 27–July 2	July 3–July 16	July 17–July 20	July 21–July 25	July 26	July 27	July 28	July 29	July 30	July 31	Aug. 1	Net
France			− 6				− 22	−380	− 971	− 143	− 16	−1538
Continent		− 7						−275		− 572		− 854
Belgium						− 50		− 41		− 548		− 639
Within Empire	+185			−280					− 150	− 80	−100	− 610
Egypt		+ 45						−465	− 100			− 335
Switzerland									− 60			− 60
Germany		+ 20										+ 20
United States	+ 70											+ 70
South America		+165		+186		+201			+ 174			+ 803
Bars Purchased	+128	+815		+124		+118		+250	+ 73	+ 139	+ 56	+1703
Net	+460	+993	+ 39	+ 30	0	+269	− 22	−911	−1034	−1204	− 60	−1440
Daily Average	+ 92.0	+ 71.0	+ 9.8	+ 6.0	0	+269.0	− 22.0	−911.0	−1034.0	−1204.0	− 60.0	—
Intensity of Perceived Hostility	3.46	3.66	3.79	4.17	4.52	4.46	5.10	5.18	5.48	5.70	6.42	—

Spearman rank-order correlation: rising hostility-exflux of gold:

$$n \quad r \quad P$$
$$11 \quad +.85 \quad <.01$$

During the period July 27–August 1, gold shipments to Europe account for 75.7 per cent of *gross* outflow and for 102 per cent of *net* gold exports. Again these figures may well be conservative; the final destination of gold shipped to Switzerland, for example, almost certainly included some of the continental belligerents.

Finally, there is strong, although indirect, evidence that much of the gold was recalled by the governments of the major powers involved in the crisis. An examination of the weekly statements of the European national banks (Table 3) reveals sharp increases in gold reserves during the crisis period. While the figures in that Table reflect internal stockpiling of gold—the German bank, for example was relieved of the necessity to honor withdrawals in gold after the outbreak of war[15]—they also suggest that major financial institutions on the Continent had been in large part responsible for the run on gold in London.

THE PRICES OF SECURITIES

The data analyzed here consist of twenty of the most important stocks and bonds for Serbia, Russia, France, Germany, Austria-Hungary, England, and Belgium, traded on the London, St. Petersburg, Paris, Berlin, Vienna and Brussels exchanges. To facilitate interpretation, the price of each security is given as a percentage of its value during the pre-crisis week (June 20–26). The index is the average value for the twenty securities. When the composite index is compared to the fluctuations in the intensity of perceived hostility, there is again an evident similarity. The decrease in perceived hostility on July 27 is matched by a slight rise in the value of securities. Some individual shares of those nations most intimately involved in the Austro-Serbian dispute rose quite markedly—Serbian Bonds (2.5%), Russian Bonds (2.5%), and Austrian Credit Shares (1.7%). Subsequently there was a virtual collapse in prices, corresponding to the rise in perceived hostility. The figures on the extent of the collapse in the last few days of the crisis are actually stated conservatively. In the first place, many of the quoted prices were, according to observers, nominal and thus higher than the actual price for which one could sell his securities (*Economist*, August 1, 1914, p. 231). Secondly, for the purpose of the index, the price of a security that was no longer traded—usually due to the closing of various exchanges[16]—are carried through July 30 at the last quoted price.

Again a question might be raised regarding the relationship between the falling price of securities and the European crisis. For purposes of comparison the price movements of the securities of traditionally neutral nations—Sweden and Switzerland—were analyzed (Table 5). The value of these stocks and bonds were unusually stable, falling less than one per cent during the crisis.

15. For some days prior to the outbreak of war German banks paid out only 20 per cent of demands in gold; on the declaration of "The State of Threatening Danger of War" (July 31), payments in gold were stopped altogether. On August 5 the Austro-Hungarian Bank Act, which required two-fifths gold backing for currency, was suspended (*Economist* Aug. 1, 1914, p. 229; Aug. 14, 1914, p. 320; Dec. 19, 1914 [Special War Supplement], p. 13).

16. The closing dates of the various European exchanges were as follows: Vienna (July 27), Budapest (July 27), Brussels (July 27), Berlin (July 29), St. Petersburg (July 30), Paris (July 30), London (July 31). The closing of the Barcelona Bourse on July 28, however, was attributed to "free fighting between members" (*Economist*, Aug. 1, 1914, p. 220).

TABLE 3. *Gold Reserves of National Banks*[a]

Bank of	Gold Reserves	On	Gold Reserves	On	No. of Days	Net Increase	Ave. Daily Increase
France	£159,028,000	June 25	£165,654,000	July 30	35	+ £6,626,000	£189,314
Belgium	£13,451,000	June 25	£15,980,000	Aug. 6	42	+ £2,529,000	£60,214
Germany	£63,712,200[b]	July 2	£75,426,000	Aug. 15	44	+ £11,713,800	£266,223
Russia	£159,575,000	June 29	£160,204,000	Aug. 4	36	+ £629,000	£17,472

[a]No figures are available for the Austro-Hungarian bank after July 23, 1914.
[b]1,306.1 million marks, converted in pounds at the rate of 20.50 m./£.

142

TABLE 4. Securities of Prospective Belligerents (June 20–26 = 100)

Security	June 27–July 2	July 3–July 16	July 17–July 20	July 21–July 25	July 26	July 27	July 28	July 29	July 30
Serbia—4% Bond	99.0	96.2	92.0	89.8	87.2	89.7	87.6	83.5	83.5
Serbia—Monopoles	98.8	98.0	98.9	97.3	96.6	95.5	93.6	92.5	92.5
Banque Internationale	98.8	97.8	95.6	91.2	89.0	89.0	85.8		
Baku	100.2	100.1	99.0	96.0	94.4	94.4	92.0		
Moscow—Kazan	97.2	96.0	93.3	92.6	93.1	93.1	88.6		
Russian—4½% 1909	99.8	99.9	98.0	95.8	91.5	94.0			
Russia—4% Bonds	100.1	98.3	97.5	96.5	93.8	91.5	90.2	89.1	89.1
Austria Credit Shares	99.5	97.8	97.2	95.5	92.8	94.5	93.5	94.3	92.7
Austria—4% Gold	99.8	99.9	99.7	99.0	98.1				
Hungary—4% Gold	99.6	98.5	98.0	97.5	94.3				
Hungarian Bonds	101.0	97.2	97.0	94.7	91.4	90.1	89.0	89.0	89.0
Germany—3% Imperial	99.7	99.2	98.8	97.8	96.5	95.9	95.8	94.8	94.8
3% Prussian Consols	99.7	99.2	98.8	97.7	96.4	97.0	96.9	94.7	
General Electric	99.9	99.8	98.1	94.7	91.2	92.1	91.2	88.9	86.9
France—3% Loan	99.0	98.9	97.8	96.5	93.8	93.7	92.9	92.9	
3½% French Loan	100.0	99.9	99.7	97.0	93.6	94.4	94.4	93.1	
Bank of France	100.0	99.4	98.7	98.0	97.5	97.5	97.5	94.8	
British Consols—2½%	99.8	101.1	101.3	100.3	98.4	96.8	95.8	94.8	93.1
Port of London B 4%	100.3	100.8	99.0	98.9	98.5	97.9	97.9	95.9	95.9
Bank of Brussels	99.9	99.5	98.5	97.6	97.0	97.0	97.9		
Index	99.6	98.9	97.8	96.2	94.2	94.3	93.3	92.5	92.1

143

TABLE 5. *Securities of Prospective Neutrals (June 20–26 = 100)*

Security	June 27–July 2	July 3–July 16	July 17–July 20	July 21–July 25	July 26	July 27	July 28	July 29	July 30	July 31
Sweden 3%	100.0	100.0	100.0	100.0	100.0	100.0	100.0	100.0	100.0	100.0
Sweden 3½%	99.7	97.9	98.4	98.5	99.2	98.3	98.0	98.0	98.0	98.2
Switzerland Chemin de Fer	100.3	99.6	99.5	99.5	99.5	99.5	99.5	99.5	99.5	99.5
Index	100.00	99.17	99.30	99.33	99.57	99.27	99.17	99.17	99.17	99.23

Spearman rank-order correlations: rising hostility–falling securities prices:

	n	r	P
Securities index (Neutrals)	10	+ .520	n.s.
Securities index (Belligerents)	9	+1.000	$<.01$

Average loss in value-securities of:

Serbia	12.0%	Germany	7.9%
Russia	10.1%	France	6.4%
Hungary	8.4%	Great Britain	5.5%

Austria	4.6%
Belgium	3.0%
Sweden	0.9%
Switzerland	0.5%

In contrast, the paper losses in values of the stocks and bonds of the major participants in the crisis were staggering. In the ten-day period ending July 30, the value of 387 representative British stocks fell by £188,000,000. By July 25, the value of the securities of twenty-three German industrial firms had dropped from £79,000,000 to £65,900,000—and the worst was yet to come! In one sense the "cost" of the war reached catastrophic proportions even before the first shot was fired (*Economist*, August 1, 1914, p. 229; August 29, 1914, p. 383).[17] Thus the comparison with the securities of belligerents and neutrals during the crisis strongly suggests that the virtual collapse of prices during July 1914 was directly related to rising international tensions.[18]

If financial indices such as gold flow, the stock market, and others are sensitive to crises, why bother with the perceptual data? The primary reason is that economic indicators respond to a variety of stimuli—some economic, some political, some social. The stock market "crashes" of 1929 and 1962, for example, were probably related more to internal rather than international factors, and recent sales of gold by the Soviet Union are largely a response to agricultural difficulties. Thus, analyzing financial data may be useful; but taken *alone*, these figures are clearly not sufficient for understanding political events within the international system.

RELATING PERCEPTION AND MILITARY ACTION

The next step was to test the basic interaction ($S-r : s-R$) model with the data. Students of conflict have frequently asserted that parties acting in crisis situations reveal more or less consistent patterns of rising tensions and escalation leading to violence (Boulding, 1962; Richardson, 1960a). Within the context of international politics, the line of reasoning can be summarized as follows: If state A—correctly or incorrectly—perceives itself threatened by state B, there is a high probability that A will respond with threats of hostile action. As state B begins to perceive this hostility directed toward itself, it is probable that B, too, will behave in a hostile (and defensive) fashion. This threatening behavior by B will confirm for A that its initial perceptions were correct, and A will be inclined to increase its hostile (and defensive) activity. Thereafter, the exchanges between the two parties will become increasingly negative, threatening, and injurious (North, 1962).

An initial and partial test of this sequence of interaction was carried out by correlating perceptual, or affective, data from 1914 with the spiral of military mobilizations just prior to the outbreak of World War I (North, *et al.*, 1964). The findings suggest that mobilizations accounted for a considerable part—but by no means all—of the variance in hostility. There was a steady rise in hostility *prior to* any acts of mobilization, and thus, to some degree, the decision makers

17. Some contemporary accounts of the various exchanges describe somthing of the atmosphere in which trading took place. Price losses "exceed anything that has happened in the past." "The Market has become completely demoralized, the chief factors being the Eastern situation." "A panic on the Bourse, on which prices fell below any recorded since 1895" (*Economist*, July 18, 1914, p. 126; July 25, 1914, p. 173; Dec. 19, 1914, p. 13).

18. Similar results were found when perceptions of hostility were correlated with wheat futures ($r = + .98$), the exchange rates for the German mark ($r = + .93$), and the Austrian krone ($r = + .98$); and, official ($r = + .97$) and market ($r = + .83$) interest rates (Holsti and North, 1965).

were responding to verbal threats and diplomatic moves, rather than to troop movements, in earlier phases of the crisis. This study thus revealed the necessity of correlating perceptual data with other types of action data. It also underscored the importance of testing hypotheses in other crisis situations, since there was little in the 1914 data to suggest under what conditions the exchange of threats leads to "de-escalation," as appears to have happened in the October, 1962, Cuban crisis, rather than to a conflict spiral.

The action data (S and R in the model) were expanded to include all events of a military character involving nations in the 1914 crisis either as agents or targets of actions. These were gathered from standard military histories of the period (Edmunds, 1937; McEntee, 1937; Frothingham, 1924) and such usually reliable newspapers as the *New Tork Times, Times* (London), and *Le Temps* (Paris). Wherever possible the reports were verified in an authoritative history of the crisis (Albertini, 1953). If serious doubt existed about the accuracy of an item— in the closing days of the crisis newspapers were filled with many unsubstantiated charges and countercharges—the item was discarded. As with the documentary data, the action data were coded in a uniform format; that is, according to the *agent* of action, the *action*, and the *target* of action. Unless the target of action was *explicit*, it was coded as general. The coding yielded three hundred and fifty-four military actions, of which the following are examples:

Agent	Action	Target
French Chamber	approves a 3-year military law	(general)
German fleet	leaves Norway for home ports	(general)
Austrian army	bombarded	Belgrade
Churchill (Britain)	orders shadowing in the Mediterranean of	two German battle-cruisers
Germany	declares war on	France

These dates were also scaled by Q-Sorting on a scale of less-to-more violence.[19] A summary of the action data, both in terms of frequency and intensity, for the entire crisis is found in Table 6.

For purposes of combining action and perceptual data in the $S–r : s–R$ model, both the s and r stages in the model are operationalized solely in terms of the hostility variable. Previous studies involving multivariant analysis, which have revealed hostility to be the best predictor of action, are supported in the present study. With violence of action as the dependent variable, only the rank-order correlation coefficient for hostility ($r_s = .66$) is statistically significant (Table 7).[20] A convenient starting point is to assume congruence across the $S–r : s–R$ model.

19. The inter-judge reliability coefficient was .84. With the help of Lincoln Moses and Joseph Kadane of the Stanford Department of Statistics, the authors are developing techniques of scaling action data which will bypass the difficulties inherent in the Q-Sort—for example, the noncomparability of two independent samples. For a further discussion, see Holsti, *et al.*, 1964a, Chap. 2).

20. Extensive correlational and multiple regression analyses of all perceptual variables have been made against various types of independent behavioral data. The latter include a prescaled chronology of the 1914 crisis; a series of key economic indicators such as gold flow, securities prices, and commodity futures; and mobilization data. Each analysis revealed that hostility is clearly the variable best predicting behavioral changes.

TABLE 6. *Summary Table of Military Action Data Scaled for Intensity of Violence*

Agent Nation	Target Nation								
	Austria-Hungary	Germany	England	France	Russia	Serbia	All Others	General	Total
Austria-Hungary	0.00	0.00	0.00	0.00	4.50	6.33	6.00	5.43	5.01
	(0)	(0)	(0)	(0)	(1)	(29)	(1)	(23)	(54)
Germany	0.00	0.00	5.50	6.81	6.00	4.75	6.00	4.62	5.26
	(0)	(0)	(4)	(16)	(11)	(2)	(4)	(57)	(94)
England	0.00	6.25	0.00	0.00	0.00	0.00	7.00	4.38	4.62
	(0)	(4)	(0)	(0)	(0)	(0)	(1)	(36)	(41)
France	0.00	5.00	0.00	0.00	0.00	0.00	0.00	3.84	4.08
	(0)	(13)	(0)	(0)	(0)	(0)	(0)	(51)	(64)
Russia	6.43	6.29	0.00	1.00	0.00	0.00	0.00	5.31	5.52
	(7)	(7)	(0)	(1)	(0)	(0)	(0)	(35)	(50)
Serbia	4.64	0.00	0.00	0.00	4.00	0.00	2.50	5.94	5.09
	(7)	(0)	(0)	(0)	(1)	(0)	(1)	(8)	(17)
All Others	0.00	0.00	0.00	0.00	0.00	7.00	0.00	4.30	4.38
	(0)	(0)	(0)	(0)	(0)	(1)	(0)	(33)	(34)
Total	5.54	5.58	5.50	6.47	5.73	6.25	5.64	4.60	5.01
	(14)	(24)	(4)	(17)	(13)	(32)	(7)	(243)	(354)

Top number is the average intensity of violence in the actions of the agent nation directed toward the target nation, measured on a Q-Sort scale of 1 to 9. Number in parentheses is frequency of actions which were coded for each agent-target relationship.

In these terms it is postulated—however tentatively—that a given amount of violence (or any other quality which the investigator wishes to measure) in an environmental stimulus (S) will yield an appropriate level of expressed affective response (r) which, in turn, will stimulate an expressed "intent" (s) of like affective loading and a response (R) at about the same level of violence as the original stimulus (S). Where data from historical crisis situations provide incongruent patterns across the model, other sources of variance must be sought to account for the discrepancy between the expected and obtained relationship.

Perceptual and action data are divided to correspond to two coalitions for the purposes of testing hypotheses across the $S-r$: $s-R$ model: the Triple Entente (England, France, Russia) and the Dual Alliance (Austria-Hungary, Germany). An examination of the data in Tables 8 and 9 raises some questions about the classical theories of international relations which are built on a simple $S-R$ model: There is a rather consistent lack of congruence in the actions of the two alliances. Under certain circumstances we may be able to predict any nation's reactions quite accurately if we know the behavior input it experiences. There is an extremely high probability that a full-scale nuclear attack by the United States or the Soviet Union on the other would elicit a similar response. Unfortunately, as Kenneth Boulding has pointed out, we are far less certain that the use of *rewards* at the international level will lead to reciprocation (Boulding, 1959).

TABLE 7. *Average Intensity Level of Perceptual and Action Variables—Dual Alliance and Triple Entente*

Perceptual Variables	June 27–July 2	July 3–July 16	July 17–July 20	July 21–July 25	July 26	July 27	July 28	July 29	July 30	July 31	Aug. 1–Aug. 2	Aug. 3–Aug. 4
Hostility:												
Dual Alliance	3.46	3.63	3.79	4.13	4.84	4.09	4.83	4.99	5.50	5.80	6.89	6.42
Triple Entente	3.67	4.22	4.00	4.25	5.07	4.93	5.61	5.42	5.44	5.58	5.70	6.10
Friendship:												
Dual Alliance	4.79	5.22	4.19	4.61	5.27	5.17	5.60	4.85	5.25	5.95	5.53	4.95
Triple Entente	0.00	6.10	6.00	5.00	4.50	4.10	4.64	4.40	4.77	5.23	4.24	5.46
Frustration:												
Dual Alliance	4.93	4.45	3.90	5.33	5.97	4.62	4.49	4.65	5.84	6.22	4.39	6.00
Triple Entente	3.33	4.60	4.33	5.50	4.83	5.46	4.78	5.19	4.78	4.61	4.78	4.42
Satisfaction:												
Dual Alliance	2.91	5.83	4.05	2.58	5.33	4.83	3.33	0.00	4.67	5.90	6.00	5.83
Triple Entente	0.00	5.25	5.67	4.22	4.83	4.55	6.17	4.95	5.00	6.00	5.47	6.21
Change Status Quo:												
Dual Alliance	6.45	5.27	4.92	4.89	4.42	4.49	4.79	4.85	5.46	5.55	5.51	5.71
Triple Entente	5.25	3.75	4.72	4.80	4.74	4.51	4.75	4.88	4.58	4.77	4.81	5.17
Behavioral Variable												
Violent Behavior:												
Dual Alliance	4.25	3.00	2.83	5.38	5.37	5.87	6.06	4.64	5.10	6.30	5.58	6.08
Triple Entente	4.38	2.58	2.62	4.28	3.68	4.95	4.68	5.07	4.60	5.50	5.90	6.03

Spearman rank-order correlations ($N = 24$)

	Viol.	C.S.Q.	Satis.	Frust.	Frsp.
Hostility	.663[a]	.157	.603[a]	.308	.161
Friendship	.187	−.047	.445[b]	−.063	
Frustration	.321	.059	−.036		
Satisfaction	.318	−.004			
Change Status Quo	.257				

Significance Levels   [a] = .001   [b] = .05

148

TABLE 8. *Average Intensity Levels of Violence and Perceived Hostility—Triple Entente (England, France, Russia)*

Time Period	Level of Other Coalition's Violent Behavior (S)[a]	Perception of Other Coalition's Hostility: Self as Target (r)	Perception of Hostility Toward Other Coalition: Self as Agent (s)	Level of Own Violent Behavior (R)
June 27–July 2	4.25	2.67	0.00	4.38
July 3–16	4.25	0.00	0.00	2.58
July 17–20	3.00	0.00	3.67	2.62
July 21–25	2.83	0.00	0.00	4.28
July 26	5.38	6.00	0.00	3.68
July 27	5.37	0.00	0.00	4.95
July 28	5.87	0.00	7.33	4.68
July 29	6.06	5.33	3.40	5.07
July 30	4.64	5.33	4.89	4.60
July 31	5.10	6.43	5.00	5.50
Aug. 1–2	6.30	6.19	3.97	5.90
Aug. 3–4	5.88	6.98	6.17	6.03

[a]The level of input behavior (S) is equivalent to the reaction (R) of the Dual Alliance during the previous time period.

TABLE 9. *Average Intensity Levels of Violence and Perceived Hostility—Dual Alliance (Austria-Hungary, Germany)*

Time Period	Level of Other Coalition's Violent Behavior (S)[a]	Perception of Other Coalition's Hostility: Self as Target (r)	Perception of Hostility Toward Other Coalition: Self as Agent (s)	Level of Own Violent Behavior (R)
June 27–July 2	4.38	3.98	3.55	4.25
July 3–16	4.38	3.93	3.39	3.00
July 17–20	2.58	4.08	2.92	2.83
July 21–25	2.62	4.45	3.66	5.38
July 26	4.28	4.87	3.89	5.37
July 27	3.68	4.10	3.97	5.87
July 28	4.95	5.16	4.42	6.06
July 29	4.68	4.89	4.79	4.64
July 30	5.07	6.62	4.25	5.10
July 31	4.60	5.48	6.29	6.30
Aug. 1–2	5.50	7.00	7.19	5.88
Aug. 3–4	5.90	6.50	5.70	6.08

[a]The level of input behavior (S) is equivalent to the reaction (R) of the Triple Entente during the previous time period.

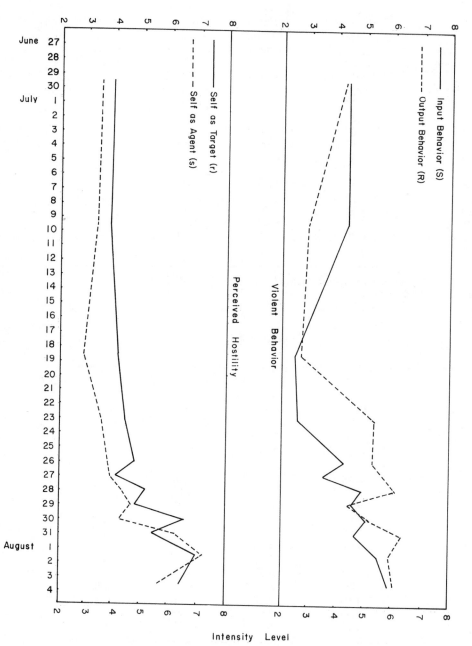

FIGURE 2. *Intensity level of violence and perceived hostility—dual alliance.*

150

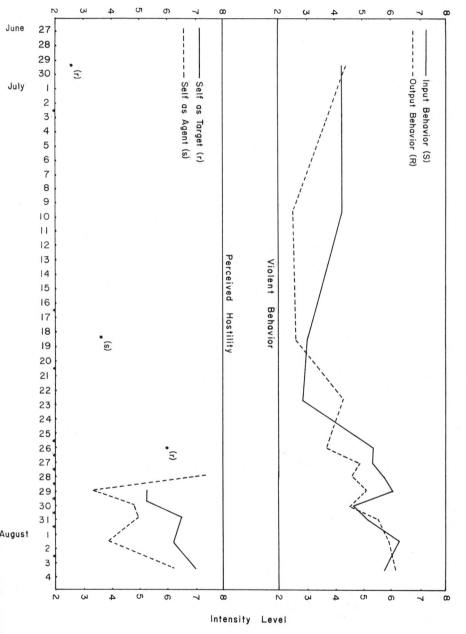

FIGURE 3. *Intensity level of violence and perceived hostility—triple entente.*

Intensity Level

151

Previous studies have suggested that in situations where two or more actor-nations are minimally engaged or involved in an interaction, the environmental stimulus (S) may yield an accurate prediction of an actor-nation's response (R). Stated somewhat differently, S may be the best predictor of R in circumstances where the actor-nations perceive that neither the penalties nor the rewards are likely to be of any great significance (Zaninovich, 1964).

The first hypothesis specifies the conditions under which the degree of congruence between S and R is high or low.

The correlation between input action (S) and policy response (R) will be better in a situation of low involvement than in one of high involvement.

This suggests that in the *low* involvement situation, the analysis of perceptions (s and r) may be less crucial, and that "objective" criteria may give the analyst adequate information. Rummel's (1964a) findings that domestic data predict state behavior fairly well—except under conditions of high conflict—can be interpreted as lending support to this hypothesis.

Of the two coalitions engaged in the crisis, the Triple Entente was engaged for a much shorter period. During the month between June 27 and July 27, that coalition revealed a total of only 40 perceptions of hostility compared to 171 for the Dual Alliance; in the late period (July 28 to August 4) the figures were 229 and 270 respectively.[21] This certainly coincides with the historians' consensus.

As suggested by the hypothesis, the degree of congruence between S and R for the less-engaged coalition, the Triple Entente, is considerably lower ($r_s = .463$) than that for the Dual Alliance ($r_s = .678$). Several explanations are possible. First, at least two members of the Triple Entente—England and France—acted (R) with a high level of violence only relatively late in the crisis period, withholding action until the threat (S) from the Dual Alliance was quite clearly defined.

On the other hand, the actions of the Dual Alliance—and particularly Austria-Hungary's actions in the early and middle part of the crisis period leading to a hoped-for local war—were not commensurate with the level of violence displayed by either Serbia or other members of the Triple Entente. There were two overlapping crises which became one at midnight August 4. The first was the result of a rather deliberately planned local war that had little to do with the actions of the other major powers and in which the members of the Triple Entente were only minimally engaged; the second resulted in an unplanned escalation into general war, engulfing all the nations.

A second hypothesis including the S and R (action) stages of the model is concerned not only with congruence or lack of congruence, but with the direction of differences.

In a situation of low involvement, policy response (R) will tend to be at a lower level of violence than the input action (S), whereas in a high-involvement situation, the policy response (R) will tend to be at a higher level of violence than the input action (S).

In terms of the events of 1914, the hypothesis suggests that the nations of the Triple Entente would under-respond to actions from the other side, whereas those of the Dual Alliance would be over-reacting to the threat from the Triple Entente. A Mann-Whitney U Test (Siegel, 1956, pp. 116–127) to compare the magnitude

21. $x^2 = 45.8$, and with $df = 1$, $P = < .001$.

TABLE 11. *Difference in Intensity Between Input Behavior (S) and Output Behavior (R) for the Triple Entente and Dual Alliance*

| Period | Dual Alliance | | Triple Entente | |
	S Minus R^a	Rank	S Minus R^a	Rank
June 27–July 2	0.13	9	−0.13	13
July 3–16	1.38	3	1.67	2
July 17–20	−0.25	16	0.38	8
July 21–25	−2.76	24	−1.45	21
July 26	−1.09	19	1.70	1
July 27	−2.19	23	0.42	6
July 28	−1.21	20	1.19	4
July 29	0.04	10.5	0.99	5
July 30	−0.03	12	0.04	10.5
July 31	−1.70	22	−0.40	18
Aug. 1–2	−0.38	17	0.40	7
Aug. 3–4	−0.18	15	−0.15	14
		$\Sigma = 190.5 = R_2$		$\Sigma = 109.5 = R_1$

$$U = 222 - 190.5 = 31.5$$
$$P = < .025$$

[a]The difference between the level of violence in the actions of the opposing coalitions (S) and level of violence in the resulting action response (R). Positive values indicate *under-reaction* to the actions of the other coalition, whereas negative values indicate *over-reaction*. Values for S and R derived from Tables 8 and 9.

of the difference between input (S) and output (R) action reveals that the values for the Dual Alliance are indeed consistently negative (indicating over-reaction), whereas those of the Triple Entente are positive (under-reaction) on balance (Table 11).[22]

The inability to predict reactions (R) solely on the basis of action (S) suggests an examination of the relationship between action, perceptual, and situational variables.

Where such lack of congruence between input and output action exists, the intervening perceptions may perform either an accelerating or decelerating function. This suggests the hypothesis that

In the low-involvement situation, r will tend to be at a lower level than S, whereas in the high-involvement situation, R will tend to be higher than S.

Intuitively the hypothesis makes sense. In a period of relative calm and low involvement, perceptual distortion will probably tend in the direction of under-perception; one may even be lulled into a false sense of security by failing to perceive a real threat. The British and French reaction to Nazi Germany—until the

22. The Mann-Whitney U Test of systematic differences between two variables was applied to the results in Tables 11–14 in order to take account of the *magnitude* as well as the *direction* of differences. Significance levels computed from Siegel's Table K (1956, pp. 274–277).

aggressive actions of Hitler became so unambiguous that even Chamberlain and
Daladier perceived the danger—is a case in point. During a period of intense
stress, on the other hand, when all fingers are near or on the trigger, even the
most innocent action may be perceived as a threat of great magnitude. This
pattern is much like that exhibited by Kaiser Wilhelm during the intense crisis
leading up to World War I. Although possessor of the world's second ranking
navy, at one point he perceived the presence of a few Russian torpedo boats in
the Baltic as adequate cause for alerting the entire German fleet (Montgelas and
Schücking, 1924, p. 223).

The hypothesis is supported by the 1914 data. Table 12 reveals the difference
between the level of input action (S) and perceptions of those actions (r). The
leaders of the Dual Alliance consistently overperceived the level of violence in
the actions of the Triple Entente. On the other hand, the Triple Entente tended to
underperceive the actions of the other coalition.

The same hypothesis can also be tested in a somewhat different way. The first
six periods (June 27–July 27) have been described as those in which the members
of the Dual Alliance were highly involved with the events in the Balkans, whereas
those of the Triple Entente were not. On the other hand, during the culminating
periods of the crisis (July 28–August 4), nations in both alliances were being
drawn into war. Thus, if the hypothesis is correct, differences in the way in which

TABLE 12. *Difference in Intensity Between Input Behavior (S) and Perceptions of Input
Behavior (r) for the Triple Entente and Dual Alliance*

| Period | Dual Alliance | | Triple Entente | |
	S Minus r^a	Rank	S Minus r^a	Rank
June 27–July 2	0.40	9	1.58	6
July 3–16	0.45	8	4.25	3
July 17–20	−1.50	21.5	3.00	4
July 21–25	−1.83	24	2.83	5
July 26	−0.59	14	−0.62	16
July 27	−0.42	13	5.37	2
July 28	−0.21	11.5	5.87	1
July 29	−0.21	11.5	0.73	7
July 30	−1.55	23	−0.69	17
July 31	−0.88	18	−1.33	20
Aug. 1–2	−1.50	21.5	0.11	10
Aug. 3–4	−0.60	15	−1.10	19
		$\Sigma = 190 = R_1$		$\Sigma = 110 = R_2$

$$U = 222 - 190 = 32$$
$$P = < .025$$

[a]The difference between the level of violence in the actions of the opposing coalition (S)
and one's perception (r) of the hostility of those actions. Positive values indicate *under-perception*
of the other coalition's action, whereas negative values indicate *over-perception*. Values for S
and r derived from Tables 8 and 9.

actions (S) are perceived (r) by nations of the two coalitions should be greatest during the early stages of the crisis. When the data in Table 12 are re-analyzed in this manner, the hypothesis is again supported. The difference between the two coalitions in regard to the S–r link during the early period is statistically significant ($U = 4$, $p = .013$), whereas in the later period it is not ($U = 11$, $p = $ n.s.).

A further hypothesis within the model relates perceptions of one's own intent with perceptions of the intent of others. Boulding (1959), Osgood (1962), and many others have pointed to the propensity of nations to perceive their own intentions in the best light possible, while attributing more hostile motives to those of others.

To the extent that there is a difference between perceptions of the other's policy (r) and statements of own intent (s), perceptions of hostility in r will tend to be higher than in s in *both* the low-involvement and the high-involvement situations.

The figures in Table 13 support the hypothesis both in that the level of perceived hostility for (r) is consistently higher than for (s), and in that there is no significant difference between the two coalitions.

The final intervening perceptual link in the model is that between the perception

TABLE 13. *Differences in Intensity Between Perceptions of Input Behavior (r) and Output Behavior (s) for the Triple Entente and Dual Alliance*

Period	Dual Alliance		Triple Entente	
	r Minus s[a]	Rank	r Minus s[a]	Rank
June 27–July 2	0.43	15	2.67	2
July 3–16	0.54	13	0.00	19
July 17–20	1.16	7	−3.67	23
July 21–25	0.79	11	0.00	19
July 26	0.98	8	6.00	1
July 27	0.13	16	0.00	19
July 28	0.74	12	−7.33	24
July 29	0.10	17	1.93	5
July 30	2.37	3	0.44	14
July 31	−0.81	22	1.43	6
Aug. 1–2	−0.19	21	2.22	4
Aug. 3–4	0.80	10	0.81	9

$$\Sigma = 155 = R_1 \qquad \Sigma = 145 = R_2$$
$$U = 222 - 155 = 67$$
$$P = \text{n.s.}$$

[a]The difference between perceptions of the other coalition's hostility (r) and one's statements of hostility toward the other coalition (s). Positive values indicate that the other coalition is perceived as more hostile than oneself. Negative values indicate one's expressions of hostility are greater than the perceived hostility of the other coalition. Values for r and s derived from Tables 8 and 9.

of one's own behavior (s) and the level of violence in the actual response (R). The hypothesis is that

> In the situation of low involvement, statements of intent (s) will tend to be higher than action responses (R), whereas in the high-involvement situation, s will tend to be lower than R.

Again there is at least intuitive support for the hypothesis. In a situation of high involvement, whether the action is essentially cooperative or conflictual, the effort one makes often far surpasses stated intent. The efforts of war-torn Western European nations after 1945 toward rebuilding economies, establishing supranational organizations, and contributing to the defense of Europe during the period of most severe Soviet threat undoubtedly exceeded the plans and intentions of most leaders. In the case where one feels little stress, on the other hand, the propensity of promises to run ahead of performance appears enhanced. The subsequent European unwillingness to raise NATO divisions, even to the promised and planned level can, at least in part, be attributed to a situation of less likelihood of massive Soviet invasion of Western Europe.

Table 14, however, reveals that there is, in fact, no difference between the two coalitions in regard to the s–R linkage. In both cases, R is consistently higher than s; that is, the states in both coalitions tended to react at a higher level of violence than suggested by the statements of intent by their various leaders.

TABLE 14. *Differences in Intensity Between Perceptions of Output Behavior (s) and Output Behavior (R) for the Triple Entente and Dual Alliance*

Period	Dual Alliance		Triple Entente	
	s Minus R^a	Rank	s Minus R^a	Rank
June 27–July 2	−0.70	12	−4.38	23
July 3–16	0.39	4	−2.58	20
July 17–20	0.09	8	1.05	3
July 21–25	−1.72	17	−4.28	22
July 26	−1.48	14	−3.68	21
July 27	−1.90	18	−4.95	24
July 28	−1.64	15	2.65	1
July 29	0.15	6	−1.67	16
July 30	−0.85	13	0.29	5
July 31	−0.01	9	−0.50	11
Aug. 1–2	1.31	2	−1.93	19
Aug. 3–4	−0.38	10	0.14	7

$$\Sigma = 128 = R_2 \qquad\qquad \Sigma = 172 = R_1$$

$$U = 222 - 172 = 50$$
$$P = \text{n.s.}$$

[a] The difference between the hostility of expressions of intent toward the other coalition (s) and the violence of actions carried out (R). Positive values indicate expressions of intent at a higher level than execution of policy, whereas negative values indicate actions which exceed statements of intent. Values for s and R derived from Tables 8 and 9.

SUMMARY OF FINDINGS

The analysis of the 1914 crisis began with an assumption basic to most traditional theories of international politics—that is, the assumption of congruence between input (*S*) and output (*R*) action. The data revealed, however, a significant difference between the two coalitions corresponding to the different levels of involvement in the situation. Congruence between (*S*) and (*R*) was high for the members of the Triple Entente, which became involved only very late in the crisis. The level of congruence was much lower for the nations of the Dual Alliance, which were engaged for essentially the entire crisis period.

Having failed to account for the escalation from a local incident to a general war with only the action variables, the perceptual variables (*r*) and (*s*) were analyzed. The various links across the model were examined and no significant difference between the two coalitions in regard to the *s–R* step was found: (*R*) was higher than (*s*) in both cases. As predicted, there was little difference between the Triple Entente and Dual Alliance in the *r–s* link, both perceiving themselves as less hostile than the other coalition. A significant difference did appear at the *S–r* step, however. The leaders of the Dual Alliance consistently over-perceived the actions of the Triple Entente. Thus the *S–r* link served a "magnifying" function. The decision-makers of the Triple Entente, on the other hand, tended to under-perceive the actions of the Dual Alliance. This difference in perceiving the environment (the *S–r* link) is consistent with the pronounced tendency of the Dual Alliance to respond at a higher level of violence than the Triple Entente.

CONCLUSION

A major drawback to the type of research embodied in the study of the 1914 crisis is found in the very nature of the research techniques used. Even elementary forms of content analysis, such as frequency counts, require extensive expenditure of scarce research resources. Moreover, the coding and scaling of documents are tasks requiring a high level of skill but offering intellectual reward for only a limited time. And such work is painstakingly slow; the costs of data-generation necessarily limit research to only a few cases. Thus the social scientist with an interest in undertaking comparable and cumulative studies of international political behavior has been faced with a dilemma: is it preferable to continue analyses of a few cases in great depth, or to analyze more cases, but at the cost of bypassing the perceptual data?

Recent developments in programming high-speed computers—such as the IBM 7090—for content analysis, have gone a long way toward solving the dilemma (Stone, *et al.*, 1962). The Studies in International Conflict and Integration have adapted the "General Inquirer" system of automated content analysis for continuing analyses such as those of the 1914 crisis (Holsti, 1964). This technique permits a substantial reduction of manual effort, while materially increasing speed, reliability, and flexibility of analysis.

The basic unit for quantitative measurement under the General Inquirer system continues to be the theme—that is, perceiver–perceived–attitude/action–target. The Stanford Political Dictionary serves as the tool for rating of these perceptual units according to three dimensions: positive affect-negative affect; strong-weak; active-passive. The three correspond to the *evaluative, potency,* and *activity* factors which are primary in human cognition irrespective of culture (Osgood, *et al.*, 1957; Suci, 1957; Osgood, 1962; Kumata and Schramm, 1956). The dictionary thus reflects the proposition that when decision makers perceive themselves, other nations, or events—or any stimulus—the most relevant discriminations are made in a milieu defined by these three factors. With the development of this technique of content analysis, further cases can be investigated with far greater ease and confidence. These have included analyses of the October 1962 Cuban missile crisis (Holsti, *et al.*, 1965), Sino-Soviet relations (Holsti, 1966) and Communist bloc integration (Hopmann, 1966) during periods of high and low international tensions.

The present study of the 1914 crisis has encompassed—within the context of developing an empirical theory—an analysis of the processes of escalation from a single incident through a planned war to an unplanned world war. To what extent are the findings, and the analytical framework employed here, relevant for the study of situations removed both in time and space?

In general there are indications that, the more intense the interaction between the parties, the more important it is to incorporate perceptual data into the analysis. Or, to state this somewhat differently, in a situation of low involvement, one may be able to predict a nation's action responses to environmental stimuli rather accurately without recourse to the perceptions of its decision makers. On the other hand, in a period of crisis marked by high involvement and rising intensity—as in the weeks prior to August 1914—the role of perception becomes increasingly important.

More specifically, it was found that the manner in which one party—or, as in this case, one coalition—perceived the actions of the other party was the crucial link between perception and action. The findings from the study of the Cuban missile crisis are relevant in this respect. In comparing the events of October 1962 with those in the summer of 1914, some important differences emerge. The members of the Dual Alliance—the more highly involved coalition— in 1914 consistently over-perceived the level of violence in actions taken by members of the Triple Entente. British, French, and Russian decision makers, on the other hand, under-perceived the level of violence in the actions of the Dual Alliance. Moreover, whereas there was a significant difference between the two coalitions during the early phase of the crisis—when members of the Dual Alliance were more highly involved with the events in the Balkans than were members of the Triple Entente—this difference disappeared as *all* nations were being drawn into war. In terms of the $S-r : s-R$ model, this relationship between one coalition's actions, the other coalition's perceptions of those actions, and the resulting policies was apparently the crucial one.

In the Cuban crisis, however, both sides tended to perceive rather accurately the nature of the adversary's actions, and then proceeded to act at an "appropriate" level; that is, as the level of violence or potential violence in the adversary's actions diminished, perceptions of those actions increased in positive affect and decreased in negative affect, and the level of violence in the resulting policies also decreased. Thus, unlike the situation in 1914, efforts by either party to delay or reverse the escalation were generally perceived as such, and were responded to in like manner. Whether the different patterns of action and perception found in the 1914 and Cuban cases will consistently be found to distinguish crises that escalate and de-escalate, of course, can only be determined through continuing research.

Charles A. McClelland

Access to Berlin:
The Quantity and Variety of
Events, 1948-1963[1]

Acute international crises have been among the most prominent recurring phenomena of post–World War II international relations. The long series of these affairs dating from 1946 is recognized at once simply from a recital of place names: Iran, Greece, Berlin, Korea, Indochina, Suez, Quemoy, the Congo, and Cuba among others. From a layman's point of view or even from a foreign affairs practitioner's point of view, there is not much mystery about an international crisis. When a crisis appears, the news is suddenly dominated by its events, officials and commentators call it by name and talk about its significance, and, after it has lapsed, it achieves a definite shape in books and articles about it. Each crisis takes its place in the tentative history of the times.

On the other hand, the word *crisis* has become extremely common in the discussions on world affairs, to the extent that some official statement or some newspaper report can almost be depended upon to label every active international conflict as a crisis. Further, a long-sustained conflict in some part of the world may be given an overall characterization as a crisis. For example, the authors of a recent book on the Berlin Wall offer the comment, "It is fascinating to observe how the 'Berlin Crisis' is a barometer of Russian fortunes in the Cold War," and they cite the remark of an unnamed West Berlin official, "What Americans must understand is that there is *always* a Berlin crisis. The Russians see to that" (Heller and Heller, 1962, pp. 15, 16). The result from usage is that *crisis* has become virtually a synonym for *trouble* in international relations. Thus, from the standpoint of theory and research in international relations, a definite problem of defining acute international crises has arisen. What would be desirable would be a definition which would state that when

1. The writer wishes to express his appreciation to Randolph Siverson, John Sullivan, Warren Phillips, and Dan Harrison—students, past and present—who have participated and assisted in the series of studies of crises.

such and such events and conditions appear, a crisis exists; when these events and conditions are not present, there is no crisis.

THEORY AND THE RESEARCH PROBLEM

This paper is concerned with the analysis of acute international crises in the Cold War era. It is based on the theoretical proposition that a crisis is, in some way, a "change of state" in the flow of international political actions. It must be some kind of identifiable departure from a pre-existing and temporary status quo in the stream of events of international relations (McClelland, 1964a, p. 203). If a "change of state" does occur with the onset of a genuine international crisis, then it should be possible to detect that change. A convincing approach would be to measure the flow of events and to establish when and how the shift occurs.

An unpublished paper which has analyzed the flow of publicly reported events related to the conflict in the Taiwan Straits area in the period of 1954–1959 has identified the "change of state" occurring with two acute crises in that period and locale (Sullivan, 1964). Through an accident, the collected data that undergirded that research were lost, and a new study will need to be carried out, therefore, to reconfirm the findings. The major results from this aborted study will be cited later, nevertheless. Here, a replication of Sullivan's investigation will be reported using a different series of international conflicts and a different period of historical time.

The replication, based on data related to the struggle to maintain Allied access to Berlin between 1948 and 1963, takes advantage of a segment of "systems theory" which states, in the jargon of that approach, that systems under stress will load or strain their sub-systems (Miller, 1956, pp. 52–63). In other words, a part or a component in a complex system—the latter being, in the case at hand, the full range of interwoven activities of international relations in Berlin, Germany, and Europe relating to the Western-Soviet conflict—will be expected to respond to important disturbances in the system. If the *system* is disturbed enough to "change state," the related sub-system will also be disturbed enough to "change state." It does not follow necessarily that a local disturbance that upsets and activates the sub-system will throw the whole system into action. The greater system should be found to activate the lesser sub-system, however. Hence, the research that will be reported here was organized as carefully as possible to isolate a sub-system from its larger system. This was done in order to reduce the expanse of the data to be analyzed and also to permit the investigation of the part-to-whole relationship.

The sub-system is constituted by "local" events which either have (1) challenged directly the Western position in Berlin and on the access routes, or (2) have been defense measures mounted against these challenges. Included are such events as interferences, harassments, and delays on the established routes between West Germany and Berlin, and the responses to these troubles; arrests and detainments of personnel connected with the occupation forces (East and West) in Berlin; disputes between the military and civil authorities of the occupation, West versus East; and the decrees, decisions, and regulations affecting Western freedom of movement and communication to and from, as well as within, the city. Excluded are the events of "high diplomacy" of the world's capitals and the other numerous events of international relations that have given the "local" occurrences their significance, in the full historical sense. In a word, the stream of action designated and isolated as a sub-system has been defined and treated technically rather than historically.

A third theoretical interest here is to test, to some extent, several propositions about acute international crises that were set forth earlier (McClelland, 1961, pp. 197–200). These propositions are the following:

1.   That acute international crises are "short burst" affairs and are marked by an unusual volume and intensity of events.

2.   That the general trend in acute international crises will be found to be toward "routinizing" crisis behaviors; toward dealing with the risks, troubles, and dangers involved by means of increasingly "standard" techniques.

3.   That in the interplay of a crisis, the participants will be reluctant to allow the level of violence to increase beyond the level present at the onset of the crisis.

To summarize, the immediate interests which have stimulated and guided the empirical research on the struggle to maintain Western access to Berlin over a period of sixteen years are three in number. The research questions are as follows:

1.   Can a "change of state" be detected in the activities of a system in the transition from a non-crisis period to a crisis period?

2.   Can a designated sub-system that is part of a more general system of action be shown to be responsive to significant disturbances of the general system?

3.   Can the three statements about international crisis behavior which were specified above be confirmed or belied by a study of a body of relevant historical information?

A question of some importance should be raised at this point. It may well be asked, why should anyone go to the trouble of demonstrating a definition of international crises in terms of a change of state in an international system or of inquiring into the responsiveness of a sub-system to change in a system? Although acute international crises may be interesting in themselves and important to the practical concerns of war and peace, it is essential, from the standpoint of the development of theories of the international system, to show the usefulness of crisis studies in the setting of more comprehensive theoretical concerns. The gradual emergence of system perspectives for the study of international relations has now led to the positive identification of two large divisions of theory and research, each of which probably will require a full generation of intensive empirical investigations and theoretical probings to realize the potential in the approach. Foreign policy analysis (the study of the field in the perspective of the actor) and international system analysis (the study of the field in the perspective of interactions—of their structure, process, and performance) are the two basic divisions of the international relations discipline, and it should be apparent that the topic of international crises might be approached in terms of reference of either analysis. The present study belongs in the area of system interaction analysis.

The interest in crises begins to fall into place in a general conception of international system analysis as soon as it is realized that the interflowing activities of the actors in the system must achieve one kind of pattern or structure at one time and different kinds at other times. Part of the intermixture of actor behaviors must tend to be recurring, while part must be expected to lie outside the realm of what has previously been familiar. It is in the detailed tracing of the *performance* of a specified system that the investigator might hope to find the indicators of structure and process and, what is still more important, the evidence of variations over time in these two fundamental properties of systems. The significant variation in the flow of action in a system is the central interest of international system analysis. Further, the complexity of international relations is such that one should hardly expect to discover a simple set of indicators of the changing configurations in a system's performance. Thus, the long-term objective of both theory and research on the international system is not to find out *everything* about the system; it is only to construct an appropriately complex and sufficiently accurate set of *performance indicators* so that "readings" of the state of the system can be taken at any time. At some future date, the rearranging and testing of different combinations of indicators probably will become a major research preoccupation. Meanwhile, the task is to begin the construction, one at a time, of possible indicators in the expectation that, sooner or later, they will be assembled and used in an effective composite form for measurement.

A fairly obvious beginning choice is to select two conspicuous "states" or conditions of the international system—of non-crisis and crisis—and to approach the reported events of appropriate historical time periods with two simple questions in hand: (1) do the numbers of reported acts in relevant categories reflect changes which, in turn, indicate a change of state in the system, and (2) do the combinations of types of acts reflect changes to indicate a change of state in the system? In the beginning, it seems best to deal with gross indicators such as volume and variety and with crude categories such as non-crisis and crisis. And, at the outset, it seems advisable to evaluate such tests as may be made of performance characteristics of the international system with the help of "the common understanding," with the expectation that, as the work progresses, cumulative results will reduce our reliance upon "common sense" appraisals.

Ordinarily, one prefers to cast the main problems in a piece of research in operational form so that it can be said, at the end, whether or not the observed phenomena as defined by the terms of the inquiry conform to the original assertions. For reasons that will be given, the procedure of "operationalizing" has not been performed explicitly in the present study. Thus, it was not stated, for example, that an acute international crisis occurring in the structure of the contemporary Cold War system is defined by at least a tripling of the volume of reported relevant acts above the level of the six months preceding the occurrence of the crisis, and by more than a two-thirds activation of all the types of behavior categorized as possible. The prime reason for posing only some "research questions" is that the reported research and the crisis studies preceding it have been regarded as no more than the "test-borings" of a preliminary survey.

To characterize the acute international crisis as a particular type of international behavior and to define it as a recurring condition in the international system as indicated by the measures of volume and variety would be, in effect, to furnish the answer before anyone is certain that the proper question has been formulated. It seems very important not to suggest premature simplifications of what is obviously going to be a complex explanation. In addition, nothing should be done which might diminish the attention that must be given to the creation, eventually, of a number of different indicators of international system performance. Literally scores of international behavior studies, designed and arranged to cross-cut one another from several theoretical starting points, probably will be needed before we can begin to describe with confidence how the international system works, given the presence of certain specified conditions and a certain composite of indicators which are sensitive to changes in the state of the system. For the present, it is idle to look for definitive theoretical statements or for decisive research results. All that we can be sure about are the difficulties in the subject matter and the impressive problems in the approach to international system analysis.

SOME METHODOLOGICAL DIFFICULTIES

Before any further discussion of research procedures, it will be well to note some of the obstacles facing this type of inquiry and to review a few of the objections and criticisms that may be raised against it.

In the perspective of the older school of scientific historiography (that is, in the Ranke tradition of painstaking research and recovery of all extant evidence), it would be judged a waste of time and effort to make a study of the Berlin crises from the sources of information that now are available to the public. Proper historical procedure would be to wait until the masses of government documents of the period are released and then to make a thorough study of *all* the available data including memoirs, diaries, correspondence, state documents, and other contemporary sources. Careful notes would be made for each piece of information studied, and from these notes the historian would write an account of what occurred, reconstructing the past "as it really was" as closely as his knowledge, insight, and literary abilities would permit. The historian of the older school would want to establish not only an accurate picture of "all" the events, but also the motivations and the behind-the-scenes moves of all the important participants. He would be dissatisfied with such interim accounts as those by Davison (1958) and Smith (1963), which are forced to fill in gaps in the evidence with logical speculations.

Not only are the data employed in this analysis of the Berlin access problem incomplete, but they were explicitly selected as well to *exclude* the material that might suggest and explain motivations behind the decisions and actions of the major participants. Further, *all* the data used were drawn from a single source, namely the *New York Times Index*. Not even the newspaper, itself, was read in gathering the facts.[2] These are serious weaknesses from the standpoint of historical method; the reports of events were collected only in order

2. To make some display of self-defense, the writer admits that he read newspaper accounts and studied the works of Davison (1958), Clay (1950), Howley (1950), Murphy (1964), Smith (1963), Speier (1961), Heller and Heller (1961 and 1962), and Windsor (1963).

that they could be arranged in chronological order, coded according to types of action, and then counted. Just how far away from meticulous historical accuracy this work stands can be shown easily by noting the sources of information loss and contaminating factors. Of all the relevant events that occurred, only some were recorded by anybody; of all the events recorded anywhere, one American newspaper (however special it is as a "newspaper of record") printed only a part; and of all the relevant information printed in the newspaper, only a part was indexed (such shortcoming must be assumed on principle according to the nature of any indexing). Further losses and distortions were inflicted, no doubt, in our gathering and categorizing of the materials that were taken from the *New York Times Index*.

A total of 1,791 reported events survived all this damaging treatment, and each one of the items was thereupon counted as if it were of the same significance and had the same weight as all the others. Thus, the Soviet order that finally closed the roads, railroads, and canals between West Germany and Berlin on June 24, 1948, was treated as no more and no less weighty than the accusation of July 19, 1953, leveled by the Soviet High Commissioner, Semyenov, that American planes were dropping anti-Soviet leaflets on Soviet air fields near Berlin. Of course, not all historical events are of the same magnitude and significance; the equal treatment that we have given to all events has a special purpose not related to the weighing of events in the historian's manner.

These numerous defects are to be viewed with concern if not with dismay; yet, if any patterning can be discerned from the surviving data, it *may* indicate a powerful redundancy in the public communication of contemporary international relations. Further, it must be pointed out and emphasized that, although historical materials are being used, they are not employed in this study for the normal purposes of historiography. Rather, we shall be searching only for *indicators* of what happened, not for all the events themselves. If, in the last analysis, it is only the behavior of the indexers of the *New York Times* that traces faithfully the ups and downs of international events, that will be a satisfactory discovery. While it is deplorable that public sources of information of international events are so uncertain and incomplete, students of international relations have little alternative but to use the materials at hand with an awareness of their defects. No more can be said in advance to meet the criticisms of historians.

Another major difficulty arises from insights into the nature of acute international crises. During the past five years, "crisis management" has become an important topic in the study of international relations and national security affairs. Behind this preoccupation is the idea that an acute crisis is a special situation both as to practical policy planning and the analysis of its advent and its demobilization. The assumption is made easily that the behaviors of the participants change during crises and are different from those of non-crisis times. In particular, it is thought that the military role is enlarged and becomes especially significant during acute crises.

The chief objection to assuming that crisis behavior is different from non-crisis behavior rests on the observation that crises are mainly psychological occurrences. It is pointed out correctly that a given act committed at one moment and in a certain context is provocative, while at another time and in a different setting, it may be merely irritating. A statement by the head of state on one occasion will be dismissed in other governments as bluster directed strictly to the home audience, while at another time it will be taken as a serious threat. Military movements and exercises may be "routine," as they are almost always described, or they may constitute important warnings to the enemy. Much depends on the context of the event and on how it is perceived by others, and mistakes can be made in the perception of the intent behind the act.

The general argument, then, is that the psychological character of acute international crises makes "crisis management" a most unlikely undertaking. No matter how carefully a government might carry out its crisis planning, the plan would be likely to miscarry in action because of the vast variety of contexts in international relations and because of the great uncertainties as to the perceptions that will take shape in the minds of the other participants. The same difficulties would be encountered in attempting to plan against an opponent's plan. Hence, the entire matter of crisis management must be considered a snare and delusion if it is set apart in any way from the normal, day-to-day analysis of international politics and the regular execution of foreign policy. To the extent that the essence of any international crisis is its psychological component, the scholarly interest in examining historical data for patterns or other regular activities peculiar to crises must also be regarded as misguided. At best, the research that would promise some useful results would be some type of content analysis of diplomatic messages and statements which might register to a limited extent the perceptions of national actors.

This line of thinking, carried to its logical extreme, will lead one to conclude that international politics is so complex and enigmatic that any research-based policy planning is absurd and also that the practice of diplomacy is a rare and personal art based on subtle combinations of insight, wisdom, and experience.

The contrary view of the nature of crises and of many other occurrences in the international system deserves as much attention, perhaps, as the thesis that the international system is almost too complex and subtle to be understood by human minds. The opposing argument simply is that behind the welter of events there is a large amount of repetition and rule-bound behavior in international politics. It is the tendency toward some consistency of action that gives the promise that the international system may be managed. This writer has noted elsewhere that "the international system is more malleable, less complex, slower to react to error, more subject to guidance, and more capable of directed change than we have usually thought . . ." (McClelland, 1964b, p. 76). If the psychological element plays a large role in international politics, statecraft is also a matter of choosing lines of action from among limited numbers of open alternative courses, according to calculations based largely on past actions of the actors of the international system. What the practitioners of foreign affairs seem to do is to make decisions on the basis of their recognition of patterns and trends in recent sequences of international interactions.

There exist many intermediate positions between the opposing contentions over the basic nature of the international system. It would seem that determined research efforts should lead to more precise statements of the dispute, if not to its termination. If researchers will press ahead in the analysis of how governments actually behave in various types of international situations, perhaps the differences between those who believe that the international system is almost too complex to understand and those who think the international system only appears to be overwhelmingly complex can be lessened according to evidence. At any rate, the international crisis provides a good subject for study not only because of its prominence in recent international relations but also because it offers an opportunity to examine in detail the characteristics of international interaction.

THE DESIGN OF THE INQUIRY

The Berlin situation between 1948 and the present time offers several outstanding advantages from the standpoint of international relations research. Although many changes have occurred in the positions of the actors and in the arrangements of the relationships among them, the basic situation has been unchanged since the beginning. That is, the four-power occupation of Berlin set up a classical conflict structure in international relations where the holding of territorial position by one side against the displacing efforts of the other side has been the essence of the situation. As everyone is aware, the three Western powers—the British, the Americans, the French, and, in due course, the West Berliners and West Germans—have constituted one side of the conflict while the Russians, the East Berliners, and the East Germans have occupied the opposing role.

From the Western standpoint, the steady objective has been to hold the physical position in the three sectors of West Berlin, to continue to claim the right to joint occupancy of all of Berlin, and to foresee and forestall moves by the East that would lead to the indirect or automatic ejection of the West from its position. From the Eastern standpoint, the steady objective has been to act in ways that would promise an immediate or eventual elimination of the Western presence in Berlin and a full incorporation of the entire city with the administration of the Soviet Zone of Germany or, in later years, with that of East Germany. The limitations on the behaviors of both sides have been balanced fairly evenly by the temptations presented to both sides. Again, the factor of steadiness is an interesting and important feature of the situation.

Since July 1945 when the Western Allies traded the territory they occupied in Thuringia, Saxony, and Saxony-Anhalt for the access to their sectors of Berlin, the West has been limited in its actions by its inherently weak and vulnerable position in Berlin. Existence in an enclave buried a hundred miles inside the Soviet-controlled zone of Germany has led many times to the temptation to give up that position. The very vulnerability of the position often has offset the temptation to withdraw, however, due to the obvious and highly public loss of prestige that would be likely to ensue. As the history of the occupation developed, reinforcing reasons for staying on have amplified the loss-of-prestige consideration.

On the Soviet side, the dominating position in Berlin held from the outset by the Soviet Union has encouraged the notion that the Western forces could be pushed out of the city at any time by direct physical force. This temptation has been offset persistently by the Soviet contemplation of the "larger systemic consequences" that might follow from a drastic dislodgement of the West in Berlin. In the earlier years, the West displayed, in part, some of these larger consequences by demonstrating its control over East-West travel and trade. The threat of general war has played a deterring role against drastic Soviet moves, as well.

In brief, during the span of the sixteen-year period under study here, the contending parties in Berlin have been confronted by a single and basic situation which has been hedged in by compelling restraints against "final" actions. Without any formal or explicit specification, a threshold of allowable action has come into being. At times, both sides have pressed hard against the threshold and, at other times, both sides have backed away to a safe distance from this intangible but existing line.

While the "solution of the Berlin problem" has been a perennial subject of high diplomacy, the "local" concern of the authorities and leaders of the contending parties in the arena of Berlin has been the struggle with the threshold—on the one hand, to protect it against breakthroughs by the other side and, on the other hand, to manipulate it for self-advantage and self-protection. The sub-system of the "local" interplay of moves and countermoves with respect to the Berlin access should be described in terms of activities occurring in the vicinity of this threshold.[3]

The obvious design for an inquiry is to mobilize the historical data in ways that will locate the threshold and that will describe the actions that have occurred close to and far from its region. Three different analyses are given below. The first is simply an abbreviated historical résumé illustrating the access phenomena of actions and responses which occurred in the span of time between 1948 and 1963. The second is a reckoning of the amounts and percentages of action engaged in by the opposing sides of East and West in the period, as reflected by the particular data at hand. The third is an information measurement which develops indicators of where the threshold has been and of the occasions on which actions have moved close to it.

Since the intent of the inquiry has been to carry out every step of the research in an open and public fashion, the step-by-step process followed in the study will be described. The initial step was to draw out of the *New York Times Index* all those reported items that had a direct and immediate bearing on the Western position in Berlin, the access routes, and Eastern actions with respect to that position. Each item was written on a card with the date, page, and column references to the newspaper. The actual language of the indexers was copied in almost all instances. As already noted, the selection process was methodologically weak, and no resources were available even to make the checks which might be possible on the reliability of the selections of facts. Almost twice as many cards were written as were finally included. The test of the sorting was simply to apply the question, "Does this item relate directly to moves made in the East-West action for position and access either to and from Berlin or within Berlin?" As was stated above, 1,791 items were retained to constitute the body of data to be analyzed. (The writer will make available on request the chronological listing of these items and their codings.)

The second step was to code or translate the language given on each card according to the most appropriate "fit" to one of eighteen different categories

3. A model of conflict and trading and their respective ranges is relevant to the local Berlin situation and is given in Boulding (1962, pp. 1–18). The bargaining range is highly restricted according to our data on the Berlin access struggle.

of actions. Which of the two opposing sides (East, West) was the source of the action was also written on each card. To offset somewhat the dangers of further contamination of the data, the eighteen types of action were made to conform as closely as possible to the language used by the *Index* compilers. Synonym lists were also developed as shown below. No reliability check was made for this coding, but given the need and the resources, this operation might still be carried out from the data. The eighteen categories with some synonyms are as follows:

Accede	agree, give consent, approve, permit, fail to enforce, admit, praise, drop a demand, comply, apologize
Withdraw	release, relent, retreat, avoid contact
Request	ask, petition, query
Propose	suggest, urge
Bargain	make a contingent offer, counterpropose, hold forth an "if this . . . then that" indulgence
Convey	announce, preannounce, hint, predict, forecast, promise, comment, explain, assure, air views, reiterate
Abstain	fail to respond, refuse to state position, be inactive
Protest	complain, counterprotest, object
Reject	turn down, spurn, ridicule, refuse to accede
Deny	contradict the other's assertion
Accuse	censure, indict, "score"
Demand	insist, issue statement calling on other party to respond in the "must" form
Warn	advise other of forthcoming risk or deprivation
Threaten	issue ultimatum, state a warning in the form of "unless . . . then . . . "
Decree	issue order that controls or deprives the other, institute depriving regulation or rule, assert policy that damages or deprives the other
Demonstrate	carry out physical act that protests, demands, warns, and/or threatens the other, move forces, mobilize, show strength
Force	seize, arrest, detain other's persons, execute rule, decree, regulation, or policy in some physical manner, take territory, commit physical act to disadvantage the other with no physical resistance of opposing group
Attack	exert force violently against resistance of the other, kill, injure, destroy, employ military or police force against active resistance, shoot down, hit

Although the list is arranged to specify a range of actions running from co-operation-coordination through bargaining to extreme conflict, the study does not make much use of the spectrum of acts and it does not depend on any assumptions about interval-distances between types of actions.

The next task was the tabulation of the coded items to show the frequency of occurrence of each type of action, for each of the two sides, and for several different time periods. The numbers of actions in each category were recorded for each month and each year from January 1, 1948, through December 31, 1963. Percentages were figured for each category for the first eight-year period (1948–1955), for the second eight-year period (1956–1963), and for the entire sixteen years (1948–1963). Percentages were also developed for each month of selected periods. On the basis of these data, observations will be offered later concerning the shifting volume of different classes of activity during the periods that were studied.

The subsequent step of the investigation requires a more detailed description of its rationale and its processes, since the ideas behind it will not be familiar to all readers. In scanning the numbers of occurrences of different kinds of action over a long period of time, one has some difficulty in arriving at clear conclusions about tendencies and trends. The changes in quantities in some time periods stand out and can be distinguished readily, but often the meanings of the numbers tend to be obscured. One of the things that would be profitable to discern would be the patterns and sequences of successions of actions of one side and the responses of the other side. How to do this most effectively still remains an unsolved problem.

An attractive alternative is to raise the question of how the opposing actors "mix" their behaviors over a specified length of time. This is sensible particularly because it promises to give a clue to any changes of the action "mix" when we know from "common knowledge" that an acute crisis has occurred. For example, one might well expect that marked increases in forceful and violent actions would appear during "crisis" periods. Further, in the cooling-off or demobilization phases of a crisis, it might be hypothesized that *increases* in the categories of "request," "propose," and "bargain" and *decreases* in "force" and "attack" should be manifested; simple statistical procedures should reflect shifts in such distributions. Our procedure was to turn to another means of measurement, however. We put to use, probably for the second time for this type of data, the technique of measuring "information potential."

INFORMATION MEASUREMENTS

The interested reader is referred to the discussions by Pierce (1961), Garner (1962), and Osgood and Wilson (1961) for more competent and more complete explanations of the logic of information measurement than we shall be able to give. The main ideas are, however, as follows.

In a situation that is steady in its demands on the participants, and where the range of *possible* actions and responses is known, information measurement can be used. We assumed that the Berlin access situation meets these requirements.[4] The scheme of placing all actions in eighteen categories establishes such a range of possible actions and responses. At any given moment for either the East or the West, we can expect one of two conditions to exist: the party will either commit one of the eighteen acts or it will not. The behavior of the party will be either in an "on" or "off" state (that is, involved in the commission of an act or not so involved). Some awkward questions might be asked. How long is a moment? How many moments occur in a period of time such as a day, a week, a month, or a year? Can two or more types of actions occur in one moment? These can be set aside, however, in favor of more "practical" questions, such as how many acts did, in fact, occur during a time period in each of the eighteen categories? For example, from the data,

4. See the above discussion of the limitations and temptations which confront both sides in the Berlin situation.

we can answer the question of how many "ons" were emitted by the West in 1956. The answer is seven; there were two "withdraws," one "request," one "propose," two "protests," one "accuse," and all the remaining categories were in the "off" condition. This shows that we can say something about the "mix" of Western behaviors in 1956. One way to compare one period of time with another period is to convert the numbers of occurrences to percentages. It will be remembered that in the tabulation, this figuring was done for: some months, all years, the two eight-year periods, and for the entire period of sixteen years.

The next important question is to ask whether or not these percentages (which, remember, for either party and for any particular time period show, in ensemble, the mix of actions) can be manipulated further to develop any clear evidence. The answer is that more can be accomplished by starting from the beginning and thinking about how things would stand if all that was known was that a party was capable of emitting an "on" in any of the eighteen categories. Given a sufficiently large number of "upcoming" actions, the chances would be that any one of the eighteen might turn "on" at the next moment. Even with complete ignorance of the actual situation, one can do some intelligent guessing. With eighteen possible categories, the likelihood that any particular one would be activated by pure chance would be a little more than five times in one hundred instances. Another important question is, if *somebody* knew which ones of the eighteen were in the "on" condition but *you* did not, how many guesses would you need, using the best procedures, to ascertain which were "on"? The answer, interestingly, is that you would need only four or five guesses to get the right answer. If there were only eight categories to choose from, you would need three guesses. If there were forty different categories, you would require only about five or six guesses.

To get this answer (four or five guesses) for the equal probability mix of eighteen categories, one merely consults a listing of numbers called "Log Base$_2$ Table Showing $-p$ Log$_2$ p Values," reads off from there the "$-p$ Log$_2$ p" value for the percentage (5.55 per cent), and multiplies that figure by the number of categories (eighteen in the case at hand). The result of the multiplication is 4.1364 according to the table that was used and extrapolated (Garner, 1962), and this figure is called the value of "maximum uncertainty" in the information jargon. The units are named "bits" of potential information; remember that the units suggest the number of best guesses it would take to find out what has happened in the mix of behaviors. The conversion from percentages to the appropriate values of the logarithms to the base of two (the system of counting by two's as contrasted to the usual method of counting by groups of ten) has some advantages. First, it allows a summarization of each batch of data by a single number—according to the "best guess" criterion as described above. Second, the simple summing up of the logarithmic values within each batch of data takes the place of somewhat more complicated statistical operations that would have to be carried out if one wished to compare one distribution of percentages with another. The logarithms have the effect of increasing the influence of the less frequently occurring items in a distribution and of decreasing the influence of the more frequently occurring items. Our computation of the "real life mix" of action types for the West in 1960 is given below to show the detailed steps.

TABLE 1. *The Tabulation and Calculation of Information Data: an Illustration Using the Western Performance in 1960*

	No. of Actions	%	$-p \log_2 p$ value
Accede	0	0	0
Withdraw	4	12.1	.3671
Request	0	0	0
Propose	0	0	0
Bargain	0	0	0
Convey	3	9.0	.3127
Abstain	0	0	0
Protest	3	9.0	.3127
Reject	3	9.0	.3127
Deny	3	9.0	.3127
Accuse	4	12.1	.3671
Demand	0	0	0
Warn	3	9.0	.3127
Threaten	2	6.0	.2435
Decree	6	18.1	.4453
Demonstrate	2	6.0	.2435
Force	0	0	0
Attack	0	0	0
Total	33	99.3	3.2317

When records of the actual performance of a system have been kept over a considerable number of time periods, the possibility arises of foretelling the future to some extent. Whether or not a prediction is in order depends on how the system has performed. The actual percentages of happenings (as illustrated above for 1960) in the several categories, when these have been converted to the sums of their "bits" (call this "absolute uncertainty"), might drop to the neighborhood of 1.000. Then, only one or two questions would be required to interpret what the mix of behaviors is. If the system ran for many time periods with such a number, our confidence in predicting what would come next would increase accordingly. Of course, there might be disappointments. To illustrate a situation, we can consider the data for the West in the years 1956-1960:

	1956	1957	1958	1959	1960
Number of Acts	7	7	7	22	33
Absolute uncertainty	2.2332	1.3780	2.2332	3.0303	3.2317

The variations in the sums of the bits are too great to permit any reasonable forecasts for 1961. The West as an "emitting system" does not show an obedient pattern of action, year after year, that would build confidence for predicting. Perhaps it is the system that runs too inconsistently, or perhaps one-year periods are too long to allow a sensitive registering of the results. It has been found, in fact, that the period of one month provides a better basis for such analyses. All that we can gather from the figures for 1956–1960, above, is that some knowledge of the actual performance reduces the number of needed guesses—information reduces uncertainty—below the number needed when we know nothing at all about the actual performance. The difference between maximum uncertainty (4.1364) and absolute uncertainty for 1959 (3.0303—see above) shows that the increased information at hand about 1959 lessens uncertainty in assessing the situation.

A way to reflect the relationship of maximum uncertainty (no performance data known) and absolute uncertainty (some knowledge of performance) is to take the ratio of the two. The resulting number, called "relative uncertainty," provides a yardstick against which one can measure the results of different runs of data. The relative uncertainty index also becomes a convenient description for the information status of a whole time period. Thus, the relative uncertainty figures (signified as H rel.) for the two years, 1959 and 1960 are:

$$1959$$

$$\frac{3.0303}{4.1364} \text{ equals } .732 \ H \text{ rel.}$$

$$1960$$

$$\frac{1.3780}{4.1364} \text{ equals } .333 \ H \text{ rel.}$$

It is relative uncertainty that will be used below in reporting the "variety" of the actions of East and West in several periods of "crisis" and "non-crisis." Although a brief account has been given here of the ideas and steps of information calculation, it may be well to restate a part of the description in another form. Until one becomes accustomed to the approach, its features tend to be elusive.

Maximum uncertainty, which is given by summing the bits for each of the equal probability percentages (when no performance knowledge is available), is a way of stating "what *could happen*." If we imagine an observer watching a succession of different events, we might appreciate his "maximum uncertainty" when he tells us he "can't make heads or tails of what is going on." Our advice to him could only be to keep on watching, to observe the different kinds of happenings, and, if he is unable to figure out anything better, to assume that things are disorderly (that is, unpatterned) and that one happening is as likely to appear as another.

When the summing of bits for actual percentages of a performance record has yielded a number for absolute uncertainty, the result expresses "what *did* happen" in information terms. Here, our observer has begun to "make some sense" out of the succession of different events. As he has been watching, he has noted that some kinds of happenings reappear more frequently than others. He notes, perhaps, that some events are very rare, while some others are very common. He is relatively surprised when an uncommon event appears and is quite "unsurprised" by the common occurrences. In a word, he has been acquiring and using "information." The language seems inept, but we can say that the observer is now dealing with "absolute uncertainty" only and is better off than at the beginning when he had to assume the condition of "maximum uncertainty."

The ratio of the absolute to the maximum (the relative uncertainty) states in effect "what could happen but didn't." As the ratio approaches 1.000, it suggests not only that almost everything that could happen has been occurring but also that the behaviors have shown increasing signs of disorderliness. The information measures do not tell us what the particular lack of ordering is, but they do give us a technical indication of a large amount of "variety" in the emissions. As the ratio decreases toward .000, the suggestion is that (1) there may be present a large amount of highly patterned and repetitive behavior and limited variety in the action, *or* (2) very little is occurring. In the international relations data studied, it can be seen from inspection that the information measure of variety and order is not completely independent of the measure of volume of activity. No attempt was made in the present effort to calculate the extent of interdependence. It is clear enough, however, that the lower figures of absolute uncertainty (such as the 2.2332 for 1956 and the 1.3780 for 1957) result from the small numbers of occurrences in the time periods.

On the basis of this observation, month-to-month calculations were made only for those periods when the numbers of occurrences of one party or the other were fifteen or more per month. In evaluating the remaining "quiet" periods, we were inclined to believe Rosenau's suggestion (1963, p. 115) that international systems do not persist at all times but, to the contrary, frequently cease to function altogether. At these extinction times, there appears to have been no threshold to put boundaries on the conflict system of East and West in the access struggle, simply because nothing much was happening. In the active periods the threshold idea seems to be quite viable, however. The more specific results of the inquiry will now be summarized.

AN HISTORICAL RÉSUMÉ

The struggle to hold the Allied position in Berlin began earlier than 1948. In his account of the first years of American military government in the city, *Berlin Command*, Colonel Frank Howley has described many episodes of conflict with the Russians in the early period of 1945–1947. Howley recalled being halted on the road to Berlin by a Russian colonel (Howley, 1950, p. 30):

> The Colonel sidled over to the window again, took another look and asked, "How many vehicles, officers, and men do you have?"
> "Roughly, 500 officers and men and 120 vehicles," I replied promptly.
> "The agreement," he said coldly, "says 37 officers, 50 vehicles and 175 men."
> "What agreement?" I asked blankly.
> "The Berlin agreement," he told me.
> I thought that one over for a while. I hadn't heard of any such agreement. "Perhaps you are confusing some offhand estimate made by one of our officers as to what we would need with an actual agreement," I suggested.
> "There is an actual agreement," he said flatly.
> At that, I felt the hairs rising on the back of my neck.

Encounters of this general type occurred thousands of times during the following two decades and with varying outcomes.

In 1945, the three Western Allied forces had to battle to establish themselves in their sectors against Soviet opposition and obstruction. "Zhukov informed the British and American generals that the Soviet Union considered access to Berlin as a privilege which they were granting the Allies, not a right to which they were entitled." (Smith, 1963, p. 83). From the beginning, the Allied authorities were embroiled endlessly in disputes and confrontations with the Soviet command and the Soviet-controlled city administration. There is a consensus of opinion on two points about the early period. The first is that a stabilization of relationships failed to develop in 1946 and 1947 in the quadripartite governing of Berlin, and the second is that 1948 saw the first serious and sustained Soviet challenge to the Western right to remain in Berlin (Davison, 1958, pp. 62–78; Smith, 1963, pp. 100–105).

In April and May of 1948, the Soviet authorities established new regulations dealing with traffic to and from West Germany and Berlin; began to stop trains, barges, and trucks along the East-West routes; increased the numbers of border guards and Soviet troops stationed in and near the city; complained of Allied violations of "air safety" in the corridors; increased their own air activity; began a propaganda campaign aimed at driving out the Western forces; proposed or hinted at forthcoming changes in access arrangements; and engaged in some direct military confrontations, such as the "showdown" of American and Soviet troops early in April at the German Railway Administration Building (Howley, 150, pp. 162–163).

These movements were connected, without question, with larger developments in Germany and Europe such as the London Conference, the arrangement for Bizonia, the Czechoslovakian coup, and the various revolutionary communist agitations throughout Western Europe in that year.

In June 1948, the Western decision to institute the currency reform was countered immediately by the Soviet stoppage of all ground transportation between the West and Berlin. The Allied response was to launch the airlift and to impose an economic counterblockade on East-West trade. An extremely complicated struggle that ranged from the "buzzing" of Allied transport aircraft by Soviet fighters to a bitter contest of Berliner against Berliner for control of the city's administrative machinery then developed. The latter conflict came to a climax in December 1948 and resulted in the East-West division of the municipal government. Early in 1949, the activity related to the access to Berlin that had been intense in 1948 subsided into a stalemate of blockade versus airlift. Due to the diplomatic negotiations in New York, an agreement to end the blockade and the counterblockade was reached on May 12, 1949 by the occupying powers. This arrangement hinged on further agreements to be worked out at a Foreign Ministers' conference scheduled for Paris in June. The lifting of the blockades on May 12, 1949, may be considered the end of the first Berlin crisis; its period was from June 24, 1948, to May 12, 1949.

The immediate aftermath of the lifting of the blockade was the reimposition of a partial blockade by the Soviet Union as early as May 19, 1949. These interferences, which were complicated by a railway strike that, in turn, was not unrelated to the access struggle, continued through the rest of the year.

Events then began to fall into a pattern that was to continue for a long period. The developments of July 9–16, 1949, were typical of many later episodes. On July 9, the Soviet guards stopped Berlin-bound trucks near Lübeck and at four border checkpoints. Allied protests were met with further Soviet interference and obstruction on the roads. On July 13, the American army organized a sixty-truck convoy to run from Helmstedt to Berlin to test and challenge the renewed Soviet curbs on the autobahn traffic. Soviet spokesmen argued that the Western truck drivers were responsible for the trouble and that the interferences were only actions taken against black-market operations. Nevertheless, the Western convoy was allowed to pass the checkpoints without hindrance, and on July 15, the Soviet Union claimed that truck traffic was normal. On July 16, the East established a new checkpoint outside West Berlin for the purpose of stopping German trucks and confiscating any West German marks carried by their drivers. The harassment technique of "seize" and "let go" became very familiar. The Western response typically was to make frequent protests and occasional demonstrations against the interference.

Early in 1951, a "little cold war" was waged between the East and West over canal and other waterway transportation—a very important artery for carrying heavy and bulky goods. The Soviet authorities held Western barges, while the British detained East German barges in retaliation. Strong protests were issued by both sides and efforts were made to reach agreements on barge traffic. Nothing was settled with any finality, however; similar seizures and retaliations reoccurred during 1952 and 1955.

In 1952, the American military authorities engaged in a trial of strength with the Russians over the right to operate Allied highway patrols along the autobahns to West Germany. The Soviets stubbornly and successfully resisted the patrol operations by enforcing their claim to exclusive control of the roads. In June 1952, the British sealed off a building in West Berlin that housed a Soviet radio station. This military action was taken amid violent Soviet protests, but it was a retaliatory act against the protested closing off by the Soviet Union of several small Western communities located at the extreme border of West Berlin. These little enclaves (such as Steinstücken), quite often became the pawns in the challenges to access.

Throughout the nineteen fifties, there were frequent arrests, detainments, protests, and releases involving military personnel of both sides for various alleged and real offenses. The most common instances involved Allied soldiers who were arrested for unauthorized and unofficial crossings into the Soviet sector. In April 1952, two Soviet jet fighters fired at and crippled an Air France plane, injuring two passengers. This incident led to a sharp exchange of protests and accusations by both sides. Incidents of a serious nature merely punctuated the long series of difficulties imposed by Soviet forces on Allied planes flying through the corridors. The favorite device was the "buzzing" of aircraft and airfields by Soviet fighter aircraft. Artillery practice, parachute jumps, cross-corridor Soviet flights, blinding of landing airplanes with searchlights, and accusations by the Soviet authorities of Allied violations of flying safety were other common methods of harassment in the air.

In 1953, other serious air incidents occurred, including the shooting down of a British Lincoln bomber in or near the air corridor between Hamburg and Berlin. The ensuing dispute led to a series of discussions between East and West over air safety and the regulation of corridor flights. During 1953, numerous Soviet and East German restrictions were imposed on movements of persons within Berlin before, during, and after the East German uprising of that year.

After 1953, events related to the access situation became less frequent. Occasional Soviet stoppages on the highways and railroad lines continued to occur, and the detainment of persons continued. A few air corridor harassments were reported as well. Attempts were made by both sides at this time to negotiate the easing of interzonal and intersector travel restraints, but these efforts were offset by Eastern impositions of new regulations on travel passes for Germans and of taxes on highway trucks. Perhaps the most important new development, beginning in 1955, was the ostentatious handing over of authority in access matters to the East German regime, accompanied by the Soviet contention that, in the future, the West would have to deal not with the Soviet Union but with the East German authorities over access problems. This theme was to become a major weapon brandished at the West during the "Deadline Crisis" of 1958–1959, and later, as well.

The rising tension of the cold war that began to mount in 1957 (Smith, 1963, p. 151) fails to be reflected in our data on the subject of Berlin access. Smith interprets the Soviet challenging of an American military convoy at Babelsberg on June 23, 1958, as a significant indicator of the increase of Soviet pressure on the West, however. Other incidents in the following month are cited by Smith (1963, pp. 160–161) as further supporting evidence of increasing tensions. Although our data do not show it, these events may well have been the forewarnings of the diplomatic storm that broke in November 1958.

Late in November, a virtual ultimatum was delivered to the West by Nikita Khrushchev. In notes delivered to the United States, Great Britain, and France on November 27, 1958, he announced a deadline of six months for the carrying out of specified changes in the status of Berlin, including the end of the occupation (withdrawal of the Western forces), and the conversion of Berlin to a free city. Otherwise, Khrushchev threatened, the Soviet Union would conclude its own settlement with the East Germans and unilaterally end the occupation. The flurry of activities at the high diplomatic level that followed during the first five months of 1959 would probably qualify as a "crisis" according to the volume and variety criteria that are suggested in this paper. The "sub-system" materials for the Berlin access situation fail to register in this way, however. Instead, a few typical autobahn incidents, a few detentions, and stiff dispute over rights in the air corridor are all that we have recorded for the year 1959.

If May 11, 1959, the day of the convening of the Geneva Foreign Ministers' conference and the main Western response to the Khrushchev ultimatum, is taken as the end of the Deadline Crisis, the sub-system of the Berlin access must be found to be non-responsive to its major system. Here, the "common understanding" that there *was* a serious crisis in 1958–1959 probably should be taken as the basis of the conclusion that the sub-system was insensitive—a finding which invalidates one hypothesis of this research. Here also is a demonstration of the earlier statement that only multiples of indicators of international system performance will be likely to give satisfactory results. There are, however, other possible reasons for the failure of our data to reflect the Deadline Crisis.

It can be argued, on the other hand, that the November 1958–May 1959 affair was but the beginning of a continuing crisis that took its full form only in August of 1961. With all the historical context removed, nothing unusual or remarkable can be discerned in the Berlin access arena until June of 1961. Beginning in June, signs of Soviet and American military mobilizations began to appear in the record, along with accusations and counter-accusations of threatening military buildups. New efforts were made by the East Germans in July to stem the tide of refugees running from East to West. On August 12 there was a single report of an airplane incident involving Eastern harassment by means of searchlights. On August 13, the East began to build the wall.

Immediately, an extraordinary number of events initiated by both East and West and bearing on the access to Berlin began to unfold. Most of the actions in August 1961 were directly related to the closing of the East-West Berlin boundary and to specific incidents associated with the closure. A blizzard of warnings, threats, protests, demands, and military demonstrations arose during the last two weeks of August.

In September, an encounter developed over air corridor rights because of the East German claim to control this traffic and a strong rejection of the claim by the Western powers. While the air corridor conflict festered on into October, the troubles in Berlin were increased by a number of detentions of Westerners by the East German police and a considerable amount of violence at the wall. There was great discontentment in West Berlin over the apparent lack of determination of the West to strike back and to protect its position. A series of actions beginning with the Lightner incident brought the access problem to the fore and raised East-West tensions to a high pitch. The deputy chief of the United States Mission in Berlin, Allen Lightner, attempted to cross the sector border into East Berlin on October 22. He was stopped and his identification papers were demanded by the East German police. Since 1945, occupation personnel travelling in official vehicles had passed between the sectors of Berlin without showing identification papers. Lightner refused to submit to the East German inspection and, after several attempts that were backed by American military demonstrations, Lightner had his way and went, uninspected, into the east sector of the city. During the next few days further tests of the right to enter the east sector were made in the midst of protests, accusations, and threats. The climax was reached when Soviet and American tanks drew up and confronted each other for sixteen hours at the boundary at Checkpoint Charlie on October 27 and 28. The mutual pullback of the tanks reduced the tension, but further incidents similar to the Lightner episode took place in December. Involved were a State Department official, Howard Trivers, and some civilian aides of General Watson. During the same period, military convoys were delayed on a number of occasions on the highways, but no serious blocking of access took place.

During the months of February and March, 1962, a sustained and aggressive Soviet interference with Allied air traffic was staged. A new form of harassment was the dropping of metal chaff to interfere with the effectiveness of radar equipment in the Allied aircraft. Air incidents were reported in July, August, and September, 1962. Allied traffic on the autobahns was obstructed sporadically during 1962, the most serious occurrences taking place in October and November.

In 1963, something resembling a return to the "normalcy" of the late 1950's developed in the Berlin access situation. There were air incidents in April, May, June, and November that drew Western protests. Minor highway delays and stoppages took place in May, June, and September. In October and November, 1963, several delays of convoys at the Marienborn and Babelsberg checkpoints over "troop counts" were more serious and involved some military confrontations. A stiff attitude to demonstrate the Allied right of free access was shown in these incidents.

It should be noted that the foregoing historical review suffers the double misfortune of including neither an adequate interpretation of the broader settings in which the access events occurred nor a detailed account of the access events themselves. The dilemma of the historical description is that it becomes unduly lengthy (as well as dull) if it really recounts detailed historical happenings and that, if it is mainly an interpretation offered in the effort to convey the significance of a complex stream of events, it loses its specificity with respect to the reports of events. Perhaps the chief value of the abbreviated account given is in the slight setting it provides for considering the following quantitative data.

QUANTITY AND VARIETY OF ACCESS EVENTS: FINDINGS

It is well to recall here that the reasons for collecting the Berlin access data have to do with some theoretical questions. By aggregating the data and then examining the results, the investigator hoped to be able to link these abstract and general questions to a portion of the facts about the "real world." The first and perhaps most important objective was to seek out a means of identifying an acute international crisis. The approach was to propose that a change of state in the system would be observable when a crisis occurs. The general understanding appears to be that three crises have occurred in the Berlin situation: the Blockade Crisis of June 1948–May 1949, the Deadline Crisis of November 1958–May 1959, and the Wall Crisis that began on August 13, 1961.

Inspection of the access material when the reported events have been compiled to show yearly totals in East and West categories reveals that 1948 and 1961 were by far the "busiest" years of the period. Table 2 gives these annual totals of numbers of events. On the simple basis of the volume of the happenings, it can be said that 1948 and 1961 were crisis years. Judged by the criterion of gross volume, the Deadline Crisis was not a crisis, however. A scanning of the totals for each year suggests another idea. The access data fall into about three

TABLE 2. *The Volume of East and West Activity in the Berlin Access Situation Computed on the Annual Basis (Numbers of recorded acts are shown)*

	1948	1949	1950	1951	1952	1953	1954	1955
West	144	44	57	39	69	36	16	27
East	210	81	87	61	128	58	22	38
Total	354	125	144	100	197	94	38	65

	1956	1957	1958	1959	1960	1961	1962	1963
West	7	7	7	22	33	135	63	23
East	10	11	14	23	43	149	88	39
Total	17	18	21	45	76	284	151	62

groups: (1) of crisis activity—in 1948 and 1961—(2) of sub-system activity—in 1949, 1950, 1951, 1952, and 1962 and (3) of sub-system inactivity or extinction —in 1954, 1955, 1956, 1958, and 1963. If seventy-five acts should be considered as the threshold, then 1960 might be called a threshold year.

Although it does not relate to the change-of-state problem, one may note in passing that, according to the data, the East has always pursued the access problem more actively than the West. Over the sixteen-year period, 59.3 per cent of the acts were initiated by the East, while 40.7 per cent arose on the side of the West. This relative passivity of the West might be associated with the common criticism that Western policy in the Cold War has been to react rather than to seize the lead. It should be remembered, however, not only that the West constantly has held the weaker physical position in Berlin but more especially that the East has been faced, by the logic of the situation, with the puzzle of how to dislodge the West by "allowable means." It follows, then, that seizing the initiative has been up to the East on almost all occasions. This role is not necessarily advantageous (McClelland, 1964a, p. 203).

When the measure of relative uncertainty is applied to the annual data with the change-of-state question in mind, the results are less clear-cut than was the case in the measure of volume of activity. In the evaluation of the uncertainty numbers, one should keep in mind the following possible meanings. An acute crisis should be expected to be a turbulent time, and the participants would not be anticipated as acting in routine ways. More of the things that *could* be happening, should be found to be happening. The party under the greater pressure should be trying "everything in the book" to discover means of dealing with the situation. Therefore, high relative uncertainty numbers should be the tell-tale sign of the presence of crisis. The annual relative uncertainty figures for East and West during the sixteen years are given in Table 3.

These numbers do not tell us clearly that 1948 and 1961 were crisis years.

TABLE 3. *Relative Uncertainty Computed on the Annual Basis for the Berlin Access Situation*

	1948	1949	1950	1951	1952	1953	1954	1955
West H rel.[a]	.927	.869	.764	.899	.792	.812	.628	.734
East H rel.	.873	.740	.649	.736	.658	.795	.670	.694
Difference	+.054	+.129	+.115	+.163	+.134	+.017	−.042	+.040

	1956	1957	1958	1959	1960	1961	1962	1963
West H rel.	.540	.278	.540	.657	.782	.781	.829	.658
East H rel.	.527	.452	.501	.712	.746	.812	.812	.668
Difference	+.013	−.174	+.039	−.055	+.036	−.031	+.017	−.010

[a] H rel. equals $\frac{H_{abs.}}{H_{max.}}$. The ratio of information actually yielded by events to the information yielded under an equal probability assumption for the occurrence of events, shown as "relative uncertainty."

Table 4. *Relative Uncertainty Computed on the Monthly Basis in the Taiwan Straits Situation*

	Jan.	Feb.	Mar.	Apr.	May	June	July	Aug.	Sept.	Oct.	Nov.	Dec.
1954												
H rel.[a]			.333	.307	.380	.240	.601	.703	.630	.736	.706	.705
1955												
H rel.	.807	.740	.734	.814	.751	.618	.732	.506	.786	.532	.240	.573
1958												
H rel.				.454	.333	.000	.747	.556	.749	.834	.742	.452
1959												
H rel.	.555	.597	.640	.333	.253	.289						

[a] H rel. is the ratio of information actually yielded by events to the information yielded under an equal probability assumption for the occurrence of events, shown as "relative uncertainty."

They do show that during these two years the East utilized a greater variety of available methods of action than at any other time, excepting 1962. The East's threshold of crisis appears to be about .800, but better estimates will be proposed later in the discussion. The West, on the other hand, utilized a large portion of the available means at these times (spectacularly in 1948), but in other years, as in 1949, 1951, 1953, and 1962, the West was just as resourceful —or confused. Due to the small numbers of occurrences in the inactive years of the fifties, it is probably wise to ignore altogether the ratios for 1956, 1957, and 1958. Further, there is a need to look more closely at relative uncertainty for shorter time periods than a year. A year is a long time, and telescoping all of a year's events into a single figure proves not to be a very discriminating procedure.

We may glean a little more information of interest from the row of figures in Table 3 showing "Difference." These numbers merely are the differences in the ratios of East and West, year by year, so that a plus number shows when West expressed more variety of behavior than East and a minus shows vice versa. It is to be noted that the West, in most years, emitted a greater variety of actions than the East. Does this prove that the East followed a more settled and surer course of action than the West? Or, does it indicate that the West tried harder and more flexibly to discover a *modus vivendi* in the access struggle? Perhaps, the observation means only that the West has had to cope with a more difficult problem and has searched more widely for solutions. This seems to be a highly speculative matter; two conclusions to be proposed are more certain. First, the eight years of 1948–1955 reveal a greater total difference than the second eight-year period. This is a bit of evidence that fits the research question about the tendency toward routinizing behavior in an extended crisis situation. It will be mentioned again, below. Second, it is interesting that over the years the differences tend to become smaller. This suggests strongly that the two sides responded to each other more directly as time passed. They appear to have coupled their behaviors more closely on a "meet-and-match" basis in the later period.

Let us look more carefully now at the volume and variety of acts by turning to monthly calculations. The identification of crisis in terms of change of state is still the focus of attention. Sullivan (1964, p. 23) in working with an eight-category scheme of "maximum uncertainty" for the Taiwan Straits data used monthly computations and concluded that a variety figure of .600 identified the crisis threshold level approximately. His tables show, however, that he may have been overly cautious in this judgment and that .700 may well be taken as the breakover level to crisis. Part of his summarized data is reproduced to illustrate this conclusion. According to common knowledge, there have been two Taiwan Straits crises—one at the end of 1954 and the beginning of 1955 and the second at Quemoy in late 1958.

The underlined figures in Table 4 bracket the periods that would define a crisis by the .700 rule, and especially with respect to the Quemoy affair, they fit well with the common interpretation of when the crises occurred. It will be noted that, in addition, the charting shows a few isolated .700's.

Our replication using the Berlin material will now be set forth. The access data for the volume of happenings identify several "clusters" or time periods in which the numbers of acts per month exceed fifteen. These are as follows:

1. April–May 1948 (preblockade crisis)
2. June–December 1948 (Blockade crisis)
3. April–July 1949 (Blockade Crisis and aftermath)
4. January–July 1950 (active access period)
5. May–December 1952 (active access period)
6. September–November 1960 (active access period)
7. June–December 1961 (Wall Crisis)
8. September–November 1962 (active access period)

For the analysis by months and for the remaining discussion of the change-of-state problem, only the data for the time periods shown in the list are used. Table 5 contains the data.

TABLE 5. *Numbers of Acts and Relative Uncertainty Figures Computed on the Monthly Basis: The Berlin Access Situation*

1. Pre-crisis, 1948

		Apr.	May
No. of Acts:	West	33	11
No. of Acts:	East	41	10
H rel.[a]	West	.784	.744
H rel.	East	.738	.754

2. Blockade Crisis, 1948

		June	July	Aug.	Sept.	Oct.	Nov.	Dec.
No. of Acts:	West	21	22	14	12	11	9	16
No. of Acts:	East	27	41	21	19	28	3	17
H rel.	West	.711	.689	.607	.607	.641	.630	.462
H rel.	East	.610	.833	.716	.547	.750	.383	.684

3. Blockade Crisis and Aftermath, 1949

		Apr.	May	June	July
No. of Acts:	West	5	13	4	5
No. of Acts:	East	15	19	8	22
H rel.	West	.561	.610	.362	.464
H rel.	East	.605	.572	.581	.449

4. Active Access Period, 1950

		Jan.	Feb.	Mar.	Apr.	May	June	July
No. of Acts:	West	6	9	1	1	6	11	4
No. of Acts:	East	14	16	2	1	13	10	8
H rel.	West	.646	.530	.000	.000	.431	.408	.362
H rel.	East	.646	.543	.000	.000	.441	.609	.420

5. Active Access Period, 1952

		May	June	July	Aug.	Sept.	Oct.	Nov.	Dec.
No. of Acts:	West	8	17	9	6	7	8	2	7
No. of Acts:	East	19	29	18	3	13	10	4	15
H rel.	West	.460	.619	.604	.462	.445	.581	.241	.471
H rel.	East	.696	.654	.661	.383	.463	.520	.241	.657

TABLE 5 (*cont.*)

6. Active Access Period, 1960

		Sept.	Oct.	Nov.
No. of Acts:	West	19	7	1
No. of Acts:	East	21	8	3
H rel.	West	.693	.513	.000
H rel.	East	.693	.520	.000

7. Wall Crisis, 1961

		June	July	Aug.	Sept.	Oct.	Nov.	Dec.
No. of Acts:	West	6	1	47	22	23	13	19
No. of Acts:	East	4	8	59	36	16	10	17
H rel.	West	.302	.000	.737	.762	.647	.606	.599
H rel.	East	.360	.420	.731	.766	.641	.494	.607

8. Active Access Period, 1962

		Sept.	Oct.	Nov.
No. of Acts:	West	9	4	2
No. of Acts:	East	15	4	5
H rel.	West	.615	.483	.100
H rel.	East	.489	.362	.331

ª *H* rel. is the ratio of information actually yielded by events to the information yielded under an equal probability assumption for the occurrence of events, shown as "relative uncertainty."

The underlined numbers for the Berlin access case, like those shown for the Taiwan Straits case, bracket periods when one or the other of the protagonists performed above the .700 crisis threshold. A comparison of the two sets of data, indicating that the .700 rule will undergird an operational definition of an acute international crisis, anchors our most important finding. Our conclusion is the same as Sullivan's: a measurable change of state takes place in the transition from a non-crisis situation to a crisis situation. Like the volume criterion, the variety measure turns out to be in accord with the common understanding of when the Blockade and Wall Crises took place. It is to be noted that the Deadline period not only fails to appear at the crisis level but also that it does not even qualify as an "active access period." There are three alternative explanations possible: either the Deadline episode was not a crisis; there was a crisis, but the sub-system failed to respond to it; or our data for the period are seriously defective, when, otherwise, the recognized flaws do not seem to matter in the analysis.

The "active access periods" tend to vary in the region of the .600's and blend in at the same level as the tailings-off or demobilizations of acute crises. The outstanding exceptions in all of the tabulation are the April-May 1948 phenomena. Here the crisis level, according to the .700 variety rule, was reached *before* the blockade. A reasonable conclusion would be that a genuine pre-blockade crisis took place at that time. A quotation of some length from a cable sent by General Clay on March 5, 1948, and a related comment by Jean Edward Smith (1963, pp. 101–102) are highly germane to this evaluation. As quoted in Smith, Clay wrote:

For some months, based on logical analysis I have felt and held that war was unlikely for at least two years. Within the last few weeks, I have felt a subtle change in Soviet attitude which I cannot define but which now gives me a feeling that it may come with dramatic suddenness. I cannot support this change in my own thinking with any data or outward evidence in relationships other than to describe it as a feeling of a new tenseness in every individual with whom we have official relations.

Smith then has commented:

In notifying Washington that something was up, General Clay was acting purely on his own initiative. The intelligence reports which he saw daily contained nothing to arouse suspicion, and on the surface, the water was still calm. This was one of the rare cases in recent American history when the responsible Commander on the spot has not only sensed something that the intelligence "experts" had overlooked but dared to communicate this feeling to his superiors.

In Washington, Clay's telegram caused intense alarm.

It may yet be that methods will be developed and applied which will sometimes improve on the practical wisdom of diplomacy and on orthodox intelligence gathering. The present finding from a small segment of research is that the performance records of the international system should be studied closely from several different perspectives. It appears possible to squeeze out of that information certain regularities that otherwise stand a good chance of being overlooked.

The second research question—can a sub-system be discovered to be responsive to its more general system—has already been answered in the preceding discussion. The responsiveness noted in 1948 and 1961 in the sub-system confirms the idea; however, some confidence is taken away by the lack of evidence of responsiveness to the events of 1958–1959. Clearly, the Deadline Crisis is a research challenge and it needs some further study.

The third research question as stated at the outset had three elements: (1) are crises "short burst" affairs, (2) are they progressively routinized, and (3) does the level of violence fail to rise during a crisis? The figures for both volume and variety suggest that the Blockade and Wall Crises were intense phenomena for only short periods—three months would seem to be about the duration.

Some indirect evidence in support of the routinizing tendency appears in the research. The general trend toward decreasing variety in the actions of both parties and their tendency to couple their behaviors more closely are pieces of supporting evidence that were cited earlier. Both volume and variety in the Wall Crisis turn out to be at a lower level than during the Blockade Crisis. The underlying principle is that a situation which becomes increasingly a "known quantity" will be dealt with in increasingly routinized fashion. The administrative approach, at its ultimate, is to dispatch a problem by dealing with it as a type and by solving it by a formula. If we divide the total span between 1948 and 1963 into two periods of eight years each, we find that Eastern and Western acts were 685 and 433 respectively for the first period, and 377 and 297 for the second. Of the 1,791 acts undertaken by both sides, 62.7 per cent of them occurred in the first period and 37.3 per cent in the second period of 1956–1963. Decline in variety appears for the West; however, variety increased for the East in the second period. Considering all the other measures, one can make out at least a weak case for the routinization of the actions of the East.

The last question to ask of the data concerns the shift of behavior in crises toward extreme conflict and violence. It has been shown previously by the figures for relative uncertainty that the *mix* of actions does, indeed, change in crises toward greater variety. The remaining concern is to find out if the mix tends toward the more violent end of the cooperation-conflict scale. One test would be to compare the three categories of "demonstrate," "force," and "attack," in which one would expect military and police participation to be prominent, for the two situations of crisis and *active* non-crisis. We found that among 447 acts in the non-crisis active periods, 139 (31.1 per cent) were of the "demonstrative, force, attack" type, and of the 526 acts in the crisis period, 191 (36.3 per cent) were of this type. The increase in such conflictful behavior from non-crisis to crisis periods toward violence is a little over 5 per cent. A shift (against the hypothesis) does appear, but it is not spectacular in this body of evidence. More direct means for measuring and assessing levels of violence than have been used here can be conceived. Obviously, more study could be given to this problem.

A CONCLUDING COMMENT

The problem of the context probably is the most significant difficulty related to the study reported here. As soon as the synthesis of historical description is set aside, the question becomes acute as to how to place quantitative findings such as those reviewed above in a proper setting. Whether the student is interested in international crises or in some other analytically separated part of international behavior, the need to establish the larger appropriate context appears. The systems approach has forced the levels of analysis concern into the open, and it has also given some hints on how to cope with the problem in theory and research. We now instruct ourselves that the international system is to be conceived somewhat in the form of the Chinese box. When the outer box is removed, there will be found next a related and smaller box (or sub-system). Down to some lower practical limit, yet smaller boxes within smaller boxes will be uncovered, according to the systems strategy.

In this research, we have tried to locate and isolate one of the smaller boxes that rests inside the more capacious limits of the international relations of Berlin. Additional and interesting sub-systems can be found, without any question. All such sub-systems can be considered as related, just as we can be certain that the Berlin crises have been related to larger systems of German and European international relations. The trouble is that we are aware of these larger relationships which establish the contexts of events, but we tend to be perplexed about how to study them in any other mode than historical interpretation. Once we have taken the trouble to quantify and analyze some aspects of the performance of a given sub-system of international relations, it will not do simply to guess about the context. It might be best to think of the kind of inquiry that has been reported here as only a single strand which eventually will need to be woven with many other strands. The weaving should be done according to strict and orderly procedures. Thus, bit by bit, the wider context might be built, in the weaving of many strands.

There are important limitations on analyses of historical events by non-historical methods. Only some of these limitations were reviewed early in the discussion. Despite the difficulties, it has seemed worthwhile to pursue "transac-

tional analyses" of the performances of the international system in the expectation not of displacing or destroying other approaches to knowledge but rather
of adding to and enriching what we feel "we know for sure" through experience,
intuition, and historical study. Transactional research can be extended in many
directions other than that taken here. It is hoped that the time is not far away
when transactional studies of the international system will be commonplace.

How is the log. tran. formation justified? why not simply use variance?

Rudolph J. Rummel

The Relationship Between National Attributes and Foreign Conflict Behavior[1]

INTRODUCTION

International relations can be conceived of as a *system* of behavior. This *behavioral system* is defined in terms of the *interdependence* of the foreign official and unofficial acts of nations and is *bounded* by a set of *dimensions* that delineate the patterns of occurrence among these acts. These dimensions define the *state of the system* at any one time.

The international behavioral system is imbedded in an *attribute* system that is bounded by the dimensions or variation in the characteristics of nations. Economic development, size, totalitarianism, and geographic distance are examples of such dimensions.

Within either of these systems it is possible to locate a nation in terms of its *magnitude* on a particular dimension or in its relative *distance* from other nations.[2]

This possibility suggests a number of fascinating questions. Is the magnitude of a nation's position on the attribute dimensions, say economic development, related to its magnitude on the behavior dimensions, such as conflict? Does the difference in magnitude on the attribute dimensions underlie the behavior of nations toward each other? Is there a mathematical function connecting the behavior to the attribute system? Is the behavioral system a sub-system or an overlay of the attribute system?

The first question will be the focus here. Particularly, the question will be narrowed to foreign conflict behavior. That is, does the magnitude of involvement of a nation along the conflict dimensions of the behavioral system relate to any of its magnitudes on the attribute dimensions of nations?

1. This paper stems from a larger project on the Dimensionality of Nations, and is supported by the National Science Foundation under grant NSF-GS-536.
2. For the mathematical structure and operationalization of the theory presented here, see Rummel (1965).

TABLE 1. *Correlations Between Foreign Conflict Behavior 1955–1957 and 1955 National Characteristics*[a]

Foreign Conflict Behavior[a]

Variable No.[b]	Machine No.	National Characteristics	Antiforeign Demonstrations 145	Negative Sanctions 146	Protests 147	Severance of Diplomatic Relations 148	Ambassadors Expelled or Recalled 149	Other Diplom. Officials Exp. or Recalled 150	Threats 151	Military Action 152	Wars 153	Troop Movements 154	Mobilizations 155	Accusations 156	Killed 157
		AGRICULTURE													
1	105	Agr. Workers/Econ. Active Pop.													
2	2	Agr. Prod./GNP						−30 (63)			−30 (63)				
3	1	Agr. Pop./Pop.													
		ARTS AND CULTURE													
5	3	Motion Picture Attendance/Pop.			30 (61)										
6	126	Book Titles/Pop.				−39 (35)		49 (35)							
7	137	Library Circulation/Pop.													
		COMMUNICATIONS													
8	15	Newspaper Circulation/Pop.													
9	4	Newsprint Consumption/Pop.				−35 (63)									
10	14	No. Illiterate/Pop. > 10 yrs. old				33 (59)									
11	112	Telephones/Pop.													
12	114	Domestic Mail/Pop.													
13	113	Radio Receivers/Pop.						31 (75)							
		DEMOGRAPHIC													
14	7	Annual Rate of Pop. Increase	31 (77)												
15	27	0–15 Age Group in Pop./Pop.			−33 (58)			−38 (58)							
16	123	Pop./Arable Land					31 (72)			31 (72)					
17	6	Pop./National Land Area													
18	5	Population			38 (77)				32 (77)			49 (77)		36 (77)	
19	8	Births/Pop.													
20	9	Pop. in Cities > 20,000 Pop./Pop.						33 (74)							
21	10	Primacy Measure: Pop. of lg. City/Pop. of 4 lg. Cities												−32 (75)	

TABLE 1.—*continued*

Foreign Conflict Behavior[a]

Variable No.[b]	Machine No.	National Characteristics	Anti-foreign Demonstrations 145	Negative Sanctions 146	Protests 147	Severance of Diplomatic Relations 148	Ambassadors Expelled or Recalled 149	Other Diplom. Officials Exp. or Recalled 150	Threats 151	Military Action 152	Wars 153	Troop Movements 154	Mobilizations 155	Accusations 156	Killed 157
		ECONOMIC													
22	11	GNP			42 (72)	−35 (72)		37 (72)	30 (72)			43 (72)			
23	127	GNP/Pop.						31 (72)							
24	30	Fixed Capital Formation/Pop.													
25	33	Manufacturing/GNP													
26	29	Public Admin. + Defense Exp./Pop.				31 (47)			31 (47)	39 (47)	37 (47)			40 (47)	39 (47)
28	32	Cost of Living Index													
29a	138	National Income			40 (65)	−40 (39)		32 (65)	31 (65)			45 (65)			
30	38	Food Exp./Total Private Exp.													
31	90	% Increase in NI/% Pop. Increase						−30 (49)							
32	28	Econ. Active Pop./Pop.													
33	31	Unemployed/Econ. Active Pop.													
34	40	GINI No. (area under Lorenz curve for Land)					−40 (39)								
35	41	% Pop. with 50% of Land													
36	42	Lorenz Curve Slope at 95% of Land Ownership													
		EDUCATION													
37	46	Educ. Exp. by Gov't/Gov't Exp.													
38	44	Pupils in Primary Sch'l/Primary Sch'l Teachers													
39	43	Pupils in Primary Sch'l/5-14 Age Group													
40	45	Pupils in Secondary & Higher Ed./Pop.													

189

TABLE 1.—continued
Foreign Conflict Behavior[a]

Variable No.[b]	Machine No.	National Characteristics	Anti-foreign Demonstrations 145	Negative Sanctions 146	Protests 147	Severance of Diplomatic Relations 148	Ambassadors Expelled or Recalled 149	Other Diplom. Officials Exp. or Recalled 150	Threats 151	Military Action 152	Wars 153	Troop Movements 154	Mobilizations 155	Accusations 156	Killed 157
		GEOGRAPHICAL													
41	48	National Area										38 (77)			
42	47	Arable National Land			30 (75)			32 (75)	31 (75)			49 (75)			
43	88	Arable Land/Total Land Area													
44	49	Average Temperature						−37 (67)							
45	50	Average Rainfall				−39 (67)		−33 (67)							
46	111	Coast Line Length/$\sqrt{\text{Area}}$													
		HEALTH													
47	56	Infant Deaths/Live Births				−46 (34)		40 (34)							
48	55	Pop./Physicians				−34 (45)									
49	89	Proteins/Calories													
50	53	Calories Consumed Minus Calories Req'd/Cal. Req'd													
51	39	Sugar Supply/Pop.													
52	54	Pop./Hospital Beds													
53	34	Life Expectancy at Birth				−31 (54)		42 (54)							
54	35	Tuberculosis Deaths/Pop.													
55	36	Typhoid Deaths/Pop.													
56	52	Cancer Deaths/Pop.						32 (50)							
57	51	Heart Disease Deaths/Pop.				−32 (49)		33 (49)							
58	37	Accidental Deaths/Pop.													
		HISTORY													
59	21	Age of Country	−33 (77)												

Table 1.—*continued*
Foreign Conflict Behavior[a]

Variable No.[b]	Machine No.	National Characteristics	Anti-foreign Demonstrations 145	Negative Sanctions 146	Protests 147	Severance of Diplomatic Relations 148	Ambassadors Expelled or Recalled 149	Other Diplom. Officials Exp. or Recalled 150	Threats 151	Military Action 152	Wars 153	Troop Movements 154	Mobilizations 155	Accusations 156	Killed 157
		MILITARY													
60	135	Defense Expenditure	32 (64)	37 (64)	48 (64)			45 (64)	43 (64)		31 (64)	51 (64)		45 (64)	
61	143	Defense Exp./Gov't. Exp.		44 (67)		39 (67)		31 (67)	35 (67)	36 (67)		37 (67)		43 (67)	31 (67)
62	144	No. in Military/Pop.						32 (75)						40 (75)	
63	139	Pop. × Energy Production			35 (74)			34 (74)				32 (74)			
64	57	No. in Military	32 (75)		45 (75)			35 (75)	39 (75)			55 (75)		55 (75)	35 (75)
		POLITICAL													
65	19	Freedom of Opposition													
66	20	Voting System													
67	58	Political Centralization	32 (36)		41 (36)		−30 (77)	38 (36)				37 (36)		36 (36)	
68	61	Federalist, Unitary													
69	109	Tax Revenue/Total Revenue													
70	110	Excise & Customs Revenue/Total Revenue													
71	16	Press Censorship													
72	59	Legality of Gov't Change													
73	18	Legitimacy of Present Gov't.													
74	17	Average Age of Last Two Gov'ts.													
75	136	Defense Expenditure/GNP		38 (67)	33 (67)	34 (67)		39 (67)	45 (67)	33 (67)		43 (67)		57 (67)	39 (67
76	128	Gov't Expenditure/GNP													
77	104	Gov't Revenue/Gov't Exp.													
78	60	No. Political Parties													
78a	22	Political Development	−35 (71)		32 (72)				34 (72)			43 (72)		32 (72)	
		RESOURCES													
79	62	Total Energy Resources Potentially Available													
80	115	Energy Resources Potentially Available/Pop.													

191

TABLE 1.—continued

Foreign Conflict Behavior[a]

Variable No.[b]	Machine No.	National Characteristics	Anti-foreign Demonstrations 145	Negative Sanctions 146	Protests 147	Severance of Diplomatic Relations 148	Ambassadors Expelled or Recalled 149	Other Diplom. Officials Exp. or Recalled 150	Threats 151	Military Action 152	Wars 153	Troop Movements 154	Mobilizations 155	Accusations 156	Killed 157
		SCIENCE AND TECHNOLOGY													
81	107	Science Book Titles/Book Titles			38 (58)			46 (58)							
82	12	Total Energy Consumption			35 (74)			39 (74)				33 (74)			
83	116	Energy Consumption/Pop.						35 (74)							
84	13	Electricity Generation			32 (74)			33 (74)							
85	134	Total Energy Production/Pop.						32 (74)							
86	65	Total Energy Production			32 (74)			36 (74)							
87	67	Steel Production			39 (50)			33 (50)				38 (50)			
88	141	Industrial Output/Workers				−39 (44)		31 (44)				34 (44)			
89	63	No. of Students in Sci. and Eng./ No. Students in Higher Education													
		SOCIAL													
90	66	Religious Groups > 1% Pop.													
91	118	Pop. Largest Religious Group/Pop.								33 (65)					
92	70	Ethnic Groups > 1% Pop.													
93	120	Pop. Largest Ethnic Group/Pop.													
94	69	Language Groups > 1% Pop.										−31 (58)		33 (63)	32 (63)
95	119	Pop. Largest Language Group/Pop.													
97	67	Nationality Groups > 1% Pop.													
98	117	Native Born/Pop.													
99	23	Negro Pop./Pop.					30 (59)								
100	25	Mongolian Pop./Pop.													
101	24	Caucasian Pop./Pop.						35 (60)							
103	71	% Dwelling Units with Piped Water			32 (31)										
104	72	Divorces/Marriages		32 (37)				34 (37)						38 (37)	
105	26	Marriages/Pop.			39 (60)			43 (60)	30 (60)		30 (60)			32 (60)	
106	121	No. Emp'd Mfg./Pop.													
107	68	National Holidays per Yr.			−39 (75)				−33 (75)			−35 (75)		−45 (75)	−33 (75)

Table 1.—continued
Foreign Conflict Behavior[a]

Variable No.[b]	Machine No.	National Characteristics	Anti-foreign Demonstrations 145	Negative Sanctions 146	Protests 147	Severance of Diplomatic Relations 148	Ambassadors Expelled or Recalled 149	Other Diplom. Officials Exp. or Recalled 150	Threats 151	Military Action 152	Wars 153	Troop Movements 154	Mobilizations 155	Accusations 156	Killed 157
		TRANSPORTATION													
108	75	Road Length/National Land Area													
109	77	RR Length per Person to Pop. distance[d]													
110	76	Railroad Length/National Land Area													
111	78	Railroad Length													
112	129	Railway Freight/Railroad Length			53 (60)			38 (60)	38 (60)		36 (60)	50 (60)		40 (60)	33 (60)
113	125	Railroad Freight/Pop.			33 (63)			36 (63)							
114	122	Vehicles in Use/Pop.		30 (73)								34 (56)			
115	74	Vehicles in Use						32 (73)							
116	140	Air-Passenger Km./Pop.		34 (56)											
117	73	Air-Passenger Kilometers													
118	147	Seaborne Goods Loaded and Unloaded/GNP													
119	130	Seaborne Goods Loaded and Unloaded													
		VALUES													
120	108	Religious Book Titles/Book Titles		31 (58)									31 (58)		
121	98	Religious Holidays per year													
122	101	Buddhist Pop./Pop.													
123	99	Roman Catholic Pop./Pop.						33 (72)	40 (70)			−34 (75)		−35 (72)	
124	100	Protestant Pop./Pop.				47 (70)				38 (70)				42 (70)	
125	102	Mohammedan, Pop./Pop.				−44 (70)									
126	103	Female Students/Total Students													
127	106	Female Workers/Econ. Active Pop.													
128	97	Minimum Voting Age													

TABLE 1.—continued
Foreign Conflict Behavior[a]

Variable No.[b]	Machine No.	National Characteristics	Anti-foreign Demonstrations 145	Negative Sanctions 146	Protests 147	Severance of Diplomatic Relations 148	Ambassadors Expelled or Recalled 149	Other Diplom. Officials Exp. or Recalled 150	Threats 151	Military Action 152	Wars 153	Troop Movements 154	Mobilizations 155	Accusations 156	Killed 157
129	95	Monarchy or Not													
130	124	Communist Party Membership/Pop.													
131	96	Students in Law/College Students													
132	91	Achievement Desire	37 (37)				42 (37)							36 (37)	
133	92	Need for Affiliation													
134	93	Need for Power									−30 (37)		−36 (37)		−30 (37)
135	94	Other-Directedness Rank													
		DOMESTIC CONFLICT													
136	79	Assassinations													
137	80	General Strikes													
138	81	Guerrilla Warfare													
139	82	Major Government Crises													
140	83	Purges	36 (77)			32 (77)				30 (77)					
141	84	Riots													
142	85	Revolutions							36 (77)						
143	86	Anti-Government Demonstrations	38 (77)											35 (77)	
144	87	Domestic Killed													34 (77)
		FOREIGN CONFLICT													
145	168	Anti-Foreign Demonstrations	100 (77)	53 (77)	39 (77)	36 (77)			50 (77)	33 (77)		39 (77)		46 (77)	35 (77)
146	169	Negative Sanctions	53 (77)	100 (77)	47 (77)	33 (77)		33 (77)	64 (77)	35 (77)		45 (77)	38 (77)	48 (77)	30 (77)
147	170	Protests	39 (77)	47 (77)	100 (77)			47 (77)	66 (77)	39 (77)	51 (77)	63 (77)	46 (77)	69 (77)	52 (77)
148	171	Severence of Diplomatic Relations	36 (77)	33 (77)		100 (77)			38 (77)	54 (77)				39 (77)	31 (77)
149	172	Ambassadors Expelled or Recalled					100 (77)								
150	173	Other Diplomatic Officials Expelled or Recalled		33 (77)	47 (77)			100 (77)	50 (77)		33 (77)	43 (77)		45 (77)	32 (77)

TABLE 1.—*continued*
Foreign Conflict Behavior[a]

Variable No.[b]	Machine No.	National Characteristics	Anti-foreign Demonstrations 145	Negative Sanctions 146	Protests 147	Severance of Diplomatic Relations 148	Ambassadors Expelled or Recalled 149	Other Diplom. Officials Exp. or Recalled 150	Threats 151	Military Action 152	Wars 153	Troop Movements 154	Mobilizations 155	Accusations 156	Killed 157
151	174	Threats	50 (77)	64 (77)	66 (77)	38 (77)		50 (7)	100 (77)	62 (77)	55 (77)	68 (77)	55 (77)	81 (77)	63 (77)
152	175	Military Action	33 (77)	35 (77)	39 (77)	54 (77)			62 (77)	100 (77)	38 (77)	45 (77)	54 (77)	65 (77)	72 (77)
153	176	Wars			51 (77)			33 (77)	55 (77)	38 (77)	100 (77)	32 (77)	37 (77)	56 (77)	77 (77)
154	177	Troop Movements	39 (77)	45 (77)	63 (77)			43 (77)	68 (77)	45 (77)	32 (77)	100 (77)	30 (77)	62 (77)	53 (77)
155	178	Mobilizations		38 (77)	46 (77)				55 (77)	54 (77)	37 (77)	30 (77)	100 (77)	46 (77)	41 (77)
156	179	Acusations	46 (77)	48 (77)	69 (77)	39 (77)		45 (77)	81 (77)	65 (77)	56 (77)	62 (77)	46 (77)	100 (77)	70 (77)
157	180	Foreign Killed	35 (77)	30 (77)	52 (77)	31 (77)		32 (77)	63 (77)	72 (77)	77 (77)	53 (77)	41 (77)	70 (77)	100 (77)
		COLLABORATION													
160	155	Economic Aid Received					−44 (46)								
161	221	Aid Received/GNP[2] per Cap			−44 (42)		−35 (42)	−46 (42)	−42 (42)		−40 (42)	−50 (42)			
162	225	IFC & IBRD Subscription/GNP[2] per Cap				33 (77)									
163	194	Balance of Official Donations												33 (58)	
164	229	Balance of Donations/Gold Stock													
165	223	Tech. Ass't. Contributions/GNP[2] per Cap				33 (76)									
166	156	Technical Assistance Contributions		43 (77)	46 (77)			43 (77)	41 (77)			39 (77)			
167	222	Tech. Ass't. Received/GNP[2] per Cap		32 (77)	39 (77)	35 (75)									
168	149	Tech. Ass't. Received	31 (77)	34 (77)	31 (77)	43 (77)		33 (77)				37 (77)			
169	152	No. of Treaties													
170	153	Military Treaties													
171	150	Multi-Lateral Treaties													
172	154	Military Treaties/(All Treaties + 1)													
173	148	Acceptance of ICJ													
		COLONIALISM													
174	158	Colonies or Not													
175	226	National Area/(Nat'l+Terr. Area)													
176	227	National Pop./(Nat'l+Terr. Pop.)													
177	157	National + Terr. Pop.	31 (76)		39(76)				33 (76)		−30 (77)	48 (76)		38 (76)	

Table 1.—*continued*
Foreign Conflict Behavior[a]

Variable No.[b]	Machine No.	National Characteristics	Anti-foreign Demon-strations 145	Negative Sanc-tions 146	Protests 147	Sever-ance of Diplo-matic Rela-tions 148	Ambas-sadors Expelled or Recalled 149	Other Diplom. Officials Exp. or Recalled 150	Threats 151	Military Action 152	Wars 153	Troop Move-ments 154	Mobili-zations 155	Accu-sations 156	Killed 157
		IR COMMUNICATION													
178	219	Foreign Mail Sent & Rec'd		31 (44)	34 (44)							32 (44)			
179	217	Foreign Mail Sent & Rec'd/Pop.													
180	220	Foreign Mail Sent/Mail Sent & Rec'd													
181	142	Foreign Titles Trans./Domestic Bk. Titles	−46 (34)	−32 (34)					−31 (34)			−35 (34)			
		DIPLOMATIC													
182	151	Embassies & Legations in Other Countries		31 (64)	43 (64)			31 (67)	32 (64)			33 (64)			
183	182	Embassies & Legations in Country		35 (66)				35 (66)				37 (66)			
		INTERNATIONAL ORGANIZATION													
184	181	U.N. Representatives	38 (57)	36 (57)	41 (57)			42 (57)	44 (57)		35 (57)	55 (57)		48 (57)	44 (57)
185	159	IGO's of Which a Member													
186	160	NGO's of Which a Member		31 (77)											
187	183	Inter'l Org. H.Q. in Country													
188	167	Culture NGO/NGO					32 (77)								
189	224	UN Delinquencies/Assessment													
190	184	UN Assessment/Total Assessment	45 (56)	35 (56)	45 (56)			53 (56)	37 (56)			48 (56)		35 (56)	31 (56)
191	164	Science NGO/NGO	35 (77)		44 (77)			49 (77)							
192	163	Law NGO/NGO													
193	162	Peace & Friendship NGO/NGO													
194	161	Religion NGO/NGO													
195	165	Medicine NGO/NGO													
196	166	Education NGO/NGO													

TABLE 1.—continued
Foreign Conflict Behavior[a]

Variable No.[b]	Machine No.	National Characteristics	Anti-foreign Demonstrations 145	Negative Sanctions 146	Protests 147	Severance of Diplomatic Relations 148	Ambassadors Expelled or Recalled 149	Other Diplom. Officials Exp. or Recalled 150	Threats 151	Military Action 152	Wars 153	Troop Movements 154	Mobilizations 155	Accusations 156	Killed 157
		INTERNATIONAL POLITICS													
197	186	Bloc Prominence	48 (77)	51 (77)	52 (77)			34 (77)	63 (77)	34 (77)	45 (77)	65 (77)	31 (77)	53 (77)	50 (77)
198	185	Bloc Allegiance													
199	188	British Commonwealth Membership													
200	187	Neutral or Not													
201	211	Western Bloc Trade/(Communist & W. Trade)						−39 (68)			−33 (68)				
202	189	U.S. Aid/(U.S. & U.S.S.R. Aid)	32 (60)					−35 (64)							
203	190	U.S. Economic Aid Rec'd													
204	132	English Titles Trans./All Trans.			−43 (25)			−36 (25)						−40 (25)	
205	133	Russian Titles Trans./All Trans.						30 (33)							
206	131	Eng. Titles Trans./(Russian & Eng. Titles Trans.)			−48 (23)			−31 (23)						−31 (23)	
207	193	Net % Votes with U.S. in UN													
208	192	Net % Votes with U.S.S.R. in UN												−32 (56)	
		POLITICAL GEOGRAPHY													
209	196	Nations Contiguous										31 (77)		32 (77)	
210	191	Air Distance from U.S.					−31 (76)								
211	195	Air Distance from U.S.S.R.													
212	213	Air Distance from U.S./(Air Distance from U.S.S.R. & U.S.)			36 (75)		−34 (75)	31 (75)						35 (75)	

TABLE 1.—continued
Foreign Conflict Behavior[a]

Variable No.[b]	Machine No.	National Characteristics	Anti-foreign Demonstrations 145	Negative Sanctions 146	Protests 147	Severance of Diplomatic Relations 148	Ambassadors Expelled or Recalled 149	Other Diplom. Officials Exp. or Recalled 150	Threats 151	Military Action 152	Wars 153	Troop Movements 154	Mobilizations 155	Accusations 156	Killed 157
		POPULATION MOVEMENT													
213	199	Immigrants	31 (51)				30 (51)		36 (51)						
214	215	Immigrants/Pop.												31 (32)	−31 (41)
215	214	Emmigrants/Pop.			40 (32)							−33 (41)			
216	207	Immigrants/Migrants													
217	201	No. of Foreign Visitors													
218	216	Foreign Visitors/Pop.													
219	197	T & R Fellowships Received													
220	198	T & R Fellowship Recipients in Country		32 (77)		30 (77)									
221	200	Foreign College Students in Country	32 (53)		42 (53)				30 (53)		39 (53)	44 (53)			
222	212	Foreign College Students/College Students													
		TRADE													
223	145	Trade			37 (71)			35 (71)							
224	203	Exports			35 (72)			30 (72)							
225	208	Imports/Trade			−36 (70)										
226	202	Raw Material Exports/Exports													
227	228	Balance of Payments/Gold Stock													
228	218	Exports/GNP	−32 (68)												
229	206	Leading Exports/Exports													
230	209	Agr. Exports/Exports			−44 (56)			−36 (56)							
231	210	Agr. Exports/Agr. Trade			−30 (51)										
232	204	Import Duties/Imports													
233	205	Balance of Investments					−30 (61)								
234	230	Balance of Investments/Gold Stock												−37 (56)	
235	146	Trade/GNP										−30 (57)			
		Percent variation accounted for by all 229 variables[c]	53%	55%	71%	57%	44%	53%	83%	68%	53%	75%	51%	85%	69%

198

[a]The number heading each column is that of the foreign conflict behavior variable. Decimals are omitted from the correlations and only correlations greater or equal to an absolute value of .30 are shown. Figures in parentheses refer to the number of nations on which the correlation coefficient was calculated. All correlations are product-moment.

[b]Total number of variables is 230. The variable numbers of those dropped during the data collection stage are omitted from the table.

[c]These are approximate figures and represent the sum of the communalities, h^2, calculated from fifteen factors extracted from the full correlation matrix with unities in the principal diagonal. The communalities are slightly inflated due to the correlation matrix being calculated from a data matrix with about 17 per cent missing data. The factors used in calculating the communalities were all those with positive eigenvalues.

[d]This is a weighting of R.R. length per person by population density.

Before an answer to this question can be posed, several preliminary remarks are necessary. First, the question is concerned with conflict *behavior*, and not a conflict *situation*. The former involves a definite act of a nation with regard to another in a situation of conflict. Such a situation is indicated by the existence of mutually incompatible goals or values between nations and the perception of this incompatibility. While conflict behavior takes place within a conflict situation, the latter may exist without any physical manifestation. A nation, for example, may be incapable of acting or may be deterred from doing so because of the consequences.

Second, the question assumes the existence of a conflict behavior *dimension* of the behavioral system. As far as research has gone, this dimension exists. A factor analysis of ninety-four international relations measures, most of them behavioral, for eighty-two nations on 1955 data yielded a conflict behavior dimension clearly correlated with such acts as threats, accusations, protests, military action, and war. (Rummel, 1964.)

Third, the question assumes the existence of attribute dimensions of nations. Several factor analyses by others[3] have shown the existence of *economic development* and *size* as such attribute dimensions. In particular, a large-scale factor analysis, discussed below, of 230 substantive variables by the author and colleagues (Rummel, Sawyer, Guetzkow, and Tanter, 1967) for 82 nations on 1955 data delineated several relevant orthogonal[4] dimensions, among which were also *economic development* and *size* (power bases).

Finally, the question of the relationship between conflict behavior magnitude and attribute dimensions assumes of an answer a research context. A fund of empirical findings systematically organized is a necessity if an answer beyond our intuition or purely personal experience is to be provided. While the brief mention of the factor studies above suggests such a fund, the nature of the main research to be drawn on should be described in terms of the work of the Dimensionality of Nations Project (DON).[5]

DON PROJECT

The DON Project was initiated in the summer of 1962 to determine the dimensions of variation of nations on their political, economic, social, cultural, and behavioral characteristics. Data were collected on 230 variables, among which were thirteen foreign conflict behavior measures: (1) anti-foreign demonstrations, (2) negative sanctions, (3) protests, (4) severance of diplomatic relations with other countries, (5) ambassadors expelled or recalled, (6) diplomatic officials of less than ambassadorial rank expelled or recalled, (7) threats, (8) military action, (9) wars, (10) troop movements, (11) mobilizations, (12) accusations, and (13) nationals killed in foreign violence. Their definitions and raw and transformed

3. Those by Cattell (1949), Cattell and colleagues (1951), Berry (1960, 1961a), and Russett (in this volume) are particularly notable.

4. When rotated to an oblique solution, the correlations between the dimensions remained small. The orthogonal solution, therefore, is accepted as the best fit to the data.

5. For a more complete description of the project than that to be given here and, in particular, for a description of the research design for the study of dyadic relations between nations, see Rummel (1965a).

data are given in a previous study (Rummel, 1963).[6] The other 217 *non-conflict* variables are listed by conceptual domain in Table 1, which gives the correlations between the conflict and non-conflict variables.[7]

Four separate analyses have been applied to the data. The thirteen foreign conflict behavior variables were intercorrelated[8] and factor analyzed[9] separately and with nine domestic conflict variables (Rummel, 1963b).[10] The foreign conflict

6. The thirteen foreign conflict measures that were selected had to meet five criteria: (1) be capable of empirical delineation, (2) define an act or occurrence of sufficient interest to be generally reported, (3) be applicable to all nations to avoid logically necessary (rather than empirical) correlations, (4) be as diverse as possible to cover the greatest possible range of conflict behavior, and (5) be an act of occurrence with respect to seven or more nations to prevent the correlations from being dependent on too few such happenings (this reduces the possibility of aberrations influencing general conclusions). In order to avoid further logically necessary correlations, each of these measures is defined in a way to make them mutually exclusive and each datum collected under the definitions was used only once.

The initial data collection involved a larger and slightly different set of measures than the thirteen given here. Data were collected for the three years, 1955–1957, from the *New York Times Index, Keesing's Contemporary Archives, Facts on File, Brittanica Book of the Year,* and *New International Yearbook.* The data collection process involved recording each datum on a separate index card. A description of the conflict act or occurrence was given, as well as the date, nation, source, and data collector. In the process of data collection, some of the definitions had to be revised, some measures were dropped, and some new ones were suggested. At the conclusion of the initial data collection, I screened the resulting several thousand index cards according to the criteria above and the definitions used. The process delineated the thirteen measures discussed in this paper as the most catholic and operational indices of foreign conflict behavior.

Before analysis, the data on these measures were tested for (1) the effect of *systematic error* due to censorship in a nation and (2) the influence of world interest in a nation. The conclusion was that such sources of error would probably have little effect on the correlations resulting from the analysis. Moreover, the stability of the data in mirroring long-run conflict patterns was assessed by (1) correlating them with similar data (1825–1946) collected by Lewis Fry Richardson, and (2) comparing the correlations among several of the thirteen conflict measures with correlations found by Raymond Cattell among data (1837–1937) on similar measures. In both cases, the patterns in the data were found to be highly similar, suggesting a high level of stability. The results of these tests for systematic error and stability and a further finding of high intercorrelations among several of the conflict measures (reducing the likelihood of random error influencing the correlations) suggest that the data used in this paper are tapping substantive meaning.

7. The data for the thirteen conflict behavior variables were collected on 77 nations for the years 1955–1957. For the other 217 variables, data generally were collected for the mid-1950's for 82 nations, with missing data running to approximately 17 per cent for the whole 230 variable data matrix. These data were analyzed for degree of normality and for extreme values; where necessary and possible, transformations were applied to remove such extreme values or to normalize the distributions in accord with the requirements of the statistical model to be employed. For more precise information on data-handling and -transformations, see Rummel, Sawyer, Guetzkow, and Tanter (1967).

8. To "intercorrelate" means to assess the degree and direction of relationship between two variables. The product moment coefficient has been used throughout for this purpose. See Ezekiel and Fox (1959).

9. Factor analysis *and* rotation are techniques for determining what clusters or groups of relationships exist among the set of variables being analyzed. For an introduction to the technique, see Fruchter (1954) and Cattell (1952). For an excellent technical discussion see Harman (1960). A philosophy, interpretation,. and methodological discussion of factor analysis, with examples from cross-national data, is given by Rummel (1967).

10. This part of the analysis has been replicated with similar results by Raymond Tanter (1966) using 1958–1960 foreign and domestic conflict data.

variables were then regressed[11] upon dimensions of national characteristics (Rummel, 1964a). A factor analysis, mentioned above, was completed on the 94 international relations variables shown in Table 1, and which included the thirteen foreign conflict variables (Rummel, 1964). And a subsequent factor analysis on all the 230 (plus six error measures) was completed through orthogonal and oblique rotation.[12]

A report on the DON analysis of the 230 variables and results is currently in preparation (Rummel, Sawyer, Guetzkow, and Tanter, 1967). Here it should suffice to sketch in the relevant results of this analysis and of the others emerging from DON.

The factor analysis of the foreign and domestic conflict variables together brought out two very distinct primary dimensions of behavior—one of domestic conflict and the other of foreign conflict. A regression of the foreign conflict dimensions, onto separately obtained domestic conflict dimensions, further substantiated this independence for the 1955–1957 data.

This independence was not as clear, however, in the later study in which the presence or absence of subversion in a nation in terms of guerrilla warfare and assassinations was found to have a small negative relationship to foreign conflict behavior. This study also determined that among the variables of technological or economic development, demographic conditions, and size, adverse demographic conditions was most independently related to foreign conflict. All the relationships, however, were very small. This independence between internal-external conflict behavior has been further investigated by Richard Chadwick (1963) and Raymond Tanter (1966). The former worked with the 1955–1957 data and found that the independence held up when the *annual* data were analyzed, with and without lag conditions being introduced. Tanter collected a new set of data, 1958–1960, and similarly found through factor analysis, regression analysis, and lagging that the internal-external conflict behavior of nations were largely independent.

Turning to other DON studies, the above-mentioned factor analysis of the 94 international relations variables brought out three major orthogonal dimensions—cooperation, conflict, and aid—and four intermediary dimensions—ideology, popularity, Latin American, and migrations—of international relations in the mid-1950's (Rummel, 1964).

When all 230 variables were included together in one factor analysis and rotated to orthogonal and oblique solutions, the following interpretable dimensions emerged: economic development, power bases (size), political (totalitarianism), foreign conflict behavior, density, Catholic culture, domestic conflict behavior, linguistic ethnic homogeneity, and trade to GNP ratio.

THE HYPOTHESES

In terms of the purpose here, a distinction between conflict behavior and situation has been drawn, and evidence for the existence of a conflict behavior dimen-

---

11. To "regress" means, in part, to determine how well the data on one variable can be predicted from the data on a set of variables. See Ezekiel and Fox (1959).

12. *Orthogonal* rotation means giving a better fit of the factors to the clusters of relationships they represent, with the restriction that the correlation (cosine) between the factors will be zero. In *oblique* rotation the factors may become correlated if this gives a better fit to the data.

sion and dimensions of attribute space has been offered. Moreover, the DON project has been described as the research context for answering the questions as to the relation between the magnitude of a nation's position on the attribute dimensions and its conflict behavior magnitude.

The question originally raised now can be given greater specificity as a set of hypotheses about the relation between attributes and conflict behavior. Rather than restricting the attributes to those defined as dimensions in empirical analyses, the theory will be loosened to accommodate characteristics that have often been posed as conditions of (causing, explaining, predicting) foreign conflict. Indeed, the nature, sources and conditions of international conflict have been a central concern of students of international relations.[13] Some of this interest has been manifested in attempts to make the study of such conflict theoretically,[14] and in particular, empirically more systematic.[15] The latter will be drawn on where possible to supplement the DON findings.

The hypotheses to be tested[16] relate the foreign conflict behavior of a nation to:

Hypothesis 1: The level of economic or technological development of a nation.
Hypothesis 2: The level of international communications or transaction of a nation.
Hypothesis 3: The amount of cooperation of a nation with others.
Hypothesis 4: The totalitarianism of a nation's government.
Hypothesis 5: The power of a nation.
Hypothesis 6: The instability of a nation.
Hypothesis 7: The military capabilities of a nation.
Hypothesis 8: The psychological motivations of a nation's people.
Hypothesis 9: The values of a nation.
Hypothesis 10: The number of borders of a nation.
Hypothesis 11: The *interaction* of combinations of the above characteristics, such as economic development, instability, and totalitarianism.

It should be noted that the hypotheses are not phrased in the language of the theory discussed in the introduction. To do so would have obscured the familiar quality of the hypotheses. The reader of the conflict literature probably has come across them in several verbal guises; each has, at one time or another, been advocated as an explanation or condition of international conflict behavior. Few of them, unfortunately, have been systematically tested.

TESTING THE HYPOTHESES

Each hypothesis states a definite relationship between attribute and behavior. For such a relationship to exist, however, the attribute and behavior must be

13. See the analyses of selected international relations texts by Boulding (1964) and Snyder (1961).

14. See, for example, Schelling (1960), Boulding (1962), Rapoport (1960), and Richardson (1960a).

15. See, for example, Richardson (1960b), Smoker (1963a, 1963b), Sorokin (1937), and Weiss (1963). The growing concern with making the study of international conflict more systematic and empirical is seen in the crop of current dissertations by Alker (1963), Haas (1964), Tanter (1966), and Zinnes (1963).

16. Technically speaking, the hypotheses are not being "tested," since they were not stated before data were collected and analyzed. Nonetheless, the outcome of relating *ex post facto* hypotheses to systematic results is largely the same. Positive results add a small measure of confirmation while negative instances thunder against the hypotheses.

concomitant. That is, a correlation should be found between the two. The "tests," therefore, will largely consist of screening systematically obtained results for such correlations.

> *Hypothesis 1. The level of economic or technical development of a nation is highly related to its foreign conflict behavior.*

This hypothesis finds little confirmation from the DON results. An economic development dimension emerged from the 230 variable factor analysis, and was defined in terms of such variables as telephones per capita (.95),[17] GNP per capita (.91), energy consumption per capita (.90), and percentage agricultural population (−.92). Relevant to the hypothesis is the fact that not one of the foreign conflict measured has as much as 10 per cent of its variation associated with the dimension. This lack of relationship can be seen in Table 1. The correlations of the economic development variables, such as those mentioned above, with the thirteen conflict variables are almost all less than | .30 | .[18] Of those few greater than | .30 | , the highest are .35, which are between GNP per capita (number 23) and the severance of diplomatic relations, and between energy consumption per capita (number 83) and diplomatic officials of lesser than ambassadorial rank expelled or recalled. The squaring of the correlation coefficients times one hundred would make them more meaningful, since it would indicate the percentage of variation two variables have in common. Thus, the most variation the economic development variables share with foreign conflict is 12.2 per cent.

This finding dovetails with the regression of the foreign conflict measures upon dimensions coming out of a separate factor analysis by Brian Berry (1960, 1961a).[19] He factor analyzed forty-three variables for ninety-five countries for mid-1950 data and extracted a technological dimension accounting for about 84 per cent of the variation among his variables. Those variables which best defined the dimensions were percentage of energy used for commercial purposes, commercial energy consumed per capita, KWH of electricity per capita, and fiber consumption per capita. The correlations of this dimension with each of the foreign conflict behavior variables are generally near zero, with the highest being that between level of technology and expelling or recalling diplomatic officials of lesser than ambassadorial rank (.27). Thus, the most variation in foreign conflict behavior, 1955–1957, that level of technology accounted for was 7.3 per cent.[20]

---

17. Numbers in parentheses refer to the correlation of the variable with the dimension. These numbers squared indicate the percentage of total variation that a variable has in common with a dimension.

18. The vertical bars | .30 | mean "an absolute value of" .30.

19. These regressions are reported in Rummel (1964a).

20. The concern here is with a cross-sectional hypothesis, that is, the relationship between levels of economic development or technology and foreign conflict across nations at a point in time. Thus, longitudinal analyses are not relevant, since a relationship found in longitudinal data may drop out when the data are considered cross-sectionally, and vice versa. (On this point see Duncan, Cuzzort, and Duncan, 1961). For their interest, however, several longitudinal studies might be mentioned here. Pitirim Sorokin (1937) plotted frequencies of data on technology and war over centuries and found that war occurred most often when technology was most rapidly increasing. Michael Haas (1964), however, found little relationship (Spearman's rank-order correlation) between annual increments in KWH electricity per capita, telephones per capita, and wars for the period 1900–1960. Rummel also found (1961) a lack

The studies of Cattell (1949) and Cattell and colleagues (1951, 1965)[21] also are relevant to the hypothesis. In the 1949 study, data largely for the years 1837–1937 on seventy-two variables for sixty-nine nations were factor analyzed. The 1951 study was a repeat of this analysis, but eliminated nations with much missing data. Since the results of the 1949 and 1951 studies were similar, only the former will be discussed. The third study (1965) was a fifty-one-variable, fifty-two-nation factor analysis of data for the mid-1950's. This study and the 1949 one included data on several foreign conflict variables—homicides and war deaths, number of wars, and foreign clashes—and on a large number of economic development and technological variables, such as national income per capita, telephones per capita, and railway length per capita.

The result of the 1949 analysis was that war and political clashes with other nations for the years 1837–1937 was largely independent of economic and technological development. In the 1965 analysis, homicide and war deaths, and political clashes, as well as defense expenditures did not come out on a dimension similar to economic development, indicating again a large measure of independence.

So far as I am aware, the above findings are the only systematic evidence available relevant to the hypothesis. But what evidence there is seems to point quite strongly to there being *little relationship between a nation's economic development or level of technology and its foreign conflict behavior.*

> *Hypothesis 2. The level of international communications or transactions of a nation are highly related to its foreign conflict behavior.*

If communications are defined in terms of international mail, and transactions in terms of economic aid and various trade measures such as imports plus exports, ratio of exports to GNP, ratio of leading exports to exports, and so forth, then the DON results lend little credence to the hypothesis. Nor would they if the meaning of "communications" and "transactions" was expanded to include diplomatic representation, signing of treaties, and membership in international organizations.

In the ninety-four variable international relations study, the factor which accounted for most of the common variation (22.2 per cent) of nations on all the variables was a *cooperation* dimension, involving all the transaction and communication variables. Trade (.95), foreign mail (.81), embassies and legations in other countries (.92), treaties (.74), and membership in intergovernmental organizations (.70), were highly correlated with, and thus defined, the dimension. An *aid* dimension came out on the seventh factor, and was defined largely in terms of technical assistance and relief fellowships received, ratio of IFC and IBRD subscriptions to GNP^2 per capita,[22] and American aid received. With

---

of relationship (product moment and Spearman's rank-order correlation) between number of inventions and wars, battles, number killed, and number of nations involved in war from 1648 to 1900. The longitudinal, or *P*-technique, factor analyses of Cecil Gibb (1956) of Australia and Raymond Cattell and Marvin Adelson (1951) of the United States showed little relationship between economic or technological growth and measures which could index levels of foreign conflict. A later *P*-technique study of England by Cattell (1953), however, did bring out a high relationship between economic growth and defense budgets.

21. The findings of the 1965 study are also given in Gorsuch (1962).

22. The measure IFC and IBRD subscriptions/GNP^2 per capita is arithmetically equivalent to IFC and IBRD *per capita*/GNP *per capita*.

both these dimensions, the foreign conflict variables had very low correlations. When the IR variables were included with 136 other substantive variables and factored,[23] the relationship between communication and transaction variables was not increased. The general lack of relationship between international communication (numbered 178–181) and transaction (numbered 223–235) variables on the one hand and 1955–1957 foreign conflict on the other can be seen in Table 1. Of these correlations, almost all are less than $|.30|$. Of the few that are greater, the highest is for foreign titles translated to domestic book titles and anti-foreign demonstrations ($-.46$). That is, the highest percentage of variation that communications and transactions have in common with foreign conflict is little more than 21 per cent. Not unappreciable, to be sure, but considering all the variables hardly sufficient to substantiate the central role given communication and transaction in the conflict literature.

One of the factors extracted by Berry (1961a, 1960) in his ninety-five-nation, forty-three-variable analysis was a *contrast in income and external relations* dimension. This dimension involved trade variables, but its correlation with the 1955–1957 foreign conflict data was found to be very low. Most of the product moment correlations were near zero, and the highest was with protests (.38), or 14.4 per cent variance in common.

Here, the available empirical evidence seems to suggest *that a nation's international communications and transactions have little relationship to its conflict behavior.*[24]

> *Hypothesis 3. The amount of cooperation of a nation with others is highly related to its conflict behavior.*

If we can define cooperation in terms of the working together of a nation with others to achieve a common goal, then cooperation can be indexed by such variables as membership in international organizations, treaties, aid, and diplomatic representation. In fact, almost the same variables which could be used to index communications and transactions could be used to index cooperation. Therefore, the results related to the previous hypothesis can also be cited here. It should suffice to point out that in the 94 variable study a dimension largely composed of highly correlated cooperation variables emerged independent of a dimension of foreign conflict, and that in the 230 variable study these variables maintained their independence of the conflict measures.

The 1965 study of Cattell and Gorsuch included among their fifty-one variables an international aid index and UNICEF contributions per capita. These variables separated out in the factor analysis onto dimensions different from homicide and war deaths, defense expenditures, and foreign political clashes.

So far the evidence seems to lend little credence to the hypothesis. But there is one positive finding. In the 1949 study of Cattell, trade for 1837–1937 was included as a variable. Its correlation with war is about .62 and with foreign

---

23. It might be thought that the larger analysis would be redundant with regard to the findings of the 94 IR variables. This is hardly the case, since in the larger study the interrelationship of the 94 IR variables with the 136 domestic characteristics must be taken into account.

24. Although not relevant to the hypothesis since he was dealing with dyadic relations between nations, Lewis Richardson's (1960a) finding that international trade does not have the pacifying and unifying effect that he had anticipated is quite interesting.

political clashes about .76,[25] and it came out highly loaded with the two conflict variables on the same factor. What this means is that war, foreign political clashes, and treaties of a nation were highly related to each other during the years 1837–1937. Unfortunately, no other cooperation-like measures were included in the 1949 study.

Because of this one positive finding we should be less inclined to negate the hypothesis than we were in the case of the first two. Nonetheless, the evidence of correlating and factoring a large number of cooperation-like measures is that *the amount of cooperation of a nation, with the possible exception of signing treaties, has little relationship to its foreign conflict behavior.*

> *Hypothesis 4. The totalitarianism of a government is highly related to its foreign conflict behavior.*

Table 1 gives a number of political measures, some indexing a nation's degree of totalitarianism. The latter variables are freedom of opposition (number 65), voting system[26] (number 66), and press censorship (number 71). As can be seen from the table, these measures have no correlation with the conflict variables exceeding | .30 | .

Since the lack of correlation may be due to other influences, such as economic development or domestic instability intervening to depress the relationship, the best indication of how totalitarianism and foreign conflict are related is the DON 230 variable factor analysis. The factor analysis partials out intervening influences and brings out, on a common factor, variables with these influences removed. The 230 variable analysis delineated a political dimension encompassing the measures of totalitarianism mentioned above, and independent of the foreign conflict dimension. This implies that the lack of relationship between foreign conflict and totalitarianism is not the result of intervening influences.

Cattell and Gorsuch included number of political parties and news censorship in their 1965 analysis. Both variables also came out on the same factor, a factor different from the ones to which homicides and war deaths and foreign political clashes were related. The 1949 study of Cattell and associates likewise included censorship and number of political parties, but for the years 1927–1939. The correlation of censorship with foreign political clashes was about −.05 and with war about −.01. That of number of political parties was −.15 and −.14, respectively. In the factor analysis, the foreign conflict variables came out on the same factor, but apart from the two political variables.

Thus, the empirical evidence available is, without exception, negative with regard to this hypothesis.[27] Rather, it seems that *the degree of totalitarianism of a government has little relationship to its foreign conflict behavior.*

25. Only approximate correlations can be given. The correlation matrix of the 1949 study was neither included in the publication nor filed with the American Documents Institute. That for the 1951 study was, however, and it is from this matrix that these correlations were taken.

26. Defined as one party without effective primary, one party with effective primary, multiparty with ban on extreme parties, and multiparty without a ban.

27. By this time the thought may have occurred to the reader that something is wrong with the 1955–1957 conflict data. The possibility was discussed and tested for in Rummel (1963) with the conclusion that systematic error would probably not distort analyses using such data. That a high amount of random error is causing the lack of relationships is argued against by the high correlations among the conflict variables themselves and their high loadings on the same factor. The possibility that this might be a method factor resulting from techniques of data collection is discussed in Rummel (1964b) and found unlikely. For similar testing of the 1958–1960 conflict behavior data, see Tanter (1966).

Hypothesis 5.   The power of a nation is highly related to its foreign conflict behavior.

If we were to define the power of a nation in terms of its physical size (number 41), population size (number 18), GNP (number 22), resources (number 79), railways (number 111), military personnel (number 64), total defense expenditures (number 60), and political centralization (number 67), then one could by looking at Table 1 get some idea as to how power correlates with foreign conflict behavior for 1955–1957. As with the previous hypothesis, the correlations are generally less than | .30 | . Of those that are greater, the highest correlation is .55 between military personnel and both troop movements and accusations, or 30.2 per cent variation in common. This correlation is due to the influence of other variables, for when the 230 variables were all factored, these power variables came out highly correlated with the same dimension (thus named a power dimension), and with which the conflict variables have little correlation.

Cattell and Gorsuch included population size and national area in their 1965 study. As with the DON analysis, these variables loaded on the same factor apart from homicide and war deaths and foreign political clashes. Moreover, the 1949 study of Cattell included population and area with the same results. The correlations between population size and foreign political clashes was .36 and for war .11. Those of area were .22 and .08, respectively.

For this hypothesis also, the results appear to point in only one direction. That is, *there is little relationship between a nation's power and its foreign conflict behavior.*

Hypothesis 6.   The instability of a nation is highly related to its foreign conflict behavior.

A nation's instability can be defined in such terms as riots, demonstrations, revolutions, and so on. Nine such variables were included in the several DON analyses and are given in Table 1 under the domestic conflict domain. The results of these studies, which largely indicated a lack of relationship between foreign conflict and domestic instability, were discussed in the DON project section above, and will not be considered further here.

Both the 1949 and 1965 studies of Cattell, Cattell and Gorsuch included riots and revolutions as separate variables. In addition, assassinations were included in the 1949 analysis. The results in both cases were that domestic instability and foreign conflict had little relationship.[28] The 1949 analysis found that war, 1837–1937, correlated .48 with riots, .18 with assassinations, and −.10 with revolutions. Foreign clashes had a correlation of .49 with riots, .28 with assassinations, and .15 with revolutions.[29]

In spite of the widely held view that nations experiencing domestic instability will have more foreign conflict than others, the empirical findings imply otherwise. Rather, the situation seems to be that *domestic instability has little relation to a nation's foreign conflict behavior.*

Hypothesis 7.   The military capabilities of a nation are highly related to its foreign conflict behavior.

28. In his massive work, Pitirim Sorokin (1937) plotted revolutions and war against each other across the centuries. He found little relationship between the two longitudinally.

29. As reported in Michael Haas (1964, p. 21, n. 67) on the basis of a letter from Cattell, Haas found that internal stress and war over time were related—a relationship magnified for agrarian and industrializing societies, and mitigated for industrialized ones.

An often-held belief is that armaments lead to foreign conflict. One way of indexing armaments and testing this assertion is in terms of defense expenditures and military personnel. Table 1 gives the correlation of these two variables (numbered 60 and 64, respectively) with foreign conflict behavior. As can be seen from the table, they have a number of correlations between .30 and .55, indicating a certain amount of relationship with general foreign conflict behavior.

This relationship can be seen in better perspective, however, when these military capabilities variables and conflict measures are included in a factor analysis with a number of other variables whose interactions might be accounting for the correlations. In the DON 230 variable factor analysis the capability variables were mainly related to the aforementioned power dimension—a correlation of .83 for defense expenditures and .73 for military personnel. Both their correlations with the foreign conflict behavior dimension, which it will be recalled was independent of the power dimension, was .32. In other words, "armaments" has about 10 per cent of its variation in common with foreign conflict behavior, 1955–1957. This is hardly a great amount, considering the causative weight often given to armaments.

Rather than defining armaments as absolute total defense expenditures and military personnel, one might operationalize the concept in relative terms as the ratio of defense expenditures to government expenditures and ratio of military personnel to population. These variables (number 61 and 62, respectively) are given in Table 1 and were included in the 230 variable analysis. The result was that the ratio of defense expenditures to government expenditures had a higher correlation, .47, with the foreign conflict behavior dimension than with any of the other fourteen dimensions, while the ratio of military personnel to population had its second highest correlation, .39, with the dimension.

The generality of this finding is qualified, however, when other studies are considered. Cattell included the same ratios in his 1949 study on 1927–1937 data, but for him, the ratios loaded on factors different from the one with which war and foreign clashes variables were highly related. The latter factor for the oblique rotation, moreover, had very low correlations (cosines) with the factors (−.10 and .06) upon which were loaded the defense expenditure and military personnel ratios. This finding is qualified considerably, however, by these relationships being between 1837–1937 conflict data and 1927–1937 data on the ratios. The 1962 study, however, included data for the 1950's on the defense expenditure ratio, homicides and war deaths, and foreign clashes, with results that confirm the 1949 findings. The defense ratio loaded highly on a separate factor. The correlation with the conflict factor was also a low −.02.

Another study is that of Lewis Richardson (1960a). In the first chapters of his analysis he explicitly tested the hypothesis of concern here, that the extent to which a country was prepared for war would help keep it out of war or, if involved in war, would reduce its losses. To test this, he correlated the pre-war defense expenditures per capita of twenty-one nations involved in World War I with their war losses per capita. His correlation was .15 when empires were considered as wholes, and .23 when empires were represented by their metropolitan centers—a finding of very little relationship. Unfortunately, his design tests more the degree to which armaments keep down war losses than the relationship between armaments and getting involved in a war. To test the latter he should have used all nations, or a random sample of them, whether involved in war or not.

On the basis of the above studies, then, the score card shows a finding of a small, but not negligible, relationship in the DON analysis between the ratio of military capabilities and foreign conflict behavior, and a finding of a *lack* of relationship in the Cattell (1949), Cattell, *et al.* (1965), and Richardson studies. The 1949 and Richardson studies bear considerable qualification, however, as pointed out above.

Considering the empirical findings when armament is defined absolutely or as a ratio, the general but not unambiguous finding is negative.[30] The ambiguity is between a small, say 20 per cent, relationship and none at all, and not between a high versus low relationship. The evidence unambiguously points to the latter alternative—*that the military capabilities of a nation have little relationship to its foreign conflict behavior.*

> *Hypothesis 8. The psychological motivations of a nation's people are highly related to its foreign conflict behavior.*

David McClelland in his pioneering study, *The Achieving Society* (1961), developed four measures of psychological motivation: achievement desire, desire for affiliation with others, desire for power, and other-directedness. He collected data on these measures for a large number of nations through a content analysis of children's readers. These data were published in his book and subsequently included in the DON 230 variable analysis; the measures are numbered 132–135 in Table 1. Their general lack of correlation with the conflict data can be seen from the Table, a lack of relationship which held up in the 230 variable factor analysis. Their correlations with the foreign conflict behavior factor were .25, .27, −.23, and −.01, respectively. The highest percentage of variation in common with the dimension was that for achievement desire, 7.3 per cent—not very high.[31] It might be concluded, therefore, with reference to the indices used here, that *psychological motivation has little relationship to a nations' foreign conflict behavior.*

> *Hypothesis 9. The values of a nation are highly related to its foreign conflict behavior.*

A number of value indices were included in the DON 230 variable analysis. In Table 1 they are numbered 120–131. Other variables not explicitly included under the value domain might be considered as highly value laden, such as variables 3 (traditionalism), 173 (internationalism), and 198, 200, 207, and 208 (ideology). As can be seen from the Table, their correlations with conflict behavior are all very low. This lack of relationship was emphasized when all 230 variables were factored. The result was that the value measures had practically no relationship to the foreign conflict behavior dimension.

The by-now-familiar 1949 and 1965 studies of Cattell and associates likewise

---

30. Some theoretical studies using empirical data have considered the reciprocal effects of defense expenditure ratios on increasing or decreasing the movement towards war. See, for example, Richardson (1960a, Chaps. 2 and 3) and Smoker (1963a, 1963b). These findings are of a high relationship or "locking in" (to borrow a very expressive idea from Anatol Rapoport) of the defense ratios of nations in a conflict situation. These results are not relevant to the hypothesis being considered here, where the concern is with the total foreign conflict behavior of a nation against *all* others.

31. Compare this finding with the often-expressed view that nations are involved in foreign conflict because of a "national drive for power."

have a number of value-type measures. The ones included in both analyses were the four ratios of Protestants, Mohammedans, Catholics, and Buddhists to population. Those included separately in the 1949 study were measures of religion or civil sanction to marriage, extent of legalization and practice of sterilization of the eugenically unfit, minimum legal marriage age, freedom from restriction on divorce, prostitution licensed as opposed to being forbidden, and extent of polygamy in marriage customs.[32] The result of the 1949 factor analysis was that *not one* of these value-type measures loaded on a factor with wars and foreign political clashes. The highest correlation that the oblique factors loading the value measures had with the "conflict" dimension was − .25.

Turning to the 1965 study, it included, in addition to the religion ratios, concern over traffic in persons and prostitutes, use of forced labor, ratio of illegitimate births, number of religious books, and number of scientific books. Of these variables, the ratio of illegitimate births was the only one loading (− .36) on the same factor with foreign clashes (.56), and even that loading was relatively low. The highest correlations of the factor with clashes on it with other factors containing value measures were − .38, − .35, and − .39.

The hypothesis about values hardly finds much confirmation from the above three analyses. Rather, *it seems that the values of a nation have little relationship to its foreign conflict behavior.*

> *Hypothesis 10. The number of borders of a nation are highly related to its foreign conflict behavior.*

A variable included in the 230 variable factor analysis was the number of territorial borders of a nation. It is variable 209 in Table 1. The highest correlation it has with any of the conflict behavior variables is .32 with accusations. Its loading on the foreign conflict behavior factor is .21, or a variation of 4.4 per cent in common with conflict.

This is a much different finding than that of Richardson (1960a, Chap. 5, Sec. 4). He correlated the number of borders of thirty-three nations with their number of wars, 1825–1946, and found a correlation of .77, or more than 59 per cent of their variation in common—the first truly good empirical evidence for any of the hypotheses discussed so far!

Why is there a difference between the two findings, one with respect to foreign conflict behavior including wars, 1955–1957, and the other for wars, 1825–1946? One possible explanation is that conflict behavior in the short run is unrepresentative of such behavior in the long run. This hardly holds up under inspection, however, for when one correlates wars and wars plus military actions, 1955–1957, with Richardson's number of wars, 1825–1946, the correlation turns out to be .87 and .81, respectively. Another possibility is that the number of borders has changed over time, while the frequency of involvement in foreign conflict has remained almost the same. The borders for most of the countries included in Richardson's study, however, such as Colombia, Mexico, France, Spain, Denmark, Sweden, and Portugal, have remained very much the same. Consequently, the difference in findings may be due to the inclusion of forty-four more nations in the DON analysis than Richardson's study. The greater generality, therefore, of the DON

---

32. The fact that one can include such qualitative measures in a factor analysis should be pointed out to those who insist on a quantitative-qualitative dichotomy in political-sociological research.

results should be given weight in assessing the different findings. Nonetheless, the different results should not be completely explained away in terms of sample size, but rather should be further investigated in future empirical studies.

In the meantime, the hypothesis should be considered neither confirmed nor disproved, since *the evidence is ambiguous as to there being a relationship between the number of a nation's borders and its foreign conflict behavior.*

> *Hypothesis 11. The interaction of combinations of characteristics of a nation, such as economic development, instability, and totalitarianism, is highly related to its conflict behavior.*

Before discussing this hypothesis, two methodological facets of factor analysis should be noted. First, as mentioned above, the variables that come out highly correlated with the same factor do so by virtue of having variation in common *after* the linear effects of other variables have been partialled out. The way this is done mathematically is by calculating a first factor that accounts for as much of the variation among the variables in a correlation matrix as possible. The variation accounted for by this factor is then subtracted out of the correlation matrix (partialled out) and a subsequent factor calculated. Then its variation is subtracted out, and so forth, until the only variation remaining in the correlation matrix can be ascribed to error. The result is that variables appearing on a common factor do so after effects of variables appearing on previous factors have been removed. An example might illustrate this process. Race could obscure a relationship between income, education, and residence, such that the intercorrelations among these variables might be low. When these variables are included in a factor analysis with other socioeconomic variables and a variable defining race, a racial factor would probably appear.[33] With the variation due to this racial factor removed from the correlation matrix, the interrelations between income, education, and residence, should stand out clearly.

A second facet of factor analysis is that although the factor model involves the linear combination of factors,[34] the factors themselves may involve highly complex relations. Thus, the economic development factor, for example, might involve a complicated polynomial relationship among the economic variables, even though the factor itself is only linearly related to each variable.[35] Moreover, if the variation of nations on a variable is due to a complex relationship among several factors, then this variable will have loadings or correlations on these factors. For example, if the variation in membership in international governmental organizations (IGO) is due to their economic development (E), their power (P), and degree of totalitarianism (T), such that

$$\text{IGO Membership} = \alpha \frac{E^2 P}{T}$$

---

33. One did appear, as a matter of fact, in a factor analysis of American states by Hofstaetter (1951).

34 The factor model is

$$\vec{X}_j = \alpha_{j1}\vec{F}_1 + \alpha_{j2}\vec{F}_2 + \ldots + \alpha_{jK}\vec{F}_K + \alpha_{jU}\vec{F}_U \quad ,$$

where $\vec{X}_j$, the variable, is the jth column vector of the data matrix; the coefficients, α, are the loadings of the variable, X_j, on the factor; $\vec{F}$ is a column vector of factor scores; and $\vec{F}^U$ is a unique factor specific to $\vec{X}_j$.

35. This point is discussed at length in "The Factor Model," in Rummel (1966).

or any other complex function, then IGO should have a high correlation with each of these factors, and not just one of them.[36]

These facets of factor analysis allow us to discuss the hypothesis in terms of the DON analysis and the 1949 and 1965 studies of Cattell, Cattell and Gorsuch. In all three factor analyses, variables were included which would index almost all the hypotheses considered in this paper in matrices of 230, 72, and 51 variables. Yet, in spite of the partialling out of the linear effects of other variables through the factoring process, these variables indexing the hypothesis did not generally come out separately or together in common on a factor with the foreign conflict variables. Moreover, if linear combinations of these variables were strongly related to conflict[37] behavior, they should come out on the same factor with conflict, which does not happen in any one of the three studies.

What about a non-linear complex relationship among the factors underlying conflict behavior? Since factors such as economic development, size, power, totalitarianism, and domestic instability emerged in the three studies,[38] this question can be answered negatively. In the three studies, the conflict behavior variables had very low, if at all different from zero, loadings on these factors.

What all the foregoing indicates, in terms of the hypothesis considered, then, is that *the hypothesized correlates of foreign conflict behavior acting singly or in combination or with the effects of other variables controlled are little related to a nation's foreign conflict behavior.*

DISCUSSION

The findings have been almost entirely negative for the nations and time periods covered. This should not lead to despair, however, since science advances through proposing hypotheses and theories and falsifying them. One should not stop at falsification, nonetheless, but should try to answer such questions as "Why the negative findings?" and "Where do we go from here?"

All the hypotheses have been concerned with relating a nation's position on a dimension of the attribute system to its *magnitude* along a conflict dimension of the behavioral system. As far as conflict is concerned, the evidence suggests that magnitudes within the two systems are not highly related. In other words, the characteristics of a nation are not highly predictive of the intensity of its involvement in foreign conflict.

I would suggest that the lack of correlation is due to the initial question which framed the relationship as one between magnitudes in the two systems. This is

---

36. See Thurstone's box problem (1947, pp. 140 ff. and *passim*). The three factors he delineates for a sample of boxes are height (z), width (y), and length (x). Note that variables which are functions of these factors, such as $\sqrt{x^2 + y^2 + z^2}$ load highly on all three factors. Those which are only functions of two of them, such as the function xy, load only on x and y factors.

37. In the regression sense, that is, $\vec{Y} = \alpha_0 + \alpha_1\vec{X_1} + \alpha_2\vec{X_2} + \ldots + \alpha_n\vec{X_n} + \vec{X_U}$ where vector $\vec{Y}$ is a foreign conflict variable and the $\vec{X}$'s are the hypothetical correlates of conflict behavior. The vector, $\vec{X_U}$, are the residuals. The assumption here is that the regression weights would all be significant.

38. They were labeled differently in the 1949 and 1965 studies, however. Part of the publication of the 230 variable analysis (Rummel, Sawyer, Guetzkow, and Tanter, 1967) results will be devoted to systematically comparing the factors of the different studies.

the same as saying that the total behavior of an individual in a social group is highly related to his personality characteristics. Place an individual in different groups and his behavior will shift as a function of his personality differences with members of the group. That is, relative *distances* on personality dimensions between individuals influence behavior more than the actual characteristics themselves.

Likewise, for nations it is social, economic, political, and geographic *distances*[39] that influence international behavior. Differences in technological levels, values, power, and perception of the international order relate to the "moves" that nations direct toward each other. The crucial concepts within the two systems deal not with magnitudes, but with *distance* between nations in the attribute system[40] and *directed* behavior between nations in the behavioral system. What should be measured in the latter system is not the location of a particular nation on the conflict behavior dimension, but rather the position of a *pair* of nations (dyad) on this dimension in terms of their behavior toward each other.

The behavioral system of nations should then be conceived of as a space of dyads who have a location in the system defined in part by cooperation and conflict dimensions. The attribute system is then connected to the behavioral system by the distances between nations on the attribute dimensions. Within this theoretical framework, which I call a social field theory, one might posit that the position of a dyad along the conflict dimension is a function of the distance between the two nations on value, economic development, power, and geographic dimensions. While some empirical evidence exists,[41] the explicit empirical test of this theory, however, will have to be the focus of another paper.[42]

39. See Wright (1942, Chap. 35). Note particularly Wright (1942, p. 1282, n. 66, n. 67) which is the first explicit theoretical use of the concept of distance. Two streams of thought, the *theoretical*, represented by Wright, and the *mathematical*, represented by developments in factor analysis and computer technology, can now be married in terms of distances between nations in multidimensional space.

40. The concept of "distance" is operationalizable in terms of the space spanned by the attribute dimensions. The technical aspects with examples are given in Rummel (1967).

41. See Pool (1951), Russett (1963), Richardson (1960a), Smoker (1963a, 1963b), North, *et al.* (1963), and Zinnes (1963).

42. The full theory is developed in Rummel (1965). Application of the theory is made to domestic conflict behavior rather than foreign.

Michael Haas

Social Change and National Aggressiveness, 1900–1960[1]

INTRODUCTION

In international systems, unit actors, whether empires, city-states, or nation-states, articulate goals based on such general considerations as "the national interest." Resources within countries usually are too limited to provide sufficient prosperity, security, and prestige, so in order to secure these aims, states make demands in the international political arena. When a country's articulated policy is accepted by others, it may be called a "rule" of interstate behavior. The scope of such rules varies from bilateral treaties or informal understandings to multilateral arrangements and customs. But world resources are also finite, so objectives of one actor often conflict with those of other actors.

Non-resolution of conflict is probably more frequent than its resolution in international systems. Non-resolution occurs when conflicting goals are suppressed, become obsolete, are withdrawn, or are not settled because their attainment can be postponed (Koch, North, and Zinnes, 1960; Wright, 1951). To resolve incompatibilities in articulated demands means to adopt common rules governing state behavior. Conflict is handled by applying one or more techniques of statecraft—diplomatic, psychological, and economic, or subversion and sabotage, and military means (see Sprout and Sprout, 1962). Were cost the main

1. The author gratefully acknowledges the assistance of Richard Carter, Heinz Eulau, Robert North, and Wilbur Schramm in their guidance of an earlier effort (Haas, 1964) from which this paper is derived. The study was financed by a Ford Foundation grant administered by the Stanford Studies on International Conflict and Integration and by NSF Grant 6P948 administered by the Stanford Computation Center. Helpful suggestions regarding this condensation were made by Karl Deutsch and J. David Singer; for support in its preparation, I am indebted to the Office of Research Administration, University of Hawaii.

criterion in selecting foreign policy techniques, nonviolent and verbal methods would be preferred to violent and physical conflict resolution. Nevertheless, a significant problem in the study of international relations is to ascertain conditions under which the latter are selected. Specifically: Why do some decision makers employ military means more than others? Why do states go to war when they do instead of at other times? Factors that account for international aggression and preparation for war need to be determined.

APPROACHES TO THE STUDY OF WAR

The classical explanation in nineteenth-century sociological theory for the use of the military tool of statecraft has not been completely adequate. Such thinkers as Auguste Comte and Herbert Spencer believed that military conquests characterize poor, agrarian societies, whereas industrializing countries desire stable international systems in order to achieve enrichment more efficiently through economic production (Silberner, 1946). However, Richardson (1960b) demonstrates that while wars have increased greatly in destructiveness since 1820, their frequency per unit time has not declined significantly. The spectacular industrial progress of the last two centuries, though related to the magnitude of war damage, appears to be noncorrelated with frequency of outbreak of war.

Why has international aggression continued? Speculation on the subject is conducted on three levels of analysis—the individual, the international, and the societal (Waltz, 1959; Singer, 1961b). The approach that centers on *man* breaks down into a focus on rationality (calculation) or irrationality (emotion) (North, 1962a). The international *system* approach claims that so long as legitimized order does not exist in the world polity, war and the threat of war remain as relatively unambiguous means for powerful states to obtain acceptance of their articulated goals. The *societal*[2] approach links cultural and social characteristics of states with propensities for warfare; its interests are in war as a tool of internal state-craft and on the societal preconditions to international aggression. In support of the three approaches, empirical research has been scanty, non-cumulative, and often difficult to interpret.

Two studies using the individual as the unit of analysis are not consistent. According to Abel (1941), rational calculation is observed prior to twenty-five major wars, including World War I, with no evidence of emotional tensions or irrational motives. But Robert North and his associates find that Austrian decision makers, humiliated by the assassination of Archduke Ferdinand in 1914, triggered World War I despite their knowledge of the inferior military strength of the Central Powers (Zinnes, North, and Koch, 1961; Holsti and North, 1965).

Because war is a symptom of an unstable international system, recent systemic analyses are relevant to the second approach to the study of war. For Kaplan (1957) stability is related to the extent of integration of units, so stability is insured by arrangements that establish cross-cutting role functions among

2. A *social* characteristic is a property of an interpersonal, interactional system; a *societal* characteristic is an aggregate feature of a larger system composed of many social groups within a fixed territorial boundary, usually a nation-state. A *systemic* property is a characteristic of a whole system, whereas a societal characteristic is the sum of its parts (English and English, 1958, pp. 506–507, 510, 540).

international actors. The most unstable system is the unit-veto system, followed in descending order by the bipolar and balance-of-power systems, to the more stable universal and hierarchical systems. In a detailed history analysis by Rosecrance (1963), systemic instability is associated with intense ideological cleavages, periods of military preponderance of one or more states, and a scarcity of unappropriated environmental resources.[3] Bipolar systems are unstable, according to his analysis; one type of multipolar system is stable, two unstable; and a unipolar and tripolar system are stable. Both Kaplan and Rosecrance, however, are criticized on various grounds in an article by Waltz (1964), who finds much stability in bipolarity.

Studies of relations between societal factors and international aggression lack consistency and precision in treatment of individual variables. One form of analysis, dealing with consequences of war, may be called the *functional* approach. The use of war by an elite to solidify its rule has been acknowledged by many observers. But non-elites also can profit from wartime disruption to seize power, so the functional societal approach to war does not lead very far.

In the *prerequisites* approach, societal conditions that must be present before a state will be tempted to embark upon war are isolated. More attention has been given to social conflict than to other societal conditions, such as stress and strain. In two longitudinal studies, "internal disturbances" cluster more often immediately before, during, and after periods of war than in peaceful eras (Lee, 1931; Sorokin, 1937). Recent factor analyses reveal that indicators of internationally aggressive behavior are independent of such examples of internal conflict behavior as revolutions and major governmental crises (Cattell, 1949; Rummel, 1963; Tanter, 1964).[4] The findings might be reconcilable, inasmuch as they use different kinds of analysis and refer to different sets of countries and time periods. But there could be a third factor or set of factors that underlie both war and revolution. Since stress and strain are more fundamental features of systems than conflict,[5] their analysis would seem profitable. However, there has been no systematic study of the relation between the use of the military tool of state-craft and societal stress and strain.[6] The purpose of the present study is to fill in this research gap.

STATEMENT OF THE PROBLEM

The first step in an analysis of the relation between variables is to define the terms in light of a theoretical framework or conceptual scheme. The second step is to operationalize key concepts by choosing valid indicators. Types of data and the ways in which they are to be manipulated are specified, justified, and the investigation proceeds. Findings are used to check the theoretical springboard.

3. Rosecrance also mentions a non-systemic factor, insecurity of tenure of the national elite, as a fourth factor associated with instability of international systems.

4. "Riots" appears on the same dimension with "war" and "foreign clashes" in two studies (Cattell, 1949; Chadwick, 1963), but in reanalyses "riots" drops out (Cattell, Bruel, and Hartman, 1951; Rummel, 1963).

5. Formal definitions of "stress" and "strain" are presented below.

6. The only such study is qualitative and impressionistic (Durbin and Bowlby, 1939). For studies on effects of stress and strain in individuals on their social behavior, another inter-systemic question, see Dollard, *et al.* (1939) and Grinker and Spiegel (1963).

Relevant Theory

If the dependent variable is a particular type of internation conflict resolution, and the independent variable is a set of societal factors, system theory is an appropriate broad-gauge context within which the present study falls. Is there a relation between two systemic levels, such as the national and the international? Are domestic societal characteristics predictors of international activity? Do states' foreign policies reflect social and cultural conditions within borders? If so, the organic conception of society (Cooley, 1927; Spiegel, 1959), assumed by the classical sociologists who postulated a connection between war and industrial growth, would be sustained: the societal system would be demonstrated to influence the international. If, on the other hand, the two systemic levels turn out to be unrelated, one could say that the course of foreign affairs has a high degree of systemic autonomy, wherein decision-making elites are detached from domestic politics and can independently calculate and execute strategies that commit their countries internationally. The latter view is held, for example, by those who argue that foreign-policy-making is inherently undemocratic (Lerche, 1959, pp. 45–46; Lippmann, 1943).

From the standpoint of structural-functional theory, the research problem could be stated in a different manner. If there is a coherent world polity, then the functions of articulation, aggregation, socialization, recruitment, transaction, rule-making, rule-applying, and rule-supervising are performed by the actors within the international arena (Almond, 1960; Haas, 1965a). If one actor employs military means of conflict resolution, then he is attempting to impose his proposed (articulated) interests onto other actors as rules of international behavior. Domestic stress and strain, meanwhile, are factors in internal socialization of international decision makers. When participation in international affairs by decision makers is a learning experience, external socialization takes place. If their socialization is largely intra-national, only domestic social norms, belief systems, and attitudes applied in domestic politics are transferred to the international level; external socialization predominates when decision makers consider only factors located outside their borders. If certain societal conditions were highly and positively related to the use of military means, it would be consistent to say that intra-national socialization guides attempt to make rules violently in international politics; low correlations would indicate that international experiences may be dominant in the socialization of foreign policy decision makers.[7]

---

7. More concretely, if urbanization is highly correlated with war frequency, then urban pressures doubtless are *more* influential than rural pressures in foreign policy making. Both urban and rural factors still might account for a considerable portion of elite behavior, however, so a more precise set of indicators of these pressures would be needed to determine the *extent* to which each separately accounts for a state's international behavior. If correlations are consistently near zero for all sorts of domestic factors, then domestic socialization is unimportant. To be complete, a test of types of pressures from international systems on foreign policy elites would be needed, though one would suspect that international and intranational considerations might tend to displace each other, except under two conditions. The first condition is that elite behavior is random, which is certainly unlikely. The second is that domestic pressures and foreign constraints dictate the same policies, in which case a constant would equally boost both inter-national and intra-national correlations with behavior in foreign affairs.

Definition of Terms

The meaning of the dependent variable, *use of military tool of statecraft*, is fairly clear. Examples of instruments of physical coercion employed by agents of a state include arms buildups, preparations for war, troop movements, and mobilizations, as well as overt combat between military forces.

The distinction between "stress" and "strain" is more subtle. *Stress* refers to "a force, applied to a system, sufficient to cause strain or distortion in the system, or when very great, to alter it into a new form" (English and English, 1958, p. 529). *Strain*, or systemic malintegration, exists in a system whose parts are out of phase with each other, or move in opposite directions. To illustrate the two concepts, an example may be taken from physics: when a weight is placed on top of a spring, the weight is the external source of stress, and the strain is the effect on the spring, which is contracting to carry the new load while expanding toward its former length (Horvath, 1959, p. 203). The terms may be clarified by pointing out typical behavioral responses to stress and strain. Stress leads to individual anxiety, tension, and paralysis; societally it leads to an overload or jamming in institutionalized and informal mechanisms of adjusting to the environment. Social mobilization, a concept developed by Deutsch (1953, 1961), is in part a process of developing effective mechanisms for coping with stress throughout society. When some of these newer devices demand contradictory role orientations, or when they fail to operate because older processes have not been terminated, strain emerges. In the United States, for example, the reward of social mobility is one of the newer techniques of industrialization, designed to encourage enterprising persons to take short-term risks for long-term benefits which may accrue when the process of economic modernization is accelerated. The upper strata of society, however, monopolize wealth and control admission to their social status; the reward of upward mobility, consequently, is unattainable for most persons. The objective of increasing one's socioeconomic position remains highly valued, while there is a restriction on access to means to that end (Merton, 1957). Strain situations of this type can be endured, if one is prepared to strive toward socially unattainable but culturally desirable goals in a philosophic manner; yet many individuals find that their attachment either to ends or means is so great that they prefer to engage in behavior deviating from cultural norms. Examples of deviance include drug and alcohol addiction, criminal activity, hypochondria and mental illness, self-mutilation and suicide, strikes, riots, demonstrations, and revolutions. If national aggressiveness is related to societal strain, then one would expect rates of deviance to be on the upswing as a decision to go to war is made by a state's decision makers.

DATA COLLECTION

A major problem of method in international relations research dealing with such large aggregate units as nation-states is sample selection. The countries and years must be so chosen that results are generalizable to the entire international system. Possible indicators also must be evaluated with respect to standard criteria of measuring instruments. Finally, the appropriate statistical techniques need to be specified and justified.

Sample Selection

A proposition about internal influences on external behavior of states is universal in scope, so a lengthy time span is desirable. Aggregate data before 1900 are quite scarce and unreliable, and current figures take about two years to be compiled and published. The years studied herein, accordingly, fall between 1900 and 1960.

The sample should be restricted further to countries with complete reliable statistics. Another consideration is to prevent artificial homogenization of results by avoiding contiguous countries, just as survey researchers are instructed to skip at least one house between interviews in a residential district. Finally, only sovereign states, with control over their own foreign affairs, are included.

The countries chosen are Australia, Finland (after 1918), France, Germany (now West Germany), Great Britain (excluding Ireland), Japan (home islands), Norway, Spain, Switzerland, and the United States. Spain, France, Germany, and Switzerland are contiguous, though the Alps and Pyrenees serve as barriers reducing the element of propinquity. Industrialized and Western states are overrepresented, a factor to be taken into account in making inferences from the findings.

Evaluation of Data

The procedure in selecting indices is to appraise them in terms of such criteria as availability, sensitivity, reliability, comparability, and validity. All of the proposed indicators are available and sensitive: they are located in standard statistical yearbooks,[8] and they vary sufficiently over time to permit fine discrimination in the cases analyzed. Such sources provide much reliability and comparability,[9] though they doubtless suffer from some underreporting.

Demonstration of the validity criterion involves more elaborate discussion, so its definition is in order. _Validity_ exists when an indicator in fact taps the dimension which one desires to measure (theoretical validity) and is highly correlated with another close but independent index (empirical validity) (English and English, 1958, p. 575). Each indicator is assessed in terms of the validity criterion in the following three sections.

Validation of Stress Indicators

Because index construction is itself a sampling problem, the specification of universes of possible indicators for each independent and dependent variable comes first. An exhaustive, mutually exclusive categorization of types of stress, therefore, precedes the discussion of indicators.

8. The main sources are the statistical yearbooks of the League of Nations (1930–1940) and the United Nations (1948–1962a, 1948–1962b). National statistical yearbooks and more limited international collections were also consulted. Machine computations were performed on the IBM 7090 from two BALGOL programs taking missing data into account.

9. For an extended discussion of the reliability and comparability of each indicator used in this study, see Haas (1964).

Stress sources may be classified into two groups—foreign and domestic. Foreign stress comes from outside a society; domestic stress is internal to the country, present due to an imperfect linkage of one sub-system with another. A study of the effect of systemic properties of international systems on foreign policy would consider external stress sources. Because the present inquiry focuses on societal factors only, indicators are needed for domestic stress sources. The two measures chosen are unemployment and rate of industrialization. Both represent stress sources within societal systems that start in the economic sub-system and spill over into the social sub-system.

Unemployment percentages usually are computed by taking the mean of twelve monthly figures reporting the percentage of the total work force out of a job and seeking employment. Such figures are most accurate where labor force sample surveys are conducted, as in Finland, Japan, and the United States today (International Labor Office, 1960, pp. 178–179; Russett, *et al.*, 1964, pp. 187–188). The reliability of figures elsewhere is a function of the extent to which those looking for work report to offices which collect labor statistics. "Labor force" definitions also vary widely. Unemployment insurance office statistics, nearly as reliable as survey data, are the source for most other countries in the present sample, though only the less representative figures of trade unions are available for France, Great Britain, and Norway before 1918.

Rate of industrialization is computed by taking yearly increments in per-capita kwh productions of electricity. Large increments in electricity measure growth in production of economic goods and in the capacity to produce "modern material culture." Electricity statistics are regarded generally as very reliable and comparable (D. McClelland, 1961).

To validate the two indices of stress, it is necessary to know that they are societally disorganizing and that they are antecedent conditions of some examples of deviant behavior. Unemployment is economically painful to society insofar as production and distribution of necessities is endangered; it indicates both distress of the economy and of individual breadwinners. Unemployment challenges the system's ability to effect readjustment. When economic collapse persists, social conflict can sharpen into revolutionary behavior (Brinton, 1952; Davies, 1962). Those who are politically mobilized increasingly vote for extremist parties as unemployment mounts (Kornhauser, 1959, p. 161). The politically apathetic unemployed person withdraws from social activities; if removed from situations wherein social pressures against deviance normally operate, the individual out of work often resorts to alcoholism, promiscuity, or suicide (Bakke, 1940; Bloodworth, 1933; Eisenberg and Lazarsfeld, 1938; Komarovski, 1940; Zawadski and Lazarsfeld, 1935; Breed, 1963; Chodorkoff, 1961; Straus and Bacon, 1951).

The electricity production indicator measures the extent of technological change. If economic growth is too rapid to be absorbed within existing institutions, and members of large societies are not consulted individually concerning each decision to modernize,[10] they are unprepared for restructuring of social communication and for psychological adjustments appropriate to new role situations. Very rapid economic change typically produces intolerable social change, except in the so-called "mature" economies, where such change is more routinized. When men compare themselves unfavorably with former

10. For a case study of non-stressful rapid change in a small community, see Redfield (1950).

members of their same social stratum whose skills in various stages of industrialization are suddenly more valued, those feeling such deprivation tend to become
alienated. Deviant social behavior is an escape for those who cannot keep pace
with modernizing trends (Brutzkus, 1953; Cantril, 1958; Durkheim, 1951;
Einaudi, Domenach, and Garoschi, 1951; Kornhauser, 1959; McNeil, 1959).

Validation of Strain Indicators

Types of strain so differ from culture to culture that strain is studied more
systematically by means of a classification of orientations or responses to strain.
Of the two basic types of reactions, conformity and deviance, only the latter is of
interest; conformity is present where strain is absent or unperceived. Deviance
may be divided, adapting a scheme of Parsons (1959), into active (rebellious)
and passive (withdrawn) orientations on one axis, and into foci on social objects
(norms and institutions) or on persons on a second axis; four pure types are
derived thereby. According to the logic of the Parsonian framework, passive
personality types are expected to manifest escapism vis-à-vis social norms or
institutions and self-damaging tendencies vis-à-vis other persons, while active
types would tend to engage in conflict and assault, respectively.

Indicators are proposed for each type of deviance except rebelliousness with
respect to norms, because this constitutes social conflict behavior, which has been
excluded from the scope of this inquiry.[11] *Homicide* represents rebelliousness
directed at social targets; *suicide* is a passive orientation to strain directed at a
person; *alcoholism* is a withdrawal with respect to social norms.

Deaths from each cause are computed in a rate form—the total number
dead per hundred thousand of the population. Mortality statistics are reliable
to the extent that there is competent medical certification of causes of death.
Urbanized countries have more trustworthy figures than less socially mobilized
countries, where an individual's exposure to government bureaucracies is infrequent (Hauser and Duncan, 1959, p. 65). Very little, however, is known about
types of bias in mortality figures, and one can hardly be overly skeptical about
such statistics until these error sources have been analyzed more systematically
(Gibbs, 1961, p. 228). If only systematic error is involved, there is no serious
problem in drawing inferences in this study. If rural and Catholic countries,
for example, consistently underreport suicides, then yearly increases and decreases
in suicides still will reflect underlying social trends, though the magnitude of
the trends will be attenuated somewhat. With more accurate figures the finding
that fewer suicides occur in rural and Catholic countries (Durkheim, 1951)
would remain.

To validate these three indicators, we must show that they are inconsistent
with cultural norms and that they increase with heightened social stress. In
addition, their correspondence to the Parsonian classification needs to be
demonstrated.

Homicide, suicide, and alcoholism are disapproved in all the cultures of the
sample; in most, they are illegal. One of the three may be a culturally anticipated

---

11. The findings in two recent studies indicate that internationally conflictual behavior is
not strongly related to domestic social conflict (Rummel, 1963; Tanter, 1964). For a
reinterpretation of the two studies, see Haas (1965b).

reaction of a person trapped by role conflict, but the behavior still is perceived to be deviant.

Since the appearance in 1897 of Emile Durkheim's classic, *Suicide*, all three indicators have been treated as consequences of the inability of individuals to adjust to changing roles in eras of "breaches in the social equilibrium" (Durkheim, 1951, p. 47). In a recent study, the three are found to be forms of deviance which are present among alienated persons but absent among the nonalienated (Nettler, 1959).

Suicide and alcoholism are withdrawal responses of those living in the highly structured milieu of the city or the bureaucracy, but who reside in skid-row rooming houses, are declining in status, or are unmarried (Bailey, 1961; Breed, 1963; Cavan, 1928; Durkheim, 1951; Gillin, 1952; Gold, 1958; Harlan, 1950; Lottier, 1938; Popham and Schmidt, 1962; Porterfield, 1952, 1958; Schmid, 1926, 1933). Social controls are less visible and effective for persons in these categories, so their reactions to stress can deviate from cultural norms more easily.

If the source of anxiety is personalized, the inadequacy of a passive individual in dealing with others leads to self-doubt, and suicide is more probable than alcoholism. If rules of job situations are perceived as impersonal sources of frustration, the individual's attention is directed toward containing spontaneity in order to comply with social norms; as the attraction of an inhibition-free existence becomes more intense, the exhilarating effects of alcohol lead to overindulgence and compulsive drinking (Bacon, 1945; Chotlos and Deiter, 1959; Jones, 1963; Straus and Bacon, 1951).

Homicide is a more active and rebellious response to strain. Rural areas and slums of cities, where most homicides occur, are the least highly structured milieus of a society. If an individual in such a setting experiences frustration, the obvious panacea may appear to be the removal of the most immediately visible sources of stress: individuals are assaulted when social conditions are personalized, so homicide is felt to be a way of alleviating intolerable living conditions (Bell, 1953; Gillin, 1952; Masor, 1961).

Validation of Dependent Variable Indicators

Military tools of statecraft can be divided into violent and nonviolent categories. The most obvious technique is warfare, so *participation in war* is one indicator. An example of a nonviolent military tool is a preparation for war or a threat to go to war. Yearly *military expenditures*, as a percentage of total government expenditures, will serve as an index of levels of warlike preparations, or of the relative importance of military means to a state. "Participation in war" is measured in two ways. First of all, the *frequency of entry into international aggression* is counted for each country. Because findings could be completely reversed if applicable to victims of wars, rather than to initiators, an *aggressiveness* indicator is necessary. Accordingly, a deck of 3×5-inch cards was prepared, one for each instance in which one of the ten countries in the sample entered war in the twentieth century. Each card contained brief descriptions of events leading up to one country's decision to go to war, including pretexts for war, if any (Haas, 1964, App. D). Names of countries were masked by inserting names of states of the United States in order to prevent any bias on the part of scalers detecting situations involved. Eight West Coast experts on international relations were asked to scale the deck of cards, by putting each card in one of nine positions, from one, for "not very aggressive," to nine, for "very aggressive." Since the aim of the exercise was to discriminate between countries along an aggressiveness continuum, the eight ratings per card were summed and averaged for use in correlational computations.

The obvious problem in validating a military expenditures indicator is to deal with the problem of defensive preparations. Most decision makers, of course, claim to act in strictly defensive terms. The spiraling arms races of 1909–1914 and 1929–1939 have been analyzed in detail by Richardson (1960a): participants in the arms races before the world wars maintained much higher military expenditure levels than nonparticipants. There were two exceptions, nevertheless: before World War II Spain's army was needed internally, and Swiss militarization was an instance of successful deterrence (Table 1). Germany and Japan,

TABLE 1. *Military Expenditure Levels* (*in mean per cent of total yearly budgets during prewar periods*)

	Aggressors[a]	Nonaggressive Participants	Nonparticipants in War
1900–1918			
Range	33 − 51.6	28.8 − 53	19.8 − 30.6
Median	42.3	40.9	20.8
N^b	2	4	3
1919–1945			
Range	14.5 − 34.4	12.1 − 26.2	25.6 − 31.9
Median	24.5	20.9	28.8
N	2	6	2
1946–1960			
Range	23.4 − 30	18 − 55.6	5.8 − 36.7
Median	26.7	18.7	24.7
N	2	3	5

[a]An "aggressor" is considered to be a country whose entry into war was rated by scalers to be above 4.5 on the nine-point aggressiveness scale.

[b]The number of cases does not add up to 10 in this time period because Finland failed to achieve independence until 1917.

the two major modern aggressors, consistently had higher expenditure levels than less aggressive countries. Present military preparations are justified in terms of defense and deterrence, but it is perhaps no coincidence that France and Great Britain, aggressors in the 1956 Suez invasion, invest more governmental resources for military purposes than do Australia and Norway, supporters of the United Nations efforts in Korea. The United States spends more of its budget for military purposes because of its position as leader of the Western bloc in a bipolar world. The high level of arms expenditures reported in Table 1 among nonparticipants in war since 1946 may seem surprising. Two countries account

[handwritten marginalia: There are numerous other factors to account for this]

[handwritten note at bottom: not, of course, because we're aggressive.]

for this result: Spain and Switzerland continue to place high priority on army expenditures.

Another aspect of the military expenditures indicator is that, as war approaches, aggressors increase military expenditures at a faster pace than nonaggressors and nonparticipants. One illustration is the period before World War II (Table 2), when only Great Britain among the nonaggressors was increasing its military

TABLE 2. *Annual Increments in Percentages of Governmental Expenditures for Military Purposes Before World War II*

	1935–6	1936–7	1937–8	Agressiveness[b]
Axis Powers				
Germany[a]	6.1	10.2	7.8	7.9
Japan[a]	−0.4	12.5	6.6	8.1
Allied Powers				
Australia	0.8	1.5	3.8	2.6
France	−4.2	1.2	−1.4	2.9
Great Britain	5.8	8.2	11.1	2.9
United States	−0.1	1.3	3.1	4.5
Other Belligerents				
Finland	0.1	0.9	4.6	2.9
Norway	0.3	0.1	−1.7	1.0
Nonbelligerents				
Spain	0.9	1.8	—[c]	0.0
Switzerland	−1.6	1.8	2.1	0.0

[a]Expressed as a percentage of national income; all other figures are given in percentage of total budget.

[b]Figures in this column represent only the average rating of each country on the nine-point aggressiveness scale, from 1 for "not very aggressive" to 9 for "very aggressive." A score of 0 indicates a country which did not participate in World War II.

[c]No data available.

budget percentages to keep pace with Germany, the European country most consciously preparing for attack. Great Britain in the interwar period played the role of leader of the allied countries, much as the United States now heads the Western bloc, so the onus for significant defensive preparations then fell to the government in London.

DATA ANALYSIS

To prove that x is related to y, the correlation coefficient is the most useful descriptive device. Two types of linear correlations appear warranted by the data analyzed in the present study. In all three cases the purpose of the correlation coefficient is both to quantify the form of the relationship, whether direct or inverse, and the degree to which one variable is a predictor of the other, as interpreted from the magnitude of the correlation. The most precise of the correlational formulas is Pearson's product-moment correlation (r); it can be used when, within a single country, yearly values for two variables are distributed in a normal, bell-shaped distribution curve. If several countries are compared, and values for two variables are not normally distributed across the countries, Spearman's rank-difference correlation (rho) may be used if a mathematical transformation of the values into a normal distribution is not possible, though rho tends to yield lower correlation magnitudes than r (McNemar, 1955, p. 209.)

Interpretation of the correlation coefficient is a further problem. Statisticians in general suggest the use of significance tests only to measure the degree to which findings depart from chance levels within a random sample of a population. When a sample is not random, as in this inquiry, statistical significance figures indicate merely the degree to which correlations might remain stable were there a larger sample size. A standard significance test is available for rho; because underreporting of data used herein leads to attenuated correlations, the significance level of .10 is used undoubtedly in presenting results. For r, the measure r^2 is used to estimate the percentage of the variance in one variable which can be accounted for by the second variable. Social significance is more important than statistical significance, and the former will be inferred when results are consistent across all countries studied (Haas, 1962).

More specifically, within each country r is used to find relationships between all variables except the lone discrete indicator, "aggressiveness." The mean values of each country on each of the eight variables are used in rho correlations. Causation, hence, might be difficult to unravel with Pearsonian correlations. To determine whether the proposed independent variables might produce effects in the dependent variable, figures should be time-lagged for computing Pearsonian correlations. An assumption can be built into the research design that it takes a certain amount of time for the independent variables to make themselves felt in the system before changes in the dependent variables will show up. But how can one know how long such a process takes? Two considerations suggest a three-year time lag, whereby suicides of 1957, for example, are matched with military expenditures of 1960. First of all, product-moment correlations assume homoscedasticity, a condition which exists when arrays of two linearly related variables are concentrated, rather than dispersed. In drawing scatter diagrams of several possible time lags, it was discovered that the homoscedasticity assumption is met best for three-year time lags. Second, defense budgets usually appropriate some money which is to be spent several years later; indeed, the tendency to appropriate funds within the scope of long-range plans is a characteristic feature of modern budgeting (Mosher, 1954). Though it may be only a coincidence, it has been observed that both Australian (Schaffer, 1963, p. 238) and American (Huntington, 1961, p. 116) defense policy is reviewed triennially.

Over all correlations based on statistics of ten countries for a sixty-one-year period may be useful for a summary, but they have little theoretical import here. The empirical unit of analysis is the sovereign nation-state, so at least ten sets of correlation coefficients are desired—one per country. An inspection of fluctuations in each variable within a single state from 1900 to 1960, however, reveals clearly that there are about three eras when deviance rates vary around steady-state levels. These periods, 1900 to 1918, 1919 to 1945, and 1946 to 1960, are separated by major wars at the conclusion of which the international system, as well as the countries themselves, changed considerably. It seems reasonable, therefore, to trifurcate the sample timewise, yielding twenty-nine sub-samples.[12]

Correlations between all variables were computed on the IBM 7090. Product-moment correlations between suicides and homicides for the 1900–1914 period, for example, were computed separately within each of the sub-samples. To summarize overall findings, across all twenty-nine cases, the median *r* is reported below, since means with such a small sample might be more subject to distortions of a few cases than medians. In computing rho correlations entries for each country consisted of mean values on suicide and homicide during each time period. Statistics of war years are excluded, because the hypotheses being tested deal with origins of war.

DIMENSIONALITY

Another methodological problem is to determine whether indicators within each of the three categories—stress, strain, and use of military means—can be treated as homogeneous units. In a factor analysis of about eighty variables, including seven of the eight used herein, no two were located on the same dimension (Cattell, 1949). Results of an interchangeability check with the data used in this study reveal low intercorrelations, mostly below the .50 level, which indicates that less than 25 per cent of the variance in one variable is accounted for by another (Table 3).

TABLE 3. *Intercorrelations Among Variables* (*Median of all Pearsonian correlations to left of diagonal*; *rho correlations to right*; *N in parentheses*)

	1	2	3	4	5	6	7	8
STRESS								
1. Unemployment		.43 (15)						
2. Industrialization	−.28 (15)							
STRAIN								
3. Suicides				.15 (26)	.27 (26)			
4. Homicides			−.03 (26)		.38ₐ (24)			
5. Alcoholism Deaths			.34 (26)	.27 (24)				
MILITARY BEHAVIOR								
6. Expenditures							.40ᵃ (27)	.37 (14)
7. War Frequency								.21 (14)
8. War Aggressiveness								

ᵃSignificant at .10 level.

12. There would be thirty nation-eras in the sample were it not for the fact that Finland did not become independent until 1917.

The two indicators of stress are inversely related, and they account for about 25 per cent of each other's variance. Clearly, initial levels of industrialization affect this correlation. Advanced industrialized countries are capable of absorbing rapid economic progress without much of a corresponding upset in employment patterns. Unemployment levels were higher for the 1919–1945 period than for the 1946–1960 period, and industrialization has increased over time. The two measures will be treated hereafter as reciprocals, therefore.

The three forms of deviance are related to each other positively, but the only statistically significant correlation, between homicides and alcoholism, reveals that but 15 per cent of the variance in one variable can be attributed to variation in another (see Nettler, 1959; Rudin, 1963). It may be of interest to note that, in almost every country studied, suicides were more frequent than deaths due to alcoholism and homicides combined; the only exceptions were during revolutions and wartime, when homicides could be found as well on the battlefield (Table 4).

TABLE 4. *Rounded Mean Suicide, Homicide and Alcoholism Death Rates (per 100,000 population)*

Country	Time Period	Suicides	Homicides	Alcoholism
Australia	1906–1914	12.3	1.94	3.72
	1919–1939	11.7	1.61	1.61
	1946–1960	10.5	1.36	2.08
Finland[a]	1919–1939	17.3	7.33	1.70
	1946–1960	18.5	3.24	0.38
France	1900–1914	21.5	——[b]	——[b]
	1919–1939	18.8	1.81	2.20
	1946–1960	15.3	1.25	7.58
Germany	1900–1914	21.6	2.09	——[b]
	1919–1939	25.6	1.98	0.62
	1946–1960	19.2	0.97	0.27
Great Britain	1900–1914	9.5	0.84	5.34
	1919–1939	11.3	0.56	0.41
	1946–1960	10.4	0.59	0.12
Japan	1900–1914	18.0	——[b]	0.49
	1919–1937	20.6	0.65	0.59
	1955–1960	22.9	2.10	0.21
Norway	1906–1918	4.7	0.82	0.50
	1919–1940	6.2	0.73	0.33
	1946–1960	7.0	0.41	0.30
Spain	1900–1918	3.9	——[b]	1.71
	1919–1945	5.3	14.50	1.52
	1946–1960	8.6	1.33	0.91
Switzerland	1900–1918	22.4	2.25	5.40
	1919–1945	24.7	1.51	5.36
	1946–1960	22.0	0.95	3.23
United States	1900–1917	15.0	5.21	5.70
	1919–1941	13.8	8.15	3.76
	1946–1960	10.6	5.01	1.53

[a]Finland was not fully sovereign until 1917.
[b]No data available.

Finally, countries with high levels of military expenditures are involved often in war, and their involvement is more likely to be aggressive. The highest of the correlations permits one to predict only 16 per cent of the variance in one variable from a second variable. Thus the three measures tap somewhat different aspects of the warlike behavior concept.

In short, each set of indicators has theoretical and empirical validity. Each of the three sets of variables contains measures that represent several dimensions within each theoretical concept. Lacking a large number of indicators on each of the dimensions, there is of course no guarantee that a single indicator is not an erratic measure of the concept being operationalized.

With the restrictions of the study in mind, it is now possible to begin an analysis of results. Each limiting feature of the research design serves as a boundary condition in generalizing from the findings.

RESULTS

In reporting results, empirical findings are stated first, then interpreted. Stress is treated initially, then strain, and a framework containing both components is applied later to the analysis of military means of international conflict resolution. Broader-gauge implications are explored in the following section.

Stress

If stress is related to international military behavior, one would expect that unemployment would be high where arms expenditures, war participation, and aggressiveness are also high. Looking first at Spearman correlations, we find instead that unemployment is unrelated to military budgets, and countries with high unemployment are involved infrequently in war (Table 5). But since unemployment is correlated with *nonaggressive* war participation, two explanations are plausible. Either unemployment so weakens states that they are easy prey for aggressors, or such countries decide to support attacked allies as an escape from stress. The reason for no relationship between unemployment and

TABLE 5. *Correlations Between Stress and Military Behavior (Median of all Pearsonian correlations to left of diagonal; rho correlations to right; N in parentheses)*

	1	2	6	7	8
STRESS					
1. Unemployment			−.02	.33	−.64
			(18)	(16)	(9)
2. Industrialization			.17	−.32	.51
			(20)	(20)	(10)
MILITARY BEHAVIOR					
6. Expenditures	−.08	.17			
	(20)	(20)			
7. War Frequency					
8. War Aggressiveness					

military expenditures is that militarization is a means of providing more jobs to the unemployed.

For most countries, upswings in military expenditures are preceded by upswings in industrialization levels and by downswings in unemployment, according to product-moment correlation medians. The industrialization indicator behaves in an opposite manner, as expected.

Two independent types of foreign policy responses to economic stress appear, therefore, to be operating. There is an inverse relation between stress and militarization among countries that fight wars, but a direct relation for those not entering international aggression. Several interpretations could be made from these results. It would appear that once unemployment is a social problem, several distinct patterns of state behavior are possible:

1. Countries that do not successfully use mechanisms for coping with stress
   (a) soon enage in war (outlet theory), or
   (b) eventually can be attacked (disunity theory).
2. Countries that successfully use mechanisms for coping with stress
   (a) increase armaments and externalize aggression (arms race theory), or
   (b) restructure the economic system and use deterrence strategy (preoccupation theory).

These types are neither exhaustive nor completely mutually exclusive, but they do occur frequently.

In order to appreciate more fully the type of stimulus to which war is a response, it is useful to look at some specific representative cases. Turning first to those in which war served as an outlet to domestic crisis, there are three examples: Australia in 1914, Germany in 1914, and Japan in 1931. The key factor in interpreting these cases is, of course, the time lag between the year of a peak in unemployment and the year of war entry. If a country goes to war very soon after unemployment mounts, the aim may be to use international aggression as an outlet or safety valve. Countries with almost a zero time lag between a peak in unemployment and its decision to go to war are classified, therefore, as engaging in *outlet* wars. Of the cases so classified, each of the countries might have avoided war: Australia could have ignored the plight of attacked European countries; Germany did not have to send the "blank check" to Austria; Japanese military leaders attacked Manchuria without consulting leaders of the government.

Turning to the *disunity* category (United States in 1917, France in 1939, Norway in 1940, and United States again in 1941), it will be recalled that Norway and France suffered a long period of unresolved economic dislocation in the depression years, and they were in no condition to resist Hitler's invasion. The United States' entry into the two world wars is somewhat similar: it cut back military expenditures during periods of unemployment, and it was attacked in part because the aggressor regarded it as too weak or cowardly to fight back. The Germans in 1917 and the Japanese in 1941, we now know, miscalculated.

The *arms race* pattern (France and Britain in 1914; Japan in 1937; Australia, Germany, and Britain in 1939; and Britain again in 1956) is that of increasing armaments in order to decrease unemployment; however, when the increase is directed at another country in particular, it leads to a war in which the militarized countries share responsibility.

The *deterrence-preoccupation* situation (Norway, 1909–1918, 1949–1960,

Switzerland, 1909–1918, 1933–1944, and 1950–1960; Australia, 1948–1960; and United States, 1948–1950 and 1953–1960) is characterized by reduction of unemployment with militarization, but the country did not end up in war except in case of the most obvious self-defense. Switzerland is the clearest case of successful deterrence. The United States failed to deter in 1950, whereupon Australia, Norway, and other countries sent assistance.[13]

To some extent the finding that many countries fall into the last two categories may be an artifact of a small sample and of the propinquity of European states: economic depressions tend to be worldwide, and the Germans triggered an arms race, so seven of the ten sample countries in the 1930's followed suit by increasing defense measures, thus reducing unemployment. The alternative of slowly coping with economic crisis at home while ignoring sources of trouble abroad, was seriously entertained only by the United States, a country protected by the vast expanse of two oceans; Spain needed less military expenditures after its revolution was terminated; and Norway could not afford a military establishment. In other words, unemployment *can* be reduced without drastic military measures, and even some increases in defense expenditures do not lead to war in every case. Comparing twenty-two cases of countries where unemployment is dropping off, in only seven are military expenditures rising; in thirteen they hold steady, and in two cases they fall off. And whereas these expenditures rise or hold steady in five and seven cases respectively of eventual aggression, they only rise or hold steady in two and six cases respectively where war did not eventuate.

To conclude that there are several ideal-typical paths from stress to war or peace cannot be entirely satisfactory until each path is related to additional variables. Observation of trends in their frequency over time leads to some speculation on the nature of economic growth, social change, and international aggression. "Outlet" wars are most common in the earliest period, when industrialization is lowest, and "arms race" wars occur mainly in the interwar years. "Disunity" wars decrease over time, while "deterrence" situations increase. If these trends continue, the industrial growth of the twentieth century may bring an end to war as an immediate escape from internal difficulties. As economic systems were being brought under political control, it was possible to militarize as a means of providing new jobs for those economically dislocated; yet the tensions of a depression crisis and the desire for world supremacy on the part of the newest industrial powers, Germany and Japan, meant that the interwar arms race resulted in war. Currently the techniques of welfare economists make it possible to bypass war as a solution to the stress of unemployment. That economists today can effectively prevent and adjust economic difficulties is consistent with the absence of major wars in the third time period, though with correlations ranging from .02 to .64 it is clear that other factors are involved. Some of the additional factors may be related to strain.

Strain

If stress persists, the social environment becomes disorganized. Strain in the system exists when it is difficult for an individual to conform to rules of social

---

13. The Korean War is excluded from correlation computations, since assistance to the Republic of Korea was prescribed as a universalistic rule of interstate behavior by the United Nations; in other war situations aggression was more clearly a case of rule-breaking behavior.

behavior because they no longer seem to operate to his benefit. If strain is the major variable which sorts out resolvable stress from intolerable stress, it may be a useful concept in distinguishing countries that support military means to gain international ends from those that are more peaceful.

To check this initial hypothesis about intolerable stress, stress and strain variables are intercorrelated (Table 6). As expected, strain almost without

TABLE 6. *Correlations Between Stress and Strain Indicators (Median of all Pearsonian correlations to left of diagonal; rho correlations to right; N in parentheses)*

	1	2	3	4	5
STRESS					
1. Unemployment			.17	.28	.45[a]
			(20)	(17)	(18)
2. Industrialization			.21	−.22	−.34
			(20)	(17)	(18)
STRAIN					
3. Suicides	.50	−.11			
	(21)	(20)			
4. Homicides	.12	−.12			
	(20)	(20)			
5. Alcoholism Deaths	−.28	−.28			
	(17)	(19)			

[a]Significant at .10 level.

exception is related positively to unemployment and related negatively to in-dustrialization rate. There is some deviant behavior in non-stressful times, but much less than during times of high stress. The finding that the median product-moment correlation for all countries between alcoholism deaths and unemployment is −.28 appears to be an artifact of a small sample, since one of the two figures adjacent to the median is as distant as +.02. Stress, in short, means increased suicides or homicides; but, despite the fact that countries with many deaths from alcoholism are prone to the most serious economic crises, there is no consistent trend in alcoholism mortality associated with yearly rises and falls in unemployment levels. The damage done to the liver of chronic alcoholics does not produce death in the same year as crises due to unemployment.

If stress appears to produce strain, and stress also is positively correlated with the use of military techniques of statecraft, one might anticipate that strain could be a better predictor of warlike behavior than stress. Results in part bear out this expectation (Table 7). With one exception, to be considered below, high strain is associated with high magnitudes in military expenditures, high frequency of participation in war, and aggressiveness in the pursuit of wars. Considering only states that enter war, the findings are strengthened. Countries engaged in inter-national aggression have higher levels of suicides and more military expenditures

TABLE 7. *Correlations Between Strain and Military Behavior (Median of all Pearsonian correlations to left of diagonal; rho correlations to right; N in parentheses)*

	3	4	5	6	7	8
STRAIN						
3. Suicides				.18	.02	.47[a]
				(27)	(27)	(14)
4. Homicides				.05	−.11	.08
				(24)	(24)	(12)
5. Alcoholism Deaths				.51[a]	.14	.03
				(25)	(26)	(12)
MILITARY BEHAVIOR						
6. Expenditures	.29	−.20	−.18			
	(29)	(24)	(25)			
7. War Frequency						
8. War Aggressiveness						

[a]Significant at .10 level.

than countries that stay out of war, and the Pearsonian correlation between suicides and arms expenses has more homoscedasticity for cases in which countries enter wars. Deaths due to alcoholism, too, are highest where international military behavior is prevalent. Homicide is found to be higher where war aggressiveness and military expenditure levels are high, though the correlations are near zero; but homicides are inversely related to frequency of war participation, which is not expected.

Considering the Pearsonian correlations, the time-lagged effect of fluctuations in strain indicators on changes in military expenditures is positive for suicide, but negative for alcoholism and homicide: as suicides increase, military expenditures also go up, but societies with rising rates of alcoholism and homicide tend to cut back military preparations. The most likely explanation for this incongruity is to be found in a theory of societal mechanisms for coping with deviance. Suicide has few societally costly consequences, except to insurance companies; it is not handled preventively in a systematic manner. Alcoholism and homicide, on the other hand, may indicate the degree of lawlessness in a society, wherein ordinary informal deterrents on crime do not operate. Police authorities may receive a larger share of government budgets if they can point to mounting lawlessness, or the army may be assigned policing roles. Countries with large rural populations, where homicide is more prevalent than suicide or alcoholism, currently have armies playing just such "interventionist" roles in political systems (Banks and Textor, 1963). Because the maintenance of internal peace has a higher priority than external policies, military expenditures are reduced if the effects of increasing alcoholism and homicides are costly to remedy. When crime is brought under some degree of control, military expenditures can resume their climb; but if strain is not contained, revolution or invasion would appear to be possible.

Another way of approaching strain is to determine how quickly it appears to be reflected in warlike behavior. As with the discussion of stress, we may divide responses to strain into two categories, those where war breaks out when deviance rates suddenly undergo a dramatic upswing, and those where war occurs when increasing deviance already has reached a maximum and starts to decline. The former is the case of war as a means of tension *release*; the latter is called *mediated* strain, since some processes must have intervened before the outbreak of war to reduce violent forms of deviance (Table 8).

There appears to be little preponderance of one type of war in relation to deviant behavior. Compared to homicides, both alcoholism and suicides are somewhat more often on the decline when war breaks out. What is perhaps more

TABLE 8.   *Wars as Responses to Strain*

Type of Deviance	Type of War	Cases
Suicide	Release	Japan 1904
		Germany 1914
		Japan 1914
		Japan 1931
		Germany 1939
		Finland 1940
		Great Britain 1956
	Mediated	France 1914
		Great Britain 1914
		Australia 1914
		United States 1917
		France 1939
		Great Britain 1939
		Australia 1939
		United States 1941
Alcoholism	Release	France 1956
	Mediated	Great Britain 1914
		Japan 1937
		Finland 1940
		United States 1941
		Great Britain 1956
Homicide	Release	Germany 1914
		United States 1917
		France 1956
	Mediated	Germany 1939
		Great Britain 1939
		Finland 1940
		United States 1941

significant is that "release" wars are most common in earlier parts of the twentieth century, and "mediated" war situations characterize more recent times.

An expansion of the coping-mechanisms theory is required to explain these results. One possibility is that alcoholic and suicidal deviance is the object of more effective police surveillance than the behavior of aggressive persons; this does not seem immediately plausible, and it would be inconsistent with the formulation presented earlier. Another interpretation is that militarization provides more of a tension release for alcoholics and potential self-destroyers than for those who commit murders. If the latter is the case, strata with high propensities to overconsume alcohol or engage in self-destruction are located in greater proximity to strain-reducing devices than strata prone to assaultive behavior. A clarification of the class basis of deviant behavior, accordingly, is in order.

Suicide is common among upper- and lower-status urbanites; alcoholism, in middle-class urbanites; homicide, among lower-status slum and rural dwellers (Alpert, 1950; Durkheim, 1951; Gibbs and Martin, 1964; Harlan, 1950; Henry and Short, 1954; McCord, McCord, and Gudeman, 1960; Popham and Schmidt, 1962; Porterfield, 1958; Powell, 1958; Riley and Marden, 1947). The positive correlation between suicides and deaths due to alcohol with the use of the military tool of statecraft doubtless reflects the preponderance of upper- and middle-status persons in decision-making bodies, and since upper-status persons have self-doubt and suicidal tendencies as they sense the impending danger of an arms race, suicide rates will increase with military expenditures. Middle-status persons may drink until world crises divert their attention from personal problems; finding it possible to displace their frustrations on external targets, they can give up the bottle to follow avidly the course of events. Lower-status persons do not pay much attention to public affairs, so their attitudes toward international relations are too superficial to satisfy psychological needs.

Turning to the functions war serves to a country, we can suggest that a "release" war arises if lower- or middle-status persons exert pressure for immediate displacement of aggression. "Mediated" wars occur when decision makers and the relatively well-informed strata are in a position to militarize or to execute an economic restructuring which temporarily can relieve strain-ridden societies.

"Cultural Alternatives" Analysis

It might be objected that much of the analysis hitherto has rested on the questionable premise that absolute magnitudes of deviance measure severity of strain. A country with twenty suicides per hundred thousand of its population in a year may not necessarily have more strain than a country with a suicide rate of ten per hundred thousand. According to Robert Bales (1946), the probability of a deviant act is a function of four factors:

1. Traditional attitudes of the culture toward that act.
2. The amount of stress present.
3. A culture's tolerance-of-stress threshold.
4. The number of culturally available deviant acts (= traditional cultural attitudes toward other deviant acts).

Each of the postulates is intuitively plausible. Although traditional attitudes toward deviance are assumed above to be the same among all countries studied, degree of disapproval of suicide is undoubtedly higher in Catholic Spain than in Shinto Japan, currently the lowest and highest in suicide rates of the ten-country sample. Secondly, unemployment, one type of objective stress condition, positively correlates with strain in this inquiry. Cultures differ in tolerance of stress, thirdly, since the product-moment correlation between suicide and unemployment varies from $+.91$ for Australia to $-.38$ for Great Britain, both in the 1946–1960 period. Fourthly, the notion of cultural alternatives may be tested in relation to suicide, as follows: first, let us assume that total violent deviance is the sum of deaths due to alcoholism, suicide, and homicide; then, if suicide magnitudes are high where the other two kinds of deviance contribute a small percentage to total deviance, the inference is that suicide is chosen most where functionally equivalent violent alternatives, such as compulsive alcoholism and homicide, are less culturally available. As anticipated, there is a rank difference (rho) correlation of $+.31$ between suicide magnitudes and percentage of total violent deviance accounted for by suicides. Bales's theory is, therefore, consistent with the data of this inquiry.

An application of the "threshold" and "cultural alternatives" concepts is fruitful in studying international military behavior. Results are consistent with expectations, but correlations are low (Table 9). Taking the correlation between suicide and unemployment to indicate the intolerability of stress, we can say that if economic stress is unbearable in a country, its government is likely to militarize; its participation in war is high but defensive. Presence of cultural alternatives to suicide, here defined operationally as a condition in which there

TABLE 9. *Rho Correlations Between Balesian Factors and Military Behavior*

	Military Behavior Indicators[a]		
	6	7	8
Lack of alternatives to suicide	.44	.14	−.07
	(23)	(23)	(11)
Suicides-unemployment *r*	.07	.13	−.20
	(18)	(18)	(6)

[a]For key to variable numbers, see Table 7.

is a low proportion of suicide deaths as compared with alcoholism and homicide fatalities, entails reduced militarism. Arms buildups and wars are more likely as suicide becomes the only culturally possible deviant act, though in many cases these are defensive wars. The three countries where suicides constitute 90 per cent of violent-aggressive deviance are Germany, Great Britain, and Japan; the proportion is lower than 75 per cent in Australia, Spain, and the United States. Although the former set have been more aggressive than the latter, when all countries are included in the computation of Spearman's correlation, the apparent direct, linear relation at the two tails of the distribution is washed out.

Cultural alternatives analysis can assess as well the relative contributions of alcoholism and homicide. Where homicides are more prevalent than alcoholism deaths, as in Finland, Norway, Spain, and the United States, military expenditure levels are low, and war participation is less common; wars of such countries, nevertheless, are very aggressive (Table 10). If deaths from alcoholism are more

TABLE 10. *Rho Correlations Between Warlike Behavior and Relative Prevalence of Homicides and Alcoholism Deaths*

	Military Behavior Indicators[a]		
	6	7	8
Homicides/Alcoholism Deaths	−.50[b]	−.29	.11
	(23)	(23)	(11)

[a]For key to variable numbers, see Table 7.
[b]Significant at .10 level.

prevalent than homicides, as in Australia, France, and Switzerland, use of the military tool of statecraft is more frequent but defensive. Such findings would seem to apply to differences between urbanized countries, which have high rates of alcoholism, and rural countries, where homicide is most frequent (Table 11). Evidently mechanisms for coping with strain are quite different in rural as opposed to urban settings. In the following section, this suggestion is explored more systematically.

THEORETICAL IMPLICATIONS

Results of this investigation have relevance to a refinement of system theory and to a functional approach to international relations. Since the sample is

TABLE. 11. *Correlations Between Deviance and Urbanism*

	Percentage of Workers Employed Nonagriculturally	
	rho	N
Suicides	−.07	18
Alcoholism Death Rates	.12	18
Homicides	−.31	18
Total	−.16	18
Percentage of Deviance Due to		
Suicides	.12	18
Homicides/Alcoholism Deaths	−.29	18

neither complete nor representative of the universe of cases, and the correlations are usually low, any conclusions at this stage might be premature. Interpretations are stated in ideal-type form to facilitate further empirical testing.

A Theory of Coping Mechanisms

That stress and strain in a societal system might spill over into state behavior on the international level is consistent with the evidence presented above. The connecting links, however, are internal to societal systems. To place the elements into a dynamic model, a continuum from rural to urban societies is a convenient starting point (see Riggs, 1957, 1964; Modelski, 1961). A convenient way of treating changing levels of urbanization longitudinally is to speak of a five-stage process.

A completely rural society is called Type I; a totally urban society is Type V; these are ideal constructs. Intermediate positions are Types II, III, and IV (Table 12). Forms of deviance, using Parsons' (1959, Chap. 7) scheme, can be associated with each point on the continuum. Because revolutions and homicides are associated with rural settings, and suicides and alcoholism most prevalent in urban milieus, active orientations are located toward the rural end; passivity,

TABLE 12.   *Deviance and the Rural-Urban Continuum*

Types of Societies	Deviant Orientations (Parsons)	Main Deviant Acts	Main Types of Wars	Examples
I. Rural-Agricultural	Active-Person Focused	Homicides	Outlet	Nomadic Tribes
II. Rural and Semi-Industrial	Active-Norm Focused	Homicides Suicides	Outlet Disunity	Finland 1900–1960 Japan 1900–1945 Norway 1900–1918 Spain 1900–1960
III. Mixed Rural-Urban	Passive-Norm Focused	Alcoholism Suicides	Arms Race	Australia 1900–1960 France 1900–1960 Germany 1900–1918 Japan 1946–1960 Norway 1919–1960 Switzerland 1900–1945 United States 1900–1918
IV. Mostly Urban-Industrial	Passive-Person Focused	Suicides	Arms Race Deterrence	Germany 1919–1960 Great Britain 1900–1960 Switzerland 1946–1960 United States 1919–1960
V. Fully Urban-Industrial	None (Conformity)	None (Conformity)	Deterrence	Orwell's 1984

toward the urban end. In Type V, it is postulated that stress is eliminated before it is strainful, so conformity is its model orientation. This pattern is presented in Table 12, with cutting points between II-III and III-IV at 50 and 75 per cent of the nonagricultural work force, respectively.[14]

The next problem is to fit coping mechanisms into the picture. "Outlet" wars are related to lack of mechanisms in rural and semi-industrial countries for handling stress directly; "arms race" wars are associated with the use of militarization as a means of dealing with economic crisis in the mixed societies; "deterrence" involves mostly urban-industrial states. Accordingly, it may be argued that there are at least five distinct causal chains linking stress conditions with the use of military means of international conflict resolution, one corresponding to each type. An extended examination of the process of coping with stress, consequently, is in order.

Perception of stress is the first stage in coping with it. Where institutionalized stress perception agencies, such as the President's Council of Economic Advisers, investigate economic fluctuations almost continuously (Types IV, V), stress is spotted quickly. In the completely urban society (Type V), prompt and successful action reduces stress, returning the system to equilibrium; the economic excuse for war ends. In the mostly urban society (Type IV), much of the stress is resolved, though a residual amount remains. If mechanisms of stress perception are inadequate (Types II, III) or nonexistent (Type I), stress goes unnoticed until it passes the culture's tolerance limits. If stress is unendurable, strain mounts. Waiting for informal social perception of strain to trigger demands for relief is an inefficient way to conduct an economic system, and by the time action in Types II and III is taken to adjust the economy it may be too late socially. The reason for the frequent inability to adjust economic systems in a period of social unrest is that social integration is itself a precondition to the efficient operation of an economy (Deutsch, 1953). When strain is very intense, the disintegration of both economy and society already have become politically explosive: social problems become self-feeding. To relieve himself of societally structured sources of strain is beyond the capacity of the atomized individual. Behavior which reduces accumulated psychological frustration, such as rebellion (Types I, II) and withdrawal (Types III, IV), is societally dysfunctional. Rebellious persons violate social norms, while many persons who withdraw may engage in petty crimes while intoxicated (Jellinek, 1946). Another set of societal mechanisms is mobilized to cope with increased lawlessness, as crime against persons (Type II) or crimes against property associated with alcoholism (Type III) increase. Demands for police activity are made to stop "crime waves." If the police force is organized inefficiently (Type II), crime continues, lynching occurs (Mintz, 1946), or an escape in foreign conquest is sought. If the crime is not checked, revolution may be approaching (Brinton, 1952), or the country will be too disunited to defend itself against invasion. If the police force is efficient (Types II, IV), a "crackdown" deters both alcoholism and homicide. Social strains, at the root of the problem, are unaffected by stepped-up law enforcement; indeed, more

14. For data on rates of deviance, see Table 4. The percentages of the work force employed non-agriculturally from the 1930's to the 1950's are the following: Australia, 79–86; Finland, 57–54; France, 64–72; Germany, 74–79; Great Britain, 94–95; Japan, 31–42; Norway, 65–74; Spain, 48–50; Switzerland, 79–83; United States, 82–87. For current figures, see Russett, *et al.* (1964, Table 50).

restrictions on conduct increase frustration and aggressiveness. More desperate means of coping with strain are entertained as crime rates drop; social conflict becomes overt. Revolution against the government is one outcome (Type II). Targets for displaced aggression may be singled out for immediate attack (Type II) or for rapid "defensive" preparations (Type III).

Though economic crises are infrequent in Type IV, strain arises nevertheless due to the rigidity of a highly structured, efficient milieu of industrial, urban society. When a passive individual cannot achieve culturally approved goals by using socially legitimate methods, the reaction is one of personal inadequacy. Suicide is the most common violent behavioral response to urban strain. Displaced aggression can be helpful in reducing personal anxiety. Lack of potency in social affairs, according to the findings presented above, is associated with a desire for strong military buildups of states. Participation in war can be postponed indefinitely once the feeling of adequate national security is shared within the population; war satisfies no further needs for passive persons.

In short, stress induces mostly rural societies to seek immediate relief, whether in warfare, revolution, or scapegoating, because complex and effective stress-coping mechanisms are unavailable. Societies in early stages of modernization wait until serious social problems compel them to deal with both economic stress and social strain, whereupon an arms race alone appears to put men back to work while channeling aggressions towards targets less internally destructive. Societies in later periods of industrialization handle economic stress and social conflict almost in a routine fashion. Feelings of inadequacy in an increasingly well-structured social environment lead to withdrawal, because constant changes in role situations overtax adjustment abilities. Reactions of mostly industrial countries to international events are stereotyped, geared toward neutralization of the external environment by such stock devices as deterrent forces (C. McClelland, 1961). In the ideal-typical stage of completely urban industrial societies, stress and strain are reduced almost automatically; change is routinized. Revolution is unnecessary and impossible, and war comes only if initiated elsewhere in the international system.

The above model is consistent with most of the evidence presented herein, but it can only be offered as tentative if based on just ten countries, and correlation coefficients which exceed .40 only nine times. A further problem is that data are more cross-sectional than longitudinal. Several countries are placed along discrete positions on a continuum, but few countries move very far along it during the years 1900 to 1960. The urbanization and modernization processes, nevertheless, do not appear to involve continuous, linear trends for the ten countries, because wars and depressions upset apparently regular patterns in growth and extinction of rates of deviance (Hart, 1946). Such a consideration leads to the unorthodox conclusion that an ideal-type formulation which links several discrete stages of economic modernization to social deviance and international aggression may portray interrelationships more precisely than a continuous, organismic model of economic growth. A brief overview of longitudinal trends in each of the ten countries, accordingly, may serve to demonstrate that the above theory of coping mechanisms does in fact describe dynamic processes accurately.

The countries which were semi-industrial (Type II) in 1900 were Finland, Japan, Norway, and Spain; all have industrialized throughout the century, especially Japan and Norway. Though higher in homicides in the earlier years, they have had increasing suicides and decreasing homicides, and deaths from alcoholism among those remaining at stage two have remained almost constant. Military expenditures were very low for all these countries except Japan in 1900, and they rose up to the 1940's; their arms expenditures have since dropped to lower levels. Japan, the most spectacular industrializer, was involved most frequently in economic setbacks and in aggressive war participation. Finland and Norway were too poor to cope with severe unemployment crises, and they preferred to stay out of war, if possible. Spain had had such a serious problem of internal disunity that its economic development lagged along with its international involvements.

Countries with mixed agrarian-industrial economies (Type III) in 1900 included Australia, France, Germany, Switzerland, and the United States. In the interwar period they were joined by Japan and Norway; Germany, Switzerland, and the United States entered the Type IV urban-industrial stage later in the century. When the century began all Type III countries had rather high rates of alcoholism and suicides; as their industrialization proceeded, suicides increased, while alcoholism and homicides declined. Some reversals in these trends have appeared since 1946: suicides have decreased in countries advancing to the next stage; alcoholism deaths have increased in Australia, France, and Switzerland, which remain Type III cases. Most of the deviance trends have been related directly to unemployment fluctuations. Levels of military expenditures were intermediate for these countries in 1900, and they were all highly responsive to arms races. Entering most of the major wars, their degree of "aggressiveness" was neither negligible nor enormous, with the exception of the most rapid industrializers, Germany, Japan, and, after World War II, France.

The only mostly urban-industrial country in 1900 was Great Britain; as the century progressed, Germany, Switzerland, and the United States were able to employ almost as many persons in nonagricultural occupations as England. Deviance death rates have declined for all of the countries, as they have attained the highly urban-industrial plateau, though the magnitudes are still high in comparison with Type II countries. Unemployment, meanwhile, ceases to be a problem within Type IV countries. The only two cases of negative Pearsonian correlations between suicides and unemployment are the United States and Great Britain since 1946; four of the seven negative correlations with homicides are among advanced countries, though only two of the seven negative correlations between alcoholism deaths and unemployment are for countries of Type IV. If the theory herein proposed is to have general applicability, these apparently anomalous cases must be explained. The correlation magnitudes are not high, so sampling error may have crept in. Another possibility is that stress in Type IV countries does lead to strain, but that it is channeled in other ways, to forms of behavior which are less socially dysfunctional. This notion has considerable support. If societies and economies become very complex, a recent study has demonstrated, suicide, homicide, and compulsive alcoholism are less socially available, but deaths due to ulcers and hypertension increase. Rudin (1963) found that the "need for power" is related to violent-demonstrative death rates (rho = .41) and the "need for achievement" correlates (rho = .66) with deaths due to inhibition and repression. Needs for instrumental power and mastery prevail in the Type III country, whereas needs for tangible achievement are more significant in the Type IV country, it would appear.

In general, the longitudinal case analysis corresponds to the aggregated, cross-sectional comparative analysis. The notion of types of stages of urbanization appears to be useful in accounting for international aggression.

Structural-Functional Theory

The main implication of the findings presented above for a functional theory of international relations is to support the hypothesis that socialization style affects the rule-making style of actors in the world polity. Specifically, domestic socialization is influential with regard to the use of military means of international conflict resolution. In urban countries pressures are more effective and continuous than in rural countries.

Countries with many homicides (Types I, II) do not appear consistently to try to impose rules of inter-state behavior; the association is at a chance level. Internal malintegration of rural countries encourages decision makers to display non-aligned, non-involved, and only occasionally warlike patterns of behavior.

Modernizing states (Type III) differ from more "mature" industrializing countries in several respects. In states that are just beginning to industrialize rapidly, desire for great-power leadership status increases; with aspiration levels raised, rules of the international system made by other states may appear constricting. In order to change the rules of the system, it is necessary to challenge existing leaders (Organski, 1958). Impatient to achieve dominant positions, such countries tighten internal controls on deviance while militarizing; both actions are employed consciously to increase the capacity to shape international as well as national rules. Though warfare could be avoided by negotiations and appeasement of challenging powers, the arms races generated in the process can reach intolerable limits. International aggression is utilized to resolve both specific conflicts over international rules and general leadership recruitment rivalries.

Advanced industrializing countries (Type IV) are accustomed to dealing with domestic stress by organizational devices and manipulations of the economic system. At one point in a system, faith in rational bargaining internally may be transferred to patience in dealing with foreign affairs by diplomacy. At another point in a system, conflict is resolved less rationally: just as rigidity follows from personal anxiety, increasing military preparations are employed as a means of providing national security against "unpredictable" international opponents. Socialized by these two kinds of processes, the advanced urban state desires that rules be made under a "peace through strength" formula. War is not welcomed within most of the strata of the country; since these countries usually can obtain their ends nationally and internationally, they do not need war for any goal-attaining purpose.

The hypothetical fully industrial state (Type V) adjusts stress and strain in a regularized fashion. Because internal maintenance is not a major problem, its decision makers can appraise the international scene with care; patient, peaceful consideration of a problem is possible. Defensive measures are taken with the aim of deterring aggression or of adhering to rules of the international system established by universalistic intergovernmental organizations.

SUMMARY AND CONCLUSION

To review, the major hypothesis researched was whether a state's international behavior is related to its internal societal characteristics; in structural-functional terms, the question posed is whether a style of rule-making is related to socialization style—whether military techniques are used by foreign policy elites who are attuned to domestic considerations. Indicators of three concepts, domestic stress and strain, and use of military tools of statecraft, were selected and intercorrelated. Results are the following:

1. The hypothesis that stress precedes international military behavior is not well supported. Countries with high unemployment do go to war very frequently, but not aggressively, and military expenditures are independent of levels of unemployment. Looking more closely at the cases studied, a pattern emerged. In rural countries, war often comes immediately after an unemployment crisis, and inasmuch as the time intervening between the crisis and the outbreak of war is short, there are no large-scale military preparations. In urbanized countries, war comes after a period of militarization, which in turn is triggered by an unemployment peak.

2. Economic stress appears to produce social strain. High unemployment is associated with high levels of suicide, homicide, and alcoholism death rates.

3. Deviance is linked to the use of the military tool of statecraft. All three forms of violent deviance are high in magnitude among belligerent countries: suicide increases precede upswings in military expenditures; but if homicide or alcoholism deaths increase, military expenditures decline. It was speculated that this inconsistency in direction of correlation is due to the visibility and controllability of deviance. There are no obvious aspects of the etiology of suicides to prevent by police surveillance, whereas both initiators of homicides and compulsive alcoholics are more active in their behavior, and more prone, therefore, to be deterred or arrested by stepped-up law enforcement.

4. If suicide is much more common than other violent deviance in a country, military expenditures climb, war participation is more frequent, but wars are less aggressively entered.

5. Changing patterns in deviance are related as well to military behavior. As alcoholism displaces homicide as a more frequent form of deviance in a country, military expenditures are increased, and wars are entered more often but less aggressively.

6. The findings are related to another variable—urban industrialism and rural agrarianism. Ruralism is associated with assaultive deviance, low military expenditure levels, and aggressiveness in deciding on war, but there is only a fifty-fifty chance that a rural country beset by stress will go to war. Transitional industrial-urbanism brings more suicides and alcoholism, militarization, and frequent but non-aggressive war participation. As industrialization is more complete, deviance and warlike behavior taper off.

Several aspects of the study limit its generalizability and suggest further research. To maximize the length of the historical sweep to a sixty-one-year sample, available data dictated a sample of ten countries and nine indicators. With broad classifications in theoretical explanations, and by using the comparative method for testing correlational hypotheses, the scope of the inferences is broadened beyond the immediate data. Another consideration is the magnitude of correlations; since few approach 1.0, it is clear that other factors account for much of warlike behavior in international systems.

Within these boundaries it is still possible to conclude that the classical nineteenth-century sociologists were correct in predicting an end to war through industrialization, though their utopia of modernized society is farther away than was anticipated. Social costs of economic change have meant increased social deviance, which few theorists foresaw. When rural lower-status persons are in the majority, they are apathetic about international events, but they may react suddenly to compel decision makers to embark upon war. In industrializing countries, uprooted persons lacking close family and friendship ties provide a base of support for militarization. In some cases a military posture may prevent a war, but often defensive and relatively unaggressive wars instead may be the outcome of arms races. As industrialization proceeds, war is less necessary for solving internal problems.

The advice of a United Nations Secretary-General applying these results to new states in the world, therefore, would be to urge continued industrialization in order to reach smoothly functioning internal social and economic systems. The process of industrialization has been harsh to individuals in the past, because extreme economic fluctuations have produced periods of crisis in which deviance has flourished, so it is possible to contend that an international system composed of rural countries would be preferable to a system containing industrializing countries, which often find that war is inescapable. The data do support the hypothesis that rural international systems are more peaceful than transitional industrial international systems. By using the principles of welfare economics, however, it is now possible to mitigate the impact of economic dips by devices built into a society; similarly, the welfare or service state is developing to a point where violent and aggressive deviance may be kept under control. As soon as a few industrial countries have experimented with such techniques, it will be possible for other industrial powers to adopt them. Industrialization may no longer be such a painful process. Highly structured societies, however, are created by the introduction of such techniques; in such countries there is increased inhibition and repression. Even though war may be discarded as a device for handling domestic problems, the prices of such a peace may be the stale overconformity of *Brave New World* or of *1984*. The authoritarian aspects of modernization may be avoided if the earliest changes in social organization are brought about slowly, with maximum opportunity for public discussion and consent. As the quality and scope of education increase, there are higher rates of learning within the population. Because a high learning rate entails speedy and painless adjustment to change, economic developments one day might proceed without such a high level of social deviance and with a decreased likelihood of violence on the international horizon.

Three

The Systemic Level

J. David Singer and Melvin Small

Alliance Aggregation and the Onset of War, 1815-1945[1]

A FRAMEWORK FOR INQUIRY

In any search for the "causes" of international war, there are at least four possible levels of analysis at which we might focus our attention: the individual, the sub-national interest group, the nation, and the international system. Furthermore, each of these four possible classes of empirical referent may be examined in terms of its *structural* attributes or in terms of its *behavior*. That is, the individual, the interest group, the nation, or the system is an object of analysis which reveals relatively *static* properties such as size, composition, organization, power, or capacity for change, and relatively *dynamic* properties such as activity level, aggressiveness, cooperativeness, responsiveness, initiative, or communicativeness. In addition to these two sets of attributes, an individual or a social organization will reveal *relationship* attributes vis-à-vis other actors at the same or other levels of organizational complexity. Nations, for example, may be geographically near or distant, more or less interdependent economically, politically hostile or friendly, ethnically or industrially similar, and so forth. In sum, we may look for the causes of war in structure, behavior, or relationship at—or across—many levels of social organization. Combining these three classes of variables with the four suggested levels of analysis, we can postulate at least twelve different classes of information one might examine in any systematic search for those factors most often associated with war.

Of course, the moment these twelve categories are filled in with illustrative

1. This study is part of a larger project on the correlates of war, supported by the Carnegie Corporation of New York and the Center for Research on Conflict Resolution at the University of Michigan. We are also grateful to Anatol Rapoport and Keith Smith with whom we consulted often on conceptual as well as methodological problems. For his efficient aid in data analysis, our thanks go also to Wen Chao Hsieh.

247

variables, it becomes evident that the structural-behaviorial-relational trichoto-
mization is not always clear-cut; one might argue, for example, that an individual
personality attribute, such as rigidity, or a national one, such as autocracy, is more
a behavioral than a structural property. At the least, we must recognize that we
may have to infer one set of attributes from the observation of another set.

Regardless of the level of organization (or class of variable) at which we look,
we must make at least two epistemological assumptions: (1) that explanatory
variables will be found in more than one place, the exact number being a function
of one's theoretical predilections; and (2) that the interaction of two or more
such classes of variables will have more explanatory power than the mere correlation of any single class of variable with our dependent variable: the incidence of
war. Which particular levels or classes one gives priority to is likewise a matter of
individual judgment, with two considerations deserving attention in that selection.
First, there is the question of parsimony, and this should lead to a preference for
variables that are at the more general rather than the more idiosyncratic end of
the continuum. Second, certain classes of possible predictors to events such as
war seem to get considerable attention in the scholarly literature, at the expense
of others of intuitively equal significance. On the basis of these considerations,
and with the intention of turning later to other possible predictors (and combinations thereof) we focus here on one cluster of *structural* variables at the *systemic*
level of analysis: alliance aggregation.

ALLIANCE AGGREGATION AS A PREDICTOR TO WAR

Without going into the quagmire of terminological and normative dispute
which has characterized much of the theoretical literature on the balance of
power, we can nevertheless note that its defense or justification clearly rests on
the assumption that the stability of the international system can be maintained
without reliance on superordinate political institutions.[2] In the words of Kaplan
(1957), it postulates a system which is "sub-system dominant"; that is, one in
which most authority is found at the national actor, or sub-systemic level, rather
than at the supranational or systemic level. The same notion is conveyed by the
international lawyers' distinction between a system in which most of the authority
lines are horizontal and one in which they tend to be vertical in direction (Falk,
1959).

In the absence of significant legal or political institutions at the supranational
level, the preservation of relative stability and the survival of the nations are
seen as depending upon the presence or absence of one or more of the following
phenomena, depending in turn upon the theoretical predilections or national
outlook of the observer: For the nations themselves, the phenomena are their
restraint and limit of ambition, their similarity of values, their approximate
parity, the absence of permanent friendships and hostilities, or their willingness

2. Almost all textbooks in the field devote some space to an effort to systematize balance-
of-power concepts, with varying degrees of success. In addition, there are several theoretical
efforts, among which are Claude (1962), Gareau (1962), Haas (1953), Kaplan (1957), Liska
(1962), Deutsch and Singer (1964), and Waltz (1964). Three important efforts to examine the
international system in the historical context are Gulick (1955), Langer (1931), and Rosecrance
(1963).

to coalesce against a challenger. For the system, these conditions might be the absence of alliances, the presence of a minimum number of alliance coalitions, the approximate parity of the coalitions, the fluidity and impermanence of these coalitions, or a high level of normative consensus. That some of these requirements are vague and that others are inconsistent seems not to discourage those who consider supranational institutions as unnecessary. In one fashion or another, they would rely upon what might be characterized as the diplomatic equivalent of Adam Smith's "invisible hand," a mechanism whereby the individual pursuit of individual interests redounds to the advantage and stability of the community as a whole.

Central to this notion is the understanding that the invisible or unseen hand will function only to the extent that all nations are free to deal and interact with all others as their national interests dictate. Thus, it is assumed that every dyadic relationship will be a mixture of the cooperative and the conflictful, with political, economic, ideological, and other issues all producing different interest configurations for each possible pair of nations. The net effect, it is believed, is such a welter of cross-cutting ties and such a shifting of friendships and hostilities that no single set of interests can create a self-aggravating and self-reinforcing division or cleavage among the nations; A and B may well have competitive economic interests in the Middle East, but harmonious strategic interests in the Caribbean, while B and C's political interests may coincide in regard to West Africa and clash in an international organization setting.

It follows from this sort of a model that anything which restrains or inhibits free or vigorous pursuit of the separate national interests will limit the efficacy of the stabilizing mechanism. And among those arrangements seen as most likely to so inhibit that pursuit are formal alliances. Nations in the same alliance are less free to compete with their allies in such spheres of incompatibility, and less free to cooperate with outsiders in areas of overlapping interests.[3] Just how *much* freedom to pursue normal interests is lost by an allied nation is, of course, most difficult to measure. Although some approximation of the degree of inhibition— or loss of interaction opportunity—can be gleaned from the text and associated documents of a given alliance treaty, a fuller appreciation would require a laborious examination of the treaty's context, and the motivations, relative power, and performance of the signatory nations. Despite the obvious simplifications, however, a differentiation based on the documents themselves is not without some merit, and we will therefore distinguish all the alliances examined as to whether they are military, neutrality, or entente commitments; the specific coding rules are outlined in a later section.

Be that as it may, if each alliance commitment reduces, to *some* degree, the normal interaction opportunities available to the total system, and the loss of such interaction opportunities is supposed to inhibit the efficacy of the balance-of-power mechanism, we should find that as the system's interaction opportunities diminish, war will increase in frequency, magnitude, or severity. Moreover, if the

---

3. A recent statement which explicitly expresses these restraints is that by Secretary Rusk in regard to Soviet-American arms control negotiations: "Of course, anything that involves our NATO allies would have to be discussed fully with our NATO allies. We could not, for example, make arrangements ourselves, nor even could the four NATO members now sitting at Geneva be able to make arrangements on control posts throughout the NATO alliance without fullest consideration in NATO."

alliance configurations show less and less partial overlap, and they instead increasingly reinforce a tendency toward a very few (but large-sized) coalitions, the system's loss of interaction opportunities becomes even more severe. Carried to its extreme condition, this tendency culminates in a completely bipolarized system, with interaction opportunities reduced (theoretically, at least) to one; each nation would then have only friends or foes, and few relationships in between these two extremes. On the other hand, if there are no alliances in the system at all, these interaction opportunities will be equal to the total number of pairs or dyads possible with a given total number of nations in the system; this would be equal to $N(N - 1)/2$.

There are, of course, several other lines of reasoning by which one might be led to predict that alliance commitments will negatively affect the stability of the international system, but they are largely variations on the present theme and several have been presented elsewhere (Deutsch and Singer, 1964). Thus, rather than dwell any longer here on the plausible reasons why alliance aggregation *should* correlate with the onset of war, it might be more useful to ascertain the extent to which it does. In order to put this proposition to the historical test, however, a number of preliminary steps are essential. These are the following:

1. Articulate the hypothesis in the various forms it might reasonably take.
2. Delineate the empirical world in time and space from which the evidence will be gathered.
3. Describe the procedures by which the chaotic welter of historical fact is converted into data.
4. Present the raw data which emerge from the above operations.

Once those steps have been completed, we can move on to:

5. Ascertain the strength and direction of any correlations which would tend to confirm or disconfirm the various hypotheses.
6. Interpret the results of this search for correlations.

In the sections which follow, the above procedures will be described in appropriate detail.

THE BASIC HYPOTHESES

Having articulated the reasons for examining the relationship between alliance aggregation and war, we can now spell out in more detail the hypotheses to be tested. In the next section, we can then move on to a specification of the procedures by which the key variables were converted from their widely scattered verbal state to collated and codified numerical form.

The hypotheses may be thought of as falling into two general classes, both of which belong to the systemic level of analysis. The first concerns alliance aggregation and the consequent loss of interaction opportunities in general; that is, it ignores the specific nature of the alliance configurations which are produced, and looks merely at the system's aggregate loss of such normal opportunities. The second of these is as concerned with the specific configurations as it is with the aggregate loss of normal dyadic interaction, and focuses on the extent to which the alliance commitments produce a bipolarized system. Bipolarization may thus be thought of as a special case of alliance aggregation.

Alliance Aggregation and the Magnitude or Severity of War

Looking first at the matter of general alliance configurations, and the extent to which they reduce normal interaction opportunities, we may articulate the first basic hypothesis: *The greater the number of alliance commitments in the system, the more war the system will experience.* The second hypothesis pays more attention to specific alliance configurations, and thus reads: *The closer to pure bipolarity the system is, the more war it will experience.*

In order to put these propositions to the test, we must first identify the empirical world within which the postulated relationships are to be sought. Let us describe and justify the world which we have selected, but a preliminary indication of the basic procedure might best precede that. Basically, the method to be employed is a trend analysis. After developing several different measures of alliance aggregation and several measures of the onset of war, we will examine the extent to which the two sets of variables rise and fall together over time.

As to the empirical domain in which the longitudinal data will be compared, the problem is to examine a span of time which is not restricted to the all-too-recent, and therefore most salient, period upon which much theorizing in international relations seems to be based. On the other hand, if we go too far back we may well find ourselves examining international environments of such disparity that generalizations embracing them become foolish and irrelevant. For the contemporary scholar, there does seem to be a chronological cutting point which provides a sufficiently extensive empirical world while nevertheless permitting a reasonable degree of comparability. We refer to the period opening with what we normally recognize as the beginning of the modern international system (the Congress of Vienna) and closing with the Japanese surrender in Tokyo Bay. Despite the many changes in the pattern and process of international relations during that 130-year period, we find a remarkable constancy. The national state was the dominant actor and the most relevant form of social organization; world politics were dominated by a handful of European powers; the Napoleonic reliance upon the citizen's army endured, with all of its implications for public involvement in diplomacy; the concept of state sovereignty remained relatively unchallenged; and while technological innovation went on apace, the period postdates the smoothbore and predates the nuclear-missile combination. In sum, it seems reasonable to conclude that this period provides an appropriate mixture of stability and transition from which generalization would be legitimate. As to whether such generalization might be extended beyond 1945 and into the present, we would be skeptical, but this is, of course, an empirical question, and one to which we will return in our conclusion.

Stated in the preceding rather general form, the hypotheses immediately raise a number of important conceptual and methodological problems. In addition to the procedures for operationalizing "number of alliance commitments" or "closer to pure bipolarity" (the independent variables) and "more war" (the dependent variable)—and these will be articulated in the next section—there are three relevant concerns of substance: (1) the time lag between the presence of a given number or percentage of alliance commitments and its effect in the form of international war; (2) the differentiation between separate regions of the world, especially between the "central" and the "peripheral" portions of the system; and (3) the differentiation between distinctive time periods in our 130 years, especially that between the nineteenth and twentieth centuries.

Let us look first at the matter of time lag. If, indeed, there *is* any relationship between the loss of interaction opportunities and war, that relationship must take a certain amount of time to make itself felt; the system certainly cannot be expected to respond immediately to a specific increase or decrease in inter-action opportunities. Not only do we not find in the literature any compelling reason for assuming a given response time, but that response time might well differ for, let us say, different decades.[4] Consequently, each year's interaction opportunity measures have been correlated with the war indices for not only the following year ($Y + 1$), but for the following three ($Y + 3$) and five years ($Y + 5$) as well; for example, if a given alliance aggregation index for 1851 is relatively high, we want to know whether its effect is felt by 1852, by 1854, or 1856. That is, our dependent variables for 1851 will reflect the amount of war which began in 1852, the amount which began between the beginning of 1852 and the end of 1854, and the amount which began between the beginning of 1852 and the end of 1856.

Two points of clarification are in order here. First, note that we are distinguishing between the amount of war which *began* in the specified time period, regardless of how long it endured, and the amount of war which the system experienced during that period. Second, we are looking at the amount of war which began at any time *within* three time periods of increasing length: within one, three, or five years, not during 1852, or 1854, or 1856 alone. Thus all forms of the basic hypothesis will be tested under three different chronological conditions.

Beyond the refinement of the hypothesis in order to account for varying time lags, we should also refine it to permit its testing within several different time- and space-bound worlds. That is, if we recognize the extent to which theorizing about diplomatic history has been dominated by European-centered scholars and practitioners from the Western world, it seems prudent to wonder whether a given relationship might be found in one region but not in another. Combining that awareness with a recognition that it was not until relatively recent times that the international system could be treated as a more or less single and inter-dependent one, it makes perfect sense to look for a point in time at which the non-European nations "joined" that central system. The most reasonable such point seems to be that which closed out World War I and marked the birth of the League of Nations; this organization, while its pretensions to universality were never fulfilled, quite explicitly included many non-European members and concerned itself with all continents. Thus, while treating the post-1920 system as a single one, we look upon the pre-1920 epoch as having both a central, Europe-oriented system and a peripheral one. Consequently, all sets of correlations will be examined in two systemic contexts. The first will be called the *total system* and will include all "independent" nations which existed during any part of the entire 130-year period. The second context will be one in which we "shuck

---

4. One admittedly intuitive analysis concludes, for example, that "the decision to wage war precedes by one to five years the outbreak of hostilities" (Abel, 1941).

off" the peripheral nations prior to 1920, in order to eliminate the statistical "noise" generated by the less important and least active nations. This we will call the *central system*, and its composition is the same as the total system's for the final 25 years, but smaller for the first 105 years.

Further, we do not restrict attributed membership in the central system to European nations only, nor do all European nations fall into the central category for the pre-League period. In order to qualify for inclusion in the central system during that earlier period, a nation must either be located in Europe or deeply involved in relatively durable relationships with European nations. Given the difficulty of operationalizing this latter phenomenon and given the high degree of consensus among historians, we have adhered closely to that consensus.[5] To be more specific, we have *excluded* a number of European nations from our pre-League central system in line with the following criteria. Outside of Prussia and Austria, the German states are excluded because their 1815 treaty of confederation sharply restricts their diplomatic independence; for example, they are prohibited, formally and effectively, from alliances which might be directed at other members of the confederation. As for the Italian states other than Sardinia, they, too, enjoy few of the perquisites of real independence prior to their unification in 1860. Modena, Parma, Tuscany, and the Two Sicilies are closely linked by dynastic ties to Austria and turn out to be little more than satellites of Vienna. As to the Papal States, the French and Austrian guarantees effectively preclude them from any significant degree of normal diplomatic interplay.[6]

Turning to the considerations which led us to *include* several non-European nations in (and exclude others from) the pre-League central system, only a few political entities even qualify (by population and recognition criteria) as independent nations at all (if we forget Latin America for the moment) and almost none of these are regularly involved in Continental diplomacy or with the Continental powers abroad. In Asia and Africa, for example, only China, Japan, Persia, Siam, Ethiopia, Korea, and Morocco meet the population and diplomatic recognition requirements between 1815 and 1920.[7] They are, of course, considerably more independent than the subordinate German and Italian states, and they do occasionally interact with the European powers (for example, Persia in the 1850's and Siam in the 1880's), but they remain largely unrelated to the wars and treaties of Continental diplomacy. China and Japan, however,

---

5. For a full description of the operations by which nations were coded and classified, see Singer and Small (1966a).

6. There are, of course, a fair number of additional German and Italian states, but they fail to meet our population threshold of 500,000; the classification criteria are discussed below.

7. The population threshold of 500,000 was only established after a fairly exhaustive list of political entities was compiled and it then became evident that almost no nation of a lesser population revealed itself as an active participant. As to recognition, we found that Britain and France almost invariably led the way to recognition by a majority of members of the European state system. Thus, we get a parsimonious criterion which produces almost exactly the same results as would one requiring, let us say, 50 per cent of the major power members of the European system to serve as legitimizers; actually these two constituted 40 per cent of that group until 1860 and from then until 1895 they constituted 33 per cent. Moreover, only Britain and France had sufficiently strong interest in Latin America to justify extending diplomatic recognition to nations in that area. By recognition we mean the accreditation of a representative at or above the rank of chargé d'affaires; neither the consul nor the diplomatic agent qualifies under this scheme.

are brought into our central system in 1895 as a consequence of the Sino-Japanese War. As to Western Hemisphere nations, the same considerations apply. Aside from the United States after the Spanish-American War, the Americas are even less involved in Continental affairs than the Asian and African nations. Between 1815 and our cutoff date of 1920 there are no alliance ties with a European power and there are only two international wars involving Europe in Latin America: that between France and Mexico in 1862–1867 and that involving Spain with Bolivia, Chile, and Peru in 1865–1866. And there are no cases of Latin American nations engaging in European wars.[8]

In sum, then, we treat the post-1920 international system as a relatively interdependent one, but divide the pre-League system into two parts: the central and the peripheral. The search for correlations between alliance aggregation and war is thus conducted in two somewhat different empirical worlds so that we may, in one, ignore those political entities which qualify as independent nations, but which may hardly be thought of as active participants in international politics. For the pre-League period, then, the following nations are treated as members of the *central system,* as of the year indicated; it should be noted that Sardinia, Prussia, and Serbia become, respectively, Italy in 1860, Germany in 1871, and Yugoslavia in 1919, and that Austria and Hungary are treated as a single nation until 1918. Those in the left-hand column are members throughout the entire period.

Austria-Hungary	Greece–1828
Denmark	Belgium–1830
England	Serbia–1878
France	Romania–1878
Holland	China–1895
Portugal	Japan–1895
Prussia	United States–1899
Russia	Norway–1905
Sardinia	Bulgaria–1908
Spain	Albania–1914
Sweden	Czechoslovakia–1919
Switzerland	Poland–1919
Turkey	Finland–1919

The following nations are excluded from the pre-1920 central system and treated as members of the *peripheral system* only, between the dates shown. The earlier date marks its qualification as a sovereign nation and the latter, if any, marks either its disqualification (via federation for the seven German and the five Italian states or annexation for Morocco and Siam) or its entry into the central system (marked by an asterisk); needless to say, the precise date at which the population criterion was met cannot always be shown, and others might select a year or two later or earlier.

8. Moreover, there were only three Latin American alliances (Ecuador-Peru, 1860–1861; Colombia-Ecuador, 1864–1865; and Bolivia-Peru, 1873–1883) which met our criteria of formality, population of the signatories, and consummation in peace time. In general, see Burr (1955).

Baden, 1815–1870
Bavaria, 1815–1870
Hanover, 1838–1870
Hesse-Electoral, 1815–1866
Hesse-Grand Ducal, 1815–1867
Mecklenburg-Schwerin, 1843–1867
Saxony, 1815–1867
Württemberg, 1815–1870
Modena, 1842–1860
Papal States, 1815–1860
Parma, 1851–1860
Tuscany, 1815–1860
Two Sicilies, 1815–1861
Morocco, 1847–1911
Korea, 1888–1905
Ethiopia, 1898
Persia, 1855
United States, 1815–1899*
China, 1860–1895*
Japan, 1860–1895*

Brazil, 1826
Colombia, 1831
Mexico, 1831
Peru, 1837
Chile, 1839
Argentina, 1841
Venezuela, 1841
Bolivia, 1848
Guatemala, 1849
Ecuador, 1854
Haiti, 1859
Salvador, 1875
Uruguay, 1882
Santo Domingo, 1887
Siam, 1887
Paraguay, 1896
Honduras, 1899
Nicaragua, 1900

Turning to the post-1920 setting, in which we drop the distinction between central and peripheral systems, we find the following additional (not previously listed) nation members and their dates of qualification for entry into the total system:

Estonia, 1920
Latvia, 1920
Lithuania, 1920
Hungary, 1920
Luxembourg, 1920
Liberia, 1920
South Africa, 1920
Australia, 1920
New Zealand, 1920
Canada, 1920

Afghanistan, 1920
Nepal, 1920
Mongolia, 1921
Costa Rica, 1920
Panama, 1920
Ireland, 1921
Saudi Arabia, 1927
Iraq, 1932
Yemen, 1934
Cuba, 1934
Egypt, 1936

In addition to these spatial differentiations, a case can be made for an explicit chronological differentiation. Contemporary theoreticians are, all other things being approximately equal, more likely to argue from recent than from remote diplomatic events. Therefore, they may well be basing their postulated correlation between alliance aggregation and war on twentieth century diplomatic history while tending to forget the nineteenth. To ascertain whether or not this has been the case, we have explicitly divided our 130 year epoch from Vienna to Tokyo Bay into two distinct periods, with the turn of the century marking the break. As to selecting this cutoff point rather than one closer to the midpoint, a number of considerations seemed relevant. First of all, there seemed to be an appreciable qualitative difference between World War I and the wars that preceded it. And bearing in mind the fact that time lags of up to five years are used, we must of necessity use a cutoff year no later than 1908. Secondly, the period *prior* to World War I is markedly different from that preceding most other wars, in that it produced a sharp and clear confrontation between the Central Powers and the

Allies, and this bipolarization was well under way by 1902. To be sure, some of the alliances contracted before 1899 (Triple and Dual alliances) transcend both periods, but in order to evaluate their effects, we would have had to go back to 1879. Had we chosen this date, we would have eliminated from the nineteenth-century pattern those several interesting, though ephemeral, configurations of the 1879 to 1899 period which had little relationship to the post-1900 world. Moreover, only after 1900 does the rate of alliance activity show that marked increase which culminates in the grouping of France, England, Russia, and Japan into several interlocking alliances and ententes which by 1908 had resolved itself into the pre-World War I bipolarization.

Finally, there appears to be a marked difference in the amount and rate of diplomatic and military activity between the nineteenth and twentieth centuries, so that while 1899 does not represent an exact chronological midpoint, it is probable that the 85 years prior to 1900 represent an approximate equivalent of the 45 post-century years in terms of "diplomatic time."

To summarize this part of the discussion, then, our hypothesis will actually be put to the test in eighteen different forms, in order to differentiate among: (1) three different time lags, for (2) six different time-space systems. In matrix form, we would want to show the correlation between our several alliance indices and wars beginning for each of the spatial-temporal cells in the chart below:

		Time Lags or Spans		
Period	System	$Y + 1$	$Y + 3$	$Y + 5$
1815–1945	Central only			
1815–1945	Total			
1815–1899	Central only			
1815–1899	Total			
1900–1945	Central only			
1900–1945	Total			

Alliance Aggregation and the Frequency of War

Up to this point we have been discussing a relationship which, however interesting, may possibly not be getting at the basic theoretical proposition. That is, we have been assuming that any positive relationship existing between aggregate alliance commitments and war would be revealed in the correlation between our various alliance indices in a given year and certain indices of the *magnitude* or *severity* of war in certain years immediately following. It could be argued that the existence of a statistically significant correlation between interaction oppotunity losses and the severity or magnitude of war is really, by indirection, a *dis*confirmation of the hypothesis. The reasoning might be that not only do magnitude or severity seldom covary with frequency, but that they are more likely to vary inversely. A glance at figures for sickness, auto or industrial accidents, or battle casualties for example, would show that the *least* serious events occur most frequently, and that in their most disastrous form these phenomena occur much less often. As a matter of fact, this is precisely what Richardson (1960) found in his *Statistics of Deadly Quarrels*. Classifying deaths on the basis of a $\log_{10}$ scale, he found that in 282 cases of mass violence between 1820 and 1945, deaths were distributed as follows:

$$3 \pm \tfrac{1}{2} - 188 \qquad 6 \pm \tfrac{1}{2} - 5$$
$$4 \pm \tfrac{1}{2} - 63 \qquad 7 \pm \tfrac{1}{2} - 2$$
$$5 \pm \tfrac{1}{2} - 24$$

Likewise, if we look at his observed frequency of ninety-one wars classified by the number of participants, a similar distribution holds:

2–42	7–3
3–24	8–2
4– 8	9–1
5– 7	10–0
6– 3	20–1

Our own results reveal the same pattern, even though our more stringent criteria for war produced a much smaller number of cases. Whether the seriousness of war is measured in terms of number of participants, duration, or battle-connected military deaths, the same inverse correlation between frequency and seriousness is found, as shown in Table 1.[9]

TABLE 1. *Frequency Distribution of all International Wars, 1815–1945, by Size, Duration, Magnitude, and Severity (N = 41)*

	No. of Participants		Months Duration		Magnitude in Nation-Months		Severity: Battle Deaths in Thous.	
	Range	Freq.	Range	Freq.	Range	Freq.	Range	Freq.
High	21–26	1	61–84	2	750 +	1	10,000 +	1
Med.-High	16–20	0	46–60	4	151–750	3	1001–10,000	1
Medium	11–15	1	31–45	1	31–150	8	101–1000	7
Med.-Low	6–10	2	16–30	5	5–30	25	11–100	13
Low	1–5	37	0.5–15	29	1–5	4	1–10	19

Given this rather critical observation, it certainly behooves us to pay as much attention to the correlations between interaction opportunity and the *frequency* of war as to those between such phenomena and the *magnitude* or *severity* of war. This we shall do in the sections which follow.

OPERATIONALIZING THE VARIABLES

In order to put any hypothesis to the empirical test, of course, one must at the very least demonstrate a correlation between the independent and dependent variables. Though a positive correlation between alliance aggregation and war, high enough not to have occurred by sheer chance, cannot be interpreted as a demonstration of any causal connection, the search for such a correlation is a necessary first step. That the presence or absence of covariation between alliances

9. This is a very simple and a-theoretical presentation of such distributions. For an indication of the theoretical implication of "mere" distributions, see Horvath and Foster (1963), Weiss (1963), Smoker (1964), and Denton (1966).

and war is not a mere artifact requires considerable subsequent analysis, but the first order of business, and that which concerns us here, is whether the hypothesized correlations are indeed borne out by the historical evidence.

This enterprise, in turn, cannot be launched until the constructs have been operationalized—until the researcher has converted the ambiguous verbal labels into variables whose shifting presence or absence or strength can be repeatedly observed and recorded. That is, we must devise explicit and visible procedures by which the welter of events and conditions may be coded, sorted, and classified in so reliable a fashion that other scholars will, in applying the identical coding procedures to the same body of information, come up with almost exactly the same data. Whether these highly reliable procedures do, however, produce data which index the qualitative variables we seek is another matter. Whereas the relative *reliability* of our measures is easily established, their *validity* always remains a matter of some dispute. Recognizing, then, that the search for operational (or machine-readable) variables may well lead to the observation of phenomena quite remote from those about which we seek to generalize, let us turn to the procedures used here.

Magnitude and Severity of War: the Dependent Variables

Before examining the frequency and distribution of our *independent* variables, we had better know what it is they are supposed to be predicting to. In the overall project of which this study is a small part, war is one of the major dependent variables; the object is to ascertain which structural, relational, and behavioral phenomena at which levels of social organization most strongly correlate with war. War, however, means many things to many people, and as a consequence, some definition and operationalization are essential; a full and detailed treatment of the problem is presented elsewhere (Singer and Small, forthcoming), but a brief recapitulation is clearly in order here.

First of all, there are many deadly quarrels (to borrow Richardson's quaint phrase) which are not normally thought of as war: riots, murders, assassinations, pogroms, executions, duels, punitive expeditions, retaliatory strikes, and so on. Even when the deadly quarrel endures and involves nations, many ambiguities remain. How many nations must be involved, for how long, and with how many men or arms? And what is a nation? Secondly, even if we agree upon the meaning of war, there are several different classes of war, each having different relevance to the search for meaningful generalization about the international system.

In order to handle these ambiguities and inconsistencies, a two-step coding procedure was used. First, adapting from the schema found in *A Study of War* (Wright, 1942, App. 20) four classes of war were differentiated: international, imperial, colonial, and civil. The criterion here is strictly one of the political-legal status of the participants. Thus, an *international* war is one in which at least one participant on each side is an independent and sovereign member of the international system, with a population exceeding 500,000 and enjoying diplomatic recognition from our two legitimizers, Britain and France. If only *one* side includes one or more independent system members, then the war is classified as imperial or colonial, depending on the political status of the adversaries, as follows. When the dominant (and usually there is only one) adversary is a more or less independent political entity, but *not* a qualified system member by our criteria, the war is classified as *imperial;* examples might be Serbia before 1878, Persia before 1855, or a Pathan tribe. When the dominant adversary is an entity which not only fails to qualify as a system member but which is also an ethnically different people formerly or presently under the suzerainty of the system member(s) against which it is fighting, the war is seen as *colonial;* examples of such wars might be the Russo-Polish ones of 1831 and 1863 or the Spanish-Cuban of 1868–1878. Wars of this latter category would generally fall, in contemporary parlance, under the rubric of wars of national independence. Finally, a *civil* (or internal) war is one between a system member's government and such sub-national factions as are able to engage in armed resistance, insurgency, or revolution. Of course, any war may *become* an international war by the intervention of one or more independent members of the international system, and the classification of a war may therefore change between its onset and its termination.[10]

However, not all international wars are of equal interest to us here, nor is reliable information on all of them available. Thus, we exclude those wars in which the best estimate of total battle-connected deaths is less than 1,000.[11] Using these criteria of war type and casualty threshold, we find that there were forty-one international wars in the total international system between 1815 and 1945; if we ignore the pre-Versailles peripheral system, that number drops to twenty-four.

Having identified those international wars which interest the student of international relations as he examines the effects of alliance patterns, the next point to note is that these wars differ markedly in their duration, magnitude, and intensity. Thus, the correlation of alliance aggregation with mere war frequency would be of limited interest (if not downright misleading) and further gradation is clearly necessary. This gradation is achieved in the first instance by use of the nation-months-of-war measure, so that the simple *magnitude* of each war is the sum of the months which all nations individually experienced as participants in the war; other political entities, even though they participate in a qualifying war, do not contribute to that war's nation-months if they fail to meet the recognition and population criteria for system membership.

A second-order refinement is also necessary, on the recognition that a nineteenth or twentieth century British war-month holds rather different implications for the international system than, for example, a Bulgarian war-month. This differentiation could be recognized by introducing several different factors as modifiers. We might want to classify the nations by power, status, or size, and then weight their nation-months by the consequent absolute or relative score. But no such satisfactory index yet exists, especially when it must be applied not only to the early nineteenth century but to many non-European powers for which

---

10. There is a rapidly burgeoning literature on the subject and it reminds us that very few civil wars remain purely internal for any length of time. See Rosenau (1964), Modelski (1961), and Eckstein (1963).

11. This figure permits us to eliminate many border skirmishes, brief interventions, punitive expeditions, blockades, and bombardments of marginal interest to the international relations student, yet excludes no international war. Where our confidence levels were low and the deaths were estimated to be nearly 1,000, we did, however, include the wars. Three examples of such an occurrence were the French invasion of Spain in 1823, the conquest of the Papal States in 1860, and Spain versus Peru, Chile, and Ecuador in 1866.

we have little accurate data at present. We have, therefore, resorted to the simple distinction between major and minor powers and calculated their wars and nation-months of war separately. Though the major-minor dichotomy may be too primitive for some theoretical purposes and not too readily operationalized, diplomatic historians have found it quite useful for centuries. Moreover, despite the invisibility of their criteria, they show near unanimity in the classification results.[12] Thus, our major powers and the dates during which they enjoyed that status are:

Austria-Hungary, 1815–1918
Prussia or Germany, 1815–1918, 1925–1945
Russia, 1815–1917, 1922–1945
France, 1815–1940
Britain, 1815–1945
Japan, 1895–1945
United States, 1899–1945
Italy, 1860–1943

A final point regarding our nation-months (magnitude) measure concerns the chronological placing of our forty-one wars. It should be reiterated here that our major concern must be not with the amount of war *going on* in the given year or years following each year's level of alliance aggregation in the system, but with the amount of war which *commenced* within that one-, three-, or five-year period. Our interest is in measures reflecting the *onset* of war. That most of the nation-months of World War II, for example, occurred during 1942 and 1943 is of much less interest in this study than the fact that they commenced in 1939.

In addition to nation-months as an index of the magnitude of war, at least one other factor seems to justify consideration. That factor we will call *severity* and it will be measured by the number of battle-connected deaths of military personnel sustained by all participants in any given war. As with the identification and classification of our wars, a full treatment of the problems encountered in locating, evaluating, and converting the casualty information into reliable data is provided in the aforementioned paper, and again only a brief summary is offered here. There have, of course, been several prior efforts to collect data on war casualties (Bodart, 1916; Dumas, 1923; Sorokin, 1937; Klingberg, 1945; Richardson, 1960; and Urlanis, 1960), but none provides a fully satisfactory compilation, even for the primitive statistical purposes encountered in this undertaking. All are partially guilty of employing either shifting or invisible criteria of classification, and as a consequence, several different sets of such figures were collected and then our own best estimates finally used. For each nation in each international war, we calculated (and estimated) two types of deaths: (1) military personnel who died, or were reported as permanently missing, as a consequence of malicious acts of the enemy; and (2) military personnel who died from accidents, wounds, disease, or exposure during the period of hostilities. Note that, in partial contradistinction to Richardson's criteria, we did *not* include: (1) civilians of participating nations who died as a result of enemy actions (and to have included this category in our World War II figures would not have changed

---

12.   Some might quarrel with our use of the historians' consensus on the classification of nations into major and minor. One significant point of assurance is found in Morgenthau where approximately the same major-power listing as ours is used (1956, p. 324).

appreciably the fact that almost half of all deaths in our forty-one wars were accounted for by this single holocaust); (2) such civilians who died from exposure or disease; (3) neutral civilians; and (4) those children who might have been born had there been no war. Battle-connected deaths of military personnel, thus, will provide our index of each war's severity.[13]

To summarize this section, then, our raw data are presented in Table 2. Note that *wars* are the items listed, and that in order to use these data for our purposes they must be transformed so as to show the magnitude and severity of all international wars which began in each of our 130 years. The results of that transformation as well as more detailed data and procedures are in a forthcoming statistical handbook.

Alliance Aggregation: The Independent Variable

Shifting our attention now from the outcome, or dependent variable, to the predictor, or independent variable, what procedures might be used to operationalize and quantify the extent to which alliance commitments reduced the interaction opportunities available to the international system? The problem here is somewhat more complex than that confronted in regard to the magnitude and severity of war, since a modest inferential leap is required. Referring back to the rationale behind our general hypotheses, we argued there that the effect of each alliance of any type was to reduce the extent to which the pluralistic, self-regulating mechanism could operate effectively. And two different lines of reasoning were suggested, depending upon the intervening constructs selected. In one, we concentrated upon the loss of interaction opportunity due to aggregate alliance commitments of all nations in the system; this may be thought of as a simple subtractive procedure. In the other, we examined the loss of interaction opportunity due to the bipolarizing effect of these alliance commitments. To put it briefly, there should be a difference between the effects of a structure which reflects a crazy-quilt pattern of all sorts of overlapping alliance membership and one in which that membership approaches or reaches a state in which only a very few easily distinguishable coalitions merge. There may, of course, be a close interdependence between these two conceptually distinct conditions, since it is perfectly plausible to assume that alliance-building is by and large an activity directed *against* other nations and other existing or anticipated alliances. If such is the case, then, the mere aggregation of alliance commitments may well move the system in the direction of some minimum number of coalitions and hence *toward* bipolarity. We will revert to this matter when we present our data, and will then have some evidence for the extent to which these two conditions covary.

Returning, then, to our operationalizing procedures, let us look first at the aggregate measure of interaction opportunity loss, in its various forms. Perhaps the most orderly procedure would be to begin with an overview of the large number of alliance ties that interest us in an analysis such as this. The typology is based upon: (1) the nature of the obligation or commitment undertaken

---

13. As to civilian and military deaths from non-battlefield engagements, the major possible source is the siege. During the period under study, however, there were few sieges which led to an appreciable number of deaths; see Hargreaves (1948).

TABLE 2. *International Wars by Duration, Magnitude, and Severity: 1815-1945*

Name of War and Participants	Dates	International System			Each Nation		National Dates (if different)
		Duration (Months)	Nation Months	Battle Deaths (thousands)	Duration (Months)	Battle Deaths (thousands)	
1. Franco-Spanish	4/7/23–11/13/23	7	14	1			
France					7	.4	
Spain					7	.6	
2. Russo-Turkish	4/26/28–9/14/29	16.5	33	130			
Russia					16.5	50	
Turkey					16.5	80	
3. Mexican	5/12/46–2/12/48	21	42	17			
Mexico*					21	6	
U.S.A.*					21	11	
4. Austro-Sardinian	3/24/48–8/9/48, 3/20/49–3/23/49	4.5	9	9			
Austria					4.5	5.6	
Sardinia (incl. Ital. rebels)					4.5	3.4	
5. Danish	4/10/48–8/26/48, 3/25/49–7/10/49	8	16	6			
Denmark					8	3.5	
Prussia					8	2.5	
6. Roman	4/30/49, 5/8/49–7/1/49	2	7	2.2			
Austria					2	.1	5/8/49–7/1/49
France					1	.5	4/30/49, 6/3/49–
Papal States*					2	1.5	[7/1/49
Two Sicilies*					2	.1	5/8/49–7/1/49
7. La Plata	7/19/51–2/3/52	6.5	13	1.3			
Argentina*					6.5	.8	
Brazil*					6.5	.5	
8. Crimean	10/23/53–3/1/56	28	115.5	264.2			
England					23	22	3/31/54–3/1/56
France					23	95	3/31/54–3/1/56
Russia					28	100	
Sardinia					13.5	2.2	1/10/55–3/1/56
Turkey					28	45	
9. Persian	10/25/56–3/14/57	4.5	9	2			
England					4.5	.5	
Persia*					4.5	1.5	
10. Italian	4/29/59–7/12/59	2.5	7	22.5			
Austria					2.5	12.5	
France					2	7.5	5/3/59–7/12/59
Sardinia					2.5	2.5	
11. Moroccan	10/22/59–3/26/60	5	10	10			
Morocco*					5	6	
Spain					5	4	
12. Roman	9/11/60 – 9/29/60	.5	1	1			
Italy					.5	.3	
Papal States*					.5	.7	

*Indicates peripheral system nation.

[a]Number includes central system nation-months only in Austro-Prussian and Franco-Prussian Wars.

[b]All foreign losses insignificant in Boxer Rebellion.

[c]Vichy 11/30/40–1/31/41, 11/8/42–11/11/42.

TABLE 2.—*continued*

Name of War and Participants	Dates	International System			Each Nation		National Dates (if different)
		Duration (Months)	Nation Months	Battle Deaths (thousands)	Duration (Months)	Battle Deaths (thousands)	
13. Sicilian	10/15/60–1/19/61	3	6	1			
Italy					3	.6	
Two Sicilies*					3	.4	
14. Mexican Expedition	4/16/62–2/5/67	57.5	115	20			
France					57.5	8	
Mexico*					57.5	12	
15. Colombian	11/22/63–12/6/63	.5	1	1			
Colombia*					.5	.3	
Ecuador*					.5	.7	
16. Schleswig-Holstein	2/1/64–4/25/64, 6/25/64–7/20/64	4	12	4.5			
Austria					4	.5	
Denmark					4	3	
Prussia					4	1	
17. Spanish	10/25/65–5/9/66	6.5	17	1			
Chile*					6.5	.1	
Peru*					4	.6	1/14/66–5/9/66
Spain					6.5	.3	
18. Austro-Prussian	6/15/66–7/26/66	1.5	15.5	36.1			
Austria			4.5ᵃ		1.5	20	
Baden*					1.5	.1	
Bavaria*					1.5	.5	
Hanover*					.5	.5	6/15/66–6/29/66
Hesse-Electoral*					1.5	.1	
Hesse-Grand Ducal*					1.5	.1	
Italy					1.5	4	
Mecklenburg-Schwerin*					1.5	.1	
Prussia					1.5	10	
Saxony*					1.5	.6	
Württemberg*					1.5	.1	
19. Franco-Prussian	7/19/70–2/26/71	7	26.5	187.5			
Baden*			14ᵃ		4	1	7/19/70–11/22/70
Bavaria*					4	5.5	7/19/70–11/15/70
France					7	140	
Prussia					7	40	
Württemberg*					4.5	1	7/19/70–11/25/70
20. Russo-Turkish	4/12/77–1/3/78	8.5	17	285			
Russia					8.5	120	
Turkey					8.5	165	
21. Pacific	2/14/79–12/11/83	58	170.5	14			
Bolivia*					58	1	
Chile*					58	3	
Peru*					54.5	10	4/5/79–10/20/83
22. Central American	3/28/85–4/15/85	.5	1	1			
Guatemala*					.5	.8	
Salvador*					.5	.2	
23. Sino-Japanese	8/1/94–3/30/95	8	16	15			
China*					8	10	
Japan*					8	5	

TABLE 2.—*continued*

Name of War and Participants	Dates	International System			Each Nation		National Dates (if different)
		Duration (Months)	Nation Months	Battle Deaths (thousands)	Duration (Months)	Battle Deaths (thousands)	
24. Greco-Turkish	2/15/97–5/19/97	3	6	2			
Greece					3	6	
Turkey					3	1.4	
25. Spanish-American	4/2/98–8/12/98	4	8	10			
Spain					4	5	
U.S.A.*					4	5	
26. Boxer	6/17/00–8/25/00	2	18	2			
China					2	1.5[b]	
Austria					2		
England					2		
France					2		
Germany					2		
Italy					2		
Japan					2		
Russia					2		
U.S.A.					2		
27. Russo-Japanese	2/8/04–9/15/05	19	38	130			
Japan					19	85	
Russia					19	45	
28. Central American	5/27/06–7/20/06	2	6	1			
Guatemala*					2	.4	
Honduras*					2	.3	
Salvador*					2	.3	
29. Central American	2/19/07–4/23/07	2	6	1			
Honduras*					2	.3	
Nicaragua*					2	.4	
Salvador*					2	.3	
30. Moroccan	7/7/09–3/23/10	8.5	17	10			
Morocco*					8.5	8	
Spain					8.5	2	
31. Italo-Turkish	9/29/11–10/18/12	12.5	25	20			
Italy					12.5	6	
Turkey					12.5	14	
32. 1st Balkan	10/17/12–4/19/13	6	20	82			
Bulgaria					4	32	}10/17/12–12/3/12,
Serbia (& Montenegro)					4	15	}2/3/13–4/19/13
Greece					6	5	
Turkey					6	30	
33. 2nd Balkan	6/30/13–7/30/13	1	4	61			
Bulgaria					1	18	
Greece					1	2.5	
Romania					.5	1.5	7/11/13–7/30/13
Serbia					1	18.5	
Turkey					.5	20	7/15/13–7/30/13

TABLE 2.—*continued*

Name of War and Participants	Dates	International System			Each Nation		National Dates (if different)
		Duration (Month)	Nation Months	Battle Deaths (thousands)	Duration (Months)	Battle Deaths (thousands)	
34. World War I	7/29/14–11/11/18	51.5	606.5	10,000			
Austria					51	1,200	7/29/14–11/3/18
Belgium					51	87.5	8/4/14–11/11/18
Bulgaria					35.5	14	10/12/15–9/29/18
England					51	908	8/5/14–11/11/18
France					51	1,350	8/3/14–11/11/18
Germany					51.5	1,800	8/1/14–11/11/18
Greece					16.5	5	6/29/17–11/11/18
Italy					41.5	650	5/23/15–11/11/18
Japan					50.5	.3	8/23/14–11/11/18
Portugal					32.5	7	3/1/16–11/11/18
Romania					15.5	335	8/27/16–12/9/17
Russia					40	1,700	8/1/14–12/5/17
Serbia					51.5	48	
Turkey					48.5	325	10/28/14–11/11/18
U.S.A.					19	126	4/17/17–11/11/18
35. Greco-Turkish	5/5/19–10/11/22	41	82	50			
Greece					41	30	
Turkey					41	20	
36. Chaco	5/12/28–12/19/33, 1/8/34–6/12/35	84	168	130			
Bolivia					84	80	
Paraguay					84	50	
37. Sino-Japanese	12/19/31–5/6/33	16.5	33	60			
China					16.5	50	
Japan					16.5	10	
38. Italo-Ethiopian	10/3/35–5/9/36	7	14	20			
Ethiopia					7	16	
Italy					7	4	
39. Sino-Japanese	7/7/37–12/7/41	53	106	1,000			
China					53	750	
Japan					53	250	
40. Russo-Finnish	11/30/39–3/12/40	3.5	7	90			
Finland					3.5	40	
Russia					3.5	50	
41. World War II	9/1/39–8/14/45	71.5	910	16,000			
Australia					71.5	23	9/3/39–8/14/45
Belgium					.5	7.8	5/10/40–5/28/40
Brazil					10	.1	7/6/44–5/7/45
Bulgaria					34.5	10	12/8/41–10/28/44
Canada					71	37.5	9/10/39–8/14/45
China					44	1,350	12/7/41–8/14/45
England					71.5	270	9/3/39–8/14/45
Ethiopia					5.5	5	1/24/41–7/3/41
Finland					39	42	6/25/41–9/19/44
France					19.5	210	9/3/39–6/22/40, 10/23/44–8/14/45[c]

TABLE 2.—*continued*

Name of War and Participants	Dates	International System			Each Nation		National Dates (if different)
		Duration (Months)	Nation Months	Battle Deaths (thousands)	Duration (Months)	Battle Deaths (thousands)	
Germany					68	3,500	9/1/39–5/7/45
Greece					6	25	10/25/40–4/23/41
Holland					.5	6.2	5/10/40–5/14/40
Hungary					43	40	6/27/41–1/20/45
Italy					57	77	6/10/40–9/2/43, 10/18/43–5/7/45
Japan					44	1,000	12/7/41–8/14/45
Mexico					3.5	.1	5/1/45–8/14/45
New Zealand					71.5	10	9/3/39–8/14/45
Norway					2	1	4/9/40–6/9/40
Poland					1	320	9/1/39–9/27/39
Romania					39	300	6/22/41–9/13/44
Russia					47	7,500	6/22/41–5/7/45, 8/8/45–8/14/45
South Africa					71	6.8	9/6/39–8/14/45
Thailand					45	.1	11/30/40–1/31/41, 1/25/42–8/14/45
U.S.A.					44	292	12/7/41–8/14/45
Yugoslavia					.5	410	4/6/41–4/17/41

toward one ally by another; and (2) the nature of the signatories in terms of whether they are major or minor' powers.

At to the first dimension, three classes of alliance commitment are considered. Class I, which will be called a *defense pact,* commits each signatory to intervene with military force on behalf of the other(s). Class II, which is called here a *neutrality or non-aggression pact,* commits each to refrain from military intervention against any of the other signatories in the event that they become engaged in war. Class III, labeled *entente,* merely requires that the signatories consult with one another in the contingent eventuality. It should be noted here that these classifications are based upon the treaty text itself and not upon the way in which the alliance was adhered to in actual practice.[14]

Perhaps a brief justification of our reliance on written alliances in general and their texts in particular is in order. Admittedly, other phenomena would reveal more fully the friendship-hostility, close-distant, or dependent-independent dimensions of international relationships, but two considerations are relevant here. First, it seems perfectly reasonable to assume that the decision to undertake such an alliance commitment does indeed reflect and respond to many of these more specific, prior relationships. Moreover, one cannot argue that the commit-

14. Elsewhere, we not only spell out the coding rules in greater detail and with illustrations, but give the voluminous bibliography from which our basic information was drawn; see Singer and Small (1966b).

ments are undertaken in a frivolous manner, with little awareness of the implications or little intent to honor them. On the basis of our earlier analysis of such commitments, we found, for example, a significant positive correlation between alliance membership and war involvement on the side of the alliance partner. Second, there are some serious obstacles to getting at the more complex phenomena surrounding alliance formation. For example, much of this could be ascertained via content analysis of diplomatic communications, yet the availability of all, or a representative sample of, such documents is problematical; and that method is still a costly and time-consuming one. Moreover, other research groups are moving ahead on the "automation" of content analysis, and there is little point in duplicating that important pioneering venture at this juncture (Holsti, *et al.*, 1964).

Turning to the second dimension, there is the matter of the signatories' power status. Here our interest is in whether a given alliance tie—and every multilateral alliance is treated, for analytical purposes, as if it were a number of separate bilateral ones—is between two major powers or between two minors, or between a major and a minor. Combining the two sets of dimensions, then, we see that nine types of bilateral alliance commitment are possible.[15]

As should be quite evident by now, it is no simple matter to identify all alliances of all relevant types for 130 years and ascertain their scope, membership, and duration. For a study of this type, based as it is on what aims to be the complete population of events rather than a sample thereof, this requirement is mandatory. Let us summarize, therefore, the coding rules which are developed in greater detail in the above-cited paper. First, only those alliance commitments embodied in a formal, written treaty, convention, or executive agreement were included, whether or not it was secret at the time. Among those which were excluded were (1) collective security agreements, such as the League Covenant and the United Nations Charter; (2) charters and constitutions of international organizations such as those of the Universal Postal Union, International Labour Organization, or the Danube River Commission; (3) treaties of guarantee to which all relevant powers registered their assent, such as the Belgian Neutrality Agreement of 1839, the Washington Conference Treaties of 1921–1922, and the Locarno Pacts of 1925; (4) agreements limited to general rules of behavior, such as the Kellogg-Briand Pact and the Geneva Conventions; (5) alliances which were consummated during, or less than three months before, a war in which any of the signatories participated, unless the alliance endured beyond the formal treaty of peace; (6) any alliances contracted during the two world wars, whether or not the signatories were belligerents; and (7) any alliance which did not include at least two members of our system.

In addition to these problems of ambiguity regarding inclusion or exclusion, there was the matter of chronological coverage. The effective inception date is almost always stipulated in the text or associated documents; if not, the date of ratification was used. In those few cases for which formal termination is not clear,

15. Though some scholars tend to differentiate between an alliance and a coalition, the distinction seems unimportant. Gulick, for example, defines an alliance as a "bilateral or trilateral agreement for offensive or defensive purposes," and then defines a coalition as "a similar agreement signed by four or more powers or a conjunction of several alliances directed toward the same end" (1955, p. 78). He alludes to other distinctions, but they make the difference no clearer.

TABLE 3. *Inter-Nation Alliances, 1815–1939, with Commitment Class and Dates*

Members	Incept.	Termin.	Class	Members	Incept.	Termin.	Class
Austria Baden* Bavaria* Hesse-Electoral* Hesse-Grand Ducal* Prussia Saxony* Württemberg* Hanover* Mecklenburg- Schwerin*	6/1815–1848, 1850 1838** 1843**	1866	1	Austria Parma*	1851	1859	1
				France Sardinia	1/1859	1859	1
Austria England Prussia Russia France	11/1815 11/1818	1823	1	Modena* Parma* Tuscany*	?/1859	1860	1
				Ecuador* Peru*	1/1860	1861(?)	1
England France Russia	7/1827	1830	3	England France Spain	10/1861	1862	3
Russia Turkey	7/1833	1840	1	Prussia Russia	2/1863	1864	1
				Colombia* Ecuador*	1/1864	1865(?)	1
Austria Prussia Russia	10/1833–1848, 1850	1854	3	Baden* Prussia	8/1866	1870	1
England France Portugal Spain	4/1834–1840, 1841	1846	1	Prussia Wurtemberg*	8/1866	1870	1
				Bavaria* Prussia	8/1866	1870	1
Austria England Prussia Russia Turkey	7/1840	1840	1	Bolivia* Peru*	2/1873	1883	1
				Austria Germany Russia	10/1873	1878	3
England Russia	6/1844	1846 (1853?)	3	Austria Russia	1/1877	1878	2
Austria Modena*	12/1847	1859	1	England Turkey	6/1878	1880	1

Classes of alliance are: 1-Defense Pact; 2-Neutrality or Nonagression Pact; 3-Entente.
    Inception dates show month and year, but termination dates cannot be ascertained with the same precision; where no consensus exists for that date, an alternate year (?) is also shown.
    Comma between dates indicates temporary break in the alliance.
    Brackets indicate that one or more bilateral alliances were merged in a new and larger grouping.

    *Indicates that nation belongs to peripheral system only.

    **Indicates that nation qualified for system membership *after* joining alliance, i.e. this date.

    ***Indicates that the same nations negotiated a new alliance of another class, effective this date.

TABLE 3.—*continued*

Members	Incept.	Termin.	Class	Members	Incept.	Termin.	Class
Austria Germany Italy	10/1879 5/1882	1914	1	France Spain	10/1904	1914	3
Austria Germany Russia	6/1881	1887	2	England Spain	5/1907	1914	3
				France Japan	6/1907	1914	3
Austria Serbia	6/1881, 1889***	1889 1895	2 1	Japan Russia	7/1907	1914	3
Austria Germany Romania Italy	10/1883 5/1888	1914	1	England Russia	8/1907	1914	3
				Japan U.S.A.	10/1908	1909	3
Germany Russia	6/1887	1890	2	Italy Russia	10/1909	1914	3
Austria England Italy	2/1887	1895 (1897?)	3	Bulgaria Serbia	3/1912	1913	1
Austria Italy Spain	5/1887	1895	2	Bulgaria Greece	5/1912	1913	1
France Russia	8/1891, 1894***	1894 1914	3 1	Greece Serbia	6/1913	1914	1
China Russia	5/1896	1902(?)	1	Czechoslov. Yugoslavia	8/1920	1933	1
Japan Russia	6/1896	1903	3	Czechoslov. Romania	4/1921	1933	1
Austria Russia	5/1897	1908	3	Romania Yugoslavia	6/1921	1933	1
England Portugal	10/1899	1914	1	Czechoslov. Romania Yugoslavia	2/1933	1939	1
France Italy	12/1900, 7/1902***	1902 1914	3 2	Belgium France	9/1920	1936	1
England Japan	1/1902	1921	1	France Poland	2/1921	1939 (1934?)	1
England France	4/1904	1914	3	Poland Romania	3/1921	1939	1

TABLE 3.—*continued*

Members	Incept.	Termin.	Class	Members	Incept.	Termin.	Class
Afghanistan Turkey	3/1921	1939	1	Persia Russia	10/1927	1939	2
Persia Turkey	4/1926	1937	2	Greece Romania	3/1928	1934	2
Afghanistan Persia	11/1927	1937	2	Greece Turkey	10/1930	1934	2
Afghanistan Iraq Persia Turkey	9/1937	1939	2	Romania Turkey	10/1933	1934	2
Austria Czechoslovakia	12/1921	1927	2	Turkey Yugoslavia	11/1933	1934	2
Estonia Latvia	11/1923	1939	1	Greece Romania Turkey Yugoslavia	2/1934	1939	1
Czechoslovakia France	1/1924, 1925***	1924 1939	3 1	Greece Italy	2/1928	1938	2
Italy Yugoslavia	1/1924	1927	2	Italy Turkey	5/1928	1938	2
Czechoslovakia Italy	7/1924	1930	3	Hungary Turkey	1/1929	1939	2
Russia Turkey	12/1925	1939	2	Bulgaria Turkey	3/1929	1938	2
Germany Russia	4/1926	1936	2	Bulgaria Greece Romania Turkey Yugoslavia	7/1938	1939	2
France Romania	6/1926	1939	2				
Afghanistan Russia	8/1926	1939	2	France Turkey	2/1930	1939	2
Lithuania Russia	9/1926	1939	2	England Iraq	1932	1939	1
Italy Romania	9/1926	1930	3	Finland Russia	1/1932	1939	2
Albania Italy	11/1926, 1927***	1927 1939	3 1	Latvia Russia	2/1932	1939	2
France Yugoslavia	1/1927	1939	2	Estonia Russia	5/1932	1939	2
Hungary Italy	4/1927	1939	2	Poland Russia	7/1932	1939	2

TABLE 3.—*continued*

Members	Incept.	Termin.	Class
France	11/1932,	1935	2
Russia	1935***	1939	1
England	6/1933	1936(?)	3
France			
Germany			
Italy			
Italy	9/1933	1939	2
Russia			
Argentina	10/1933	1939	2
Brazil			
Chile			
Mexico			
Paraguay			
Uruguay			
Colombia	4/1934		
Panama	11/1936		
Finland	2/1938		
Germany	1/1934	1939	2
Poland			
Austria	3/1934	1938	3
Hungary			
Italy			
Estonia	8/1934	1939	3
Latvia			
Lithuania			
France	4/1935	1938	3
Italy			
Czechoslovakia	5/1935	1939	1
Russia			
Mongolia	3/1936	1939	1
Russia			
Egypt	10/1936	1939	1
England			
Germany	11/1936	1939	3
Japan			
Italy	11/1937		

Members	Incept.	Termin.	Class
Argentina	12/1936	1939	3
Bolivia			
Brazil			
Chile			
Colombia			
Costa Rica			
Cuba			
Dominican Republic			
Ecuador			
Guatemala			
Haiti			
Honduras			
Mexico			
Nicaragua			
Panama			
Paraguay			
Peru			
Salvador			
U.S.A.			
Uruguay			
Venezuela			
Italy	3/1937	1939	2
Yugoslavia			
Arabia	4/1937	1939	1
Yemen			
China	8/1937	1939	2
Russia			
France	12/1938	1939	3
Germany			
Portugal	3/1939	1939	2
Spain			
Germany	5/1939	1939	1
Italy			
Denmark	5/1939	1939	2
Germany			
Estonia	6/1939	1939	2
Germany			
Germany	6/1939	1939	2
Latvia			

we have relied upon a consensus of the historical monographs available. Finally, renewals were not counted as separate treaties unless the specific commitments were changed, as from entente to defensive alliance. The hundred and twelve alliances which met our criteria are shown in Table 3, along with the effective dates and the class of commitment undertaken by the signatories.

Once all of the relevant alliances were discovered, classified, and counted, it was a simple matter to complete the operationalization of our aggregate interaction opportunity indices. For each year, we merely converted the raw numbers of each type of alliance into a percentage figure, so that we ended up with a list of the five following independent variables:

1. Percentage of all nations having at least one alliance *of any class* with any type of nation, major or minor.
2. Percentage of all nations having at least one *defensive* pact with any type of nation.
3. Percentage of *major* powers having at least one alliance *of any class* with another major power.
4. Percentage of major powers having at least one *defensive* pact with another major.
5. Percentage of major powers having at least one alliance *of any class* with any *minor* power.

In addition to these five measures of aggregate interaction opportunity loss[16] we also sought a measure of the extent to which the various alliances created a degree of bipolarity in the system for each year. Here the procedure was a bit more complicated, and to balance off manageability with relevance, the computations were only made for *defensive* pacts among *major* powers. The first step was to calculate the maximum number of dyads that could be formed from among the population of major powers, using the formula $\frac{N(N-1)}{2}$. Then we calculated the percentage of these which had been exhausted, via the following steps. All defensive pact links were counted and the target(s), if any, of each identified; either a single nation or all members of a given alliance can be classified as targets. Next, we eliminated all linkages that were no longer possible: (1) those between members within each alliance; (2) those between members of opposing alliances; and (3) those between a target nation and all members of the alliance directed against that target nation. For any nation which was neither a target nor an alliance member, the maximum number of linkages still open was then counted, using the rule that it might contract an alliance with other non-allied or non-target nations, plus either all members of the largest alliance, or all the non-allied target(s), whichever was the larger number. Once the number of feasible remaining defensive alliance links was ascertained, that number was divided into the original number that would have been possible in the absence of any such alliances, to give the percentage of major power defensive alliance ties exhausted.

One problem that confronted us was the occasional ambiguity regarding the

---

16. We also gathered data for neutrality pacts and ententes, but further refinements of those measures is called for in order to handle the problem of which alliance commitment takes precedence when a nation belongs to alliances of different classes. Findings based on those measures will be reported subsequently.

target nation of a given alliance. That is, in 48 of our 130 years, there was sufficient disagreement among historians as to whether or not there is any target at all. In those cases, we computed an alternative bipolarity index. As in other places where professional consensus was used in place of a costly and complex operationalizing procedure, our authorities are identified in the basic descriptive article (Singer and Small, 1966b). In the tables, therefore, two sets of bipolarity indices and two sets of correlations are shown, and in the next section the intercorrelations between them are also shown. Let us illustrate (Figure 1) this procedure by reference to the alliance configuration of 1913; in that year, there were eight major powers, offering a maximum of twenty-eight possible linkages.

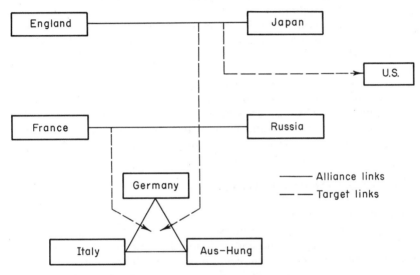

FIGURE 1. *Major Power Alliance Configurations, 1913*

In the diagram, we see that twenty-one (or 75 per cent) of those twenty-eight possible linkages were exhausted by alliances or by the logic of the targets as follows

By Alliance (5)	*By Target* (14)	
England-Japan	England-Italy	France-Germany
France-Russia	England-Germany	France-Austria
Austria-Germany	England-Austria	Russia-Italy
Austria-Italy	Japan-Italy	Russia-Germany
Germany-Italy	Japan-Germany	Russia-Austria
	Japan-Austria	Japan-United States
	France-Italy	England-United States

Two (2) more linkages are exhausted because if the United States allied with Germany, Austria-Hungary, and Italy, it obviously could no longer ally with France and Russia.

Before leaving this section, one more procedure needs to be described. Just as we ran correlations for three different time lags during which the onset of war could be measured, we felt that there was no *a priori* justification for assuming that our alliance data for a single year gave us the best independent variable. It could just as readily be argued that the system's alliance patterns are best reflected in their average magnitude over a longer period of time; for example, the duration of a given configuration might be as important as its magnitude. Therefore, three separate indices for each year and each independent variable were computed, showing that year's index, an average for that year plus the two preceding years, and an average for that year plus the four preceding years. Thus, for 1908 we have indicators on the independent variable side for 1908, the 1906–1908 average, and the 1904–1908 average. While all correlations have been run, only the three-year average is reported. (The remaining figures may be requested from the authors.)

These, then, represent our effort to convert the chaotic welter of historical facts or impressions on wars and alliances into relatively operational and machine-readable variables. The rigorous social scientist may well argue that intuition and apparent consensus among historians was permitted too large a role, while the diplomatic historian may hold that we have forced a large number of discrete events and unique relationships into too few Procrustean categories. Be that as it may, we have sought the most reasonable balance between reliability and validity, and urge others to examine and perhaps improve upon, the detailed coding procedures outlined in the two descriptive papers cited earlier.

OBSERVED CORRELATIONS

With our operationalizing procedures out of the way, and our raw data's legitimacy more or less established, we can now turn to the many alternative correlations which were sought and/or found. Because of our uncertainty as to which represented the best measure and because of the low marginal cost of the additional measures, we developed and gathered data on a multiplicity of indices for both the dependent and the independent variables. Therefore, prior to an examination of the correlations between our independent and dependent variables, it might be helpful to look *within* each of these groups, summarize their inter-correlations, and ascertain the extent to which each of our seven independent variables and our five dependent ones seem to be measuring the same phenomena.

Comparing the Dependent Variables

It will be recalled that we collected our data in such form as to permit the measurement of both the amount of war *underway* in any given year and the amount which *began* in any given year. In this study, however, concerned as we are with the extent to which alliance aggregation predicts to the *onset* of war, we will only present the data showing the number, magnitude, and severity of wars *beginning* in a given year. For a number of theoretical and methodological reasons, the underway data will be reserved for a separate and later paper.

The reader will also recall that the exploratory nature of the study demanded that we allow three different time lags during which a given alliance pattern's "effects" could be measured. That is, uncertain as to how long it took for the hypothesized consequences of alliances to be felt, we gathered data to show the effects within one year, within three years, and within five years following each year's alliance configuration. Thus, if we are looking, for example, at the alliance data for 1868, those various indices were all correlated with the data for wars which began in 1869, which began between January 1869 and December 1871, and those which began between January 1869 and December 1873. Once these data were in, however, it became clear that, if any alliance effects were to be found, they had largely made themselves felt within three years, especially in the twentieth century.[17] Thus, only the $Y + 3$ correlations will be shown in the Tables here.

TABLE 4. *Correlations Among Dependent Variables: The Onset of War within Three Years of each Year's Alliance Aggregations, 1815–1945*

	Total System				Central System			
	N-M War Begun—All	N-M War Begun—Majors	Battle Deaths—All	Battle Deaths—Majors	N-M War Begun—All	N-M War Begun—Majors	Battle Deaths—All	Battle Deaths—Majors
N-M War Begun—All								
N-M War Begun—Majors	95				96			
Battle Deaths—All	97	96			98	97		
Battle Deaths—Majors	97	97	99		98	98	99	
No. Wars Begun	34	35	28	27	52	54	49	47

As Table 4 reveals, whether we look at the total international system or the central system alone, there is indeed an impressively high correlation among most of these dependent variable indicators.[18] It is patently evident that we were overly concerned. That is, whether we look at the total system or the central system, and whether we look at all nations or major ones only, the correlation coefficient between nation-months and battle deaths is only a shade less than one. (Unity, of course, would show that the indices were all measuring precisely the same thing.) The only low, but nevertheless still significant, correlations are between the magnitude and severity measures on one hand and the frequency ones on the other. Given the distributions described earlier, this was to be expected.

17. An interesting point emerges when these various time lags are examined carefully. In the nineteenth century, the effects are seldom fully evident until five years have elapsed, whereas three years suffice in the twentieth century. This pattern strongly suggests that, in contrast to "real" time, "diplomatic" time has indeed speeded up in more recent years. In a subsequent paper, we will report a number of other indications of this time compression tendency. A suggestive treatment of this problem in social science is Moore (1963).

18. A statistical note is in order here. We recognize that our observations do not satisfy the requirements which most statisticians would demand in order to speak of levels of significance. First, we are not sampling here, but are observing the entire population of events. Second our indices—annual readings of alliance aggregation and war onset—obviously are not independent

(continued overleaf)

Comparing the Independent Variables

Comparing the alliance aggregation figures to one another is a somewhat more complex matter than that involving the war data. Here, we have not only the standard spatial and chronological subsets, but the various combinations of signatory status and alliance class. Further, there is the distinction between aggregate commitments and those which generate our two alternative indices of bipolarity. In addition to these latter, which, as indicated earlier, are based solely on the polarization among the major powers, there are (1) all classes of alliance among all nations; (2) all classes of alliance among major powers; (3) defense

TABLE 5. *Correlations Among Independent Variables: Annual Alliance Aggregations, 1815–1839*

	Total System						Central System Only					
	% Nations in Alliance	% Nations in Defense Pact	% Majors in Alliance	% Majors in Defense Pact	% Major Allied with Minors	Major Bilateral Defense Exhausted–a	% Nations in Alliance	% Nations in Defense Pact	% Majors in Alliance	% Majors in Defense Pact	% Majors Allied with Minors	Major Bilateral Defense Exhausted–a
% Nations in Defense Pact	*74*						*80*					
% Majors in Alliance	*50*	*53*					*77*	*74*				
% Majors in Defense Pact	*32*	*60*	*81*				*58*	*83*	*81*			
% Majors Allied with Minors	*64*	*61*	*64*	*59*			*80*	*70*	42	33		
Major Bilateral Defense Exhausted—a	00	–01	*47*	*57*	26		*54*	*53*	*47*	*57*	*51*	
Major Bilateral Defense Exhausted–b	*45*	*50*	*60*	*68*	*67*	*58*	*57*	*70*	*60*	*68*	48	*58*

of one another from year to year. Third, the distributions are not "normally" distributed, and any normalizing transformation would have distorted a perfectly satisfactory scale. However, one must use some objective and quantitative benchmark by which "strong" relationships may be differentiated from "weak" ones, and by which one may classify these observed relationships as compelling or not. Thus, we have used the Pearson product-moment correlation as our measure of the strength of the observed relationships and gone on to scrutinize each such correlation value (r) to ascertain whether or not we might call it strong or weak. For that purpose, we use Fisher's exact test of statistical significance (two-tailed to allow for negative correlations) and treat all r's that exceed the requirements for an .01 level of significance with a given N as strong. For the nineteenth century and an N of 85, that threshold is .25, and for the twentieth and an N of only 45, the threshold requirement goes up to a coincidental .45; values meeting these levels are italicized. Note that r's are rounded off to only two places and that the decimal point is omitted.

pacts among all; (4) defense pacts among majors; and (5) all alliances between majors and minors. As noted earlier, we are not examining here the extent to which neutrality pacts and ententes "predict to" war, inasmuch as the count on these is somewhat misleading; that is, neutrality or entente commitments were counted only when no defense pact existed between the nations in any dyad. In other words, only the highest class of commitment between each pair was counted.

As Table 5 reveals, there exists a very impressive intercorrelation among these several alliance measures. In the central system, every indicator correlates strongly with every other, and in the total system, the only absence of correlation is that between the initial and the alternative bipolarity figures on the one hand, and the all-allied and all-in-defense-pact figures, on the other. This lack of significant correlation need not surprise us, given the fact that the bipolarity measures reflect major power cleavages only. Again, but to a considerably lesser extent than with war, we are tapping approximately the same structural phenomena.

Having digressed for the important purpose of ascertaining the extent to which our many different measures tend to tap the same phenomena, we may now move on to the primary concern of the study: the extent to which alliance aggregation in its various forms predicts to war.

Total System, 1815–1945

In order to make more comprehensible the many pairs of correlations within our six different systemic settings, a brief recapitulation would seem to be in order. The correlations will be so presented in the separate tables as to identify: (1) the international system or portion thereof which is under examination; (2) the time period for which it is being examined; (3) the specific independent variables being used; and (4) the specific dependent variables. As we indicated earlier, a great many more correlations were run than are reported here; among those not shown here are (1) eight of the nine r values for each cross-correlation, with only the three-year average for alliance indices and the three-year lag for war indices correlated in the text and accompanying tables; (2) all neutrality pact and entente data, with only the defense pact and all alliance class categories shown in the text; and (3) all data dealing with war actually underway, with only the data on *onset* of war shown in the text. Contrary to some practice, we will include all r values in each table, even those which are not equivalent to statistically significant levels; those which equal or exceed the .01 level requirement will be italicized. As to sequence, we begin with the total system for the entire 1815–1945 period, and then drop the peripheral nations and concentrate on the central system only for the same full period. Next we look at the total system in the nineteenth century, and then move on to the central system only for that eighty-five-year period. Finally, we examine the twentieth century total system and central system in that order.

Turning, then, to our first and most comprehensive empirical world—that of the total international system for the entire 1815–1945 period (shown in Table 6)—we find one set of consistently high correlations. That is, the grossest of the independent variables—percentage of *all* nations in at least one alliance of *any* class—shows significant correlations with all four of the magnitude and severity indicators, but not with the number of wars beginning within three years. On the major power side, however, no such findings emerge. As a matter of fact there are no other sufficiently high *r* values at all for this total system-entire period setting, although the major with minor correlation approaches that level.

TABLE 6. *Total System, 1815–1945: Correlations Between Alliance Indicators and Magnitude, Severity, and Frequency of War Beginning Within Three Years*

	% of All in Any Alliance	% of All in Defense Pact	% of Majors in Any Alliance	% of Majors in Defense Pact	% of Majors with Minor	Bipolarity Initial	Bipolarity Alternate
Nation-Months War—All	30	−05	05	06	17	08	13
Nation-Months War—Majors	28	−01	10	04	22	14	18
Battle Deaths for All	34	−01	11	01	21	15	19
Battle Deaths for Majors	31	−01	12	04	21	17	21
Number of Wars	07	−01	06	04	18	−03	01

Central System, 1815–1945

Let us now take the first of several steps in the direction of increasingly restrictive empirical worlds, and shuck off all the peripheral system nations, leaving the central system only, but still for the entire time period. The picture is pretty

TABLE 7. *Central System, 1815–1945: Correlations Between Alliance Indicators and Magnitude, Severity, and Frequency of War Beginning Within Three Years*

	% of All in Any Alliance	% of All in Defense Pact	% of Majors in Any Alliance	% of Majors in Defense Pact	% of Majors with Minor	Bipolarity Initial	Bipolarity Alternate
Nation-Months War—All	33	11	06	−02	34	12	16
Nation-Months War—Majors	34	14	11	03	34	15	13
Battle Deaths for All	35	12	11	01	34	15	18
Battle Deaths for Majors	35	14	12	04	34	17	20
Number of Wars	19	07	05	−03	28	−07	16

much the same, as we see in Table 7; that is, the percentage of all nations in any class of alliance correlates strongly with all four magnitude (nation-months of war) and severity (battle deaths) indices. Again, defense pacts among all, or among majors only, do not show a high covariation; but in this more restrictive setting, the percentage of majors having at least one alliance of any kind with a minor power does predict significantly to all the war measures. Note that even the frequency measure correlates, albeit modestly, with the major-minor measure, but not with any of the other alliance indicators.

Total System, 1815–1899

As suggested in a previous section, it seemed useful to inquire as to whether the relationship between alliance commitments and war might be stronger or weaker in different epochs; thus we have not only divided our total population into central and total systems, but have also divided it into nineteenth and twentieth century systems. Let us therefore shift from the full population (that is, total system, entire 130-year period) and examine the total system up through 1899 only. A brief glance at Table 8 indicates that this concentration upon the nineteenth-century total system exercises a striking effect on our correlations. That is, we no longer find alliance aggregation in general predicting to war, and those *r*'s that are close to significant are all in the *negative* direction. And when we move over to include major powers only, their general alliance involvement does indeed show a strong—but negative—correlation with both the severity measures; the same holds for major-minor alliances vis-à-vis battle deaths for all. As to our initial bipolarity measure, we find relatively strong correlations vis-à-vis one of the magnitude measures and both of the severity measures.

Although the statistically alert reader may already anticipate what our *post-*1900 correlations will look like, it would be premature either to present them

TABLE 8. *Total System, 1815–1899: Correlations Between Alliance Indicators and Magnitude, Severity and Frequency of War Beginning Within Three Years*

	% of All in Any Alliance	% of All in Defense Pact	% of Majors in Any Alliance	% of Majors in Defense Pact	% of Majors with Minor	Bipolarity Initial	Bipolarity Alternate
Nation-Months War—All	−16	−16	−23	−34	−21	−32	−23
Nation-Months War—Majors	−04	01	−26	−14	−01	−23	−19
Battle Deaths for All	−27	−23	−38	−42	−33	−33	−28
Battle Deaths for Majors	−26	−19	−41	−38	−27	−30	−25
Number of Wars	−00	01	−10	−05	05	−21	−12

next or to offer an interpretation of the above rather consistent negative correlations. Rather, let us stay in the same nineteenth-century time frame, but again shuck off the nations of the peripheral system and look exclusively at the nineteenth century central, or European, state system.

Central System, 1815–1899

TABLE 9. *Central System, 1815-1899: Correlations between Alliance Indicators and Magnitude, Severity and Frequency of War Beginning Within Three Years*

	% of All in Any Alliance	% of All in Defense Pact	% of Majors in Any Alliance	% of Majors in Defense Pact	% of Majors with Minor	Bipolarity Initial	Bipolarity Alternate
Nation-Months War—All	−19	−14	−15	−08	−16	−19	−14
Nation-Months War—Majors	−20	−14	−19	−09	−13	−17	−16
Battle Deaths for All	−45	−45	−44	−45	−33	−34	−30
Battle Deaths for Majors	−46	−41	−48	−42	−30	−32	−28
Number of Wars	−05	−02	−03	07	−04	−20	−06

Here, as Table 9 makes evident, the same nineteenth century pattern continues. That is, all of the strong correlations are in the negative direction, with the severity indices against most sensitive to alliance aggregation. Worth observing is that every one of the alliance indicators correlates strongly and inversely with all battle deaths and with major-power battle deaths arising from war beginning within three years of the alliance condition.

Total System, 1900–1945

We can now look at some of the evidence that should have been anticipated once the nineteenth century data were contrasted to data for the entire period. That is, if alliances and war show some modest positive correlations for the entire 130 years and somewhat stronger, but *negative* correlations for the first 85 years, we may logically expect positive and somewhat stronger *r*'s for the twentieth century data. This indeed is what we find, despite the fact that our N of only 45 years raises the *r*-value requirement to a coincidental .45. Thus, the percentage of all nations in any class of alliance, as well as in defense facts, correlates highly with all four magnitude and severity measures in every case but one (.43 with nation-months of war for all). Likewise, the major-minor figure predicts well to three of these four dependent variables. On the bipolarity side, however, none of the correlations are high enough to be interesting.

TABLE 10. *Total System, 1900–1945: Correlations Between Alliance Indicators and Magnitude, Severity, and Frequency of War Beginning Within Three Years*

	% of All in Any Alliance	% of All in Defense Pact	% of Majors in Any Alliance	% of Majors in Defense Pact	% of Majors with Minor	Bipolarity Initial	Bipolarity Alternate
Nation-Months War—All	53	43	24	05	43	15	28
Nation-Months War—Majors	46	48	35	16	47	24	36
Battle Deaths for All	56	48	29	08	46	19	31
Battle Deaths for Majors	51	48	31	13	45	23	36
Number of Wars	18	29	50	26	54	27	26

It is possible that the 2 WW's completely distort these correlations, due to their vast magnitude.

Central System, 1900–1945

Turning to the last of our empirical worlds, the pattern is essentially the same for the central as for the total twentieth century system. Though defense pacts among all do not predict to war compellingly in this case, alliances in general among all do, as do major-minor alliances in three of the four cases. Again, the bipolarity correlations are all moderately in this direction, but as in the total system, they still fail to satisfy the .01 requirements.

TABLE 11. *Central System, 1900–1945: Correlations Between Alliance Indicators and Magnitide, Severity, and Frequency of War Beginning Within Three Years*

	% of All in Any Alliance	% of All in Defense Pact	% of Majors in Any Alliance	% of Majors in Defense Pact	% of Majors with Minor	Bipolarity Initial	Bipolarity Alternate
Nation-Months War—All	45	04	23	05	42	14	27
Nation-Months War—Majors	49	17	35	18	47	24	36
Battle Deaths for All	50	09	29	09	46	19	32
Battle Deaths for Majors	50	13	31	14	45	23	36
Number of Wars	25	−02	24	−05	40	−05	02

SUMMARY AND INTERPRETATION

Given the material with which we worked, the data-making operations, and the observed correlations between and among our many variables, what can we now say regarding the basic hypothesis? Do alliance aggregations in general, or bipolarity tendencies in particular, correlate in any meaningful way with the onset of international war in the nineteenth and twentieth centuries?

Assuming that our measures are as valid and reliable as claimed, the evidence seems to be relatively unambiguous. We say relatively because there are two quite distinct and incompatible patterns, but the incompatibility is easily resolved by dividing the entire historical epoch into two periods. That is, if we look at the twentieth century segment only, the hypothesis is rather strongly confirmed. (Taking the seven independent variable indicators and the four measures of war magnitude and war severity, for both the central and the total systems, we have fifty-six opportunities for a strong positive correlation to appear. Our results show such a correlation on seventeen of these occasions.) Looking first at the alliance aggregation measures, for both the central and the total systems, we find that the percentage of all nations in the system having at least one alliance with any other nation predicts to the amount of war on all eight of the possible occasions. And the percentage of major powers having at least one alliance with a minor does likewise on six of the eight possible occasions. Defense pact aggregation does so on three of the eight possible occasions. Combining this powerful tendency with the fact that there are quite a few more correlations that are only slightly weaker and that not a single negative correlation appears, we may only conclude that the well-accepted hypothesis has indeed been borne out by our historical evidence.

Does the hypothesis do as well in an earlier epoch? Clearly not. To the contrary, on all eight of the possible occasions for a positive correlation to turn up between gross alliance aggregation and the magnitude or severity of war in the nineteenth century, the correlation was negative. And if the same matrix were constructed for defense pacts, seven of the eight turn out to be negative. Furthermore, if we look at all classes of alliance among major powers only for the nineteenth century, all eight correlations are again negative, four of them stongly so. Even if we focus on major-power defense pacts for both of these nineteenth century systems, five of the eight negative correlations meet our rather stringent threshold criteria. Finally, all eight of the war correlations with major-minor alliance percentages are negative, three at the .01 equivalent level. The observed relationship between alliance aggregation and the onset of war in the nineteenth century, then, is clearly a negative one, and shows a distribution which is diametrically opposed to, and almost as strong as, that found for the twentieth century.

To what extent is the alliance aggregation pattern repeated when we try to predict to war from *bipolarity*? In general, the same tendencies appear, but with somewhat lower coefficient values. That is, if we look at both the initial and the alternative indices of major-power bipolarization, and correlate them with our four magnitude and severity indices in both forms (central and total) of the twentieth century system, all sixteen r's are positive, but only twelve of these are in significance ranges better than .1 (not .01). Any doubt as to the general tendency is dispelled, however, when we examine the nineteenth century total and central systems. As with alliance aggregation, every one of the r values is negative, with eight of the sixteen meeting the .01-level requirement.

Given the extraordinarily low probability of such correlations occurring in such consistent form by sheer chance, we have no choice but to conclude that alliance aggregation and bipolarization do indeed have a meaningful relation to the onset of war. But it is important to note the theoretical implications of these relationships. It is certainly clear that formal alliance patterns do not exercise a uniform impact over time. To the contrary, both alliance aggregation and bipolarity covary strongly with the amount of war that follows within three years during the twentieth century, and correlate *inversely* to almost the same degree during the nineteenth century.

Regardless of the war-onset measure we use, the pattern is similar. Whether it is nation-months of war or battle-connected deaths, whether the data are for the total system or the central one only, and whether they reflect all members of the system or major powers only, when alliance aggregation or bipolarity in the nineteenth century increases, the amount of war experienced by the system goes down, and vice versa. And in the twentieth century, the greater the alliance aggregation or bipolarity in the system, the more war it experiences.

Now the cautious or skeptical reader may say that "it depends" upon what we mean by "amount of war," and ask whether the same picture emerges when we look at the sheer *number* of wars. As a matter of fact, it does, but not quite as impressively. That is, almost all of our independent variables correlate negatively with the number of wars beginning within the $Y + 3$ period during the nineteenth century, and positively during the twentieth century. And the five exceptions out of the fourteen opportunities are barely perceptible: we find r's of .01, .05, and .07 for the nineteenth, and $-.02$ and $-.05$ for the twentieth. Moreover, if there were any concern that it is the sheer magnitude and severity of the two world wars that accounts for the twentieth century positive correlation, it should be noted that when the *number* of wars begun is used as the dependent variable, the r values for percentage of all nations in alliances of any class are .18 and .25. For all major power alliances, these are .50 and .24, and for major-minor alliances, they are .54 and .40, for the total and central systems respectively.[19] In sum, whether we measure amount by number of wars, the nation-months involved, or battle deaths incurred, alliance aggregation and bipolarity predict strongly away from war in the nineteenth century and even more strongly toward it in the twentieth. One might say that those who generalize about the effects of alliance activity—and most postulate a destabilizing effect, especially in regard to bipolarity—have been so preoccupied with more recent history that they have neglected the patterns which obtained in an earlier, but by no means incomparable, period; one recent exception is Waltz (1964).

It is obvious that correlation and causality are rather different things, and that correlation at a high level is *necessary* to the establishment of a causal relationship, but not at all *sufficient*. Unless a logically tight and empirically correct linkage between the independent variables and the dependent ones can be presented, and competing explanations can be disconfirmed, we have established something less than causality. Thus, it seems appropriate to conclude on a cautious note, by indicating the sorts of substantive and methodological questions which remain.

For example, are we able to demonstrate a close empirical and chronological connection between specific alliances and specific wars? At this juncture, our

19. To be doubly sure, we also ran these correlations *without* the World War years, with only a minor reduction in the coefficients resulting.

data are not in the form which would permit a direct answer, but we do have some results of a tangential nature. That is, if we look at the frequency with which a given nation belongs to any alliance within three years prior to any war, and compare that figure to the frequency with which it participates in any war, we find that for all 82 of our nations over the 130 year period, the correlation is .60; and for the 67 central-system members, the figure is a very high .72. But this still doesn't establish a causal connection. Again, there is the simple, but not unreasonable, argument that national decision makers will tend to step up their alliance-building activities as they perceive the probability of war to be rising. This might well account for our twentieth century correlations, and we have, as yet, produced no evidence to contravene the hypothesis.

Beyond this, even though we have uncovered a compelling relationship between alliances and the onset of war, the magnitude of that relation still remains an empirical question, and it may well be that other factors will account for much more of the variance than these two sets of variables. As a matter of fact, if we use the statistical rule of thumb which permits us to say that the amount of variance accounted for by a given independent variable—the coefficient of determination—is approximately the square of the product-moment correlation, we see how limited the alliance effect may be. With the twentieth century (positive) correlations averaging out at .29 and the nineteenth century (negative) ones averaging out at .26, these alliance factors may be interpreted as accounting for somewhere between 8.4 and 6.8 per cent of the variance.[20]

Furthermore, a number of qualifications and caveats regarding some of our independent variables come to mind. As to the five different alliance aggregation indices, we did indeed cover a wide range of possibilities, using all classes of alliance, as well as defense pacts alone, using all nations as well as major powers alone, using six different spatio-temporal forms of the international system, and using nine different lead and lag combinations, but the exploration nevertheless remains incomplete. Again, though we have gathered data on neutrality pacts and on ententes, data on these classes of alliance have not been processed for use here, and it may well be that their presence and absence might shed further light on the alliance-war relationship. Another possibility worth examining might be that of changes in alliance aggregation; that is, each year's increments or decrements vis-à-vis the previous year or years might reveal a discernible pattern that either strengthens or challenges the tendency discovered in this study. Likewise, an investigation into the rates of change might produce some valuable results. Finally, a closely related systemic property is that of the number of individual alliance changes and shifts made in a given year or more by all nations in the system. This measure we call lateral mobility, and some preliminary work on it is already underway.

Similar thoughts occur when our bipolarity measures are considered. First of all, the measure itself reflects the degree of cleavage among major powers only, and while one would intuitively expect the total system to partially parallel the major power sub-system, we have no hard evidence that it does. Moreover, the measure is by no means as compelling an indicator of bipolarization as it might be. Since embarking on this project we have discovered in the sociometry and graph theory literature some promising alternative operations by which such cleavage might be measured; some of these operations require that we first develop a better

20. Another way of saying this is to reiterate that bivariate analyses can seldom explain (account for) highly complex and obviously multivariate social phenomena.

procedure for identifying alliance targets, while others do not.[21] In the same vein, it immediately occurs to us that bipolarity by itself may not be as interesting or compelling a predictor as when it is combined with one or more additional variables. For example, it might well pay to examine the joint effects of polarity and parity: is high bipolarity more likely to precede the onset of war when the two coalitions are approximately equal in power and capability or when a clear disparity exists?

Or, it might well be that the traditional theory overlooks a simple but crucial element: can the invisible hand ever function within so small a population? Certainly a large numerical discrepancy exists between the thousands of buyers and sellers in an economic marketplace and the eighty-two actors in our pre-1945 total system or the one hundred-twenty-odd ones in the postwar system. It might turn out that hypotheses generated from models of oligopoly or duopoly will stand the empirical test more successfully than those generated by a free and open market model.

Then, again, there is the matter of structural or cultural context. Is it not possible that the structural variable utilized here—alliance aggregation—is in turn responsive to other systemic properties, and that its predictive power is a function of its interaction with such variables? To put it another way, are nations as likely to respond to short- and middle-range security requirements and make alliances on that basis alone, when the diplomatic culture is increasingly ideological or less homogeneous, or when the structure of the system is more rigid or its supra-national aspects are increasing? Similarly, it can be argued that our approach is entirely too formal, and that emphasis might better be placed on other indices of international relationship: diplomatic communication, trade, tourism, or less formal and perhaps unwritten indicators of reciprocal committment. Though these suggestions would carry us beyond our immediate concern here, they are certainly well taken.

A final concern is that raised in a thoughtful but as yet unpublished critique (Zinnes, 1966) regarding the extent to which this analysis really "tested the balance of power theory." As the title of this paper and its specific sections makes clear, we are not testing *the theory*, but only one basic proposition which we believe can be deduced from it; moreover, to grace the conceptual and empirical chaos of the balance of power literature with the label "theory" is much too generous. Within that critique, however, a specific problem of considerable importance *is* raised, and it merits a brief discussion. As we understand the criticism, it concerns the validity of our independent variable, and questions whether our alliance aggregation and alliance involvement indicators really reflect the diminution of cross-pressures as implied in our theoretical argument. Our argument, it will be recalled, is that each alliance committment undertaken by a nation reduces its interaction opportunities, and thus the interaction opportunities available to the entire system; as these diminish, we reason that the allied nation is now "less free to compete with its new allies and less free to cooperate with non-allies." The randomized cross-pressures on it give way, to some extent, to pressures that are likely to be more discriminatory and systematic. That is, the nation is now less likely to treat all others in a neutral fashion, but will tend to remove some of them from the neutral category and treat them more nearly as friends or as opponents. Given

21. See, for example, Harary (1961), Coleman (1964), Rapoport (1963), Rapoport and Horvath (1961), Berge (1962), and Flament (1963).

what we know about reciprocity in diplomatic behavior, it follows that those nations which are now treated in a non-random fashion will respond more or less in kind. The original randomized pressures (impinging on it from many directions) will now come in upon the newly-allied nation from more parallel or polarized directions, with a net loss of pluralistic cross-pressures in the system as a whole.

The criticism is that this model, while a reasonable interpretation of the classical formulation, ignores the fact that cross-pressures are *not* reduced unless the "nations belong to one and only one alliance." (Zinnes, 1966, p. 7). It goes on further to contend that in only 22 of our 130 years does that condition hold, and that our various indicators are therefore not theoretically valid. The assertion here, as we understand it, is that multiple alliance commitments do not necessarily diminish the cross-pressures, and may, under some conditions, even increase them. While the question is an empirical one, neither we nor others have yet sought to test it against evidence, and we must therefore fall back on logical analysis. In principle we would expect the assertion to hold in only an extremely limited set of cases: those in which a nation belongs to two alliances which are clearly *directed against one another*. And the only case in our population which clearly satisfies this unlikely condition is that of Italy, which belonged to both the Triple Alliance and the Entente (in a fragile sort of way) during the period leading up to World War I.

Even if there were other cases of such multiple membership in conflicting alliance groupings, however, the criticism would not hold. That is, it would only hold if the international system were composed solely of those two alliance memberships; as long as the system is larger than the five nations hypothesized in the critique, the assertion fails to stand. This is so because the allied nation, in its dealings with nations outside the two conflicting alliances, will not be as free as a non-allied nation would be in dealing with these more remote system members. In sum, we consider our independent and our intervening variables to be valid, and therefore remain satisfied that we have indeed examined a proposition which is central to the classical balance of power paradigm.[22]

These considerations bring us, therefore, back to the points raised at the outset of the paper. In any search for the "causes" of war, the quest for correlates may lead us not only into attributes of the international system, but into attributes of the more war-prone nations, their pre-conflict and pre-war relationships, and their pre-war behavior and interaction. It is our working assumption that any theory of the causes of war will include all four sets of independent variables. But we urge that considerable exploration of systemic properties be given high priority. Unless we understand the environment within which inter-nation conflict occurs, and can ascertain the approximate effect of that environment, there is no meaningful way of establishing the controls which are essential to any experimental inquiry. And if we look upon this quantitative approach to diplomatic history as a sequence of ex post facto, natural world experiment, the importance of such controls cannot be exaggerated.

22. Furthermore, even though our alliance aggregation index is not responsive to multiple memberships, the alliance *involvement* index presented in an earlier paper *is*, and the correlations between the two indicators when applied to all nations in any alliances and to all in defense pacts are .90 and .87 respectively (Singer and Small, 1966b, p. 20).

[handwritten annotation at bottom:] moderating intra-alliance disputes & making inter-alliance war more costly — ∴ less desirable. This does appear to account for 19th cent. data. C-P's alone are not adequate.

[handwritten annotation in left margin:] This is meant to some JC-P, different alliance also. Strong probability that alliance formation far from increas likelihood of conflict thus diminished C-P's function to foster hostilities by One interpretation of the 6 O/P system is that alliance formation — far from increas likelihood of conflict thus diminished C-P's function to foster hostilities by

Hayward Alker, Jr., and Donald Puchala

Trends in Economic Partnership: The North Atlantic Area, 1928–1963[1]

INTRODUCTION

Questions raised by a political scientist studying economic interactions in the North Atlantic Area are somewhat different, though not totally so, from the questions raised by economists looking at the same phenomena. Looking at the Common Market as an ongoing institution, for example, political scientists focus on the political impact of steps toward economic integration, while the economist may be more interested in their economic effects: whether or not trade liberalization has changed the price and cost structures of member countries, or the volume and direction of trade among EEC countries and between them and the rest of the world. The two concerns are closely linked in that political consequences of the Common Market in part depend on whether or not economic theories of comparative cost and comparative advantage have been actualized by the lowering of tariffs within the EEC and their standardization with respect to non-EEC members.[2]

As political scientists, we have chosen to focus on the political implications of trends in gross trading relationships in the North Atlantic Area. Such an approach requires a satisfactory way of describing changes in the level of

1. Research utilized in this chapter was supported in part by the United States Arms Control and Disarmament Agency. Any judgments or opinions expressed herein are those of the authors and do not necessarily reflect the views of the United States Arms Control and Disarmament Agency or any other department or agency of the U.S. government.
2. General theories of international trade and economics are explored by Kindleberger (1958) pp. 85–572. In addition, international trade theory has been admirably summarized by Haberler (1961). Specific work on the theory of international economic integration has been carried on by Balassa et al. (1961), by Streeten (1961), and by Scitovsky (1958). A valuable dialogue on the economic aspects and impacts of integration in western Europe is to be found in the alternative views of Balassa (1961) and Myrdal (1956), pp. 56–71.

economic transactions between and among nations, as well as a theoretical statement as to the relationship between changes in economic relationships and changes in political ones. If, as will be argued here, the level of economic interaction between nations can serve as a reliable *indicator* of their degree of political integration, then we may gain some insight into the political integration process among Common Market countries by looking at changes in the level of economic relationships among them.

Transaction Flows and Community Formation

Communities at the national and international level are populations whose members share and value common identities, and whose mutual goal attainment and conflict resolution procedures are expected to work in a peaceful fashion.[3] Synonymously, we speak of such peaceful collectivities as integrated communities and their conflict resolution procedures as integrative processes.

Economic, social, and political interchanges among members within a national or international community are typically more intense, more rewarding, and more enduring than those for individuals or nations not within the same community. Because intense, enduring, and rewarding transactions are a characteristic of international or supranational communities, we may use measures for the extent of economic transactions—in particular, trade—as one among many *indicators* of the existence of international community.[4]

Other indicators would include investment patterns, verbal communications, the existence of authoritative and legitimate supranational political institutions, and elite and mass attitudes and practices regarding the community in question. The validity of any of these indicators does not depend, it should be noted, on the degree of its causal significance for the continued existence of the community in question. Economics may or may not cause particular political relationships; but economic indicators may in either case help us describe the directions in which these relationships are moving.

Changing the discussion from communities already in existence to communities in the process of decay or formation, we may also expect that patterns of international trade will usually serve as valid and reliable indices of stability and change in an international political climate. This claim is only as valid as the theories of international community formation which point to the importance of communication and interaction in the integration process.[5] Increased assurance about such indicators comes also from provisional tests of such an approach (as to be given hereafter in a discussion of the European interwar period).

Even when they have distinguished between causal and indicator variables, critics of the transaction flows approach have argued that the high levels of

3. Deutsch (1957), pp. 5–9. For alternative—though not contradictory—definitions of "international community" see Etzioni (1963), pp. 407–421 and Hoffman (1963) pp. 521–549.
4. Deutsch (1964), pp. 75–97 and Russett (1963), pp. 26–62. A major study employing the transaction flows approach is Deutsch and Savage (forthcoming). These studies rarely suggest that the same simple linear or even ordinal relationships between economic *RA*'s and political integration are always possible without some further attention to the historical context of the nation pairs or groups involved. Therefore in the present study we shall try to explain the various relationships suggested by our analyses verbally rather than statistically.
5. Deutsch (1957), pp. 54–55: Etzioni, *op. cit.*

international transactions might rather be of disintegrative significance.[6] Cases in point might include the high level of diplomatic or economic exchanges preceding the outbreak of wars, such as Japanese purchases of American steel in the 1930's, or exploitive colonial relationships, such as the double exodus of Frenchmen and francs during and shortly after the Algerian insurrection.

Looking at the content of these particular transactions helps make clear a number of more or less implicit assumptions underlying the transaction flow approach to measuring international community formation, First, even among highly interdependent economies, or communications partners, we must assume *the principal actors to be autonomous enough to be able to initiate or to refuse transactions.* Dependent territories raise a host of special problems which call for special treatment and interpretation when transaction flow analysis is applied. Second, in order to be sure that both parties benefit mutually from their interchanges, we would require evidence of *voluntarily agreed upon reciprocal relationships of a continuing nature.* This is to say, the analysis of transactions in their relevance to international community formation derives from the assumption that *beneficial communication must span a period of several years and that such communication must take on a variety of peaceful forms.* Thus Japanese purchases of American steel received no reciprocal response by the United States. Diplomatic communications explosions before the outbreak of war are seldom more than several months' duration. French-Algerian and Algerian-French transactions before, during, and after the revolt fell into a "special" category of metropolitan-dependency communications where "abnormal" transaction patterns might be expected and could be meaningfully interpreted.

From this discussion, it appears that an appropriate strategy for using gross trading relationships to indicate degrees of international community would include the following points. Close economic ties of a continuing or increasing nature are likely to indicate the existence or emergence of integrative processes. Such a structuring of economic relationships along particular lines will more certainly indicate integrative processes if there is additional evidence to suggest the predominance of noncoercive inducements for participating in such transactions. Reciprocal patterns of special attention among members of a potential community also encourage trust in the validity of transactional indicators. *Finally, independent tests should be used to corroborate inferences based largely on economic transactions. The use of multiple indicators of intense, enduring, and rewarding relationships helps to prevent the reification of any one imperfect indicator.*[7]

6. In particular see Hoffmann (1960), pp. 45 ff.

7. It should be noted here that though we discuss only observed trends in international economic transactions and draw our conclusions from these observations, the particular observations represent only one set considered in the context of a much broader body of research now in progress and directed toward answering questions concerning community formation in western Europe. The basic design of this larger body of research establishes a scheme for the "multi-indicator" validation of our conclusions. In this larger body of research we also consider trends in various other ranges of international communication—social, cultural, institutional, and so on—as well as trends in intra-European and transatlantic interpolitics, and trends in western European attitudes, opinions, and foreign policies. Preliminary conclusions drawn from such "multi-indicator" research are to be found in Puchala (1965). Trends in foreign policy cohesiveness of western Europeans are also discussed in Alker and Russett (1965).

Theoretical guidelines for multi-indicator research are discussed in Campbell and Fiske (1959), pp. 81–105 and in Peak (1953), pp. 243–299.

Having argued for the usefulness of trading relationships as an indicator of international community, we must now turn to a more careful discussion of ways of measuring the extent of economic partnerships among nations.

MEASURING TRANSACTION FLOWS

We are interested in the extent to which international economic partnerships are strengthened or destroyed over a period of time within a particular nation or region or between nations or regions. That is, we would like to know who is trading with whom, how intensely, how reciprocally, and why. Moreover, did the "whos" and "whoms" change over time, and what does the pattern of stability or change suggest about the environment of international relations and the possibility of international community formation?

Several problems of measuring the level of economic transactions can be obviated by the use of appropriate statistical procedures. One of these is the inaccuracy of gross trade figures as measures of economic relationships between nations of very different economic capacities. Ten million dollars of trade between England and France is but a small part of each nation's total trade; ten million dollars of trade between Ireland and Iceland, however, is a much larger share of their respective total trade figures. A "contextually-defined"[8] measure of trading interaction that takes these total trade figures into account, would better reflect the significance for particular pairs of nations of transactions totaling a certain fixed amount. That is, gross effects due to the size of the foreign trade sector for each country being studied should be removed in order to detect the degree of special attention given by one country to another.

A second problem concerns domestic economic transactions. The statement that most nations trade internally a good deal more than they do externally, although true, does not help measure the specificity of choices among economic partners. It does suggest, however, that relatively high trade interactions will be economically and politically more significant for nations whose economies depend more heavily on foreign commerce. Such possibilities might be examined once measures of international partnership have been derived. On the other hand, omitting internal trade from a measure of the degree of trading relationship between two nations has several advantages. As we shall see below, it helps clarify the meaning of a nation's tendency to trade with nations other than itself. It also makes possible a much simpler answer to the question "Who trades with whom?" when referring to international regions as well as individual nations. Measures of the relative cohesiveness and separateness of regional economic groupings are essential data for the study of international community formation.

After controlling for total trade and internal trade, one can attribute remaining levels of international transactions to a great variety of causes. Economic logic— comparative advantage, product complementarity, economic distance, etc.— accounts in large part for the directions and intensities of international trade flows. But, such factors as geographic proximity; ethnic, cultural, or linguistic similarity; traditional affinities; and formal international political linkages and commitments also help to determine trade flows. To try to *control* for all these

8. Snyder (1962), p. 129.

variables and extract just those transactions representing "pure" community would be unwise for, operationally, "community" means the whole inventory of affinities and ties. Integrative processes are more likely to work *through* such things as geographic, cultural, and economic proximity and complementarity rather than *around* them. The desire to determine the relative importance of each of these factors as determinants of economic partnerships should not distract us from the utility of a highly general summary index of a whole variety of cultural, economic and political affinities and integrative processes.

A Null Model for Analysis of Flows

The decisions to control only for gross size effects and to omit from consideration "internal trade" in measuring economic partnership between nations led Savage and Deutsch to develop the following "null model" for studying international transactions.[9] Essentially, they wanted to know *whether the trade between two countries was more or less than the amount that would be expected knowing only the share of exports and imports received by each country, disallowing internal trade.* The main feature of a model for calculating trade expectations based only on propensities to export and import is the rule of "origin-destination independence": knowing which country a bundle of goods came from would help but little to determine its destination. If transactions were essentially random in this fashion, they would not be evidence of a particularized form of economic partnership. We do not expect such a model to reproduce exactly actual world trade patterns; hence, our use of the phrase "null model". Moreover, and more important, *deviations* from the null model should offer a useful way to *measure the extent of nonrandom trading partnerships for nations or regions.* That is, stronger national and regional trading partnerships appear as positive deviations from "null model" patterns, while trading relationships between nations isolated from one another show up as negative deviations from the randomly expected pattern.

Looking at the Savage-Deutsch scheme analytically, we see that their null model derives the *expected* trade between nations i and j (symbolically T_{ij}) according to the formula in equation (1):

$$T_{ij} = S \cdot P_i \cdot Q_j \cdot T \qquad \text{(if } i \neq j) \qquad (1)$$
$$T_{ij} = 0 \qquad \text{(if } i = j)$$

Starting from the right, we should interpret T as total trade for all N countries, P_i and Q_j as "theoretical tendencies" for nation i to export, and for nation j to import, any particular bundle of goods. P_i and Q_j are derived by an iterative procedure from i's fraction of total exports and j's fraction of total imports respectively. S is a constant defined to compensate for the fact that self-trade from any country to itself may not occur and has therefore been eliminated in the calculations of the P_i's and Q_j's specifically,

$$S = \frac{1}{1 - \sum_i P_i Q_i} \qquad (2)$$

9. Savage and Deutsch (1960), pp. 551–572, cf. also, Alker (1962), pp. 498–499. For a clear survey of recent developments in the statistical theory of transaction flows models, see also Goodman (1964), pp. 176–186.

The Greek letter $\sum$ (capital "sigma") indicates a summation of the PQ products; the index i means the summation is for all nations i ($i = 1, 2, \ldots, N$) being considered.

Savage and Deutsch measure deviations from their null model in fractional terms. They define a Relative Acceptance coefficient for countries i and j (RA_{ij}) to describe the extent that the acceptance by j of the exports of i exceed the expectations of the null model. Using T_{ij} to symbolize actual trade from country i to country j, RA_{ij} is defined as in equation (3):

$$RA_{ij} = \frac{T_{ij} - \hat{T}_{ij}}{\hat{T}_{ij}} \qquad (i \neq j) \tag{3}$$

$$(RA_{ij} \text{ is undefined if } i = j)$$

Notice how RA's range between -1.00, when no trade occurs, to zero, in which case trade equals that amount expected by the null model, to any arbitrarily high value, depending upon how large T_{ij} is, compared to $\hat{T}_{ij}$. An RA of 2.00, for example, would indicate actual trade 200 per cent greater than our null model expectations.

How should we define a Relative Acceptance coefficient for a regional group of countries so as to be able to study national links with regions, interregional partnership, and regional cohesiveness or exclusiveness? Because of the "origin-destination independence" rule, calculating *regional* propensities to export and import is completely straightforward. P's and Q's for the relevant group of nations can be added together without affecting the probability of a particular bundle coming from or going to a particular nation. Actual transactions can be subtracted from null expectations of regional transactions, once these null expectations have been defined using regional P's and Q's. Thus for trade from nation i to region k, we sum actual and expected transactions to all countries j belonging to region k (ϵ, "epsilon," should be read "is a member of"):

$$T_{ik} = \sum_{\substack{j \epsilon k \\ j \neq i}} T_{ij}$$

$$\hat{T}_{ik} = \sum_{\substack{j \epsilon k \\ j \neq i}} SP_i Q_j T \tag{4}$$

$$RA_{ik} = \frac{T_{ik} - \hat{T}_{ik}}{\hat{T}_{ik}}$$

Because internal trade is not to be considered, if country i is a member of region k, it is excluded from the summations defining T_{ik} and $\hat{T}_{ik}$; that is the meaning of the equation $j \neq i$ below the summation signs in equation series (4). It should be clear to the reader that RA_{ki} for trade *from* region k *to* nation i can be defined in a way very similar to RA_{ik}.

It remains only to define a Relative Acceptance coefficient for trade within or between regions. Formulas for these cases can be presented in terms of two hypothetical regions k and k'. Actual or expected trade between k and k' is calculated by summing all actual or expected trade from countries i in k to countries j in k', again disallowing any trade going from a country back to itself:

$$T_{kk'} = \sum_{\substack{i\varepsilon k \\ i \ne j}} \sum_{j\varepsilon k'} T_{ij}$$

$$\hat{T}_{kk'} = \sum_{\substack{i\varepsilon k \\ i \ne j}} \sum_{j\varepsilon k'} SP_i \, Q_j \, T \tag{5}$$

$$RA_{kk'} = \frac{T_{kk'} - \hat{T}_{kk'}}{\hat{T}_{kk'}}$$

RA_{kk}, the relative absorption of region k's own trade by itself is calculated by the same formulas as in equation series (5) for trade among nations in a single region. Within a region, RA's only make sense, however, when there are at least two countries; otherwise we know from equations (1) and (3) that RA_{kk} is undefined.

Using the preceding formulas, Relative Acceptance coefficients for trade among fifteen countries and five regions in the North Atlantic Area, as well as a residual rest-of-the-world category, were computed for 1928, 1948, 1951, 1954, 1959, 1962, and 1963. Using these coefficients as measures of the degree of economic partnership among nations and regions, we can now begin to answer questions concerning international community formation in the North Atlantic Area. These include (1) whether an international community—or communities— might now be forming in the North Atlantic Area, and (2) which countries and peoples these communities embrace and exclude.

Our principal concern will be with trends in relative acceptances of international trade since the interwar period. A new look at Savage and Deutsch's original 1928 data and computations will serve both to indicate the relevance of economic transactions in making political inferences and as a benchmark for further analyses. As to time scale, long-run trends to be considered are those that developed between the interwar and postwar periods, while short-run trends are those occurring during the 1950's.

THE "NORMALCY" OF THE INTERWAR PERIOD—1928

Europe was at peace during the 1920's but subsequent events have shown that this was a peace without security. The conflagration of the century's second decade was past; its horrors were still remembered; yet the passions that had nursed the war's fury were only temporarily dormant. Because the "normalcy" of the interwar period's international relations was superficial, we should expect that the lines of antagonism etched into the map of Europe before 1914 and renewed in 1939 would be visible in interwar patterns of intra-European economic relations.

We shall see that, in general, trade flows in the North Atlantic Area in 1928, the last predepression year of the interwar period,[10] did reflect economic and political disunity within the region. The five Scandinavian countries were a

10. We have chosen to base our analysis of interwar "normalcy" on one of the few years in which economic relations were suffering neither from postwar economic adjustments or the effects of the Depression beginning in 1929. The availability of the Savage-Deutsch calculations, and their remarkable similarity to political patterns that become more obvious ten years later also suggested re-examining these results.

TABLE 1. *The Relative Acceptance of International Trade in the North Atlantic Area 1928*[a]

	U.K.	U.S.	Can.	Ire.	Reg. 1	Germ.	France	BLx.	Neth.	Italy	Reg. 2	Switz.	Reg. 3	Rest of World
U.K.		—.47	—.01	4.66	—.14	—.35	—.26	—.10	—.20	—.44	—.29	—.41	.07	.29
U.S.	—.20		3.13	—.71	.34	—.22	—.30	—.36	—.26	—.04	—.24	—.86	—.22	.01
Can.	.75	1.81		.63	1.14	—.69	—.83	—.34	—.05	—.43	—.56	—.97	—.55	—.54
Ire.	4.31	—.96	—.93		1.80	—.95	—.95	—.91	—1.00	—1.00	—.95	—.82	—1.00	—.96
Reg. 1	.11	.00	1.64	1.49	.36	—.34	—.35	—.27	—.21	—.26	—.31	—.69	—.16	.04
Germ.	—.51	—.53	—.87	—.81	—.56		.03	.22	1.70	.43	.51	1.81	1.42	.15
France	—.21	—.57	—.67	—.85	—.40	.01		3.85	—.25	.34	.60	2.83	—.54	—.002
BLx.	—.05	—.39	—.68	—.51	—.25	.30	1.17		3.01	.25	.85	.59	—.04	.31
Neth.	—.17	—.72	—.77	—.62	—.27	1.23	.02	1.91		—.39	.78	—.19	—.42	—.25
Italy	—.48	—.19	—.92	—.80	—.43	.29	.56	—.39	.68		.13	3.41	.60	.25
Reg. 2	—.30	—.50	—.79	—.77	—.44	.32	.28	1.48	.99	.22		1.90	.41	.02
Switz.	—.21	—.28	—.51	—.82	—.28	.71	.24	—.33	—.21	1.14	.57		—.06	—.01
Reg. 3	.88	—.45	—.86	—.69	.18	.74	—.41	—.36	—.18	.53	.56	5.27		.57
Rest of World	.04	.35	—.79	—.82	.04	.12	.24	—.48	—.30	.14		—.41	—.45	

Key: Region 1 = Anglo-American Region (U.K., U.S., Canada, Ireland); Region 2 = Current EEC members (the "six," Germany, France, Italy, the Netherlands, Belgium-Luxembourg); Region 3 = Scandinavia (Denmark, Sweden, Norway, Finland, Iceland); Rest of world is a composite "region" accounting for all remaining world trade.
[a]*Source:* I. Richard Savage and Karl W. Deutsch, *op. cit.,* pp. 564 and 568.

trading community, but no other group in the North Atlantic Area formed such a bloc. Intra-regional trading on the Continent—at least in the West—was marked by isolated paired partnerships, by dominantly unidirectional trade-flows and by the near or actual isolation of major potential economic partners. Germany in 1928 was not a part of western Europe economically. Furthermore, England was economically isolated from most of continental Europe, and neither England nor the continental countries shared any economic partnership with North America. *Relative economic isolation rather than relative partnership defined the 1928 pattern of trade-flows in the North Atlantic Area.* More details supporting these general impressions are gained by considering the 1928 interwar *RA* matrix in Table 1.

Scandinavian Unity

For simplicity at this point Scandinavia is scored only as a region and not as five separate countries—Denmark, Sweden, Norway, Finland, and Iceland. The high economic cohesion of this region is indicated by the within-region *RA* of 5.27 in Table 1. That is, trade among the Scandinavian countries was 527 per cent of null model expectations. No other intra-region *RA* coefficient in the diagonal of Table 1 comes even close to this level of internal transactions, a level high enough to be called an "economic community" in describing Scandinavia's extensive economic interdependence.

Precursors of the Six

Lack of economic integration among the "six" in 1928 was symptomatic of the more general lack of economic community in continental Western Europe as a whole. Although the over all regional *RA* of .57 is moderately positive, it is apparent from the variety of negative figures for pairs of nations that no comprehensive pattern of reciprocal economic partnerships linked France, Germany, Italy, the Netherlands, and Belgium-Luxembourg in 1928. That is to say, in 1928 there were six distinct countries, and there was some economic interaction among them, *but there was no "six."* The German-Dutch relationship was strong (*RA* = 1.70, 1.23) as was the Benelux partnership (*RA* = 3.01, 1.91) and the Franco-Belgian tie (*RA* = 3.85, 1.17). However, *there was no partnership between the two largest countries, France and Germany (RA = 0.03, −.01)*, none between France and the Netherlands (*RA* = −.25, .02), and only a weak partnership between Germany and Belgium-Luxembourg (*RA* = .22, .30), even though these countries all shared common borders. Furthermore, in 1928 Italy found no major partners in any of the countries that were destined to become its supranational associates in the 1950's. Nor did any of the future "six" export to Italy in significantly greater than expected volumes. Isolation between Italy and the Benelux countries, for example, was both mutual and extreme in 1928.

As alluded to above, economically in 1928 Germany was not a part of western Europe. No major German economic partners (except perhaps the Netherlands) were to be found in the west. German isolation from western Europe, and especially from France and many of the future EEC countries, was underlined in

1928 by the fact that German economic ties were to the north and east rather than in the west. Whereas German relative acceptance of trade from the future EEC group was only .32 in 1928, German relative acceptance of trade from Scandinavia was .74. At the same time German exports to the future EEC group were 51 per cent more than expected, while German exports to Scandinavia were 142 per cent higher.

Relative to intra-Scandinavian economic integration, these trading relationships between Scandinavia and Germany in 1928 were not especially impressive, nor were they as reciprocal as Scandinavian exporters might have wished. Nonetheless, German-Scandinavian ties in 1928 were clearly stronger than either German or Scandinavian ties with the western continental countries. In a political focus here we see the possibility that some neutral relationships, such as Sweden opted for during World War II, might easily have been perceived as profitable by the Scandinavian countries concerned, as long as territorial acquisitiveness or other strategic considerations did not override satisfactory economic partnerships. Then too, and far less subtly, one might interpret German relations with the western continental countries during the interwar period as a situation wherein economic isolation only symbolized a more general social, cultural, and political chasm.

Still considering the position of Germany in the fragmented economic network of interwar Europe, data not displayed in Table 1 lead us to believe that German exporters found outlets in eastern Europe nearly as lucrative as those in the west, while German importers found better sources in the east than in the west. In 1928, nearly one-fifth of German exports went to eastern Europe and 13 per cent of German imports came from that area. During the same year about 25 per cent of German exports went to France, Italy, Belgium-Luxembourg, and the Netherlands combined, but only 9 per cent of the German imports came from these countries.[11] Therefore in 1928 the German economic partnership with the east was, percentagewise, at least as strong as its partnership with the "six", and had we computed relative acceptance scores for trade flows between Germany and eastern Europe, it would most likely have turned out that the German partnership with the east was a good deal stronger than its partnership with the west during the interwar period.[12]

The English-Speaking World

Moving from the continent to Great Britain, three patterns were apparent in British economic relations in 1928: (1) Britain was economically isolated from western Europe, (2) Britain was similarly economically isolated from the United States, and (3) a greater than expected volume of British exports flowed to the "rest of the world" outside the North Atlantic Area, but this flow was not matched by a volume of imports from that area significantly greater than expected. A

11. League of Nations (1930), pp. 10, 35, 53, 146, 235, 246, 287.
12. It was not practicable to compute the relative acceptance scores on trade flows with the eastern European countries because the basic fifteen-country "North Atlantic" matrices had already been computed when the German-east European relationship became apparent. Current research plans call for the expansion of the basic matrix to include eastern Europe.

non-reciprocal relationship between Britain and the Empire thus seems to be indicated.

With the exceptions of its agricultural imports from Denmark and a weak trading partnership with Norway, the United Kingdom's general economic relationship with the rest of western Europe in the interwar period was marked by meager interactions. Britain's relative acceptance of imports from the "six" plus Switzerland was −.30 in 1928, while this group's acceptance of imports from Great Britain at that time was similarly −.30. The same pattern held in interwar British economic relationships with the countries destined to become the European Economic Community. British exports to the "six" in 1928 flowed in volumes 29 per cent lower than expected; imports from the area were 30 per cent lower than randomly expected.

Nor was there any notable economic partnership between Britain and North America during the interwar period. The Canadians exported substantial quantities of primary products to Great Britain, but Britain found no extensive export outlets in Canada. More important, all trade flowing between Great Britain and the United States during the interwar period flowed in volumes significantly lower than might be expected. It may be true that a traditional cultural affinity binds the United Kingdom to the United States, but this affinity, if it existed in 1928, did not reflect itself in an Anglo-American economic partnership.

On the other hand, Britain in 1928 exported in greater than expected volumes to areas outside the North Atlantic Area. (The British *RA* score of .29 was the highest export score to the "rest of the world" recorded for any single country in 1928. This *RA* score represented a flow of 54.7 per cent of total British exports.) This suggests that Britain was probably using colonial markets to sell finished goods, while foodstuffs came to Britain from Canada and Denmark and low-priced raw materials came from the colonies. The British in the interwar period neither sought nor needed trade partnerships with other industrial countries in western Europe.

Interwar Disunity in Retrospect

Looking back, one could argue that the economic patterns of 1928 reflected in several ways the political patterns of 1913 and in others presaged the political developments of the 1930's. Except possibly for the Scandinavian region, there were no enduring pluralistic security communities in Europe during the interwar period. Neither was there an integrated economic community on the continent at that time. Germany was not integrated into any western trading system in 1928; the Franco-German border seemed as much an obstacle to German trade in 1928 as it had to German armies in 1913. France also found no economic reason to be responsive to Germany. In the same way, Britain was economically isolated from all of western Europe in the interwar period. Is it then surprising that British attention throughout this era focused mainly upon its world empire, and on its European neighbors only when their actions affected this empire? Then, too, the United States, with its Latin American economic ties, in the interwar period was as isolated from western Europe economically as it professed to be isolated politically.

None of the major countries of the North Atlantic Area—the United States, England, France, and Germany—had multiple ties with the rest of Europe (note how all RA's for each of these countries to and from the rest of the world are positive) or close ties with each other (note how the highest of 12 RA's among them is .03). Each had its primary areas of economic concern—Latin America, Empire, colonies, northern and eastern Europe; each lived and traded in a world apart from the others. *The patterns of relative economic acceptance remarkably reflect the picture of political disunity in the North Atlantic Area during the interwar period. This being the case, we might suspect that new economic patterns in the postwar era will also reflect something of the era's new international politics.*

TRENDS FROM INTERWAR TO POSTWAR PERIODS

Hypotheses

The literature on European integration, as well as our sense of historical perspective, suggests a variety of possible changes in the pattern of trade-flows in the North Atlantic Area between the interwar and the postwar period. First, *the "six" might have come into being*—that is, not only appeared on paper but joined in real economic partnership. This would have been the case if (1) all or most of the patterns of economic isolation observed among the "six" in 1928 transformed into patterns of economic partnership during the 1950's, and (2) some of the partnerships observed between EEC countries and non-EEC countries in 1928 weakened or dissolved as intra-EEC partnerships intensified. This is to say that, in terms of relative acceptance patterns, the emergence of the "six" as an economic community would be defined by increased partnership within the group and a related isolation of other countries or groups of countries. To find "economic integration" in the RA pattern for the "six" then, we would look for both *community* and *confinement.*[13]

Second, *western Europe may have come out of the war and the postwar recovery period substantially more economically integrated* than it had been during the interwar period, and this integration may not have been limited to the "six." This possible course of economic evolution stems from the hypothesis that the liberalizations of the OEEC, together with the sealing off of eastern markets, have had a greater impact upon western European economic behavior than the supranationality of the communities, and that in fact all of western Europe has emerged as an expansive, responsive, and intensive trading community. Evidence supporting this hypothesis would have to show that (1) intra-European partnerships intensified in the postwar period, and (2) barriers among the continental countries, as well as barriers between France and Scandinavia, Italy and Scandinavia, and Great Britain and the continent, all apparent in 1928, failed to reappear in mid-century trading patterns.

Another alternative pattern to be considered would be *the emergence of a*

13. Liska (1964), pp. 32, 51–55; Etzioni, *op. cit.* For a similar kind of analysis of the reactions of newly independent nations on the world scene, see Lasswell (1951). It should be noted that when RA coefficients for trade among a certain group of nations are highly positive (thus indicating considerable economic partnership or political community), RA's with other nations will necessarily tend to be below zero (thus indicating some kind of isolation or confinement).

"Continental" trading community including France, Germany, Italy, the Benelux countries, Switzerland and Scandinavia, but excluding Great Britain.

It is also possible (but unlikely) that the entire North Atlantic Area emerged as an economic community after World War II and that transatlantic partnerships strengthened along with continental partnerships.

Finally, after World War II, the *North Atlantic Area may have returned to the economic "normalcy" of the interwar period*, with disunity renewed, barriers rebuilt, and patterns of scattered isolated partnerships restored. This last pattern also seems unlikely because East-West partnership became impossible after 1948. Nevertheless, the "no change" hypothesis is worth consideration because some important vestiges of the 1928 pattern may have carried into the 1950's.

It turns out that almost all of these hypotheses about the postwar pattern of relative acceptance in the North Atlantic Area are partly validated by the data, but by different data recorded at different times during the 1948 to 1963 period. The over-all pattern of economic interaction in the postwar period is exceedingly complex, but not in the least contradictory. There *was* a period of all-western European economic partnership; there *was* a period of relapse when it looked as if western Europe might return to the "normalcy" of 1928; and finally, there *was* a period during which the "six" appeared to be emerging as an integrated economic community.

To understand the evolution of the postwar pattern, attention in analysis should again focus upon key channels, that is, those points in the patterns which define major shifts and continuities in economic behavior over time. Particular attention might be paid to the German position in the postwar European trading system, to the interrelationships among the "six," and to the interrelationships among non-EEC members. At the same time interpretations and explanations should consider (1) the impact of the postwar recovery and of Marshall Plan aid and guidance upon intra-European economic partnerships, (2) trading patterns among the "six", (3) the impact of supranationalism among the "six" upon economic relations between them and other European countries, and (4) the impact of the Common Market upon economic relations among countries not participating in the supranational experiment.

Most of the basic data for our subsequent analysis is contained in Table 2 or Figure 1.[14] These displays allow us to study time-series changes in *RA*'s from the interwar period data for 1928 reported in Table 1 until 1963, the last postwar year for which *RA*'s have been calculated.

The Effects of War and the Marshall Plan

We can summarize trends in economic partnership from 1928 through 1951 by looking first at national *RA*'s to and from the rest of the world outside the North Atlantic Area, secondly at regional *RA*'s, and thirdly by focusing on inter-regional *RA*'s, all of which are recorded in Table 2. Of the three regions in Table 2,

14. In recording the relative acceptance pattern for 1928 we used the matrix of scores published by Savage and Deutsch, *op. cit.*, pp. 564, 568. They list their source as the League of Nations (1930). In computing the relative acceptance patterns for 1948, 1951, 1954, 1957, 1959, 1962, and 1963, we used international trade statistics compiled by the United Nations (various years). Results for 1962 were sufficiently similar to those for 1963 not to require reproduction here.

TABLE 2. *The Relative Acceptance of International Trade in the North Atlantic Area, 1928, 1948, 1954, 1957, 1959, 1963*[a]

From	To	U.K.	U.S.	Can.	Ire.	Reg. 1	Germ.	France	BLx.	Neth.	Italy	Reg. 2	Switz.	Reg. 3	Rest of World
U.K.	1928		-.5	-.0	4.7	-.1	-.4	-.3	-.1	-.2	-.4	-.3	-.4	.1	.3
	1948		-.8	-.2	3.8	-.5	-.4	-.6	-.3	-.2	-.7	-.4	-.4	.4	.4
	1954		-.6	-.1	5.1	-.4	-.5	-.5	-.4	-.1	-.3	-.4	-.4	.7	.3
	1957		-.5	.0	6.0	-.2	-.6	-.6	-.3	-.1	-.4	-.4	-.4	.6	.3
	1959		-.4	.0	4.8	-.2	-.5	-.5	-.5	-.1	-.3	-.4	-.2	.5	.3
	1963		-.4	-.1	4.6	-.2	-.3	-.3	-.3	-.1	-.3	-.3	-.2	.6	.2
U.S.	1928	-.2		3.1	-.7	.3	-.2	-.3	-.4	.1	.0	-.2	-.9	-.2	.0
	1948	-.7		1.9	-.6	-.1	1.5	-.3	-.2	-.3	-.6	-.1	-.2	-.4	.1
	1954	-.6		2.9	-.7	.4	-.4	-.5	-.4	-.3	-.3	-.4	-.3	-.7	.1
	1957	-.6		2.2	-.8	.3	-.4	-.5	-.4	-.4	-.1	-.4	-.3	-.6	.2
	1959	-.6		2.3	-.7	.4	-.6	-.7	-.5	-.3	-.3	-.5	-.5	-.6	.2
	1963	-.5		2.5	-.7	.4	-.6	-.6	-.5	-.3	-.4	-.5	-.5	-.6	.3
Can.	1928	.8	1.8		-.6	1.1	-.7	-.8	-.3	-.1	-.4	-.6	-.9	-.6	-.5
	1948	.8	2.1		-.6	1.4	-.9	-.7	-.7	-.5	-.6	-.7	-.6	-.8	-.6
	1954	.3	2.8		-.6	1.7	-.6	-.8	-.6	-.8	-.8	-.7	-.6	-.8	-.7
	1957	.4	3.2		-.6	1.9	-.6	-.8	-.6	-.6	-.6	-.6	-.7	-.7	-.7
	1959	.4	2.7		-.7	1.7	-.7	-.8	-.7	-.7	-.8	-.7	-.7	-.7	-.7
	1963	.6	2.6		-.8	1.7	-.7	-.8	-.7	-.7	-.8	-.8	-.8	-.7	-.4
Ire.	1928	4.3	-.9	.9		1.8	-.9	-.9	-.9	-1.0	-1.0	-.9	-.8	-1.0	-.9
	1948	4.9	-.9	.9		1.5	-1.0	-.9	-.3	.2	-.9	-.6	-.9	-.9	-.9
	1954	6.3	-.9	.9		1.7	-.7	-.9	-.6	-.8	-.9	-.8	-.9	-.8	-.9
	1957	6.5	-.8	.9		1.8	-.6	-.7	-.8	-.8	-.8	-.7	-.9	-.8	-.8
	1959	5.9	-.5	.8		1.6	-.7	-.8	-.8	-.8	-.8	-.7	-.9	-.8	-.7
	1963	7.1	-.5	.6		1.9	-.7	-.7	-.8	-.8	-.8	-.8	-.8	-.9	-.7

TABLE 2—continued

To:	U.K.	U.S.	Can.	Ire.	Reg. 1	Germ.	France	BLx.	Neth.	Italy	Reg. 2	Switz.	Reg. 3	Rest of World
From:														
Reg. 1														
1928	.1	.0	1.6	1.5	.4	— .3	— .4	— .3	— .2	— .3	— .3	— .7	— .2	.0
1948	— .3	.1	1.2	.7	.1	— .6	— .4	— .3	— .3	.0	— .2	— .3	— .2	— .1
1954	— .3	.5	1.8	1.2	.5	— .5	— .6	— .4	— .3	— .4	— .4	— .4	— .2	— .1
1957	— .3	.7	1.5	1.0	.5	— .5	— .6	— .4	— .3	— .3	— .4	— .4	— .3	— .1
1959	— .3	.7	1.5	.9	.5	— .6	— .6	— .5	— .3	— .4	— .5	— .4	— .3	— .1
1963	— .2	.6	1.7	.7	.5	— .5	— .5	— .5	— .3	— .4	— .5	— .4	— .3	— .2
Germ.														
1928	— .5	— .5	— .9	— .8	— .6		.0	.2	1.7	.4	.5	1.8	1.4	.2
1948	.1	— .7	— .9	— .9	— .4		3.8	4.0	2.7	.4	3.0	2.9	1.5	.9
1954	— .7	— .6	— .9	— .4	— .7		.3	1.2	1.2	.9	.9	2.2	1.6	— .1
1957	— .7	— .5	— .8	— .5	— .6		.4	1.1	1.4	.7	.8	2.9	1.3	— .1
1959	— .7	— .5	— .8	— .5	— .6		.6	.8	1.2	.7	.8	2.2	1.2	— .1
1963	— .6	— .5	— .8	— .4	— .6		.7	.8	1.0	.6	.8	2.3	.8	.2
France														
1928	— .2	— .6	— .7	— .9	— .4	.0		3.9	— .3	.3	.6	2.8	— .5	.0
1948	— .4	— .8	— .9	— .9	— .7	1.0		1.6	.4	.6	.7	1.5	— .2	.3
1954	— .5	— .8	— .9	— .8	— .6	.5		1.2	— .4	.3	.4	1.5	— .1	.4
1957	— .5	— .6	— .9	— .6	— .6	.6		1.5	— .2	.3	.5	2.1	— .2	.2
1959	— .6	— .5	— .8	— .7	— .6	.5		1.1	— .3	.5	.5	1.3	— .3	.3
1963	— .5	— .7	— .9	— .6	— .6	.7		1.4	— .3	.6	.6	1.9	— .4	.0
BLx.														
1928	— .1	— .4	— .7	— .5	— .3	.3	1.2		3.0	— .3	.9	.6	.0	— .3
1948	— .4	— .6	— .8	— .3	— .6	.8	.7		4.0	— .3	1.3	2.2	.9	— .2
1954	— .5	— .8	— .8	— .3	— .5	.7	.9		4.1	— .1	1.4	.8	.5	— .3
1957	— .5	— .4	— .6	— .2	— .5	.4	1.0		5.3	— .4	1.4	.9	.3	— .4
1959	— .5	— .2	— .8	— .3	— .4	.6	.9		4.9	— .1	1.3	.6	.1	— .4
1963	— .5	— .5	— .8	— .5	— .5	.7	1.0		3.0	— .2	1.0	.1	— .3	— .2

301

TABLE 2.—continued

To:	U.K.	U.S.	Can.	Ire.	Reg. 1	Germ.	France	BLx.	Neth.	Italy	Reg. 2	Switz.	Reg. 3	Rest of World
From-														
Neths.														
1928	.2	—.7	—.8	—.6	—.3	1.2	.0	1.9		—.4	.8	.2	.4	—.3
1948	.1	—.8	—.9	—.1	—.4	.5	.6	3.9		—.1	1.2	1.2	1.3	—.3
1954	—.1	—.6	—.9	—.1	—.4	1.8	—.2	3.4		—.3	1.1	.5	1.0	—.3
1957	.0	—.6	—.9	—.2	—.4	1.6	—.1	4.1		—.2	1.2	.7	1.0	—.4
1959	.0	—.7	—.9	—.1	—.5	1.6	.1	3.6		—.1	1.3	.4	.8	—.4
1963	—.1	—.8	—.9	—.3	—.5	1.4	.2	2.7		.3	.9	.0	.2	—.2
Italy														
1928	—.5	—.2	—.9	—.8	—.4	.3	.6	—.4	—.7		.1	3.4	—	.3
1948	—.3	—.5	—.9	—.8	—.4	—.1	.1	—.1	—.3		—.1	2.7	.6	.2
1954	—.3	—.5	—.9	—.7	—.5	1.0	.2	—.2	—.3		.3	3.8	.5	.1
1957	—.4	—.3	—.8	—.7	—.5	1.0	.2	—.2	—.4		.3	4.1	—.1	.1
1959	—.3	—.3	—.8	—.8	—.4	1.0	.3	—.2	—.3		.4	3.2	—.2	.0
1963	—.4	—.4	—.8	—.7	—.5	.9	.7	.0	—.2		.5	2.1	.3	.0
Reg. 2														
1928	—.3	—.5	.0	—.7	—.4	.3	.3	1.5	1.0	.2	.6	1.9	.4	.0
1948	—.2	—.7	—.9	—.6	—.5	.6	1.0	2.1	1.7	—.3	1.1	2.0	.8	—.1
1954	—.5	—.6	—.9	—.5	—.6	.9	.3	1.4	1.0	.4	.8	1.8	.7	—.0
1957	—.5	—.5	—.8	—.5	—.6	.8	.4	1.5	1.4	.3	.8	2.3	.6	—.1
1959	—.5	—.4	—.8	—.5	—.5	.9	.5	1.2	1.2	.4	.8	1.7	.5	—.1
1963	—.5	—.6	—.8	—.5	—.6	.9	.7	1.2	.9	.3	.8	1.5	.1	—.1
Switz.														
1928	—.2	—.3	—.5	—.8	—.3	.7	.2	—.3	—.2	1.1	.4		—	—.0
1948	—.7	—.2	—.8	—.8	—.5	.3	.7	2.3	1.1	1.2	1.1		.3	—.1
1954	—.6	—.2	—.7	—.6	—.4	1.1	.5	.4	—.0	1.9	.8		.3	—.1
1957	—.4	—.3	—.8	—.7	—.4	.9	.3	.4	.1	1.0	.6		.2	—.0
1959	—.5	—.3	—.6	—.8	—.4	1.1	.5	.2	.1	1.7	.8		.2	—.1
1963	—.3	—.3	—.7	—.5	—.3	.9	.6	.0	—.1	1.0	.6		.3	.3

TABLE 2—*continued*

To:	UK.	US.	Can.	Ire.	Reg. 1	Germ.	France	BLx.	Neth.	Italy.	Reg. 2	Switz.	Reg. 3	Rest of World
From:														
Reg. 3														
1928	.9	—.5	—.9	—.7	.2	.7	—.4	—.4	—.2	—.5	.1	—.6	5.3	—.6
1948	.5	—.6	—.9	—.4	.2	.3	—.1	1.0	1.3	—.1	.4	—.2	3.1	—.3
1954	.9	—.6	—.9	—.1	—.1	1.0	—.2	—.0	.0	—.0	.2	—.3	2.7	—.3
1957	.7	—.6	—.9	—.3	—.2	.7	—.3	—.1	.0	—.2	.1	—.3	2.3	—.1
1959	.8	—.5	—.9	—.3	—.1	.9	—.3	—.1	—.1	—.1	.3	—.3	2.9	—.4
1963	1.0	—.5	—.8	—.3	—.1	.6	.1	—.2	.0	—.2	.1	—.1	3.9	—.5
Rest of World														
1928	.0	.4	—.8	—.8	.0	.1	.2	—.5	—.3	.1	.0	—.4	—.5	
1948	.3	.2	—.6	—.4	.1	—.7	.2	—.2	—.3	.0	—.1	—.2	—.2	
1954	.3	.2	—.7	—.7	.1	—.1	.4	—.3	—.2	.1	.0	—.6	—.4	
1957	.3	.1	—.5	—.5	.1	.0	.4	—.3	—.3	.1	.0	—.7	—.2	
1959	.4	.1	—.5	—.4	.1	.0	.3	—.2	—.4	.1	.0	—.6	—.3	
1963	.3	.3	—.5	—.1	.2	—.1	.0	—.3	—.3	.2	—.1	—.8	—.2	

Key: Region 1 = Anglo-American Region (U.K., U.S., Canada, Ireland); Region 2 = Current EEC members (Germany, France, Italy, the Netherlands, Belgium-Luxembourg); Region 3 = Scandinavia (Denmark, Sweden, Norway, Finland, Iceland); Rest of World = Remaining countries of the world considered as a single trading partner.
[a] *Source:* See note 14.

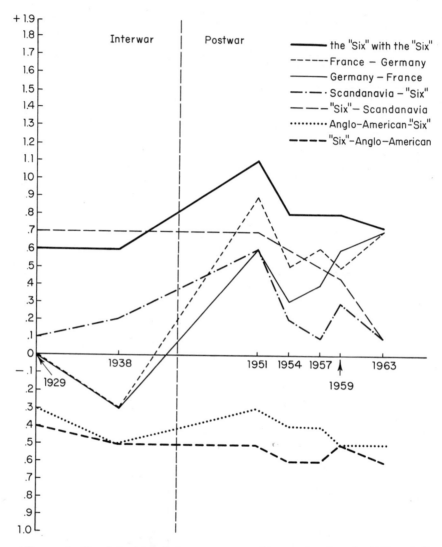

FIGURE 1. *Trends in the relative acceptance of international trade, 1928 to 1963.*

both the English-speaking nations and the Scandinavians decreased their within-region *RA*'s over time, the former group from a modest .4 to an even more modest .1, the latter from an extremely high 5.3 to a still extremely strong 3.1. More interesting than either of these changes, however, is the rather dramatic increase (from 60 per cent above null expectations to 110 per cent above null expectations) of the "six." Other summary measures of trade between regions and with the non-Atlantic world show few dramatic changes, except for German withdrawal from non-Atlantic relationships, and increased west European ties with Scandinavia.

Highlights of the 1928–1951 changes and trends are portrayed in Figure 1.[15]
On the continent, a new Franco-German economic partnership in the postwar
period appears to account for the markedly increased trading among the "six".
Whereas in 1938 the French traded with the Germans in volumes 27 per cent lower
than would be expected under the *RA* null model, by 1951 they were trading with
the Germans in volumes 93 per cent greater than would be expected. Similarly,
whereas in 1938 the Germans traded with the French in volumes 25 per cent
lower than expected, by 1951 they were trading with the French in volumes 59
per cent greater than expected—a remarkable restructuring of economic relationships. Also on the continent, Frenchmen and Dutchmen were trading with one
another in 1948 in volumes 50 per cent greater than null expectations. This
Franco-Dutch economic partnership in the early postwar era replaced that
Franco-Dutch economic isolation noted in the 1928 pattern. Interwar isolation
was also superseded by partnership in the early postwar era in relations between
Scandinavia and the continental countries to the south. Relative acceptance
scores for trading between Scandinavia and the "six" edged up from .1 and .7
in 1928 to .6 and .7 in 1951. In sum then, the intra-European pattern of economic
relative acceptance in the early postwar period, and changes between the interwar
and the postwar period, suggest a "Continental" economic community in the
offing. Strong ties were apparent among the "six" and important ties linked the
"six" to Scandinavia. Moreover, continued British and American isolation from
economic partnership with western Europe suggested that the economic network
emerging in the early postwar period was strictly a "Continental" one and
not an "Atlantic Community" system.

   *These changes in trading relationships between 1928 and 1951 appear to reflect
major European political realignment brought about by the conclusion of World War
II and subsequent American foreign policy.* From 1948 to 1951, the Marshall
Plan era, American aid efforts were directed toward European recovery on a
continental rather than a national plane. Marshall Plan directors and early
OEEC administrators strove to allocate American aid so as to encourage intra-
European economic interaction, while discouraging movement toward national
economic autarchy. The goal was an economically interdependent Europe and
not simply a cluster of economically viable nation-states. As the figures indicate,
this goal was apparently realized in the late 1940's and early 1950's—as long as
Marshall Plan administrators wielded influence in European economics. Once
again, European trading partnerships appear to indicate paramount political
relationships. The fact that they were partly imposed by the United States
(and thus not wholly autonomous or reciprocal) for only a short period of time
should lead one to question their validity as indicators of a potential, enduring
political community.

   As both current and subsequent observers have noted, *the economic interdependence of the immediate postwar era was sufficiently artificial not to generate
or to sustain an integrated European community.* The period of the late 1940's
and the early 1950's was a period of acute dollar shortage in the western European
balance of payments. To remedy the situation, European governments, with

---

15. Data sources for Figure 1 include those cited in footnote 14, above. We are also grateful
to Savage and Deutsch for permission to use 1938 *RA*'s taken from their forthcoming *Tides
Among Nations*.

American acquiescence, introduced systematic discriminations against dollar-area trade—that is, trade with the United States and the rest of North and South America. In the same period after 1950, Europeans moved to facilitate intra-European trade through the multiple clearance system of the European Payments Union. In terms of relative acceptance analysis, the net result of this abnormal world trading situation in the late 1940's and early 1950's was to set intra-European RA scores artificially high. High RA scores in 1948 resulted in part from externally imposed non-autonomous trading relationships among continental Europeans as well as from abnormal self-exclusion efforts by dollar-area partners to discourage across-Atlantic relationships (notice how American RA's with the "six" and with Scandinavia *declined* between 1928 and 1948).

But the significance of the "1948 peak" in economic "Europeanism" must not be obscured by these special economic conditions. Europe—all of western Europe, including Scandinavia—was much more an integrated trading community in the period 1948 to 1951 than it had been before or has been since. *The multiple economic partnership among the "six" was stronger during the Marshall Plan era (1948–1951) than it ever had been in the interwar period or ever has been in any other part of the postwar era.* Their relative acceptance of intra-regional trade was .57 in 1928, 1.0 in 1948, 1.1 in 1951, and never higher than .8 between 1954 and 1963. Europeans were more "European" economically during the late 1940's and early 1950's than they are even in the contemporary period of restricted supranational economic institutions, in which their foreign policies have also evidently become more dissimilar.

THE POSTWAR PERIOD: INTEGRATION WITHIN DISINTEGRATION

A Partial Return to Prewar Normalcy

The period 1952 to 1954 marked the end of the only era in the twentieth century when *all* of western Europe (excluding Great Britain) appeared to be moving toward economic integration. During this period a return to economic "normalcy" reminiscent of the interwar period can be observed in the patterns of economic interaction. Looking once more at Figure 1, we see how many of the trend lines seem to straighten out after the major peaks of the Marshall Plan era. The summary RA for all trade among the "six," for example, leveled off after the 1951 peak in a range about 30 per cent higher than the prewar level. Anglo-American ties with the "six" also appeared to be continuing their downward trend. Perhaps the most dramatic change from the "Europeanization" of the Marshall Plan era, however, is the decreasing value of Scandinavian-"six" RA's from .1 and .7 in 1948 to .1 and .1 in 1963. Scandinavian exporters lost heavily on southern continental markets between 1948 and 1963.

By 1954 the Marshall Plan had ended, the European Payments Union had outlived its usefulness, the dollar shortage had been largely remedied, and OEEC programs called for liberalization, thereby encouraging the lifting of restrictions against extra-European trade. From the relative acceptance figures it appears that, with few exceptions, Europeans by the mid-fifties were again seeking out traditional foreign markets, welcoming traditional customers, and in general restructuring their economic behavior vis-à-vis other countries into a pattern of scattered national partnerships remarkably similar to the pattern of 1928. Germany in particular greatly reduced its introversion from the non-Atlantic world by reducing its "rest of the world" RA's from $-.9$, $-.7$ in 1948 to $-.1$, $-.1$ in 1954—much the same levels as found in the prewar period.

Many of the new economic partnerships born during the Marshall Plan era had also slackened by 1954. The regional linkage between Scandinavia and the "six" reached a peak intensity during the era and then weakened considerably. Within the "six," the Franco-Dutch partnership, fairly strong during the Marshall Plan era, had disappeared by 1954, and the Franco-German partnership which had been extremely strong during the era also dropped off considerably. On the other hand, the German-Dutch, Franco-Belgian, and Benelux partnerships, observed in 1928, were still strong in 1954, as was the German partnership with Scandinavia. All of these lingering partnerships were reminiscent of the interwar pattern. In addition, Italy's isolation from the Benelux countries and French isolation from the Netherlands, both notable in 1928, had also reappeared by 1954. Finally, since relationships between Great Britain and the continent did not change substantially between 1928 and 1948, or between 1948 and 1954, the pattern of British economic isolation from western Europe was still apparent in the mid-1950's, thereby making the 1954 pattern of relative acceptances even more similar to the pattern of 1928.

The Beginnings of Economic Supranationalism

To say the era of *all-western European* economic integration had come to an end after 1952 is not to say that movement toward economic integration in Europe had ceased altogether. The period 1952 to 1954 marked the introduction of Europe's first experiment in economic supranationalism, the European Coal and Steel Community, as a first step toward the geographical confinement of European economic integration. As far as economic partnerships were concerned, the impact of the opening of the ECSC in 1952 was more symbolic than substantive. A potential system of preferential economic partnerships among the "six" was defined on paper between 1950 and 1952, but no actual restructuring of economic partnerships within the ECSC area could be observed until about 1957.

However, by 1957, a number of interesting shifts had occurred in the pattern of economic interaction among the "six", reflecting emerging political relationships. First, intraregional relative acceptance within the EEC perimeter was up slightly, but perhaps meaningfully, if this small jump marked the opening of a new upward trend after the decline between 1951 and 1954. Second, the Franco-German partnership, which had all but disappeared after the Marshall Plan era, appeared to be increasing in intensity again after 1954. Whereas in 1954 Germans accepted French imports in volumes 50 per cent greater than expected under the null model, in 1957 they accepted French imports in volumes 60 per cent greater. Similarly, whereas in 1954 the French accepted German imports in volumes 30 per cent greater than null expectations, in 1957 they accepted German imports in volumes 40 per cent greater. Third, there were hints in the French and Dutch figures in 1957 that France and the Netherlands might have begun to move from economic isolation back to economic partnership. (This trend was suggested by decreased Franco-Dutch isolation rather than increased partnership.)

By 1959 Italy's integration into the "six" could also be observed. The Franco-Italian partnership was intensifying and the German-Italian partnership remained high (since 1954 Italy exported to Germany 100 per cent more than null expectations and imported about 50 per cent more). Even Italian ties with the Benelux countries were beginning to increase. Between 1954 and 1959 there were a number of internal trends which appeared to point toward the emergence of the "six" as a strong multiple economic partnership, or an integrated economic community.

The Confinement of the "Six"

At the same time there were a number of external trends in economic relationships among non-EEC countries and in economic relationships between EEC countries and non-EEC countries that pointed to the *confinement* of the "six" as an externally distinct trading community. That is, there was economic restructuring along the periphery of the EEC—or what was to be the EEC in 1958—that underlined the distinctiveness of the EEC group. Most notable among these trends were (1) increased French withdrawal from non-European trading ties; (2) the declining economic partnership between the "six" and Scandinavia after 1951, and, in particular, German and Benelux withdrawal from their Scandinavian ties; (3) Scandinavia's turn outward to Great Britain and inward upon itself; and (4) intensifying economic relations between both Great Britain and Scandinavia and Switzerland. While many of these trends were only beginning to make themselves apparent during the 1954 to 1957 period, they were much more discernible in the relative acceptance figures between 1959 and 1963.

As evidenced in Figure 2, however, France's withdrawal from world empire

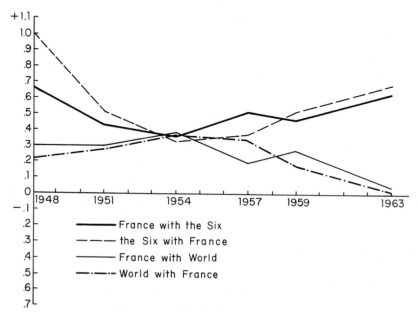

FIGURE 2. *French economic interaction with the "six" and with the rest of the world, 1948, 1951, 1954, 1957, 1959, and 1963.*

appears to have been cushioned by the opening of new markets in Europe to replace old ones in the rest of the world. Even though the year 1954 saw France defeat EDC, Figure 2 suggests it to have been the last point at which French ties with the "six" were exceeded by partnerships with the rest of the world. Since 1954, French reciprocal ties with the "six" have steadily increased from RA's of about .4 to ones near .8, while French external ties have declined in the direction of null expectations.

The end of the "Continental" trading system of the early postwar era was nowhere symbolized more abruptly than in the declining economic partnership between the "six" and Scandinavia. As Table 2 shows, the EEC's relative acceptance of imports from Scandinavia dropped steadily from .4 in 1948 to .1 in 1963. At the same time, Scandinavian acceptance of imports from the EEC dropped from .8 to .1 during the same period. These patterns resulted largely from Germany's progressive withdrawal from Scandinavian markets, Scandinavia's weakened position on German markets, and from the disappearance, after 1957, of some fairly strong Dutch-Scandinavian and Belgian-Scandinavian trade-flows of preceding years.

It seems that between 1928 and 1963 German buyers and sellers completed an about-face in their preference for markets, turning from the east and the north and to the west and the south. Political reasons are apparent. First of all the cold war had cut off both German eastern lands and German eastern markets. Secondly, the Federal Republic's postwar economic and political engagement on the continent tended to disrupt her traditionally strong ties to the north and the east. Between 1954 and 1959 Germany, for the first time in the twentieth century, appeared to be entering a *western* economic system. In the same manner, but on a lesser scale, the Belgians and the Dutch also executed a change of partners between 1954 and 1963, the Belgians turning from the Scandinavians to the Germans, and the Dutch from the Scandinavians to the French.

But the Scandinavians were also changing economic partners during the 1959 to 1963 period. Relative acceptance scores show that, while partnerships between the "six" and its periphery slackened during the 1950's, partnerships among countries geographically flanking the "six" developed and strengthened. As we saw in Figure 1, the relative acceptance of Scandinavian trade by EEC markets had already dropped to .1 in 1957. RA's remained only slightly positive through 1963.

Between 1954 and 1963, western Europe had begun to split into two trading areas—the ECC and its periphery. While EEC countries were abandoning traditional partnerships in Scandinavia, Scandinavian buyers and sellers turned inward to strengthen intra-Scandinavian economic bonds (within-region RA's rose from 2.7 in 1954 to 3.9 in 1963) and outward toward Great Britain and other non-ECC countries. The Anglo-Scandinavian partnership, traditionally a weak relationship, began to gain in intensity after 1957. There was also a rise in British relative acceptance of imports from Scandinavia between 1957 and 1959 (.67 to .84) and a reciprocal rise in Scandinavian relative acceptance of imports from Great Britain between 1959 and 1963 (.45 to .59).

The last element in the development of a Europe at "sixes and sevens"[16] during the latter part of the 1950's was the increase of Switzerland's trading ties

16. The phrase "sixes and sevens" refers of course to the six countries of the Common Market and the seven countries of the EFTA. This latter group is the one we allude to when we speak of the "periphery" of the EEC. See Benoit (1961).

with England and Scandinavia. Just as increased Scandinavian integration began to flank the EEC on the north and a growing Anglo-Scandinavian partnership began to flank the "six" on the west, new Swiss-Scandinavian and Anglo-Swiss economic links were beginning to mark the EEC's confinement along the east and the south. The evidence in support of this proposition is by no means conclusive, partly because Swiss-"six" *RA*'s remain as high as, or higher than, Anglo-Swiss and Swiss-Scandinavian relationships. Swiss-Scandinavian and Anglo-Swiss relations show declining trends in isolation, rather than trends in intensifying partnership. Nevertheless these trends do point in the direction of stronger and more reciprocal economic partnerships along the periphery of the EEC. Then too, the figures marking Swiss relations with the EEC suggest a declining partnership. Between 1957 and 1963 the traditionally intense Swiss partnership with the "six" showed some signs of weakening. While the EEC's acceptance of Swiss exports remained fairly constant, Swiss acceptance of EEC exports declined markedly from 2.31 in 1957 to 1.53 in 1963, a new low *RA* score for the twentieth century in this channel.

The increasing confinement of the "six" from the outside was, for the most part, continuing right into 1963. *However, this was not the case for the internal development of the EEC partnership.* Within the EEC, 1959 was another "peak" year. Since that time, and despite greatly increased economic prosperity, western European economic relations have remained relatively unchanged. In terms of economic partnership, as defined by relative acceptance scores, the "six" were as integrated in 1957 as they were in 1963. Their relationship was no more "special" in 1963 than in 1957. Moreover, they were really more integrated, though less isolated from non-community members, in 1948 than in 1957. Economic integration within the "six" lost ground after 1951, regained some between 1954 and 1959, and then stopped. *Confinement* has moved along since 1957, but *community* has lagged behind.

THE IMPACT OF THE COMMON MARKET

It will be remembered that the EEC was born on Benelux initiative out of what appeared to many to be the ruins of the European unification movement, set back as it was in 1954 by the defeat of the EDC. In 1957 the Treaty of Rome committed France, Germany, Italy, and the Benelux countries ultimately to abolish all international trade restrictions within their community, while at the same time providing for supranational policy-making to cushion economic transitions and to guide liberalizations.[17] The Common Market was opened in 1958, and substantial trade liberalization has already taken place.[18] What has all of this meant in terms of intra-European trade flows, economic partnerships, and economic and political integration?

The Formalization of Previously Developed Economic Partnerships

One major conclusion of the preceding section was that national preferences for trading partnerships did not shift appreciably among EEC members after the Common Market came into being. The Common Market, it seems, served

17. Shanks and Lambert (1962), pp. 43–186, and Kitzinger (1963), pp. 21–96.
18. *Ibid.*, and Shanks and Lambert (1962), pp. 56–79.

rather to formalize and institutionalize a number of previous long-term and short-term patterns of partnerships and isolation. The most important of these partnerships were among the "six" themselves. Also observed were the decrease of French *RA*'s with the rest of the world and lessening German preference for Scandinavian transactions. Only the trend toward cohesiveness among European nations *on the periphery of the EEC* seems to have come *after* the formation of the Common Market.

On the other hand, politically, the Rome treaty introduced a new symbol into European minds. After 1957 western Europeans both inside the EEC and without could view the world in a new perspective. France, Germany, Italy, and the Benelux nations had, by their agreement to enter the EEC, symbolically become something more than, and something different from, six neighboring nations. The treaty gave the supranational experiment on the Continent a new name. Member countries gained a new distinctiveness.

The United States and Great Britain, who had long been relatively isolated economically from German, French, Italian, and Benelux markets and who had long kept their own markets relatively isolated from the Continent, were confronted in 1958 with the fact that they might be no longer isolated simply from six national markets, but now from a vast supranational market. In the years after 1958, both the British and the Americans came to discover that attempts to reverse their isolation from the Continent became more difficult as the supranational market became an enduring part of European economic life.

The Economic Boom

The transaction-flows model explicitly distinguishes between expanding *volumes* of international trade and redirected trading *partnerships*. It also explicitly controls for internal trading relationships related to the production of the national product. An overall assessment of economic relationships during the Common Market years would be remiss if it did not examine what in several ways have been the most significant *changes* in postwar European economic relationships— changes in the volume of both international and intranational transactions.

European supranational economic institutions overseeing the "six" have, at least since 1957, been presiding over one of the greatest economic booms in modern history. It has been argued that the trade liberalization policies of the EEC could have helped western Europeans to reap the profits of their postwar economic boom by opening mass markets to expanding industries. This first possible impact of the Common Market—call it the boom impact—has most certainly occurred. Documentary evidence flows from the international trade reports of the EEC countries, from EEC agencies, and from all international bodies which record trends in international economics. Tables 3, 4, and 5 provide a quick summary of the boom impact at the EEC's inception.

Table 3 shows notable increases in national imports and exports for EEC countries, ranging from an 83 per cent increase in imports for Belgium-Luxembourg between 1958 and 1963, and a 260 per cent increase in imports for Italy during the same period, to a 98 per cent increase in exports for the Netherlands from 1958 to 1963, and a 194 per cent increase in exports for Italy over the five-year period. *For the EEC as a whole, imports rose by 131 per cent and exports rose by 132 per cent in the five-year period between 1958 and 1963.*

TABLE 3. *Indices of International Trade Flows 1958–1963;*
Intra–EEC Commerce, (1958 = 100)

	Imports					
	Germany	France	BLx.	Neth.	Italy	EEC
1958	100	100	100	100	100	100
1959	129	110	110	115	130	119
1960	159	150	129	136	190	149
1961	180	171	146	165	223	172
1962	210	205	158	176	275	197
1963	228	254	183	203	360	231

	Exports					
	Germany	France	BLx.	Neth.	Italy	EEC
1958	100	100	100	100	100	100
1959	113	134	110	119	132	119
1960	140	179	138	138	177	149
1961	167	213	151	153	214	173
1962	187	238	178	168	267	197
1963	226	272	213	198	294	232

[a]A. Sturmthal, *National Income and Growth Rates in Western Europe*, 1964 (manuscript).

TABLE 4. *Indices of International Trade Flows, 1958–1963;*
Extra–EEC Commerce, (1958 = 100)

	Imports					
	Germany	France	BLx.	Neth.	Italy	EEC
1958	100	100	100	100	100	100
1959	110	84	108	103	97	100
1960	129	101	123	117	135	120
1961	137	104	124	123	145	126
1962	151	114	133	126	165	138
1963	158	127	144	136	200	152

	Exports					
	Germany	France	BLx.	Neth.	Italy	EEC
1958	100	100	100	100	100	100
1959	110	103	106	106	107	107
1960	125	120	111	115	130	122
1961	135	120	109	119	146	128
1962	137	116	111	123	154	129
1963	143	125	113	123	165	135

[a]A. Sturmthal, *National Income and Growth Rates in Western Europe*, 1964 (manuscript).

TABLE 5. *Indices of International Trade Flows, 1953–1963;*
Intra/Extra–EEC Commerce, (1953 = 100)

	Imports		
	Intra-EEC	Extra-EEC	Intra-Extra
1953	100	100	0
1954	115	109	6
1955	140	125	15
1956	160	146	14
1957	177	162	15
1958	171	147	24
1959	204	147	57
1960	256	177	79
1961	296	186	110
1962	339	203	136
1963	397	224	173

	Exports		
	Intra-EEC	Extra-EEC	Intra-Extra
1953	100	100	0
1954	115	110	5
1955	139	126	13
1956	159	135	24
1957	177	151	29
1958	170	158	12
1959	202	164	38
1960	253	194	59
1961	294	203	91
1962	336	205	131
1963	394	214	180

[a]A. Sturmthal, *National Income and Growth Rates in Western Europe*, 1964 (manuscript).

Table 4 indicates clearly that the postwar economic expansion in western Europe was not limited to intra-EEC expansion, but was also marked by rising levels of trade flowing between EEC and non-EEC European countries. However, dividing the intra-EEC by extra-EEC figures—as is done in Table 5—shows that import and export expansions was a great deal more impressive within the EEC than on the continent as a whole. As Sturmthal points out, "1959 clearly marks a break in the evolution of EEC trade. While extra-EEC trade progresses at a moderate rate, trade relations among EEC partners intensified at about twice that rate. As the figures stand, they indicate that the EEC had considerable effect upon the foreign trade relations of its members."[19]

19. Sturmthal (1965).

An Increasing EEC Share of World Trade

The mathematical reason why such prodigious increases in extra-EEC and especially intra-EEC trade have not been reflected in *increased* economic partnerships within the EEC is simply that expected transactions have kept up with changes in actual transactions. Since null expectations of trade were calculated solely on the basis of each nation's *share* of world exports and of world imports, the necessary conclusion is that the "six" have dramatically increased their share of world trade.

One of the major "spill-over" effects of the economic boom has been the increased economic and political power of the "six." Besides being able to project an image of economically successful supranationalism, a larger share of world trade gives the "six" more economic leverage in bargaining with other individual nations. As the Kennedy Round negotiations have shown, an economically united group of nations with a common policy, a total population and national product approaching that of the United States, has more leverage at the bargaining table than six separate and smaller entities.

The growing political independence of the "six" in the western camp, buttressed as it is by growing economic might, has been demonstrated on a number of occasions in recent years. First the American Trade Expansion Act of 1962 has not lived up to the expectations of the Kennedy administration "grand designers,"[20] largely because the "six" have thus far been loath to accept the American invitation for expanded transatlantic trade. Europeans can now afford to wait for bigger American economic "carrots" because the American economic "stick" is losing its credibility in booming western Europe. Not only has the Common Market bolstered the European regional position in international political affairs, but membership in the Common Market has also bolstered the national status of major EEC members. For example, French objections to the MLF, her veto of the British bid for membership in the EEC, her views on the reorganization of NATO, and De Gaulle's independent stands on Vietnam would have been unlikely during the era of the Marshall Plan. Even when her Common Market partners disagree, France is less economically dependent upon, and can afford to stand against, the United States. What is currently true of France may become increasingly true of West Germany also.

The Growing Economic Interdependence of the "Six"

During the 1950's, economic growth rates of the member nations of the Common Market were about twice as high as those of the United States and the United Kingdom.[21] Growth rates of 7.2 per cent for Germany, 4.2 per cent for France, and 5.9 per cent for Italy, although impressive, in no way match the doubling of external trade relationships that have taken place in the last four or five years. The appropriate inference is again hidden by the transactions-flow

20. Kraft (1962), pp. 15–80.
21. Growth rates for national GNP's were computed from statistics compiled by the United Nations and published in United Nations (1959), pp. 19, 80, 86, 114, 140, 156, 228, 235, and United Nations (1963), pp. 90, 98, 138, 162, 177, 271, and 279. Growth rates during the 1950's for the "six" as compared with the United States and Great Britain were as follows:

analyses. External trading relationships have been an increasingly large part of EEC national economies. This growing economic interdependence among Common Market countries is perhaps the most significant spill-over of enduring and moderately high economic partnerships. An internationally shared economic development is perhaps the surest sign of the achievement of supranational economic and political integration.

This seems to cast considerable doubt on the utility of null-model to say the least — if not on economic indicators generally.

CONCLUSIONS

Perhaps it is too early to draw conclusions about economic and political integration in western Europe and to project findings into the future. However, a number of tentative observations about Europe's future can be made while a number of findings concerning Europe's past are underlined.

1. There was a notable structural change in economic interaction in the North Atlantic Area between the inter-war and the post-war period. Western Europe emerged from World War II more economically and politically "European" than it had ever been in the inter-war period. Between 1948 and 1951 Scandinavia was linked to the southern European nations, and these southern Continentals were economically linked to one another more intensely than ever before or since.

2. The period of *all-western European* partnership is over. It appears to have ended with the end of massive Marshall Plan aid and with the demise of the EDC. There has been as much economic *dis*integration in Europe since 1951 as there has been integration. Many western European partnerships of the Marshall Plan era were more imposed than autonomously inspired. Economic integration between the "six" and Scandinavia and between the "six" and Great Britain now appears to be out of question. Current chances for political federation between these states also appear to be small.

3. There has been a noticeable increase in the normally weak economic partnerships among non-EEC countries in the post-war era. Whether these new ties represent more than defensive reactions to the economic supranationalism of the "six" will be shown by any future trends toward future *positive* and enduring partnerships among the members of the European Free Trade Association. Such an economic confinement of the "six" might turn out to be politically meaningful in that it could focus the self-attention and stimulate the self-awareness and distinctiveness among peoples within the EEC or among those on its periphery. In this sense economic confinement reflects and might ultimately

Time Period	Country	Growth Rate[a]
52–59	Belgium	2.6
52–60	France	4.2
52–60	Fed. Republic	7.2
52–60	Italy	5.9
52–60	Netherlands	4.8
53–58	Luxembourg	3.3
52–60	United States	2.6
52–60	United Kingdom	2.7

[a]GNP at constant market prices.

contribute to political integration. Such a mutual identification process might be a necessary preliminary step to forming building blocks for some distant European federation.

4. The peoples of the "six" have yet to build a community from their confinement. Despite the new supranational framework, members of the "six" have grown no closer to one another in their economic relations structurally in the early 1960's than they were already in the early 1950's. On the basis of the relative acceptance figures one cannot argue that economic integration among the "six" has been moving forward. Moreover, in light of the *RA* scores' demonstrated relevance as an indicator of international political affinity, we are not greatly surprised that movement toward political unity among the "six" dramatically bogged down between 1962 and 1966. The French boycott of the EEC Council of Ministers between July 1965 and February 1966 has left EEC "community spirit" at a low ebb. Unless further structural change intensifies the economic partnership, movement toward political unity among the "six" seems unlikely.

5. Going beyond levels of economic partnerships, three trends were observed that in some way could be considered spill-over effects of the sustained economic partnerships of the last five to ten years. First of all, since the beginning of the economic boom in the early 1950's, the "six" have grown faster economically than either the United States or the collective membership of the European Free Trade Association. Secondly, the European share of world trade has increased considerably both because of its economic boom and because of its lessened trade barriers. As a result of this tremendous trade expansion, Common Market countries have become more economically independent, External trade has taken an increasingly large share of domestic European national products into the international arena.

6. The question of the EEC's political future depends to a considerable extent on the continuation of its current economic progress. Present supranational institutions have been able to survive and even to promote the strains of extremely rapid economic growth. To retreat from this increased regional interdependence of economies of scale made possible by the Common Market would be extremely unsettling. Nevertheless analysis has shown that partnerships within the EEC have been difficult to insure even in a prosperous and expansive boom period (within-region *RA* scores for the "six" have not increased since 1959). Therefore, some questions that must be asked concerning economic integration among the "six" are: What might happen to the EEC partnership in the event of an economic down-turn or recession? Will national foreign trade sectors suffer first and most severely from the down-turn? Will the EEC Commission come up with a new "supranational" anti-recession policy that will work effectively to both curb the recession and keep the EEC partnership intact? Or might we again expect a return to the economic "normalcy" and the fragmented Europe of the interwar period?

Bruce M. Russett

Delineating International Regions[1]

REGIONS AND POLITICAL THEORY

What is a Region?

According to some Frenchmen, "L'Afrique commence aux Pyrénées." Most Spaniards would probably not agree, but the search for a cultural (rather than a geographic) definition of Europe is not a simple one. In "western Europe" and "Africa" we have two regions which seem, in matters of political and social importance, to be relatively homogenous within themselves but different from each other. But how would we draw the boundaries so as to maximize the similarity within each group and minimize that between them? In the words of a recent article, "Where Is the Middle East?" (Davison, 1964): does it extend from Morocco to Pakistan, or should the line be drawn somewhere between? What do we do about Israel which, though right in the middle of any geographic delimitation of the region, still does not quite fit? Or within the United States: Where is the South? Does it include Texas? Kentucky? And what difference does it make to the politics of a state if it is more, or less, "southern"?

There are, of course, no simple answers to these questions. Different definitions and different criteria will produce different regions, and no two analysts may fully agree as to what the appropriate criteria are. This is a problem which has vexed social scientists, both students of international relations and observers of national social and political systems, for decades. In the late 1930's very substantial

1. This paper is part of the research of the Yale Political Data Program, supported by a grant from the National Science Foundation. An early draft was presented to the International Political Science Association in Geneva, Sept. 1964. I am grateful to Hayward Alker, Robert Hefner, James Lingoes, Rudolph Rummel, Raymond Tanter, Charles Wrigley, and others for comments, and to Lutz Erbring, Robert Grey, and Joel Jutkowitz for research assistance.

research was done on the matter within the United States, but, the various questions involved were never fully answered, and nothing comparable to that effort has been devoted to delineating regions of the world. But since the matter is not trivial in either its theoretical or its policy implications, I would like to explore it here in a tentative manner.

Some Criteria

First we must face certain problems. *How do we define a region*? One possibility is simply to identify an area divided from another by geographic barriers, a definition thus by *isolation* or separateness. One might find a natural region, such as a river valley or a plain. But virtually all social scientists, including geographers, would reject this definition. A region, they might say, must be composed of units with common characteristics. Regions should be areas of relative *homogeneity*. This might still be defined in physiographic terms: "any portion of the earth's surface whose physical conditions are similar," for example (Vance, 1951, p. 123). More common, however, is a homogeneity of economic and social structure. Or, the composite social region is thought to combine "a relatively large degree of homogeneity measured by a relatively large number of indices available for a relatively large number of purposes or classifications. This means it must comprehend both the natural factors and the social factors" (Odum and Moore, 1938, p. 30).

A perceptive critic of the regionalism concept replies, however, "Regionalism is not one thing but many things. The failure to discriminate the many distinct factors that underlie the emergence and persistence of regions is a serious fault of present-day research. Areas of homogeneity have been mistakenly represented as areas of integration" (Wirth, 1951, p. 392). Rupert Vance (1951, p. 123) quotes a geographer's reference to "an *ensemble de rapports* between man and the natural milieu." Thus, regions are sometimes explicitly defined by *interdependence*, as nodes within which a higher degree of mutual dependence exists than in relationships outside that area; within which people are bound together by common interests. This easily leads to a definition of a region according to *loyalties* or patriotism, "An area of which the inhabitants instinctively feel themselves a part" (Vance, 1951, p. 123). Nor is this the end of the possibilities. A "region" may also be an areal unit defined by an *ad hoc problem*. One suspects that "Southeast Asia's" principal claim to regional status with many Americans is simply the threat posed to the whole area by China. This leads to yet another definition: "A device for effecting *control*" (National Resources Committee, 1935, p. 139). According to some distinguished analysts, "Regionalism provides an economy for the decentralization of political power" (Odum and Moore, 1938, p. 27).

We thus find a combination of description and prescription in the approach of some "regionalists." This certainly was true of Odum and Moore, who advocated the delegation to regional authorities—especially one for the American Southeast— of political functions which they thought could properly be carried out neither by the federal nor by state governments. The same prescriptive orientation is evident in many international relations writings. Much talk, both by scholars and premiers, about regional (for example, Latin-American, Arab) political integration is based upon a presumed homogeneity, or interdependence, or loyalties, which may exist only in the mind of the beholder.[2] The United Nations Charter explicitly allows for security arrangements under regional agreements; NATO is often described as coming under a rather loose interpretation of "regional" in this context.

If we finally settle upon a definition or group of definitions—perhaps homogeneity, or homogeneity plus interdependence plus geographical separateness— we come to the problem of methods for *delineating regions*. The problem, in effect, is one of making the definition operational. If *separateness* is a primary criterion, physiographical indices might be included, or longitude and latitude incorporated into the analysis. If *homogeneity* is important, climatic conditions might be included. Crop and manufacturing areas might be relevant. The ethnic composition of the populace could be taken into account, as could the level of economic development, the history of the area, and its religious divisions. Frederick Jackson Turner, in emphasizing the political aspects of American regionalism, defined a "section" as a group of states contending with other groups. As measures he suggested homogeneity of votes by Congressmen, or areas defined by relative homogeneity of vote in presidential and state elections (Turner, 1932, p. 288). Perhaps if *interdependence* is to be a major criterion, the patterns of newspaper circulation (to the papers of which central city do outlying regions subscribe?), or mail, trade, or rail-traffic patterns would be good indicators. Or if patriotism or *loyalty* is considered the key, one might use survey research to ask a large number of residents, especially of the presumed border areas, of what region they considered themselves to be members.

Most of the large-scale empirical efforts to delineate regions have in fact made use of a wide variety of indices, though they have chiefly emphasized those which might be expected to measure homogeneity. In using a number of variables one can take advantage of the fact that "cultural traits" are correlated among themselves. If no cultural trait were related to any other, a region would have to be determined by a single trait and would have no meaning except in terms of that trait. On the other hand, "while the natural and cultural landscape often coincide they also often clash" (Wirth, 1951, p. 385). And, in addition, different measures of the cultural landscape itself may clash as often as they correlate. "The continental United States cannot be divided into a single set of sizable regions which meet perfectly all the standards of hypothetical regionality. Compromise is indicated. . . . A region may be delineated upon the basis of many factors, and its extent varies with the factor or factors selected for generalization" (National Resources Committee, 1935, pp. 123, 145). In the Appendix to its report, the National Resources Committee gives over one hundred maps for what it describes as "proto-regions," that is, single-factor regions. The factors in this case are the definitions applied by federal administrative agencies—virtually all are differently delineated. Again according to Louis Wirth (1951, p. 389),

> Short of considering the whole world as a single region . . . there is no other regional arrangement of lesser scope that will fully satisfy the many interests that clamor for recognition. The best we can do is to make the most reasonable compromises we can invent, which means weighting some functions more heavily than others, and to keep our lines of demarcation flexible enough so that they can be adjusted to changing needs and possibilities.[3]

2. See the criticism by George Lundberg (1942) of Nicholas Spykman (1942) and others.
3. Though recognizing that different indices will identify different regions at present, Walter Isard (1956) hopes that advances in theory will make possible the delineation of a "true" set of regions on which all the important indices will agree.

Odum and Moore (1938, pp. 447–448) conclude, "The mere grouping together of facts and indices of difference does not give us an organic regional entity, but simply gives us a description, an inventory of what has happened and what *is* under the given forces, which must of course be duly analyzed." In the end, the criteria "must be chosen not by chance, but in close relation to the definition of the region as a functional unit" (Riemer, 1943, p. 279). Perhaps we return to some idea of interdependence.

If there is no agreement about indices for delineation, even more clearly there is no consensus on the *proper magnitude* of a "region." Again according to the National Resources Committee (1935, p. 145),

The term "region" is not commonly applied to small areas, but there seems to be some disagreement as to whether it should be applied to very large sections such as the Middle West, the South, etc., or to smaller subdivisions of these, as for instance, the Corn Belt, the Industrial Piedmont, the Chicago metropolitan area, etc.

If states (or nations) are taken as the basic sub-unit from which regions are to be built up, there is clearly a lower limit to the size of a region. Some such political unit is most often used as the building block, not necessarily because such a course is theoretically most desirable, but because satisfactory data are not readily accessible for smaller units. Even so, no consensus on size exists. The size criterion might in large part determine whether "Latin America" emerged as a single region or was divided into several groups, like Central America, tropic South America, and temperate South America.

Finally, there is the sticky problem of *identifying the boundaries* of various regions. If one uses separateness or isolation as a major element in the definition of regions this problem may not be difficult, but otherwise it is. "It seems to be agreed that regional boundaries are usually indefinite, being zones rather than lines. In the majority of instances, therefore, any boundaries which may be drawn will be necessarily arbitrary" (National Resources Committee, 1935, p. 145). "The characteristics of a region should be most pronounced in its interior.... Regions end in transition, seldom in definite boundaries" (Finch, 1939, p. 14). Hence we are sure that France is in western Europe, however defined, but it is hard to know where to put Finland.

International Regions and International Integration

In this paper I would like to explore and suggest some answers to five general questions. I emphasize that these are to be tentative answers; only a small portion of the data that might appropriately be brought to bear on the problem can be discussed here. Other data, measuring other social, economic, or political dimensions, would almost surely change our answers somewhat. Also, alternative techniques for identifying groups or clusters should be explored. These are the central questions: (1) How many groups ("regions") are necessary for an adequate summary description of the similarities and differences among types of national political and social systems? (2) What countries are to be found in which groups? (3) How do these groups compare with the groupings, including the areal groupings we call regions, now in use by social scientists? (4) What are the discriminating variables for distinguishing groups in general, and in distinguishing between specific groups? (5) What is the relevance of our groupings to theories of international politics?

Political integration at the international level, particularly the union of formerly independent states, has been the subject of extensive research in recent years. We still know little enough about the necessary prerequisites for successful integration, or in what sequence they need occur, but various authors have identified several conditions as very important. Perhaps among others they include a degree of cultural homogeneity, interdependence, and the existence of formal institutions with substantial "spill-over."[4]

The first two of these conditions coincide closely with two of our suggested definitions of a region. We shall delineate international regions by each criterion, compare their congruence, and then further compare them with areas where past or present supra-national or inter-governmental political institutions exist. In so doing we should be able to identify certain areas of the world where the potential for further integration is high, and perhaps point out other areas where, despite present or projected institutions, some apparent preconditions seem weak or absent. We cannot, of course, say whether the degree of homogeneity or interdependence we find is sufficient to support a given level of integration, but we can point out areas of more and less, and note important discontinuities.

Our conclusions should be relevant to several different approaches to the organization of world politics. There is a rather widespread view that international integration on the "regional" level is more likely to succeed than is the worldwide imposition of a powerful political institution. Certainly there is a long and honorable tradition in the profession which regards regionalism as the proper basis for world order, an alternative both to fragmentation and to universalistic solutions.[5] Sometimes regional federations are urged not as an alternative but as stepping stones or building blocks which might later be dissolved, or perhaps even be maintained within a world union. The latter version is to be seen in a policy statement of the British Movement of Federal Union, calling for regional units as "constituent and permanent elements of a World Government structure" (cited in de Rusett, 1950, p. 159). This leads easily to the view that regional organizations must be a basic element in a multi-level wider union, sharing the load and handling issues about which there is sufficient regional but not worldwide consensus.[6]

This study will not attempt to support or refute any of these contentions, nor will it offer any new empirical evidence about the value of particular factors in aiding or hindering the process of integration. But whatever the purpose behind any advocacy of regional unity, it will help to indicate how one might delineate a region so that, in the light of our current theories, the chances of success may be maximized.

REGIONS OF HOMOGENEITY

A Factor Analysis of Social and Cultural Variables

The first set of data used in this analysis is applied to finding areas of homogeneity, and is derived from data presented in the *World Handbook of Political*

4. On the importance of these three conditions, and their interrelations, see, among others, Deutsch, *et al.* (1957), Etzioni (1962, 1963, 1965), Haas (1957, 1958), and Russett (1963).

5. An early advocate would be Spykman (1942); most of the current advocates of European or Atlantic union would probably also belong here.

6. E. H. Carr (1945) held this view in his influential work. Other representatives of this school are discussed by Claude (1959), and Etzioni (1964) also expounds it.

and Social Indicators (Russett, *et al.*, 1964).[7] In the *Handbook*, seventy variables (for up to a hundred and thirty-three countries each) were correlated with each other; they were selected to provide information on a wide variety of social, cultural, political, and economic conditions. Though it is easy to think of other variables that might have been included, many would correlate quite highly with some already in the *Handbook*, and I believe we were reasonably catholic in our tastes.

In order to produce, for this analysis, a set of data with fairly complete information, I limited the study to fifty-four variables on eighty-two countries in the late 1950's. The countries included most of the world's sovereign states and major colonies, except for sub-Saharan Africa, about which too few data were available. Several data were added to the *Handbook* collection from other sources and, where necessary, the values for missing data were estimated, so that there were no missing observations apparent in the analysis.[8] I intended, however, not simply to use fifty-four indicators which happened to be available, but to analyze national variation on those variables that were not purely idiosyncratic, bore some relation to basic patterns of social and cultural variation across nations, and seemed relevant to theories of political integration. Hence some method of finding the underlying patterns of association among the variables was required. Factor analysis seemed to be the appropriate method. In the most common type of factor analysis every variable is correlated with every other variable, using a product-moment correlation. Those variables which show high correlations among themselves and very low correlation with other variables point to a single underlying dimension, or *factor*. The factors themselves are uncorrelated with (orthogonal to) each other.

In this study I was able to reduce the fifty-four separate variables to five orthogonally rotated dimensions which together accounted for 60 per cent of the total variation (variance) in the original variables. Table 1 presents the list of variables with their "loadings" (the correlations of the *particular* variable with the broader *factor* or dimension) on each of the five factors. At the top of each column is a label for the dimension it seems to be measuring, and the percentage of the total variance accounted for by the factor.[9] For emphasis, factor loadings of .50 or higher are underlined with solid lines, and loadings between .30 and .50 with dashed lines.

---

7. Fuller definitions of the variables and discussions of reliability are to be found in the *Handbook*. As done there, some variables were subjected to a logarithmic transformation to make the distributions more normal. If the distributions were very skewed (non-normal) the outliers (extreme values) would affect the correlation disproportionately.

8. One method of estimation was multiple regression. Where it was inapplicable it was often necessary to use the mean observation for countries with data. If a logarithmic transformation had been applied it was the mean logarithm that was employed. Less than 15 per cent of all observations had to be estimated, however. The effect of erroneous estimates, if random, would be to reduce the correlations among variables.

9. Each factor has an eigenvalue which tells how much of the total variance in the fifty-four variables is explained by the factor. It is computed by summing the squared coefficients of correlation of each variable with the factor. Since each variable has a variance equal to unity, dividing the eigenvalue by the number of variables tells us the percentage of the total variance that is explained by each factor. By a procedure known as "rotation" to a "simple structure," one obtains factors which tend to have either very high or very low correlations with the variables, thus making it easy to identify those variables which contribute most to a substantive interpretation of the factor.

TABLE 1. *Basic Socio-cultural Dimensions*

Variable	Factor 1 Economic Development 31%	Factor 2 Communism 11%	Factor 3 Size 7%	Factor 4 Catholic Culture 5%	Factor 5 Intensive Agriculture 6%
1. GNP per Capita	.94	−.00	.06	.09	−.04
2. Newspapers per 1,000 Population	.93	.13	−.03	.06	−.01
3. Non-agricultural Workers as % of Wage and Salary Earners	.93	.00	.05	−.05	.03
4. Life Expectancy	.92	.09	−.01	−.02	.10
5. % Labor Force in Agriculture	−.89	.12	−.02	−.04	−.12
6. Radios per 1,000 Population	.88	.09	−.04	.26	−.14
7. Domestic Mail per Capita	.87	.11	.10	−.09	.07
8. % of GNP from Agriculture	−.85	.04	.03	−.07	—.08
9. Inhabitants per Hospital Bed	−.85	−.18	.16	−.11	.10
10. % Labor Force in Industry	.85	.19	.09	−.06	.04
11. Primary and Secondary School Pupils as % of Population	.83	.12	−.08	−.08	.11
12. % Adults Literate	.82	.21	.07	.07	.07
13. Births per 1,000 Population	−.82	−.26	−.16	.05	−.17
14. Wage and Salary Earners as % of Working Age Population	.80	.07	−.05	−.04	−.07

The "principal components" method of factor analysis was used, and the dimensions shown in Table 1 are the orthogonally rotated factors. All ten factors with eigenvalues greater than one were rotated. In all factor analyses in this chapter unities were inserted in the principal diagonal. For a discussion of the technique see Harman (1960). Factor analysis has for some time been used in regional analysis as a tool for condensing a large number of variables into a manageable number of summary dimensions. See Kendall (1939), Hagood, Danilevsky, and Beum (1941), Hagood (1943), Cattell and his associates (1949, 1951, 1965), Berry (1960, 1961b), Moser and Scott (1961), Thompson and Sufrin (1964), and Gregg and Banks (1965). As a method for research in international politics its acceptance is more recent; for examples and further references see Alker (1964), Alker and Russett (1965), and Rummel (1963). For a valuable review of other methods of regional delineation see Duncan, Cuzzort, and Duncan (1961), pp. 128–160.

TABLE 1.—*continued*

Variable	Factor 1 Economic Development 31%	Factor 2 Communism 11%	Factor 3 Size 7%	Factor 4 Catholic Culture 5%	Factor 5 Intensive Agriculture 6%
15. % of Population in Cities	.77	−.09	.05	−.14	−.11
16. Television Sets per 1,000 Population	.70	−.01	.26	.35	−.03
17. Foreign Mail per Capita	.68	−.09	−.30	−.05	.22
18. Cinema Attendance per Capita	.67	.26	−.09	−.03	−.03
19. Inhabitants per Physician	−.62	−.05	−.09	−.23	−.08
20. Investment as % of GNP	.60	.44	−.20	−.12	−.21
21. % of Population of Working Age	.58	.30	.29	−.03	.16
22. Deaths from Political Violence	−.55	−.02	−.12	.23	−.22
23. Students in Higher Education as % Population	.53	−.03	.42	.18	−.04
24. Radios per 1,000 Population—% Annual Increase	.52	.12	.27	.24	.05
25. Annual Rate of Population Increase	−.52	−.31	−.11	−.02	−.23
26. Infant Mortality Rate	−.52	.03	.13	−.07	−.14
27. Private Consumption as % of GNP	−.47	−.30	−.06	.28	.20
28. Speakers of Dominant Language as % of Population	.44	−.06	−.17	.30	−.00
29. Moslems as % of Population	−.42	−.05	−.13	−.35	.05
30. Female Workers as % of Labor Force	.37	.30	.06	−.00	−.05
31. Communist Votes as % of All Votes	−.01	.96	.14	.03	.00
32. Central Government Expenditure as % GNP	.11	.95	.08	−.03	.04

TABLE 1.—*continued*

Variable	Factor 1 Economic Development 31%	Factor 2 Communism 11%	Factor 3 Size 7%	Factor 4 Catholic Culture 5%	Factor 5 Intensive Agriculture 6%
33. Central Government Revenue as % GNP	.12	.94	.11	−.01	.06
34. Non-communist Secular Votes as % All Votes	−.05	−.92	−.14	−.05	−.15
35. GNP per Capita— %Annual Increase	.31	.61	.10	−.06	.28
36. Votes as % of Voting Age Population	.41	.59	−.02	−.17	.01
37. Inhabitants per Hospital Bed—% Annual Change	.23	−.30	−.09	.15	−.07
38. Total Population	−.14	.15	.93	−.12	.06
39. Gross National Product	.35	.15	.89	−.07	.05
40. Area	−.11	.01	.74	−.06	.59
41. Foreign Trade as % of GNP	.15	−.38	−.66	−.03	.08
42. Defense Expenditures as % of GNP	−.02	.22	.41	−.09	.21
43. Roman Catholics as % of Population	.04	−.13	−.11	.87	.02
44. All Christians as % of Population	.47	.01	−.17	.68	−.09
45. Socialist Vote as % of All Votes	.31	−.29	−.14	−.53	.18
46. Population Density	.02	.16	−.03	−.02	.90
47. Population per Hectare Agricultural Land	−.07	.06	−.03	−.05	.89
48. Foreign Mail Sent/ Foreign Mail Received	.18	.19	−.05	.08	.45
49. Inequality of Farm Land Distribution	−.23	−.12	−.24	.35	−.42

TABLE 1.—*continued*

Variable	Factor 1 Economic Development 31%	Factor 2 Communism 11%	Factor 3 Size 7%	Factor 4 Catholic Culture 5%	Factor 5 Intensive Agriculture 6%
50. Religious Party Vote as % of All Votes	.09	−.13	−.00	.10	.37
51. % Labor Force in Agriculture—% Annual Change	.18	.07	.22	.08	.31
52. Military Personnel as % Working Age Population	.13	.20	.04	−.27	.30
53. Executive Stability	.04	−.04	−.21	−.05	−.01
54 % of Farms Rented	−.03	−.09	.08	−.01	.15

The first factor is labeled "Economic Development," from the variables which load heavily on (are highly correlated with) it. They include GNP per capita (variable 1); newspapers (2) and radios (6) per capita; life expectancy (4); labor force in industry (10); pupils in primary and secondary school (11); literacy (12); urbanization (15); infant mortality rate (26); and, with high negative correlations, percentage of GNP from agriculture (8) and labor force in agriculture (5); hospital beds (9) and physicians (19) per capita; and birth rate (13). It is remarkable, in fact, how high these correlations are for so many variables. Virtually any one of them would, by itself, form a reasonable measure of economic development. Together in this factor they account for 31 per cent of the total variance in the Table.

The second factor is clearly a measure of *communist influence*. Variables which load highly on it include votes for communist parties (31) and a negative correlation with non-communist secular votes (34); government expenditure (32) and revenue (33) (including those of publicly owned enterprises); the rate of increase of GNP per capita (35); and total voting turnout (36). The third factor may best be called simply *size*. Correlated with it are total population (38); total GNP (39); and area (40). Foreign trade as a percentage of GNP (41) is negatively correlated with size.[10] Factor four is for convenience labeled "Catholic Culture," because of the religious variable loading most highly on it (43). Other high loadings include those for all Christians as a percentage of population (44) and votes for socialist parties (45). The latter, plus the moderately high loadings of television ownership (16), speakers of dominant language (28), Moslems as a percentage of population (negative, 29), and land inequality (49), indicate that a fairly broad cultural phenomenon, rather than a purely religious one, is being measured.

Finally, factor five has been called "Intensive Agriculture" (to contrast with *extensive* agriculture). Variables loading highly on it include overall population density (46) and density as related to agricultural land (47) and, negatively, area (40). One might call the dimension simply "density," except for the fact that inequality of land distribution (49) is rather negatively correlated with it, emphasizing that in sparsely settled countries there are not only small family farms but a number of great estates as well. Though it is hard to find a perfect label, it is clear that a pattern of agriculture is the dimension involved here, a pattern that may have important roots and consequences in the general structure of a society. The latter interpretation is supported by the correlations between .30 and .50 of a number of other variables (48, 50–52) with it.[10]

These are the five most important factors; no other accounted for as much as 5 per cent of the variance. Furthermore no other factor had more than one variable with a loading as high as .65 on it, and in most cases they defied clear substantive interpretations. I decided, therefore, to work only with these five dimensions in attempting to delineate homogeneous regions. Yet even this seemed not quite right, for "size" is not usually considered in such delineations. For most purposes—though perhaps not in the interplay of international power politics—Luxembourg would be thought of as similar to Belgium or Germany; it is not less "European" for being small and weak. Thus in the interests of agreement with most notions of what cultural or social variables are relevant to political integration and to the delineation of regions I discarded the size factor (number three). This also seemed to serve the interests of parsimony, providing that an adequate identification of regions could be achieved without it.

We have, then, four basic dimensions of national variation being represented: a measure of wealth and standards of living, one of political and economic institutions, a measure of agriculture and land-use patterns, and one concerned with religious culture. While there are of course other kinds of variables and dimensions we might wish to see included, possibly some which might have given broader political or religious factors, these seem adequate for an exploratory study. Furthermore, they correspond quite closely to the factors that have emerged from a variety of other studies. I shall give a detailed report in a later study (Russett, 1967) on a rigorous comparison of these dimensions with those from seven cross-national analyses of a wide variety of indices (Cattell, 1949; Cattell, Breul, and Hartman, 1951; Cattell and Gorsuch, 1965; Berry, 1961a; Gregg and Banks, 1965; Robinson, 1965; and Rummel *et al.*, 1967). Three of our original five factors (economic development, size, and intensive agriculture) very closely resemble those found in each of the other seven analyses; the correspondence between the other two (communism and Catholic culture) and dimensions in other analyses was less, but still substantial, with a factor related to ours always present. Considering the wide variation in data sources and types used in these analyses—Gregg and Banks, for example, used dichotomized variables derived from judgmental coding; Robinson used data coded on a 0–10 ordinal scale; in Cattell's earlier two studies the data had to come from pre-World War II League of Nations sources with serious reliability problems—the overall correspondence is gratifying. Although we might well have added other variables, the dimensions we have are neither fortuitous, unique to this study, nor theoretically irrelevant.

Factor analysis was originally devised by psychologists, and at that by

---

10. Lack of space prevents fuller discussion of the implications of these correlations, but see Russett, *et al.* (1964).

psychologists who were interested more in general dimensions of mental ability ("vectors of the mind") than in individual persons. Thus it was, and still is, most commonly used as a method for finding correlations among tests, in a matrix where each item (test-taker, or in our application a country) is a row and each variable (test or socio-cultural index) is a column. But by turning the table 90 degrees the countries become columns and the indices become rows. When this transposed matrix is factored the correlations identify countries with similar patterns on the variables and the factors point to clusters of similar countries. The term Q-analysis is usually used to distinguish this procedure from the more common technique (R-analysis) employed earlier, but the mathematical procedures are just the same. Q-analysis has by now been used rather frequently in other disciplines, though to my knowledge the only published applications to comparative or international politics are those of Banks and Gregg (1965) and my own on voting in the United Nations (Russett, 1966).

I transposed the matrix for a Q-analysis, but in keeping with the preceding discussion I employed only those socio-cultural indices which were fairly highly correlated (.60 or greater) with one of the four dimensions identified as relevant to our concern with regional delineation and integration. Use of only these twenty-nine variables seemed a reasonable compromise between brute empiricism (throwing in every available cross-national index) and an *a priori* specification of a few individual *indicators*—not just broad dimensions—as crucial to integration (a procedure that would not be supportable in the still amorphous state of contemporary theory). This second analysis tells us what countries are like each other over a variety of indicators. It provides the number of factors (dimensions) necessary for grouping the countries, and the relative importance of each. We can discover which countries load most heavily on each factor and give them a descriptive "regional" name or names. The factors and "clusters" of countries need not be identical. A factor might be bipolar, with one cluster of countries having very high positive loadings on it and another group of countries with high negative loadings. Or, as is in fact the case below, a cluster may be identified by its members' moderately high loadings on two separate factors. But the Q-analysis does give us a parsimonious way of looking in detail at the configuration. Table 2 shows four rotated factors, and five clusters, so derived, as well as a few countries at the end which are not closely identified with any single grouping.

TABLE 2. *Regions of Socio-cultural Homogeneity*

	Factor 1 23%	Factor 2 27%	Factor 3 22%	Factor 4 9%
		"*Afro-Asia*"		
Tunisia	.92	−.06	.28	−.03
Iraq	.91	−.13	.21	−.09
Iran	.90	−.09	.22	−.11
Malaya	.88	.16	.13	−.09
Turkey	.88	.06	.20	.06
Morocco	.87	−.07	.28	−.12
India	.87	−.27	.24	−.12

TABLE 2.—*continued*

	Factor 1 23%	Factor 2 27%	Factor 3 22%	Factor 4 9%
Thailand	.86	−.06	.27	.02
South Korea	.85	−.02	.21	−.00
Burma	.84	−.27	.23	.00
Syria	.84	−.05	.26	−.19
Jordan	.84	−.04	.19	−.05
Taiwan	.84	.12	.04	−.05
Ceylon	.84	.18	.21	.01
Indonesia	.82	−.25	.18	−.01
Pakistan	.79	−.35	.24	−.25
Egypt	.76	−.05	.14	−.08
Algeria	.75	.01	.33	.05
Mauritius	.60	.25	.25	−.11
Lebanon	.50	.25	.29	−.11

"Western Community"

	Factor 1 23%	Factor 2 27%	Factor 3 22%	Factor 4 9%
Denmark	.04	.98	.01	−.05
Sweden	−.05	.97	−.03	.05
Norway	.06	.94	.05	.14
United Kingdom	−.10	.93	−.12	−.14
United States	−.01	.93	−.02	−.18
Switzerland	−.12	.93	.09	.00
West Germany	−.21	.91	.00	.06
Finland	.11	.91	.09	.26
Canada	−.10	.89	.20	−.10
Netherlands	−.06	.89	.04	.16
France	−.22	.87	.30	.10
New Zealand	−.04	.85	−.06	−.12
Iceland	.02	.82	.12	.08
Australia	−.16	.81	−.03	−.19
Belgium	−.27	.81	.24	.02
Austria	−.29	.78	.25	.14
Luxembourg	−.31	.77	.26	.05
Cyprus	.44	.75	.26	.13
Ireland	−.11	.74	.50	−.01
Argentina	−.19	.74	.51	−.24
Japan	.36	.73	−.25	.12
Greece	.42	.67	.32	.15
Italy	−.27	.66	.38	.20
Israel	.26	.63	−.34	−.03
Malta	−.04	.61	.42	−.03
Trinidad and Tobago	.25	.54	.10	−.12

TABLE 2.—*continued*

	Factor 1 23%	Factor 2 27%	Factor 3 22%	Factor 4 9%
"Latin America"				
Colombia	.16	.15	.95	−.04
Honduras	.34	−.06	.92	−.09
Nicaragua	.31	−.04	.92	−.05
Ecuador	.25	.05	.90	−.12
Guatemala	.34	−.06	.90	−.09
El Salvador	.34	.06	.90	−.09
Dominican Republic	.31	.02	.89	−.06
Peru	.22	.17	.88	−.11
Costa Rica	.23	.28	.87	−.01
Mexico	.20	.10	.87	−.19
Brazil	.21	.28	.87	−.17
Bolivia	.30	−.12	.86	−.14
Paraguay	.26	.01	.85	−.08
Panama	.20	.39	.82	−.10
Philippines	.43	.10	.81	−.08
Venezuela	−.08	.35	.67	−.14
"Semi-Developed Latins"				
Uruguay	−.17	.64	.51	−.08
Puerto Rico	.05	.59	.60	−.02
Cuba	.01	.56	.74	−.14
Spain	.01	.54	.65	−.01
Portugal	.13	.53	.73	.08
Chile	−.11	.49	.64	−.11
"Eastern Europe"				
Romania	−.03	−.00	−.15	.97
Yugoslavia	.02	−.08	−.04	.95
Bulgaria	−.04	.00	−.29	.92
Poland	−.41	.03	.17	.83
Albania	.30	−.41	−.19	.78
Hungary	−.53	.24	−.20	.73
Czechoslovakia	−.50	.30	−.26	.71
East Germany	−.36	.42	−.39	.66
U.S.S.R.	−.22	.18	−.55	.66
Unclassifiable				
Haiti	.58	−.34	.66	−.06
Jamaica	.42	.47	.50	.11
British Guiana	.43	.44	.29	.04
South Africa	.49	.52	.14	−.07
China	.44	−.63	−.17	.53

The Regions and Their Characteristics

Except possibly for the fourth one, each of these groupings is readily identifiable as very similar to a "region" in common parlance. Group one, for instance, corresponds quite closely to Asia and the Arab states, with few exceptions. Of the countries physically located on the Asian continent, its periphery, or Saharan Africa, only Japan, the Philippines, Israel, and China are missing.

Table 3 will help explain why some countries were included and others excluded from the groups which emerged inductively from the Q-analysis. It gives the factor scores for each country on the four socio-cultural dimensions originally derived from the *Handbook* (the dimensions, omitting size, given in Table 1 and used in the selection of indicators for the Q-analysis). A factor score is a composite index built up from a country's values on the original indicators, with each indicator weighted by a coefficient which corresponds roughly to that indicator's contribution to the underlying factor. Thus it gives us a measure of "economic development," for instance, that is related to the original data but as a composite index is less subject to error or idiosyncratic variation on particular indicators. But because they are composites they must be interpreted as rough and general indicators rather than as precise measures. It is not hard to point out where particular rankings might seem more plausible if reversed. This is part of the price one pays for using a composite index (though the same problem often arises, from measurement error, even in simple indicators). Except that it would complicate communication, there is much to be said for simply labeling the factors, X, Y, and Z. Otherwise one risks the fallacy of misplaced concreteness: for example, the argument that the factor scores must somehow be wrong because Argentina is "really" more Catholic than Uruguay, not less so. "Catholic culture" is a useful and descriptive label, but still an imperfect one for the underlying dimensions being measured. The factor scores themselves of course do not enter into the actual Q-analysis.

These factor scores have been standardized with a mean for the entire world of zero and a standard deviation of unity. At the head of each grouping in Table 3 we give the mean and standard deviation of each set of factor scores for the group. The smaller the standard deviation the greater the group's homogeneity on that dimension. Thus we can easily see the profile of the "Afro-Asian" group; very underdeveloped, moderately non-communist, decidedly not Catholic in culture, and in which population densities and agricultural patterns may vary rather widely.

Although abstractly Turkey might have been considered a candidate for a European grouping, actually it fits the Afro-Asian profile almost perfectly. And Lebanon, as the wealthiest Middle Eastern country in our sample, and with a population that is one-half Christian, barely makes the cluster. Several other countries which might have been expected to group with the other Asian states do not. Japan and Israel both load more highly on the dimension that identifies the "Western Community" than on the Afro-Asian one—each is economically much more developed (by three and four standard deviations above the mean respectively) than the typical Asian nation. And the Philippines, predominantly Roman Catholic in religion and heavily influenced by the colonial rule of Spain and the United States, is on these dimensions more like a Latin American than an Asian country. China, listed with the unclassifiables at the end, is in political ways

TABLE 3. *Countries' Factor Scores on Socio-cultural Dimensions*

	Factor 1 Economic Development	Factor 2 Communism	Factor 3 Intensive Agriculture	Factor 4 Catholic culture
		"Afro-Asia"		
Mean	−0.93	−0.36	0.27	−0.85
Standard deviation	0.56	0.37	0.89	0.56
Tunisia	−0.89	−0.27	−0.24	−0.47
Iraq	−0.81	−0.27	−0.57	−0.76
Iran	−0.90	−0.18	−0.90	−1.09
Malaya	−0.50	−0.50	0.23	−1.12
Turkey	−0.84	−0.36	0.22	−0.77
Morocco	−1.03	−0.56	−0.21	−0.77
India	−1.77	−0.61	0.73	−1.20
Thailand	−1.43	−0.50	0.25	−1.13
South Korea	−1.07	−0.64	1.72	−0.15
Burma	−1.56	0.04	−0.30	−1.92
Syria	−0.67	−0.53	−0.80	−0.75
Jordan	−0.71	0.24	0.23	−1.02
Taiwan	−0.06	−0.54	2.07	−1.54
Ceylon	−0.79	−0.56	0.62	−1.50
Indonesia	−1.77	0.41	0.16	−1.17
Pakistan	−2.05	−1.01	0.60	−0.85
Egypt	−0.46	−1.01	1.07	0.54
Algeria	−1.00	0.53	−1.50	−0.61
Mauritius	−0.37	−0.02	1.45	−0.72
Lebanon	0.07	−0.36	0.49	0.11
		"Western Community"		
Mean	1.15	−0.31	−0.14	−0.28
Standard deviation	0.45	0.38	1.24	0.88
Denmark	1.37	−.084	0.59	−1.05
Sweden	1.55	−0.41	−0.16	−0.13
Norway	1.29	−0.33	−0.16	−1.05
United Kingdom	1.78	−0.63	0.70	−0.92
United States	1.90	−1.11	−0.87	0.54
Switzerland	1.37	−0.81	1.00	−0.21
West Germany	1.51	−0.00	1.11	0.18
Finland	0.93	−0.01	−0.50	−0.82
Canada	1.47	−0.93	−1.33	−0.01
Netherlands	1.34	0.00	1.85	0.08
France	1.18	−0.11	0.55	0.32
New Zealand	1.57	−0.37	−1.30	−1.39
Iceland	1.01	−0.19	−2.27	−1.00
Australia	1.74	−0.56	−2.86	−1.39
Belgium	1.26	−0.29	1.87	0.56

TABLE 3.—*continued*

	Factor 1 Economic Development	Factor 2 Communism	Factor 3 Intensive Agriculture	Factor 4 Catholic culture
Austria	1.10	0.29	0.80	0.50
Luxembourg	1.31	0.14	0.87	0.51
Cyprus	0.40	−0.39	−0.02	−0.44
Ireland	0.77	−0.52	0.21	0.52
Argentina	0.79	−0.72	−1.88	−0.87
Japan	0.77	−0.12	1.13	−1.79
Greece	0.18	−0.32	0.44	−0.24
Italy	0.75	0.57	1.02	1.28
Israel	1.24	0.19	0.27	−1.43
Malta	0.64	−0.37	−1.54	1.09
Trinidad and Tobago	0.58	−0.11	0.44	−1.03

"Latin America"

Mean	−0.66	−0.40	−0.55	1.20
Standard deviation	0.38	0.27	0.66	0.30
Colombia	−0.58	−0.28	−0.91	1.83
Honduras	−1.09	−0.45	−0.54	1.42
Nicaragua	−0.76	−0.08	−0.48	0.97
Ecuador	−0.74	−0.34	−0.28	1.21
Guatemala	−1.18	−0.43	0.02	1.32
El Salvador	−0.70	−0.55	0.21	1.47
Dominican Republic	−0.70	−0.25	0.14	1.38
Peru	−0.55	−0.33	−0.97	1.07
Costa Rica	−0.41	−0.37	−0.65	1.29
Mexico	−0.44	−0.70	−0.24	1.28
Brazil	−0.32	−0.83	−0.71	1.12
Bolivia	−1.10	−0.06	−1.94	0.85
Paraguay	−0.75	−0.52	−0.94	0.98
Panama	−0.41	−0.61	−0.37	1.19
Philippines	−1.18	−0.82	0.65	0.44
Venezuela	0.35	0.19	−1.74	1.38

"Semi-Developed Latins"

Mean	0.23	−0.47	0.24	1.11
Standard deviation	0.21	0.14	0.95	0.12
Uruguay	0.62	−0.34	−1.54	1.09
Puerto Rico	0.09	−0.40	1.23	1.03
Cuba	0.14	−0.28	−0.16	1.27
Spain	0.39	−0.66	0.78	0.94
Portugal	0.01	−0.60	1.11	1.10
Chile	0.12	−0.56	−0.01	1.27

TABLE 3.—*continued*

	Factor 1 Economic Development	Factor 2 Communism	Factor 3 Intensive Agriculture	Factor 4 Catholic culture
		"Eastern Europe"		
Mean	0.20	2.55	−0.01	0.18
Standard deviation	0.57	0.21	0.63	0.74
Romania	−0.17	2.72	0.15	0.23
Yugoslavia	−0.22	2.36	0.38	−0.37
Bulgaria	0.11	2.74	0.11	0.14
Poland	0.06	2.17	0.54	0.98
Albania	−0.82	2.76	−0.06	−0.78
Hungary	0.46	2.45	−0.17	1.16
Czechoslovakia	0.71	2.42	0.11	0.43
East Germany	1.02	2.72	0.42	0.72
U.S.S.R.	0.66	2.58	−1.58	−0.92
		Unclassifiable		
Haiti	−1.87	0.03	0.68	0.12
Jamaica	−0.21	−0.29	0.53	−0.84
British Guiana	0.15	−0.26	−1.17	−0.92
South Africa	−0.04	−0.47	−1.44	−0.86
China	−1.83	2.48	−0.14	−0.69

like her fellow communist states, but is economically much more backward.

The second grouping is best described by some term like "Western Community." Leaving aside for the moment a few countries in the fourth group ("Semi-Developed Latins"), it includes all the states of Western Europe, North America, and Oceania. And in addition to Israel and the European or European-settled nations it includes, fairly far down in the list, Japan and Trinidad. From Table 3 we can see that these states vary substantially on the intensive agriculture and Catholic culture dimensions, but are characterized by moderately low communism scores and, uniformly, by a high level of economic development. The presence of Japan is especially noteworthy. On three of the four original dimensions Japan's profile shows quite a close approximation (within a standard deviation of the mean) to the countries of Europe and North America. Japan's economic prosperity has brought her to a per capita income level not far below the other industrial states, and Japan is the only member of the Organization for Economic Cooperation and Development from outside the geographically-defined area of the North Atlantic. Only Japan's very non-Catholic culture keeps her from a more central position in the cluster, and provides a loading, albeit fairly low on the first factor, which in Table 2 is identified with "Afro-Asia." Greece and Cyprus have some affinity for the "Afro-Asia" factor, but still come in here toward the bottom. This "Western Community" of developed industrialized nations makes no distinction between Western Europe and the English-speaking states, or between neutrals and NATO allies. In their modest way these findings support the advocate of "Atlantic Union" against the Gaullist notion of a Europe "from the Atlantic to the Urals." Along with British Guiana and Jamaica, South Africa loads about as highly on the first factor as on the second, and is put with the unclassifiables. It is of course, precisely the efforts of its white government to keep the country from becoming "Afro-Asian" that has produced the present political tension.

Although there are some important exclusions, the third cluster, "Latin America," includes only Western Hemisphere countries and the Philippines. But several of the twenty republics of Central and South America are missing. Haiti's absence is readily understandable. Its level of economic development is two standard deviations below the Latin American mean, and is actually well under the average even for Asia. It also ranks comparatively low on Catholic culture (Voodoo?), has a higher population density than most Western Hemisphere states, and even rates moderately high on Communism. (Perhaps its above-average score on "Communism" is typical of certain kinds of non-communist but authoritarian regimes. Haiti's score does not, of course, approach that of nations which actually have communist governments.)

Also missing from this group are all the political units which have, or had until recently, colonial governments. Trinidad, relatively well developed and non-Catholic, fits uneasily at the end of the "Western Community" listing. Most relevant to the exclusion of British Guiana is its score on Catholic culture, eight standard deviations below the Latin American mean. The same is true of Jamaica, which joins British Guiana among the unclassifiables. Like the other countries at the bottom of the table, they were left separate because they had two or more loadings above .40, the higher of which, when squared, was less than twice the magnitude of the smaller one squared. That is, the proportion of the variance accounted for by the more important factor was less than two times that accounted for by a second. These states cannot as a result be placed unambiguously in a single cluster.

Most commonly, in a factor analysis of this sort, the factors can be used to identify groups of countries with relative ease. But several countries in this analysis are distinguished by the way in which they load more or less equally on the same two factors, those which above picked out the "Latin American" and "Western Community" states. This is illustrated in Figure 1, a scattergram with the positions of the countries on the two competing factors plotted between the axes. The vertical axis represents the percentage of variance (100 times the factor loading squared) accounted for by Factor 2, and the horizontal axis the percentage explained by Factor 3. All the countries with loadings of .40 or higher on *both* factors are represented, as well as several others for reference.

In some instances one factor accounts for three or more times as much of a country's variance as does the other, and when this happens there is little question as to where the nation should be grouped. This applies, for instance, to Venezuela, which I unhesitatingly assigned to the "Latin American" cluster. Any country which occupies a position either between the vertical axis and the sloping solid line to its right, or between the horizontal axis and the sloping solid line above it, has this variance ratio of more than three to one. The sloping dashed lines to the right and above the solid ones respectively mark the gray area where the variance ratio is over two to one. Although the countries occupying this space are distinctly

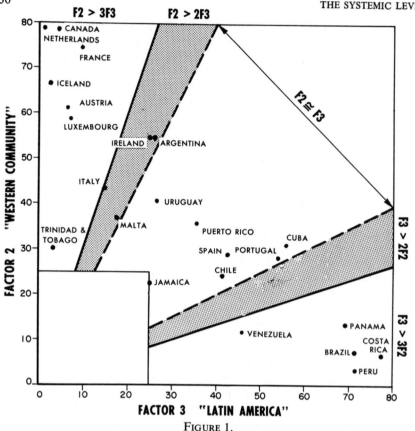

FIGURE 1.

more marginal than ones lying closer to the axes, it is usually not unreasonable still to assign them as weak members of the group whose factor accounts for more than twice as much variance as any other. Accordingly I did so with Argentina, Ireland, Italy, and Malta, putting them too with the "Western Community." And states which have less than 25 per cent of their variance accounted for by either of these factors would fall into the square at the lower left of the diagram which has been left empty.

But six states go into the area where the percentage of the variance explained by the more powerful factor is less than twice that of the other. They are Portugal and Spain from Europe, Cuba and Puerto Rico from the Caribbean, and Chile and Uruguay from South America. All share much the same "Catholic culture" as the "Latin American" states, but their level of economic development is appreciably higher though short of the "Western Community" mean. The presence of the poor Iberian states, bearers of Latin culture to the New World, is instructive if not really surprising. In a sense the French proverb should be revised to declare, "Latin America begins at the Pyrenees." We shall treat this as a separate group even though it is not as distinct from either the "Latin Americans" or the "Western Community" as the latter two are from each other. The label "Semi-Developed Latins" is awkward and probably the least satisfying, intuitively, of the inductive classifications so far encountered here. Jamaica is shown on the graph but ought not to be considered part of the cluster. Its case shows the limitations of a three-dimensional presentation. Had we a third dimension, depth, represented here we would see that Jamaica is kept distinct by a moderately high loading also on the "Afro-Asia" factor.

Finally, we come to the "Eastern European" group, which could with some justice be equated with the communist countries.[11] "Communism" is of course the most sharply discriminating dimension for this group, but a middle level of economic development, and fairly low Catholic culture are also typical features. As with all the other clusters, there is a wide variation in agricultural patterns and the mean of the scores from the "Intensive Agriculture" factor is neither very high nor very low. On all of them the group is quite homogeneous (with low standard deviations). Yugoslavia is not notably different, by these criteria, from any of the countries under more immediate Russian influence. Mainland China, however, is put with the unclassifiables because of its high loading also on the factor identified with "Afro-Asia" and high *negative* loading on the "Western Community" factor. And note that China's backward satellite Albania, though in the "Eastern Europe" group, itself has quite a high loading on the "Afro-Asian" factor, much higher than that of any other Eastern European state.

There have been a few peculiarities, but despite them we have found that, by purely inductive techniques, using indicators identified with only four cultural dimensions, we can classify, with a high degree of plausibility, the world's polities into "regions." Four factors, which find five groupings, account for 80 per cent of the variance. (Nine factors with eigenvalues greater than one were rotated, but only the first four accounted for as much as 3 per cent of the variance.) This occurs without the injection of any *a priori* judgments as to the number of regions which should be found, or what those regions should be. We did not include, as we might have, some explicitly geographical variables (like longitude and latitude) in the analysis. We have, of course, been using the geographic term "region" loosely. For historical reasons regions and sociocultural groupings often coincide, but they need not. Yet in four of the five cases the "regions" which emerged from our analysis do correspond to generally recognizable geographic groupings, and all make substantial cultural sense.

Where there are exceptions to common usage it is usually possible to explain them, and in explaining them to add something to our understanding of international and comparative politics. Haiti's absence from the Latin American cluster, for instance, made substantial sense, as did Japan's absence from Asia. Both of these cases suggest something about their political and social systems.

The regions found here coincide rather well with those found by Berry (1960, 1961a) from the examination of countries' scores on an economic and a demographic scale, but the use in this chapter of more dimensions, and explicitly political-cultural ones, allows much better differentiation than Berry achieved. Cattell (1950) also found similar regions, though with more unclassifiable countries and more countries seemingly classified erroneously. The difference there is attributable both to a difference in method (a clustering procedure) and to his use of prewar data. The regions in addition correspond quite closely to those obtained by several previous cluster and other analyses of my own. I have never been fully satisfied with any of the clustering techniques offered, yet the similarity of the

11. The data used here antedate the Castro regime in Cuba.

clusters here with both of my own previous attempts and others' indicates a substantial degree of cross-method validation.[12]

On grounds of theory or methodology one could, of course, conceive of more and differently defined groups. Other methods must still be explored. Four cultural dimensions produce these groupings; more dimensions would surely help to distinguish further subgroups. It would be desirable to know whether, by some salient political or social dimensions, one could divide the Middle Eastern states from the rest of Asia. If we had data, we would want to know what makes Africa different from Asia; subdivision of the Western Community or Latin American groups would also be revealing.

REGIONS OF INTERDEPENDENCE

A Measure of Economic Interdependence

A shift from our focus on homogeneity may help with these problems. Nations which are very different culturally may nevertheless be highly interdependent (for instance, a colony and its mother country). Thus we can obtain a different perspective by examining nations' patterns of exports and imports to look for "regions" of economic interdependence. In this context it is difficult to find a perfect index of interdependence. One might simply look at the total *value* of trade between two countries, or the *percentage* their mutual commerce is of their total trade, using high values, or high percentages, as indicators of interdependence. But the trouble here is the *size* effect—most countries will have both a high value and a high percentage of their trade with countries like the United States and the United Kingdom which account for a large proportion of total world trade. In some respects this would be proper—much of the world *is* interdependent with the American and British economies. Though no longer quite so true, it used to be said that when America sneezed Europe caught pneumonia.

Another and perhaps more satisfactory index, however, controls for the size effect, essentially by hypothesizing that the proportion of A's exports which go to B will correspond to the mean of the proportion of A's exports in all world exports and the proportion of B's imports in all world imports. Thus if the United States contributes 26 per cent of all world exports and Britain takes 18 per cent of all world imports, we "expect" Britain to take 22 per cent of American exports[13].

12. The chief fault of the clustering routines is that they usually are irreversible. That is, they build up groups by minimizing within-group variation *at any given stage*, with the limitation that a group, once formed, cannot be decomposed at a later stage in the hierarchy. By treating previously-formed groups as givens they cannot allow for the possibility that splitting up tentatively-formed groups and rebuilding them in different combinations might produce even less within-group variation. See, for example, the method described by Ward and Hook (1963).

One other procedure I tried was to construct a matrix of socio-cultural "distances" from the factor scores in Table 3. The distance between two countries was the square root of the squared differences between their factor scores, summed across all four factors. The distances can be converted into "proximities" with a range of zero to one and used as an input to a direct factor analysis as though they were correlation coefficients. While direct factor analysis is a common and accepted procedure, there is reason to think that it is not fully appropriate for Euclidean distances, with the result that it may somewhat distort the configuration and dimensionality. Accordingly I have not published those results here.

13. For the proper formulas and a full discussion of this "expected" value, see Savage and Deutsch (1960), with a correction to the published version by Alker (1962); see also Goodman (1963).

Given the "expected" values it is possible to compute a *ratio* of *actual* to *expected* exports, or what might be called an index of relative acceptance of one country for another's exports. This relative acceptance index is computed as follows:

$$RA_{ij} = \frac{A_{ij} - E_{ij}}{E_{ij}}$$

where A is the *actual* value of trade, E the *expected* value, i a subscript for an exporting country, and j a subscript for an importing country. This formula produces RA's ranging from infinity for very high trade to -1.00 for no trade between two countries, with .00 indicating an actual value which is precisely that "expected" by the model. Since for computing product moment correlations the variables should be approximately normally distributed, the RA's were subjected to a logarithmic transformation. This still does not produce a fully normalized distribution, but here I am only using the factor analysis as the first step in a search, and I want it to weight extremes at the tail (closeness) somewhat more heavily. The trade data used here are from the United Nations (1957), and the original RA's were computed by Savage and Deutsch.

Use of the RA as the index of interdependence suffers from one serious defect— it does not take into account the volume of the trade. Two countries might trade with each other more than "expected" but, if both were small countries or countries which conducted little international trade, the total volume, and the interdependence effect, might be small. An alternative procedure would be to measure interdependence by their mutual trade as a proportion of the importing or exporting country's GNP. I have done this elsewhere (Russett, 1965, Chap. 3, and 1967), with similar but hardly identical results. But the theoretical question is different in each case, and in the context of this paper we can be especially interested in the personal contacts and communication that go with a high RA index, and so use it rather than trade proportion or dollar value as the interdependence index.

Finally, it should be emphasized that data on trade in commodities give only an incomplete measure of economic interdependence. A full analysis would require data on investment, foreign aid, receipts from shipping, tourism, and other "invisibles." Nevertheless, because these items typically account for only about 25 per cent of total foreign exchange receipts, the omission is perhaps not too serious.

It should be clear that in this instance the "expected" values are those given by a *null* model, not a *predictive* one. It says nothing about the effect on trading patterns of the international division of labor, or distance, or transportation costs, or political or cultural ties, or governmental restrictions. It merely gives us *a base against which to measure deviations* from the null model, deviations which indicate interdependence, or a lack of it, *to be explained by substantive theory.*

Two Factor Analyses of Trading Patterns

With these revised RA's we were in a position to use factor analysis to identify groups of countries with similar (highly correlated) trading patterns. Two countries which trade closely with the same third countries will load heavily on the same factor. Note, however, that this is not necessarily the same as saying that the two countries are *interdependent*. To be interdependent they must of course trade with *each other*, but with the factor analysis it is possible, if they trade in a similar enough fashion with the rest of the world, for them to load heavily on the same factor even if they do *not* trade much with each other. To some extent this was corrected by including for all self-choices a value equal to the largest *RA* in the entire matrix. But this only tends to reduce the danger, and it is essential after finding countries with high loadings on the same factor to look closely at their detailed trading relationships before asserting that one has found an interdependent group. Several examples below will show individual countries which seemed, by their factor scores, to be interdependent with a group, but on close examination proved merely to be similar.

Furthermore, note that the *RA*'s are not symmetrical; exports of A to B are treated separately from A's imports from B. Pakistan, for example, exports heavily to Communist China but takes relatively few imports from it. This is an important item of information, since one reasonable definition of interdependence would demand high trade in both exports and imports between two nations. Thus it was necessary to perform two factor analyses, one in which countries' exporting *RA*'s were treated as variables and imports as observations, and once *vice versa*. Interdependent groups were tentatively identified only in those instances where the basic pattern of factor loadings was similar in both analyses.[14]

The economic data used in the following analysis are for 1954; the set of countries is the same as used in the previous analysis except that we have trade data for Indochina, Saudi Arabia, and Sudan, and data were unavailable for Jordan, Malta, Puerto Rico, Luxembourg (combined with Belgium), and the Soviet Bloc states of eastern Europe. But even with the N reduced, we found a substantially larger number of groups, and found a much greater tendency for countries to load rather highly on two or more different factors. In each of the factor analyses there were thirteen factors accounting for 3 per cent or more of the total variance; no rotated factor accounted for more than 7.5 per cent of the variance, and the thirteen together accounted for only 65 per cent of the total variance in one analysis and 64 per cent in the other. In part this may be due to random errors in the data (countries not bothering to report any trade with small countries, trade which though small in volume might be substantial with respect to expected value); it seems more likely to indicate a fragmentation of the world in terms of patterns of economic interdependence.

The method of presentation here differs from that employed previously. The two full 72×13 matrices of countries' factor loadings would be very difficult to

14. This procedure, using data on countries' "choices" of trading partners, resembles the analysis of sociometric information. Duncan MacRae, Jr. (1960) performed a direct factor analysis on a set of non-symmetrical sociometric data derived from asking prison inmates to name their friends and allowing the men to appear in the matrix both as choosers and as chosen. He found, however, a somewhat more nearly reciprocal pattern of relationships than those discovered here from trading patterns. A similar analysis was made by Wright and Evitts (1961). Other methods than factor analysis might be used to find interdependent groups. Some are cited by MacRae (1960). The HIDECS procedure of Alexander (1963) and Alexander and Manheim (1963) could do so but can use only dichotomized (high-trade, low-trade) variables. Another possibility is the set of methods for linkage analysis developed by McQuitty (1964). A different definition of interdependence, however, might well accept a triangular relationship in lieu of reciprocal pairs. In my longer study (Russett, 1967) I have used *direct* factor analysis to find in one step countries that are truly interdependent rather than merely possess similar trade patterns.

interpret. More important, as indicated above the factor analysis here must be just the first of two steps; individual *RA*'s must be inspected and factor loadings on each of the two analyses must be compared to identify true cases of inter-dependence as distinguished from similarity. In fact, three of the groups in each analysis were discarded as failing one of these tests. (The percentage of variance accounted for by the factor was in every case below 4.0). Eight groups are shown below, with the rows for exporting countries and the columns for importers. Countries' closest importing and exporting partners in the entire world have been ranked numerically, and each cell contains room for two entries: the upper half for an exporting partner, the lower half for an importing country. In each table the rankings were carried to *N* minus one (*N* being the number of countries in the group) and partners which did not rank this high, but with whom trade was nevertheless greater than "expected," are indicated by an asterisk. Less than "expected" trade is indicated by an empty cell. This method allows the reader quickly to see the instances in which interdependence is greatest, and to identify the countries whose group membership is most marginal. Finally, under the name of each country is its factor loading on either exporting (country names read vertically) or importing (country names read horizontally) factor analyses.

Thus in Table 4 to find the country to which Mexico is closest as an exporter, one would read *across* the *upper* half of the Mexico *row* to Costa Rica, which ranks as the number one recipient of Mexican exports. But treating Costa Rica as importer and reading *down* the Costa Rica *column* in the *lower* half of each cell one sees that Mexico is only her second closest partner with Panama first. And the fact that Mexico is much more interdependent with the group as an exporter than as an importer is shown by all the empty cells reading vertically, and substantiated by its much higher factor loading (.60) with this factor in the exporting matrix than in the importing one (.32). Note, however, that because of the effect of similarity or non-similarity in trade with non-members of the group, the factor loadings will not necessarily coincide exactly with the degree of inter-dependence indicated by the cell entries.

The Regions and their Characteristics

Our first substantive findings concern the group which in the previous section was labeled "Latin America." With the trade data we find no such continent- or hemisphere-wide grouping, but instead three separate sets. The first, illustrated in Table 4, is labeled "Central America Plus United States."

The core group of interdependent countries is composed of El Salvador, Honduras, Nicaragua, Costa Rica, and Guatemala. In most cases they trade heavily with each other, though Guatemala is a partial exception. Mexico is closely bound to the group as an exporter, but the Mexicans apparently find little to import from their southern neighbors. Perhaps this situation is due to Mexico's status as a moderately industrialized country with manufactured goods to sell, while at the same time producing agricultural goods very similar to those in Central America. Although sometimes included in the area called Central America, Panama is very peripheral when economic interdependence is the criterion. Panama trades heavily only with its immediate neighbor Costa Rica. Very strikingly, however, the United States appears as a major market and source of goods for all these countries. They share not only relative interdependence among themselves, but a common trading pattern with the Colossus of the North. The United States factor loadings for this group are nevertheless only moderately high; its world trading connections are much wider and more varied than are those of the Central American states.

TABLE 4. *"Central America Plus United States"*

To / From	El Salvador .92	Honduras .84	Nicaragua .78	Costa Rica .61	Guatemala .67	Mexico .32	Panama .35	United States .29
El Salvador .91	X	1 1	2 1	7 6	3 1			4 6
Honduras .80	1 1	X		2 2	3 3			4 3
Nicaragua .78	1 2	2 2	X	* 3			* 4	6 *
Costa Rica .73	2 4	3 3	6 4	X			1 1	4 *
Guatemala .69	1 3				X		7	2 5
Mexico .60	7 6	4 5	5 5	1 2	* 5	X		2 4
Panama .25				1 1			X	2 1
United States .49	* 5	7 4	* 2	* 4	* 3	2 1	4 2	X

The five most closely linked countries in this table are precisely those that originally belonged to the Federation of Central America. All recently joined in the Central American Common Market, though Costa Rica entered only eighteen months after the group was first formed. Costa Rica's tardiness may partly be explained by her close trading ties with other Latin American countries (see Table 5). Mexico's rather peripheral status is emphasized by her decision to join not the Central American group but the Latin American Free Trade Association, composed of South American states.

TABLE 5. *"Northern South America Plus United States"*

To From	Panama .78	Colombia .71	Ecuador .65	Costa Rica .64	Peru .46	Venezuela .44	United States .36
Panama .76	X	5	3 2	1 1		4 2	2 1
Colombia .74	6	X	5				1 2
Ecuador .67	5 6	1 1	X				3 *
Costa Rica .42	1 1	* 3		X			4 *
Peru .36		* 5	3 1		X		5 *
Venezuela .23						X	6 *
United States .30	4 2	* 2	* 3	* 3	* 3	* 1	X

The second Latin group is composed of several states from the northern part of South America, plus Panama, Costa Rica, and again the United States. Once more we have a core group—Panama, Colombia, Ecuador, and Costa Rica. Panama clearly fits this group much better than it does the one in the previous table. The first three are quite interdependent, as is Costa Rica with Panama and Colombia but not more distant Ecuador. At one time these first three nations were united in the state of Gran Colombia, as was Venezuela. The Table here shows that, although Venezuela has moderate loadings on these factors, it really is not part of an interdependent group and should be excluded; Peru, with exporting ties to Ecuador and Colombia, is a more marginal case. Once more the United States is grouped with Latins by close ties, and again its factor loadings are kept fairly low by a wider world trading pattern.

Finally we come to a group that can clearly be labeled "South American." Here the core is composed of the four most southern states—Argentina, Chile, Uruguay, and Paraguay. Four others—Bolivia, Peru, Brazil, and Ecuador—are rather peripheral, usually trading with the core countries but not necessarily with each other. Several of the peripheral ones are also linked to other groups—Peru and Ecuador to the group in Table 5, Brazil to several European countries (see below). All except Bolivia have joined the Latin American Free Trade Association, as have Colombia and Mexico, two countries which do not trade much with the core group.

TABLE 6. *"South America"*

To From	Argentina .78	Chile .69	Uruguay .74	Paraguay .70	Bolivia .68	Peru .65	Brazil .52	Ecuador .37
Argentina .78	X	3 2		2 2	4 2	5 1	6 3	
Chile .72	1 2	X	2 3		3 3	* 4	* *	6 4
Uruguay .66			X	1 1	4 5		2 1	
Paraguay .59	1 1		2 1	X				
Bolivia .63		3		4	X		5	
Peru .74	7 6	1 1	6 5		2 1	X		3 1
Brazil .51	2 3	3 7	1 2				X	
Ecuador .42	6 *	1 3		3 4				X

For Latin America, therefore, we find not one interdependent region as a whole, but three distinct groupings of states. Geographical contiguity is important in defining the groups, for each member has a land boundary with one or more others (United States excepted), but geography does not tell us precisely where the boundaries between one group and the next will be. For that we must go to history, current political ties, or economics. Also, the United States, though not a *Latin* American, clearly emerges as interdependent with most of the countries. Finally, there are a number of absent states. The Caribbean republics are linked to no group; they trade heavily with the United States, but not with each other or with the continental countries. The same is true of Venezuela. Nor are the colonies—Jamaica, Trinidad, and British Guiana—joined by economic bonds to Latin America. Their close ties are with Canada or outside the hemisphere. (A partial exception is the high volume of trade between Venezuela and Trinidad, directly off the Venezuelan coast.) These, it should be noted, are states which also failed to group with Latin America according to the homogeneity criteria applied in the previous section of this paper. Politics and culture, as well as geography, are substantial influences in the delimitation of interdependent regions.

TABLE 7. *"East Asia"*

To *From*	South Korea .77	Taiwan .83	Japan .63	Philip- pines .47	Saudi Arabia .31
South Korea .72	X	3 3	1 2		
Taiwan .61	3 2	X	1 1	* *	2 3
Japan .40	2 1	1 1	X	* 2	* *
Philippines .49	3 4		1 *	X	
Saudi Arabia .45		* 4	2 5	* 3	X

Moving on, we find that the countries previously classified as "Asia" break down into no fewer than five distinct groupings of interdependence. One, shown in Table 7, can be identified as "East Asia," because it includes as its core South Korea, Taiwan, and Japan, with the Philippines slightly marginal. These four countries all are fairly proximate to each other, and in addition the first three were members of the former Japanese Empire. It is rather surprising to find Saudi Arabia with this group, but substantial interdependence of that country with the "East Asians" is apparent. Saudi Arabia serves as a major source of oil to most of them, and in addition imports both from Japan and Taiwan.

The next group can perhaps best be called "Southeast Asia." All but Burma and Japan border on the South China Sea. Excepting only pairs involving old Indochina and Burma, six of the seven show very high interdependence. Even Communist China exports heavily to three other members, though its imports from them are slightly less substantial. But China's *total* importing pattern is rather different from the rest of the group's, as indicated by its low loading on the factor in the import analysis (only .18). (The difference would be even greater if our analysis had been able to include trade data for other communist countries, with which China, but not most other Asians, trade heavily.)

Next we have a group labeled Middle East. Its core is composed of Arab countries, though Iraq is somewhat to the fringe of the core and Sudan is definitely outside. All the core but Egypt was part of the Turkish Empire until 1914, though

Turkey now trades heavily only with her immediate neighbors, Syria and Lebanon, and does not even make the Table. Iran, India (but not Pakistan), and the Mediterranean countries of Italy, Cyprus, and Greece also trade fairly heavily with the Arabs, as does Belgium with several. A sub-group is formed by Sudan plus Italy, Cyprus, and Greece (who are part of a larger grouping in Table 8). Notable by their absence are the three former French Arab countries—Algeria, Morocco, and Tunisia.

TABLE 8. *"Southeast Asia"*

To / From	Thailand .83	Indonesia .81	Malaya .79	Indochina .60	Burma .57	Japan .34	China .18
Thailand .77	X	4	2	6	*	3	
		3	1	4	6	4	
Indonesia .77	3	X	1	5		4	
	5		2	6			
Malaya .72	1	2	X	4	3	*	*
	2	4		3	3	5	*
Indochina .65	4		1	X		3	6
	4		3			*	
Burma .61		3	5		X	4	
		1	5			3	
Japan .51	5	3	*	*	4	X	*
	1	2	*	*	2		5
China .60		*	4	3		6	X
		*	4	2		*	

One other small Asian group, not shown in tabular form, would be composed of the states of the Indian sub-continent: India, Pakistan, and Ceylon, together with a country quite outside the geographical and cultural area, the United Kingdom. The tie among these nations obviously is associated with the former political rule of Britain over them. Yet it is not broadened into a general British Commonwealth grouping. There is another small core of Britain, Australia, and New Zealand, and Australia to some degree joins these two fairly small groups by substantial trade with India and Ceylon, but otherwise all resemblance to a large independent Commonwealth group ceases. Many countries—British Guiana, Canada, Jamaica, South Africa, Sudan, and Trinidad—with present or former ties to Great Britain do indeed trade heavily with the mother country, but only to a very limited degree with each other. Except for Australia and the ex-British India area, any attempt to picture the commercial relations among the Commonwealth states would look essentially like a wheel with spokes radiating out from the United Kingdom to each of the one-time colonies, but with no network of mutual links among the countries around the rim. In this key respect,

TABLE 9. *"Middle East"*

From \ *To*	Lebanon .83	Syria .85	Saudi Arabia .78	Egypt .50	Iraq .73	Iran .58	India .37	Sudan .34	Italy .40	Cyprus .39	Greece .27	Belgium .38
Lebanon	X	2	1	5	4	7			10	3	6	9
.87		1	1	1	1	5			*	1	3	7
Syria	1	X	2	10	3	4			9	*		8
.87	1		2	*	2	4			*	*		5
Saudia Arabia	11	3	X	5			6		4			
.57	10	3		5			4		2			
Egypt	4	7	1	X			3		9	*		
.58	2	6	5				2		8	*		
Iraq	8	1	6		X				2			*
.68	11	2	8						1			*
Iran	3	6			2	X	9		7			
.59	3	7			3		8		*			
India		*	5	10	*	7	X	3		*		
.39		*	7	*	7	6		1		11		
Sudan	8		2	1			5	X	6	4	7	
.58	*		4	2			6		7	6	6	
Italy	10	5	*	7	*	*	*	11	X	9	1	
.31	9	4	*	7	8	*	*	4		3	1	
Cyprus	5			2				1	7	X	10	
.35	4	11		4				2	*			
Greece	*	*	5	6		-		11	3	1	X	
.40	*	*	5	6				7	3	4		
Belgium	10	*			*						8	X
.29	*	*			*						10	

plus the absence of any clear-cut grouping in the socio-cultural analysis of the preceding section, we see the failure of the Commonwealth to forge new bonds to replace those of empire.[15]

TABLE 10. *"Northwest Europe"*

From \ To	Norway .74	Iceland .79	Denmark .65	Sweden .65	Finland .67	Spain .63	Portugal .54	Netherlands .35	West Germany .31	Ireland .43	Israel .44	Brazil .45
Norway .80	X	6 / 6	1 / 1	2 / 1	4 / 5	5 / 10	11 / *		8 /		* / 11	9 / 7
Iceland .79	3 / 2	X	6 / 5	* / *	2 / 2	4 / 4	1 / 1		* / *	9 / 5	5 / 4	10 / 10
Denmark .71	2 / 3	1 / 3	X	3 / 2	6 / 9				5 / 8			8 / 11
Sweden .70	1 / 1	4 / 5	2 / 2	X	3 / 7	* / *	* / *	11 / 10	5 / *	11		8 / 8
Finland .59	* / *	1 / 1	3 / 6	* / *	X	10 / *		* / *	11 / *	7 / 4	6 / 6	* / *
Spain .58	7 / 10	1 / 2	* / *	* / 9	8 / 10	X			6 / 10	* / 9		* / *
Portugal .43	11 / *			9 / *		3 / 9	X		7 / *	10 / 8	4 / 7	
Netherlands .45	5 / 8	9 / 7	6 / 8	2 / 4	3 / 8	* / *	* / *	X	4 / 7	10		
West Germany .41	10 / 4	* / 8	6 / 4	4 / 3	* / *	* / *	11 / 6	* / 5	X		3 / 5	* / *
Ireland .33				10	3	2	11		8	X		
Israel .39	6 / 5	4 / 4	11 / *	10 / 10	2 / 1						X	
Brazil .37	* / *	* / 9	10 / 10	9 / 6	3 / 4	7 / 11			6 / *			X

15. This pattern—close links between a metropolitan country and dependent (or formerly dependent) states, but not among the dependent states themselves—is much like that identified in mid-eighteenth century Colonial America by Richard Merritt (1966).

In the case of another former empire, however—the French Union—we do find something very much more like an interdependent group. All the French territories in this analysis naturally traded with France, but in addition the three North African colonies (Algeria, Morocco, and Tunisia) also showed a high level of transactions among themselves. Even Indochina, though marginal, imported heavily from Algeria and Morocco as well as from France.

By the trade ties criterion there is no group that corresponds satisfactorily with the "Western Community" socio-cultural group. Two major segments, however, do seem identifiable. Table 10 shows one which we shall label "Northwest Europe," though that geographical identification is not entirely apt. The heart of this group is to be found in Scandinavia, with all five Nordic states trading very heavily with one another. Most of the other countries represented in this table are there because they conduct a high level of commerce with these Scandinavian states, and sometimes with the rest of these non-Nordic countries as well. West Germany fits the pattern very well on this basis as, more surprisingly, do two very non-Nordic nations—Spain and Brazil. Of the other peripheral members, Israel and the Netherlands export a great deal to Scandinavia, but import less; Portugal trades with some, but not all, of the northern countries; and Ireland is distinctly peripheral and might better be dropped from the Table. Note that all of Ireland's export cells are filled only in the upper half. This indicates that though these countries are among the principal recipients of Ireland's exports (Sweden ranks second) the volume in question is *less* than the "expected" value. If the volume were greater than "expected," the bottom half of the cell, showing Ireland's status as a source of Swedish imports, would also have a rank number, or at the least an asterisk.

Thus we have an interdependent core in Scandinavia (including Denmark) and a more marginal group of countries who trade much with Scandinavia but not necessarily among themselves. On the whole, there is also a substantial amount of trade within the sub-group Spain-Portugal-Netherlands-Germany, with only 25 per cent of the cells empty.

Table 11 may be called, and again in quotation marks, "Eastern Mediterranean." Six of the first seven, plus Egypt, are Mediterranean states, and it should be remembered that most of landlocked Austria's overseas commerce must move through Adriatic ports. With almost equal justification the group might be labeled "Central Europe" in recognition of the presence of Switzerland and West Germany. Brazil and Finland, of course, fit neither of these titles, but they are on the fringe. Turkey, Yugoslavia, Greece, Israel, and Austria together form a very tightly knit center, with Italy, Cyprus, and West Germany not far outside. Germany, Italy, Austria, and Switzerland form something of a sub-group among themselves. Egypt also would fit the main group rather well, except for the total absence of trade between it and Israel. Finland and Brazil are definitely at the edges; only about half of their trade pairs show greater than "expected" commerce. All but four (Egypt, Turkey, Yugoslavia, and Brazil) loaded above .60 on the "Western Community" factor in the socio-cultural analysis.

Neither in this nor in the previous table does there emerge a group corresponding to the European Economic Community. Belgium-Luxembourg, France, Italy, and Greece (associate member) are absent from Table 10; Belgium-Luxembourg, the Netherlands, and France from Table 11. Also, neither the United States nor the states of the Old Commonwealth appear in either table. As we have seen, the United States' closest links are with the Western Hemisphere; Britain, Australia and New Zealand trade heavily among themselves and, except for New Zealand, with most of the newer Commonwealth countries. To a degree

TABLE 11. *"Eastern Mediterranean"*

From \ To	Turkey .78	Yugoslavia .80	Greece .71	Israel .73	Austria .77	Italy .48	Cyprus .63	West Germany .41	Switzerland .55	Egypt .45	Finland .50	Brazil .31
Turkey .80	X	2 / 1	* / *	1 / 1	8 / 7	9 / *	7 / 8	6 / 5	* / 10	10 / *	4 / 3	
Yugoslavia .78	1 / 2	X	3 / 2	4 / 2	2 / 1	5 / 5	* / *	8 / 4	10 / 6	11 / *		
Greece .71	* / 10	7 / 5	X	10 / 8	2 / 4	3 / 4	1 / 4	4 / 2		6 / 6	8 / 7	9 / 5
Israel .71	1 / 1	5 / 3	9 / 9	X	7 / 8		3 / 2		* / *		2 / 1	
Austria .61	6 / 9	1 / 2	4 / 4	11 / *	X	2 / 2	10 / 11	3 / 3	5 / 4	8 / *		
Italy .51	8 / 4	6 / 4	1 / 1		3 / 3	X	9 / 7	* / *	4 / 1	7 / 7		* / *
Cyprus .52			10	4 / 3	9 / 9	7 / *	X	3 / 1		2 / 4		
West Germany .37	9 / 7	7 / 7	8 / 6	3 / 5	1 / 2	* / *		X	2 / 2	* / *	* / *	* / *
Switzerland .35	* / 11	* / 11		* / *	2 / 5	3 / 6		7 / 11	X	5 / 8		* / *
Egypt .33		* / 8			8 / 6	9 / 7	* / *	* / *	11 / 7	X		
Finland .41	4 / 6			6 / 6				11 / *		5 / 9	X	* / *
Brazil .41	* / *	* / 10			11	* / *		6 / *			3 / 4	X

this situation has changed since 1954, as some of the bonds within the Common Market have become tighter.

DIFFERENT TYPES OF REGIONS: THEIR CONGRUENCE AND SOME IMPLICATIONS

We have by no means exhausted possible indices or criteria for identifying regions. Those suggested here should be tested more thoroughly, and should also be systematically compared with politically relevant regions, both formal groups such as those delineated by alliances or other treaties, and with informal groups such as countries which caucus or vote together on certain issues in the United Nations. Yet we are in a position to make some tentative comments on the prospects for political integration in some of these areas.

It might well be argued that the amount of homogeneity demanded in this analysis is too little to result in successful integration, that more rigorous demands, such as a common language or similar political systems, should be made. Whether or not this is true, we at least have identified a number of instances where countries are quite different culturally from other members of a potentially integrated unit with which they are sometimes identified. The affinities of Portugal and Spain for Latin America, and the low loading of Greece on the "Western Community" factor, emphasize the potential difficulty of incorporating these states into a European union. And one wonders about the long-run consequences of Turkey's sharp differences from Western Europe. Even Japan might be a better candidate for some rather broadly defined union.

If we go beyond a fairly weak test of homogeneity to demand interdependence as well, the result is to break the world down into many smaller regions. No European, or Latin American, or Asia-wide grouping emerges; that is, none of the most obvious geographical groups approaches what we have suggested are some of the requisites for integration. In Latin America there are perhaps potential groups in Central America plus Mexico, the southern half of South America, and parts of former Gran Colombia. Venezuela and the Caribbean states would be excluded. In Asia there are possibilities in Southeast Asia (the East Asia group is rather heterogeneous culturally for a union that is freely chosen rather than imposed by one member—for example, Japan before World War II) and several of the Arab countries. The former Maghreb states of North Africa would also seem to have these prerequisites. In Europe the situation is more complex, and we must treat the data more cautiously because of the substantial increases in the volume of intra-European trade if not in the *RA*'s that have occurred since 1954. Even so, the economic separation of Britain from the Continent is clear. And the Commonwealth fails the tests of both homogeneity and interdependence.

Finally we may look for regions which possess, in addition to homogeneity and interdependence, existing intergovernmental institutions. Etzioni (1964) suggests the following low-to-high ordering for spill-over effects associated with various kinds of institutions: 1. narrowly functional organizations; 2. tariff unions; 3. military organizations; 4. economic unions (common markets); 5. political unions. Concentrating primarily on the trade groups (because in this paper the trade groups are smaller than the cultural ones) we find only a few organizations, other than functional ones, with which they are reasonably co-extensive. In Latin America there is the Central American Common Market and the Latin American Free Trade Association, though both have yet to prove themselves as politically effective institutions. In Asia there is the Arab League, although it includes the former French Arab states as well as the economically interdependent group. Among European countries there is the core group represented in the Nordic Council. The European Common Market includes some, but not all, of the states which in 1954 traded heavily among themselves. Yet common markets—particularly this one—undoubtedly have the power to create far greater interdependence than that with which they began. An important next step is the investigation of how homogeneity, interdependence, and institutions interact.

Selected Bibliography

If we consider four possible combinations of disciplinary background and research method as complementary avenues to a science of international politics, it turns out that only *one* of those combinations is reflected in this particular volume. Using the disciplinary background and viewpoint of the author as one dimension, and the extent to which the work generates new data or creatively transforms existing data as the other, three of our four cells are *not* represented here: (1) data-generating work by socio-psychological scientists; (2) essentially conceptual work by these same people; and (3) essentially conceptual, nonquantitative work by political scientists (and historians). The purpose of the bibliography, then, is to indicate not only what additional quantitative research has been done by international relations scholars, but also the extent to which they have used the findings and concepts (rather than the methods) of other behavioral sciences, and the extent to which scholars from those disciplines have contributed to our discipline in both empirical and conceptual terms.

This fourfold listing is not, of course, exhaustive. On the substantive side, it omits such relevant disciplines as anthropology, economics, and geography. Next, no journal articles are listed, since the number of those which use behavioral science concepts but generate no data are too numerous, and those which do generate data are readily found in a handful of places. Most well-known of these is the *Journal of Conflict Resolution*, published by the University of Michigan Center for Research on Conflict Resolution since 1957. A relatively new journal, equally important on the data-making side, is the *Journal of Peace Research*, published by the Peace Research Institute in Oslo since 1964. Also very recent and important are the annual *Peace Research Society Papers*, initiated in 1964 by the Department of Regional Science at the University of Pennsylvania. In addition to these three, there are those well-established journals which occasionally publish quantitative work in international politics: *World Politics*, *International Organization*, *Background*, and *American Political Science Review*.

Another omission is that of research emanating from the comparative politics field; even though much of that work is, or could be, relevant to our concerns, only those studies which are highly innovative or which present large bodies of data are listed. Still another important omission is the empirical (as well as the conceptual) literature on attitude formation and public opinion by social psychologists, unless directly concerned with international politics; much of that work is reported in *Conflict Resolution*, as well as in *Public Opinion Quarterly* and the *Journal of Abnormal and Social Psychology* (title changed to *Journal of Personality and Social Psychology* in 1965). Nor have we listed work which still exists in unpublished form: memoranda, preliminary reports, working papers, and so forth. Although the research most relevant to the purposes of this volume is to be found primarily in that form today, it is too scattered and fugitive to be helpful in a bibliography such as this. However, much of it is referred to in the studies reported here, and an increasing portion of it should soon begin to appear in book and article form.

Also left out is the vast traditional literature produced by international relations scholars over a long period of time. Much of it is conceptually creative and factually rich, and little of it can be summarily dismissed; but almost all of it is pre-operational. Its inclusion here would, of course, be either spatially impossible or whimsically selective, and would contribute but little to the purposes of the volume.

In summary, then, four classes of published books and monographs are represented here. First (I-A) there are studies comparable to those prepared for this volume: conducted by political scientists and historians and largely valuable for the measures they devise and the new data which they generate and analyze. Second (I-B), there are those by the same class of authors and which are also thought of as essentially scientific in outlook; they utilize or discuss the concepts, data, and methods of the behavioral sciences, but generate little if any new data. Some in this class may, however, analyze data generated by others, especially in the public opinion and voting field. For the third category (II-A) we shift over to work reflecting the outlook of sociologists and psychologists, and list the data-generating research; most of this, as might be expected, is from social psychology, and deals largely with opinions and attitudes toward international affairs. Finally in the fourth group (II-B) are the studies and symposiums (including a few special issues of concerned journals) in which these "non-political" behavioral scientists discuss or apply their expertise as it relates to our area of concern. Let it be emphasized in closing that these distinctions are by no means clear and operational; moreover, we may hope that they will, before too long, be further obliterated by a growing trend toward the interdisciplinary and toward an increasingly intimate linkage between the conceptual and the empirical.

I. POLITICAL SCIENCE AND HISTORY

A. *STUDIES WHICH GENERATE NEW DATA*

Alker, Hayward, Jr., and Bruce M. Russett. *World Politics in the General Assembly.* New Haven, Conn.: Yale Univ. Press, 1965.

Almond, Gabriel, and Sidney Verba. *The Civic Culture: Political Attitudes and Democracy in Five Nations.* Princeton, N.J.: Princeton Univ. Press, 1963.

Banks, Arthur S., and Robert B. Textor. *Cross-Polity Survey.* Cambridge, Mass.: MIT Press, 1963.

Deutsch, Karl W. *Nationalism and Social Communication: An Inquiry into the Foundations of Nationality.* Cambridge, Mass.: Technology Press, 1953 and 1966.

———, and Lewis J. Edinger. *Germany Rejoins the Powers.* Stanford, Calif.: Stanford Univ. Press, 1959.

Grassmuck, George. *Sectional Biases in Congress on Foreign Policy.* Baltimore, Md.: Johns Hopkins Press, 1951.

Haas, Ernst B. *Beyond the Nation-State: Functionalism and International Organization.* Stanford, Calif.: Stanford Univ. Press, 1964.

————. *Consensus Formation in the Council of Europe.* Berkeley, Calif.: Univ. of California Press, 1960.

————. *The Uniting of Europe: Political, Social and Economic Forces, 1950–57.* Stanford, Calif.: Stanford Univ. Press, 1958.

Hovet, Thomas. *Africa in the United Nations.* Evanston, Ill.: Northwestern Univ. Press, 1963.

————. *Bloc Politics in the United Nations.* Cambridge, Mass.: Harvard Univ. Press, 1960.

Jewell, Malcolm. *Senatorial Politics and Foreign Policy.* Lexington, Ky.: Univ. of Kentucky Press, 1962.

Lasswell, Harold D., *et al. World Revolutionary Elites.* Cambridge, Mass.: MIT Press, 1965.

Lerche, Charles. *The Uncertain South: Its Changing Patterns of Politics in Foreign Policy.* Chicago: Quadrangle Books, 1964.

Merritt, Richard L., and Stein Rokkan (eds.). *Comparing Nations: The Use of Quantitative Data in Cross-National Research.* New Haven, Conn.: Yale Univ. Press, 1965.

Pool, Ithiel de Sola. *The Prestige Papers.* Stanford, Calif.: Stanford Univ. Press, 1952.

————, with collaboration of Harold D. Lasswell, Daniel Lerner, *et al. Symbols of Internationalism.* Stanford, Calif.: Stanford Univ. Press, 1951.

Richardson, Lewis F. *Arms and Insecurity.* Chicago: Quadrangle Books, 1960.

————, *Statistics of Deadly Quarrels.* Chicago: Quadrangle Books, 1960.

Rieselbach, Leroy N. *The Roots of Isolationism.* Indianapolis: Bobbs-Merrill, 1967.

Riggs, Robert E. *Politics in the United Nations.* Urbana, Ill.: Univ. of Illinois Press, 1958.

Robinson, James A. *Congress and Foreign Policy-Making: A Study in Legislative Influence and Initiative.* Homewood, Ill.: Dorsey Press, 1962.

Rosenau, James N. *National Leadership and Foreign Policy: A Case Study in the Mobilization of Public Support.* Princeton, N.J.: Princeton Univ. Press, 1963.

Rummel, Rudolph J., *et al. Dimensions of Nations.* Evanston, Ill.: Northwestern Univ. Press (Forthcoming, 1967, 2 vols.).

Russett, Bruce. *Community and Contention: Britain and America in the Twentieth Century.* Cambridge, Mass.: MIT Press, 1963.

————. *Trends in World Politics.* New York: Macmillan, 1965.

————, Hayward Alker, Karl Deutsch, and Harold Lasswell. *World Handbook of Political and Social Indicators.* New Haven, Conn.: Yale Univ. Press, 1964.

Wright, Quincy. *A Study of War.* 2 vols. Chicago: Univ. of Chicago Press, 1942.

B. *STUDIES WHICH ARE LARGELY CONCEPTUAL*

Alker, Hayward R. *Mathematics and Politics.* New York: Macmillan, 1965.

Almond, Gabriel. *The American People and Foreign Policy.* New York: Harcourt, Brace, 1950.

Cohen, Bernard C. *The Political Process and Foreign Policy: The Making of the Japanese Peace Settlement.* Princeton, N.J.: Princeton Univ. Press, 1957.

Deutsch, Karl W. *Political Community at the International Level: Problems of Definition and Measurement.* New York: Doubleday, 1954.

————. *Nerves of Government.* New York: Free Press, 1963.

————, *et al. Political Community in the North Atlantic Area.* Princeton, N.J.: Princeton Univ. Press, 1956.

Dunn, Frederick S. *War and the Minds of Men.* New York: Harper & Row, 1950.

Jacob, P. E., and J. V. Toscano (eds.). *The Integration of Political Communities*. Philadelphia: J. B. Lippincott, 1964.

Kaplan, Morton. *System and Process in International Politics*. New York: John Wiley, 1957.

Knorr, Klaus, and Sidney Verba (eds.). *The International System: Theoretical Essays*. Princeton, N.J.: Princeton Univ. Press, 1961.

Lasswell, Harold D. *World Politics and Personal Insecurity*. New York: McGraw-Hill, 1935.

McClelland, Charles A. *Theory and the International System*. New York: Macmillan, 1966.

North, Robert C., Ole R. Holsti, M. George Zaninovich and Dina A. Zinnes. *Content Analysis: A Handbook with Applications for the Study of International Crisis*. Evanston, Ill.: Northwestern Univ. Press, 1963.

Pool, Ithiel de Sola. *Communication and Values in Relation to War and Peace*. New York: Institute for International Order, 1961.

Riker, William H. *The Theory of Political Coalitions*. New Haven, Conn.: Yale Univ. Press, 1962.

Rock, Vincent P. *A Strategy of Interdependence: A Program for the Control of Conflict Between the United States and the Soviet Union*. New York: Scribner's, 1964.

Rosecrance, Richard. *Action and Reaction in World Politics*. Boston: Little, Brown, 1963.

Rosenau, James N. (ed.). *International Politics and Foreign Policy: A Reader in Research and Theory*. New York: Free Press, 1961.

Snyder, Richard C., H. W. Bruck, and Burton Sapin. *Foreign Policy Decision Making: An Approach to the Study of International Politics*. New York: Free Press, 1962.

———, and James A. Robinson. *National and International Decision-Making*. New York: Institute for International Order, 1961.

Sorokin, Pitirim A. *Social and Cultural Dynamics*. 4 vols. New York: American Book, 1937, Vol. III.

Van Wagenen, Richard W. *Research in the International Organization Field: Some Notes on a Possible Focus*. Princeton, N.J.: Princeton Univ. Center for Research in World Political Institutions, 1952.

Wright, Quincy, W. Fred Cottrell, and Ch. Boasson. *Research for Peace*. Amsterdam: North-Holland Publishing Company, 1954.

II. PSYCHOLOGY AND SOCIOLOGY

A. *STUDIES WHICH GENERATE NEW DATA*

Angell, Robert C. *The Creeping Vine of Peace*. Princeton, N.J.: Van Nostrand, forthcoming.

Bauer, Raymond A., Ithiel de S. Pool, and Lewis A. Dexter. *American Business and Public Policy: The Politics of Foreign Trade*. New York: Atherton Press, 1963.

Buchanan, William, H. E. Krugman, and Richard W. Van Wagenen. *An International Police Force and Public Opinion: Polled Opinion in the United States, 1939–1953*. Princeton, N.J.: Princeton Univ., Center for Research on World Political Institutions, 1954.

———, and Hadley Cantril. *How Nations See Each Other: A Study in Public Opinion*. Urbana, Ill.: Univ. of Illinois Press, 1952.

Cantril, Hadley. *The Pattern of Human Concerns*. New Brunswick, N.J.: Rutgers Univ. Press, 1966.

Christiansen, Bjorn. *Attitudes toward Foreign Affairs as a Function of Personality*. Oslo: Oslo Univ. Press, 1959.

Cottrell, Leonard S., Jr., and Sylvia Eberhart. *American Opinion on World Affairs in the Atomic Age*. Princeton, N.J.: Princeton Univ. Press, 1948.

Eisenstadt, Samuel N. *Political Systems of Empires*. New York: Free Press, 1962.

Etzioni, Amitai. *Political Unification: A Comparative Analysis of Leaders and Forces*. New York: Holt, Rinehart and Winston, 1965.

Free, Lloyd A. *Six Allies and a Neutral*. New York: Free Press, 1959.

George, Alexander L. *Propaganda Analysis: A Study of Inferences Made from Nazi Propaganda in World War II*. Evanston, Ill.: Row, Peterson, 1959.

Hero, Alfred O. *The Southerner and World Affairs*. Baton Rouge, La.: Louisiana State Univ. Press, 1965.

Janowitz, Morris. *The Professional Soldier*. New York: Free Press, 1960.

Paul, John and Jerome Laulicht. *In Your Opinion: Leaders' and Voters' Attitudes on Defense and Disarmament*. Clarkson, Ont.: Canadian Peace Research Institute, 1963.

Withey, Stephen, and William Scott. *The United States and the United Nations: The Public View*. New York: Manhattan Publishing Co., 1958.

B. *STUDIES WHICH ARE LARGELY CONCEPTUAL*

Bernard, Jessie, T. H. Pear, Raymond Aron, and Robert C. Angell. *The Nature of Conflict: Studies on the Sociological Aspects of International Tensions*. Paris: UNESCO, 1957.

Bernard, Luther L. *War and Its Causes*. New York: Henry Holt, 1944.

Boulding, Kenneth E. *Conflict and Defense: A General Theory*. New York: Harper, 1962.

Bramson, L., and G. W. Goethals (eds.). *War: Studies from Psychology, Sociology, and Anthropology*. New York: Basic Books, 1964.

Cantril, Hadley (ed.). *Tensions That Cause Wars*. Urbana, Ill.: Univ. of Illinois Press, 1950.

Daugherty, W. E., and Morris Janowitz (eds.). *A Psychological Warfare Casebook*. Baltimore: Johns Hopkins Press, 1958.

Doob, Leonard W. *Patriotism and Nationalism*. New Haven, Conn.: Yale Univ. Press, 1964.

Durbin, E. F. M., and J. Bowlby. *Personal Aggressiveness and War*. London: Kegan Paul, 1939.

Fisher, Roger (ed.). *International Conflict and Behavioral Science: The Craigville Papers*. New York: Basic Books, 1964.

Glover, Edward. *War, Sadism and Pacifism*. London: Allen & Unwin, 1935.

Guetzkow, Harold. *Multiple Loyalties*. Princeton, N.J.: Princeton Univ. Center for Research on World Political Institutions, 1955.

———. Chadwick F. Alger, Richard A. Brody, Robert C. Noel, and Richard C. Snyder. *Simulation in International Relations: Developments for Research and Teaching*. Englewood Cliffs, N.J.: Prentice-Hall, 1963.

Hero, Alfred O. *Americans in World Affairs*. Boston: World Peace Foundation, 1959.

———. *Mass Media and World Affairs*. Boston: World Peace Foundation, 1959.

———. *Opinion Leaders in American Communities*. Boston: World Peace Foundation, 1959.

———. *Voluntary Organizations in World Affairs Communication*. Boston: World Peace Foundation, 1960.

International Communications Research. Vol. XVI, No. 4 (Winter 1952–1953) of *Public Opinion Quarterly*.

Isaacs, Harold. *Scratches on Our Minds*. New York: John Day, 1958.

Jackson, Elmore. *Meeting of Minds: A Way to Peace through Mediation*. New York: McGraw-Hill, 1952.

Kelman, Herbert C. (ed.). *International Behavior: A Social-Psychological Analysis.* New York: Holt, Rinehart, & Winston, 1965.

──────. *Relevance of Social Research in War Prevention—A Symposium, Journal of Human Relations,* Spring 1954.

──────. *Research Approaches to the Study of War and Peace,* Vol. XI, No. 1 (1955) of *Journal of Social Issues.*

Kisker, George W. (ed.). *World Tension: The Psychopathology of International Relations.* Englewood Cliffs, N.J.: Prentice-Hall, 1951.

Klineberg, Otto. *The Human Dimension in International Relations:* New York: Holt, Rhinehart, and Winston, 1964.

──────. *Tensions Affecting International Understanding: A Survey of Research.* New York: Social Science Research Council, 1950.

Lentz, Theodore F. *Towards a Science of Peace: Turning Point in Human Destiny.* London: Halcyon Press, 1955.

McNeil, Elton B. (ed.). *The Nature of Human Conflict.* Englewood Cliffs, N.J.: Prentice-Hall, 1965.

May, Mark. *A Social Psychology of War and Peace.* New Haven, Conn.: Yale Univ. Press, 1943.

Murphy, Gardner (ed.). *Human Nature and Enduring Peace.* Boston: Houghton-Mifflin, 1945.

Nef, John U. *War and Human Progress.* Cambridge, Mass.: Harvard Univ. Press, 1950.

Nielsen, Gerhard S. (ed.). *Psychology and International Affairs: Can We Contribute?* Copenhagen, Denmark: International Congress of Applied Psychology, 1962.

Ogburn, William F. (ed.). *Technology and International Relations.* Chicago: Univ. of Chicago Press, 1949.

Osgood, Charles E. *An Alternative to War or Surrender.* Urbana, Ill.: Univ. of Illinois Press, 1962.

Pear, T. H. (ed.). *Psychological Factors of Peace and War.* New York: Philosophical Library, 1950.

Rapoport, Anatol. *Fights, Games and Debates.* Ann Arbor, Mich.: Univ. of Michigan Press, 1960.

Schelling, Thomas C. *The Strategy of Conflict.* Cambridge, Mass.: Harvard Univ. Press, 1960.

Singer, J. David (ed.). *Human Behavior and International Politics.* Chicago: Rand McNally, 1965.

Stanton, Alfred H., and Stewart E. Perry (eds.). *Personality and Political Crisis: New Perspectives from Social Science and Psychiatry for the Study of War and Politics.* New York: Free Press, 1951.

Strachey, Alix. *The Unconscious Motives of War.* New York: International Universities Press, 1957.

Tolman, Edward C. *Drives Toward War.* New York: Appleton-Century-Crofts, 1942.

Turney-High, H. H. *Primitive War: Its Practice and Concepts.* Columbia, S.C.: Univ. of South Carolina Press, 1949.

West, Ranyard. *Psychology and World Order.* London: Penguin, 1945.

Wright, Q., W. M. Evan, and M. Deutsch (eds.). *Preventing World War III: Some Proposals.* New York: Simon & Schuster, 1962.

Zawodny, J. K. (ed.). *Man and International Relations,* San Francisco: Chandler, 1966.

Combined References

The bibliographic references for each of the ten papers have been combined and placed here in order to: (a) make them more easily available to the reader than if they were hidden away between the separate papers; (b) provide a fairly extensive and representative list of the materials most heavily used in current quantitative research; and (c) save space.

Abel, Theodore. "The Element of Decision in the Pattern of War," *American Sociological Review*, VI (Dec. 1941), pp. 853–859.

Abelson, Robert P. "A Derivation of Richardson's Equations," *Journal of Conflict Resolution*, VII (1963), pp. 13–15.

Ackoff, Russell L. "Systems, Organizations, and Interdisciplinary Research," *General Systems*, V (1960), pp. 1–8.

Adams, Sherman. *Firsthand Report: The Story of the Eisenhower Administration.* New York: Harper & Row, 1961.

Albertini, Luigi. *The Origins of the War of 1914.* 3 vols. New York: Oxford Univ. Press, 1953.

Alexander, Christopher. *HIDECS 3: Four Computer Programs for the Hierarchical Decomposition of a Set Which Has an Associated Linear Graph.* Cambridge, Mass.: Civil Engineering Systems Laboratory, M.I.T., 1963.

———, and Marvin L. Manheim. *HIDECS 2: A Computer Program for the Hierarchical Decomposition of a Set Which Has an Associated Linear Graph.* Cambridge, Mass.: Civil Engineering Systems Laboratory, M.I.T., 1963.

Alger, Chadwick F. "Private Conversation in Public Diplomacy: A Microscopic Analysis of One Hundred and Twenty-four Minutes in the United Nations Security Council." Evanson, Ill.: Northwestern Univerity, International Relations Program 1961, (mimeo).

———. "Participation in the United Nations as a Learning Experience," *Public Opinion Quarterly*, XXVII (Fall 1963), pp. 412–426.

———. "Interaction and Negotiation in a Committee of the United Nations General Assembly," *Peace Research Society (International) Papers*, Vol. V, 1966a, pp. 141–160.

———. "Negotiation, Regional Groups, Interaction, and Public Debate in the Development of Consensus in the United Nations General Assembly," paper presented to Sixth World Congress of Sociology, International Sociology Association, Evian, France, September, 1966b.

Alker, Hayward R., Jr. "An IBM 709 Program for the Gross Analysis of Transaction Flows," *Behavioral Science*, VII, No. 4 (Oct. 1962), pp. 498–499.

———. "Dimensions of Voting in the United Nations." Ph.D. Dissertation, Yale Univ. 1963.

———. "Dimensions of Conflict in the General Assembly," *American Political Science Review*, LVIII, 3 (1964).

———. *Mathematics and Politics*. New York: Macmillan, 1965.

———, and Bruce M. Russett. *World Politics in the General Assembly*. New Haven, Conn.: Yale Univ. Press, 1965.

Almond, Gabriel A. "Introduction: A Functional Approach to Comparative Politics," in Gabriel A. Almond and James S. Coleman (eds.). *The Politics of the Developing Areas*. Princeton, N.J.: Princeton Univ. Press, 1960.

Alpert, Harry. "Suicides and Homicides," *American Sociological Review*, XV (1950), p. 673.

Angell, Robert C. "Governments and Peoples as Foci for Peace-Oriented Research," *Journal of Social Issues*, XI (1955).

Austro-Hungarian Monarchy, Ministerium des K. and k. Hauses und des Aeusseren. *Oesterreich-Ungarns Aussenpolitik von der bosnischen Krise, 1908, bis zum Kriegsausbruch 1914. Diplomatische Aktenstücke des Oesterreich-ungarischen Ministeriums des Aeusseren*, Ludwig Bittner and Alfred Pribram (eds.) Vienna and Leipzig, 1930, Vol. VIII.

Bacon, Selden D. "Alcohol and Complex Society," Ch. 14 in Yale Univ. Center for Alcoholic Studies (ed.), *Alcohol, Science and Society*. New Haven, Conn.: *Quarterly Journal of Studies on Alcohol*, 1945, pp. 179–200.

Bailey, Margaret B. "Alcoholism and Marriage. A Review of Research and Professional Literature," *Quarterly Journal of Studies on Alcohol*, XXII (1961), pp. 81–97.

Bakke, E. Wight. *Citizens Without Work*. New Haven, Conn.: Yale Univ. Press, 1940.

Balassa, B. *The Theory of Economic Integration*. Homewood, Ill.: Richard D. Irwin, 1961.

———, T. Scitovsky, and A. Lamfalussy, "Europe's Progress: Due to the Common Market?" *Lloyds Bank Review*, New Series No. 62 (Oct. 1961).

Bales, Robert F. "Cultural Differences in Rates of Alcoholism," *Quarterly Journal of Studies on Alcohol*, VI (1946), pp. 480–499.

———. *Interaction Process Analysis: A Method for the Study of Small Groups*. Cambridge, Mass.: Addison-Wesley, 1950.

Banks, Arthur S., and Robert B. Textor. *A Cross-Polity Survey*. Cambridge, Mass.: MIT Press, 1963.

———, and Phillip M. Gregg. "Grouping Political Systems: Q-Factor Analysis of a Cross-Polity Survey," *American Behavioral Scientist*, IX, No. 3 (1965), pp. 3–6.

Bates, A. P. "Some Sociometric Aspects of Social Rankings in a Small Face-to-Face Group," *Sociometry*, XV (1952), pp. 330–341.

Bell, Daniel. "Crime as an American Way of Life," *Antioch Review*, XIII (1952), pp. 131–154.

Benoit, Emile. *Europe at Sixes and Sevens*. New York: Columbia Univ. Press, 1961.

Berelson, Bernard. *Content Analysis in Communication Research*. New York: Free Press, 1952.

———. "Content Analysis," in Gardner Lindzey (ed.). *Handbook of Social Psychology*. Cambridge, Mass.: Addison-Wesley, 1954.

———, and Gary Steiner. *Human Behavior; An Inventory of Scientific Findings*. New York: Harcourt, Brace, 1964.

Berge, Claude. *The Theory of Graphs*. London: Methuen, 1962.

Berry, Brian J. L. "An Inductive Approach to the Regionalization of Economic Development." in Norton Ginsburg (ed.), *Essays on Geography and Economic Development,* Chicago: Univ. of Chicago Press, 1960.

———. "Basic Patterns of Economic Development," in Norton Ginsburg (ed.), *Atlas of Economic Development.* Chicago: Univ. of Chicago Press,1961a.

———. "A Method for Deriving Multi-factor Uniform Regions," *Polish Geographer,* 33, 2 (1961b), pp. 263–79.

Bisco, Ralph L. "Social Science Data Archives: A Review of Developments," *American Political Science Review,* LX (1966), pp. 93–109.

Block, Jack. *The Q-Sort Method in Personality Assessment and Psychiatric Research.* Springfield, Ill.: Charles Thomas, 1961.

Bloodworth, Jessie A. *Social Consequences of Prolonged Unemployment.* Minneapolis: Univ. of Minnesota Press, 1933.

Bodart, Gaston. *Losses of Life in Modern Wars.* Oxford: Clarendon, 1916.

Borgatta, Ed. F., and R. F. Bales, "Sociometric Status Patterns and Characteristics of Interaction," *Journal of Psychology,* XLIII (1956), pp. 289–297.

Boulding, Kenneth E. *Conflict and Defense.* New York: Harper and Row, 1962.

———. "The Content of International Studies in College: A Review," *Journal of Conflict Resolution,* VIII (1964), pp. 65–71.

———. "National Images and International Systems," *Journal of Conflict Resolution,* III (1959), pp. 120–131.

Breed, Warren. "Occupational Mobility and Suicide among White Males," *American Sociological Review,* XXVIII (1963), pp. 179–188.

Brim, Orville G. "Socialization Through the Life Cycle," *Items,* XVIII (March 1964), pp. 1–5.

Brinton, Crane. *The Anatomy of Revolution.* Englewood Cliffs, N.J.: Prentice-Hall, 1952.

Brody, Richard A. "Cognition and Behavior: A Model of International Relations," in O. J. Harvey (ed.), *Experience Structure, and Adaptation.* New York: Springer Publishing, 1966.

———. "Some Systemic Effects of the Spread of Nuclear Weapons Technology: A Study Through Simulation of a Multi-Nuclear Future," *Journal of Conflict Resolution,* VII (Dec. 1963), pp. 663–753.

Brutzkus, Boris. "The Historical Peculiarities of the Social and Economic Development of Russia," in Reinhard Bendix and Seymour M. Lipset (eds.), *Class, Status and Power.* New York: Free Press, 1953.

Bülow, Prince Bernhard von. *Memoirs of Prince von Bülow.* Boston: Little, Brown 1932.

Burr, Robert N. "The Balance of Power in Nineteenth Century South America: An Exploratory Essay," *Hispanic American Historical Review,* XXV (Feb. 1955), pp. 37–60.

Campbell, Donald T., and D. W. Fiske. "Convergent and Discriminant Validation by the Multitrait-Multimethod Matrix," *Psychological Bulletin,* LVI, No. 2 (March 1959), pp. 81–105.

Cantril, Hadley. *Public Opinion 1935–1946.* Princeton, N.J.: Princeton Univ. Press, 1951.

Carleton, William G. *The Revolution in American Foreign Policy: Its Global Range.* New York: Random House, 1963.

Carr, E. H. *Nationalism and After.* London: Macmillan, 1945.

Cattell, Raymond B. "The Dimensions of Culture Patterns by Factorization of National Characters," *Journal of Abnormal and Social Psychology,* XLIV (1949), pp. 443–469.

———. "The Principal Culture Patterns Discoverable in the Syntal Dimensions of Existing Nations." *Journal of Social Psychology,* 32, 2 (1950), pp. 215–53.

Cattell, Raymond B. "A Quantitative Analysis of the Changes in Culture Pattern of Great Britain, 1837–1937, by P-Technique," *Acta Psychologica*, IX (1953), pp. 99–121.

———. *Factor Analysis*. New York: Harper, 1952.

———, H. Bruel, and H. Parker Hartman. "An Attempt at a More Refined Definition of the Cultural Dimensions of Syntality in Modern Nations," *American Sociological Review*, XVII (1951), pp. 408–421.

———, and Marvin Adelson. "The Dimensions of Social Change in the U.S.A. as Determined by P-Technique," *Social Forces*, XXX (1951), pp. 190–201.

———, and Richard Gorsuch. "The Definition and Measurement of National Morale and Morality." *Journal of Social Psychology*, LXVII, No. 1 (1965), pp. 77–96.

Cavan, Ruth Shonle. *Suicide*. Chicago: Univ. of Chicago Press, 1928.

Chadwick, Richard. "An Analysis of the Relationship of Domestic to Foreign Conflict Behavior over the Period 1955–1957." Evanston, Ill.: Northwestern Univ., 1963 (mimeo).

Chaumont, C. "The Evolutionary Aspect of International Organization and International Cooperation," *International Social Science Bulletin*, V, No. 2 (1953), pp. 257–277.

Chodorkoff, Bernard, *et al.* "Employment Characteristics of Hospitalized Alcoholics," *Quarterly Journal of Studies on Alcohol*, XXII (1961), pp. 106–110.

Chotlos, John W., and John B. Deiter. Psychological Considerations in the Etiology of Alcoholism," David J. Pittman (ed.), *Alcoholism: An Interdisciplinary Approach*. Springfield, Ill.: Charles Thomas, 1959.

Churchill, Winston S. *The World Crisis, 1911–1914*. New York: Scribner's, 1928.

Claude, Inis L., Jr. *Swords into Plowshares*, New York: Random House, 1959.

———. *Power and International Relations*. New York: Random House, 1962.

Clay, Lucius D. *Decision in Germany*. New York: Doubleday, 1950.,

Cohen, Bernard C. *The Political Process and Foreign Policy: The Making of the Japanese Peace Settlement*. Princeton, N.J.: Princeton Univ. Press, 1957.

Coleman, James. *Introduction to Mathematical Sociology*. New York: Free Press, 1964.

Collins, Barry E., and Harold Guetzkow. *A Social Psychology of Group Processes for Decision-Making*. New York: John Wiley, 1964.

Cooley, Charles H. *Social Process*. New York: Scribner's, 1927.

Crow, Wayman J. "A Study of Strategic Doctrines Using the Inter-Nation Simulation," *Journal of Conflict Resolution*, VII (1963), pp. 580–89.

———, and Lawrence N. Solomon. *A Simulation Study of Strategic Doctrines*. La Jolla, Calif.: Western Behavioral Sciences Institute, 1962.

Davies, James C. "Toward a Theory of Revolution," *American Sociological Review*, XXVII (1962), pp. 5–19.

Davison, W. Phillips. *The Berlin Blockade: A Study in Cold War Politics*. Princeton, N.J.: Princeton Univ. Press, 1958.

Denton, Frank H. "Some Regularities in International Conflict, 1820–1949," *Background*, IX, No. 4 (1966), pp. 283–96.

De Rusett, Alan. *Strengthening the Framework of Peace*. London: Royal Institute of International Affairs, 1950.

Deutsch, Karl W. *Nationalism and Social Communication*. Cambridge, Mass.: Technology Press, 1953.

———. *Political Community at the International Level: Problems of Definition and Measurement*. New York: Doubleday, 1954.

———. "Toward an Inventory of Basic Trends and Patterns in Comparative and International Politics," *American Political Science Review*, LIV (1960), pp. 34–57.

———. "Social Mobilization and Political Development," *American Political Science Review*, LV (1961), pp. 493–514.

Deutsch, Karl W. "Transaction Flows as Indicators of Political Cohesion," in Philip E. Jacob and James V. Toscano (eds.), *The Integration of Political Communities.* Philadelphia: J. P. Lippincott, 1964, pp. 75–97.

——, *et al. Political Community and the North Atlantic Area.* Princeton, N.J.: Princeton Univ. Press, 1957.

——, and J. David Singer. "Multipolar Power Systems and International Stability," *World Politics*, XVI, (April 1964), pp. 390–406.

——, J. David Singer and Keith Smith. "The Organizing Efficiency of Theories: The N/V Ratio as a Crude Rank Order Measure," *American Behavioral Scientist*, IX, No. 2 (Oct. 1965), pp. 30–33.

——, and Richard Savage. *Tides Among Nations.* (Forthcoming).

Dollard, John, *et al. Frustration and Aggression.* New Haven, Conn.: Yale Univ. Press, 1939.

Dumas, S., and K. O. Vedel-Peterson. *Losses of Life Caused by War.* Oxford: Clarendon, 1923.

Duncan, Otis, Ray P. Cuzzort, and Beverly Duncan. *Statistical Geography.* New York: Free Press, 1961.

Dunn, Frederick S. *Peace-Making and the Settlement with Japan.* Princeton, N.J.: Princeton Univ. Press, 1963.

Durbin, E. F. M., and J. Bowlby. *Personal Aggressiveness and War.* London: Kegan Paul, 1939.

Durkheim, Emile. *Suicide.* Trans. John A. Spaulding and George Simpson. New York: Free Press, 1951.

Eckstein, Harry (ed.). *Internal War: Basic Problems and Approaches.* New York: Free Press, 1963.

Economist. London, June-Aug., 1914.

Edinger, Lewis J. "Political Science and Political Biography," *Journal of Politics*, XXVI (May and Aug. 1964), pp. 423–439 and 648–676.

Edmunds, Sir James E. *Official History of the War, Military Operations: France and Belgium 1914.* 3d ed. London: Macmillan, 1937.

Einaudi, Mario, Jean-Marie Domenach, and Aldo Garoschi. *Communism in Western Europe.* Ithaca, N.Y.: Cornell Univ. Press, 1951.

Eisenberg, Philip, and Paul Lazarsfeld. "The Psychological Effects of Unemployment, *Psychological Bulletin*, XXXV (1938), pp. 358-390.

English, Horace B. and Ava C. English. *A Comprehensive Dictionary of Psychological and Psychoanalytic Terms.* N.Y.: Longmans, Green, 1958.

Etzioni, Amitai. "The Dialectics of Supranational Unification." *American Political Science Review*, LVI, No. 4 (1962), pp. 927–36.

——. "The Epigenesis of Political Communities at the International Level," *American Journal of Sociology*, LXVIII, No. 3 (Jan. 1963), pp. 407–421.

——. "Atlantic Union, the Southern Continents, and the United Nations," in Roger Fisher (ed.). *International Conflict and Behavioral Science.* New York: Basic Books, 1964.

——. *Political Unification.* New York: Holt, Rinehart, and Winston, 1965.

Eulau, Heinz. *The Behavioral Persuasion in Politics.* New York: Random House, 1963.

Ezekiel, Mordecai, and Karl A. Fox. *Methods of Correlation and Regression Analysis.* 3d ed. New York: John Wiley, 1959.

Falk, Richard. "International Jurisdiction: Horizontal and Vertical Conceptions of Legal Order," *Temple Law Quarterly*, XXXII (1959).

Fay, Sidney B. *The Origins of the World War.* New York: Macmillan, 1928.

Fenno, Richard. "The House Appropriations Committee as a Political System: The Problem of Integration," *American Political Science Review*, LVI, No. 2 (June 1962), pp. 310–324.

Fiellin, Alan. "The Functions of Informal Groups in Legislative Institutions," *Journal of Politics*, XXIV, No. 1 (Feb. 1962), pp. 77–91.

Finch, V. C. "Geographical Science and Social Philosophy." *Annals of the Association of American Geographers*, XXIX, No. 1 (1939), pp. 1–28.

Flament, Claude. *Applications of Graph Theory to Group Structure*. Englewood Cliffs, N.J.: Prentice-Hall, 1963.

France, Commission for the Publication of Documents Relative to the War of 1914. *Documents Diplomatiques Français (1871–1914)*. 3d Series, Vols. X and XI. Paris, 1936.

Francis, Wayne L. "Influence and Interaction in a State Legislative Body," *American Political Science Review*, LVI, No. 4 (Dec. 1962), pp. 953–960.

Frothingham, Thomas C. *The Naval History of the World War: Offensive Operations, 1914–1915*. Cambridge: Harvard Univ. Press, 1924.

Fruchter, Benjamin. *Introduction to Factor Analysis*. New York: Van Nostrand, 1954.

Gareau, Frederick H. *The Balance of Power and Nuclear Deterrence: A Book of Readings*. Boston, Mass.: Houghton Mifflin, 1962.

Garner, Wendell R. *Uncertainty and Structure as Psychological Concepts*. New York: John Wiley, 1962.

George, Alexander L. *Propaganda Analysis*. Evanston, Ill.: Row, Petersen, 1959.

Gibb, Cecil A. "Changes in the Cultural Pattern of Australia, 1906–1946, as Determined by P-Technique," *Journal of Social Psychology*, XLIII (1956), pp. 225–238.

Gibbs, Jack, P. "Suicide," in *Contemporary Social Problems*. Robert K. Merton and Robert A. Nisbet (eds.), New York: Harcourt, Brace, 1961.

——, and Walter T. Martin. *Status Integration and Suicide*. Eugene, Ore.: Univ. of Oregon Press, 1964.

Gillin, John L., *et al*. *Social Problems*. 4th ed. New York: Appleton-Century-Crofts, 1952.

Gold, Martin. "Suicide, Homicide, and the Socialization of Aggression," *American Journal of Sociology*, LXIII (1958), pp. 651–661.

Goodman, Leo. "Statistical Methods for the Preliminary Analysis of Transaction Flows." *Econometrica*, XXXI (1963), pp. 197–208.

——. "A Short Computer Program for the Analysis of Transaction Flows," *Behavioral Science*, IX, No. 2 (Apr. 1964), pp. 176–186.

Gorsuch, Richard L. "National Morale, Morality and Cultural Integration." M.A. Thesis, Univ. of Illinois, 1962.

Great Britain, Foreign Office, *British Documents on the Origins of the War*, 1898–1914, Vol. XI, G. P. Gooch and Harold Temperley, (eds.), London: 1926.

Gregg, Phillip M., and Arthur S. Banks. "Dimensions of Political Systems: Factor Analysis of a Cross-Polity Survey," *American Political Science Review*, LIX, No. 3 (1965), pp. 602–614.

Grinker, Roy R. and John P. Spiegel. *Men Under Stress*. New York: McGraw-Hill, 1963.

Guetzkow, Harold, Chadwick F. Alger, Richard A. Brody, Robert C. Noel, and Richard C. Snyder. *Simulation in International Relations: Developments for Research and Teaching*. Englewood Cliffs, N.J.: Prentice-Hall, 1963.

Guilford, J. P. *Fundamental Statistics in Psychology and Education*. 3d ed. New York, McGraw-Hill, 1956.

Gulick, Edward V. *Europe's Classical Balance of Power*. Ithaca, N.Y.: Cornell Univ. Press, 1955.

Haas, Ernst B. "The Balance of Power: Prescription, Concept, or Propaganda," *World Politics*, V (1953), pp. 442–477.

——. *The Uniting of Europe*. Stanford, Calif.: Stanford University Press, 1957.

——. "The Challenge of Regionalism." *International Organization*, XII, No. 3 (1958), pp. 440–48.

Haas, Ernst B. "System and Process in the International Labor Organization: A Statistical Afterthought," *World Politics*, XIV (Jan. 1962), pp. 322–352.

Haas, Michael. "Comparative Analysis," *Western Political Quarterly*, XV (1962), pp. 294–303.

———. "Some Societal Correlates of International Political Behavior." Ph.D. dissertation, Stanford Univ., 1964.

———. "A Functional Approach to International Organization," *Journal of Politics*, XXVII (1965a), pp. 498–517.

———. "Societal Approaches to the Study of War," *Journal of Peace Research*, II (1965b), pp. 308–323.

Haberler, G. *A Survey of International Trade Theory*. Princeton, N.J.: International Finance Section, Dept. of Economics, Princeton Univ. 1961.

Hadwen, John, and Johan Kaufmann. *How United Nations Decisions are Made*. Leyden: A. W. Sythoff, 1962.

Hagood, Margaret. "Statistical Methods for Delineation of Regions Applied to Data on Agriculture and Population," *Social Forces*, XXI, No. 3 (1943), pp. 287–97.

———, Nadia Danilevsky, and Corlin O. Beum. "An Examination of the Use of Factor Analysis in the Problem of Sub-regional Delineation," *Rural Sociology*, VI, No. 3 (1941), pp. 216–34.

Harary, Frank. "A Structural Analysis of the Situation in the Middle East," *Journal of Conflict Resolution*, V, No. 2 (1961), pp. 167–178.

Hargreaves, Reginald. *The Enemy at the Gate: A Book of Famous Sieges, Their Causes, Their Progress, and Their Consequences*. Harrisburg, Pa.: Stackpole, 1948.

Harlan, Edward. "Five Hundred Homicides," *Journal of Criminal Law and Criminology*, XL (1950), pp. 736–752.

Harman, Harry H. *Modern Factor Analysis*. Chicago: Univ. of Chicago Press, 1960.

Hart, Hornell. "Depression, War, and Logistic Trends," *American Journal of Sociology*, LII (1946), pp. 112–122.

Hauser, Philip M., and Otis Dudley Duncan (eds.). *The Study of Population*. Chicago: Univ. of Chicago Press, 1959.

Heller, Deane, and David Heller. *The Berlin Crisis*. Derby, Conn.: Monarch Books, 1961.

———. *The Berlin Wall*. New York: Walker & Co., 1962.

Henry, Andrew F., and James F. Short, Jr. *Suicide and Homicide*, New York: Free Press, 1954.

Hermann, Charles F., and Margaret Hermann. "On the Possible Use of Historical Data for Validation Study of Inter-Nation Simulation." Evanston, Ill.: Northwestern Univ. 1962 (mimeo).

Hill, Norman L. *Mr. Secretary of State*. New York: Random House, 1963.

Hirst, F. W. *The Political Economy of War*. New York: E. P. Dutton, 1915.

Hoffmann, Stanley (ed.). *Contemporary Theory in International Relations*. Englewood Cliffs, N.J.: Prentice-Hall, 1960.

———. "Discord in Community: The North Atlantic Area as a Partial International System," *International Organization*, XVII, No. 3 (1963), pp. 521–549.

Hofstaetter, P. R. "A Factorial Study of Culture Patterns in the U.S." *Journal of Psychology*, XXXII (1951), pp. 99–113.

Holsti, Kalevi J. "The Use of Objective Criteria for the Measurement of International Tension Levels," *Background*, VII (1963), pp. 77–96.

Holsti, Ole R. "The Belief System and National Images: A Case Study," *Journal of Conflict Resolution*, VI (Sept. 1962), pp. 244–252.

———. "The Value of International Tension Measurement," *Journal of Conflict Resolution*, VII (1963), pp. 608–617.

———. "An Adaptation of the 'General Inquirer' for the Systematic Analysis of Political Documents," *Behavioral Science*, IX (1964), pp. 382–388.

Holsti, Ole R. "The 1914 Case," *American Political Science Review*, LIX (1965), pp. 365–78.

———. "External Conflict and International Cohesion: The Sino-Soviet Case," in Philip J. Stone (ed.). *The General Inquirer: A Computer Approach to Content Analysis in the Behavioral Sciences*, Cambridge, Mass.: M.I.T., Press, 1966.

———, and Robert C. North. "History as a 'Laboratory' of Conflict," in Elton B. McNeil (ed.), *The Nature of Human Conflict*. Englewood Cliffs, N.J.: Prentice-Hall, 1964.

———, and Robert C. North. "Perceptions of Hostility and Economic Variables," in Richard L. Merritt (ed.), *Comparing Nations*. New Haven: Yale Univ. Press, 1965.

———, Richard A. Brody, and Robert C. North. *Theory and Measurement of Interstate Relations: An Application of Automated Content Analysis*. Stanford, Calif.: 1964a (mimeo).

———, Richard A. Brody, and Robert C. North. "Violence and Hostility: The Path to World War." Paper read at American Psychiatric Association Conference, Los Angeles, Calif., 1964b.

———, Richard A. Brody, and Robert C. North. "Measuring Affect and Action in International Reaction Models: Empirical Materials from the 1962 Cuban Crisis." *Peace Research Society Papers*, II (1965), pp. 170–190.

———, Joanne Loomba and Robert C. North. "Content Analysis," in Gardner Lindzey and Elliot Aronson (eds.), *The Handbook of Social Psychology*. 2d ed. Cambridge, Mass.: Addison-Wesley, 1966.

Hopmann, P. Terry. "International Conflict and Cohesion in the Communist System," Stanford University, 1966 (mimeo).

Horst, Paul. *Matrix Algebra for Social Scientists:* New York: Holt, Rinehart and Winston, 1963.

Horvath, Fred. "Phychological Stress: A Review of Definitions and Experimental Research," *General Systems*, IV (1959), pp. 203–230.

Horvath, William J., and Caxton C. Foster. "Stochastic Models of War Alliances," *Journal of Conflict Resolution*, VII, No. 2 (1963), pp. 110–116.

Hovet, Thomas, Jr. *Bloc Politics in the United States*. Cambridge, Mass.: Harvard Univ. Press, 1960.

———. *Africa in the United Nations*, Evanston, Ill.: Northwestern Univ. Press, 1963.

Howley, Frank. *Berlin Command*. New York: Putnam's, 1950.

Huntington, Samuel P. *The Common Defense: Strategic Problems in National Politics*. New York: Columbia Univ. Press, 1961.

International Court of Justice Reports, 1962. "Certain Expenses of the United Nations" (Article 17, paragraph 2 of the Charter, Advisory Opinion of 20 July 1962), pp. 151–308.

International Labour Office. *Year Book of Labour Statistics* (1960).

Isard, Walter. "Regional Science, the Concept of Region, and Regional Structure." *Papers and Proceedings of the Regional Science Association*. Cambridge, Mass.: Regional Science Association, 1956.

Jaeger, Ruth M. *Stabilization of Foreign Exchange*. New York: Isaac Goldman Co., 1922.

Janda, Kenneth. *Data Processing: Applications to Political Research*. Evanston, Ill.: Northwestern Univ. Press, 1965.

Jellinek, E. M. "Phases in the Drinking History of Alcoholics," New Haven, Conn.: Quarterly Journal of Studies on Alcohol, VII (1946).

Jones, Howard, *Alcoholic Addiction*. London: Tavistock, 1963.

Kaplan, Morton. *System and Process in International Politics*. New York: John Wiley, 1957.

Kendall, Maurice G. "The Geographical Distribution of Crop Productivity in England," *Journal of the Royal Statistical Society*, Series A., CII (1939), pp. 21–62.

Kerlinger, Fred N. *Foundations of Behavioral Research.* New York: Holt, Rinehart, & Winston, 1964.

Kindleberger, Charles P. *International Economics.* Homewood, Ill.: Irwin, 1958.

Kitzinger, U. W. *The Politics and Economics of European Integration.* New York: Praeger, 1963.

Klingberg, Frank L. *Historical Study of War Casualties.* Washington, D.C.: War Department, 1945.

Koch, Howard E., Jr., Robert C. North, and Dina A. Zinnes, "Some Theoretical Notes on Geography and International Conflict," *Journal of Conflict Resolution*, IV (1960), pp. 4–14.

Komarovsky, Mirra. *The Unemployed Man and His Family.* New York: Dryden Press, 1959.

Kornhauser, William. *The Politics of Mass Society.* New York: Free Press, 1959.

Kraft, Joseph. *The Grand Design: From Common Market to Atlantic Partnership.* New York: Harper, 1962.

Kumata, H., and Wilbur Schramm. "A Pilot Study of Cross-Cultural Methodology," *Public Opinion Quarterly*, XX (1956), pp. 229–237.

Langer, William L. *European Alliances and Alignments, 1871–1890.* New York: Knopf, 1931.

Lasswell, Harold D. *The World Revolution of Our Time.* Stanford, Calif.: Stanford Univ. Press, 1951.

Le Temps. Paris, June-Aug., 1914.

League of Nations, Economics Section, *Memorandum on International Trade and Balance of Payments*, III, Geneva, 1930.

League of Nations. *Statistical Yearbook of the League of Nations* (Published annually from 1930 to 1940).

Leavitt, Harold J., and Ronald A. Mueller. "Some Effects of Feedback on Communication," in A. Paul Hare, *et al.* (eds.), *Small Groups: Studies in Social Interaction.* New York: Knopf, 1955, pp. 414-423.

Lee, J. S. "The Periodic Recurrence of Internecine Wars in China," *China Journal of Science and Arts*, XIV (1931), pp. 111–115.

Lerche, Charles O., Jr. *Foreign Policy of the American People*, 2d ed. Englewood Cliffs, N.J.: Prentice-Hall, 1959.

Lijphart, Arend. "The Analysis of Bloc Voting in the General Assembly: A Critique and a Proposal," *American Political Science Review*, LVII, No. 4 (Dec. 1963), pp. 902–917.

Lippmann, Walter, *U.S. Foreign Policy.* Boston: Little, Brown, 1943.

Liska, George. *Nations in Alliance: The Limits of Interdependence.* Baltimore: Johns Hopkins Press, 1962.

———. *Europe Ascendant.* Baltimore: Johns Hopkins Press, 1964.

Lottier, Stuart, "Distribution of Criminal Offenses in Metropolitan Regions," *Journal of Criminal Law and Criminology*, XXIX (1938), pp. 37–50.

Lundberg, George. "Regionalism, Science, and the Peace Settlement." *Social Forces*, XXI, No. 2 (1942), pp. 131–37.

McClelland, Charles A. "The Acute International Crisis," *World Politics*, XIV (Oct. 1961), pp. 182–204.

———. "Action Structures and Communication in Two International Crises: Quemoy and Berlin," *Background*, VII (Feb. 1964a), pp. 201–215.

———. "Teaching About the Role of Law in the Cold War Era," *Proceedings of the American Society of International Law*, (1964b), pp. 68–77.

McClelland, David. *The Achieving Society.* New York: Van Nostrand, 1961.

McCord, William and Joan McCord, with Jon Gudeman. *Origins of Alcoholism.* Stanford, Calif.: Stanford Univ. Press, 1960.

McEntee, Girard L. *Military History of the World War*. New York: Scribner's, 1937.

McNeil, Elton B. "Psychology and Aggression," *Journal of Conflict Resolution*, III (1959), pp. 195–293.

McNemar, Quinn. *Psychological Statistics*. New York: John Wiley, 1955.

McQuitty, L. L. "Capabilities and Improvements of Linkage Analysis as a Clustering Method," *Educational and Psychological Measurement*, XXIV, No. 4 (1964), pp. 441–56.

MacRae, Duncan, Jr. "Director Factor Analysis of Sociometric Data," *Sociometry*, XXXIII, No. 4 (1960), pp. 360–71.

March, James G., and Herbert A. Simon. *Organizations*. New York: John Wiley, 1958.

Masor, Nathan. "Psychopathology of the Social Deviate," in Joseph S. Roucek (ed.). *Sociology of Crime*. New York: Philosophical Library, 1961.

Matthews, Donald R. *U.S. Senators and Their Worlds*. Chapel Hill, N.C.: Univ. of North Carolina Press, 1961.

Merritt, Richard. *The Growth of American Community*. New Haven, Conn.: Yale University Press, 1966.

Merton, Robert K. *Social Theory and Social Structure*. New York: Free Press, 1957.

Miller, James G., "Toward a General Theory for the Behavioral Sciences," in Leonard D. White (ed.). *The State of the Social Sciences*. Chicago: Univ. of Chicago Press, 1956.

Mintz, Alexander. "Re-examination of Correlations Between Lynchings and Economic Indices," *Journal of Abnormal and Social Psychology*, XLI (1946), pp. 154–160.

Modelski, George. "Agraria and Industria: Two Models of the International System," *World Politics*, XIV (1961a), pp. 18–43.

——. *The International Relations of Internal War*. Princeton, N.J.: Center of International Studies, 1961b.

Montgelas, Max., and Walter Schücking (eds.). *Outbreak of the World War, German Documents Collected by Karl Kautsky*. New York: Oxford Univ. Press, 1924.

Moore, W. E. "Predicting Discontinuities in Social Change," *American Sociological Review*, XXIX (June 1964), pp. 331–338.

Morgenthau, Hans J. "John Foster Dulles (1953-1959)," in Norman A. Graebner (ed.), *An Uncertain Tradition: American Secretaries of State in the Twentieth Century*. New York: McGraw-Hill, 1961.

——. *Politics among Nations*. New York: Knopf, 1956.

Mosely, Philip. "Some Techniques of Negotiation," in Raymond Dennett and Joseph E. Johnson (eds.). *Negotiating with Russians*. Boston: World Peace Foundation, 1951, pp. 271–304.

Moser, C. A. and Wolf Scott. *British Towns*. Edinburgh and London: Oliver and Boyd, 1961.

Mosher, Frederick C. *Program Budgeting*. New York: Public Administration Service, 1954.

Murphy, Robert. *Diplomat Among Warriors*. New York: Doubleday, 1964.

Myrdal, Gunnar. *An International Economy*. New York: Harper, 1956.

National Resources Committee. *Regional Factors in National Planning and Development*. Washington, D.C.: Government Printing Office, 1935.

Nettler, Gwynn. "Antisocial Sentiment and Criminality," *American Sociological Review*, XXIV (1959), pp. 202–208.

North, Robert C. "Decision-making in Crises: An Introduction," *Journal of Conflict Resolution*, VI (1962a), pp. 197–200.

——. "International Conflict and Integration: Problems of Research," in Muzafer Sherif (ed.), *Intergroup Relations and Leadership*. New York: John Wiley, 1962b.

North, Robert C., Ole R. Holsti, M. George Zaninovich, and Dina A. Zinnes. *Content Analysis: A Handbook with Application for the Study of International Crisis.* Evanston, Ill.: Northwestern Univ. Press, 1963.

———, Richard A. Brody, and Ole R. Holsti. "Some Empirical Data on the Conflict Spiral," *Peace Research Society Papers,* I (1964). pp. 1–14.

Odum, Howard W., and Harry Estill Moore. *American Regionalism: A Cultural Historical Approach to National Integration.* New York: Henry Holt, 1938.

Organski, A. F. K. *World Politics.* New York: Alfred A. Knopf, 1958.

Osgood, Charles E. *An Alternative to War or Surrender.* Urbana, Ill.: Univ. of Illinois Press, 1962a.

———. "Studies on the Generality of Affective Meaning Systems," *American Psychologist,* XVII (1962b), pp. 10–28.

———. "Suggestions for Winning the Real War with Communism," *Journal of Conflict Resolution,* III, No. 4 (1959), pp. 295–325.

———, George J. Suci, and Percy H. Tannenbaum. *The Measurement of Meaning.* Urbana, Ill.: Univ. of Illinois Press, 1957.

———, and Kellogg V. Wilson. *Some Terms and Associated Measures for Talking About Human Communication.* Urbana, Ill.: Institute of Communication Research, 1961 (mimeo).

Parsons, Talcott. *The Social System.* New York: Free Press, 1959.

———, and Edward A. Shils (eds.). *Toward A General Theory of Action.* Cambridge, Mass.: Harvard Univ. Press, 1952.

Patterson, Samuel. "Patterns of Interpersonal Relations in a State Legislative Group," *Public Opinion Quarterly,* XXIII (Spring 1959), pp. 101–109.

Peak, Helen. "Problem of Objective Observation," in Leon Festinger and Daniel Katz (eds.), *Research Methods in the Behavioral Sciences.* New York: Dryden Press, 1953, pp. 243–299.

Pierce, John R. *Symbols, Signals and Noise.* New York: Harper, 1961.

Pool, Ithiel de Sola. *Symbols of Internationalism.* Stanford, Calif.: Stanford Univ. Press, 1951.

———. *The Prestige Papers: A Survey of Their Editorials.* Stanford, Calif.: Stanford Univ. Press, 1952.

——— (ed.). *Trends in Content Analysis.* Urbana, Illinois: University of Illinois Press, 1959.

Popham, Robert E., and Wolfgang Schmidt. *A Decade of Alcoholism Research.* Toronto: Univ. of Toronto Press, 1962.

Porterfield, Austin L. "Suicide and Crime in the Social Structure of an Urban Setting: Fort Worth, 1930–1950," *American Sociological Review,* XVII (1952), pp. 341–349.

———. "Ecological Correlates of Alcoholism," *Social Problems,* V (1958), pp. 326–338.

Powell, Elwin H. "Occupation, Status, and Suicide: Toward a Redefinition of Anomie," *American Sociological Review,* XXIII (1958), pp. 131–139.

Pruitt, Dean G. "An Analysis of Responsiveness Between Nations," *Journal of Conflict Resolution,* VI (1962), pp. 5–18.

Puchala, D. J. *European Integration: Progress and Prospects,* New Haven, Conn.: Yale Univ. 1965 (mimeo).

Rapoport, Anatol. *Fights, Games, and Debates.* Ann Arbor, Mich.: Univ. of Michigan Press, 1960.

———. "Mathematical Models of Social Interaction," in R. Duncan Luce, Robert Bush and Eugene Galanter (eds.), *Handbook of Mathematical Psychology.* Vol. 2, New York: John Wiley, 1963, pp. 494–579.

———, and W. J. Horvath. "A Study of a Large Sociogram," *Behavioral Science,* VI (Oct. 1961), pp. 279–291.

Raser, John R., and Wayman J. Crow. "Winsafe II: An Inter-Nation Simulation

Study of Deterrence Postures Embodying Capacity to Delay Response." La Jolla, Calif.: Western Behavioral Sciences Institute, 1964, (mimeo).

Redfield, Robert. *A Village That Chose Progress*. Chicago: Univ. of Chicago Press, 1950.

Richardson, Lewis F. *Arms and Insecurity*. Chicago: Quadrangle, 1960a.

———. *Statistics of Deadly Quarrels*. Chicago: Quadrangle, 1960b.

Riemer, Svend. "Theoretical Aspects of Regionalism." *Social Forces*, XXI, No. 3 (1943), pp. 275–80.

Rieselbach, Leroy N. "Quantitative Techniques for Studying Voting Behavior in the U.N. General Assembly," *International Organization*, XIV (1960), pp. 291–306.

Riggs, Fred. W. "Agraria and Industria: Toward a Typology of Comparative Adminis- tration," in William Siffin (ed.), *Toward the Comparative Study of Public Administration*. Bloomington, Ind.: Univ. of Indiana Press, 1957.

———. *Administration in Developing Countries: The Theory of Prismatic Society*. Boston: Houghton Mifflin, 1964.

Riker, William H. *The Theory of Political Coalitions*. New Haven, Conn.: Yale Univ. Press, 1962.

Riley, John, W., Jr., and Charles F. Marden. "The Social Patterns of Alcohol Drink- ing," *Quarterly Journal of Studies on Alcoholism*. XV (1954), pp. 477–490.

Robinson, John. *Multidimensional Analysis as a Comparative Framework for Political Systems*. Ann Arbor, Mich.: University of Michigan, seminar paper, 1965.

Rosecrance, Richard. *Action and Reaction in World Politics*. Boston: Little, Brown, 1962.

Rosenau, James N. *The Senate and Dean Acheson: A Case Study in Legislative Attitudes*, Princeton Univ.: Ph.D. Dissertation, 1957.

———. "Senate Attitudes Toward a Secretary of State." in John Wahlke and Heinz Eulau (eds.), *Legislative Behavior: A Reader in Theory and Research*. New York: Free Press, 1959.

———. "The Functioning of International Systems," *Background*, VII (Nov. 1963) pp. 111–17.

———. *International Aspects of Civil Strife*. Princeton, N.J.: Princeton Univ. Press, 1964a.

———. "Pre-Theories and Theories of Foreign Policy," New Brunswick, N.J.: Rutgers Univ., 1964b, (mimeo).

Routt, Garland C. "Interpersonal Relationships and the Legislative Process," *American Academy of Political and Social Science Annuals*, CXCV (Jan. 1938), pp. 129–136.

Rudin, Stanley A. "What Price Glory? Psychogenic Death Rates and the Motives for Achievement and Power in 17 Countries," Paper delivered at the 17th International Congress of Psychology, Washington, D.C., Aug. 1963.

Rummel, Rudolph J. *Applied Factor Analysis*. Evanston, Ill.: Northwestern Univ. Press, 1967 (in press).

———. "Dimensions of Conflict Behavior within and between Nations," *General Systems: Yearbook of the Society for General Systems Research*, VIII (1963), pp. 1–50.

———. "Testing Some Possible Predictors of Conflict Behavior within and between Nations," *Peace Research Society Papers I*, 1964a, pp. 79–111.

———. "Dimensions of International Relations in the Mid-1950's," Yale Univ.: Dimensionality of Nations Project, 1964b (mimeo).

———. "A Field Theory of Social Action and of Political Conflict Within Nations," Yale Univ.: Dimensionality of Nations Project (mimeo), 1965a.

———. "The Dimensionality of Nations Project," in Richard Merritt and Stein Rokkan (eds.), *Comparing Nations*. New Haven, Conn.: Yale Univ. Press, 1965b.

Rummel, Rudolph J. "Technology and War: A Correlational Analysis." M.A. Thesis, Univ. of Hawaii, 1961.

———, Jack Sawyer, Harold Guetzkow, and Raymond Tanter. *Dimensions of Nations.* Evanston, Ill.: Northwestern Univ. Press, 1967 (in press).

Russett, Bruce M. "Cause, Surprise and No Escape," *Journal of Politics,* XXIV (1962), pp. 3–32.

———. *Community and Contention: Britain and America in the Twentieth Century.* Cambridge, Mass.: MIT Press, 1963.

———. *Trends in World Politics,* New York: Macmillan, 1965.

———. "Discovering Voting Groups in the United Nations," *American Political Science Review,* LX, No. 2 (1966), pp. 327–39.

———. *International Regions and the International System.* Chicago: Rand McNally, 1967 (in press).

———, with Hayward R. Alker, Karl W. Deutsch, and Harold Lasswell. *World Handbook of Political and Social Indicators.* New Haven, Conn.: Yale Univ. Press, 1964.

Russia, Komissiia po Izdaiiu Dokumentov Spokhi Imperilizma. *Mezhdunarodnve otnosheniia v ipokhu imperializma;* dokumenty iz arkhivov tsarskogo i vremennogo pravitel 'stv 1878–1917 gg., seriia III, toma IV and V. Moskva/Leningrad, IV (1931); V (1934).

Savage, I. Richard, and Karl W. Deutsch. "A Statistical Model of the Gross Analysis of Transaction Flows," *Econometrica.* XXVIII, No. 3 (July 1960), pp. 551–572.

Schaffer, B. B. "Policy and System in Defense: The Australian Case," *World Politics,* XV (1963), pp. 236–261.

Schelling, Thomas C. *The Strategy of Conflict.* Cambridge, Mass.: Harvard Univ. Press, 1960.

Schmid, Calvin. "A Study of Homicides in Seattle, 1914 to 1924," *Social Forces,* IV (1926), pp. 745–756.

———. "Suicide in Minneapolis, Minnesota, 1928–1932," *American Journal of Sociology,* XXXIX (1933), pp. 30–48.

Scitovsky, Tibor. *Economic Theory and Western European Integration.* London: Allen & Unwin, 1958.

Shanks, Michael and John Lambert. *The Common Market Today—and Tomorrow.* New York: Praeger, 1962.

Sharp, Walter. "A Check List of Subjects for Systematic Study of International Conferences," *International Social Science Bulletin,* V (1963), pp. 311–339.

Shulman, Marshall D. *Stalin's Foreign Policy Reappraised.* Cambridge, Mass.: Harvard Univ. Press, 1963.

Siegel, Sidney. *Nonparametric Statistics for the Behavioral Sciences.* New York: McGraw-Hill, 1956.

Silberner, Edmund. *The Problem of War in Nineteenth Century Economic Thought.* Trans. Alexander H. Krappe. Princeton, N.J.: Princeton Univ. Press, 1946.

Simon, Herbert A. *Administrative Behavior.* New York: Macmillan, 1958.

Singer, J. David. "The United Nations Advisory Committee on Administrative and Budgetary Questions," *Public Administration,* XXXV (1957), pp. 395–410.

———. *Financing International Organization: The United Nations Budget Process.* The Hague: Martinus Nijhoff, 1961a.

———. "The Level of Analysis Problem in International Relations," *World Politics,* XIV (1961b), pp. 77–92.

———. "Soviet and American Foreign Policy Attitudes: A Content Analysis of Elite Articulations," *Journal of Conflict Resolution,* VIII (1964), pp. 424–485.

———. "Data-Making in International Relations," *Behavioral Science,* X, No. 1 (Jan. 1965), pp. 68–80.

Singer, J. David, and Melvin Small. "The Composition and Status Ordering of the International System, 1815–1940," *World Politics*, XVIII (Jan. 1966a), pp. 236–282.

———, and Melvin Small. "Formal Alliances, 1815–1939: A Quantitative Description," *Journal of Peace Research*, III (1966b), pp. 1–32.

———, and Melvin Small. *International War, 1815–1965: A Statistical Handbook* (forthcoming).

Singer, Marshall R., and Barton Sensenig, III. "Elections within the United Nations: An Experimental Study Utilizing Statistical Analysis," *International Organization*, XVII (1963), pp. 901–925.

Smith, Jean Edward. *The Defense of Berlin*. Baltimore: Johns Hopkins, Press, 1963.

Smoker, Paul A. "A Mathematical Study of the Present Arms Race," *General Systems Research*, VIII (1963a), pp. 51–59.

———. "A Pilot Study of the Present Arms Race," *General Systems*, VIII (1963b), pp. 61–76.

———. "Fear in the Arms Race: A Mathematical Study," *Journal of Peace Research*, I (1964), pp. 55–63.

Snyder, Richard C. "Toward Greater Order in the Study of International Relations," in James N. Rosenau (ed.), *International Politics and Foreign Policy*. New York: Free Press, 1961, pp. 36–43.

———. "Some Recent Trends in International Relations Theory and Research," in Austin Ranney (ed.), *Essays on the Behavioral Study of Politics*. Urbana, Ill.: Univ. of Illinois Press, 1962.

———. "The Korean Decision (1950) and the Analysis of Crisis Decision-Making," *Working Group Reports, 1963 MORS Conference*, pp. 242–248.

———, and Glenn Paige. "The United States Decision to Resist Aggression in Korea," *Administrative Science Quarterly*, III (1958), pp. 341–378.

———, and James A. Robinson. *National and International Decision-Making*. New York: The Institute for International Order, 1961.

———, H. W. Bruck, and Burton Sapin (eds.). *Foreign Policy Decision-Making*. New York: Free Press, 1962.

Sorokin, Pitirim A. *Social and Cultural Dynamics*. Vol. 3. New York: American Book, 1937.

Speier, Hans. *Divided Berlin*. New York: Praeger: 1961.

Spiegel, John P. "A Model for Relationships among Systems," in Roy R. Grinker (ed.), *Toward a Unified Theory of Human Behavior*, New York: Basic Books, 1959.

Sprout, Harold, and Margaret Sprout. *Foundations of International Politics*. Princeton, N.J.: Van Nostrand, 1962.

Spykman, Nicholas. *American's Strategy in World Politics*. New York: Harcourt, Brace, 1942.

Stone, Philip J., Robert P. Bales, J. Zvi Namenwirth, and Daniel M. Ogilvie. "The General Inquirer: A Computer System for Content Analysis and Retrieval Based on the Sentence as a Unit of Information," *Behavioral Science*, VII (1962), pp. 484–494.

Straus, Robert, and Selden Bacon. "Alcoholism and Social Stability: A Study of Occupational Integration in 2023 Male Clinic Patients," *Quarterly Journal of Studies on Alcohol*, XII (1951), pp. 231–260.

Streeten, P. *Economic Integration*. Leyden: A. W. Sythoff, 1961.

Sturmthal, A. *National Income and Growth Rates in Western Europe*. New Haven, Conn.: Yale Univ. 1965 (mimeo).

Suci, George J. *An Investigation of the Similarity Between the Semantic Spaces of Five Different Cultures*. Report for the Southwest Project in Comparative Psycholinguistics, 1957.

Sullivan, John D. *Quemoy and Matsu: A Systematic Analysis.* Los Angeles, Calif., May 1964 (mimeo).

Suppes, Patrick and Joseph L. Zinnes, "Basic Measurement Theory," in R. Duncan Luce, Robert R. Bush, and Eugene Galanter, (eds.). *Handbook of Mathematical Psychology,* New York: John Wiley, 1963, pp. 1–76.

Tanter, Raymond. *Dimensions of Conflict Behavior within and between Nations, 1958–1960.* Bloomington, Ind.: Indiana Univ., Ph.D. Thesis, 1964.

Thompson, John, S. Sufrin, P. Gould, and M. Buck. "Toward a Geography of Economic Health: The Case of New York State," in John Friedmann and William Alonso (eds.). *Regional Development and Planning: A Reader.* Cambridge, Mass: MIT Press, 1964, pp. 187–206.

Times. London, June-Aug., 1914.

Turner, Frederick Jackson. *The Significance of Sections in United States History.* New York: Henry Holt, 1932.

UNESCO. *The Technique of International Conferences. A Progress Report on Research Problems and Methods,* Paris, France, 1951.

United Nations. Statistical Papers, series T., Vol. 8, No. 7. *Direction of International Trade.* New York: United Nations, 1957.

United Nations, General Assembly, Seventeenth Session, Fifth Committee, *Official Records,* 914th meeting to 983rd meeting (Oct. 1 to Dec. 20, 1962).

United Nations, Statistical Office. *Direction of International Trade.* New York: N.Y., Annual.

———. Department of Economics and Social Affairs. *Yearbook of National Account Statistics, 1958.* New York, 1959.

———. *Yearbook of National Account Statistics, 1962.* New York, 1963.

———. *Demographic Yearbook.* (Annual from 1948 to 1962.)

———. *Statistical Yearbook.* (Annual from 1948 to 1962.)

United States Congress, *Congressional Record.* Washington, D.C.: Government Printing Office, XCXII (1956).

———. Senate, Committee on Government Operations. *Organizing for National Security: Inquiry of the Subcommittee on National Policy Machinery* (Vol. I: Hearings). Washington, D.C.: Government Printing Office, 1961.

Urlanis, Boris T. *Volny i Narodonaselenie Evropy.* (*Wars and the Population of Europe*). Moscow: Government Publishing House, 1960.

Vance, Rupert B. "The Regional Concept as a Tool for Social Research," in Merrill Jensen (ed.). *Regionalism in America.* Madison, Wis.: University of Wisconsi Press, 1951.

Wahlke, John C., Heinz Eulau, William Buchanan, and Leroy C. Ferguson. *The Legislative System: Explorations in Legislative Behavior.* New York: John Wiley, 1962.

Wall Street Journal. June-Aug., 1914.

Waltz, Kenneth N. *Man, the State, and War.* New York: Columbia Univ. Press, 1959.

———. "The Stability of a Biplolar World," *Daedalus,* XCIII (1964), pp. 881–909.

Ward, Joe H. and Marion Hook. "Application of an Hierarchical Grouping Procedure to a Problem of Grouping Profiles," *Educational and Psychological Measurement,* XXIII, No. 1 (1963), pp. 69–81.

Weiss, Herbert K. "Stochastic Models for the Duration and Magnitude of a 'Deadly Quarrel'," *Operations Research,* XI (Jan.-Feb. 1963), pp. 101–121.

Windsor, Philip. *City on Leave: A History of Berlin 1945–1962.* London: Chatto, 1963.

Wirth, Louis. "Limitations of Regionalism" in Merrill Jensen (ed.). *Regionalism in America.* Madison, Wis.: University of Wisconsin Press, 1951.

Wolfers, Arnold. (ed.), *Discord and Collaboration.* Baltimore: Johns Hopkins Univ. Press, 1962.

Wright, B., and M. Evitts, "Direct Factor Analysis in Sociometry," *Sociometry,* 24, 1 (1961), pp. 82–98.

Wright, Quincy. "Design for a Research Proposal on International Conflict and the Factors Causing Their Aggravation or Amelioration," *Western Political Quarterly*, X (1957), pp. 263–275.

———. "The Nature of Conflict," *Western Political Quarterly*, IV (1951), pp. 193–209.

———. *Problems of Stability and Progress in International Relations*. Berkeley, Calif.: Univ. of California Press, 1954.

———. *The Study of International Relations*. New York: Appleton, 1955.

———. *A Study of War*. 2 Vols. Chicago: Univ. of Chicago Press, 1942.

Zaninovich, George, "An Empirical Theory of State Response: The Sino-Soviet Case," Stanford Univ.: Ph.D. dissertation, 1964 (mimeo).

Zawadzki, Bohan, and Paul Lazarsfeld. "The Psychological Consequences of Unemployment," *Journal of Social Psychology*, VI (1935), pp. 224–251.

Zinnes, Dina A., Robert C. North, and Howard E. Koch, Jr. "Capability, Threat and the Outbreak of War," in James N. Rosenau (ed).), *International Politics and Foreign Policy: A Reader in Research and Theory*. New York: Free Press, 1961.

———. "Expression and Perception of Hostility in Inter-State Relations." Stanford Univ.: Ph.D. dissertation, 1963a.

———. "Documents as a Source of Data," in Robert C. North, Ole R. Holsti, M. George Zaninovich and Dina A. Zinnes, *Content Analysis*. Evanston, Ill. Northwestern University Press, 1963b, pp. 17–36.

———. "Pair Comparison Scaling in International Relations," in Robert C. North, Ole R. Holsti, M. George Zaninovich and Dina A. Zinnes. *Content Analysis*. Evanston, Ill.: Northwestern University Press, 1963c, pp. 79–89.

———. "Testing a Balance of Power Theory," Bloomington, Ind.: Indiana Univ., 1966 (mimeo).

Indices

Subject Index

While the indexes found in scholarly books have as their major purpose the location of references to specific entities, events, and conditions, they can also tell the reader something about the theoretical scheme which informs and shapes the study. They *can* do so, but since most indexes are prepared by someone other than the volume's author or editor, they seldom do. This weakness in conceptual organization, combined with the typical author's indifference to the matter, usually produces an index of extremely limited value. Normally, the reader must try a variety of index entries before turning up the item he is after, and then only after wading through a number of utterly irrelevant passages. Moreover, no two books on the same general topic are likely to use indexing schemes that are sufficiently similar to permit comparison and cumulativeness across different, but related, studies.

With these considerations in mind, I decided to depart from tradition here, and try a somewhat different approach. It becomes increasingly apparent that the international politics field can, by certain timely innovations of a mechanical nature, avoid much of the chaos and consequent losses of comparability that have hampered our sister disciplines. By profiting from their experiences, we can markedly increase the efficiency of our research community, especially in regard to enhancing the cumulativeness and interdependence of our findings. One way to do this, it seems, is to move toward a fairly uniform classification scheme, not only for archival purposes and abstracts, but for indexes as well. In a forthcoming book, I outline a taxonomy that comes quite close to being theoretically neutral (if not quite a-theoretical) as well as relatively operational, and it could conceivably provide one such uniform storage and retrieval scheme.

To apply that scheme to a single man's work is, however, hardly a test of its general applicability, and it therefore seemed appropriate to try it here, where a number of very distinctive orientations and empirical domains are represented.

While the scheme is fairly self-evident, a brief summary might not be amiss. Basically, every reference that is likely to interest the social scientist may be thought of as some condition or event involving some social unit or entity. Thus, each reference here is found in the cell marked by the intersection of a particular entity (or class of entities) with the appropriate condition or event. The entity rows are listed in the left-hand column, beginning at the extra-national level and descending through the national and intra-national levels to the individual.

All levels can be thought of as having entities that are either highly organized, structured, and institutionalized (called "formal" here), or quite loose, unstructured and perhaps little more than a mere aggregation; these latter are called "informal." These entities may also be essentially governmental and official (ranging from foreign ministries to semi-governmental central banks) or quite private and non-governmental, such as professional associations, labor unions in some nations, or an ethnic group. Thus, at every level there could be entries for all four combinations. At this stage, however, there has been very little research dealing with the role of entities which are informal, and even less concerning those which are non-governmental, and this volume reflects that current lack of attention. Therefore, at the extra-national level, the reader will find a few inter-governmental entities of an informal nature (such as European powers, underdeveloped nations, or Moslem nations), but no non-governmental ones at either the formal (such as International Political Science Association, Catholic Church, or World Veterans Association) or the informal (such as all opponents of conference diplomacy) end of the spectrum. And at the intra-national level, the governmental-formal (such as a foreign ministry or central bank) combination was again most frequent, with no entries at all for governmental-informal (such as the "inner circle" or Washington "establishment"), non-governmental-formal (such as the League to Enforce the Peace, or Council on Foreign Relations), or the non-governmental-informal (such as those who are medically unfit for military service or all tool manufacturers who export to East Africa).

Shifting from the entities to the conditions or events which they might experience, we note that any entity may, first of all, be described or compared to others in terms of certain attributes; these are cited in the first column. In the second column are references to the bonds, links, and relationships—and therefore interdependence—which any entity has with others. Finally, column three includes all references to the behavior which any entity manifests (or is the object of) and to the interaction sequences which arise out of such discrete behavioral events.

We have found that every important reference in all ten studies can be readily placed in one of the many (but finite) cells formed by the intersection of the entity rows with the phenomena columns. While nothing of significance appears to have been omitted, several types of reference have been included in more than one cell. These double entries arise because, for example, we often observe the relationship among entities at one level in order to infer and describe the attributes of the next higher system level. Likewise, we often operationalize a relationship by counting the interaction sequences of a given type which occur between the entities whose relationship is being described. In sum, this indexing scheme clearly shows certain weaknesses, but if it permits the reader to retrieve needed information as readily as it permitted us to store it, and if it turns out to provide a model for future storage and retrieval systems—be it the index of a single book or a more general sort of data and finding archive—the enterprise will have been worth the effort. Any suggestions for its modification or replacement, as well as reports of its utility, will be most welcome.

CLASS OR NAME OF ENTITY	Entity Attributes or Comparisons	Interdependence Between and Among Entities	Behavior and Interaction of Entities
NATIONAL AND INTRA-NATIONAL LEVEL Governmental—Formal (cont.)			
Malta	329, 332-3, 336		
Manchuria			230
Mauritius	329		
Mecklenburg-Schwerin	253, 255	268	263
Mexico	254-5, 330, 333, 341	271, 341-2	262-3, 266
U.N. delegation			60-1, 71, 73
Modena	253, 255	268	
Mongolia	255	271	
U.N. delegation			58
Morocco	253-5, 328, 332	349	262, 346
Nepal	255		
U.N. delegation			60, 62, 66-7, 73
Netherlands	254, 295, 329, 332-3	294-6, 299, 305, 307, 348-9	266, 294-6, 300-3, 307, 309, 312-3, 349
U.N. delegation			59-62, 65-7, 70, 72-3, 83
New Zealand	255, 329, 332-3	346, 350	266
U.N. delegation			59-62, 65, 70, 73
Nicaragua	255, 330, 333	271, 341-2	264
Nigeria: U.N. delegation			66-7, 72-3, 78
Norway	221-4, 237-42, 254, 329, 332-3	294, 348-9	221-4, 266, 294-5, 297, 300-3
U.N. delegation			59-60, 66-7, 70, 72
Pakistan	329	346	340, 346
U.N. delegation			60-1, 66-7, 73, 78
Panama	255, 330, 333	271, 343	346
Papal States	253, 255		259n, 262
Paraguay	255, 330, 333	271	265, 343-4
Parma	253, 255	268	
Persia (see Iran)			
Peru	254-5, 330, 333	254n, 268, 271, 343-4	259n, 263
Philippines	330-1, 334	345	
Poland	254, 330, 334	269-71	259, 266
U.N. delegation			58-60, 66-7, 78
Portugal	254, 330, 333, 336, 351	268-9, 271, 348-9	265
Prussia	253-4	268	260, 262-6, 273
Puerto Rico	330, 333, 336		
Rumania	254, 330, 334	269-70	97, 264-6
U.N. delegation			58-60, 66-7, 78

CLASS OR NAME OF ENTITY	Entity Attributes or Comparisons	Interdependence Between and Among Entities	Behavior and Interaction of Entities
Non-Governmental—Informal No References			
INDIVIDUALS AND ROLES Austria-Hungary: Political elites Berchtold			88, 92, 94, 135
Conrad			135
Forgach			88, 135
Francis Ferdinand			123, 139
Franz Joseph			88, 135
Hoyos			135
Macchio			88, 135
Sturgkh			88, 135
Tisza			88, 135
France: Political elites Berthelot			88, 135
Bienvenu-Martin			88, 135
Daladier			154
DeGaulle	22		49, 314
DeMargerie			88
Delcassé			88
Doumergue			88
Ferry			135
Jonnart			88
Messimy			135
Pichon			88
Poincaré			88, 135
Viviani			88, 135
Germany: Political elites Bethmann-Hollweg			88, 134n, 135
Bülow			134n
Hitler			124, 133, 154
Jagow			88, 135
Kaiser Wilhelm II			88, 93, 135, 137, 139, 139n, 154
Moltke			135
Stumm			135
Zimmerman			88, 135
Princip, Gavrilo			123
Serbia: Political elites Alexander, Crown Prince			88
Pashitch			88
Patchou			88
United Kingdom: Political elites Asquith			88, 135

Author Index

The authors (individual, multiple, or institutional) of all works cited in this volume are listed in alphabetical order. When more than one author is responsible for a given item, EACH *one is listed separately.*

Abel, Theodore, 124, 136, 216, 252n
Abelson, Robert P., 126
Ackoff, Russell L., 126
Adams, Sherman, 31n
Adelson, Marvin, 205n, 323
Albertini, Luigi, 124, 134, 146
Alexander, Christopher, 340n
Alger, Chadwick, 63n, 82n, 83
Alker, Hayward R., 6, 7n, 12, 20, 203n, 221, 239n, 289n, 291n, 321-2, 322n, 323, 338n
Almond, Gabriel A., 218
Angell, Robert C., 127
Austro-Hungarian Monarchy, Ministerium des K. and k. Hauses und des Aeusseren, 89n, 134
Alpert, Harry, 235

Bacon, Selden D., 221, 223
Bailey, Margaret B., 223
Bakke, E. Wight, 221
Balassa, Bela, 287n
Bales, Robert F., 57, 81, 157, 235
Banks, Arthur S., 12, 233, 323, 327, 328
Bates, Alan P., 81
Bell, Daniel, 223
Benoit, Emile, 309n
Berelson, Bernard, 12, 90, 138
Berge, Claude, 285n
Berry, Brian J. L., 200n, 204, 206, 323n, 327, 337
Beum, Corlin O., 323
Bisco, Ralph L., 11n
Bittner, Ludwig, 89n, 139
Block, Jack, 137, 137n
Bloodworth, Jessie A., 221
Bodart, Gaston, 260
Borgatta, Edgar F., 81
Boulding, Kenneth E., 126, 145, 147, 155, 167n, 203n
Bowlby, John, 217n
Breed, Warren, 221, 223
Brim, Orville G., 23
Brinton, Crane, 221, 239

Brody, Richard A., 128n, 130, 131, 145, 146n, 158, 267
Bruck, H. W., 127, 128n, 131, 133
Bruel, H., 200n, 205, 217, 323, 327
Brutzkus, Boris, 222
Buchanan, William, 30n
Buck, M., 323
Bülow, Bernhard von, 134n
Burr, Robert N., 254n

Campbell, Donald T., 289n
Cantril, Hadley, 12, 222
Carleton, William G., 22n
Carr, E. H., 321n
Cattell, Raymond B., 200n, 201n, 205, 205n, 206, 207, 208, 209, 210, 213, 217, 217n, 227, 323, 327, 337
Cavan, Ruth Shonle, 223
Chadwick, Richard, 202, 217n
Chaumont, C., 63, 63n
Chodorkoff, Bernard, *et al.*, 221
Chotlos, John W., 223
Churchill, Winston S., 139n
Claude, Inis L., 248n, 321n
Clay, Lucius D., 163n
Cohen, Bernard C., 29
Coleman, James, 285n
Collins, Barry E., 81
Cooley, Charles H., 218
Crow, Wayman J., 130, 131
Cuzzort, Ray P., 204n, 323

Danilevsky, Nadia, 323
Davies, James C., 221
Davison, W. Phillips, 163, 163n, 174, 317
Deiter, John B., 223
De Rusett, Alan, 321
Denton, Frank, 257n
Deutsch, Karl W., 6, 8n, 12, 130, 134, 219, 221, 239, 239n, 248n, 250, 288n, 291, 291n, 292, 293, 293n, 294, 299n, 305n, 321-2, 321n, 322n, 338n, 339
Dollard, John, *et al.*, 217n
Domenach, Jean-Marie, 222

391